PREFACE

Every subject has ▮▮▮▮▮▮▮ e one that becomes a household ▮▮▮▮▮▮ d records, you think of *Guinnes* ▮▮▮▮▮▮ of anatomy, *Gray's*; of music ▮▮▮▮▮▮ -language dictionaries, *Webster* a▮▮ ▮▮▮▮▮.

And whenever somebody thinks of law dictionaries, *Black's* seems inevitably to come to mind. Henry Campbell Black (1860–1927) first published his magnum opus in 1891, and his achievement might easily be taken for granted today. He entered a crowded field, for there were many law dictionaries then in print—several more major ones, in fact, than there are now. But who today, apart from the specialist, remembers the names of Anderson, Burrill, English, Kinney, Lawson, Rapalje, Sweet, Wharton, or even the better-known Bouvier?

What happened is that Henry Campbell Black's *Dictionary of Law* took the field and became incontestably supreme, partly because of his comprehensiveness, partly because of his academic standing, and partly because he had the good fortune of publishing his work with West Publishing Company.

Black's Law Dictionary has evolved over its six unabridged editions. And this pocket edition continues that evolution. Indeed, because it was compiled on modern lexicographic principles, the book you're holding is something of a radical leap forward in the evolutionary line.

Lexicographic Methods and Features

Little is known about exactly how Black and his contemporaries worked, but one thing is certain to anyone who has spent any time examining 19th-century and early-20th-century law dictionaries: a great deal of the "work" was accomplished through wholesale borrowing from other dictionaries. To cite but one example, in Bouvier (1839), Anderson (1890), Black (1891), Kinney (1893), Shumaker & Longsdorf (1901), and several other law dictionaries of the period, the phrase *disorderly house* is defined in the following word-for-word sequence: a "house the inmates of which behave so badly as to become a nuisance to the neighborhood." Hundreds of other definitions are virtually verbatim from book to book.

Although this practice of heavy borrowing is suspect today, it may be wrong to judge these early lexicographers by modern standards. They might have copied for various reasons. First, even nonspecialist lexicographers of the time commonly borrowed from each other; that is, apart from a few notable exceptions such as Samuel Johnson (1709–1784), Noah Webster (1758–1843), and James A.H. Murray (1837–1915—the first editor of the *Oxford English Dictionary*), a high percentage of entries in early English-language dictionaries were directly traceable to even earlier dictionaries. Second, dictionary editors in the legal field were trained as common-law lawyers, under the Anglo-American system of precedent. As a result, they might have thought that accuracy precluded a reconsideration of their predecessors' words—especially if the earlier dictionary-maker cited caselaw in support of a definition. And third, notions of plagiarism were much less well defined than they are today (and, in any event, have always been looser in lexicography than elsewhere).

But the result of all this is that, as the legal language has grown, law dictionaries have generally strayed further and further afield from actual legal usage. Instead of monitoring legal language for new entries—words that emerge in a given practice area, legal slang that crops up in a certain context, words that take on meanings different from their traditional ones—compilers of law dictionaries have tended to look too much at their forerunners.

PREFACE

This book, however, represents a stem-to-stern (very stern) reconsideration of legal terms—an entirely fresh edition of *Black's Law Dictionary* compiled on modern lexicographic methods. This means that my colleagues and I have done several things. We have:

- Attempted a thorough marshaling of the language of the law from original sources. Many terms make their "debut" in this edition.

- Examined the writings of specialist scholars rather than looking only at judicial decisions.

- Considered entries entirely anew rather than merely accepting what previous editions have said. We have often checked WESTLAW and other sources when trying to decide which of two competing forms now predominates in legal usage.

- Imposed analytical rigor on entries by avoiding duplicative definitions and by cataloguing and numbering senses.

- Shown pronunciations that reflect how American lawyers actually say the words and phrases—not how English lawyers used to say them (and not necessarily how Latin teachers would have us say them).

- Recorded cognate forms—for example, the verb and adjective corresponding to a given noun.

- Ensured that specialized vocabularies are included— from bankruptcy to securities law, from legal realism to critical legal studies.

As a result, this book represents a balanced and up-to-date treatment of legal terms—even within the strict confines of a "pocket" dictionary.

PREFACE

Acknowledgments

Thanks are due to many who have played a role in producing this book. As assistant editors, David Schultz and Becky McDaniel—both former law-review editors with experience as practicing lawyers—brought energy, common sense, and true dedication to the project.

Other experienced lawyers were extraordinarily helpful. Elizabeth S. Kerr read through an entire draft and supplied most of the pronunciations—all with the insight and reliability that typify everything she does. Katherine Smith worked skillfully on many entries, and Charles Dewey Cole commented helpfully on a near-final draft of the A entries.

My research assistants from Southern Methodist University School of Law helped research scores of entries. Many thanks to Lauren Chadwick, Kimberly R. Lafferty, Jennifer Berg, and Rick Prahl.

While the work progressed, I occasionally ran queries by scholars in various legal specialties, and they all responded helpfully. Many thanks to Robert E. Keeton, Richard A. Posner, Robert W. Hamilton, Geoffrey C. Hazard, Jr., Mark P. Gergen, and Charles Alan Wright.

My wife, Teo Garner, brought to this project her usual tenacity and flair. As the chief administrator of LawProse, Inc.—which housed the project and provided office space, computers, printers, photocopiers, and library facilities—she made the day-to-day operations run smoothly.

My most intense work on the book came in June 1995, when my family and I spent a month in Salzburg, Austria. The primary purpose of the trip was to advance the work on *Black's*. On his own initiative, Professor Christoph Schreuer of the University of Salzburg kindly asked his department chair to arrange an office for me at the law school. Because of his kindness—and the warm hospitality of my wife's family in Austria, the Webers and the Seyfrieds—I was able to accomplish a great deal while also managing to enjoy what must be the most congenial environment on the face of the earth.

Everyone who has worked on this project has shared a goal: to produce the most accurate, readable, and comprehensive paperback law dictionary ever published. Though we doubtless could have done better here and there, we think we have met our goal. We hope that it meets your needs.

BRYAN A. GARNER

Dallas, Texas
May 1996

*

GUIDE TO THE DICTIONARY

1. Alphabetization

All headwords, including abbreviations, are alphabetized letter by letter, not word by word. For example:

per annum
P/E ratio
per capita
percentage lease
per diem
peremptory

Numerals included in a headword precede the letter "a" and are arranged in ascending numerical order:

Rule 10b–5
Rule 11
rule absolute
rulemaking
rule of 72
rule of 78

Numerals at the beginning of a headword are alphabetized as if the numeral were spelled out:

Eighth Amendment
eight-hour law
8–K
ejection

Commas break the letter-by-letter alphabetization:

at the bar
attorney
attorney, power of
attorney-at-law
attorney-client privilege

2. Pronunciation

A word may have more than one acceptable pronunciation. When that is so, the preferred pronunciation appears first. For variably pronounced syllables, only the changed syllables are generally included. Boldface syllables receive primary stress. For example:

oligopoly (ol-ə-**gop**-ə-lee *or* ohl-), *n.*

Brackets in pronunciations indicate either an optional sound, as in *inure* (i-**n[y]oor**), or a soft schwa sound, as in *patent* (**pa**-t[ə]nt).

For quick reference, the pronunciation guide is located inside the front cover.

3. Style and Usage Tags

Archaic = old-fashioned and declining in use
Slang = very informal
Jargon = typical of stilted legal writing and easily simplified
pl. = plural
cap. = capitalized

4. Angle Brackets

Contextual illustrations of a headword are given in angle brackets:

avail, *n.* **1.** Use or advantage <of little or no avail>. **2.** (*pl.*) Profits or proceeds, esp. from a sale of property <the avails of the trust fund>.

5. Cognate Forms

This dictionary lists corresponding parts of speech. For example, under the definition of *confirmation,* the corresponding verb (*confirm*) and adjective (*confirmatory*) are listed.

Agent nouns are included only if they are irregularly formed—that is, do not end in *-er.* But agent nouns ending in *-er* are included if there is more than one acceptable form, such as *abettor* and *abetter.* Also, if the corresponding form ending in *-ee* is defined, then the agent noun ending in *-er* or *-or* is included as a separate headword. For example, *garnisher* and *garnishee* are defined at separate entries.

Adjectives ending in *-able* are included only if they are irregularly formed—for example, *abdicable.*

If a cognate form applies to only one sense of a headword, that form is denoted as follows:

> **construction,** *n.* **1.** The act of building by combining or arranging parts or elements; the thing so built. **2.** The act or process of interpreting or explaining the sense or intention of something (such as a statute, opinion, or instrument).—**construct** (corresponding to sense 1), *vb.*—**construe** (corresponding to sense 2), *vb.*

6. Cross-references

a. See

The signal "See" is used in three ways:

(1) To indicate that the definition is at another location in the dictionary. For example:

> **call loan.** See LOAN.

> **perpetuities, rule against.** See RULE AGAINST PERPETUITIES.

(2) To refer to closely related terms:

> **checks and balances.** The theory of governmental power and functions whereby each branch of government has the ability to counter the actions of any other branch, so that no single branch can control the entire government; for example, the executive can check the legislature by exercising its veto power, but the legislature can, by a sufficient majority, override any veto. See SEPARATION OF POWERS.

cognovit (kog-**noh**-vit). [Latin "the person has conceded (a debt or an action)"] An acknowledgment of debt or liability in the form of a confessed judgment; formerly, credit contracts often included a cognovit clause in which consumers agreed in advance that, if they were sued for nonpayment, they had relinquished any right to be notified of court hearings—but such clauses are generally illegal today. See *confession of judgment* under JUDGMENT.

(3) To refer to a synonymous subentry:

binding instruction. See *mandatory instruction* under JURY IN-STRUCTION.

b. Cf.

"Cf." is used to refer to related but distinguishable terms. For example:

bigamy, *n.* The act of marrying one person while legally married to another; bigamy is a criminal offense if it is committed knowingly.—**bigamous,** *adj.*—**bigamist,** *n.* Cf. POLYGAMY; MONOGAMY.

c. Also termed

The phrase "also termed" at the end of an entry signals a synonymous word or phrase. Variations on "also termed" include "formerly also termed," "also spelled," and "often shortened to."

d. Terms with multiple senses

If the cross-referenced term has multiple senses, the particular sense referred to is indicated in parentheses:

delivery bond. See BOND (2).

collateral fraud. See *extrinsic fraud* (a) under FRAUD.

7. Subentries

Many terms in this dictionary are collected by topic. For example, the different types of contracts, such as *bilateral contract* and *gratuitous contract,* are defined under the main term *contract*. If a term has more than one sense, then the corresponding subentries are placed under the appropriate sense of that term.

8. Typefaces

Most of the typefaces used in this dictionary are self-explanatory. For instance, all headwords and cognate forms are in boldface type and all subentries are italicized. As for headwords of foreign origin, those that are fully naturalized are in boldface roman type, while those that are not fully naturalized are in boldface italics. Generally, small caps are used with "See" and "Cf." cross-references. There are, however, three other uses of small caps deserving special mention:

a. Small caps refer to a synonymous headword. In the following example, the small caps suggest that you review the definition at *contiguous* for further information:

> **adjoining, *adj.*** Touching; sharing a common boundary; CONTIGUOUS.—**adjoin,** *vb.* Cf. ADJACENT.

b. Small caps also refer to the predominant form when it may be phrased or spelled in more than one way. For example, the following uses of small caps direct you to the entries at *perjury* and *payor:*

> **false swearing.** PERJURY.

> **payer.** PAYOR.

c. Small caps also refer to the spelled-out form of abbreviations (the term is defined at the spelled-out headword, not the abbreviated form). For example:

FDIC. *abbr.* FEDERAL DEPOSIT INSURANCE CORPORATION.

Federal Deposit Insurance Corporation. An independent governmental agency that insures bank deposits up to a statutory amount per depositor at each participating bank; the insurance fund is financed by a small fee paid by the participating banks.—*Abbr.* FDIC.

CONTENTS

*

BLACK'S
LAW DICTIONARY

Pocket Edition

*

A

AAA. *abbr.* **1.** AMERICAN ARBITRATION ASSOCIATION. **2.** AMERICAN ACCOUNTING ASSOCIATION. **3.** AMERICAN ACADEMY OF ACTUARIES.

AALS. *abbr.* ASSOCIATION OF AMERICAN LAW SCHOOLS.

a aver et tener ([ah-]**ah**-vər-et-**ten**-ər). [Law French] To have and to hold. See HABENDUM CLAUSE.

ABA. *abbr.* AMERICAN BAR ASSOCIATION.

abandoned property. See PROPERTY.

abandonee. One to whom property rights are relinquished; one to whom something is formally or legally abandoned.

abandonment, *n.* **1.** The act of giving up some right or interest with the intent of never claiming it again. **2.** In family law, the act of leaving children or a spouse willfully and without an intent to return. See DESERTION. **3.** In criminal law, RENUNCIATION (2). **4.** In bankruptcy law, the trustee's court-approved release of property that is burdensome or of inconsequential value to the estate, or the trustee's release of nonadministered property to the debtor when the case is closed. **5.** In contract law, RESCISSION (2). —**abandon,** *vb.*

abatable nuisance. See NUISANCE.

abatement (ə-**bayt**-mənt), *n.* **1.** The act of eliminating or nullifying <abatement of a nuisance> <abatement of a writ>. **2.** The suspension or defeat of a pending action for a reason unrelated to the merits of the claim <the defendant sought abatement of the suit because of misnomer>. See *plea in abatement* under PLEA. **3.** The act of lessening or moderating; diminution in amount or degree <abatement of the debt>. **4.** *Archaic.* The act of thrusting oneself tortiously into real estate after the owner dies and before the legal heir enters <abatement of freehold>. —**abate,** *vb.*—**abatable,** *adj.*—**abator,** *n.*

abbreviator. **1.** One who abbreviates, abridges, or shortens. **2.** In ecclesiastical law, an officer in the court of Rome appointed as assistant to the vice-chancellor for drawing up the Pope's briefs and reducing petitions, when granted, into proper form to be converted into papal bulls.

abbroachment (ə-**brohch**-mənt), *n.* The act of forestalling the market by buying wholesale merchandise to sell it at retail as the only vendor <the abbroachment by the competing supermarket put the local grocery store out of business>. —Also spelled *abbrochment*; *abbrochement.* —**abbroach,** *vb.*

abdication, *n.* The act of renouncing or abandoning privileges or duties, esp. those connected with high office <the court's abdication of its judicial responsibility>. —**abdicate,** *vb.*—**abdicable,** *adj.*—**abdicator,** *n.*

abduction, *n.* **1.** The act of leading someone away by force or fraudulent persuasion. **2.** *Archaic.* At common law, the crime of taking away a female person without her consent by use of persuasion, fraud, or violence, for the purpose of marriage, prostitution, or illicit sex. —**abduct,** *vb.*—**abductor,** *n.* See KIDNAPPING.

abet, *vb.* **1.** To encourage and assist (someone), esp. in the commission of a crime <abet a known felon>. **2.** To support (a crime) by active assistance <abet a burglary>.—**abetment,** *n.*—**abettor, abetter,** *n.* See AID AND ABET.

abeyance (ə-**bay**-əns), *n.* **1.** Temporary inactivity; suspension. **2.** In property law, a lapse in succession during which no person is vested with title. —**abeyant,** *adj.*

abide, *vb.* 1. To tolerate or withstand <the widow found it difficult to abide the pain of losing her husband>. **2.** To obey <try to abide the doctor's order to quit smoking>. **3.** To await <the death-row prisoner abides his execution>. **4.** To perform or execute (an order or judgment) <the trial court abided the appellate court's order>. **5.** To stay or dwell <the right to abide in any of the 50 states>.

ab initio (ab-I-**nish**-ee-oh), *adv.* [Latin] From the beginning <the injunction was valid *ab initio*>. Cf. IN INITIO.

abjure, *vb.* **1.** To renounce formally or on oath <abjure one's citizenship>. **2.** To avoid or abstain from <abjure one's civic duties>. —**abjuration,** *n.*—**abjuratory,** *adj.*

able-bodied seaman. In maritime law, a merchant seaman who is qualified for all seaman's duties. —Abbr. ABS. —Also termed *able seaman.*

abnormally dangerous activity. ULTRAHAZARDOUS ACTIVITY.

abode. A home; a fixed place of residence. See DOMICILE.

abolish, *vb.* To annul or destroy, esp. an ongoing practice or thing. —**abolition,** *n.*

abominable and detestable crime against nature. SODOMY.

aboriginal title. INDIAN TITLE.

abortion, *n.* The spontaneous or artificially induced expulsion of an embryo or fetus; the right of a woman to choose to end her pregnancy was first recognized in *Roe v. Wade* as a privacy right stemming from the Due Process Clause of the Fourteenth Amendment. 410 U.S. 113 (1973). —**abort,** *vb.*

above-mentioned. AFORESAID.

above-stated. AFORESAID.

abridge, *vb.* **1.** To reduce or diminish <abridge one's civil liberties>. **2.** To condense (as a book or other writing) <the author abridged the treatise before final publication>. —**abridgment,** *n.*

abrogate (**a**-brə-gayt), *vb.* To abolish (a law or custom) by formal or authoritative action; to annul or repeal. —**abrogation,** *n.*

ABS. *abbr.* ABLE-BODIED SEAMAN.

abscond, *vb.* To depart secretly or suddenly, esp. to avoid service of process; to conceal oneself. —**abscondence,** *n.*

absentee landlord. See LANDLORD.

absentee voting. See VOTING.

absolute contraband. See CONTRABAND.

absolute deed. See DEED.

absolute defense. See *real defense* under DEFENSE (4).

absolute delivery. See DELIVERY.

absolute estate. See ESTATE.

absolute law. A supposed law of nature thought to be unchanging in principle, although circumstances may vary the way in which it is applied. See NATURAL LAW.

absolute liability. See *strict liability* under LIABILITY.

absolute majority. See MAJORITY.

absolute presumption. See *conclusive presumption* under PRESUMPTION.

absolute-priority rule. In bankruptcy, the rule that a confirmable reorganization plan must provide for full payment to a class of dissenting unsecured creditors before a junior class of claimants is allowed to receive or retain anything under the plan; some jurisdictions recognize an exception to this rule when a junior class member, usu. a partner or shareholder of the debtor, contributes new capital in exchange for an interest in the debtor.

absolutism, *n.* In politics, the atmosphere surrounding a dictator whose power has no restrictions, checks, or balances; the belief in such a dictator. —**absolutist,** *adj. & n.*

absolve, *vb.* **1.** To release from an obligation, debt, or responsibility. **2.** To free from the penalties for misconduct. —**absolution,** *n.*

absorption, *n.* **1.** The act or process of including or incorporating. **2.** In international law, the merger of one nation into another, whether voluntarily or by subjugation. **3.** In a postmerger collective-bargaining agreement, a provision allowing seniority for union members in the resulting entity. **4.** The rate at which property will be leased or sold on the market at a given time. **5.** A sales method by which a manufacturer pays the seller's freight costs, which the manufacturer accounts for before quoting the seller a price. —Also termed (in sense 5) *freight absorption.* —**absorb,** *vb.*

absque hoc (ab-skwee-**hok** *or* -**hohk**). [Latin] *Archaic.* Without this; the phrase was formerly used in common-law pleading to introduce the denial of allegations. See TRAVERSE.

abstention. 1. A federal court's relinquishment of jurisdiction when necessary to avoid needless conflict with a state's administration of its own affairs. **2.** The legal principle underlying such a relinquishment of jurisdiction. Cf. COMITY.

Burford abstention. A federal court's refusal to review a state court's decision in cases involving a complex regulatory scheme and sensitive areas of state concern. *Burford v. Sun Oil Co.,* 319 U.S. 315 (1943).

Colorado River abstention. A federal court's decision to abstain while there are relevant and parallel state-court proceedings under way. *Colorado River Water Conservation Dist. v. United States,* 424 U.S. 800 (1976).

Pullman abstention. A federal court's decision to abstain in order to give the state courts an opportunity to settle an underlying state-law question whose resolution may avert the need to decide a federal constitutional question. *Railroad Comm'n v. Pullman Co.,* 312 U.S. 496 (1941).

Thibodaux abstention (**tib**-ə-doh). A federal court's decision to abstain in order to allow state courts to decide difficult issues of public importance that, if decided by the federal court, could result in unnecessary friction between state and federal authorities. *Louisiana Power & Light Co. v. City of Thibodaux*, 360 U.S. 25 (1959).

Younger abstention. **a.** A federal court's decision not to interfere with an ongoing state criminal proceeding by issuing an injunction or granting declaratory relief, unless the prosecution has been brought in bad faith or merely as harassment. *Younger v. Harris*, 401 U.S. 37 (1971). **b.** By extension, a federal court's decision not to interfere with a state-court civil proceeding used to enforce the criminal law, as to abate an obscene nuisance. See OUR FEDERALISM.

abstraction, *n.* **1.** The act of taking with the intent to injure or defraud <the abstraction of funds was made possible by the forged signature on the check>. **2.** The mental process of considering something without reference to a concrete instance <she briefly had the abstraction of giving a beggar all her money>. **3.** A theoretical idea not applied to any particular instance <an abstraction of utopia>. **4.** The act of summarizing and recording <abstraction of the judgment in Tarrant County>. —**abstract,** *vb.*—**abstractor,** *n.*

abstract of judgment. A copy or summary of a judgment that, when filed with the appropriate public office, creates a lien on the judgment debtor's nonexempt property. See *judgment lien* under LIEN.

abstract of record. An abbreviated case history that is complete enough to show an appellate court that the questions presented for review have been preserved.

abstract of title. A concise statement, usu. prepared for a mortgagee or purchaser of real property, summarizing the history of a piece of land, including all conveyances, interests, liens, and encumbrances that affect title to the property. —Also termed *brief.*

abuse, *n.* **1.** A departure from legal or reasonable use; misuse. **2.** Physical or mental maltreatment. — **abuse,** *vb.*

child abuse. An intentional or neglectful physical or emotional injury imposed on a child, including sexual molestation. See BATTERED-CHILD SYNDROME.

sexual abuse. An illegal sex act, esp. one performed against a minor by an adult. —Also termed *carnal abuse.*

spousal abuse. Physical, sexual, or psychological abuse inflicted by one spouse on the other spouse. See BATTERED-WOMAN SYNDROME.

abuse of discovery. DISCOVERY ABUSE.

abuse of discretion. 1. An adjudicator's failure to exercise sound, reasonable, and legal decision-making. **2.** An appellate court's standard for reviewing a decision that is asserted to be grossly unsound, unreasonable, or illegal. See DISCRETION.

abuse of process. MALICIOUS ABUSE OF PROCESS.

abut, *vb.* To join at a border or boundary; to share a common boundary with <the company's land in Arizona abuts the Navajo Indian reservation>. —**abutment,** *n.*

accede, *vb.* To consent or agree. — **accession,** *n.*—**accedence,** *n.*

accelerated cost-recovery system. A method of depreciation allowed for property placed in service from 1981 to 1986, whereby the cost of a fixed asset is written off for tax purposes over a prescribed period and for a fixed percentage each year; for property placed in service after 1986, the modified accelerated cost-recovery system applies. I.R.C. § 168. —Abbr. ACRS. Cf. MODIFIED ACCELERATED COST-RECOVERY SYSTEM.

accelerated-depreciation method. See DEPRECIATION METHOD.

acceleration, *n.* **1.** The shortening of the time for vesting in possession of an expectant interest. **2.** In property law, the hastening of an owner's time for enjoyment of an estate due to the failure of a preceding estate. **3.** In securities law, the SEC's expediting of a registration statement's effective date, thus bypassing the required 20-day waiting period. —**accelerate,** *vb.*

acceleration clause. A loan-agreement provision that requires the debtor to pay off the balance sooner than the regular payment date if some specified event occurs, such as failure to timely pay installments or to maintain insurance. Cf. INSECURITY CLAUSE.

acceptance, *n.* **1.** An agreement, either by express act or implied from conduct, to the terms of an offer so that a binding contract is formed; if an acceptance modifies the terms or adds new ones, it generally operates as a counteroffer. **2.** The formal receipt of and agreement to pay a negotiable instrument. **3.** A negotiable instrument, esp. a bill of exchange, that has been accepted for payment. —**accept,** *vb.*

banker's acceptance. A bill of exchange drawn on and accepted by a commercial bank; banker's acceptances are often issued to finance the sale of goods in international trade. —Abbr. BA. —Also termed *bank acceptance.*

trade acceptance. A bill of exchange for the amount of a specific purchase, drawn on and accepted by the buyer for payment at a specified time.

acceptor. A person or entity who accepts a negotiable instrument and engages to be primarily responsible for its payment or performance.

access, *n.* An opportunity or ability to enter, approach, pass to and from, or communicate with. —**access,** *vb.*

multiple access. In a paternity suit, the defense that the mother had lovers other than the defendant around the time of conception.

access easement. See EASEMENT.

accession. 1. The act of acceding or agreeing <the family's accession to the kidnapper's demands>. **2.** A coming into possession of a right or office <as promised, the state's budget was balanced within two years after the governor's accession>. **3.** In international law, the process by which a nation becomes a party to a treaty that has already been agreed on by other nations <Italy became a party to the nuclear-arms treaty by accession>. —Also termed *adherence*; *adhesion*. **4.** The acquisition of title to personal property by bestowing labor on a raw material to convert it to another thing <the owner's accession to the lumber produced from his land>. **5.** A property owner's right to all that is added to the land, naturally or by labor, including land left by floods and improvements made by others <the newly poured concrete driveway became the homeowner's property by accession>. Cf. ANNEXATION.

accessory, *n.* **1.** Something of secondary or subordinate importance. **2.** A person who aids or contributes in the commission of a crime; an accessory is usu. liable only if the crime is a felony. —**accessory,** *adj.* Cf. PRINCIPAL (2).

accessory after the fact. An accessory who knows that a crime has been committed and who helps the offender try to escape arrest or punishment; the liability of such an accessory is still treated separately under most penal statutes.

accessory at the fact. See *principal in the second degree* under PRINCIPAL (2).

accessory before the fact. An accessory who assists or encourages another to commit a crime but who is not present when the offense is actually committed; most jurisdictions have abolished this category of accessory and instead treat such an offender as an accomplice. See ACCOMPLICE.

accessory obligation. See OBLIGATION.

accessory use. See USE (1).

access to counsel. RIGHT TO COUNSEL.

accidental-death benefit. An insurance-policy provision that allows for a payment (often double the face amount of the policy) if the insured dies as a result of some mishap or sudden external force. —Abbr. ADB.

accidental killing. Homicide resulting from a lawful act performed in a lawful manner under a reasonable belief that no harm is possible. — Also termed *death by misadventure*; *homicide by misadventure*; *killing by misadventure*. See *justifiable homicide* under HOMICIDE. Cf. *involuntary manslaughter* under MANSLAUGHTER.

accident insurance. See INSURANCE.

accommodated party. See ACCOMMODATION PARTY.

accommodation, *n.* **1.** A loan or other financial favor. **2.** The act of signing an accommodation paper as surety for another. See ACCOMMODATION PAPER.

accommodation loan. See LOAN.

accommodation paper. A negotiable instrument that one party co-signs, without receiving any consideration in return, in order to act as surety for another party who remains primarily liable; such an instrument is typically used when the cosigner is more creditworthy than the principal debtor. —Also termed *accommodation bill*; *accommodation note*.

accommodation party. A person who signs a negotiable instrument for the purpose of being a surety for another party (called the *accommodated party*) to the instrument; the accommodation party can sign in any capacity (i.e., as maker, drawer, acceptor, or indorser) <the father served as an accommodation party by cosigning the bank note with his daughter>. See SURETY.

accomplice. A person who knowingly, voluntarily, and intentionally unites with the principal offender in committing a crime and thereby becomes punishable for it. See ACCESSORY. Cf. PRINCIPAL (2).

accord, *n.* **1.** An amicable arrangement between parties, esp. between peoples or nations; COMPACT; TREATY. **2.** An agreement under which an obligee promises to accept a stated performance in satisfaction of the obligor's existing duty. —Also termed (in sense 2) *executory accord*; *accord executory*.

accord, *vb.* **1.** To furnish or grant, esp. what is suitable or proper <accord the litigants a stay of costs pending appeal>. **2.** To agree <they accord in their opinions>.

accord and satisfaction. An agreement, usu. in contractual contexts, to substitute for an existing debt some alternative form of discharging that debt, coupled with the actual discharge of the debt by the substituted performance; the new agreement is called the *accord*, and the discharge is called the *satisfaction*. Cf. NOVATION; SETTLEMENT.

account, *n.* **1.** A detailed statement of the debits and credits between parties to a contract or to a fiduciary relationship; a reckoning of monetary dealings <the trustee balanced the account at the end of each month>. **2.** A course of business dealings or other relations for which records must be kept <open a brokerage account>.

account payable. (*usu. pl.*) An account reflecting a balance owed to a creditor; a debt owed by an enterprise in the normal course of business dealing. —Often shortened to *payable*. Pl. *accounts payable*.

account receivable. (*usu. pl.*) An account reflecting a balance owed by a debtor; a debt owed by a customer to an enterprise for goods or services. —Often shortened to *receivable*. Pl. *accounts receivable*.

account rendered. An account produced by the creditor and presented for the debtor's examination and acceptance.

account settled. An account with a paid balance.

account stated. **a.** A balance that parties to a transaction or settlement agree on, either expressly or by implication; the phrase also refers to the agreement itself or to the assent giving rise to the agreement. **b.** A plaintiff's claim in a suit for such a balance. **c.** *Archaic.* In equity, a defendant's plea in response to an action for an accounting; the defendant states that the balance due on the statement of the account has been discharged and that the defendant holds the plaintiff's release. —Also termed *stated account*.

assigned account. A pledge of an account receivable to a bank or factor as security for a loan.

book account. A detailed statement of debits and credits that give a history of the business transactions of an enterprise.

capital account. An account on a partnership's balance sheet representing a partner's share of the partnership capital.

closed account. An account that no further credits and debits may be added to, but that remains open for adjustment or setoff.

contra account. An account that serves to reduce the gross valuation of an asset.

escrow account. **a.** A bank account, generally held in the name of the depositor and an escrow agent, that is returnable to the depositor or paid to a third person on the fulfillment of an escrow condition. See ESCROW. **b.** See *impound account*.

impound account. An account of accumulated funds held by a lender for payment of taxes, insurance, or other periodic debts against real property. —Also termed *escrow*; *escrow account*; *reserve account*. See ESCROW.

margin account. In securities transactions, a brokerage account that allows an investor to buy or sell securities on credit, with the securities serving as collateral for the broker's loan.

open account. **a.** An unpaid or unsettled account. **b.** An account that is left open for ongoing debit and credit entries and that has a fluctuating balance until either party finds it convenient to settle and close, at which time there is a single liability.

pledged account. A mortgagor's account pledged to a lender in return for a loan bearing interest at a below-market rate.

running account. An open, unsettled account that exhibits the reciprocal demands between the parties.

3. ACCOUNTING (3) <the principal filed an action for account against his agent>. **4.** ACCOUNTING (4) <the contractor filed an action for account against the nonpaying customer>. **5.** A statement by which someone seeks to explain an event <Fred's account of the holdup differed significantly from Martha's>.

accountable, *adj.* Responsible; answerable. —**accountability,** *n.* See LIABILITY.

accountant. A person whose business is to keep books or accounts, to perform financial audits, to design and control accounting systems, and to give tax advice.

certified public accountant. An accountant who has satisfied the statutory and administrative requirements to be registered or licensed as a public accountant. —Abbr. CPA.

accountant-client privilege. See PRIVILEGE.

accounting. 1. An act or system of making up or settling accounts. **2.** A rendition of an account, either voluntarily or by court order. **3.** A legal action commenced by one who has given another money or other property to be applied in a particular way, the action being designed to compel the recipient to provide details of the debts owed to the plaintiff. —Also termed *account render*; *account.* **4.** More broadly, an action for the recovery of money for services performed, property sold and delivered, money loaned, or damages for the nonperformance of simple contracts; such an action is available when the rights of parties will be adequately protected by the payment of money. —Also termed *action on account*; *account.* **5.** In partnership law, an equitable proceeding for a complete settlement of all partnership affairs, usu. in connection with a winding up. See WINDING UP.

accounting for profits. An action for equitable relief against a person in a fiduciary relationship to recover profits taken in a breach of the relationship.

accounting method. A method for determining income and expenses for tax purposes.

accrual accounting method. An accounting method that records entries of debits and credits when the liability arises, not when the income or expense is received or disbursed.

capitalization accounting method. A method of determining an asset's present value by discounting its stream of expected future benefits at an appropriate rate.

cash-basis accounting method. The accounting system that considers only cash actually received as income, and only cash actually paid out as an expense.

completed-contract accounting method. A method of reporting profit or loss on certain long-term contracts by recognizing gross income and expenses in the tax year that the contract is completed.

cost accounting method. The practice of recording the value of assets in terms of their cost. —Also termed *cost accounting.*

direct charge-off accounting method. A system of accounting for bad debts allowing for a deduction when an account becomes partially or completely worthless.

equity accounting method. A method of accounting for long-term investment in common stock based on acquisition cost, investor income, net losses, and dividends.

fair-value accounting method. The valuation of assets at present actual or market value.

installment accounting method. A method by which a taxpayer can spread the recognition of gains from a sale of property over the payment period by computing the gross-profit percentage from the sale and applying it to each payment.

physical-inventory accounting method. A method of counting a company's goods at the close of an accounting period.

accounting period. A regular period of time used for accounting purposes; esp., a period used by a taxpayer in determining income and related tax liability.

account in trust. An account established by an individual to hold the account's assets in trust for someone else.

account payable. See ACCOUNT.

account receivable. See ACCOUNT.

account render. ACCOUNTING (3).

account stated. See ACCOUNT.

accredit, *vb.* **1.** To give official authorization or status to. **2.** To recognize (a school) as having sufficient academic standards to qualify graduates for higher education or for professional practice. **3.** In international law, to send (a person) with credentials as an envoy. —**accreditation,** *n.*

accredited investor. In a private securities offering, a knowledgeable and sophisticated person or institution not requiring the protection afforded by the disclosure provisions of the Securities Act of 1933 <the court declared the plaintiff, a wealthy business-school graduate, to be an accredited investor and dismissed the lawsuit against the stockbroker>.

accredited law school. See LAW SCHOOL.

accredited representative. See REPRESENTATIVE.

accretion (ə-**kree**-shən). **1.** The gradual accumulation of land by natural forces, esp. as alluvium is added to land situated on the bank of a river or on the seashore. Cf. ALLUVION; AVULSION (2). **2.** In civil law, the right of heirs or legatees to unite their shares of the estate with the portion of any coheirs or legatees who do not accept their portion, fail to comply with a condition, or die before the testator. **3.** Any increase in trust property other than increases ordinarily considered as income.

accroach, *vb.* To exercise power without authority; to usurp. —**accroachment,** *n.*

accrocher un procès (a-kroh-**shay**-ən-proh-**say**). [French] To stay the proceedings in a suit.

accrual, clause of. See CLAUSE OF ACCRUAL.

accrual accounting method. See ACCOUNTING METHOD.

accrue, *vb.* **1.** To come into existence as an enforceable claim; to arise <the plaintiff's cause of action for silicosis did not accrue until the plaintiff knew or had reason to know of the disease>. **2.** To accumulate periodically <the savings-account interest accrues on a monthly basis>. —**accrual,** *n.*

accrued compensation. See COMPENSATION.

accrued expense. See EXPENSE.

accrued income. See INCOME.

accrued interest. See INTEREST (3).

accruer. See CLAUSE OF ACCRUAL.

accumulated-earnings tax. See TAX.

accumulations, rule against. A rule rendering void any accumulation of income beyond the period of perpetuities.

accumulative judgment. See JUDGMENT.

accumulative legacy. See LEGACY.

accusation, *n.* **1.** A formal charge of criminal wrongdoing; the accusation is usu. presented to a court or magistrate having jurisdiction to inquire into the alleged crime. **2.** An informal statement that a person has engaged in an illegal or immoral act. —**accuse,** *vb.*—**accusatory,** *adj.*

accusatorial system. ADVERSARY SYSTEM.

accusatory body. A body, such as a grand jury, charged with the duty to hear evidence and determine whether a person should be charged with a crime.

accusatory instrument. CHARGING INSTRUMENT.

accusatory pleading. See PLEADING (1).

accusatory procedure. ADVERSARY SYSTEM.

accusatory stage. The point in a criminal proceeding when the suspect's right to counsel attaches; this occurs usu. after arrest and once interrogation begins.

accused, *n.* A person whom someone has blamed of wrongdoing <many people believed that the accused was incapable of committing such a brutal act>.

accusing jury. GRAND JURY.

acid-test ratio. QUICK-ASSET RATIO.

acknowledgment. 1. A formal declaration made in the presence of an authorized officer, such as a notary public, by someone who signs a document and says that the signature is authentic; in most states, the officer certifies that (1) he or she personally knows the document signer or has established the signer's identity through satisfactory evidence, (2) the signer appeared before the officer on the date and in the place (usu. the county) indicated, and (3) the signer acknowledged signing the document freely. Cf. VERIFICATION (1). **2.** The officer's certificate that is affixed to the document. —Also termed (in sense 2) *certificate of acknowledgment* and (loosely) *verification.*

proof of acknowledgment. An authorized officer's certification—based on a third party's testimony—that the signature of a person (who usu. does not appear before the notary) is genuine and was freely made. —Also termed *certificate of proof.*

ACLU. *abbr.* AMERICAN CIVIL LIBERTIES UNION.

acquets (ə-**kwets**). In civil law, property acquired by purchase, gift, or any way other than succession; profits or gains of property between husband and wife. —Also termed *acquest.* See COMMUNITY PROPERTY.

acquiesce (ak-wee-**es**), *vb.* To accept tacitly or passively; to give implied consent to (an act) <in the end, all the partners acquiesced in the settlement>. —**acquiescence,** *n.*—**acquiescent,** *adj.*

acquired right. See RIGHT.

acquired surplus. See SURPLUS.

acquisition, *n.* **1.** The act of gaining possession or control of something. **2.** The thing acquired. —**acquire,** *vb.*

acquittal, *n.* **1.** In criminal law, the legal certification, usu. by jury verdict, that an accused person is not guilty of the charged offense. **2.** In contract law, a release or discharge from debt or other liability; ACQUITTANCE. —**acquit**, *vb.*

acquittance, *n.* A document by which one is discharged from a debt or other obligation; a receipt or release indicating payment in full. —**acquit**, *vb.*

acre. An area of land measuring 43,-560 square feet.

ACRS. *abbr.* ACCELERATED COST-RECOVERY SYSTEM.

act, *n.* **1.** Something done or performed, esp. voluntarily; a deed. **2.** The process of doing or performing; ACTION (1). **3.** The formal product of a legislature or other deliberative body; esp., STATUTE.

actio (**ak**-tee-oh *or* -shee-). [Latin] Action; a right or claim; a lawsuit.

action. **1.** The process of doing something; conduct or behavior. **2.** The thing done; ACT (1). **3.** A civil or criminal judicial proceeding.

action in equity. An action that seeks equitable relief, such as an injunction or specific performance, as opposed to damages.

action in personam. An action determining the rights and interests of the parties themselves in the subject matter of the case. —Also termed *personal action.* See IN PERSONAM.

action in rem. An action determining the title to property and the rights of the parties, not merely among themselves, but also against all persons at any time claiming an interest in that property. See IN REM.

action on account. ACCOUNTING (4).

action on the case. TRESPASS ON THE CASE.

action quasi in rem. An action brought against the defendant personally, with jurisdiction based on an interest in property, the objective being to deal with the particular property or to subject the property to the discharge of the claims asserted. See *quasi in rem* under IN REM.

action to quiet title. A proceeding to establish a plaintiff's title to land by compelling the adverse claimant to establish a claim or be forever estopped from asserting it. —Also termed *quiet-title action.*

amicable action. See *test case* (a) under CASE.

civil action. An action brought to enforce, redress, or protect a private or civil right; a noncriminal litigation.

class action. See CLASS ACTION.

collusive action. An action between two parties who have no actual controversy, being merely for the purpose of determining a legal question or receiving a precedent that might prove favorable in related litigation.

criminal action. An action instituted by the government to punish offenses against the public.

derivative action. See DERIVATIVE ACTION.

direct action. See DIRECT ACTION.

local action. An action that can be brought only in the jurisdiction where the cause of action arose, as when the action's subject matter is a piece of real property.

matrimonial action. An action relating to the state of marriage, such as an action for separation, annulment, or divorce.

nonpersonal action. An action that proceeds within some category of territorial jurisdiction other than in personam—i.e., jurisdiction in rem, quasi in rem, or over status.

penal action. **a.** A criminal prosecution. **b.** A civil lawsuit by an aggrieved party seeking recovery of a statutory fine or a penalty, such as punitive damages.

personal action. **a.** An action brought for the recovery of debts, personal property, or damages arising from any cause. **b.** See *action in personam.*

petitory action (**ped**-i-tor-ee). An action to establish and enforce title to property independent of the right to possession.

plenary action (**plee**-nə-ree *or* **ple**-). A full hearing or trial on the merits, as opposed to a summary proceeding. Cf. *summary proceeding* under PROCEEDING.

possessory action. An action to obtain, recover, or maintain possession of property but not title to it, such as an action to evict a non-paying tenant.

real action. An action brought for the recovery of land or other real property.

representative action. **a.** CLASS ACTION. **b.** DERIVATIVE ACTION (1).

separate action. An action brought alone by each of several complainants who are all concerned in the same transaction but cannot legally join the suit.

test action. See *test case* (b) under CASE.

third-party action. An action distinct from the main claim, whereby the defendant brings in an entity that is not directly involved in the lawsuit but that may be liable to the defendant for all or part of the plaintiff's claim; a common example is an action for indemnity or contribution.

transitory action. An action that can be brought in any jurisdiction where the defendant can be personally served with process.

action, cause of. See CAUSE OF ACTION.

action, form of. See FORM OF ACTION.

action, right of. See RIGHT OF ACTION.

actionable, *adj.* Furnishing the legal ground for a lawsuit or other legal action <intentional interference with contractual relations is an actionable tort>.

active concealment. See CONCEALMENT.

active euthanasia. See EUTHANASIA.

active trust. See TRUST.

active waste. See *commissive waste* under WASTE.

act of God. An overwhelming event caused exclusively by forces of nature, without the possibility of prevention and without intervention by any human agency; examples are earthquakes, floods, and tornadoes. —Also termed *act of nature*; *act of providence*. Cf. FORCE MAJEURE.

act-of-state doctrine. The common-law principle that prevents U.S. courts from questioning the validity of a foreign country's sovereign acts within its own territory.

actual authority. See AUTHORITY.

actual bailment. See BAILMENT.

actual cash value. FAIR MARKET VALUE.

actual cause. See *but-for cause* under CAUSE (1).

actual damages. See DAMAGES.

actual delivery. See DELIVERY.

actual eviction. See EVICTION.

actual fraud. See FRAUD.

actual knowledge. See KNOWLEDGE.

actual loss. See LOSS.

actual malice. See MALICE.

actual market value. FAIR MARKET VALUE.

actual notice. See NOTICE.

actual possession. See POSSESSION.

actual seisin. See *seisin in deed* under SEISIN.

actual service. See *personal service* under SERVICE.

actual value. FAIR MARKET VALUE.

actuarial table. The organized statistical data indicating life expectancies; this type of table is usu. admissible in evidence. —Also termed *expectancy table*; *mortality table*. Cf. LIFE TABLE.

actuary, *n.* A statistician who determines the present effects of future contingent events, esp. one who calculates insurance and pension rates on the basis of experience tables. — **actuarial,** *adj.*

actus reus (**ak**-təs-**ray**-əs *or* -ree-). [Law Latin "guilty act"] The wrongful deed that comprises the physical components of a crime and that generally must be coupled with *mens rea* to establish criminal liability <the *actus reus* for theft is the taking or unlawful control over property without the owner's consent>. Cf. MENS REA.

A.D. *abbr.* ANNO DOMINI.

ADA. *abbr.* AMERICANS WITH DISABILITIES ACT.

adaptation right. A copyright holder's exclusive right to prepare derivative works based on the protected work; for example, before a movie studio can make a film version of a book it must secure the author's adaptation right. See DERIVATIVE WORK.

ADB. *abbr.* ACCIDENTAL-DEATH BENEFIT.

ad damnum **clause** (a[d]-**dam**-nəm). [Latin "to the damage"] A clause in a prayer for relief stating the amount of damages claimed. See PRAYER FOR RELIEF.

addendum. Something added, esp. to a document; a supplement.

addict (a-dikt), *n.* A person who habitually uses a substance, esp. narcotic drug. —**addict** (ə-dikt), *vb.*— **addictive,** *adj.*—**addiction,** *n.*

addictive drug. See DRUG.

ad diem (a[d]-**dee**-əm *or* -**dI**-). [Latin] At the day; at a day.

additional instruction. See JURY INSTRUCTION.

additional insured. See INSURED.

additional legacy. See LEGACY.

additional standard deduction. See DEDUCTION.

additur (a-di-tər). [Latin "it is added to"] A trial-court order, issued usu. with the defendant's consent, that increases the damages awarded by the jury to avoid a new trial on grounds of inadequate damages; the term may also refer to the increase itself, the procedure, or the court's power to make the order. —Also termed *increscitur*. Cf. REMITTITUR.

adduce, *vb.* To offer or put forward for consideration (something) as evidence or authority <adduce the engineer's expert testimony>. —**adduction,** *n.* —**adducible,** *adj.*

ademption, *n.* A testator's revocation of a bequest or legacy by disposing of the gift before the will takes effect (that is, before death). —**adeem,** *vb.* Cf. ADVANCEMENT; LAPSE (2).

adequacy test. IRREPARABLE-INJURY RULE.

adequate care. See *reasonable care* under CARE.

adequate compensation. See *just compensation* under COMPENSATION.

adequate protection. In bankruptcy law, the protection afforded to a holder of a secured claim against the debtor, such as a periodic cash payment or an additional lien <the bankruptcy court permitted the lender to foreclose on the debtor's home after finding a lack of adequate protection of the lender's property interest>. 11 U.S.C. § 361.

adequate-state-grounds doctrine. A judge-made principle that prevents the Supreme Court from reviewing a state-court decision based partially on state law if a decision on a federal issue would not change the result.

adherence. ACCESSION (3).

adhesion. ACCESSION (3).

adhesion contract. See CONTRACT.

adhesionary contract. See *adhesion contract* under CONTRACT.

adhesory contract. See *adhesion contract* under CONTRACT.

ad hoc (ad-**hok**), *adj.* [Latin "for this"] Formed for a particular purpose <the board formed an ad hoc committee to discuss funding for the new arena>—**ad hoc,** *adv.*

ad hominem (ad-**hom**-ə-nəm), *adj.* [Latin "to the person"] Appealing to personal prejudices rather than to reason; attacking an opponent's character rather than the opponent's assertions <the brief was replete with *ad hominem* attacks against opposing counsel>. —**ad hominem,** *adv.*

ad idem (ad-**I**-dəm). [Latin] To the same point or matter; of the same mind <the parties reached a consensus *ad idem* and agreed to consummate a sale>.

ad infinitum (ad-in-fə-**nIt**-əm). [Latin "without limit"] To an indefinite extent <a corporation has a duration *ad infinitum* unless the arti-

cles of incorporation specify a shorter period>.

adjacent, *adj.* Lying near or close to, but not necessarily touching. Cf. ADJOINING.

adjective law. PROCEDURAL LAW.

adjoining, *adj.* Touching; sharing a common boundary; CONTIGUOUS. —**adjoin,** *vb.* Cf. ADJACENT.

adjourn (ə-jərn), *vb.* To recess or postpone. —**adjournment,** *n.*

adjourn sine die (sI-nee-**dI**[-ee] *or* si-nay-**dee**-ay). [Latin "without day"] To postpone action of a convened court or legislative body until another time specified, or indefinitely.

adjourned summons. See SUMMONS.

adjudication (ə-joo-di-**kay**-shən), *n.* **1.** The legal process of resolving a dispute; the process of judicially deciding a case. **2.** JUDGMENT. —**adjudicate,** *vb.*—**adjudicative, adjudicatory,** *adj.*—**adjudicator,** *n.*

adjudicative fact. See FACT.

adjudicatory hearing. In administrative law, an agency proceeding in which the rights and duties of a particular person are decided after notice and opportunity to be heard. —Also termed *adjudicatory proceeding.*

adjunct (**a**-jung[k]t), *adj.* Added as an accompanying object or circumstance; attached in a subordinate or temporary capacity <an adjunct professor>. —**adjunct,** *n.*

adjure (ə-**juur**), *vb.* To charge or entreat solemnly <the President adjured the foreign government to join the alliance>. —**adjuration,** *n.*—**ad-**

juratory, *adj.*—**adjurer, adjuror,** *n.*

adjustable-rate mortgage. See MORTGAGE.

adjusted basis. See BASIS.

adjusted gross income. See INCOME.

adjusted present value. See PRESENT VALUE.

adjuster. One appointed to ascertain, arrange, or settle a matter; esp., an independent agent or employee of an insurance company who negotiates and settles claims against the insurer. —Also termed *claims adjuster.*

adjusting entry. An accounting entry made at the end of an accounting period to record previously unrecognized revenue and expenses, as well as changes in assets and liabilities.

adjustment board. An administrative agency charged with the duty to hear and determine zoning appeals. —Also termed *board of zoning appeals.*

adjustment bond. See BOND (1).

adjustment security. See SECURITY.

adjutant general (a-jə-tənt), *n.* (*usu. cap.*) **1.** The administrative head of a military unit having a general staff. **2.** An officer in charge of the National Guard of a state.

ad litem (ad-**lI**-təm). [Latin "for the suit"] For the purposes of the suit; pending the suit. See GUARDIAN AD LITEM.

admeasurement, *n.* Ascertainment, assignment, or apportionment by a fixed quantity or value, or by certain limits <the ship's admeasurement is based on its crew, engine, and capacity>. —**admeasure,** *vb.*

administration, *n.* **1.** The management or performance of the executive duties of a government, institution, or business. **2.** In public law, the practical management and direction of the executive department and its agencies. **3.** The management and settlement of the estate of an intestate decedent, or of a testator who has no executor, by a person legally appointed and supervised by the court. —**administer,** *vb.*—**administrative,** *adj.*—**administrator,** *n.*

administration cum testamento annexo (kəm-tes-tə-**men**-toh-ə-**nek**-soh). [Latin "with the will annexed"] An administration granted when a testator's will does not name any executor or when the executor named is incompetent to act, is deceased, or refuses to act. —Abbr. c.t.a.

administration de bonis non (dee-**boh**-nəs-**non**). [Latin "of the goods not administered"] An administration granted for the purpose of settling the remainder of an estate that was not administered by the former executor or administrator. —Abbr. d.b.n.

ancillary administration. An administration that is auxiliary to the administration at the place of the decedent's domicile, such as one in a foreign state, the purpose being to collect assets and pay debts in that locality.

domiciliary administration. The handling of an estate in the state where the decedent was domiciled at death.

pendente lite administration (pen-**den**-tee-**lI**-tee). An administration granted during the pendency of a suit concerning a will's validity. See PENDENTE LITE.

public administration. In some jurisdictions, an administration by an officer appointed to administer for an intestate who has left no person entitled to apply for letters (or whose possible representatives refuse to serve).

special administration. An administration with authority to deal with only some of a decedent's effects, as opposed to administering the whole estate.

administrative adjudication. The process used by an administrative agency to issue regulations through an adversary proceeding. Cf. RULE-MAKING.

administrative agency. AGENCY (3).

administrative hearing. An administrative-agency proceeding in which evidence is offered for argument or trial.

administrative law. The law governing the organization and operation of the executive branch of government (including independent agencies) and the relations of the executive with the legislature, the judiciary, and the public.

administrative-law judge. A person who presides at an administrative hearing, with the power to administer oaths, take testimony, rule on questions of evidence, and make agency determinations of fact. 5 U.S.C. § 556(c). —Abbr. ALJ. —Also termed *hearing examiner; hearing officer.*

administrative remedy. See REMEDY.

administrative rulemaking. See RULEMAKING.

administrator. 1. A person appointed by the court to manage the assets and liabilities of an intestate decedent. Cf. EXECUTOR (2). **2.** One who manages a business, public office, or agency.

administrator's deed. See DEED.

admiralty, *n.* **1.** A court that exercises jurisdiction over all maritime contracts, torts, injuries, or offenses; the federal courts are so called when exercising their admiralty jurisdiction, which is conferred by U.S. Const. art. III, § 2. —Also termed *admiralty court; maritime court.* **2.** The system of jurisprudence that has grown out of the practice of admiralty courts; MARITIME LAW. —Also termed (in sense 2) *admiralty law.* — **admiralty,** *adj.*

admiralty law. MARITIME LAW.

admissible, *adj.* **1.** Allowable; permissible <admissible evidence>. **2.** Worthy of gaining entry or being admitted <a person is admissible to the bar upon obtaining a law degree and passing the bar exam>. —**admissibility,** *n.*

admissible evidence. See EVIDENCE.

admission, *n.* A voluntary acknowledgment of the existence of facts relevant to an adversary's case. —**admit,** *vb.* Cf. CONFESSION.

admission against interest. See *declaration against interest* under DECLARATION (6).

admission by employee or agent. An admission made by a party-opponent's agent during employment and concerning a matter either within the scope of the agency or authorized by the party-opponent.

admission by silence. The failure of a party to speak after an assertion of fact by another party that, if untrue, would naturally compel a person to deny the statement.

adoptive admission. An action by a party that indicates approval of a statement made by another, and thereby acceptance of the truth of the statement.

extrajudicial admission. An admission made outside of court.

implied admission. An admission reasonably inferable from a party's action or statement, or a party's failure to act or speak. —Also termed *tacit admission.*

incidental admission. An admission made in some other connection, or involved in the admission of some other fact.

judicial admission. A formal waiver of proof that relieves an opposing party from having to prove the admitted fact and bars the party who made the admission from disputing it.

quasi-admission. An act or utterance, usu. extrajudicial, that creates an inconsistency with and discredits, to a greater or lesser degree, a present claim or other evidence of the person creating the inconsistency.

admonition, *n.* **1.** Any authoritative advice or cautions from the court to the jury regarding their duty as jurors or the admissibility of evidence for consideration <the judge's admonition that the jurors not discuss the case until they are charged>. **2.** A reprimand or cautionary statement addressed to counsel by a judge <the judge's admonition that the lawyer stop speaking out of turn>. —**admonish,** *vb.* —**admonitory,** *adj.*

adoption, *n.* **1.** In family law, the statutory process of terminating a child's legal rights and duties toward the natural parents and substituting similar rights and duties toward adoptive parents.

adoption by estoppel. An equitable adoption of a child by a person's promises and acts that preclude the person and his or her estate from denying adopted status to the child. —Also termed *equitable adoption*; *virtual adoption*.

2. In contract law, the process by which a person agrees to assume a contract that was previously made for that person's benefit, such as a newly formed corporation's acceptance of a preincorporation contract. —**adopt,** *vb.* —**adoptive,** *adj.*

adoptive admission. See ADMISSION.

ADR. *abbr.* **1.** ALTERNATIVE DISPUTE RESOLUTION. **2.** ASSET-DEPRECIATION RANGE. **3.** AMERICAN DEPOSITORY RECEIPT.

ad respondendum (ad-rə-spon-**den**-dəm). [Latin] To answer. See *capias ad respondendum* under CAPIAS; *ha-*

beas corpus ad respondendum under HABEAS CORPUS.

ad satisfaciendum (ad-sat-əs-fay-shee-**en**-dəm). [Latin] To satisfy. See *capias ad satisfaciendum* under CAPIAS.

ad testificandum (ad-tes-tə-fə-**kan**-dəm). [Latin] To testify. See *habeas corpus ad testificandum* under HABEAS CORPUS; SUBPOENA.

adult (ə-dult), *n.* A person who has attained the legal age of majority, generally 18 years of age. —Also termed *major.* —**adult,** *adj.*

adult correctional institution. PRISON.

adultery, *n.* Voluntary sexual intercourse between a married person and a person other than the offender's spouse. —**adulterous,** *adj.* Cf. FORNICATION.

adult offender. See OFFENDER.

ad valorem (ad-və-**lor**-əm), *adj.* [Latin "according to the value"] (Of a tax) proportional to the value of the thing taxed. —*ad valorem,* *adv.*

ad valorem tax. See TAX.

advance directive. 1. A durable power of attorney that takes effect upon one's incompetency and designates a surrogate decision-maker for healthcare matters. See POWER OF ATTORNEY. **2.** A legal document explaining one's wishes as to medical treatment if one becomes incompetent or unable to communicate. —Also termed *medical directive*; *physician's directive*; *written directive*. Cf. LIVING WILL.

advancement, *n.* A payment or gift to an heir (esp. a child) during one's lifetime as an advance share of one's estate, with the intention of extinguishing the heir's claim to the estate under intestacy laws. —**advance,** *vb.*

advance sheets. A softcover pamphlet containing recently reported opinions by a court or set of courts; advance sheets are published during the interim between an opinion's announcement and its inclusion in a bound volume of law reports. Cf. *slip opinion* (a) under OPINION.

adversary, *n.* An opponent; esp., opposing counsel. —**adversary, adversarial,** *adj.*

adversary procedure. ADVERSARY SYSTEM.

adversary proceeding. 1. A hearing involving a dispute between opposing parties <Judge Adams presided over the adversary proceeding between the landlord and tenant>. **2.** In bankruptcy law, a lawsuit that is brought within a bankruptcy proceeding, governed by special procedural rules, and based on conflicting claims usu. between the debtor (or the trustee) and a creditor or other interested party <the Chapter 7 trustee filed an adversary proceeding against the party who received $100,000 from the debtor one week before the bankruptcy filing>.

adversary system. A procedural system, such as the Anglo-American legal system, involving active and unhindered parties contesting with each other to put forth a case before an independent decision-maker. —Also termed *adversary procedure* and (in criminal cases) *accusatorial system* or *accusatory procedure.* Cf. INQUISITORIAL SYSTEM.

adverse easement. See *prescriptive easement* under EASEMENT.

adverse impact. DISPARATE IMPACT.

adverse-inference rule. ADVERSE-INTEREST RULE.

adverse interest. An interest that is opposed or contrary to that of another party.

adverse-interest rule. The principle that if a party fails to produce a witness who is within its power to produce and who should have been produced, the judge may instruct the jury to infer that the witness's evidence is unfavorable to the party's cause. —Also termed *empty-chair doctrine*; *adverse-inference rule.*

adverse possession. A method of acquiring title to real property by possession for a statutory period under certain conditions, such as a nonpermissive use of the land with a claim of right when that use is continuous, exclusive, hostile, open, and notorious. Cf. PRESCRIPTION (1).

adverse witness. See *hostile witness* under WITNESS.

advertising substantiation. A doctrine of the Federal Trade Commission making it an unfair and deceptive act to put out an advertisement unless the advertiser has an advance reasonable basis for believing that each claim in the advertisement is true.

advice of counsel. 1. The guidance given by lawyers to their clients. **2.** In a malicious-prosecution lawsuit, a defense requiring both a complete presentation of facts by the defendant to his or her attorney and honest compliance with the attorney's advice. **3.** A defense in which a party seeks to avoid liability by claiming that he or she acted reasonably and in good faith on the attorney's advice; such a defense usu. requires waiver of the attorney-client privilege, and the attorney cannot have knowingly participated in implementing an illegal plan.

advisement. Careful consideration; deliberation <the judge took the matter under advisement and promised a ruling by the next day>.

advising bank. See BANK.

advisory jury. See JURY.

advisory opinion. See OPINION (1).

advocate (**ad**-və-kət), *n.* **1.** A person who assists, defends, pleads, or prosecutes for another.

public advocate. An advocate who purports to represent the public at large in matters of public concern, such as utility rates or environmental quality.

2. The civil-law equivalent of a barrister, as in Scotland. See BARRISTER. —**advocate** (**ad**-və-kayt), *vb.*— **advocacy,** *n.*

aesthetic functionality. See FUNCTIONALITY.

affects doctrine. In constitutional law, the principle allowing Congress to regulate intrastate activities that have a substantial effect on interstate commerce; so called because the test is whether a given activity "affects" interstate commerce. — Also termed *effects doctrine* or (erroneously) *affectation doctrine*.

affiant (ə-**fī**-ənt). One who makes an affidavit. —Also termed *deponent*.

affidavit. A voluntary declaration of facts written down and sworn to by the declarant before an officer authorized to administer oaths; a great deal of evidence is submitted by affidavit, esp. in pretrial matters such as summary-judgment motions.

affidavit of inquiry. An affidavit, required in certain states before substituted service of process on an absent defendant, in which plaintiff's attorney or a person with knowledge of the facts indicates the defendant cannot be served within the state.

affidavit of notice. An affidavit stating that the declarant has given proper notice of hearing to other parties to the action.

poverty affidavit. An affidavit made by an indigent person seeking public assistance, appointment of counsel, waiver of court fees, or other free public services. —Also termed *pauper's affidavit; in forma pauperis affidavit; IFP affidavit*.

self-proving affidavit. An affidavit attached to a will and signed by witnesses, indicating that the testator was of sound mind and under no duress when signing the will; the effect is to make live testimony or other evidence unnecessary when the will is offered for probate.

affiliate (ə-**fil**-ee-ət), *n.* **1.** A corporation that is related to another corporation by shareholdings or other means of control. **2.** In securities law, one who controls, is controlled by, or is under common control with an issuer of a security. See CONTROL PERSON. —**affiliate** (ə-**fil**-ee-ayt), *vb.*— **affiliation,** *n.*

affiliated director. See *outside director* under DIRECTOR.

affiliated group. A chain of corporations that can elect to file a consolidated tax return because at least 80% of each corporation is owned by others in the group.

affinity. 1. A close agreement. **2.** In family law, the relation one spouse has to the blood relatives of the other spouse; relationship with in-laws.

affirmance, *n.* **1.** A ratification, re-acceptance, or confirmation. **2.** The formal approval by an appellate court of a lower court's judgment, order, or decree. —**affirm,** *vb.*

affirmation, *n.* A pledge equivalent to an oath but without reference to a supreme being or to "swearing"; while an oath is "sworn to," an affirmation is merely "affirmed," but either type of pledge may subject the person making it to the penalties for perjury. —**affirm,** *vb.*—**affirmatory,** *adj.*—**affirmant,** *n.* Cf. OATH.

affirmative action. The positive steps designed to eliminate existing and continuing discrimination, to remedy lingering effects of past discrimination, and to create systems and procedures to prevent future discrimination. See *reverse discrimination* under DISCRIMINATION.

affirmative defense. See DEFENSE (1).

affirmative easement. See EASEMENT.

affirmative relief. See RELIEF.

affirmative warranty. See WARRANTY (3).

affirmative waste. See *commissive waste* under WASTE.

affix (ə-**fiks**), *vb.* To attach, add to, or fasten on permanently. —**affixation,** *n.* See FIXTURE.

AFL-CIO. *abbr.* AMERICAN FEDERATION OF LABOR AND CONGRESS OF INDUSTRIAL ORGANIZATIONS.

aforesaid, *adj. Jargon.* Mentioned above; referred to previously. —Also termed *aforementioned; above-mentioned; above-stated; said.*

aforethought, *adj.* Thought of in advance; deliberate; premeditated <malice aforethought>. See MALICE AFORETHOUGHT.

a fortiori (ah-for-shee-**or**-ee *or* ay-for-shee-**or**-I), *adv.* [Latin] By even greater force of logic; even more so <if a 14-year-old child cannot sign a binding contract, then, *a fortiori*, a 13-year-old cannot>.

after-acquired domicile. See DOMICILE.

after-acquired property. 1. The property of a debtor that is acquired after a security transaction and becomes additional security for payment of the indebtedness. U.C.C. § 9-204. —Also termed *future-acquired property.* **2.** In bankruptcy law, property that the bankruptcy estate acquires after commencement of the case. 11 U.S.C. § 541(a)(7).

after-acquired-property clause. A mortgage provision that makes any subsequently acquired real estate subject to the mortgage.

after-acquired-title doctrine. In property law, the principle that if a person sells property that he or she does not own, but then later acquires title to that property, the title automatically vests in the buyer.

aftermarket. See *secondary market* under MARKET.

AG. *abbr.* ATTORNEY GENERAL.

agency. 1. A fiduciary relationship created by express or implied contract or by law, whereby one party (the *agent*) may act on behalf of another party (the *principal*) and bind that other party by words and actions.

agency by estoppel. An agency created by operation of law and established by a principal's actions that would reasonably lead a third person to the conclusion of an agency's existence.

exclusive agency. The right to represent a principal—esp. either to sell the principal's products or to act as the seller's real-estate agent—within a particular market free from competition. —Also termed *exclusive franchise.*

general agency. A principal's delegation to an agent, without restriction, to take all acts connected with a particular trade, business, or employment.

special agency. An agency in which the agent is authorized only to conduct a single transaction or a series of transactions not involving continuous service.

undisclosed agency. A relationship between an agent and a third party who has no knowledge that the agent is acting on a principal's behalf; the fact that the agency is undisclosed does not prohibit the third party from seeking redress from the principal or the agent.

2. An agent's place of business. **3.** A governmental body charged with implementing and administering particular legislation, such as the Federal Communications Commission. —Also termed (in sense 3) *administrative agency*; *public agency*; *regulatory agency.*

independent agency. A federal agency, commission, or board that is not under the direction of the executive, such as the Federal Trade Commission or the Environmental Protection Agency.

agency regulation. REGULATION (2).

agency shop. A business in which a union acts as an agent for the employees, regardless of their union membership.

agent. 1. One who is authorized to act for or in place of another; a representative <a professional athlete's agent>. Cf. PRINCIPAL (1); EMPLOYEE.

apparent agent. A person who reasonably appears to have authority to act for another, regardless of whether actual authority has been conferred. —Also termed *ostensible agent.*

co-agent. A person who shares with another agent the authority to act for the principal.

del credere agent. An agent who guarantees the solvency of the third party with whom the agent makes a contract for the principal.

foreign agent. A person who registers with the federal government as a lobbyist representing the interests of a foreign nation or corporation.

independent agent. An agent who exercises his or her own judgment and is subject to the principal only for the results of the work performed.

local agent. An agent appointed to act as another's (esp. a company's) representative and to transact business within a specified district.

managing agent. A person who is invested with general power that involves the exercise of judgment and discretion, as opposed to an ordinary agent who acts under the direction and control of the principal.

public agent. A person appointed to act for the public in matters pertaining to governmental administration or public business.

registered agent. A person authorized to accept service of process for another person, esp. a corporation, in a particular jurisdiction. —Also termed *resident agent.*

statutory agent. An agent designated by law to receive litigation documents and other legal notices for a nonresident corporation; in most states, the secretary of state is the statutory agent for such corporations.

stock-transfer agent. An organization that oversees and maintains records of transfers of shares for a publicly held corporation.

subagent. A person appointed by an agent to perform some duty relating to the agency. —Also termed *subservant.*

universal agent. An agent authorized to perform all acts that the principal could personally perform.

2. Something that produces an effect <an intervening agent>. See CAUSE (1).

age of capacity. The age, usu. defined by statute as 18 years, at which a person is legally capable of agreeing to a contract, executing a will, maintaining a lawsuit, or the like. —Also termed *age of majority*; *legal age*; *lawful age.* See CAPACITY.

age of consent. The age, usu. defined by statute as 16 years, at which a person is legally capable of agreeing to marriage (without parental consent) or to sexual intercourse. See CONSENT.

age of majority. 1. The age, usu. defined by statute as 18 years, at which a person attains full legal rights, esp. civil and political rights such as the right to vote. **2.** AGE OF CAPACITY.

age of reason. The age at which a person becomes able to distinguish right from wrong and is thus legally capable of committing a crime or tort; the age of reason varies from jurisdiction to jurisdiction, but 7 years is usu. the age below which a child is conclusively presumed not to have committed a crime or tort, while 14 years is usu. the age below which a rebuttable presumption applies.

aggravated, *adj.* (Of a crime) made worse or more serious by circumstances such as violence, the presence of a deadly weapon, or the intent to commit another crime

<aggravated robbery>. Cf. SIMPLE (1).

aggravated assault. See ASSAULT.

aggravated battery. See BATTERY.

aggravated robbery. See ROBBERY.

aggregate concept. An approach to taxing business organizations whereby the organization is viewed as a collection of its individual owners rather than a separate taxable entity.

aggregate income. See INCOME.

aggregation doctrine. The rule that precludes a party from totaling all claims for purposes of meeting the minimum amount necessary to give rise to federal diversity jurisdiction under the amount-in-controversy requirement. See *diversity jurisdiction* under JURISDICTION; AMOUNT IN CONTROVERSY.

aggrieved party. See PARTY.

agrarian (ə-grer-ee-ən), *adj.* Relating to land, or to a division or distribution of land. —**agrarian,** *n.*

agreed-amount clause. An insurance-policy provision that the insured will carry a stated amount of coverage.

agreed judgment. See JUDGMENT.

agreed statement of facts. See STATEMENT OF FACTS.

agreement. A mutual understanding between two or more persons regarding their relative rights and duties as to past or future performances.

binding agreement. An enforceable contract. See CONTRACT.

agreement of rescission. RESCISSION (2).

Aguilar-Spinelli **test** (a-gee-lahr-spə-**nel**-ee). In criminal procedure, a standard for determining whether hearsay (such as an informant's tip) is sufficiently reliable to establish probable cause for an arrest or search warrant; under this two-pronged test—which has been replaced by a broader, totality-of-the-circumstances approach—the reliability of both the information and the informant must be independently shown. *Aguilar v. Texas*, 378 U.S. 108 (1964); *Spinelli v. United States*, 393 U.S. 410 (1969). Cf. TOTALITY-OF-THE-CIRCUMSTANCES TEST.

AICPA. *abbr.* American Institute of Certified Public Accountants.

aid and abet, *vb.* To assist or facilitate the commission of a crime, or to promote its accomplishment; aiding and abetting is a crime in most jurisdictions. —Also termed *aid or abet.* —**aider and abettor,** *n.*

air right. The right to use all or a portion of the airspace above real property.

a.k.a. *abbr.* Also known as.

alcoholometer. BREATHALYZER.

alderman. A member of a city council or other local governing body. —Also termed *alderperson.*

aleatory (**ay**-lee-ə-tor-ee), *adj.* Dependent on uncertain contingencies. —Also termed *aleatoric.*

aleatory contract. See CONTRACT.

alegal, *adj.* Outside the sphere of law; not classifiable as being legal or illegal <the law often treats the promises of unmarried cohabitants as

contractual words rather than alegal words of commitment>. —**alegality,** *n.*

Alford **plea.** A guilty plea entered into by a defendant in connection with a plea bargain, without actually admitting guilt; this plea is not considered compelled within the language of the Fifth Amendment if the plea represents a voluntary, knowing, and intelligent choice between the available options <the defendant—realizing the strength of the prosecution's evidence and not wanting to risk receiving the death penalty—entered into an *Alford* plea>. *North Carolina v. Alford,* 400 U.S. 25 (1970).

ALI. *abbr.* AMERICAN LAW INSTITUTE.

alias, *n.* **1.** An assumed or additional name a person has used or is known by. —Also termed *assumed name.* **2.** *Archaic.* A second writ issued after the first has failed. —**alias,** *adv.*

alias execution. See EXECUTION.

alias subpoena. See SUBPOENA.

alias writ. See *alias execution* under EXECUTION.

alibi, *n.* **1.** A defense based on the physical impossibility of a defendant's guilt by placing the defendant in a location other than the scene of the crime at the relevant time. Fed. R. Crim. P. 12.1. **2.** The fact or state of having been elsewhere when an offense was committed. —**alibi,** *vb.*

alien, *n.* A person who is not a citizen of a given country; a person not owing allegiance to a particular nation. —**alienage,** *n.*

enemy alien. A citizen or subject of a country at war with the country in which the citizen or subject is living or traveling.

illegal alien. An alien who enters a country at the wrong time or place, eludes an examination by officials, obtains entry by fraud, or enters into a sham marriage to evade immigration laws. —Also termed *undocumented alien.*

nonresident alien. A person who is neither a resident nor a citizen of the U.S.

resident alien. An alien who has a legally established domicile in the U.S. Cf. NATURALIZATION.

alienation, *n.* **1.** Withdrawal from former attachment; estrangement <alienation of affections>. **2.** Conveyance or transfer of property to another <alienation of one's estate>. —**alienate,** *vb.*

alienation of affections. A tort claim for willful or malicious interference with a marriage by a third party without justification or excuse; the tort has been abolished in most states. See CONSORTIUM (1).

alimony. A court-ordered allowance that one spouse pays to the other spouse for maintenance and support while they are separated, while they are involved in a matrimonial lawsuit, or after they are divorced. —Also termed *spousal support; maintenance.*

alimony in gross. Alimony in the form of a single and definite sum not subject to modification. —Also termed *lump-sum alimony.*

alimony pendente lite (pen-**den**-tee-**li**-dee *or* pen-**den**-tay-**lee**-tay). Temporary alimony ordered by the court pending an action for divorce or separation. —Also termed *allowance pendente lite*.

permanent alimony. Alimony payable in usu. weekly or monthly installments either indefinitely or until a time specified by court order; such alimony may usu. be modified for changed circumstances of either party.

rehabilitative alimony. Alimony necessary to assist a divorced person in regaining a useful and constructive role in society through vocational or other training.

aliquot (**al**-ə-kwot), *adj.* Contained in a larger whole an exact number of times; fractional <5 is an aliquot part of 30>.

aliunde (ay-lee-**yən**-dee), *adj.* [Latin] *Jargon.* From another source; from elsewhere <evidence aliunde>. See *extrinsic evidence* under EVIDENCE.

aliunde rule. The doctrine that a verdict may not be impeached by evidence of a juror unless a foundation to introduce such evidence is first made by competent evidence from another source.

ALJ. *abbr.* ADMINISTRATIVE-LAW JUDGE.

all and singular. *Jargon.* Collectively and individually.

allegation, *n.* **1.** The act of declaring something to be true. **2.** Something declared or asserted as a matter of fact, esp. in a legal pleading; a party's formal statement of a factual matter as being true or provable, without it yet having been proved. — **allege,** *vb.*

material allegation. In a pleading, an assertion that is essential to the claim or defense <a material allegation in a battery case is harmful or offensive contact with a person>.

allegiance. **1.** A citizen's obligation of fidelity and obedience to the government or sovereign. **2.** In feudal law, a vassal's obligation to the liege lord.

***Allen* charge.** In criminal procedure, a supplemental jury instruction given by the court to encourage a deadlocked jury, after prolonged deliberations, to reach a verdict. *Allen v. United States*, 164 U.S. 492 (1896). —Also termed *dynamite charge*; *dynamite instruction*; *nitroglycerine charge*; *shotgun instruction*; *third-degree instruction*.

all-events test. A requirement that an accrual-method taxpayer must meet before reporting an item of income or expense; generally, the test requires the occurrence of all events that fix the right to receive income or incur liability.

all fours, on. See ON ALL FOURS.

all-holders rule. In corporate law, an SEC rule that prohibits a public offering by the issuer of shares to some, but less than all, of the holders of a class of shares.

alliance. **1.** A bond or union between persons, families, states, or other parties. **2.** In international law, a union or association of two or more states or nations, formed by league or treaty, esp. for jointly waging war or mutually protecting against and repelling hostile attacks. Cf. DE-TENTE; ENTENTE. See STRATEGIC ALLIANCE.

all-inclusive mortgage. See *wraparound mortgage* under MORTGAGE.

allision, *n.* In maritime law, the sudden impact of a vessel with a stationary object such as an anchored vessel or a pier. —**allide,** *vb.* Cf. COLLISION.

allocation, *n.* A designation or apportionment for a specific purpose <allocation of funds>. —**allocate,** *vb.*—**allocable,** *adj.*—**allocator,** *n.*

allocution (al-oh-**kyoo**-shən), *n.* **1.** In criminal procedure, the requirement that the trial judge formally address the defendant and ask him or her to speak in mitigation of the sentence to be imposed. **2.** Loosely, a criminal defendant's speech in mitigation of the sentence to be imposed. —**allocute,** *vb.*—**allocutory,** *adj.*

victim allocution. A crime victim's addressing the court usu. to urge a harsher sentence.

allodium (ə-**loh**-dee-əm), *n.* An estate held in fee simple absolute. —Also spelled *alodium.* —**allodial** (ə-**loh**-dee-əl), *adj.*

allograph (**al**-ə-graf or **al**-oh-graf). An agent's writing or signature for the principal.

allonge (ə-**lonj**). A piece of paper attached to a note or other negotiable instrument to make room for further indorsements.

all-or-none offering. See OFFERING.

allotment, *n.* **1.** A share or portion of something, such as property previously held in common or shares in a corporation. **2.** In American Indian law, the selection of specific land awarded to an individual allottee from a common holding. —**allot,** *vb.*

allowance. 1. A share or portion, esp. of money that is assigned or granted.

family allowance. A portion of a decedent's estate set aside by statute for a surviving spouse, children, or parents, regardless of any testamentary disposition or competing claims.

spousal allowance. A portion of a decedent's estate set aside by statute for a surviving spouse, regardless of any testamentary disposition or competing claims. —Also termed *widow's allowance; widower's allowance.*

2. A deduction.

depletion allowance. A tax deduction for the owners of oil, gas, mineral, or timber resources corresponding to the reduced value of the property resulting from the removal of the resource.

allowance pendente lite. See *alimony pendente lite* under ALIMONY.

all-risk insurance. See INSURANCE.

alluvion (ə-**l[y]oo**-vee-ən). **1.** Strictly, the flow or wash of water against a shore or riverbank. **2.** A deposit of soil, clay, or other material caused by running water; esp., in land law, an addition of land caused by the buildup of deposits from running water, the added land then belonging to the owner of the property to which it is added. —Also termed (in sense 2) *alluvium*. Cf. ACCRETION (1); AVULSION.

alluvium. ALLUVION (2).

alodium. ALLODIUM.

ALTA. *abbr.* American Land Title Association.

alter ego. A corporation used by an individual in conducting personal business, such that a court may impose personal liability by piercing the corporate veil when fraud has been perpetrated on someone dealing with the corporation. See PIERCING THE CORPORATE VEIL.

alter-ego rule. 1. In corporate law, the doctrine that shareholders will be treated as the owners of a corporation's property, or as the real parties in interest, whenever it is necessary to do so to prevent fraud or to do justice that might otherwise fail. **2.** In criminal law, the common-law doctrine limiting the use of force when defending another person to the amount of force that the other person would be privileged to use in self-defense.

alternate legacy. See LEGACY.

alternate valuation date. In tax law, the date six months after a decedent's death; generally, the estate can elect to appraise the decedent's property either on the date of the decedent's death or on the alternate valuation date. See BASIS.

alternative constituency. NON-SHAREHOLDER CONSTITUENCY.

alternative contract. See CONTRACT.

alternative dispute resolution. A procedure for settling a dispute by means other than litigation, such as arbitration, mediation, or minitrial. —Abbr. ADR.

alternative judgment. See JUDGMENT.

alternative minimum tax. See TAX.

alternative pleading. See PLEADING (2).

alternative relief. See RELIEF.

alternative remainder. See REMAINDER.

alternative writ. See WRIT.

AMA. *abbr.* American Medical Association.

amalgamation (ə-mal-gə-**may**-shən), *n.* The act of combining or uniting; consolidation <amalgamation of two small companies to form a new corporation>. —**amalgamate**, *vb.*—**amalgamator**, *n.* Cf. MERGER.

ambassador, *n.* A diplomatic officer of the highest rank, usu. designated by a government as its resident representative in a foreign state. —**ambassadorial**, *adj.*—**ambassadorship**, *n.*

ambiguity (am-bi-**gyoo**-ə-dee), *n.* An uncertainty in meaning, esp. one that is revealed by the text or by extrinsic evidence other than direct evidence of the writer's intention when that intention contradicts the plain meaning of the text. —**ambiguous**, *adj.*

latent ambiguity. An ambiguity that does not readily appear in the language of a document, but instead arises from a collateral matter when the document's terms are applied or executed <the contract contained a latent ambiguity because the shipping terms stated the goods would arrive on the ship *Peerless*, but two ships have that name>. —Also termed *extrinsic ambiguity*.

patent ambiguity (**pay**-tənt). An ambiguity that clearly appears on the face of a document, arising from the language itself <the nonperformance was excused because the two different prices expressed in the contract created a patent ambiguity>. —Also termed *intrinsic ambiguity*.

ambulatory, *adj.* **1.** Able to walk <the accident victim is still ambulatory>. **2.** Capable of being altered or revised <a will is ambulatory because it is revocable until the testator's death>.

ameliorate (ə-**meel**-[I-]yə-rayt), *vb.* **1.** To make better <the charity tries to ameliorate the conditions of the homeless>. **2.** To become better <with time, the situation ameliorated>. —**amelioration,** *n.*—**ameliorative,** *adj.*

ameliorating waste. See WASTE.

ameliorative waste. See *ameliorating waste* under WASTE.

amenable (ə-**mee**-nə-bəl *or* -**men**-), *adj.* Legally answerable; liable to being brought to judgment <amenable to process>. —**amenability,** *n.*

amend, *vb.* **1.** To put right; change <amend the order to correct a clerical error>. **2.** To add to; supplement <amend the complaint to include a new claim>. —**amendatory,** *adj.*

amended pleading. See PLEADING (1).

amended return. See TAX RETURN.

amendment. 1. A legislative change in a statute or constitution, usu. by adding provisions not in the original. **2.** The correction of an error or the supplying of an omission in a document such as a pleading or order.

a mensa et thoro (ay-**men**-sə-et-**thor**-oh). [Latin "from board and hearth"] (Of a divorce decree) effecting a separation of the parties rather than a dissolution of the marriage <a divorce *a mensa et thoro* was the usual way for a couple to separate under English law up until 1857>. See SEPARATION.

amercement (ə-**mərs**-mənt), *n.* **1.** The imposition of a fine, esp. by a court or on an official for misconduct <an amercement proceeding>. **2.** The fine so imposed <an amercement charged to the sheriff for failing to return the writ of execution>. —Also termed *amerciament.* —**amerce** (ə-**mers**), *vb.*—**amerciable** (ə-**mər**-see-ə-bəl *or* -**mər**-shə-bəl), *adj.*

American Academy of Actuaries. A national organization of actuaries who must meet specified educational requirements and have at least three years of actuarial work experience; the Academy—created in 1965 and having more than 12,500 members—promotes public awareness of the actuarial profession, represents the profession before federal and state governments, and sponsors continuing-education conferences. —Abbr. AAA. See ACTUARY.

American Accounting Association. An organization of accounting practitioners, educators, and students; the Association—founded in 1916 and now having some 10,000 members—promotes accounting as an academic discipline by sponsoring research projects and continuing-education seminars. —Abbr. AAA.

American Arbitration Association. A national organization that maintains a panel of arbitrators to hear labor and commercial disputes. —Abbr. AAA.

American Bar Association. A voluntary national organization of lawyers; among other things, it participates in law reform, law-school accreditation, and continuing legal education in an effort to improve legal services and the administration of justice. —Abbr. ABA.

American Bar Foundation. An outgrowth of the American Bar Association involved with sponsoring and funding projects in legal research, education, and social studies.

American Civil Liberties Union. A national organization whose primary purpose is to help enforce and preserve individual rights and liberties guaranteed by federal and state constitutions. —Abbr. ACLU.

American depository receipt. A receipt issued by an American bank as a substitute for stock shares in a foreign-based corporation. —Abbr. ADR. —Also termed *American depositary receipt*.

American Federation of Labor and Congress of Industrial Organizations. A voluntary affiliation of over 100 labor unions that operate autonomously yet benefit from the affiliation's establishment of broad policies for the national labor movement. —Abbr. AFL-CIO.

American Inns of Court Foundation. See INN OF COURT (2).

American Law Institute. An organization of lawyers, judges, and legal scholars who promote consistency and simplification of American law by restatements of the law and other model codes and treatises, as well as promoting continuing legal education. —Abbr. ALI.

American Lloyd's. LLOYD'S UNDERWRITERS.

American rule. The requirement that each litigant must pay its own attorney's fees, even if the party prevails in the lawsuit; the rule is subject to bad faith and other statutory and contractual exceptions. Cf. ENGLISH RULE.

American Stock Exchange. An organized stock exchange, located in New York City, for trading national corporate stocks; it often trades in the securities of young or small companies because its listing requirements are less strict than those of the NYSE. —Abbr. AMEX; ASE.

Americans with Disabilities Act. A federal statute that prohibits discrimination against physically or mentally disabled persons in employment, public services, and public accommodations (including those operated by private entities). —Abbr. ADA. 42 U.S.C. §§ 12101 et seq.

AMEX (a-meks). *abbr.* AMERICAN STOCK EXCHANGE.

amicable action. See *test case* (a) under CASE.

amicus curiae (ə-mee-kəs-k[y]oor-ee-I *or* am-I-kəs-). [Latin "friend of the court"] A person who is not a party to a lawsuit but who petitions the court to file a brief in the action because that person has a strong interest in the subject matter. —Often shortened to *amicus*. —Also termed *friend of the court.* Pl. **amici curiae.**

amnesty, *n.* A pardon extended by the government to a group or class of persons, usu. for a political offense <the 1986 Immigration Reform and Control Act provided amnesty for undocumented aliens already present in the country>. —Also termed *general pardon.* —**amnesty,** *vb.* See PARDON.

amortization (am-ərd-ə-**zay**-shən *or* -ərt-), *n.* **1.** The act or result of gradually extinguishing a debt, such as a mortgage, usu. by contributing payments of principal each time a periodic interest payment is due.

negative amortization. An increase in a loan's principal balance caused by monthly payments insufficient to pay accruing interest.

2. The act or result of apportioning the initial cost of a usu. intangible asset, such as a patent, over the asset's useful life. —**amortize,** *vb.* Cf. DEPRECIATION.

amortized loan. See LOAN.

amortized mortgage. See MORTGAGE.

amount in controversy. The damages claimed or relief demanded by the injured party in a lawsuit; for a federal court to have diversity jurisdiction, the amount in controversy must exceed $50,000. 28 U.S.C. § 1332(a). —Also termed *jurisdictional amount.* See DIVERSITY OF CITIZENSHIP.

AMT. See *alternative minimum tax* under TAX.

anaconda clause. MOTHER HUBBARD CLAUSE (1).

analogous art. See ART.

analytical jurisprudence. See JURISPRUDENCE.

anarchist, *n.* One who advocates the overthrow of organized government by force or who believes in the absence of government as a political ideal. —**anarchism** (the philosophy), *n.*

anarchy, *n.* Absence of government; lawlessness. —**anarchic,** *adj.*

anatomical gift. See GIFT.

ancestor. ASCENDANT.

ancestral estate. See ESTATE.

ancient-lights doctrine. In property law, the English common-law doctrine by which a landowner could acquire, after usu. 20 years' use, a prescriptive easement over neighboring land for the unobstructed passage of light through the landowner's windows; this doctrine is not applied in the U.S.

ancient writing. A document admissible under the Federal Rules of Evidence because its physical condition generates no doubts concerning its authenticity, it has existed for 20 or more years, and it comes from a natural, reasonable place. Fed. R. Evid. 901(b)(8). —Also termed *ancient document.*

ancillary, *adj.* Supplementary; subordinate <ancillary claims>. **—ancillarity,** *n.*

ancillary administration. See ADMINISTRATION.

ancillary bill. See *ancillary suit* under SUIT.

ancillary jurisdiction. See JURISDICTION.

ancillary proceeding. See *ancillary suit* under SUIT.

ancillary process. See *ancillary suit* under SUIT.

ancillary suit. See SUIT.

ancipitis usus. See *conditional contraband* under CONTRABAND.

and his heirs. See HEIR.

animo (**an**-ə-moh). [Latin] See ANIMUS (2).

animus (**an**-ə-məs). [Latin] **1.** Ill will; animosity. **2.** Intention; all the following Latin "animus" phrases have analogous adverbial forms beginning with "animo" (the definition merely needing "with" at the outset)—for example, *animo furandi* means "with the intent to steal," *animo testandi* means "with testamentary intention," etc.

animus belligerendi (bə-li-jə-**ren**-dee). The intention to wage war.

animus defamandi (de-fəm-**an**-day). The intention to defame.

animus donandi (doh-**nahn**-dee). The intention to give.

animus felonico (fe-**loh**-ni-koh). The intention to commit a felony.

animus furandi (f[y]uu-**ran**-dee). The intention to steal.

animus injuriandi (in-juur-ee-**an**-dee). The intention to injure.

animus revertendi (re-vər-**ten**-dee). The intention to return (to a place).

animus revocandi (re-və-**kahn**-dee). The intention to revoke (a will) <her destruction of the will indicated that she had animus revocandi>.

animus testandi (tes-**tahn**-dee). Testamentary intention.

annexation, *n.* **1.** The act of attaching; the state of being attached. **2.** In property law, the point at which a fixture becomes a part of the realty to which it is attached. **3.** In international law, a formal act by which a nation incorporates a territory within its dominion; the usual formalities of announcing annexation involve having specially commissioned officers hoist the national flag and read a proclamation. **—annex,** *vb.* Cf. ACCESSION.

Anno Domini (an-oh-**dom**-ə-nee). [Latin "in the year of the Lord"] Of the modern era by way of calculating time from the birth of Christ. — Abbr. A.D. <1776 A.D.>.

annotation, *n.* A note that explains or criticizes (usu. a case), esp. to give, in condensed form, some indication of the law as deduced from cases and statutes, as well as to point out where similar cases can be found; annotations appear, for example, in the *United States Code Annotated* (U.S.C.A.). **—annotate,** *vb.***—annotative,** *adj.***—annotator,** *n.* Cf. NOTE (2).

annual meeting. See MEETING.

annual percentage rate. See IN-TEREST RATE.

annual report. A yearly corporate financial report for shareholders and other interested parties; it includes a balance sheet, income statement, statement of changes in financial position, reconciliation of changes in owners' equity accounts, a summary of significant accounting principles, other explanatory notes, the auditor's report, and comments from management about prospects for the coming year. —Also termed *annual statement*.

annuitant (ə-n[y]oo-ət-ənt). A beneficiary of an annuity.

annuity. 1. A fixed sum of money payable periodically. **2.** A right, often acquired under a life-insurance contract, to receive fixed payments periodically for a specified duration. Cf. PENSION. **3.** A savings account with an insurance company or investment company, usu. established for retirement income; payments into the account accumulate tax-free, and the account is taxed only when the annuitant withdraws money in retirement.

annuity certain. An annuity payable over a specified period, regardless of whether the annuitant dies.

annuity due. An annuity that makes payments at the beginning of each pay period. Cf. *ordinary annuity.*

contingent annuity. **a.** An annuity that begins making payments when some future event occurs, such as the death of a person other than the annuitant. **b.** An annuity that makes an uncertain number of payments, depending on the outcome of a future event.

deferred annuity. An annuity that begins making payments on a specified date if the annuitant is alive at that time. —Also termed *deferred-payment annuity.*

fixed annuity. An annuity that guarantees fixed payments, either for life or for a specified period.

group annuity. An annuity payable to members of a group, esp. employees, who are covered by a single annuity contract, such as a group pension plan.

joint annuity. An annuity payable to two annuitants until one of them dies, at which time the annuity terminates for the survivor (unless the annuity also provides for survivorship rights). See *survivorship annuity.*

life annuity. An annuity payable only during the annuitant's lifetime, even if the annuitant dies prematurely.

nonrefund annuity. An annuity with guaranteed payments during the annuitant's life, but with no refund to anyone at death. —Also termed *straight life annuity*; *pure annuity.*

ordinary annuity. An annuity that makes payments at the end of each pay period. Cf. *annuity due.*

refund annuity. An annuity that, upon the annuitant's death, pays to the annuitant's estate the difference between the purchase price and the total payments received during the annuitant's lifetime.

straight annuity. An annuity that makes payments in fixed amounts at periodic intervals. Cf. *variable annuity.*

survivorship annuity. An annuity providing for continued payments to a survivor, usu. a spouse, after the original annuitant dies.

variable annuity. An annuity that makes payments in varying amounts depending on the success of investment strategy. Cf. *straight annuity.*

annuity bond. See BOND (1).

annulment, *n.* **1.** The act of nullifying or making void. **2.** Judicial or ecclesiastical declaration that a marriage is void; unlike a divorce, an annulment establishes that marital status never existed. Cf. DIVORCE. — **annul,** *vb.*

anomalous indorsement. See *irregular indorsement* under INDORSEMENT.

anomalous pleading. See PLEADING (1).

anonymous, *adj.* Not named or identified <the police arrested the defendant after a tip from an anonymous informant>. —**anonymity,** *n.*

answer, *n.* A defendant's first pleading that addresses the merits of the case, usu. by denying the plaintiff's allegations.

answer, *vb.* **1.** To respond to a pleading or a discovery request <the company failed to answer the interrogatories within 30 days>. **2.** To assume the liability of another <a guarantor answers for another person's debt>.

ante. [Latin] Before.

antecedent (an-tə-**seed**-[ə]nt), *adj.* Earlier; preexisting; previous. —**antecedent** (preceding thing), *n.*—**antecedence** (quality or fact of going before), *n.*

antecedent debt. See DEBT.

antedate, *vb.* **1.** To affix with a date earlier than the true date; BACKDATE (1) <antedate a check>. **2.** To precede in time <the doctrine antedates the *Smith* case by many years>. —Also termed *predate.*— **antedate,** *n.* Cf. POSTDATE.

antenuptial. PRENUPTIAL.

antenuptial agreement. PRENUPTIAL AGREEMENT.

antenuptial will. See *prenuptial will* under WILL.

anticipation. In patent law, the previous use, knowledge, documentation, or patenting of an invention; any of these will negate the invention's novelty, thereby preventing a patent or providing a defense to an infringement claim. See NOVELTY.

anticipatory breach. See BREACH OF CONTRACT.

anticipatory nuisance. See NUISANCE.

anticipatory offense. See *inchoate offense* under OFFENSE.

anticipatory repudiation. See REPUDIATION.

anticipatory search warrant. See SEARCH WARRANT.

antidilution provision. A convertible-security provision that safeguards the conversion privilege from share splits, share dividends, or other transactions that might affect the conversion ratio. See CONVERSION RATIO; DILUTION (2).

antidumping law. A statute designed to protect domestic companies by preventing the sale of foreign goods in the domestic country for less than fair value—that is, for a smaller price than they command in the foreign country. See DUMPING.

antidumping tariff. See TARIFF.

antifraud rule. RULE 10B-5.

Anti-Injunction Act. A federal statute providing that a federal court may not enjoin state-court proceedings unless an injunction is (1) expressly authorized by Congress, (2) necessary for the federal court's in rem jurisdiction, or (3) necessary to prevent relitigation of a judgment rendered by the federal court. 28 U.S.C. § 2283.

anti-john law. A criminal-law statute punishing prostitutes' customers.

antilapse statute. In the law of wills, a statute that passes a bequest to the heirs of the beneficiary if the beneficiary dies before the testator dies. —Also termed *lapse statute*; *nonlapse statute*.

antimarital-facts privilege. See *marital privilege* (b) under PRIVILEGE.

antinomy (an-**tin**-ə-mee), *n.* A contradiction in law or logic; a conflict of authority <antinomies between law and morality>. —**antinomic** (an-ti-**no**-mic), *adj.*

antitrust law. The body of law designed to protect trade and commerce from restraints, monopolies, pricefixing, and price discrimination; the principal federal antitrust laws are the Sherman Act (15 U.S.C. §§ 1-7) and the Clayton Act (15 U.S.C. §§ 12-27).

apartheid (ə-**pahr**-tIt *or* -tayt). Racial segregation; specifically, a policy of discrimination and segregation against blacks in South Africa.

a posteriori (ah-po-stir-ee-**o[ə]r**-ee *or* ay-poh-stir-ee-**or**-I), *adv.* [Latin "from what comes after"] Inductively; from the particular to the general, or from known effects to their inferred causes <as a legal analyst, she reasoned a posteriori—from countless individual cases to generalized rules that she finally arrived at>. —**a posteriori,** *adj.* Cf. A PRIORI.

apostille. CERTIFICATE OF AUTHORITY.

apparent, *adj.* Visible; manifest; obvious.

apparent agent. See AGENT.

apparent authority. See AUTHORITY.

apparent easement. See EASEMENT.

apparent heir. See *heir apparent* under HEIR.

appeal, *n.* A proceeding undertaken to reverse a decision by bringing it to a higher authority; esp., the submission of a lower court's or agency's decision to a higher court for review and possible reversal <the case is on appeal>. —**appellate,** *adj.* Cf. CERTIORARI.

consolidated appeal. An appeal in which two or more parties, whose interests were similar enough to make a joinder practicable, proceed as a single appellant.

cross-appeal. An appeal by the appellee, usu. heard at the same time as the appellant's appeal.

interlocutory appeal. An appeal that occurs before the trial court's final ruling on the entire case; some interlocutory appeals involve legal points necessary to the determination of the case, while others involve collateral orders that are wholly separate from the merits of the action.

limited appeal. An appeal from only certain portions of a decision, usu. only the adverse or unfavorable portions.

appeal, *vb.* To seek review (from a lower court's decision) by a higher court <petitioner appeals the conviction>. —**appealability,** *n.*

appealable decision. See DECISION.

appeal bond. See BOND (2).

appeal court. See *appellate court* under COURT.

appealer. *Archaic.* APPELLANT.

appeal in forma pauperis (in-for-mə-**paw**-pər-əs). An appeal by an indigent party, for whom court costs are waived. Fed. R. App. P. 24. See IN FORMA PAUPERIS.

appeals council. A commission that hears appeals of rulings by administrative-law judges in social-security matters.

appeals court. See *appellate court* under COURT.

appearance, *n.* A coming into court as a party or interested person, or as a lawyer on behalf of a party or interested person. —**appear,** *vb.*

appearance pro hac vice (proh-hak-**vIs** *or* -**vIs**-ee *or* -hahk-**vee**-chay). [Latin] An appearance in a local jurisdiction by an out-of-state lawyer for one particular case. See PRO HAC VICE.

compulsory appearance. An appearance by one who is required to appear by having been served with process.

general appearance. An appearance for general purposes, which waives a party's ability later to dispute the court's personal jurisdiction.

special appearance. An appearance only to contest the court's personal jurisdiction. —Also termed *limited appearance; appearance de bene esse.*

voluntary appearance. An appearance entered by a party's own will, without the service of process.

appearance docket. See DOCKET.

appellant (ə-**pel**-ənt). A party who appeals a lower court's decision, usu. seeking reversal of that decision. — Formerly also termed *appealer.* Cf. APPELLEE.

appellate (ə-**pel**-ət), *adj.* Of or relating to an appeal or appeals generally.

appellate court. See COURT.

appellate jurisdiction. See JURISDICTION.

appellate record. RECORD ON APPEAL.

appellate review. See REVIEW.

appellee (ap-ə-**lee**). A party against whom an appeal is taken and who responds to that appeal, usu. seeking affirmance of the lower court's decision. Cf. APPELLANT.

appellor (a-**pəl**-oh[ə]r *or* ə-**pel**-ər). *Archaic.* In English law, a person who formally accuses another of crime, challenges a jury, or informs against an accomplice.

appendant (ə-**pen**-dənt), *adj.* Attached or belonging to property as an additional but subsidiary right. —**appendant**, *n.*

appendant easement. See *easement appurtenant* under EASEMENT.

appendix. A supplementary document attached to the end of a writing <the brief includes an appendix of exhibits>. Pl. **appendixes, appendices**.

appointee. 1. One who is appointed. **2.** One who receives the benefit of a power of appointment. See POWER OF APPOINTMENT.

appointment, *n.* **1.** The act of designating a person, such as a nonelected public official, for a job or duty <Article II of the U.S. Constitution grants the President the power of appointment for principal federal officials, subject to senatorial consent>. **2.** An office occupied by someone who has been appointed <a high appointment in the federal government>. **3.** The act of disposing of property, in exercise of a power granted for that purpose <the tenant's appointment of lands>. See POWER OF APPOINTMENT. —**appoint,** *vb.*—**appointer** (corresponding to senses 1 & 2), *n.*—**appointor** (corresponding to sense 3), *n.*

apportionment, *n.* **1.** Division into proportionate shares. **2.** The act of allocating or attributing moneys or expenses in a given way, as when a taxpayer allocates part of profits to a particular tax year or part of the use of a car to a business. **3.** Distribution of legislative seats among districts that are entitled to representation. See REAPPORTIONMENT. —**apportion,** *vb.*

appraisal, *n.* The act or an instance of estimating the worth of something; valuation, esp. for tax purposes. —Also termed *appraisement.* —**appraise,** *vb.*

appraisal clause. An insurance-policy provision allowing either the insurer or the insured to demand an independent estimation of a claimed loss.

appraisal remedy. The statutory right of corporate shareholders who oppose some extraordinary corporate action (such as a merger) to have their shares judicially appraised and to demand that the corporation buy back their shares at the appraised value. —Also termed *appraisal right*; *dissenters' right*; *right of dissent and appraisal.*

appraisement. APPRAISAL.

appraiser. An impartial person selected to estimate the value of something, esp. a piece of real estate.

appreciation, *n.* An increase in value, esp. in the market value of an asset. —**appreciate,** *vb.*—**appreciable,** *adj.* Cf. DEPRECIATION.

appreciation surplus. See *revaluation surplus* under SURPLUS.

apprehension, *n.* **1.** Seizure in the name of the law; arrest <apprehension of a criminal>. **2.** Perception; comprehension <the tort of assault requires apprehension by the plaintiff of imminent contact>. **3.** Fear;

anxiety <most people approach public speaking with some apprehension>. —**apprehend,** *vb.*

appropriation, *n.* **1.** The exercise of control over property; a taking of possession. **2.** A legislative body's act of setting aside a sum of money for a public purpose. **3.** The sum of money so voted. **4.** In tort law, an invasion of privacy whereby one person takes the name or likeness of another for commercial gain. —**appropriate,** *vb.*—**appropriable,** *adj.*—**appropriator,** *n.* Cf. EXPROPRIATION; MISAPPROPRIATION.

appropriation bill. See BILL (3).

approval sale. See *sale on approval* under SALE.

approximation, doctrine of. CY PRES.

appurtenance (ə-**pərt**-[ə-]nən[t]s), *n.* Something that belongs or is attached to something else <the garden is an appurtenance to the land>. —**appurtenant,** *adj.*

appurtenant easement. See *easement appurtenant* under EASEMENT.

APR. See *annual percentage rate* under INTEREST RATE.

à prendre (ah-**pron**-dər or -drə). [French] To take; to seize. See PROFIT A PRENDRE.

a priori (ah-pree-**or**-ee *or* ay-prI-**or**-I), *adv.* [Latin "from what is before"] Deductively; from the general to the particular <as an analyst, he reasoned a priori—from seemingly self-evident propositions to particular conclusions>. —**a priori,** *adj.* Cf. A POSTERIORI.

APV. See *adjusted present value* under PRESENT VALUE.

a quo (ah-**kwoh** *or* ay-). [Latin] From which. —Also termed *a qua.* See *court a quo* under COURT.

arbiter (**ahr**-bə-tər). Anyone with the power to decide disputes, such as a judge <the Supreme Court is the final arbiter of legal disputes in the U.S.>. Cf. ARBITRATOR.

arbitrage (**ahr**-bə-trahzh), *n.* The simultaneous buying and selling of identical securities in different markets, hoping to profit from the price difference in those markets. —Also termed *space arbitrage.* —**arbitrager, arbitrageur,** *n.*

kind arbitrage. Purchase of a security that is, without restriction other than the payment of money, exchangeable or convertible within a reasonable time to a second security, with a simultaneous offsetting sale of the second security. —Also termed *convertible arbitrage.*

risk arbitrage. Arbitrage of corporate stock in a potential merger or takeover, whereby the target company's stock is bought and the acquiring company's stock is sold simultaneously.

time arbitrage. Purchase of a commodity against a present sale of the identical commodity for a future delivery; esp., the simultaneous buying and selling of securities hoping to profit from the difference in prices for immediate delivery and future delivery.

arbitrament. 1. The power to decide for oneself or others; the power to decide finally and absolutely. **2.** The act of deciding or settling a dispute that has been referred to arbitration. **3.** AWARD.

arbitration, *n.* A method of dispute resolution involving one or more neutral third parties who are chosen by or agreed to by the disputing parties, and whose decision is binding. —**arbitrate,** *vb.*—**arbitral,** *adj.* Cf. MEDIATION (1).

compulsory arbitration. Arbitration required by law or forced by law on the parties.

arbitration act. A federal or state statute providing for the submission of disputes to arbitration.

arbitration clause. A contractual provision mandating arbitration—and thereby avoiding litigation—of disputes about the contracting parties' rights and duties.

arbitration of exchange. The simultaneous buying and selling of bills of exchange in different international markets, hoping to profit from the price difference of the currencies in those markets. See ARBITRAGE; BILL OF EXCHANGE.

arbitrator, *n.* A neutral person chosen to resolve disputes between parties, esp. by means of formal arbitration. —**arbitratorship,** *n.* Cf. ARBITER.

architect's lien. See LIEN.

architectural review. DESIGN REVIEW.

architectural work. In copyright law, the design of a building, as embodied in any tangible medium of expression, including plans and drawings (which are protected as pictorial or graphic works) or the building itself (which is protected, if built after December 1, 1990, under the Berne Convention).

area bargaining. Negotiation by a union of collective-bargaining agreements with several employers in a particular geographic area.

area variance. See VARIANCE (2).

Areeda-Turner test. In antitrust law, an economic test for predatory pricing whereby a price below average variable cost is presumed to be predatory and therefore illegal; this test is widely accepted by federal courts. See PREDATORY PRICING.

arguendo (ahr-gyoo-**en**-doh). [Latin] *Jargon.* For the sake of argument <assuming arguendo that discovery procedures were correctly followed, the court still cannot grant the defendant's motion to dismiss>.

argument. 1. A statement that attempts to persuade. **2.** The act or process of attempting to persuade. See ORAL ARGUMENT.

argumentative, *adj.* **1.** Of or relating to argument or persuasion <an argumentative tone of voice>. **2.** Stating not only facts, but also inferences and conclusions drawn from facts <the judge sustained the prosecutor's objection to the argumentative question>.

arise, *vb.* **1.** To originate; to stem from <a federal claim arising under the U.S. Constitution>. **2.** To result (from) <litigation routinely arises from such accidents>. **3.** To emerge in one's consciousness; to come to one's attention <the question of appealability then arose>.

ARM. See *adjustable-rate mortgage* under MORTGAGE.

armed robbery. See ROBBERY.

armistice. TRUCE.

arms, right to bear. See RIGHT TO BEAR ARMS.

arm's-length, *adj.* Of or relating to dealings between two parties who are not related or not on close terms and who are presumed to have roughly equal bargaining power; not having a confidential relationship <an arm's-length transaction normally does not create fiduciary duties between the parties>.

arraignment, *n.* The initial step in a criminal prosecution whereby the defendant is brought before the court to hear the charges and to enter a plea. —**arraign,** *vb.* Cf. PRELIMINARY HEARING.

arrangement with creditors. In bankruptcy law, a debtor's arrangement with creditors for the settlement, satisfaction, or extension of time for payment of debts. See BANKRUPTCY PLAN.

array, *n.* **1.** A panel of potential jurors; VENIRE (1) <the array of mostly wealthy professionals seemed to favor the corporate defendant>. **2.** The jurors actually impaneled <the array hearing the case consisted of seven women and five men>. **3.** A list or roster of impaneled jurors <the plaintiff obtained a copy of the array to help prepare for voir dire>. **4.** Order; arrangement <the array of jurors from oldest to youngest>. **5.** A militia <the array organized anti-government rallies>. **6.** A large number <an array of possibilities>. **7.** A series of statistics or a group of elements <a mathematical array>.

array, *vb.* **1.** To impanel a jury for trial. **2.** To call out the names of jurors, one by one, as they are impaneled.

arrear, *n.* (*usu. pl.*) **1.** The state of being behind in the payment of a debt or the discharge of an obligation <the creditor filed a lawsuit against the debtor who was in arrears>. — Also termed *arrearage*. **2.** An unpaid or overdue debt <the creditor reached an agreement with the debtor on settling the arrears>. **3.** An unfinished duty <the arrears of work have accumulated>.

arrearage. ARREAR (1).

arrest, *n.* **1.** Any seizure or forcible restraint. **2.** The taking or keeping of a person in custody by legal authority, esp. in response to a criminal charge. —**arrest,** *vb.*

citizen's arrest. An arrest of a private person by another private person on grounds that (1) a public offense was committed in the arrester's presence, or (2) the arrester has reasonable cause to believe that the arrestee has committed a felony.

false arrest. An arrest made without proper legal authority. See FALSE IMPRISONMENT.

house arrest. See HOUSE ARREST.

malicious arrest. An arrest made without probable cause and for an improper purpose; malicious arrest can be grounds for an action for either false imprisonment or malicious prosecution.

parol arrest. An arrest ordered by a judge or magistrate from the bench, without written complaint, and executed immediately, such as an arrest of a person who breaches the peace in open court. See CONTEMPT.

warrantless arrest. An arrest, without a warrant, based on probable cause of a felony, or for a misdemeanor committed in a police officer's presence. See WARRANT.

3. In admiralty law, the taking of a ship into custody by virtue of a court's warrant.

arrest of judgment. The staying of a judgment after its entry; esp., a court's refusal to render or enforce a judgment because of a defect apparent from the record.

arrest record. 1. A form completed by a police officer when a person is arrested. **2.** A cumulative list of the instances when a person has been arrested.

arrest warrant. See WARRANT (1).

arret (ah-**ret** or -**ray**). [French] A judgment, sentence, or decree of a court with competent jurisdiction; this term is derived from French law and used in the U.S. only in Louisiana.

arrogation (ar-ə-**gay**-shən), *n.* **1.** Claiming or taking something without the right to do so <some commentators argue that limited military actions unilaterally ordered by the president are an arrogation of Congress's power to declare war>. **2.** In civil law, the adoption of an adult. — **arrogate,** *vb.*

arson, *n.* **1.** At common law, the malicious burning of someone else's dwelling house. **2.** Under modern statutes, the malicious burning of someone else's or one's own dwelling house or of anyone's commercial or industrial property. —**arsonous,** *adj.* Cf. HOUSEBURNING.

arsonable, *adj.* (Of property) of such a nature as to give rise to a charge of arson if maliciously burned <only real property, and not personal property, is arsonable>.

arson clause. An insurance-policy provision that excludes coverage of a loss due to fire if the insured intentionally started the fire.

arsonist. INCENDIARY (1).

art. 1. The methodical application of knowledge or skill in creating something. **2.** An occupation or business that requires skill; a craft. **3.** In patent law, a process or method that produces a beneficial physical effect.

analogous art. The technique or method that is reasonably related to the problem addressed by the invention, and with which the inventor is assumed to be familiar. — Also termed *pertinent art.* See NONOBVIOUSNESS.

prior art. The body of previously patented inventions that the patent office or court analyzes before granting or denying a patent to a comparable invention.

4. *Archaic.* In a seduction case, the skillful and systematic arrangement of means to coax another into having sex.

artful pleading. See PLEADING (2).

article. 1. Generally, a particular item or thing <article of clothing>. **2.** A separate and distinct part (as a clause or stipulation) of a writing, esp. in a contract, statute, or constitution <Article III>. **3.** (*pl.*) An instrument containing a set of rules or stipulations <articles of war> <articles of incorporation>. **4.** A nonfictional literary composition forming an independent part of a publication, such as a law review or journal <a well-researched article>.

Article I Court. See *legislative court* under COURT.

Article III Court. A federal court that, deriving its jurisdiction from U.S. Const. art. III, § 2, hears cases arising under the Constitution and the laws and treaties of the U.S., cases in which the U.S. is a party, and cases between the states and between citizens of different states.

articles of association. 1. ARTICLES OF INCORPORATION. **2.** A document—similar to articles of incorporation—that legally creates a nonstock or nonprofit organization.

Articles of Confederation. The instrument that governed the association of the thirteen original states from March 1, 1781 until the adoption of the U.S. Constitution.

articles of dissolution. The document that a dissolving corporation must file with the appropriate governmental agency, usu. the secretary of state, after the corporation has settled all of its debts and distributed all of its assets.

articles of impeachment. A formal document alleging the causes for removing a public official from office; it is similar to an indictment in a criminal proceeding. See IMPEACH.

articles of incorporation. The document that legally creates a corporation when filed with the appropriate governmental agency, usu. the secretary of state; the articles typically establish the corporation's purpose and duration, the rights and liabilities of shareholders and directors, and the classes of stock and other securities. —Also termed *articles of association*; *articles of organization*; *certificate of incorporation*. Cf. BYLAW (1); CHARTER (2).

articles of partnership. PARTNERSHIP AGREEMENT.

articulated pleading. See PLEADING (1).

artificial person. See PERSON.

ascendant, *n.* One who precedes in lineage, such as a parent or grandparent. —Also termed *ancestor*. —**ascendant,** *adj.* Cf. DESCENDANT.

collateral ascendant. Loosely, an aunt, uncle, or other relative who is not strictly an ancestor. —Also termed *collateral ancestor*.

ascent. The passing of an estate upwards to an heir in the ascending line. Cf. DESCENT.

ASE. *abbr.* AMERICAN STOCK EXCHANGE.

as is. In the existing condition without modification <the customer bought the car as is>; under the U.C.C., a seller can disclaim all implied warranties by stating that the goods are being sold "as is" or "with all faults." U.C.C. § 2-316(3)(a).

ask price. See *asking price* under PRICE.

asked price. See PRICE.

asking price. See PRICE.

as of. On; at—often used to signify the effective legal date of a document, as when the document is backdated or the parties sign at different times <the lease commences as of June 1>.

as of right. By virtue of a legal entitlement <the case is not one triable to a jury as of right>.

as per. *Jargon.* In accordance with; PER (3).

asportation, *n.* The act of carrying away or removing (property or a person); asportation is a necessary element of larceny. —**asport,** *vb.* See LARCENY.

assassination, *n.* The act of deliberately killing someone, esp. a public figure, usu. for hire or for political reasons. —**assassinate,** *vb.*—**assassin,** *n.*

assault, *n.* **1.** In criminal law and tort law, the threat or use of force on another that causes that person to have a reasonable apprehension of imminent harmful or offensive contact. **2.** In criminal law only, an attempt to commit battery, requiring the specific intent to cause physical injury. **3.** Loosely, a criminal battery. —**assault,** *vb.*—**assaultive,** *adj.* Cf. BATTERY.

aggravated assault. Criminal assault accompanied by circumstances that make it more severe, such as the use of a deadly weapon, the intent to commit another crime, or the intent to cause serious bodily harm.

assault with a deadly weapon. An aggravated assault in which the defendant, controlling a deadly weapon, threatens the victim with death or serious bodily injury. —Also termed *felonious assault.*

conditional assault. An assault expressing a threat on condition, such as "your money or your life."

sexual assault. **a.** Sexual intercourse with another person without that person's consent; several state statutes have abolished the crime of rape and replaced it with the offense of sexual assault. **b.** Offensive sexual contact with another person, exclusive of rape. —Also termed (in sense b) *indecent assault.* Cf. RAPE.

assault and battery. Loosely, a criminal battery. See BATTERY.

assaultee. A person who is assaulted.

assaulter. A person who assaults another.

assembly. 1. A group of persons organized and united for some common purpose.

unlawful assembly. A meeting of three or more persons who intend either to commit a violent crime or to carry out some act, lawful or unlawful, that will constitute a breach of the peace. Cf. RIOT.

2. In many states, the lower house of a legislature.

assembly, right of. See RIGHT OF ASSEMBLY.

assent, *n.* Agreement, approval, or permission. —**assent,** *vb.* See CONSENT.

mutual assent. See MUTUAL ASSENT.

assertion, *n.* A declaration or allegation. —**assert,** *vb.*—**assertor,** *n.*

assertive conduct. See CONDUCT.

assertory oath. See OATH.

assessment, *n.* **1.** Determination of the rate or amount (of something, such as a tax or damages) <assess-

ment of the losses covered by insurance>. **2.** Imposition (of something, such as a tax or fine) according to an established rate; the tax or fine so imposed <assessment of a luxury tax>.

deficiency assessment. An assessment by the I.R.S. —after administrative review and tax-court adjudication—of additional tax owed by a taxpayer who underpaid. See TAX DEFICIENCY.

jeopardy assessment. An assessment by the I.R.S. —without the usual review procedures—of additional tax owed by a taxpayer who underpaid, based on the I.R.S.'s belief that collection of the deficiency would be jeopardized by delay.

maintenance assessment. A charge for keeping an improvement in working condition or a residential property in habitable condition. — Also termed *maintenance fee*.

special assessment. The assessment of a tax on property that especially benefits from a public improvement.

3. Official valuation (of property) for purposes of taxation <assessment of the beach house>. Cf. APPRAISAL. —**assess**, *vb.*

assessment district. See DISTRICT.

assessor. 1. A person who evaluates or makes assessments, esp. for purposes of taxation. **2.** A person who advises a judge or magistrate about scientific or technical matters during a trial. See MASTER (2).

asset. 1. Generally, any item of use or value; a resource <her services were an asset to the firm>. **2.** (*pl.*) The entire property available for the payment of one's debts <assets and liabilities>.

capital asset. **a.** A long-term asset used in the operation of a business or used to produce goods or services, such as equipment, land, or an industrial plant. —Also termed *fixed asset*. **b.** For income-tax purposes, any of most assets held by a taxpayer except those assets specifically excluded by the Internal Revenue Code; major categories of noncapital assets include inventory, trade accounts, and real property used in a trade or business.

current asset. An asset that is readily convertible into cash, such as a marketable security, a note, or an account receivable. —Also termed *liquid asset*; *quick asset*.

dead asset. A worthless asset that has no realizable value, such as an uncollectible account receivable.

frozen asset. **a.** An asset that is difficult to convert into cash. —Also termed *illiquid asset*. **b.** An asset that cannot be used because of legal restrictions.

hidden asset. An asset carried on the books at a substantially reduced or understated value that is less than market value.

intangible asset. An asset that is not a physical object, such as a patent, a trademark, or goodwill.

legal asset. A decedent's asset that by law is subject to the claims of creditors or legacies. —Also termed *probate asset*.

nominal asset. An asset whose value is difficult to assess, such as a judgment or claim.

wasting asset. An asset exhausted through use or the loss of value, such as an oil well or a coal deposit.

asset allocation. The spreading of funds between different types of investments with the hope of decreasing risk and increasing return.

asset acquisition. Acquisition of a corporation by purchasing all its assets directly from the corporation itself, rather than by purchasing shares from its shareholders. Cf. SHARE ACQUISITION.

asset-based financing. See FINANCING.

asset-coverage test. In accounting, a bond-indenture restriction that permits additional borrowing only if the ratio of assets (typically net tangible assets) to debt (typically long-term debt) does not fall below a specified minimum.

asset-depreciation range. The I.R.S.'s range of depreciation lifetimes allowed for assets placed in service between 1970 and 1980 and for assets depreciated under the Modified Accelerated Cost Recovery System under the Tax Reform Act of 1986. —Abbr. ADR.

asset dividend. See DIVIDEND.

asset value. NET ASSET VALUE.

asseverate, *vb.* To state solemnly or positively; to aver. —**asseveration,** *n.* See AVERMENT.

assign, *n. (usu. pl.)* ASSIGNEE.

assigned account. See ACCOUNT.

assigned counsel. See COUNSEL.

assigned risk. See RISK.

assignee (as-ə-**nee** *or* ə-**sIn**-ee). One to whom property rights or powers are transferred by another. —Also termed *assign*.

assignee clause. A provision of the Judiciary Act of 1789 that prevented a litigant without diversity of citizenship from assigning a claim to another who did have the required diversity; in 1948 the assignee clause was replaced by 28 U.S.C. § 1359, which denies federal jurisdiction when a party is improperly or collusively joined, by assignment or otherwise, in order to invoke jurisdiction.

assigner. ASSIGNOR.

assignment, *n.* **1.** The transfer of rights or property; the rights or property so transferred <assignment of stock>. **2.** The instrument of transfer <the assignment was appended to the contract>. **3.** A task, job, or appointment <the student's math assignment> <assignment as ambassador to a foreign country>. —**assign,** *vb.*

assignment for the benefit of creditors. Assignment of a debtor's property to another person in trust so as to consolidate and liquidate the debtor's assets for payment to creditors, with any surplus being returned to the debtor; this procedure serves as a state-law substitute for federal bankruptcy proceedings.

general assignment. Assignment of a debtor's property for the benefit of all the assignor's creditors, instead of only a few. —Also termed *voluntary assignment.*

preferential assignment. See PREFER-ENTIAL TRANSFER.

assignment of errors. A specification of the trial court's alleged errors on which the appellant relies in seeking an appellate court's reversal, vacation, or modification of an adverse judgment. —Also termed *assignments of error.* See ERROR. Cf. WRIT OF ERROR.

assignment-of-rents clause. A mortgage provision or separate agreement that entitles the mortgagee to collect rents from the mortgaged premises if the mortgagor defaults.

assignor (as-ə-**nor** *or* ə-**sIn**-ər). One who transfers property rights or powers to another. —Also spelled *assigner.*

assise. ASSIZE.

assistance of counsel. Representation by a lawyer, esp. in a criminal case. See RIGHT TO COUNSEL.

effective assistance of counsel. A conscientious, meaningful legal representation, whereby the defendant is advised of all rights and the lawyer is given reasonable opportunity to perform assigned tasks.

ineffective assistance of counsel. A representation in which the lawyer cannot devote full effort to the defendant, usu. due to a conflict of interest; the Supreme Court has held that ineffective assistance of counsel denies the defendant's Sixth Amendment right.

assistance, writ of. See WRIT OF ASSISTANCE.

assisted self-determination. See *assisted suicide* under SUICIDE.

assisted suicide. See SUICIDE.

assize (ə-**sIz**), *n.* **1.** A session of a court or council. **2.** A law enacted by such a body, usu. one setting the measure, weight, or price of a thing. **3.** The procedure provided for by such an enactment. **4.** The court that hears cases involving that procedure. **5.** A jury trial. **6.** The jury's finding in such a trial. —Also spelled *assise.*

associate, *n.* **1.** A colleague or companion. **2.** A junior member of an organization or profession; esp., a lawyer in a law firm, usu. with fewer than eight years of practice, who may, upon achieving the requisite seniority, receive an offer to become a partner.

participating associate. An associate who, like a partner, shares in the firm's profits, but who does not vote on firm policy. —Abbr. P.A.

associate justice. See JUSTICE.

association. 1. The process of mentally collecting ideas, memories, or sensations. **2.** A gathering of people for a common purpose; the persons so joined. **3.** An unincorporated business organization that is not a legal entity separate from the persons who compose it; if, however, an association has sufficient corporate attributes, such as centralized management, continuity of existence, and limited liability, it may be classified and taxed as a corporation.

professional association. **a.** A group of professionals organized to practice their profession together, though not necessarily in corporate or partnership form. **b.** A group of professionals organized for education, social activity, or lobbying, such as a bar association. —Abbr. P.A.

Association of American Law Schools. An organization of law schools that have each graduated at least three annual classes of students. —Abbr. AALS.

assumed name. 1. ALIAS (1). **2.** The name under which a business operates.

assumpsit (ə-**səm[p]**-sət). [Law Latin "he undertook"; "he promised"] **1.** An express or implied promise, not under seal, by which one person undertakes to do some act or pay something to another <an assumpsit to pay a debt>. **2.** A common-law action for breach of such a promise or for breach of a contract <the creditor's assumpsit against the debtor>.

general assumpsit. An action based on the defendant's breach of an implied promise to pay a debt to the plaintiff. —Also termed *common assumpsit*; *indebitatus assumpsit*.

special assumpsit. An action based on the defendant's breach of an express contract. —Also termed *express assumpsit*.

assumption, *n.* **1.** A fact or statement taken for granted; a supposition <a logical assumption>. **2.** The act of taking (something) for or on oneself; the agreement to so take <assumption of a debt>. —**assume,** *vb.*

implied assumption. The imposition of personal liability on a land purchaser who buys subject to a mortgage and who deducts the mortgage amount from the purchase price, so that the purchaser is treated as if he or she assumed the debt.

assumption of the risk. 1. The act or an instance of a prospective plaintiff's taking on the risk of loss, injury, or damage <the skydiver's assumption of the risk>. **2.** In tort law, the principle that one who has taken on oneself the risk of loss, injury, or damage consequently cannot maintain an action against the party having caused the loss; assumption of the risk was originally an affirmative defense, but in most jurisdictions it has now been subsumed by the doctrines of contributory or comparative negligence <assumption of the risk was not a valid defense>.

assurance, *n.* **1.** Something that gives confidence; the state of being confident or secure <self-assurance>. **2.** A pledge or guarantee <adequate assurances of the borrower's solvency>. **3.** In English law, see *life insurance* under INSURANCE <she obtained assurance before traveling abroad, naming her husband as the beneficiary>. **4.** The act of transferring real property; the instrument by which it is transferred <the owner's assurance of the farm to his son>. —**assure,** *vb.*

common assurance. MUNIMENT OF TITLE.

further assurance. A covenant contained in a warranty deed whereby the grantor promises to execute any document that might be needed in the future to perfect the title that the original deed purported to transfer.

assured, *n.* INSURED.

assurer. INSURER.

asylee. A refugee applying for asylum; an asylum-seeker.

asylum. **1.** A sanctuary or shelter. **2.** Protection of usu. political refugees from arrest by a foreign jurisdiction; a nation or embassy that affords such protection. —Also termed *political asylum*. **3.** An institution for the protection and relief of the unfortunate, esp. the mentally ill.

at bar. Now before the court <the case at bar>. —Also termed *at bench*; *at the bar*.

at equity. According to equity; by, for, or in equity.

at issue. Taking opposite sides; under dispute; in question <the federal appeals courts are at issue over a question of law>.

at large. **1.** Free; unrestrained; not under control <the suspect is still at large>. **2.** Not limited to any particular place, person, matter, or question <at-large election>. **3.** Chosen by the voters of an entire political entity, such as a state, county, or city, rather than from separate districts within the entity <councilmember at large>. **4.** Not ordered in a topical way; at random <statutes at large>. **5.** Fully; in detail; in an extended form <there wasn't time to discuss the issue at large>.

at law. According to law; by, for, or in law.

at-risk rules, *n. pl.* Statutory limitations of a taxpayer's deductible losses to the amount the taxpayer could actually lose, to prevent taxpayers from sheltering income.

attach, *vb.* **1.** To annex, bind, or fasten <attach the exhibit to the pleading>. **2.** To take or seize under legal authority <attach the debtor's assets>. **3.** To become attributed; to adhere <jeopardy attaches when the jury is sworn>.

attaché (a-tə-**shay**), *n.* A person who serves as a technical adviser to an embassy.

attachment. **1.** The taking into custody of a person's property to secure a judgment or to be sold in satisfaction of a judgment. Cf. GARNISHMENT; SEQUESTRATION (1). **2.** The arrest of a person who is either in contempt of court or who is to be held as security for the payment of a judgment. **3.** A writ ordering legal seizure of property (esp. to satisfy a creditor's claim) or of a person. — Also termed *writ of attachment*. **4.** In commercial law, the creation of a security interest, occurring when the debtor agrees to the security, receives value from the secured party, and obtains rights in the collateral. U.C.C. § 9-203. Cf. PERFECTION. **5.** The act of affixing or connecting; something (as a document) that is affixed or connected to something else.

attachment bond. See BOND (2).

attachment lien. See LIEN.

attainder, *n.* At common law, the act of extinguishing a person's civil rights when sentenced to death or declared an outlaw for committing a felony or treason. —**attaint,** *vb.* See BILL OF ATTAINDER.

attempt, *n.* **1.** The act or an instance of making an effort to accomplish something, esp. without success. **2.** In criminal law, an overt act, done with the intent to commit a crime, that falls short of completing the crime; attempt is an inchoate offense distinct from the attempted crime. —Also termed (in sense 2) *offer*. Cf. CONSPIRACY; SOLICITATION (2). —**attempt**, *vb.*

attendant, *adj.* Accompanying; resulting <attendant circumstances>.

attenuation doctrine (ə-ten-yə-**way**-shən). In criminal procedure, the rule providing—as an exception to the fruit-of-the-poisonous tree doctrine—that evidence obtained by illegal means may nonetheless be admissible if the connection between the evidence and the illegal means is sufficiently attenuated or remote. See FRUIT-OF-THE-POISONOUS-TREE DOCTRINE.

attest, *vb.* **1.** To bear witness; testify <attest to the defendant's innocence>. **2.** To affirm to be true or genuine; to authenticate by signing as a witness <attest the will>. —**attestation**, *n.*—**attestative**, *adj.*

attestation clause. A provision at the end of an instrument (esp. a will) that is signed by the instrument's witnesses and that recites the formalities required by the jurisdiction in which the instrument might take effect (such as where the will might be probated). Cf. TESTIMONIUM CLAUSE.

attested copy. See *certified copy* under COPY.

attesting witness. See WITNESS.

at the bar. AT BAR.

attorney. 1. Strictly, one who is designated to transact business for another; a legal agent. —Also termed *attorney-in-fact.* **2.** One who practices

law; LAWYER. —Also termed (in sense 2) *attorney-at-law.* Cf. COUNSEL. —Abbr. atty. Pl. **attorneys.**

attorney, power of. See POWER OF ATTORNEY.

attorney-at-law. ATTORNEY (2).

attorney-client privilege. See PRIVILEGE.

attorney general. The chief law officer of a state or of the U.S., responsible for advising the government on legal matters and representing it in litigation. —Abbr. AG. Pl. **attorneys general.**

attorney in charge. See *lead counsel* under COUNSEL.

attorney-in-fact. ATTORNEY (1).

attorney malpractice. See *legal malpractice* under MALPRACTICE.

attorney of record. The lawyer who appears for a party in a lawsuit and who is entitled to receive, on the party's behalf, all pleadings and other formal documents from the court and from other parties. —Also termed *counsel of record.* See OF RECORD (1).

attorney's fees. The charge to a client for services performed for the client, such as an hourly fee, a flat fee, or a contingent fee. —Also spelled *attorneys' fees*. —Also termed *attorney fees*. Cf. RETAINER (2).

attorney's lien. See LIEN.

attorney work product. WORK PRODUCT.

attornment (ə-**tərn**-mənt), *n.* **1.** A tenant's agreement to hold the land as the tenant of a new landlord. **2.** A bailee's acknowledgment that he or she will hold the goods on behalf of someone else. —**attorn,** *vb.*

attractive nuisance. See NUISANCE.

attractive-nuisance doctrine. In tort law, the rule that a person who owns property with a dangerous instrumentality or condition that will foreseeably lure children to trespass is under a duty to protect those children from the dangerous attraction <the attractive-nuisance doctrine imposed a duty on the school to protect the children from the shallow, polluted pond on school property>. —Also termed *turntable doctrine.* See DANGEROUS INSTRUMENTALITY.

attribution, *n.* A rule or process by which a decision-maker assigns a given person's or entity's stock ownership to a related family member or entity for tax purposes when stock ownership is significant. —Also termed *stock attribution.* —**attribute,** *vb.*—**attributive,** *adj.*

atty. *abbr.* ATTORNEY.

at will. Of or relating to a legal relationship that continues until either party wishes to terminate it <tenancy at will> <at-will employee>.

at-will tenancy. See *tenancy at will* under TENANCY.

auction, *n.* A sale of property to the highest bidder. —**auction,** *vb.*—**auctioneer,** *n.*

audit, *n.* A formal examination of an individual's or organization's accounting records or financial situation. —**audit,** *vb.*—**auditor,** *n.* See GENERALLY ACCEPTED AUDITING STANDARDS.

correspondence audit. An I.R.S. audit of a taxpayer's return conducted through the mail.

field audit. An I.R.S. audit conducted at the taxpayer's business premises or lawyer's offices.

independent audit. An audit conducted by an outside person or firm not connected with the company being audited.

internal audit. An audit performed by a company's personnel to ensure that internal procedures, operations, and accounting practices are in proper order.

office audit. An I.R.S. audit of a taxpayer's return conducted in the I.R.S. agent's office.

post audit. An audit—after completion of a capital project—of funds spent on the project to assess the efficiency with which the funds were spent and to compare expected cash-flow estimates with actual cash flows.

tax audit. The review of a taxpayer's return by the I.R.S., including an examination of the taxpayer's books, vouchers, and records supporting the return. —Also termed *audit of return.*

audit opinion. See OPINION (2).

auditor. A person or firm, usu. an accountant or an accounting firm, who formally examines an individual's or entity's financial records or status.

audit trail. The chain of evidence connecting account balances to original transactions and calculations.

authentication, *n.* The act of proving that something (such as a document) is true or genuine, esp. so that it may be admitted as evidence; the condition of being so proved <authentication of the handwriting>. — **authenticate,** *vb.*—**authenticator,** *n.*

self-authentication. Authentication without extrinsic evidence of truth or genuineness; in federal courts, certain writings, such as notarized documents and certified copies of public records, may be admitted in evidence by self- authentication. Fed. R. Evid. 902.

authority. 1. The right or permission to legally act on another's behalf; the power delegated by a principal to an agent <authority to sign the contract>. See AGENCY. **2.** Governmental power or jurisdiction <within the court's authority>. **3.** A judicial or administrative decision taken as precedent <that case is good authority in Texas>. **4.** A source, such as a statute, case, or treatise, cited in support of a legal argument <the brief's table of authorities>. **5.** A governmental agency or corporation that administers a public enterprise <transit authority>.

actual authority. Authority that a principal intentionally confers on an agent, including the authority that the agent reasonably believes he or she has as a result of the agent's dealings with the principal; actual authority can be either express or implied. —Also termed *real authority.*

apparent authority. Authority that a third party reasonably believes an agent has, based on the third party's dealings with the principal; apparent authority can be created

by law even when no actual authority has been conferred. —Also termed *ostensible authority.*

authority coupled with an interest. Authority given to an agent for valuable consideration; this authority cannot be unilaterally terminated by the principal.

express authority. Authority given to the agent by explicit agreement, either orally or in writing.

implied authority. Authority given to the agent as a result of the principal's conduct, such as the principal's earlier acquiescence to the agent's actions. —Also termed *presumptive authority.*

incidental authority. Authority needed to carry out actual or apparent authority; for example, the actual authority to borrow money includes the incidental authority to sign commercial paper to effect the borrowing. —Also termed *inferred authority.*

naked authority. Authority delegated solely for the principal's benefit, without giving any consideration to the agent; this authority can be revoked by the principal at any time.

authorize, *vb.* **1.** To give legal authority; to empower <he authorized the employee to act for him>. **2.** To formally approve; to sanction <the city authorized the construction project>—**authorization,** *n.*

authorized capital stock. See *authorized stock* under STOCK.

authorized shares. See *authorized stock* under STOCK.

authorized stock. See STOCK.

authorized stock issue. See *authorized stock* under STOCK.

autocracy (aw-**tok**-rə-see), *n.* Government by one person with unlimited power and authority; monarchy. —**autocratic,** *adj.*—**autocrat,** *n.*

automatic stay. See STAY.

automatic suspension. See *automatic stay* under STAY.

automatism (aw-**tom**-ə-tiz-əm), *n.* Action or conduct occurring without will, purpose, or reasoned intention, such as sleepwalking; automatism may be asserted as a defense to negate the requisite mental state of voluntariness for commission of a crime. —**automaton,** *n.*

automobile guest statute. GUEST STATUTE.

automobile insurance. See INSURANCE.

autonomy (aw-**ton**-ə-mee), *n.* The right of self-government; a self-governing state. —**autonomous,** *adj.*

autopsy. An examination of a dead body in order to determine the cause of death, esp. in a criminal investigation. —Also termed *postmortem.*

autoptic evidence. See *demonstrative evidence* under EVIDENCE.

autrefois (oh-trə-**fwah**). [Law French] On another occasion; formerly.

autrefois acquit. A plea in bar of arraignment that the defendant has been acquitted of the offense. See DOUBLE JEOPARDY.

autrefois convict. A plea in bar of arraignment that the defendant

has been convicted of the offense. See DOUBLE JEOPARDY.

avail, *n.* **1.** Use or advantage <of little or no avail>. **2.** (*pl.*) Profits or proceeds, esp. from a sale of property <the avails of the trust fund>.

availment, *n.* The act of making use or taking advantage of something for oneself <availment of the benefits of public office>. —**avail,** *vb.*

average, *n.* **1.** A single value that represents a broad sample of subjects; esp., in mathematics, the mean, median, or mode of a series. **2.** The ordinary or typical level; the norm. **3.** In maritime law, liability for partial loss or damage to an insured ship or its cargo during a voyage; the apportionment of such liability. —**average,** *vb.* & *adj.*

general average. Average resulting from an intentional partial sacrifice of ship or cargo in order to avoid total loss; such liability is shared by all parties who had an interest in the voyage. —Also termed *gross average.*

particular average. Average resulting from an accidental partial loss or damage; such liability is borne solely by the person who suffered the loss. —Also termed *simple average.*

average daily balance. See DAILY BALANCE.

averment, *n.* A positive declaration or affirmation of fact; esp., an assertion or allegation in a pleading <the plaintiff's averment that the defendant ran a red light>. —**aver,** *vb.*

negative averment. In pleading, an averment that is negative in form but affirmative in substance and that must be proved by the alleging party; an example is the statement "she was not old enough to enter into the contract," which is more than just a simple denial. Cf. TRAVERSE.

avigational easement. See EASEMENT.

avoid, *vb. Jargon.* To render void <because the restrictive covenant was overbroad, the court avoided it>; because this legal use of *avoid* can be easily confused with the ordinary sense of the word, the verb *to void* is preferable.

avoidable-consequences doctrine. MITIGATION-OF-DAMAGES DOCTRINE.

avoidance, *n.* **1.** The act of evading or escaping <avoidance of tax liability>. See TAX AVOIDANCE. **2.** The act of refraining from (something) <avoidance of an argument>. **3.** VOIDANCE. <avoidance of the agreement>. **4.** CONFESSION AND AVOIDANCE <the defendant filed an avoidance in an attempt to avert liability>. —**avoid,** *vb.*

avowal, *n.* **1.** An open declaration. **2.** OFFER OF PROOF. —**avow,** *vb.*

avowry (ə-**vow**-ree), *n.* In common-law pleading, an acknowledgment—

in an answer to a replevin action—that one has taken property, and a justification for that taking <the defendant's avowry was based on alleged damage to the property by the plaintiff>. —**avow,** *vb.*

avulsion (ə-**vəl**-shən), *n.* **1.** Generally, a forcible detachment or separation. **2.** In land law, a sudden removal of land caused by change in a river's course or by flood; land removed by avulsion remains the property of the original owner. Cf. ALLUVION; ACCRETION (1). **3.** A tearing away of a body part surgically or accidentally. —**avulse,** *vb.*

award, *n.* A final judgment or decision, esp. one by an arbitrator or by a jury assessing damages. —Also termed *arbitrament.*

award, *vb.* To grant by formal process or by judicial decree <the company awarded the contract to the low bidder> <the jury awarded punitive damages>.

AWOL. *abbr.* Absent without leave; missing without notice or permission.

axiom, *n.* An established principle that is universally accepted within a given framework of reasoning or thinking <"innocent until proven guilty" is an age-old axiom or criminal law>. —**axiomatic,** *adj.*

B

BA. See *banker's acceptance* under ACCEPTANCE.

baby act, pleading the. *Slang.* Asserting a person's infancy as a defense to an action based on a contract made by the minor.

Baby Doe. A generic pseudonym for a very young child involved in litigation, esp. in the context of medical care.

Baby FTC Act. A state statute, modeled on the Federal Trade Commission Act, that outlaws deceptive and unfair practices.

baby-snatching. See *child-kidnapping* under KIDNAPPING.

BAC. *abbr.* Blood alcohol content. See DRIVING WHILE INTOXICATED.

backadation. BACKWARDATION.

backdate, *vb.* **1.** To put a date earlier than the actual date on (something, as an instrument); backdating does not affect an instrument's negotiability. U.C.C. § 3-113(a). Cf. POSTDATE. **2.** To make (something) retroactively valid.

back-to-back loan. See LOAN.

backwardation. In securities transactions, a fee paid by the seller so that the buyer will allow delayed delivery of the securities beyond their original delivery date. —Also termed *backadation*.

bad-boy disqualification. A person's disqualification from certain SEC-registration exemptions as a result of that person's securities-law violations.

bad check. See CHECK.

bad debt. See DEBT.

bad-debt reserve. See RESERVE.

bad faith, *n.* Dishonesty of belief or purpose <the jury found that the insurance company had settled the claim in bad faith>. —Also termed *mala fides* (**mal**-ə-**fI**-deez). —**bad-faith,** *adj.* Cf. GOOD FAITH.

badge of fraud. An act or fact that the courts generally interpret as a reliable indicator that a party to a transaction was trying to hinder or defraud the other party, such as a transfer in anticipation of litigation, a transaction outside the usual course of business, or false statements. See FRAUD.

badge of slavery. 1. Strictly, a legal disability suffered by a slave, such as the inability to vote or to own property. **2.** Broadly, any act of racial discrimination—public or private— that Congress can prohibit under the Thirteenth Amendment.

bad-man theory. The jurisprudential doctrine or belief that a bad person represents the best test of what the law actually is because that person will carefully calculate precisely what the rules allow and operate up to the rules' limits; this theory was first espoused by Oliver Wendell Holmes in his famous essay *The Path of the Law* (1897). See LEGAL REALISM.

bad title. See TITLE.

bail, *n.* **1.** Release of a prisoner on security for a future appearance <the court refused bail for the accused serial killer>. **2.** The security (such as cash or a bond) required by the court for such a release <bail is set at $500>. Cf. RECOGNIZANCE.

excessive bail. Bail that is unreasonably high considering both the offense with which the accused is charged and the risk that the accused will not appear for trial; excessive bail is prohibited by the Eighth Amendment.

3. BAILER (1) <the attorney stood as bail for her client>.

bail, *vb*. **1.** To obtain the release of (oneself or another) by providing security for future appearance <his parents bailed him out of jail>. **2.** To release (a person) after receiving such security <the court bailed the prisoner>. **3.** To place (personal property) in someone else's charge or trust <bail the goods with the warehouse>.

bail bond. See BOND (2).

bail bondsman. BAILER (1).

bailee. One to whom personal property is delivered without any change in ownership. See BAILMENT.

bailer. **1.** One who provides bail as a surety for a criminal defendant's release. —Also spelled *bailor*. —Also termed *bail bondsman*; *bailsman*. **2.** BAILOR (1).

bailiff. **1.** A court officer who maintains order with the parties, attorneys, and jury during court proceedings. **2.** A sheriff's officer who executes writs and serves processes.

bail-jumping, *n*. The criminal offense of defaulting on one's bail. — **bail-jumper,** *n*. See JUMP BAIL.

bailment. **1.** A delivery of personal property by one person (the *bailor*) to another (the *bailee*) who holds the property under an express or implied-in-fact contract. Cf. PAWN.

actual bailment. A bailment that arises from an actual or constructive delivery of property to the bailee.

bailment for hire. A bailment for which only the bailee is compensated, such as leaving one's car with a parking attendant. —Also termed *lucrative bailment*.

bailment for mutual benefit. A bailment for which the bailee is compensated and from which the bailor receives some additional benefit, such as leaving one's car with a parking attendant who will also wash the car while it is parked.

constructive bailment. A bailment that arises when the law imposes an obligation on a possessor of personal property to return the property to its rightful owner, as with an involuntary bailment.

gratuitous bailment. A bailment for which the bailee receives no compensation, such as the borrowing of a friend's car; a gratuitous bailee is liable for loss of the property only if the loss is caused by the bailee's gross negligence. —Also termed *naked bailment*.

involuntary bailment. A bailment that arises when a person accidentally—but without any negligence—leaves personal property in another's possession; an involuntary bailee who refuses to return the property to the owner can be liable for conversion. See *abandoned property*, *lost property*, *mislaid property* under PROPERTY.

2. The personal property delivered by the bailor to the bailee. **3.** The contract or legal relation resulting from such a delivery. **4.** The action of posting bail for a criminal defendant. **5.** The documentation on the posting of bail for a criminal defendant.

bailor. 1. One who delivers personal property to another as a bailment. — Also spelled *bailer*. **2.** BAILER (1).

bailout, *n.* **1.** A rescue of an entity, usu. a corporation, from financial trouble. **2.** An attempt by a business to receive favorable tax treatment of its profits, such as a conversion of ordinary income to capital gain.

bailsman. BAILER (1).

bait and switch. A sales practice whereby a store advertises a low-priced product to lure customers into the store only to induce them to buy a higher- priced product; most states prohibit the bait and switch when the original product is not really available as advertised.

balance, *vb.* **1.** To compute the difference between two sides of an account <the accountant balanced the company's books>. **2.** To equalize in weight, number, or proportion; to bring into harmony <the law firm tried to balance the ratio of associates to partners>. **3.** To offset <the judge balanced the equities before granting the motion>. —**balance,** *n.*

balance of probability. PREPONDERANCE OF THE EVIDENCE.

balance sheet. A statement of an entity's current financial position, disclosing the value of the entity's assets, liabilities, and owners' equity. —Also termed *statement of finan-*

cial condition; *statement of financial position*. Cf. INCOME STATEMENT.

balance-sheet test. See *balance-sheet insolvency* under INSOLVENCY.

balancing test. A judicial doctrine, used esp. in constitutional law, whereby a court measures competing interests—such as between individual rights and governmental powers, or between state authority and federal supremacy—and decides which interest should prevail.

balloon note. See NOTE.

balloon payment. See PAYMENT.

balloon-payment mortgage. See MORTGAGE.

ballot, *n.* **1.** The formal record of a person's vote. **2.** A list of candidates running for office. —**ballot,** *vb.*

banc (baynk *or* bon[g]k). [French] Bench. See EN BANC.

B and E. *abbr.* Breaking and entering. See BURGLARY (2).

bank. 1. A financial establishment for the deposit, loan, exchange, or issue of money and for the transmission of funds.

advising bank. A bank that gives notice of the issuance of a letter of credit by another bank. U.C.C. § 5-103(1)(e).

commercial bank. A bank authorized to receive both demand and time deposits, to engage in trust services, to issue letters of credit, to rent time-deposit boxes, and to supply similar services.

confirming bank. A bank that declares either that it will honor a letter of credit issued by another bank or that such a credit will be honored by the issuer or a third bank. U.C.C. § 5-103(1)(f).

correspondent bank. A bank that acts as an agent for another bank, or engages in an exchange of services with that bank, in a geographical area to which the other bank does not have direct access.

investment bank. A bank whose primary purpose is to acquire financing for businesses, esp. through the sale of securities; an investment bank does not accept deposits and, apart from selling securities, does not deal with the public at large. Cf. INVESTMENT BANKER.

member bank. A bank that is a member of the Federal Reserve System. —Also termed *reserve bank.* See FEDERAL RESERVE SYSTEM.

mutual savings bank. A bank that has no capital stock and in which the depositors are the owners. See SAVINGS-AND-LOAN ASSOCIATION.

national bank. A bank incorporated under federal law and governed by a charter approved by the Comptroller of the Currency.

payor bank. A bank that is requested to pay the amount of a negotiable instrument and, on the bank's acceptance, is obliged to pay that amount. —Also termed *drawee bank.*

presenting bank. A nonpayor bank that presents a negotiable instrument for payment.

savings-and-loan bank. See SAVINGS-AND-LOAN ASSOCIATION.

savings bank. A bank that receives deposits, pays interest on them, and makes certain types of loans, but does not provide checking services.

state bank. A bank chartered by a state and supervised by the state banking department and the FDIC; a state bank must follow Federal Reserve Board regulations even if it is not a member of the Federal Reserve System.

2. The office in which such an establishment conducts transactions.

bank acceptance. See *banker's acceptance* under ACCEPTANCE.

bank-account trust. See *Totten trust* under TRUST.

bankbook. PASSBOOK.

bank draft. See DRAFT.

banker's acceptance. See ACCEPTANCE.

bank note. See NOTE.

bankrupt, *n.* **1.** A person who cannot meet his or her financial obligations; an insolvent person. **2.** DEBTOR (2).

cessionary bankrupt. Archaic. A person who forfeits all property so that it may be divided among creditors; for the modern near-equivalent, see CHAPTER 7.

bankruptcy. 1. The statutory procedure, usu. triggered by insolvency, by which a person is relieved of most debts and undergoes a judicially supervised reorganization or liquidation for the benefit of that person's creditors; for various types of bankruptcy under federal law, see entries at CHAPTER. —Also termed *bankruptcy proceeding*; *bankruptcy case.* **2.** Loosely, the fact of being financially unable to pay one's debts and meet one's obligations; INSOLVENCY.

involuntary bankruptcy. Bankruptcy proceedings initiated by creditors (usu. three or more) to force the debtor to declare bankruptcy or be legally declared bankrupt. 11 U.S.C. § 303(b).

voluntary bankruptcy. Bankruptcy proceedings initiated by the debtor. 11 U.S.C. § 301.

3. The fact of having declared bankruptcy under a bankruptcy statute. **4.** The field of law dealing with the rights and entitlements of debtors and creditors in bankruptcy situations.

Bankruptcy Act. The Bankruptcy Act of 1898, which governed bankruptcy cases filed before October 1, 1979.

bankruptcy case. BANKRUPTCY (1).

Bankruptcy Code. The Bankruptcy Reform Act of 1978 (as amended and codified in 11 U.S.C.), which governs bankruptcy cases filed on or after October 1, 1979.

bankruptcy court. A federal court that is a unit of a district court and that is exclusively concerned with administering bankruptcy proceedings.

bankruptcy estate. A debtor's legal and equitable interests in property as of the commencement of a bankruptcy case.

bankruptcy judge. A judicial officer appointed by a U.S. Court of Appeals to preside over a bankruptcy court in a designated judicial district for a term of 14 years.

bankruptcy plan. A detailed program of action formulated by a debt-or or its creditors to govern the debtor's rehabilitation, continued operation or liquidation, and payment of debts; the bankruptcy court and creditors must approve the plan before it is implemented. —Also termed *plan of reorganization*; *plan.* See ARRANGEMENT WITH CREDITORS.

bankruptcy proceeding. **1.** BANKRUPTCY (1). **2.** Any judicial or procedural action—usu. in bankruptcy court—related to a bankruptcy, such as a hearing.

bankruptcy trustee. The person appointed by the U.S. Trustee and approved by the bankruptcy court to take charge of and administer the debtor's estate during bankruptcy proceedings. —Also termed *trustee in bankruptcy.* See UNITED STATES TRUSTEE.

bar, *n.* **1.** In a courtroom, the railing that encloses the area around the judge where the court's business is transacted; by extension, a similar railing in a legislative assembly <the spectator stood behind the bar>. **2.** The whole body of lawyers qualified to practice in a given court or jurisdiction; the legal profession, or an organized subset of it. <the attorney's outrageous misconduct disgraced the bar>. See BAR ASSOCIATION. **3.** A particular court or system of courts <case at bar> **4.** BAR EXAMINATION <Pendarvis passed the bar>. **5.** A preventive barrier to or the destruction of a legal action or claim; the effect of a judgment for the defendant <a bar to any new lawsuit>. Cf. MERGER (5). **6.** A plea arresting a lawsuit or legal claim <the defendant filed a bar>. See *plea in bar* under PLEA.

bar, *vb.* To prevent, esp. by legal objection <the statute of limitations barred the filing of the stale claims>.

bar association. An organization of members of the legal profession <several state bar associations sponsor superb CLE programs>.

integrated bar. A bar association in which membership is a statutory requirement for the practice of law in a given state. —Also termed *unified bar.*

bareboat charter. See CHARTER (3).

bare licensee. See LICENSEE.

bare promise. See *naked promise* under PROMISE.

bar examination. A written test that a person must pass before being licensed to practice law in a given state; the content and format of bar examinations vary from state to state. —Often shortened to *bar.*

Multistate Bar Examination. A part of every state's bar examination given in the form of a multiple-choice test covering broad legal subjects, including constitutional law, contracts, criminal law, evidence, property, and torts. —Abbr. MBE.

bar examiner. One appointed by the state to test law graduates by preparing and administering the bar examination.

bargain, *n.* An agreement between parties for the exchange of promises or performances; a bargain is not necessarily a contract because the consideration may be insufficient or the transaction may be illegal. —**bargain,** *vb.*

bargain-and-sale deed. See DEED.

bargainee. The buyer in a bargained-for exchange.

bargaining unit. A group of employees authorized to engage in collective bargaining on behalf of all the employees of one company.

bargainor. The seller in a bargained-for exchange.

barratry (**bair**-ə-tree *or* **ba[ə]r**-), *n.* **1.** Vexatious persistence in, or incitement to, litigation; barratry is a crime in most jurisdictions. **2.** In maritime law, fraudulent or grossly negligent conduct (by a master or crew) that is prejudicial to a shipowner. —**barratrous,** *adj.*—**barrator,** *n.*

barrister, *n.* In England or Northern Ireland, a lawyer who is admitted to plead at the bar and who may try or argue cases in superior courts. —**barristerial,** *adj.* Cf. SOLICITOR (4).

barter, *n.* The exchange of one commodity for another without the use of money. —**barter,** *vb.*

basement court. *Slang.* A low-level court of limited jurisdiction, such as a police court, traffic court, municipal court, or small-claims court.

basis. **1.** A fundamental principle; an underlying condition. **2.** In tax law, the value assigned to a taxpayer's investment in property and used primarily for computing gain or loss from a transfer of the property; when the assigned value represents the cost of acquiring the property, it is also called *cost basis.* —Also termed *tax basis.* Pl. **bases.**

adjusted basis. Basis increased by capital improvements and decreased by depreciation deductions.

carryover basis. The basis of property transferred by gift or in trust; carryover basis equals the transferor's basis. —Also termed *substituted basis.*

stepped-up basis. The basis of property transferred by inheritance; stepped-up basis equals the fair market value of property on the date of the decedent's death (or on the alternate valuation date).

substituted basis. **a.** The basis of property transferred in a tax-free exchange or other specified transactions. **b.** See *carryover basis.*

basis point. One-hundredth of one percent (.01%); basis points are used in computing investment yields, and in apportioning costs and figuring interest rates in real-estate transactions.

bastard. 1. A child born outside of a lawful marriage. **2.** A child born to a married woman whose husband could not possibly be the father.

bastardy. ILLEGITIMACY.

bastardy proceeding. PATERNITY SUIT.

Batson **challenge.** See CHALLENGE (1).

battered-child syndrome. The medical and psychological condition of a child who has suffered continuing injuries that could not be accidental and are therefore presumed to have been inflicted by someone close to the child.

battered-woman syndrome. The medical and psychological condition of a woman who has suffered physical, sexual, or emotional abuse at the hands of a spouse or lover; this syndrome is sometimes proposed as a justification defense for the woman's killing of the man. —Sometimes (more specifically) termed *battered-wife syndrome.*

battery, *n.* **1.** In criminal law, the application of force to another resulting in harmful or offensive contact.

aggravated battery. A criminal battery accompanied by circumstances that make it more severe, such as the use of a deadly weapon or the fact that the battery resulted in serious bodily harm.

simple battery. A criminal battery not accompanied by aggravating circumstances and not resulting in grievous bodily harm.

2. In tort law, an intentional and offensive touching of another. —**batter,** *vb.* Cf. ASSAULT.

battle of the forms. In commercial law, the conflict between the terms of standard forms exchanged between a buyer and a seller during contract negotiations; U.C.C. § 2-207 attempts to resolve battles of the forms by abandoning the common-law requirement of mirror-image acceptance and providing that an acceptance with additional terms is normally valid. See MIRROR-IMAGE RULE.

bawdy house. DISORDERLY HOUSE.

bear market. See MARKET.

bearer. A person who holds a negotiable instrument, esp. one that is marked "payable to bearer."

bearer bond. See BOND (1).

bearer document. See *bearer paper* under PAPER.

bearer instrument. See *bearer paper* under PAPER.

bearer paper. See PAPER.

beauty contest. *Slang.* A meeting at which a major legal client interviews two or more law firms to decide which firm will get its business.

belief-action distinction. In First Amendment law, the Supreme Court's distinction between allowing a person to follow any chosen belief and allowing the state to intervene if necessary to protect others from the practices of that belief.

belief-cluster. In critical legal studies, a group of unconnected ideas or opinions that appear to be related when considered together in reference to a specific subject, such as racism, sexism, or religious intolerance.

belligerent, *n.* A country involved in a war or other hostile action. — **belligerent,** *adj.*

bellum (**bel**-əm). [Latin] WAR (1).

below-market loan. See *interest-free loan* under LOAN.

bench. 1. The seat occupied by the judge in a courtroom <approach the bench>. **2.** The court considered in its official capacity <remarks from the bench>. **3.** Judges collectively <bench and bar>. **4.** The judges of a particular court <the Fifth Circuit bench>.

bench conference. SIDEBAR CONFERENCE (1).

bench memo. 1. A short brief submitted by a lawyer to a trial judge, often at the judge's request. **2.** A legal memorandum prepared by an appellate judge's law clerk to help the judge in preparing for oral argument and perhaps in drafting an opinion.

bench trial. See TRIAL.

bench warrant. See WARRANT (1).

beneficial, *adj.* **1.** Favorable; producing benefits <beneficial ruling>. **2.** Consisting in a right that derives from something other than legal title <beneficial interest in a trust>.

beneficial interest. A right or expectancy in something (such as a trust or an estate), as opposed to legal title to that thing; for example, a person with a beneficial interest in a trust receives income from the trust but does not hold legal title to the trust property.

beneficial owner. See OWNER.

beneficial use. See USE (1).

beneficiary, *n.* One who gains or benefits from something; esp., the person designated to receive something from a legal arrangement or instrument, such as the income from a trust or the proceeds from an insurance policy. —**beneficiary,** *adj.*

contingent beneficiary. The person designated in a life-insurance policy to receive the proceeds if the primary beneficiary is unable to do so. —Also termed *secondary beneficiary.*

creditor beneficiary. A third-party beneficiary whom the promisee owes a debt to be satisfied by performance of the contract.

donee beneficiary. A third-party beneficiary who is intended to receive the benefit of the contract's performance as a gift from the promisee.

incidental beneficiary. A third-party beneficiary who is not intended to benefit from a contract and thus does not acquire rights under the contract. Cf. *intended beneficiary.*

intended beneficiary. A third-party beneficiary who is intended to benefit from a contract and thus acquires rights under the contract as well as the ability to enforce the contract once those rights have vested. Cf. *incidental beneficiary.*

primary beneficiary. The person designated in a life-insurance policy to receive the proceeds when the insured dies.

third-party beneficiary. A person who is not a party to a contract but who may benefit from the contract's performance; for example, if Ann and Bob agree to a contract under which Bob will render some performance to Chris, then Chris is a third-party beneficiary.

benefit, *n.* **1.** Advantage; privilege <the benefit of owning a car>. **2.** Fruit, profit, or gain <a benefit received from the sale>.

fringe benefit. A benefit received by an employee from an employer, other than direct salary or compensation, such as insurance, a company car, or a tuition allowance. — Often shortened (esp. in pl.) to *benefit.*

general benefit. In the law of eminent domain, the whole community's benefit as a result of the taking.

pecuniary benefit. A benefit capable of monetary valuation.

special benefit. In the law of eminent domain, a benefit that accrues to the owner of the land in question and not to any others.

3. Financial assistance that is received from an employer, insurance, or a public program (such as social security) in time of sickness, disability, or unemployment <a benefit from the welfare office>. **—benefit,** *vb.*

benefit of clergy. 1. At common law, the right of a cleric not to be tried for a felony in the King's Court <in the Middle Ages, anyone who could recite the "neck verse" was granted the benefit of clergy>. **2.** Loosely, religious approval as solemnized in a church ritual <the couple had several children without benefit of clergy>.

benefit-of-the-bargain rule. The principle that a defrauded purchaser may recover the difference between the real and the fraudulently represented value of the property purchased. —Also termed *benefit-of-bargain rule.*

bequeath, *vb.* To give property (usu. personal property) by will. **—bequest, bequeathal,** *n.*

bequest, *n.* **1.** The act of giving property (usu. personal property) by will. **2.** Property (usu. personal property other than money) disposed of in a will. Cf. DEVISE; LEGACY.

conditional bequest. A bequest whose effectiveness or continuation depends on the occurrence or nonoccurrence of a particular event.

demonstrative bequest. A bequest that, by its terms, must be paid out of a specific source, such as a stock fund.

executory bequest. A bequest of a future, deferred, or contingent interest in personalty.

general bequest. A bequest payable out of the general assets of the estate.

pecuniary bequest. A bequest of money; LEGACY.

residuary bequest. A bequest of the remainder of the testator's estate, after the payment of the debts, legacies, and specific bequests. —Also termed *remainder bequest.*

specific bequest. A bequest of a specific item or cash amount.

Berne Convention. An international copyright treaty—administered by the World Intellectual Property Organization—providing that works created by citizens of one signatory nation will be protected in other signatory nations, without the need for local formalities; the U.S. ratified the Berne Convention in 1989 and modified several aspects of U.S. copyright law to comply with the treaty's terms.

best efforts. Diligent attempts to carry out an obligation; as a standard, a best-efforts obligation is stronger than a good-faith obligation <the contractor must use best efforts to complete its work within the stated time>. —Also termed *best endeavors.* Cf. DUE DILIGENCE (1); GOOD FAITH.

best-efforts underwriting. See UNDERWRITING.

best evidence. See EVIDENCE.

best-evidence rule. The evidentiary rule providing that for a party to prove the contents of a writing (or a recording or photograph), the original writing must be produced unless it is unavailable, in which case secondary evidence—such as copies, notes, or testimony—may be admitted. Fed. R. Evid. 1001-1004. —Also termed *original-writing rule; original-document rule.*

bestiality (bes-chee-**al**-i-dee *or* bees-) Sexual activity between a human and an animal. See SODOMY.

best-mode requirement. In patent law, the requirement that a patent application show the best physical method known to the inventor for using the invention.

bestow, *vb.* To convey as a gift <bestow an honor on another>. — **bestowal,** *n.*

best use. See *highest and best use* under USE.

betterment. An improvement that increases the value of real property. See IMPROVEMENT.

betterment act. A statute requiring the owner of a piece of land to compensate an occupant who, with the good-faith belief that he or she is the real owner, improves the land; the compensation usu. equals the increase in the land's value generated by the improvements. —Also termed *occupying-claimant act.*

beyond a reasonable doubt. See REASONABLE DOUBT.

BFOQ. *abbr.* BONA FIDE OCCUPATIONAL QUALIFICATION.

BFP. See *bona fide purchaser* under PURCHASER.

bias, *n.* Inclination; prejudice <the juror's bias prompted a challenge for cause>. —**bias,** *vb.*—**biased,** *adj.*

bicameral, *adj.* (Of a legislature) having two legislative bodies (usu. called the House of Representatives and the Senate); the federal government and all states except Nebraska have bicameral legislatures. —**bicameralism,** *n.*

bid, *n.* **1.** A buyer's offer to pay a specified price for something that may or may not be for sale <a bid at an auction> <a takeover bid>. **2.** A submitted price at which one will perform work or supply goods <the subcontractor's bid>. —**bid,** *vb.*

open bid. A bid that the bidder may reduce after submission in order to meet competing bids.

sealed bid. A bid that is not disclosed until all submitted bids are opened and considered simultaneously.

bid and asked. In securities transactions, a notation describing the range of prices quoted in an over-the-counter stock exchange; *bid* denotes the buying price, and *asked* denotes the selling price. See SPREAD (2).

bid price. See PRICE.

bifurcated divorce. See *divisible divorce* under DIVORCE.

bifurcated trial. See TRIAL.

bigamy, *n.* The act of marrying one person while legally married to another; bigamy is a criminal offense if it is committed knowingly. —**bigamous,** *adj.*—**bigamist,** *n.* Cf. POLYGAMY; MONOGAMY.

bilateral contract. See CONTRACT.

bilateral mistake. See *mutual mistake* (a) under MISTAKE.

bilateral monopoly. See MONOPOLY.

bill, *n.* **1.** A formal written complaint, such as a court paper requesting some specific action for reasons alleged. **2.** An equitable pleading by which a claimant brings a claim in a court of equity; before the merger of law and equity, the bill in equity was analogous to the declaration in law. —Also termed *bill in equity.* See DECLARATION (7).

bill of certiorari. A bill in equity seeking removal of an action to a higher court. See CERTIORARI.

bill of costs. A certified, itemized statement of the amount of taxable costs furnished by an attorney in an action or a suit.

bill of discovery. A bill in equity seeking disclosure of facts within the adverse party's knowledge. See DISCOVERY.

bill of exceptions. A formal written statement—signed by the trial judge and presented to the appellate court—of a party's objections or exceptions taken during trial and the grounds on which they are founded; these bills have largely been replaced by straight appeals under the Federal Rules of Civil Procedure. See EXCEPTION (1).

bill of peace. A bill in equity seeking relief from multiple suits.

bill of review. A bill in equity requesting that a court reverse or revise a prior decree.

3. A legislative proposal offered for debate before its enactment.

appropriation bill. A bill that authorizes governmental expenditures; the federal government cannot spend money unless Congress has appropriated the funds. U.S. Const. art. I, § 9, cl. 7. See APPROPRIATION (3) & (4).

engrossed bill. A bill passed by one house of the legislature.

enrolled bill. A bill passed by both houses of the legislature and signed by their presiding officers. See ENROLLED-BILL RULE.

omnibus bill. A single bill containing various distinct matters, usu. drafted in this way to force the executive either to accept all the unrelated minor provisions or to veto the major provision.

revenue bill. A bill that levies or raises taxes; federal revenue bills must originate in the House of Representatives. U.S. Const. art. I, § 7, cl. 1.

4. Loosely, an enacted statute <the GI Bill>. **5.** An itemized list of charges; INVOICE <hospital bill>. Cf. FEE STATEMENT. **6.** A bill of exchange <the bank would not honor the unsigned bill>. See DRAFT (1). **7.** A formal document or note; an instrument <bill of sale>.

billable hour. A unit of time used by an attorney to account for work performed and chargeable to a client; billable hours are usu. divided into quarters or tenths of an hour <some firms require associates to amass at least 2,100 billable hours each year>.

billa vera. [Latin] TRUE BILL.

bill in equity. BILL (2).

bill of attainder. A special legislative act prescribing capital punishment, without a trial, for a person guilty of a high offense such as treason or a felony; bills of attainder are

prohibited by U.S. Const. art. I, § 9, cl. 3. —Also termed *act of attainder*. See ATTAINDER.

bill of certiorari. See BILL (2).

bill of costs. See BILL (2).

bill of credit. LETTER OF CREDIT.

bill of discovery. See BILL (2).

bill of exceptions. See BILL (2).

bill of exchange. See DRAFT (1).

bill of indictment. The instrument presented to a grand jury for the jury's determination of whether sufficient evidence exists to formally charge the accused with a crime. See INDICTMENT; NO BILL; TRUE BILL.

bill of lading. A document of title acknowledging the receipt of goods by a carrier or by the shipper's agent. —Abbr. B/L. —Also termed *waybill.*

order bill of lading. A negotiable bill of lading stating that the goods are consigned to the order of the person named in the bill.

straight bill of lading. A nonnegotiable bill of lading that specifies a consignee to whom the carrier is contractually obligated to deliver the goods.

bill of pains and penalties. A legislative act that is similar to a bill of attainder but that prescribes punishment less severe than capital punishment; like the bill of attainder, it was abolished by the U.S. Constitution.

bill of particulars. A formal, detailed statement of the claims or charges brought by a plaintiff or a prosecutor, usu. filed in response to the defendant's request for a more specific complaint. —Also termed *statement of particulars*. See MOTION FOR MORE DEFINITE STATEMENT.

bill of peace. See BILL (2).

bill of review. See BILL (2).

bill of rights. (*usu. cap.*) A section or addendum, usu. in a constitution, defining the situations in which a politically organized society will permit free, spontaneous, and individual activity, and guaranteeing that government powers will not be used in certain ways; esp., the first 10 amendments to the U.S. Constitution.

bill of sale. An instrument for the conveyance of title to personal property. Cf. DEED.

bind, *vb.* To impose one or more legal duties on (a person or institution) <the contract binds the parties> <courts are bound by precedent>. —**binding,** *adj.*

binder. 1. In property law, a document in which the buyer and the seller of real property declare their common intention to bring about a transfer of ownership, usu. accompanied by the buyer's initial payment. **2.** Loosely, the buyer's initial payment in the sale of real property. Cf. EARNEST MONEY. **3.** In insurance, an insurer's memorandum giving the insured temporary coverage while the application for an insurance policy is being processed.

binding agreement. See AGREEMENT.

binding instruction. See *mandatory instruction* under JURY INSTRUCTION.

binding jury instruction. See JURY INSTRUCTION.

binding precedent. See PRECEDENT.

bind over, *vb.* To put (a person) under a bond or other legal obligation to do something, esp. to appear in court. —**binding over,** *n.*— **bindover,** *adj.*

bindover hearing. PRELIMINARY HEARING.

B/L. *abbr.* BILL OF LADING.

blackletter law. One or more legal principles that are fundamental and well settled. —Also termed *hornbook law.*

blacklist, *vb.* To put the name of (a person) on a list of those persons who are to be boycotted or punished <the firm blacklisted the former employee>. —**blacklist,** *n.*

blackmail, *n.* A menacing demand made without justification; EXTORTION (1). —**blackmail,** *vb.* Cf. GREENMAIL; FEEMAIL.

blackmail suit. See SUIT.

black market. See MARKET.

blanket bond. See BOND (2).

blanket mortgage. See MORTGAGE.

blanket policy. See INSURANCE POLICY.

blanket search warrant. See SEARCH WARRANT.

blank indorsement. See INDORSEMENT.

blasphemy, *n.* Irreverence toward a religious icon or something considered sacred; blasphemy was a crime at common law and remains so in some U.S. jurisdictions, but it is rarely if ever enforced because of its questionable constitutionality under the First Amendment. —**blaspheme,** *vb.*—**blasphemous,** *adj.*

blended trust. See TRUST.

blind trust. See TRUST.

bloc. A group of persons or nations aligned with a common interest or purpose, even if only temporarily <voting bloc>.

block, *n.* **1.** A municipal area enclosed by streets <three blocks away>. See LOT (1). **2.** A quantity of things bought or sold as a unit <a block of preferred shares>.

blockade. In international law, a belligerent's prevention of access to or egress from an enemy's ports by stationing ships or squadrons in such a position that they can intercept vessels attempting to approach or leave those ports; to be binding, a blockade must be effective—that is, must be maintained by a force sufficient to prevent access to the coast of the enemy.

blockage rule. In tax law, the principle that a large block of stock shares may be valued at less than the sum of the values of the individual shares because such a large block may be difficult to sell at full price.

blocked income. See INCOME.

blocking statute. A law that imposes a penalty on a national for complying with a foreign court's discovery request. —Also termed *clawback provision*.

blood, corruption of the. See CORRUPTION OF THE BLOOD.

blue-blue-ribbon jury. See *blue-ribbon jury* under JURY.

Blue Book. 1. In some states, a compilation of session laws. **2.** A volume formerly published to give parallel citation tables for a volume in the National Reporter System.

Bluebook. The citation guide—formerly titled *A Uniform System of Citation*—that is generally considered the authoritative reference for American legal citations; it is compiled by the editors of the *Columbia Law Review*, the *Harvard Law Review*, the *University of Pennsylvania Law Review*, and *The Yale Law Journal*.

blue chip, *n.* A corporate stock that is considered a safe investment because the corporation has a history of stability, consistent growth, and reliable earnings. —**blue-chip,** *adj.*

blue law. A statute regulating or prohibiting commercial activity on Sundays. —Also termed *Sunday law*; *Sunday-closing law*; *Sabbath law.*

blue-pencil test. A judicial standard sometimes applied by a court considering an illegal contractual provision and deciding whether to invalidate the whole contract or only the offending words, the standard being whether it would be possible to delete the offending words simply by running a blue pencil through them, as opposed to changing, adding, or rearranging words.

blue-ribbon jury. See JURY.

blue-sky law. A state statute establishing standards for offering and selling securities, the purpose being to protect citizens from investing in fraudulent companies.

board-certified, *adj.* (Of a lawyer) having qualified as a specialist in a given field of law <she is board-certi-

fied in civil litigation>. See BOARD OF LEGAL SPECIALIZATION.

board of directors. The governing body of a corporation elected by the shareholders and usu. comprising officers of the corporation and persons not otherwise associated with the corporation. See DIRECTOR.

staggered board of directors. A board of directors in which a fraction of the board is elected every year to serve for two or three years.

board of legal specialization. A body, usu. an arm of a state bar association, that certifies qualifying lawyers as specialists within a given field; typically, to qualify as a specialist, a lawyer must meet a specified level of experience and pass an examination.

Board of Tax Appeals. See TAX COURT, U.S..

board of zoning appeals. ADJUSTMENT BOARD.

bodily harm. See HARM.

bodily heirs. See *heirs of the body* under HEIR (1).

bodily injury. See INJURY.

body execution. CAPIAS.

bogus check. See *bad check* under CHECK.

boilerplate, *n.* **1.** Ready-made or all-purpose language that will fit in a variety of documents. **2.** Fixed or standardized contractual language that, in the view of the party whose forms contain it, is rarely subject to modification. —**boilerplate,** *adj.*

bona fide (boh-nə-fīd-ee *or* boh-nə-fīd), *adj.* [Latin "in good faith"] **1.** Made in good faith; without fraud or deceit. **2.** Sincere; genuine. See GOOD FAITH.

bona fide occupational qualification. An employment qualification that discriminates against a protected class (such as sex, religion, or national origin) but that also relates to an essential job duty and is reasonably necessary to the operations of the particular business; such a qualification is not illegal under federal employment-discrimination laws. — Abbr. BFOQ.

bona fide purchaser. See PURCHASER.

bona fides (boh-nə-fī-deez), *n.* [Latin] GOOD FAITH.

bona vacantia (boh-no-və-**kan**-shee-ə). [Latin "vacant goods"] Property not disposed of by a decedent's will and to which no relative is entitled under intestacy laws. See ESCHEAT.

bond, *n.* **1.** A long-term, interest-bearing debt instrument that is issued by a corporation or governmental entity usu. to provide for a particular financial need; esp., such an instrument in which the debt is secured by a lien on the issuer's property. Cf. DEBENTURE (2).

adjustment bond. A bond issued when a corporation is reorganized. —Also termed *reorganization bond.*

annuity bond. A bond that lacks a maturity date and that perpetually pays interest. —Also termed *consol; perpetual bond.*

bearer bond. A bond payable to the person holding it; the transfer of the bond's possession transfers its ownership. Cf. *registered bond.*

convertible bond. A bond that can be exchanged for shares in the corporation that issued the bond.

coupon bond. A bond with attached interest coupons that the holder may present to receive interest payments.

debenture bond. DEBENTURE (2).

discount bond. A bond sold at its current market value, which is less than its face value.

guaranteed bond. A bond issued by a corporation and guaranteed by an outside third party. —Also termed *endorsed bond.*

junk bond. A high-risk, high-yield bond issued by a corporation with a below-standard industry rating.

mortgage bond. A bond secured by a mortgage on the issuer's property.

municipal bond. A bond issued by a nonfederal government or governmental unit, such as a state bond to finance local improvements; the interest received from a municipal bond is generally exempt from federal, state, and local taxes. —Often shortened (in plural) to *municipals; munies.*

participating bond. A bond issued without a fixed interest obligation by a corporation that will award the holders additional payments from its profits.

redeemable bond. A bond that the issuer may call for payment. —Also termed *callable bond.*

registered bond. A bond that only the recorded holder may redeem, enjoy benefits from, or transfer to another. Cf. *bearer bond.*

revenue bond. A government bond repayable by the income from a public project.

savings bond. A nontransferable bond issued by the U.S. Government.

secured bond. A bond backed by some type of security. Cf. DEBENTURE (2).

serial bond. A bond issued concurrently with other bonds that have different maturity dates.

series bonds. A group of bonds issued under the authority of the same indenture, but publicly offered at different times and with distinct maturity dates and interest rates.

term bond. A bond issue in which all bonds mature concurrently unless previously redeemed.

Treasury bond. See TREASURY BOND.

unsecured bond. DEBENTURE (2).

2. A written promise to pay money or do some act if certain circumstances occur.

appeal bond. A bond that an appellate court may require from an appellant in a civil case to ensure payment of the costs of appeal. Fed. R. App. P. 7. Cf. *supersedeas bond.*

attachment bond. A bond that a defendant gives in order to recover attached property; the plaintiff then looks to the bond to satisfy a judgment against the defendant.

bail bond. A bond given to a court by a criminal defendant's surety, guaranteeing that the defendant will duly appear in court in the future. See BAIL.

blanket bond. **a.** A bond covering several projects that require performance bonds. **b.** See *fidelity bond.*

delivery bond. A defendant's bond guaranteeing that once the attached property is returned, he or she will surrender the property or its value in satisfaction of any adverse judgment. —Also termed *forthcoming bond.*

discharging bond. A delivery bond that not only permits a defendant to regain possession of the attached property but also releases the property from the lien of attachment. —Also termed *dissolution bond.*

fidelity bond. A bond that covers an employer or business for loss due to embezzlement, larceny, or gross negligence by an employee or other person holding a position of trust. —Also termed *blanket bond.*

judicial bond. A bond required by courts to secure a party's costs of appeal, attachment, injunction, and the like.

payment bond. A bond given by a surety to cover any fees that, because of the general contractor's default, are not paid to subcontractors or materialmen.

peace bond. A bond required by a court from a person who has breached or threatened to breach the peace. See BREACH OF THE PEACE.

penal bond. A bond requiring the obligor to pay a specified sum as a penalty if the underlying obligation is not performed. —Also termed *penal bill.*

performance bond. **a.** A third party's agreement to guarantee the completion of a construction contract upon the default of the general contractor. **b.** A bond given by a surety to ensure the timely performance of a contract. —Also termed *completion bond; surety bond.*

straw bond. A bond, usu. a bail bond, that carries either fictitious names or names of persons who are unable to pay the sum guaranteed; a worthless or inadequate bond.

supersedeas bond. A bond that a court requires from an appellant who wants to delay payment of a judgment until the appeal is over. —Often shortened to *supersedeas.* See SUPERSEDE (2). Cf. *appeal bond.*

bond, *vb.* **1.** To secure payment by providing a bond <at the creditor's insistence, Gabriel consolidated and bonded his various loans>. **2.** To provide a bond for (a person) <the company bonded its off-site workers>.

bond discount. See DISCOUNT (3).

bonded debt. See DEBT.

bond issue. See ISSUE (2).

bond premium. See PREMIUM (3).

bondsman. One who guarantees a bond; a surety.

bonum factum. [Latin] A good or proper act or deed.

bonus share. See *bonus stock* under STOCK.

bonus stock. See STOCK.

book, *vb.* To record a person's arrest in a sequential list of police arrests, with details of the person's identity (usu. including photographs and fingerprints), particulars about the alleged offense, and the name of the arresting officer.

book account. See ACCOUNT.

book entry. 1. A notation made in an accounting journal. **2.** The method of reflecting ownership of publicly traded securities whereby customers of brokerage firms receive confirmations of transactions and monthly statements, but not stock certificates. See CENTRAL CLEARING SYSTEM.

bookkeeping, *n.* The mechanical recording of debits and credits or the summarizing of financial information, usu. about a business enterprise <double-entry bookkeeping>. Cf. ACCOUNTING.

book value. The value at which an asset is carried on a company's balance sheet.

boot, *n.* **1.** In tax accounting, supplemental money or property subject to tax in an otherwise tax-free exchange. **2.** In a corporate reorganization, anything received other than the stock or securities of a controlled corporation. **3.** Cash or other consideration used to balance an otherwise unequal exchange.

bootleg, *vb.* To manufacture, reproduce, or distribute (something) illegally or without authorization <he was bootlegging copyrighted videotapes>.

bootstrap sale. See SALE.

booty. 1. In international law, movables taken from the enemy as spoils in the course of warlike operations on land. —Also termed *spoils of war.* **2.** Property taken by force or piracy; prize or loot.

bordereau (**bor**-də-roh), *n.* **1.** A description of reinsured risks. **2.** A detailed note of account. Pl. **bordereaux.** —**bordereau,** *vb.*

border search. See SEARCH.

bork, *vb. Slang.* **1.** (Of the U.S. Senate) to reject a nominee for the U.S. Supreme Court because of the nominee's unorthodox political and legal philosophy. **2.** (Of political and legal activists) to embark on a media campaign that helps pressure U.S. Senators into rejecting a president's nominee for the U.S. Supreme Court—both senses derive from the name of Robert Bork, President Reagan's unsuccessful nominee for the Court in 1987.

borough English. *Archaic.* A common-law rule of descent whereby, upon the father's death, the youngest son inherited all lands. See PRIMOGENITURE.

borrowed employee. See EMPLOYEE.

borrowed servant. See *borrowed employee* under EMPLOYEE.

borrowing statute. A legislative exception to the conflict-of-laws rule holding that a forum state must apply its own statute of limitations; a borrowing statute specifies the circumstances in which a forum state may adopt another state's statute of limitations.

boundary. A natural or artificial separation that delineates the confines of real property <the creek serves as a boundary between the two properties>. See METES AND BOUNDS.

bounty. **1.** A premium or benefit offered or given, esp. by a government, to induce a group of persons to take action or perform services <a bounty for the killing of dangerous animals>. **2.** A gift, esp. in a will; generosity in giving <the court will distribute equally the testator's bounty>.

boutique. A small specialty business; esp., a small law firm specializing in one particular aspect of law practice <a tax boutique>.

boycott, *n.* A concerted refusal to do business with a party in order to express disapproval of that party's practices. —**boycott,** *vb.* Cf. PICKETING; STRIKE.

consumer boycott. A boycott by consumers of products or services to show displeasure with the manufacturer, seller, or provider.

primary boycott. A boycott by union members who stop dealing with a former employer.

secondary boycott. A boycott of the customers or suppliers of a given business so that they will withhold their patronage for that business; for example, a group might boycott a manufacturer's goods if that manufacturer advertises on a radio station that broadcasts messages that the group finds objectionable.

***Brady* material.** Significant information or evidence that is favorable to a criminal defendant's case and that the prosecution has a duty to disclose; the prosecution's withholding of such information violates the defendant's due-process rights. *Brady v. Maryland*, 373 U.S. 83 (1963). Cf. JENCKS MATERIAL.

brain death. See DEATH.

Brandeis brief. A brief, usu. an appellate brief, that makes use of social and economic studies in addition to legal principles and citations; the brief is named after Louis D. Brandeis, a Supreme Court justice, who as an advocate filed the most famous such brief in *Muller v. Oregon*, 208 U.S. 412 (1908), in which he persuaded the Court to uphold a statute setting 10 hours as the maximum number of daily work hours for women.

breach, *n.* Violation or infraction of a law or obligation <breach of warranty> <breach of duty>. — **breach,** *vb.*

breach of close. The unlawful or unauthorized entry on another person's land; a common-law trespass. —Also termed *breaking a close.* See CLOSE.

breach of contract. Violation of a contractual obligation, either by failing to perform one's own promise or by interfering with the other party's performance.

anticipatory breach. A breach of contract caused by a party's anticipatory repudiation. —Also termed *constructive breach.* See REPUDIATION.

continuing breach. A breach of contract that endures for a considerable amount of time, or that is repeated at short intervals.

efficient breach. An intentional breach of contract and payment of damages by a party who would incur greater economic liability in performing under the contract. See EFFICIENT-BREACH THEORY.

material breach. A substantial breach of contract, usu. excusing the aggrieved party from further performance and affording it the right to sue for damages.

partial breach. A breach of contract that is less significant than a material breach and that gives the aggrieved party a right to damages but does not generally excuse that party from performance. —Also termed *immaterial breach.*

breach of duty. Violation of a legal obligation. See NEGLIGENCE.

breach of promise. Violation of a promise, esp. to marry. See HEART-BALM STATUTE.

breach of the peace. The criminal offense of creating a public disturbance or engaging in disorderly conduct, particularly by unnecessary or distracting noise. —Also termed *breach of peace; disturbing the peace; disturbance of the peace.* See DISORDERLY CONDUCT.

breaking a close. BREACH OF CLOSE.

breaking and entering. BURGLARY (2).

breaking bulk, *n.* Larceny by a bailee, esp. a carrier, who opens or reduces items delivered in bulk and then converts some of them to his or her own use. —**break bulk,** *vb.*

Breathalyzer. *Trademark.* A device used to measure the blood-alcohol content of a person's breath sample, esp. when the police suspect that the person was driving while intoxicated; Breathalyzer test results are admissible as evidence if the test was properly administered. —Also termed *alco-holometer; drunkometer; intoxilyzer; intoximeter.* —**breathalyze,** *vb.*

breathing room. *Slang.* The post-bankruptcy period during which a debtor may formulate a debt-repayment plan without harassment or interference by creditors.

brethren, *n. pl.* Brothers, esp. those considered spiritual kin (such as male colleagues on a court) <my brethren argue in the dissent that my statutory interpretation is faulty>; the use of this collegial term has naturally dwindled as more women have entered law and esp. into the judiciary. Cf. SISTREN.

breve (bree-vee). [Latin] Writ.

bribee. One who receives a bribe.

briber. One who offers a bribe.

bribery, *n.* The corrupt payment, receipt, or solicitation of a private favor for official action; bribery is a felony in most jurisdictions. —**bribe,** *vb.*—**bribe,** *n.*

commercial bribery. Corrupt dealing with the agents or employees of prospective buyers in order to secure an advantage over business competitors.

bridge loan. See LOAN.

brief, *n.* **1.** A written statement setting out the legal contentions of a party in litigation, esp. on appeal. **2.** ABSTRACT OF TITLE. —**brief,** *vb.*

bright-line rule. A judicial rule of decision that is simple, straightforward, and avoids or ignores the ambiguities or difficulties of the problems at issue.

bring to book. To arrest and try (an offender) <the fugitives were brought to book and convicted>.

brocard. An elementary legal principle or maxim, esp. one deriving from Roman law or ancient custom.

broker, *n.* An agent who acts as an intermediary or negotiator, esp. between prospective buyers and sellers. —**broker,** *vb.*

brokerage. 1. The business or office of a broker <a profitable stock brokerage>. **2.** A broker's fee <collect the brokerage after the house sells>.

broker call loan. See *call loan* under LOAN.

***Bruton* error.** A court's violation of a criminal defendant's constitutional right of confrontation by admitting into evidence a nontestifying codefendant's confession that implicates a defendant who claims innocence. *Bruton v. United States,* 391 U.S. 123 (1968).

brutum fulmen (broo-təm-fəl-mən). [Latin "inert thunder"] An empty noise; an empty threat; something ineffectual.

BTA. *abbr.* Board of Tax Appeals. See TAX COURT.

buggery, *n.* Sodomy or bestiality. —**bugger,** *vb.*—**bugger,** *n.* See SODOMY.

bugging. A form of electronic surveillance by which conversations may be electronically intercepted, overheard, and recorded, usu. covertly; eavesdropping by means of electronic technology. See WIRETAPPING.

building-and-loan association. A quasi-public corporation that accumulates funds through member contributions and lends money to the members for the purpose of purchasing or building homes. Cf. SAVINGS-AND-LOAN ASSOCIATION.

bulk transfer. A sale of a large quantity of inventory outside the ordinary course of the seller's business; bulk transfers are regulated by U.C.C. art. 6, which is designed to prevent sellers from defrauding unsecured creditors by making such transfers and dissipating the sale proceeds. —Also termed *bulk sale.*

bull market. See MARKET.

burden, *n.* **1.** A duty or responsibility <the seller's burden to insure the shipped goods>. **2.** Something that is oppressive <a burden on interstate commerce>. **3.** A restriction on the use or value of land; an encumbrance <the easement created a burden on the estate>. —**burden,** *vb.*— **burdensome,** *adj.*

burden of allegation. A party's duty to plead a matter in order for that matter to be heard in the lawsuit.

burden of persuasion. A party's duty to convince the fact-finder to view the facts in a way that favors that party; in civil cases the plaintiff's burden is usu. "by a preponderance of the evidence," while in criminal cases the prosecution's burden is "beyond a reasonable doubt."—Also termed *persuasion burden*; *risk of nonpersuasion.* —Also loosely termed *burden of proof.*

burden of production. A party's duty to introduce enough evidence to have a given issue considered by the fact-finder in the case, rather than have the issue be dismissed by the judge in a peremptory ruling, such as a nonsuit or a directed verdict. — Also termed *burden of going forward with evidence*; *burden of producing evidence*; *production burden*.

burden of proof. 1. A party's duty to prove a disputed assertion or charge; the burden of proof includes both the *burden of persuasion* and the *burden of production*. —Also termed *onus probandi*. **2.** Loosely, BURDEN OF PERSUASION.

***Burford* abstention.** See ABSTENTION.

burglary, *n.* **1.** The common-law offense of breaking and entering another's dwelling at night with the intent to commit a felony. **2.** The modern statutory offense of breaking and entering any building—not just a dwelling, and not only at night—with the intent to commit a felony. —Also termed (in sense 2) *breaking and entering*. —**burglarize, burgle,** *vb.*—**burglarious** (bər-**glair**-ee-əs), *adj.*—**burglar,** *n.* Cf. ROBBERY.

bursting-bubble theory. In the law of evidence, the principle that a presumption disappears once the presumed facts are contradicted by credible evidence.

business compulsion. See *economic duress* under DURESS.

business court. See COURT.

business cycle. The recurrent expansion and contraction of economic activity.

business guest. See GUEST.

business-interruption insurance. See INSURANCE.

business-judgment rule. In corporate law, the doctrine shielding directors and officers from liability for unprofitable or harmful corporate transactions, as long as the transactions were made in good faith, with due care, and within the directors' or officers' authority.

business-records exception. In law of evidence, a hearsay exception that provides for the admissibility of business records (such as reports or memoranda) that were prepared in the course of a regularly conducted business activity. Fed. R. Evid. 803(6).

business situs. See SITUS.

business trust. See TRUST.

bust-up merger. See MERGER.

but-for cause. See CAUSE (1).

but-for test. In tort and criminal law, the doctrine providing that causation exists only when the result would not have occurred without the party's conduct. —Also termed (in criminal law) *had-not test*. See *but-for cause* under CAUSE (1).

butts and bounds. METES AND BOUNDS.

buyer's market. See MARKET.

buying in, *n.* The buying of property by the original owner or an interested party at an auction or mortgage foreclosure sale. —**buy in,** *vb.*

buying on margin. MARGIN TRANSACTION.

buyout, *n.* The purchase of a controlling percentage of a company's shares. —**buy out,** *vb.* Cf. MERGER (7).

leveraged buyout. The purchase of a publicly held corporation's outstanding stock by its management or outside investors, financed mainly with funds borrowed from investment bankers or brokers and usu. secured by the target company's assets. —Abbr. LBO.

management buyout. **a.** A leveraged buyout of a corporation by an outside entity in which the corporation's management has a financial interest. —Abbr. MBO. **b.** GOING PRIVATE.

buy-sell agreement. 1. An arrangement between owners of a business by which the surviving owners agree to purchase the interest of a withdrawing or deceased owner. **2.** In corporate law, a share-transfer restriction that commits the shareholder to sell, and the corporation or other shareholders to buy, the shareholder's shares at a fixed price when a specified event occurs. Cf. OPTION AGREEMENT.

by-bidder. At an auction, a person employed by the seller to bid on property for the sole purpose of stimulating bidding by potential genuine buyers.

bylaw. 1. A rule or administrative provision adopted by an association or corporation for its internal governance; corporate bylaws are usu. enacted apart from the articles of incorporation. —Also termed *regulation*. **2.** ORDINANCE. —Sometimes spelled *by-law*; *byelaw*.

by operation of law. See OPERATION OF LAW.

bypass trust. See TRUST.

bystander. One who is present at a situation or event but does not participate in it; in a products-liability case, a foreseeable bystander is usu. eligible to recover along with the user or consumer of the product.

C

c. *abbr.* CIRCA.

ca. *abbr.* CIRCA.

cabala (kə-**bahl**-ə *or* **kab**-ə-lə). An esoteric or obscure doctrine.

cabinet. (*usu. cap.*) The advisory council to an executive officer, usu. the President.

kitchen cabinet. An informal body of noncabinet advisers to whom the President turns for advice.

cafeteria plan. An employee fringe-benefit plan allowing a choice of basic benefits up to a certain dollar amount.

cahoots. *Slang.* Partnership, esp. in an illegal act; collusion <the lawyer was in cahoots with her client>.

calendar, *n.* **1.** A systematized ordering of time into years, months, weeks, and days; esp., the Gregorian calendar (established in 1582), which is used throughout the Western world. **2.** A court's list of civil or criminal cases. —**calendar,** *vb.*

calendar call. A court session dedicated to determining the status of all cases awaiting trial and to assigning court dates to them.

court calendar. DOCKET (2).

special calendar. A calendar marked with court cases having established hearing dates. See *special setting* under SETTING.

call, *n.* **1.** A request or command to come or assemble; an invitation or summons. **2.** A demand for payment of money.

maintenance call. A securities broker's demand that an investor increase the money or securities put up as collateral for stock that is owned on margin and that has gone down or is likely to go down in value, so that the minimum required margin may be met.

margin call. A securities broker's demand that a customer put up money or stock as collateral when the customer purchases stock.

3. See *call option* under OPTION. **4.** A demand for the presentation of a security (esp. a bond) for redemption before the maturity date. —**call,** *vb.*

callable, *adj.* (Of a security) redeemable before maturity by the issuing corporation. See REDEMPTION.

callable bond. See *redeemable bond* under BOND (1).

callable security. See *redeemable security* under SECURITY.

called meeting. See *special meeting* under MEETING.

call loan. See LOAN.

call option. See OPTION.

call price. See PRICE.

calumny (**kal**-əm-nee), *n. Archaic.* **1.** The act of falsely and maliciously misrepresenting the words or actions of another in a way that is calculated to injure that person's reputation. **2.** A false charge or imputation. —**calumniate,** *vb.*—**calumnious,** *adj.*—**calumniator,** *n.*

camera. [Latin] Chamber; room. See IN CAMERA.

cancellation, *n.* **1.** The act or an instance of defacing or obliterating a writing (as by marking lines across it), thereby rendering it void. **2.** The act or an instance of annulling or terminating a promise or obligation. —**cancel**, *vb.*—**cancelable**, *adj.*

C & F. *abbr.* COST AND FREIGHT.

canon, *n.* **1.** A rule or principle, esp. one accepted as fundamental. **2.** (*usu. cap.*) A maxim stating in general terms the standards of professional conduct expected of lawyers; in the Model Code of Professional Responsibility, the nine Canons are elaborated by Disciplinary Rules and Ethical Considerations. **3.** A rule of ecclesiastical law. **4.** A corpus of writings. — **canonical**, *adj.*—**canonist**, *n.*

canon law. **1.** A body of Roman ecclesiastical jurisprudence that was compiled between the 12th and 14th centuries. **2.** A body of religious jurisprudence developed within a Christian church or denomination. —Also termed *church law*. See ECCLESIASTICAL LAW.

canon of construction. A rule or maxim used in interpreting legal instruments, esp. contracts and statutes; although a few states have codified the canons of construction— examples of which are *contra proferentem* and *ejusdem generis*—most jurisdictions treat the canons as mere customs not having the force of law.

canvass, *vb.* **1.** To examine in detail; scrutinize <that issue has been repeatedly canvassed by our state's courts>. **2.** To go to (voters or a voting district) in order to solicit political support; to take stock of public opinion <the candidate is actively canvassing the Western states>. — **canvass**, *n.*

cap, *n.* A set limit, such as a statutorily imposed limit on the amount one can recover in a tort action or on the amount of interest a bank can charge. —**cap**, *vb.*

capacitate, *vb.* To qualify; to make legally competent. —**capacitation**, *n.*

capacity. **1.** The role in which one performs an act <in her corporate capacity>. **2.** A legal qualification, such as legal age, that determines one's ability to sue or be sued, to enter into a binding contract, and the like <she had full capacity to bind the corporation with her signature>. **3.** The mental ability to understand the nature and effects of one's acts <his acute pain reduced his capacity to understand the hospital's admission form>. —Also termed *mental capacity*. See COMPETENCY.

diminished capacity. An impaired mental condition—short of insanity—that is caused by intoxication, trauma, or disease and that prevents the person from having the specific mental state necessary to be held responsible for a crime; the court can consider a defendant's diminished capacity when determining the degree of the offense or the severity of the punishment. —Also termed *diminished responsibility*. Cf. INSANITY.

testamentary capacity. The mental condition a person must have when preparing a will in order for the will to be considered valid; this capacity is often described as the ability to recognize the natural objects of one's bounty and the nature and extent of one's estate.

capacity defense. See DEFENSE (1).

CAPIAS

capias (**kay**-pee-əs *or* **ka**-). [Latin "that you take"] Any of various types of writs that require an officer to take a named defendant into custody. —Also termed *writ of capias*; *body execution*.

capias ad audiendum judicium (ad-o-dee-**en**-dəm-joo-**dish**-[ee]əm). [Latin "that you take to hear the judgment"] In a misdemeanor case, a writ issued to bring the defendant to hear the judgment to be imposed after having failed to appear.

capias ad respondendum (ad-ri-spon-**den**-dəm). [Latin "that you take to answer"] A writ commanding the sheriff to take the defendant into custody to enforce attendance at court. —Abbr. *ca. resp.*

capias ad satisfaciendum (ad-sat-əs-fay-shee-**en**-dəm). [Latin "that you take to satisfy"] *Archaic.* A post-judgment writ commanding the sheriff to imprison the defendant until the plaintiff's claim was satisfied. —Abbr. *ca. sa.*

capital, *n.* **1.** The total assets of a business, esp. those that help generate profits; net worth <the manufacturer bought more equipment to increase its capital>. **2.** Money or assets invested, or available for investment, in a business <the capital needed to start a new company>. **3.** The total amount or value of a corporation's stock; corporate equity <AT & T's stated capital>. See *capital stock* under STOCK.

debt capital. Funds raised by issuing bonds.

equity capital. Funds provided by a company's owners in exchange for evidence of ownership, such as stock.

fixed capital. **a.** The amount of money that is permanently invested in the business. **b.** The amount of money invested in fixed assets, such as land and machinery.

floating capital. Capital not presently invested or committed; esp., capital retained for the purpose of meeting current expenditures. —Also termed *circulating capital.*

impaired capital. Capital that is worth less than the par value of the issued stock.

legal capital. The amount of contributed capital that must, by law, stay in the firm as protection against creditors; usu. equal to the par or stated value of issued capital stock. —Also termed *stated capital.*

paid-in capital. The amount paid for the capital stock of a corporation.

risk capital. **a.** Money or property invested and exchanged for common stock in a business venture, esp. one in which the investor has no managerial control. **b.** See *venture capital.*

stated capital. **a.** See *legal capital.* **b.** The total equity of a corporation as it appears on the balance sheet.

subscribed capital. The total amount of stock or capital for which there are subscriptions (contracts of purchase).

venture capital. Funds invested in a new company or enterprise that has high risk and the potential for a high return. —Also termed *risk capital.* See SEED MONEY.

working capital. A firm's investment in current assets such as cash, inventory, or accounts receivable; working capital measures liquidity and the ability to discharge short-term liabilities.

capital, *adj.* **1.** Of or relating to economic or financial capital <capital market>. **2.** Punishable by execution; involving the death penalty <a capital offense>.

capital account. See ACCOUNT.

capital asset. See ASSET.

capital contribution. 1. Cash, property, or services contributed by partners to a partnership. **2.** Funds made available by a shareholder without increasing his or her stock holdings.

capital crime. See *capital offense* under OFFENSE.

capital expenditure. An outlay of funds for acquiring or improving a fixed asset. —Also termed *capital improvement*; *capital outlay*.

capital gain. The profit realized on selling or exchanging a capital asset. —Also termed *capital gains*.

capital-gains tax. See TAX.

capital goods. See GOODS.

capital improvement. CAPITAL EXPENDITURE.

capitalism, *n.* An economic system that depends on the private distribution of the means of production and distribution and that is driven by the individual's desire and ability to make a profit. —**capitalist,** *adj.* & *n.*

capitalization, *n.* **1.** The total amount of a corporation's long-term financing, including stock, bonds,

and retained earnings. **2.** In accounting, the recording of an expenditure with long-term benefits as an asset instead of as a current expense. **3.** A process for determining the value of property by dividing its income by a predetermined annual rate. —**capitalize,** *vb.*

thin capitalization. The financial condition of a company that is indebted to its shareholders beyond the value of shareholder equity.

undercapitalization. The financial condition of a business that does not have enough cash or patronage to carry on its business.

capitalization accounting method. See ACCOUNTING METHOD.

capitalization rate. The interest rate used in calculating the present value of future periodic payments; it is determined by dividing the net operating income for the first year by the total investment. —Also termed *cap rate*; *income yield*.

capitalization ratio. The ratio between the amount of capital raised from a particular source and the total capitalization of the firm.

capital loss. See LOSS.

capital market. See MARKET.

capital offense. See OFFENSE.

capital outlay. 1. CAPITAL EXPENDITURE. **2.** Money expended in acquiring, equipping, and promoting an enterprise.

capital punishment. DEATH PENALTY.

capital return. In tax accounting, the payments received by the taxpayer that represent the individual's cost or capital and that are therefore not taxable as income.

capital stock. See STOCK.

capital structure. The mix of debt and equity by which a corporation finances its operations.

capital surplus. See *paid-in surplus* under SURPLUS.

capitation. See *poll tax* under TAX.

capitation tax. See *poll tax* under TAX.

capitulation, *n.* **1.** The act of surrendering or giving in. **2.** In international law, an agreement for the surrender on conditions of a fortified place, or of a military or naval force; a commander may generally make such an agreement with regard to the place or force under his or her control. —**capitulate,** *vb.*—**capitulatory,** *adj.*

cap rate. CAPITALIZATION RATE.

caprice, *n.* **1.** Arbitrary or unfounded motivation. **2.** The disposition to change one's mind impulsively. —**capricious,** *adj.*

captain-of-the-ship doctrine. In medical-malpractice law, the doctrine imposing liability on a surgeon for the actions of assistants who are under the surgeon's control.

caption. 1. The introductory part of a court paper stating the names of the parties, the name of the court, the docket or file number, and the title of the action. Cf. STYLE. **2.** The arrest or seizure of a person by legal process.

care, *n.* **1.** Serious attention; heed <written with care>. **2.** In the law of negligence, the conduct demanded of a person in a given situation; typically, this involves a person's giving attention both to possible dangers, mistakes, and pitfalls and to ways of ensuring that these risks do not materialize <standard of care>. See REASONABLE PERSON.

great care. **a.** The degree of care that an ordinarily prudent person exercises in dealing with very important personal affairs. **b.** The degree of care exercised in a given situation by the person most competent to deal with the situation.

highest degree of care. **a.** The degree of care exercised commensurate with the danger involved. **b.** The degree of care applied by people in the business or profession of dealing with the given situation.

reasonable care. As a test of liability, the degree of care that an ordinarily prudent and competent person engaged in the same line of business or endeavor should exercise under similar circumstances. — Also termed *due care*; *ordinary care*; *adequate care*; *proper care.* See REASONABLE PERSON.

slight care. The degree of care a person gives to matters of minor importance; the degree of care given by a person of limited accountability.

carelessness, *n.* **1.** The fact, condition, or instance of a person's not having done what he or she ought to have done. **2.** A person's general disposition not to do something that ought to be done. —**careless,** *adj.*

ca. resp. See *capias ad respondendum* under CAPIAS.

carnal abuse. See *sexual abuse* under ABUSE.

carnal knowledge. Sexual intercourse.

carrier. 1. An individual or organization that transports passengers or goods for hire, such as a railroad or airline.

common carrier. A carrier that is required by law to convey passengers or freight, without refusal, if the approved fare or charge is paid. — Also termed *public carrier*.

private carrier. A carrier that does not accept business from the general public and is therefore not considered a common carrier.

2. INSURER.

carryback, *n.* In tax law, the provision that allows a taxpayer to apply an amount to a prior taxable year; esp., the application of a net operating loss suffered in one year to the three immediately preceding years. —**carry back,** *vb.* Cf. CARRYOVER.

carryforward, *n.* In accounting, the transfer of an entry or an amount into the next record, period, or account. —**carry forward,** *vb.*

carrying charge. 1. A cost borne by a debtor, in addition to interest, for holding the installment credit. **2.** Expenses incident to property ownership, such as taxes and upkeep.

carrying cost. See COST.

carryover, *n.* In tax law, the provision that allows a taxpayer to apply an amount to a future taxable year; esp., the application of a net operating loss suffered in one year to the years after the loss. —**carry over,** *vb.* Cf. CARRYBACK.

carryover basis. See BASIS.

carte blanche (kart-**blonsh**). [French "white card"] **1.** A signed, blank instrument that is filled out at an agent's discretion. **2.** Full discretionary power; unlimited authority.

cartel (kahr-**tel**), *n.* **1.** A combination of any producers of a product, who join together to control the production and price of the product. **2.** An association by agreement of companies or sections of companies with common interests, seeking to prevent extreme or unfair competition, allocate markets, or share knowledge. **3.** In international law, an agreement between belligerents about the means of conducting whatever relations they allow during wartime; esp., such an agreement regarding the exchange of prisoners. —Also spelled *chartel*. —**cartelize,** *vb.*

carveout, *n.* **1.** An explicit exception to a broad rule. **2.** The separation, for tax purposes, of the income derived from a property from the property itself. —**carve out,** *vb.*

ca sa. See *capias ad satisfaciendum* under CAPIAS.

case. 1. Any proceeding, action, suit, or controversy at law or in equity <the parties settled the case>.

case of first impression. A case that presents the court with issues of law that have not previously been considered within a given jurisdiction.

case reserved. A written statement of the facts proved at trial, drawn up and stipulated to by the parties, so that certain points of law can be determined upon full argument before an appellate court. —Also termed *case made*; *special case*.

case stated. A formal written statement of the facts in a case, submitted to the court jointly by the parties so that a decision may be rendered without trial. —Also termed *case agreed on*.

test case. **a.** A lawsuit brought to establish an important legal principle or right; such an action is frequently brought by the mutual consent of the parties on an agreed set of facts—when that is so, a test case is also sometimes termed *amicable action*. **b.** An action selected out of a number of suits that are based on the same facts and evidence, that raise the same question of law, and that have a common plaintiff or a common defendant; when all parties agree, the court orders a consolidation and all parties are bound by the decision in the test case. —Also termed *test action*.

2. A criminal investigation <the Manson case>. **3.** An individual suspect or convict in relation to any aspect of the criminal-justice system <the probation officer said he considers Mr. Jones a difficult case>. **4.** An argument <the debater made a compelling case for gun control>. **5.** An instance, occurrence, or situation <a case of mistaken identity> <a terminal case of cancer>. **6.** TRESPASS ON THE CASE <the actions of trover and case are not entirely defunct>.

case agreed on. See *case stated* under CASE.

casebook. A law-school textbook containing the leading cases in a field, usu. with commentary on and questions about the decisions. Cf. HORNBOOK.

caseflow. 1. The movement of cases through the judicial system, from the initial filing to the final appeal. **2.** An analysis of that movement.

case-in-chief. The part of a trial in which the party with the burden of proof presents evidence.

caselaw. The collection of reported cases that form the body of jurisprudence within a given jurisdiction. — Also spelled *case law*; *case-law*. — Also termed *decisional law*; *jurisprudence*; *organic law*.

caseload. The volume of cases assigned to a given court, agency, or individual judge or other officer.

case made. See *case reserved* under CASE.

case of first impression. See CASE.

case-or-controversy requirement. The constitutional requirement that a case, in order for a federal court to hear it, must be an actual dispute and cannot be a hypothetical scenario or a legal question presented in a vacuum. See CONTROVERSY (3).

cash, *n.* **1.** Money or its equivalent. **2.** Currency or coins, negotiable checks, and balances in bank accounts. —**cash,** *vb.*

cash-basis accounting method. See ACCOUNTING METHOD.

cash dividend. See DIVIDEND.

cash equivalent. A short-term security that is sufficiently liquid that it may be considered financially equivalent to cash.

cash-equivalent doctrine. The tax-law doctrine that requires income to be reported even if it is not cash, such as when the taxpayer barters to receive in-kind payments.

cash flow. 1. The movement of cash through a business, as a measure of profitability or liquidity. **2.** The cash generated from a business or transaction. **3.** Cash receipts minus cash disbursements for a given period. — Sometimes spelled *cashflow*.

cash flow per common share. The difference between cash flow from operations and preferred stock dividends, divided by the number of outstanding common shares.

discounted cash flow. A method of evaluating a capital investment by comparing its future income and costs with its equivalent current value. —Abbr. DCF.

incremental cash flow. The net increase in a firm's cash flow attributable to a particular capital investment.

negative cash flow. A financial situation in which one's cash needs exceed cash intake. See INSOLVENCY.

net cash flow. Cash inflow minus cash outflow.

cashier, *n*. **1.** One who collects and records payments at a business. **2.** The executive officer of a bank or trust company, who is responsible for banking transactions.

cashier, *vb*. To dismiss from service dishonorably <after three such incidents, Jones was cashiered>.

cashier's check. See CHECK.

cash merger. See MERGER.

cash out, *n*. The arrangement by a seller to receive the entire amount of equity in cash rather than retaining an interest in the property. —**cash out,** *vb*.

cash-out merger. See *cash merger* under MERGER.

cash surrender value. The amount of money that an insurance policy having cash value, such as a whole-life policy, would yield if cashed in with the insurance company. —Abbr. CSV.

cash tender offer. See TENDER OFFER.

cash value. FAIR MARKET VALUE.

cash-value option. See OPTION.

castle doctrine. The criminal-law doctrine that functions as an exception to the retreat rule by allowing a person to use deadly force to protect his or her house and its inhabitants from attack, esp. from a trespasser who intends to commit a felony or inflict serious bodily harm. —Also termed *dwelling defense*; *defense of habitation*. See RETREAT RULE.

casual ejector. The nominal or fictitious defendant in an action for ejectment. See EJECTMENT.

casual employment. See EMPLOYMENT.

casualty. 1. A serious or fatal accident. **2.** A person or thing injured, lost, or destroyed.

casualty insurance. See INSURANCE.

casualty loss. See LOSS.

casus (kas-əs *or* kahs-əs *or* kay-səs). [Latin] **1.** A chance accident or event. **2.** A case contemplated.

casus belli (bel-ee *or* -I). [Latin] An act or circumstance that provokes or justifies war.

casus fortuitus (for-tyoo-wə-təs). [Latin] **1.** A fortuitous event. **2.** A loss happening despite human effort to prevent it.

casus major. [Latin] In civil law, an extraordinary casualty.

categorical question. LEADING QUESTION.

caucus, *n.* A collection of representatives from a political party who assemble for the purpose of nominating candidates and deciding party policy. —**caucus,** *vb.*

causa (koz-ə), *conj.* [Latin] By virtue of; in contemplation of <gift *causa mortis*>.

causa, *n.* [Latin] A cause, consideration, or inducement. See CAUSE.

causa causans (koz-anz). An immediate or effective cause. See *immediate cause* under CAUSE.

causa mortis. See *gift causa mortis* under GIFT.

causa proxima (prok-si-mə). The immediate or latest cause. See *proximate cause* under CAUSE.

causa remota (re-moh-tə). A remote or indirect cause. See *remote cause* under CAUSE.

causa sine qua non (si-nay-kwah-non *or* sI-nee- *or* -kway-). A necessary or inevitable cause; the cause without which the thing cannot be. See *but-for cause* under CAUSE.

causal challenge. See *challenge for cause* under CHALLENGE (2).

causality, *n.* The principle of causal relationship; the relation between cause and effect <the foreseeability test is one of duty and of causality>. —Also termed *causation.* —**causal,** *adj.*

causation. 1. The causing or producing of an effect <the plaintiff must prove causation>. **2.** CAUSALITY.

cause, *n.* **1.** Something that produces an effect or result <the cause of the accident>. —**cause,** *vb.*

but-for cause. The cause without which the event could not have occurred. —Also termed *actual cause; cause in fact.*

concurrent cause. **a.** One of two or more causes that simultaneously create a condition that no single cause could have brought about. **b.** One of two or more causes that simultaneously create a condition that any one cause could have created alone.

immediate cause. The last event in a chain of events, though not necessarily the proximate cause of what follows. —Also termed *effective cause.*

intervening cause. An unanticipated event that comes between the initial event in a sequence and the end result, thereby altering the natural course of events that might have connected a wrongful act to an injury; if the intervening cause is strong enough to relieve the wrongdoer of any liability, it becomes a *superseding cause.* —Also termed *intervening act; indepen-*

dent intervening cause; efficient intervening cause; supervening cause; novus actus interveniens; nova causa interveniens.

procuring cause. **a.** See *proximate cause* (b). **b.** In real-estate law, the efforts of the agent or broker who effects the sale of realty and who is therefore entitled to a commission.

proximate cause. **a.** A cause that directly produces an event and without which the event would not have occurred. **b.** A cause that is legally sufficient to result in liability. —Also termed *direct cause; efficient cause; legal cause; procuring cause; producing cause; jural cause.*

remote cause. A cause that does not necessarily or immediately produce an event or injury.

superseding cause. An intervening act that the law considers sufficient to override the cause for which the original tortfeasor was responsible, thereby exonerating that tortfeasor from liability. — Also termed *sole cause.* Cf. *intervening cause.*

2. A ground for legal action <the plaintiff does not have cause to file suit>.

good cause. A legally sufficient reason; good cause is often the burden placed on a litigant (usu. by court rule or order) for showing why a request should be granted or why a violation should be excused. —Also termed *just cause; lawful cause; sufficient cause.*

probable cause. See PROBABLE CAUSE.

3. A lawsuit; a case <the court has 50 causes on the motion docket>.

cause in fact. See *but-for cause* under CAUSE (1).

cause list. DOCKET (2).

cause of action. 1. A group of operative facts, such as a harmful act, giving rise to one or more rights of action <the crash gave rise to Aronson's cause of action>. **2.** A legal theory of a lawsuit <a malpractice cause of action>. Cf. RIGHT OF ACTION. **3.** Loosely, a lawsuit <there are four defendants in the pending cause of action>.

cause célèbre (kawz-sə-**leb**[-rə]). [French "celebrated case"] A trial or decision in which the subject matter or the characters are unusual or sensational <the O.J. Simpson trial is the definitive cause célèbre of the 1990s>.

cautionary instruction. See JURY INSTRUCTION.

C.A.V. *abbr.* CURIA ADVISARI VULT.

caveat (**kav**-ee-aht). [Latin "let him or her beware"] **1.** A warning or proviso <he sold the dog to his friend with the caveat that the dog's front left leg may be broken>.

caveat emptor (**em**[**p**]-tər *or* -tor). [Latin "let the buyer beware"] A doctrine holding that purchasers buy at their own risk; modern statutes and cases have greatly limited the importance of this doctrine.

caveat venditor (**ven**-də-tər). [Latin] Let the seller beware.

2. A formal notice or warning given by a party to a court or court officer requesting a suspension of proceedings <the decedent's daughter filed a caveat stating the facts on which her will contest is based>.

caveatee (ka-vee-ə-**tee**). One whose interest is challenged by a caveat.

caveat emptor. See CAVEAT.

caveator (ka-vee-ə-**tor**). One who files a caveat, esp. to challenge the validity of a will; CONTESTANT.

caveat venditor. See CAVEAT.

CBOE. *abbr.* CHICAGO BOARD OPTIONS EXCHANGE.

CBOT. *abbr.* CHICAGO BOARD OF TRADE.

CBT. *abbr.* CHICAGO BOARD OF TRADE.

C.C. *abbr.* **1.** Circuit, city, civil, or county court. **2.** Chancery, civil, criminal, or crown cases. **3.** CIVIL CODE. **4.** CEPIA CORPUS.

C corporation. See CORPORATION.

CD. CERTIFICATE OF DEPOSIT.

cease, *vb.* **1.** To stop, forfeit, suspend, or bring to an end. **2.** To become extinct; to pass away. —**cessation** (se-**say**-shən), *n.*

cease-and-desist order. A court order or agency order prohibiting a person from continuing a particular course of conduct. See INJUNCTION; RESTRAINING ORDER.

ceasefire. TRUCE.

cede, *vb.* **1.** To surrender or relinquish. **2.** To assign or grant. —**cession,** *n.*—**cessionary,** *adj.*

ceiling price. See PRICE.

censor, *n.* **1.** A Roman officer who acted as a census taker, assessor, and reviewer of public morals. **2.** A person who inspects publications, films, and the like for objectionable content. **3.** In the armed forces, someone who reads letters and other communications and deletes material considered a threat to security. —**censor,** *vb.*—**censorial,** *adj.*—**censorship,** *n.*

censure (**sen**-shər), *n.* An official reprimand or condemnation; harsh criticism. —**censure,** *vb.*—**censorious,** *adj.*

census. The official counting of people to compile social and economic data for the political subdivision to which the people belong. Pl. **censuses.**

center-of-gravity doctrine. The rule that, in choice-of-law questions, the law of the jurisdiction with the most significant relationship to the event applies. —Also termed *significant-relationship theory*; *grouping-of-contacts theory*.

central clearing system. The modern system of clearing securities transactions in which an agent holds shares for a central clearing corporation; most transactions are reflected by book entries.

Central Intelligence Agency. A federal agency responsible for gathering, analyzing, and sometimes acting on information relating to the national security of the United States, esp. with respect to foreign intelligence and counterintelligence activities. —Abbr. CIA.

CEO. *abbr.* CHIEF EXECUTIVE OFFICER.

cepia corpus (**kay**-pee-ə-**kor**-pəs). [Latin "I have taken the body"] The return of a writ of capias by a sheriff who has arrested the defendant. — Abbr. C.C. See CAPIAS.

CERCLA (sər-klə). *abbr.* Comprehensive Environmental Response, Compensation, and Liability Act of 1980; this statute holds responsible parties liable for the cost of cleaning up hazardous waste sites. 42 U.S.C. §§ 9601 et seq. See SUPERFUND.

ceremonial marriage. See MARRIAGE (2).

cert. *abbr.* CERTIORARI.

certificate, *n.* **1.** A document in which a fact is formally attested <death certificate>. **2.** A document certifying the status or authorization of the bearer to act in a specified way <nursing certificate>. **3.** A writing made in one court, by which notice of its proceedings is given to another court, usu. by transcript <the Supreme Court dismissed the certificate from the court of appeals>.

certificate of acknowledgment. ACKNOWLEDGMENT (2).

certificate of authority. A document authenticating a notarized document that is being sent to another jurisdiction; the certificate assures the out-of-state or foreign recipient of the notarized document that the notary public has a valid commission. —Also termed *certificate of capacity; certificate of official character; certificate of authentication; certificate of prothonotary; certificate of magistracy; apostille; verification.*

certificate of deposit. 1. A certificate from a banker acknowledging the receipt of money with a promise to pay to the depositor. **2.** A bank document that evidences the exis-

tence of a time deposit that normally pays interest. —Abbr. CD.

certificate of discharge. SATISFACTION PIECE.

certificate of incorporation. 1. A document issued by the state authority (usu. the secretary of state) granting a corporation its legal existence and the right to function as a corporation. —Also termed *charter; corporate charter.* **2.** ARTICLES OF INCORPORATION.

certificate of proof. See *proof of acknowledgment* under ACKNOWLEDGMENT.

certificate of stock. STOCK CERTIFICATE.

certificate of title. A document indicating ownership of real or personal property and identifying any liens or other encumbrances.

certification, *n.* The act of authoritatively attesting. **2.** The state of having been authoritatively attested. **3.** An attested statement. **4.** The writing on the face of a check by which it is certified. **5.** One of the three methods by which a federal case may be appealed to the U.S. Supreme Court, whereby the court of appeals "certifies" a legal question on which it needs guidance in a civil or criminal case. —**certify,** *vb.*

certification mark. A trademark or servicemark used to indicate that a product or service meets certain standards of quality or regional origin; an example is the mark "Made in the USA." Cf. COLLECTIVE MARK.

certification of bargaining agent. UNION CERTIFICATION.

certification to federal court. A method by which a U.S. Court of Appeals certifies a question of law to the Supreme Court; only in rare instances will certification instead of certiorari be used to seek the Supreme Court's review. Cf. CERTIORARI.

certification to state court. The procedure by which a federal court abstains from deciding a state-law question until the highest court in the state has had an opportunity to rule on the question certified.

certified check. See CHECK.

certified copy. See COPY.

certified mail. See MAIL.

certified public accountant. See ACCOUNTANT.

certiorari (sər-sh[ee]ə-**rah**[ə]r-ee or -**rer**-ee or -**re**[ə]r-I). [Latin "to be informed"] An extraordinary writ issued by an appellate court, at its discretion, directing a lower court to deliver the record in the case for review; certiorari is used by the U.S. Supreme Court to review the cases that it wants to hear. —Abbr. cert. — Also termed *writ of certiorari.* Cf. APPEAL.

certworthy, *adj. Slang.* (Of a case or issue) deserving of review by writ of certiorari. —**certworthiness,** *n.*

cesser. The termination of a right or interest.

cession. 1. The act of relinquishing property rights. **2.** The relinquishment or transfer of land from one state to another, esp. when a state defeated in war gives up the land as part of the price of peace. **3.** The land so relinquished or transferred.

cessionary bankrupt. See BANKRUPT.

cestui que trust (**sed**-ee-kə *or* set-wee- *or* -kee). [Law French] One who possesses equitable rights in property and receives the rents, issues, and profits from it; BENEFICIARY.

cestui que use. The person for whose use and benefit property is being held by another, the other person having actual legal title and right to possession.

cestui que vie (sed-ee-kə-**vee** *or* set-wee-). The person whose life measures the duration of a trust, gift, estate, or insurance contract.

ceteris paribus (**kayd**-ər-əs-**par**-ə-bəs). [Latin] Other things being equal.

cf. *abbr.* [Latin *confer*] Compare.

C.F. *abbr.* COST AND FREIGHT.

CFR. *abbr.* CODE OF FEDERAL REGULATIONS.

CGL policy. See *comprehensive general liability policy* under INSURANCE POLICY.

ch. *abbr.* **1.** Chapter. **2.** Chancellor. **3.** Chancery. **4.** Chief.

chain-certificate method. The procedure for authenticating a foreign official record by the party seeking to admit the record as evidence at trial. Fed. R. Civ. P. 44.

chain conspiracy. See CONSPIRACY.

chain of custody. 1. The movement and location of real evidence from the time it is obtained to the time it is presented in court. **2.** The history of a chattel's possession. —Also termed *chain of possession.*

chain of title. The ownership history of a piece of land, from its original source to the present owner. —Also termed *line of title*.

chain-referred scheme. PYRAMID SCHEME.

chair. The person who presides over the meeting of a committee, convention, or assembly, or over the gathering of any other deliberative body. — Also termed *chairman*; *chairwoman*; *chairperson*.

challenge, *n.* **1.** An act or instance of formally questioning the legality or legal qualifications of a person, action, or thing <a challenge to the opposing party's expert witness>.

Batson challenge. In criminal procedure, a defendant's objection to a peremptory jury challenge whereby the defendant raises an inference that the prosecution used the peremptory challenge to exclude the juror on the basis of race (*Batson v. Kentucky*, 476 U.S. 79 (1986)); *Edmonson v. Leesville Concrete Co.* extended *Batson* challenges to civil cases. 500 U.S. 614 (1991).

2. A party's request that a judge disqualify a potential juror or an entire jury panel <the personal-injury plaintiff used his last challenge to disqualify a neurosurgeon>. —Also termed *jury challenge*. —**challenge,** *vb.*

challenge for cause. A party's challenge supported by a specified reason, that if established will automatically disqualify that juror, such as a bias or prejudice. —Also termed *causal challenge*; *general challenge*.

challenge to jury array. A challenge to the form, manner, or legality of making up a jury panel.

peremptory challenge. One of a party's limited number of challenges that need not be supported by any reason, unless it appears that the party has used such a challenge in a way that discriminates against a protected minority. —Often shortened to *peremptory*.

chamber, *n.* **1.** A room or compartment <gas chamber>. **2.** A legislative or judicial body; the hall or room where such a body conducts business <the senate chamber>. — **chamber,** *adj.*

judge's chambers. **a.** The private room or office of a judge. **b.** Any place that the judge transacts official business when not holding a session of the court. See IN CAMERA.

lower chamber. In a bicameral legislature, the larger of the two legislative bodies, such as the House of Representatives or the House of Commons.

upper chamber. In a bicameral legislature, the smaller of the two legislative bodies, such as the Senate or the House of Lords.

chamber, *vb.* (Of a judge) to sit in one's chambers at a given location <Judge Kaye chambers sometimes in New York and sometimes in Albany>.

chamber business. All of a judge's official business that is done outside the courtroom.

chamber of commerce. An association of business people and merchants who organize to promote the commercial interests of a given area and whose group is generally affiliated with the national organization of the same name.

champerty (cham-pər-tee), *n.* **1.** An agreement between a stranger to a lawsuit and a litigant by which the stranger pursues the litigant's claim as consideration for receiving part of any judgment proceeds. **2.** The act or fact of maintaining, supporting, or promoting another person's lawsuit. —**champertous,** *adj.*—**champertor,** *n.* Cf. MAINTENANCE (3).

chance, *n.* **1.** A hazard or risk. **2.** The unforeseen, uncontrollable, or unintended consequences of an act. **3.** An accident.

chancellor, *n.* **1.** A judge serving on a court of chancery. **2.** A university president or CEO of an institution of higher education. —**chancellorship,** *n.*

chance-medley. A spontaneous fight during which one participant kills another participant in self-defense. —Also termed *chaud-medley*.

chancery. 1. A court of equity. — Also termed *court of chancery*; *chancery court*. **2.** The system of jurisprudence administered in courts of equity. See EQUITY. **3.** In international law, the place where the head of diplomatic mission and staff have their offices, as distinguished from the embassy (where the ambassador lives).

chance verdict. See VERDICT.

changed circumstances. See *change of circumstances* under CIRCUMSTANCE.

change of circumstances. See CIRCUMSTANCE.

change of venue. 1. The removal of a lawsuit from one locale to another. **2.** The removal of a lawsuit begun in one court to another court in the same district, usu. because of questions of fairness. —Also termed *transfer of venue*. See VENUE.

Chapter 7. 1. The chapter of the Bankruptcy Code calling for the collection and liquidation of a debtor's property, voluntarily or by court order, to satisfy creditors. **2.** A bankruptcy case filed under this chapter. —Also termed (in sense 2) *straight bankruptcy*.

Chapter 9. The chapter of the Bankruptcy Code governing the adjustment of a municipality's debts; a case filed under this chapter.

Chapter 11. 1. The chapter of the Bankruptcy Code allowing an insolvent business, or one that is threatened with insolvency, to reorganize itself under court supervision while continuing its normal operations and restructuring its debt; although the Code does not expressly prohibit the use of Chapter 11 by an individual nonbusiness debtor, the vast majority of Chapter 11 cases involve business debtors. **2.** A business reorganization conducted under this chapter; REORGANIZATION (2).

Chapter 12. 1. The chapter of the Bankruptcy Code providing for a court- approved debt-payment relief plan for family farmers with a regular income. **2.** A bankruptcy case filed under this chapter. —Also termed (in sense 2) *family-farmer bankruptcy*.

Chapter 13. 1. The chapter of the Bankruptcy Code calling for a person's future earnings to be placed under the supervision of a trustee until all unsecured creditors are satisfied; a plan filed under this Chapter is sometimes called a *wage-earner's plan* or a *wage-earner plan*. **2.** A bankruptcy case filed under this chapter.

character evidence. See EVIDENCE.

characterization. 1. In conflict of laws, the classification, qualification, and interpretation of laws that apply to the case. **2.** The process of classifying marital property as either separate or community property.

character witness. See WITNESS.

charge, *n.* **1.** A formal accusation of a crime as a preliminary step in prosecution <a murder charge>. **2.** An instruction or command <a mother's charge to her son>. **3.** JURY CHARGE <review the charge for appealable error>. **4.** An assigned duty or task; a responsibility <the manager's charge to open and close the office>. **5.** An encumbrance, lien, or claim <a charge on property>. **6.** A person or thing entrusted to another's care <a charge of the estate>. **7.** Price, cost, or expense <free of charge>. — **charge,** vb.

charge conference. A meeting between a trial judge and the parties' attorneys in order to develop a jury charge.

chargé d' affaires (shahr-zhayd-ə-fe[ə]r). A diplomat who is the second in command in a diplomatic mission (hence, subordinate to an ambassador or minister). —Also spelled *chargé des affaires*. Pl. **chargés d' affaires.**

chargee. 1. The holder of a charge on property or of a security on a loan. **2.** One charged with a crime.

charge sheet. A police record of the names of the persons brought into custody, the nature of the accusations, and the identity of the accuser in each case.

charging instrument. A document that sets forth an accusation of a crime, usu. either an indictment or an information. —Also termed *accusatory instrument*.

charging lien. See LIEN.

charging order. In partnership law, a statutory procedure whereby an individual partner's creditor can satisfy its claim from the partner's interest in the partnership.

charitable contribution. 1. A contribution of money or property to an organization that is engaged in charitable purposes. **2.** A contribution to a qualified nonprofit charitable organization—deductible for certain tax purposes.

charitable corporation. See CORPORATION.

charitable deduction. See DEDUCTION.

charitable immunity. See IMMUNITY (2).

charitable organization. In tax law, a tax-exempt organization that (1) is created and operated exclusively for religious, scientific, literary, athletic, public-safety, or community-service purposes, (2) does not distribute net earnings for the benefit of a private shareholder or individual, and (3) does not interfere in any way with political campaigns and decision-making processes. I.R.C. § 501(c)(3). —Also termed *charity.*

charitable remainder. See REMAINDER.

charitable trust. See TRUST.

charity, *n.* **1.** CHARITABLE ORGANIZATION. **2.** Aid given to the poor, suffering, or general community for religious, educational, economic, public safety, or medical purposes. **3.** Goodwill. —**charitable,** *adj.*

charlatan (**shahr**-lə-tən), *n.* A person who pretends to have more knowledge or skill than he or she actually possesses; a quack or faker. —**charlatanism, charlatanry,** *n.*

charta (**kahr**-tə). **1.** In old English law, a charter or deed. **2.** Formerly, a signal or token by which an estate is held. **3.** In civil law, an instrument or writing. See MAGNA CARTA.

chartel. CARTEL.

charter, *n.* **1.** An instrument by which a sovereign (as a city or state) grants rights, liberties, or powers to the sovereign's subjects. **2.** A legislative act that creates a business or defines a corporate franchise. Cf. ARTICLES OF INCORPORATION.

corporate charter. **a.** CERTIFICATE OF INCORPORATION (1). **b.** A document filed with the Secretary of State upon one's incorporating a business, such as the articles of incorporation.

3. The leasing or hiring of an airplane, ship, or other vessel.

bareboat charter. A charter in which the shipowner provides only the ship, and the charterer provides the personnel, insurance, and other necessary expenses and materials.

gross charter. A charter in which the shipowner provides all the necessary expenses and personnel.

time charter. A charter for a specified period of time, rather than for a specific task or trip.

charterparty. A contract by which a ship, or some principal part of it, is leased to a merchant for the conveyance of goods on a predetermined voyage to one or more places. —Also spelled *charter-party; charter party.*—Also termed *charter agreement.*

chattel (**chat**-[ə]l). (*usu. pl.*) Movable or transferable property; any property other than freehold land, esp. personal property.

chattel personal. Tangible goods or intangible rights (as in patents, stocks, or shares).

chattel real. Personal property that concerns real property; a real-property interest that is less than a freehold or fee, such as a leasehold estate. —Also termed *real chattel.*

chattel mortgage. See MORTGAGE.

chattel paper. See PAPER.

chaud-medley (show-**med**-lee). CHANCE-MEDLEY.

check, *n.* A draft that is signed by the maker or drawer, drawn on a bank, payable on demand, and unlimited in negotiability. —Also spelled *cheque.* See DRAFT.

bad check. A check that is not honored upon proper presentation because there are insufficient funds in the account or because the account does not exist. —Also termed *worthless check*; *rubber check*; *cold check*; *bogus check*; *false check*.

cashier's check. A check drawn by a bank on itself, directed to another person, and evidencing the payee's authorization to receive from the bank the amount of money represented by the check.

certified check. The check of a depositor drawn on a bank that then guarantees the available funds for the check.

depository-transfer check. An unsigned, nonnegotiable check that is used by banks to transfer funds from the branch bank to the collection bank.

memorandum check. A check that a borrower gives to a lender for the amount of a short loan, with the understanding that it is not to be presented at the bank but will be redeemed by the maker when the loan falls due.

postdated check. A check that bears a date after the date of its issue and that is payable on or after the stated date.

raised check. A check whose face amount has been increased, usu. without the knowledge of the issuer—an act that under the U.C.C. is considered a material alteration. U.C.C. 3-407. See RAISING AN INSTRUMENT.

registered check. A check purchased at a bank and drawn on bank funds that have been set aside for that check.

stale check. A check that has been outstanding for an unreasonable time—more than six months under the U.C.C.; banks in jurisdictions adopting the U.C.C. may choose not to honor such checks. U.C.C. 4-404.

check-kiting. The illegal practice of writing a check against a bank account with insufficient funds to cover the check, in the hope that the funds from a previously deposited check will reach the account before the bank debits the amount of the outstanding check. —Also termed *kiting*.

check-off system. The procedure by which an employer deducts union dues directly from the employees' wages and remits those dues to the union.

checks and balances. The theory of governmental power and functions whereby each branch of government has the ability to counter the actions of any other branch, so that no single branch can control the entire government; for example, the executive can check the legislature by exercising its veto power, but the legislature can, by a sufficient majority, override any veto. See SEPARATION OF POWERS.

cheque. CHECK.

Chicago Board of Trade. The commodities exchange where futures contracts in a large number of agricultural products are transacted. —Abbr. CBT; CBOT.

Chicago Board Options Exchange. The predominant organized marketplace in the U.S. for trading options. —Abbr. CBOE.

chicanery (shi-**kayn**-[ə-]ree *or* chi-), *n.* Trickery; deception. —Also termed *chicane.* —**chicanerous,** *adj.*

chief, *n.* **1.** A person who is put above the rest; the leader <chief of staff>. **2.** The principal or most important part or position <commander-in-chief>. —**chief,** *adj.*

chief executive. See EXECUTIVE.

chief executive officer. A corporation's highest-ranking administrator who manages the firm on a daily basis and reports to the board of directors. —Abbr. CEO.

chief judge. See JUDGE.

chief justice. See JUSTICE.

chief magistrate. MAGISTRATE (1).

child. 1. At common law, a person who has not reached the age of 14, though the age now varies from jurisdiction to jurisdiction. **2.** A boy or girl; a young person. **3.** A son or daughter. **4.** A baby or fetus. See JUVENILE; MINOR.

neglected child. **a.** A child whose parents or legal custodians are unfit to care for him or her for reasons of cruelty, immorality, or incapacity. **b.** A child whose parents or legal custodians refuse to provide the necessary care and medical services for the child.

child abuse. See ABUSE.

child- and dependent-care tax credit. See TAX CREDIT.

child-kidnapping. See KIDNAPPING.

child-labor law. A state or federal statute that protects children by prescribing the necessary working conditions for children in a workplace.

child pornography. See PORNOGRAPHY.

child-stealing. See *child-kidnapping* under KIDNAPPING.

child support. 1. A parent's legal obligation to contribute to the economic maintenance and education of children; the obligation is enforceable both civilly and criminally. **2.** In a custody or divorce action, the money paid by one parent to the other for the expenses incurred for children of the marriage. See ALIMONY.

chill, *vb. Jargon.* To inhibit or discourage <chill a person's rights>.

chilling a sale. The act of bidders or others who combine or conspire to discourage others from attempting to buy an item so that they might buy the item themselves for a lower price.

chilling effect. In constitutional law, the result of a law or practice that seriously discourages the exercise of a constitutional right, such as the right to appeal or the right of free speech.

Chinese Wall. A screening mechanism that protects client confidences by preventing one or more lawyers within an organization from participating in any matter involving that client; this mechanism is designed to allow a lawyer to move to a new law firm without the fear of vicariously disqualifying that firm from representing certain clients.

chirograph, *n.* **1.** A written deed, subscribed and witnessed. **2.** Such a deed in two parts from a single original document separated by an indented line through the word "chirographum," each party retaining one part. —**chirographic,** *adj.*

chit. 1. A signed voucher for money received or owed, usu. for food, drink, or the like. **2.** A slip of paper with writing on it.

choate (**koh**-it), *adj.* **1.** Complete in and of itself. **2.** Having ripened or become perfected. —**choateness,** *n.* Cf. INCHOATE.

choate lien. See LIEN.

choice of evils. NECESSITY (1).

choice of jurisdiction. In conflict of laws, the choice of the state (or country) that should exercise jurisdiction over a case.

choice of law. In conflict of laws, the question of which jurisdiction's law should apply in a given case. See CONFLICT OF LAWS.

choice-of-law clause. A contractual provision by which the parties designate the state whose law will govern any disputes that may arise between the parties. Cf. FORUM-SELECTION CLAUSE.

chose (shohz), *n.* [French] A thing, whether tangible or intangible; a personal article; a chattel.

chose in action. The right to bring an action to recover a debt, money, or thing. —Also termed *thing in action.*

church court. See *ecclesiastical court* under COURT.

church law. CANON LAW (2).

churning, *n.* A stockbroker's excessive trading of a customer's account in order to earn more commissions rather than to further the customer's interests; under securities laws, the practice is illegal. —**churn,** *vb.*

CIA. *abbr.* CENTRAL INTELLIGENCE AGENCY.

C.I.F. *abbr.* COST, INSURANCE, AND FREIGHT.

CIO. *abbr.* The Congress of Industrial Organizations, which merged with the AFL in 1955. See AMERICAN FEDERATION OF LABOR AND CONGRESS OF INDUSTRIAL ORGANIZATIONS.

circa. [Latin] About or around; approximately <the book was written circa 1938-41>. —Abbr. c.; ca.

circle conspiracy. See *wheel conspiracy* under CONSPIRACY.

circuit, *n.* A judicial division in which hearings occur in several locations, as a result of which judges often travel to different courthouses; esp,, a judicial division of the United States—that is, the thirteen circuits where the U.S. Courts of Appeals sit.

circuit court. See COURT.

circuit judge. See JUDGE.

circular letter of credit. LETTER OF CREDIT.

circular note. LETTER OF CREDIT.

circulating capital. See *floating capital* under CAPITAL.

circumstance, *n.* (*usu. pl.*) An accompanying or accessory fact, event, or condition, such as a piece of evidence that indicates the probability of an event. —**circumstantial,** *adj.*

change of circumstances. In family law, the condition used to show the need for modification of a custody or support order. —Also termed *changed circumstances.*

exigent circumstances. A situation that demands unusual or immediate action and that may allow people to circumvent usual procedures, as when a neighbor breaks through a window of a burning house to save someone inside.

extraordinary circumstances. A highly unusual set of facts that are not commonly associated with a particular thing or event.

mitigating circumstances. **a.** A set of facts that do not justify or excuse an act or offense, but may reduce the degree of moral culpability and thereby reduce the damages in a civil case or the penalty in a criminal case. **b.** In contract law, an unusual or unpredictable event that prevents performance, such as a strike. —Also termed *extenuating circumstances.*

circumstantial evidence. See EVIDENCE.

citation, *n.* **1.** A court-issued writ that commands a person to appear at a certain time and place to do something demanded in the writ, or to show cause for not doing so. **2.** A police-issued order to appear before a judge on a given date to defend against the stated charge, such as a traffic ticket. **3.** A reference to a legal precedent or authority, such as a case, statute, or treatise, to substantiate or fortify a given position. — Also termed (in sense 3) *cite.* —**cite,** *vb.*—**citational, citatory,** *adj.*

parallel citation. An additional reference to a case that has been reported in more than one reporter; for example, whereas a *Bluebook* citation reads "*Morgan v. U.S.,* 304 U.S. 1 (1938)," the same reference

including parallel citations reads "*Morgan v. U.S.,* 304 U.S. 1, 58 S.Ct. 773, 82 L.Ed.2d 1129 (1938)," in which the main citation is to the *U.S. Reports* and the parallel citations are to the *Supreme Court Reporter* and to *Lawyer's Edition.*

pinpoint citation. The page on which a quotation or relevant passage appears, as opposed to the page on which a case or article begins; for example, the number 217 denotes the pinpoint citation in *Baker v. Carr,* 369 U.S. 186, 217 (1962). — Also termed *dictum page; jump citation.*

citator. A book that provides the subsequent judicial history and interpretations of reported decisions, often supplying also legislative history and interpretations of statutes, rules, and regulations.

cite. CITATION (3).

citizen, *n.* **1.** A person who, by either birth or naturalization, is a member of a political community, owing allegiance and being entitled to enjoy all the civil rights and protections of the community.

natural-born citizen. A person born within the jurisdiction of a national government.

naturalized citizen. A foreign-born person who attains citizenship by law.

2. For diversity-jurisdiction purposes, a corporation that has strong connections to a given state. —**citizenship,** *n.*

citizen-informant. A witness who, without expecting payment and with the public good in mind, comes forward and volunteers information to the police or other authorities.

citizen's arrest. See ARREST.

civic, *adj.* **1.** Of or relating to citizenship or a particular citizen <civic responsibilities>. **2.** Of or relating to a city <civic center>.

civil, *adj.* **1.** Of or relating to the state or its citizenry <civil rights>. **2.** Of or relating to private rights and remedies that are sought by action or suit, as distinct from criminal proceedings <civil litigation>. **3.** Of or relating to any of the modern legal systems derived from Roman law <Louisiana is a civil-law jurisdiction>.

civil action. See ACTION.

Civil Code. 1. The code that embodied the law of Rome. **2.** The code that embodies the law of France, from which a great part of the Louisiana civil code is derived. —Abbr. C.C. — Also termed *Code Civil*. See NAPOLEONIC CODE. **3.** A codification of non-criminal statutes.

civil commitment. See COMMITMENT.

civil conspiracy. See CONSPIRACY.

civil contempt. See CONTEMPT.

civil court. See COURT.

civil death. 1. *Archaic.* At common law, the loss of rights—such as the right to vote, to make contracts, to inherit, and to sue—by a person who has been outlawed or convicted of a serious crime, or who is considered to have left the temporal world for the spiritual by entering a monastery. **2.** In some states, the loss of rights—such as the right to vote and to hold public office—by a person serving a life sentence. Cf. *civil disability* under DISABILITY (2). **3.** The state of a corporation that has formally dissolved or become bankrupt, leaving an estate to be administered for the benefit of shareholders and creditors. —Also termed *legal death*.

civil disability. See DISABILITY (2).

civil disobedience. A deliberate but nonviolent act of lawbreaking to call attention to a particular law or set of laws of questionable legitimacy or morality.

civil disorder. A public disturbance involving three or more persons who commit acts of violence that cause immediate danger or injury to persons or property. See RIOT.

civilian, *n.* **1.** A person not enlisted in the military. **2.** A lawyer in a civil-law jurisdiction. —**civilian,** *adj.*

civil injury. See INJURY.

civil law. 1. The civil law of Rome. —Also termed *Roman law*. **2.** (*usu. cap.*) One of the two prominent systems of jurisprudence in the Western World, originally administered in the Roman Empire and still in effect in continental Europe, Latin America, Scotland, and Louisiana among other parts of the world. —Also termed *jus civile*; *Roman law*. Cf. COMMON LAW (2). **3.** The body of law imposed by the state, as opposed to moral law. **4.** The law of civil or private rights, as opposed to criminal law or administrative law.

civil liberty. (*usu. pl.*) Freedom from undue governmental interference or restraint, such as freedom of speech or religion. —Also termed *civil right*.

civil marriage. See MARRIAGE (2).

civil offense. See OFFENSE.

civil procedure. 1. The body of law that governs the methods and practices used in civil litigation, such as the Federal Rules of Civil Procedure. **2.** A particular method or practice used in carrying on civil litigation. Cf. CRIMINAL PROCEDURE.

civil right. (*usu. pl.*) **1.** The individual rights of personal liberty guaranteed by the Bill of Rights and by the 13th, 14th, 15th, and 19th Amendments, as well as by legislation such as the Voting Rights Act; civil rights include esp. the right to vote, the right of due process, and the right of equal protection under the law. **2.** CIVIL LIBERTY.

civil-rights act. One of several federal statutes enacted after the Civil War (1861-1865) and, much later, during and after the civil-rights movement of the 1950s and 1960s, with the purpose of implementing and giving further force to the basic rights guaranteed by the Constitution, and esp. prohibiting discrimination in employment and education on the basis of race, sex, religion, color, or age.

civil-rights removal. See REMOVAL.

civil service, *n.* The administrative branches of a government; the body of persons employed by these branches. **—civil servant,** *n.*

civil war. See WAR.

civil wrong. See WRONG.

civitas (siv-ə-tas). [Latin] In Roman law, a group of people living under a given body of law.

C.J. *abbr.* **1.** See *chief justice* under JUSTICE. **2.** See *chief judge* under JUDGE. **3.** See *circuit judge* under JUDGE. **4.** CORPUS JURIS.

CJE. *abbr.* CONTINUING JUDICIAL EDUCATION.

C.J.S. *abbr. Corpus Juris Secundum.*

Claflin trust. See *indestructible trust* under TRUST.

claim, *n.* **1.** The assertion of an existing right <the spouse's claim to half of the lottery winnings>. **2.** A demand for money or property to which one asserts a right <an insurance claim>.

liquidated claim. A claim concerning an amount that has been agreed on by the parties or that can be precisely determined by operation of law or by the terms of the parties' agreement.

matured claim. A claim based on a debt that is due for payment.

unliquidated claim. A claim in which the liability of the party or the amount of the claim is in dispute.

3. A cause of action; an interest or remedy recognized at law; the means by which a person can obtain a privilege, possession, or enjoyment of a right or thing <claim against the employer for wrongful termination>.

contingent claim. A claim that has not yet accrued and that is dependent on some future event that may never happen.

counterclaim. See COUNTERCLAIM.

cross-claim. See CROSS-CLAIM.

supplemental claim. A claim that is filed when further relief is sought after the original claim has already been brought.

4. Under the Bankruptcy Code, the right to payment or performance, whether or not the right is fixed, matured, disputed, or secured <the lender's priority claim>.

secured claim. A claim held by a creditor who has a lien or a right of setoff against the debtor's property.

unsecured claim. **a.** A claim held by a creditor who does not have a lien or a right of setoff against the debtor's property. **b.** A claim held by a creditor who has a lien on or right of setoff against the debtor's property worth less than the amount of the debt.

5. In patent law, a formal statement describing the novel features of an invention and defining the scope of the patent's protection <the claim failed to emphasize the significance of the new printing method>. Cf. SPECIFICATION (2). —**claim,** *vb.*— **claimant,** *n.*

claim and delivery. A claim for the recovery of specific personal property wrongfully taken or detained, as well as for any damages caused by the taking or detention; this claim derived from the common-law action of replevin.

claim dilution. In bankruptcy law, the reduction in the likelihood that a debtor's claimants will be fully repaid, including considerations of the time value of money.

claim for relief. The part of a complaint stating that if the facts are shown to be as alleged, then the plaintiff is entitled to receive the court's help in enforcing the claim.

claim-jumping. 1. The extension of the borders of a mining claim to infringe on other areas or claims. **2.** The filing of a duplicate claim to take advantage of a flaw in the original claim.

claim of ownership. 1. The possession of a piece of property with the intention of claiming it in hostility to the true owner. **2.** A party's manifest intention to take over land, regardless of title or right. —Also termed *claim of right*; *claim of title.*

claim-of-right doctrine. In tax law, the rule that any income constructively received must be reported as income, whether or not the taxpayer has an unrestricted claim to it.

claim preclusion. RES JUDICATA.

claims adjuster. ADJUSTER.

claims-consciousness, *n.* The quality characterizing a legal culture in which people have firm expectations of justice and are willing to take concrete steps to see that justice is done <claims-consciousness in the U.S. has resulted from certain social changes, not from any character deficiency>. —Also termed *rights-consciousness.* —**claims-conscious,** *adj.*

Claims Court, U.S. A federal court created in 1855 and having original, nationwide jurisdiction to render money judgments on any claim against the U.S. founded on the Constitution, a federal statute, a federal regulation, an express or implied-in-fact contract with the U.S., or any other claim for damages not sounding in tort; appeal is possible through the U.S. Court of Appeals for the Federal Circuit. —Also termed *Court of Claims*.

claims-made policy. See INSURANCE POLICY.

clandestine (klan-**des**-tən), *adj.* Secret or concealed, esp. for illegal or unauthorized purposes.

class, *n.* **1.** A group of persons, things, qualities, or activities that have common characteristics or attributes <a class of common-stock shares> <the upper-middle class>. **2.** The order or rank that persons or things are arranged in <she flew first class to Chicago>. **3.** A body of persons, uncertain in number <a class of beneficiaries>.

testamentary class. A body of beneficiaries who are uncertain in number but whose number is ascertainable in the future, when each will take an equal or other proportionate share of the gift.

4. In litigation, a group of people that have a common legal position, so that all their claims can be efficiently adjudicated in a single proceeding <a class of asbestos plaintiffs>.

settlement class. Numerous similarly situated people for whom a claimant's representative and an adversary propose a contract liquidating the claims of all class members; during the 1980s and 1990s, mass-tort defendants began using settlement classes as a means of foreclosing claims by some unknown number of future claimants.

class action. A lawsuit in which a single person or a small group of people represent by their litigation the interests of a larger group; federal procedure requires the following to maintain a class action: (1) the class must be so large that individual suits would be impracticable, (2) there must be legal or factual questions common to the class, (3) the claims or defenses of the representative parties must be typical of those of the class, and (4) the representative parties must adequately protect the interests of the class. Fed. R. Civ. P. 23. —Also termed *class suit*; *representative action*.

hybrid class action. A type of action in which the rights to be enforced are several and varied, but the object is to adjudicate claims that do or may affect the specific property in the action.

class gift. See GIFT.

class legislation. See *local and special legislation* under LEGISLATION.

class representative. See REPRESENTATIVE.

class suit. CLASS ACTION.

class voting. See VOTING.

clause. 1. ITEM (3). **2.** Loosely, any provision in a legal document.

clause of accrual. A provision, usu. found in a gift by will or in a deed between tenants in common, that grants a decedent beneficiary's shares to the surviving beneficiary. —Also termed *clause of accruer*.

clausula rebus sic stantibus. REBUS SIC STANTIBUS.

clawback, *n.* **1.** Money paid that is taken back. **2.** Tax relief that is at first granted but later annulled. — **claw back,** *vb.*

clawback provision. **a.** A penalty in the form of a tax. **b.** BLOCKING STATUTE.

Clayton Act. A federal statute—enacted in 1914 to amend the Sherman Act—that prohibits price discrimination, tying arrangements, and exclusive-dealing contracts, as well as mergers and interlocking directorates if their effect might substantially lessen competition or create a monopoly in any line of commerce. 15 U.S.C. §§ 12-27.

CLE. *abbr.* CONTINUING LEGAL EDUCATION.

clean-hands doctrine. The principle that a party cannot take advantage of his or her own wrong by seeking equitable relief or asserting an equitable defense if that party has violated an equitable principle, such as good faith; such a party is described as having "unclean hands."— Also termed *unclean-hands doctrine*.

clean-up clause. In a loan agreement, a clause that calls for a loan to be repaid in full within a given period, after which no further loans will be afforded the debtor for a specified "clean up" period.

clear and convincing evidence. See EVIDENCE.

clear and convincing proof. See *clear and convincing evidence* under EVIDENCE.

clear-and-present-danger test. In constitutional law, the doctrine allowing the government to restrict the First Amendment freedoms of speech and press if necessary to prevent immediate and severe danger to interests that the government may lawfully protect; this test was formulated by Justice Oliver Wendell Holmes in *Schenck v. United States,* 249 U.S. 47 (1919).

Clearfield Trust **doctrine.** The doctrine describing the federal courts' power to make federal common law when there is both federal lawmaking power to do so and a strong federal interest in a nationally uniform rule. *Clearfield Trust Co. v. United States,* 318 U.S. 363 (1943). Cf. ERIE DOCTRINE.

clearinghouse. **1.** A place where banks exchange checks and drafts and settle their daily balances. **2.** A stock-and-commodity exchange where the daily transactions of the brokers are cleared. **3.** Any place for the exchange of specialized information.

clearly-erroneous standard. The standard of review that an appellate court usu. applies in judging a trial court's treatment of factual issues; under this standard, a judgment is reversible if it resolves issues in a clearly erroneous manner.

clear market value. FAIR MARKET VALUE.

clear title. See TITLE.

clear-view doctrine. PLAIN-VIEW DOCTRINE.

clemency, *n.* Mercy or leniency; esp., the power of the President or a governor to pardon or commute a criminal sentence. —Also termed *executive clemency.* —**clement,** *adj.* See PARDON; COMMUTATION.

clergy, benefit of. See BENEFIT OF CLERGY.

clerical error. See ERROR.

clerk, *n.* **1.** A public official whose duties include keeping records or accounts. **2.** A court officer responsible for filing papers, issuing process, and keeping records of court proceedings as generally specified by rule or statute. —Also termed *clerk of court.* **3.** An employee who performs general office work. **4.** A law student who assists a lawyer or judge with legal research, writing, and other tasks. — Also termed *law clerk*; *extern*; or (depending on the time of year) *summer associate.* See INTERN.

clerk of the corporation. SECRETARY.

client, *n.* A person or entity that employs a professional for advice or help in that professional's line of work. —**cliental,** *adj.*

client's privilege. See *attorney-client privilege* under PRIVILEGE.

client state. A nation that is obliged in some degree to share in the control of its external relations with some foreign power or powers. Cf. SOVEREIGN STATE.

Clifford **trust.** See TRUST.

clog on the equity of redemption. An agreement or condition that prevents a mortgagor who defaults from getting back the property free from encumbrance upon paying the debt or performing the obligation for which the security was given. See REDEMPTION.

close, *n.* **1.** An enclosed portion of land. **2.** The interest of a person in a particular piece of land, enclosed or not. **3.** The final price of a stock at the end of the exchange's trading day.

close-connectedness doctrine. A doctrine used by some courts to deny holder-in-due-course status to an assignee of a negotiable note if the assignee is too closely connected to the original holder-mortgagee. —Also termed *close-connection doctrine.*

close corporation. See CORPORATION.

closed account. See ACCOUNT.

closed corporation. See *close corporation* under CORPORATION.

closed-end fund. See MUTUAL FUND.

closed-end mortgage. See MORTGAGE.

closed mortgage. See MORTGAGE.

closed shop. A workplace in which the employees must be members of a particular union to work there; in most cases, closed shops are illegal under the Taft-Hartley Act. —Also termed *union shop.* See RIGHT-TO-WORK LAW. Cf. OPEN SHOP; *closed union* under UNION.

closed union. See UNION.

closely held corporation. See *close corporation* under CORPORATION.

closing. In the sale of real estate, the final transaction between the buyer and seller, whereby the conveyancing documents are concluded and the money and property transferred. —Also termed *settlement.*

closing argument. In a trial, a lawyer's final statement to the judge or jury before deliberation begins, in which the lawyer requests the judge or jury to consider the evidence and to apply the law in his or her client's favor; usu. in a jury trial, the judge afterwards charges the jury. —Also termed *closing statement*; *final argument*; *jury summation*; *summing up*.

closing costs. In a real-estate transaction, the expenses that must be paid in addition to the purchase price.

closing statement. 1. CLOSING ARGUMENT. **2.** A written breakdown of the costs involved in a particular real-estate transaction, usu. prepared by a lender or an escrow agent. — Also termed *settlement sheet*; *settlement statement*.

cloture (**kloh**-chər), *n.* The procedure of ending debate in a legislative body and calling for an immediate vote. —**cloture,** *vb.*

cloud on title. A defect or potential defect in the owner's title to a piece of land arising from some claim or encumbrance, such as a lien, an easement, or a court order. See QUIET-TITLE ACTION.

CLS. *abbr.* CRITICAL LEGAL STUDIES.

CLSer. See CRIT.

cluster zoning. See ZONING.

c/o. *abbr.* Care of.

coadjutor, *n.* A coworker or assistant, esp. one appointed to assist a bishop who, because of age or infirmity, is unable to perform his duties. —**coadjutor,** *adj.*

co-agent. See AGENT.

Coase Theorem. An economic proposition describing the relationship between legal rules about entitlements and economic efficiency; the theorem holds that if there are no transaction costs—such as the costs of bargaining or acquiring information—then any legal rule will produce an efficient result.

coconspirator's exception. An exception to the hearsay rule whereby one conspirator's acts and statements, if made in furtherance of the conspiracy, are admissible against a defendant even if the statements are made in the defendant's absence. See HEARSAY.

C.O.D. *abbr.* **1.** Cash on delivery; collect on delivery. **2.** Costs on delivery. **3.** Cash on demand. —Sometimes written *c.o.d.*

code. 1. A systematic collection or revision of laws, rules, or regulations <the Uniform Commercial Code>. **2.** (*usu. cap.*) The collection of laws and constitutions made by order of the Roman Emperor Justinian and first authoritatively published in 534 A.D.; contained in 12 books, the Code is one of four works that make up the *Corpus Juris Civilis.* —Also termed (in sense 2) *Legal Code.* See CODEX; CORPUS JURIS CIVILIS.

Code Civil. CIVIL CODE (2).

codefendant. One of two or more defendants sued in the same litigation or charged with the same crime. —Also termed *joint defendant.*

Code Napoléon. NAPOLEONIC CODE.

Code of Federal Regulations. The annual collection of executive-agency regulations published in the daily Federal Register, combined with previously issued regulations that are still in effect. —Abbr. CFR.

Code of Military Justice. The collection of substantive and procedural rules governing the discipline of members of the armed forces. 10 U.S.C. §§ 801 et seq. —Also termed *Uniform Code of Military Justice* (UCMJ).

Code of Professional Responsibility. See MODEL CODE OF PROFESSIONAL RESPONSIBILITY.

code pleading. See PLEADING (2).

codex (**koh**-deks). [Latin] *Archaic*. **1.** A code, esp. the Justinian Code. **2.** A book written on paper or parchment; esp., a volume of an ancient text.

codicil (**kod**-ə-səl *or* -sil). A supplement or addition to a will, not necessarily disposing of the entire estate but modifying, explaining, or otherwise qualifying the will in some way.

codification, *n*. The process of compiling, arranging, and systematizing the laws of a given jurisdiction into an ordered code; the resulting code. —**codify,** *vb*.—**codifier,** *n*.

codifying statute. See STATUTE.

coemption, *n*. **1.** The act of purchasing the whole quantity of any commodity. **2.** *Archaic*. A Roman-law marriage under which the husband gains contractual rights over the wife. —**coemptional, coemptive,** *adj*.

coercion, *n*. **1.** Compulsion by force or threat; an act such as signing a will is not legally valid if done under coercion. **2.** Constraint by subjugation. —**coerce,** *vb*.—**coercive,** *adj*.—**coercer,** *n*.

criminal coercion. Coercion with the purpose of restricting another's freedom of action by threatening to commit a criminal act against that person or by doing any of the following: (1) threatening to accuse that person of having committed a criminal act, (2) threatening to expose a secret that either would subject the victim to hatred, contempt, or ridicule, or would impair the victim's credit or goodwill, or (3) taking or withholding official actions or causing an official to take or withhold action.

coercion, doctrine of. *Archaic*. A common-law rule holding a husband responsible for his wife's offenses that are committed in his presence; the rule is based on the presumption that a husband exercises influence over his wife.

coercive relief. See RELIEF.

coexecutor. One who is a joint executor of an estate with one or more others.

cogent (**koh**-jənt), *adj*. Compelling or convincing <utterly cogent reasoning>. —**cogency,** *n*.

cognation, *n*. **1.** Relationship by blood rather than by marriage. **2.** Relationship between persons or things of the same or similar nature; likeness. —**cognate,** *adj*.—**cognate,** *n*.

cognate offense. See OFFENSE.

cognitive test. In connection with the insanity defense, a test of the defendant's ability to know certain things, specifically the nature of his or her conduct and whether the conduct was right or wrong.

cognizable (**kog**-ni-zə-bəl), *adj*. **1.** Capable of being known or considered; comprehensible <why the decedent omitted his daughter from the will is not cognizable>. **2.** Capable of being judicially tried or examined before a designated tribunal <these personal-injury claims are not cognizable before the Court of Claims>. **3.** Capable of being defined and limited <the number of Christian Scientists in the county is cognizable>. **—cognize,** *vb.***—cognizance,** *n.*

cognizable group. In the criminal-jury selection process, an identifiable group of people whose common interests cannot be represented by another group, so that jury selection would be unconstitutional without representation by this group.

cognovit (kog-**noh**-vit). [Latin "the person has conceded (a debt or an action)"] An acknowledgment of debt or liability in the form of a confessed judgment; formerly, credit contracts often included a cognovit clause in which consumers agreed in advance that, if they were sued for nonpayment, they had relinquished any right to be notified of court hearings—but such clauses are generally illegal today. See *confession of judgment* under JUDGMENT.

cognovit clause. A clause, outlawed or restricted in most states, by which the debtor agrees to jurisdiction in certain courts, waives notice requirements, and authorizes the entry of an adverse judgment in the event of a default or breach; a promissory note containing such a clause is termed a *cognovit note.*

cognovit judgment. See JUDGMENT.

cohabitation, *n.* The fact or state of living together, esp. as partners in life, usu. with the suggestion of sexual relations. **—cohabit,** *vb.***—cohabitative,** *adj.***—cohabitant,** *n.*

illicit cohabitation. At common law, the act of a man and a woman openly living together without being married to each other. —Also termed *lewd and lascivious cohabitation.*

matrimonial cohabitation. The living together of husband and wife.

notorious cohabitation. Open cohabitation that is considered illegal under statutes that are now rarely enforced.

coheir. One of two or more persons to whom an inheritance descends. See HEIR.

Cohen **doctrine.** COLLATERAL-ORDER DOCTRINE.

coif (koif). A white linen headpiece formerly worn by barristers of high standing in common-law courts; the rank or order of serjeants-at-law. See ORDER OF THE COIF.

coinsurance. See INSURANCE.

cold blood. A killer's state of mind when committing a willful and premeditated homicide <a shooting in cold blood>. See COOL BLOOD. Cf. HEAT OF PASSION.

cold check. See *bad check* under CHECK.

collateral, *n.* **1.** A person collaterally related to a decedent. **2.** Property that is pledged as security against a debt. —Also termed (in sense 2) *collateral security.*

cross-collateral. **a.** Security given by all parties to a contract. **b.** In bankruptcy, bargained-for security that protects a creditor's postpetition extension of credit in addition to the creditor's prepetition unsecured claims which, as a result of such security, obtain priority over other creditors' prepetition unsecured claims; only some courts allow this procedure, which is known as *cross-collateralization*.

collateral, *adj.* **1.** Supplementary; accompanying, but secondary and subordinate to <whether or not the accident victim was wearing a seatbelt is a collateral issue>. **2.** Not direct in line, but on a parallel or diverging line <my uncle is in my collateral line of descent>. Cf. LINEAL. —**collaterality,** *n.*

collateral ancestor. See *collateral ascendant* under ASCENDANT.

collateral ascendant. See ASCENDANT.

collateral attack. An impermissible attack on a judgment outside the proceeding in which the judgment was rendered, the purpose being to impeach or overturn the judgment. — Also termed *indirect attack*. Cf. DIRECT ATTACK.

collateral consanguinity. See CONSANGUINITY.

collateral defense. See DEFENSE (1).

collateral estoppel. An affirmative defense barring a party from relitigating an issue determined against that party in an earlier action, even if the second action differs significantly from the earlier one. —Also termed *issue preclusion*; *direct estoppel*; *estoppel by judgment*. Cf. RES JUDICATA.

defensive collateral estoppel. Estoppel asserted by a defendant to prevent a plaintiff from relitigating an is-sue previously lost against another defendant.

offensive collateral estoppel. Estoppel asserted by a plaintiff to prevent a defendant from relitigating an issue previously lost against another plaintiff.

collateral fraud. See *extrinsic fraud* (a) under FRAUD.

collateral heir. See HEIR.

collateral-inheritance tax. See TAX.

collateralize, *vb.* **1.** To serve as collateral for <the purchased property collateralized the loan agreement>. **2.** To make (a loan) secure with collateral <the creditor insisted that the loan be collateralized>. —**collateralization,** *n.*

collateral line. See LINE.

collateral loan. See *secured loan* under LOAN.

collateral negligence. See NEGLIGENCE.

collateral-negligence doctrine. The rule holding that one who employs an independent contractor is not liable for physical harm that the contractor causes if (1) the contractor's negligence consists solely in the improper manner in which the contractor does the work, (2) the risk of harm created is not normal to the work, and (3) the employer had no reason to contemplate the contractor's negligence when the contract was made.

collateral note. See *secured note* under NOTE.

collateral-order doctrine. A doctrine allowing appeal from an interlocutory order that conclusively determines an issue wholly separate from the merits of the action and that is effectively unreviewable on appeal from a final judgment. —Also termed *Cohen doctrine* (from *Cohen v. Beneficial Indus. Loan Corp.* 337 U.S. 541 (1949)). See *appealable decision* under DECISION.

collateral proceeding. See PROCEEDING.

collateral security. 1. See SECURITY. **2.** COLLATERAL (2).

collateral-source rule. In tort law, the doctrine holding that if an injured party receives compensation for its injuries from a source independent of the tortfeasor, such as insurance proceeds, the payment should not be deducted from the damages that the tortfeasor would otherwise have to pay.

collateral use. See USE (1).

collation (ko-**lay**-shən *or* koh-), *n.* **1.** The comparison of a copy with its original to ascertain its correctness; the report of the officer who made the comparison. **2.** An estimate of the value of advancements made by an intestate to his or her children in order that the entire estate may be divided in accordance with the intestacy statute. —**collate**, *vb.* —**collator**, *n.*

collective bargaining. Negotiations between an employer and the representatives of organized employees for the purpose of determining the conditions of the employment, such as wages, hours, and fringe benefits.

collective mark. A trademark or servicemark used by an association, union, or other group either to indicate the group's products or services or to signify membership in the group; collective marks—such as "Realtor" or "American Peanut Farmers"—can be federally registered under the Lanham Act. Cf. CERTIFICATION MARK.

collision. In maritime law, the sudden impact of two moving vessels. Cf. ALLISION.

colloquium (kə-**loh**-kwee-əm). In a defamation action, the plaintiff's offer of extrinsic evidence establishing that the alleged defamatory statement referred to the plaintiff even though the statement did not explicitly mention the plaintiff. Pl. **colloquiums, colloquia.** Cf. INDUCEMENT (4); INNUENDO (2).

collusion, *n.* An agreement between two or more persons to defraud another or to obtain something forbidden by law; for example, before the creation of the no- fault doctrine in divorce proceedings, the husband and wife might agree to make it appear that one of them had committed an act that was grounds for divorce. —**collude,** *vb.* —**collusive,** *adj.* —**colluder,** *n.*

collusive action. See ACTION.

collusive joinder. See JOINDER.

colony, *n.* A group of people who live in a new territory but retain ties with their parent country; the territory inhabited by such a group. —**colonize,** *vb.* —**colonial,** *adj.*

colonial law. The body of law in force in the thirteen original U.S. colonies before the Declaration of Independence.

color, *n.* Appearance, guise, or semblance; esp., the appearance of a legal claim to a right, authority, or office <color of title> <under color of state law>. —**colorable,** *adj.*

***Colorado River* abstention.** See ABSTENTION.

comaker. One who participates jointly in borrowing money on a promissory note; esp., one who acts as surety under a note if the maker defaults. —Also termed *cosigner.* Cf. MAKER.

comes now. *Jargon.* Traditionally, the standard commencement in pleadings <Comes now the plaintiff, Gilbert Lewis, by and through his attorneys of record, and would show unto the court the following>; for a plural subject, the phrase is *come now* <Come now the plaintiffs, Bob and Louise Smith>. —Also termed *now comes.* —Sometimes shortened to *comes* <Comes the State of Tennessee>.

comingle. COMMINGLE.

comity (**kom**-ə-tee). Courtesy among political entities (as nations, states, or courts of different jurisdictions), involving esp. mutual recognition of legislative, executive, and judicial acts. Cf. ABSTENTION.

judicial comity. The respect a court of one state or jurisdiction shows to another state or jurisdiction in giving effect to the other's laws and judicial decisions.

commencement. INTRODUCTORY CLAUSE.

comment, *n.* **1.** NOTE (2). **2.** An explanatory statement made by the drafters of a particular statute, code section, or rule. —**commentator,** *n.*

commentators. POSTGLOSSATORS.

commenter. One who comments; esp. one who sends comments to an agency about a proposed administrative rule or regulation. See NOTICE-AND-COMMENT PERIOD.

comment on the evidence. A statement made to the jury by the judge or by counsel on the probative value of the evidence presented; lawyers typically make such comments in closing argument—and judges may make such comments in federal court—but judges in most states are not permitted to do so when examining a witness, instructing the jury, and the like (in which case the comment is sometimes termed an *impermissible comment on the evidence*).

comment period. NOTICE-AND-COMMENT PERIOD.

commerce. The exchange of goods and services, esp. on a large scale involving transportation between cities, states, and nations.

interstate commerce. Trade and other business activities between persons located in different states; esp., traffic in goods and travel of persons between states.

intrastate commerce. Commerce that begins and ends entirely within the borders of a single state.

Commerce Clause. U.S. Const. art. I, § 8, cl. 3, which gives Congress the exclusive power to regulate commerce among the states, with foreign nations, and with Indian tribes.

Dormant Commerce Clause. The constitutional principle that the

Commerce Clause prevents state regulation of interstate commercial activity even when Congress has not acted under its Commerce Clause power to regulate that activity.

commercia belli (ko-**mer**-see-ah-**bel**-I). Contracts between nations at war, or between the subjects of nations at war, under which arrangements for nonhostile dealings are made.

commercial bank. See BANK.

commercial bribery. See BRIBERY.

commercial division. See *business court* under COURT.

commercial domicile. See DOMICILE.

commercial frustration. See FRUSTRATION.

commercial general liability policy. See *comprehensive general liability policy* under INSURANCE POLICY.

commercial impracticability. See IMPRACTICABILITY.

commercial insurance. See INSURANCE.

commercial law. 1. The substantive law dealing with the sale and distribution of goods, the financing of credit transactions on the security of the goods sold, and negotiable instruments; most American commercial law is governed by the Uniform Commercial Code. —Also termed *mercantile law.* **2.** LAW MERCHANT.

commercial letter of credit. See LETTER OF CREDIT.

commercial loan. See LOAN.

commercial paper. See PAPER.

commercial speech. See SPEECH.

commingle, *vb.* To put together in one mass, as when one mixes separate funds or properties into a common fund. —Also spelled *comingle.* — **commingling,** *n.*

commissary, *n.* **1.** A person who is delegated or commissioned to perform some duty usu. as a representative of a superior. **2.** A general store, esp. on a military base; also, a lunchroom. —**commissary,** *adj.*

commission, *n.* **1.** A warrant or authority, from the government or a court, that empowers the person named to execute official acts <the student received his commission to the U.S. Navy after graduation>. **2.** The authority under which a person transacts business for another <the client gave her attorney express commission to sign the contract>. **3.** A body of persons acting under lawful authority to perform certain public services <the Federal Communications Commission>. **4.** In criminal law, the action of doing or perpetrating (as a crime) <the perpetrator fled to Mexico after commission of the assault>. **5.** A fee paid to an agent or employee for a particular transaction, usu. as a percentage of the money received from the transaction <a real-estate agent's commission>.

commission del credere (del-**krayd**-ə-ray). The guaranty of a buyer's debt by the seller's agent.

commissioner. 1. A person who directs a commission; a member of a commission. **2.** The administrative head of an organization, such as a professional sport.

county commissioner. A county officer charged usu. with the management of the county's financial affairs, its police regulations, and its corporate business. —Also termed *county supervisor.*

court commissioner. An officer appointed by the court esp. to hear and report facts, or to conduct judicial sales and report.

commissioner's court. See COURT.

commission plan. A form of municipal government whereby both legislative and executive power is vested in a small group of elected officials; today, commission plans are used only in a few cities.

commission to examine a witness. A judicial commission directing that a witness who is beyond the court's territorial jurisdiction be deposed. Cf. LETTER OF REQUEST.

commissive waste. See WASTE.

commitment, *n.* **1.** An agreement to do something in the future, esp. to assume a financial obligation <the shipper had a firm commitment>. **2.** The action of entrusting or giving in charge <commitment of money to the bank>. **3.** The action of consigning a person to a penal or mental institution <commitment of the felon to prison>. **4.** The order directing an officer to take a person to a penal or mental institution <the judge signed the commitment after ruling that it was in the best interest of the troubled teen>. —**commit,** *vb.*

civil commitment. A confinement order for a person who is ill, incompetent, drug-addicted, or the like, as contrasted with the criminal commitment of a sentencing; the confinement itself.

committee. 1. (kə-**mi**-dee) A body of persons on whom the consideration, determination, or management of a matter is conferred <the bill was sent to legislative committee>. **2.** (kom-i-**tee**) A person who is civilly committed, usu. to a psychiatric hospital <the board determined that the committee was dangerous and should not be released>. **3.** (kom-i-**tee**) The guardian for the person so committed <the patient's lawyer objected to the appointment of the committee>.

committing magistrate. See MAGISTRATE.

commodity. 1. An economic good, esp. a raw material or an agricultural product. **2.** An article of trade or commerce.

commodity option. See OPTION.

common, *n.* **1.** A legal right to use another person's property, such as an easement. See PROFIT A PRENDRE. **2.** A tract of land set aside for use by the general public. —**common,** *adj.*

common and notorious thief. See *common thief* under THIEF.

common area. 1. In landlord-tenant law, the portion of the leased premises that all tenants may use and over which the landlord retains control and responsibility. **2.** An area in common ownership and common use by the residents of a condominium, subdivision, or planned-unit development.

common assumpsit. See *general assumpsit* under ASSUMPSIT.

common assurance. MUNIMENT OF TITLE.

common carrier. See CARRIER.

common cost. See *indirect cost* under COST.

common court. See COURT.

common descriptive name. GENERIC NAME.

common design. 1. The intention by two or more people to commit an unlawful act. **2.** The intention of committing more than one crime. **3.** The general design or layout of plots of land surrounding a particular tract. —Also termed *common scheme*; *common plan*. See ZONING.

common disaster. A situation in which two or more persons with related property interests (such as an insured and the beneficiary) die at the same time, with no way to tell who died first. See SIMULTANEOUS-DEATH ACT.

common-enemy doctrine. In property law, the rule that a landowner has the right to repel or divert surface waters as necessary (such as during a flood), without having to consider the consequences to other landowners; the doctrine takes its name from the idea that the water is every landowner's common enemy.

common enterprise. JOINT ENTERPRISE.

common error. In copyright law, a mistake found in both a copyrighted work and an alleged infringement, the mistake being persuasive evidence of unauthorized copying.

common-fund doctrine. The rule that a plaintiff or attorney whose efforts create, discover, increase, or preserve a fund to which others also have a claim, is entitled to recover the litigation costs from that fund.

common intendment. See INTENDMENT.

common-interest doctrine. See *joint-defense privilege* under PRIVILEGE.

common jury. See *petit jury* under JURY.

common law. 1. The body of law derived from judicial decisions and opinions, rather than from statutes or constitutions; CASELAW <federal common law>. **2.** The body of law based on the English legal system, as distinct from a civil-law system <all states except Louisiana have the common law as their legal system>. Cf. CIVIL LAW (2). **3.** General law common to the country as a whole, as opposed to special law that has only local application <the issue is whether the common law trumps our jurisdiction's local rules>. **4.** The body of law to which no constitution or statute applies <the common law used by lawyers to settle disputes>.

common-law copyright. See COPYRIGHT.

common-law crime. See CRIME.

common-law fraud. See *promissory fraud* under FRAUD.

common-law marriage. See MARRIAGE (1).

common-law trust. See *business trust* under TRUST.

common market. See MARKET.

common mistake. See *mutual mistake* (b) under MISTAKE.

common nuisance. See *public nuisance* under NUISANCE.

common plan. COMMON DESIGN.

common plea. See PLEA.

common property. See PROPERTY.

common scheme. COMMON DESIGN.

common-situs picketing. See PICKETING.

common stock. See STOCK.

common tenancy. See *tenancy in common* under TENANCY.

common thief. See THIEF.

commonweal. The general welfare; the common good.

commonwealth. 1. A nation, state, or other political unit <the Commonwealth of Pennsylvania>. **2.** A political unit that has local autonomy but is voluntarily united with the U.S. <Puerto Rico and the Northern Mariana Islands are commonwealths>. Cf. DEPENDENCY; TERRITORY. **3.** A loose association of countries that recognize one sovereign as their head <the British Commonwealth>. — Abbr. Commw.

commorientes (kə-mor-ee-**en**-teez). **1.** Persons who die at the same time, such as spouses who die in an accident. **2.** In Louisiana, the rule of succession regarding such persons. See *simultaneous death* under DEATH; SIMULTANEOUS-DEATH ACT.

commune (**kom**-yoon), *n.* A community of people who share property.

communication. 1. In the law of evidence, any writing or conversation between people. **2.** In constitutional law, actions protected under the Fifth Amendment's right against self-incrimination.

confidential communication. A statement made within a certain protected relationship—such as husband-wife, attorney-client, or priest-penitent—and therefore legally protected from forced disclosure.

privileged communication. A communication that is protected from forced disclosure by a legal privilege. See PRIVILEGE (3).

communitization, *n.* In oil-and-gas law, the aggregating of small tracts sufficient for the granting of a well permit under applicable rules for the spacing of wells. —Also termed *pooling.* —**communitize,** *vb.* Cf. UNITIZATION.

community. 1. A neighborhood, vicinity, or locality. **2.** A society or body of persons with similar rights or interests. **3.** A collection of common interests that arise from an association.

community property. Property owned in common by husband and wife as a result of its having been acquired during the marriage by means other than gift or inheritance, each spouse holding a one-half interest in the property; the nine community-property states are Arizona, California, Idaho, Louisiana, Nevada, New Mexico, Texas, Washington, and Wisconsin. See *marital property* under PROPERTY. Cf. SEPARATE PROPERTY.

commutation, *n.* **1.** Generally, an exchange or replacement. **2.** In criminal law, the executive's substitution in a particular case of a less severe form of punishment for a more severe form that has already been judicially imposed. Cf. PARDON; RE-

PRIEVE. **3.** In commercial and civil law, the substitution of one form of payment for the other. **—commute,** *vb.*—**commutative,** *adj.*

commuted value. 1. In taxation and for the assessment of damages, the present value of a future interest in property. **2.** The value of future payments when discounted to present value.

Commw. *abbr.* COMMONWEALTH.

compact, *n.* An agreement or covenant between two or more parties, esp. between governments or states.

interstate compact. A voluntary agreement between states enacted into law in the participating states upon federal congressional approval.

Compact Clause. U.S. Const. art. I, § 10, cl. 3, which disallows a state from entering into a contract with another state or a foreign country without congressional approval.

company. A corporation—or, less commonly, an association, partnership, or union—that carries on a commercial or industrial enterprise.

holding company. A company formed to control other companies, usu. confining its role to owning stock and supervising management.

investment company. A company formed to acquire and manage a portfolio of diverse assets by investing money collected from different sources. —Also termed *investment trust.* See REAL-ESTATE INVESTMENT TRUST; MUTUAL FUND.

joint-stock company. **a.** An unincorporated association of individuals possessing common capital, the capital being contributed by the members and divided into shares, of which each member possesses a number of shares proportionate to his or her investment. **b.** A partnership in which the capital is divided into shares that are transferable without the express consent of the co-partners. —Also termed *joint-stock association*; *stock association.*

limited company. A company in which the liability of each shareholder is limited to the amount individually invested, such as a corporation.

limited-liability company. A company—statutorily authorized in certain states—that is characterized by limited liability, management by members or managers, and limitations on ownership transfer. — Abbr. L.L.C. —Also termed *limited-liability corporation.*

personal holding company. A holding company subject to special taxes and that usu. has a limited number of shareholders, with most of its revenue originating from passive income such as dividends, interest, rent, and royalties.

reporting company. See REPORTING COMPANY.

title company. A company that examines real-estate titles for any encumbrances, claims, or other flaws. See TITLE SEARCH.

trust company. A company that acts as a trustee for individuals and entities and that sometimes also operates as a commercial bank. See TITLE.

company union. See UNION.

comparative fault. See *comparative negligence* under NEGLIGENCE.

comparative-impairment test. In choice-of-law analysis, a test that asks which of two or more forums would have its policies most impaired by not having its law applied to the case.

comparative interpretation. A method for interpreting statutes by which parts of the statute are compared to each other, and the statute as a whole is compared to other documents from the same source on a similar subject.

comparative jurisprudence. See JURISPRUDENCE.

comparative law. See *comparative jurisprudence* under JURISPRUDENCE.

comparative negligence. See NEGLIGENCE.

comparative-negligence doctrine. The tort-law principle that reduces a plaintiff's recovery proportionally to his or her fault in the damage, rather than barring recovery completely; most states have statutorily adopted the comparative-negligence doctrine. See NEGLIGENCE. Cf. CONTRIBUTORY-NEGLIGENCE DOCTRINE.

comparative-rectitude doctrine. In family law, before the advent of no-fault divorce, the rule providing that when both parties to a divorce show grounds for divorce, the party least at fault is granted the requested relief.

comparator. Something with which something else is compared <the fe-male plaintiffs alleged illegal wage discrimination and contrasted their pay with that of male comparators>.

compelling-state-interest test. In constitutional law, a method for determining the validity of a law that seems to encroach on constitutional rights, whereby the government's interest in the law is balanced against the individual's constitutional right to be free of the law, and only if the government's interest is strong enough will the law be upheld; the compelling-state-interest test is used most commonly in equal-protection analysis when the disputed law requires strict scrutiny. See STRICT SCRUTINY.

compensable, *adj.* Able or entitled to be compensated for <a compensable injury>. —Also termed *recompensable.*

compensable injury. See INJURY.

compensating balance. The amount of money a borrower from a bank is required to keep on deposit as a condition for a loan or a line of credit.

compensatio (kom-pən-**say**-sh[ee]oh). [Latin "weighing; balancing"] In civil law, a defendant's claim to have the plaintiff's demand reduced by the amount owed by the plaintiff to the defendant. See SET-OFF.

compensation, *n.* **1.** Remuneration for services rendered; salary or wages. **2.** Payment of damages, or any other act that a court orders to be done by a person who has caused injury to another and must therefore make the other whole. —**compen-**

sate, *vb.*—**compensatory, compensational,** *adj.*

accrued compensation. Remuneration that has been earned but not yet paid.

deferred compensation. **a.** Payment for work performed, paid in the future or when some future event occurs. **b.** An employee's earnings that are taxed when received or distributed and not when earned, such as contributions to a qualified pension or profit-sharing plan.

just compensation. Under the Fifth Amendment, a fair payment by the government for property it has taken under eminent domain— usu. the fair market value of the property, so that the owner is no worse off after the taking. —Also termed *adequate compensation.*

unreasonable compensation. Under the Internal Revenue Code, pay that is out of proportion with the actual services rendered and therefore not deductible.

compensatory damages. See *actual damages* under DAMAGES.

competence, *n.* **1.** A basic or minimal ability to do something; qualification, esp. to testify <competence of a witness>. **2.** The capacity of an official body to do something <the court's competence to enter a valid judgment>. **3.** Admissibility <competence of the evidence>. —**competent,** *adj.* Cf. COMPETENCY.

competency, *n.* The mental ability to understand problems and make decisions; in the context of a criminal defendant's ability to stand trial, competency includes the capacity to understand the proceedings, to con-

sult meaningfully with counsel, and to assist in the defense. —**competent,** *adj.* Cf. COMPETENCE.

competent evidence. See EVIDENCE.

competent witness. See WITNESS.

competition, perfect. See PERFECT COMPETITION.

compilation, *n.* **1.** A collection of literary works arranged in some way. **2.** A collection of statutes, updated and arranged to facilitate their use. —**compile,** *vb.*

complainant. The party who brings a legal complaint against another; esp., the plaintiff in a civil suit.

complaint. 1. The initial pleading that starts a civil action and states the grounds for the court's jurisdiction, the plaintiff's claim, and the demand for relief; in some jurisdictions, this pleading is labeled a petition. **2.** In criminal law, a formal charge accusing a person of an offense. Cf. INDICTMENT; INFORMATION.

amended complaint. A complaint that modifies and replaces the initial complaint by bringing to notice relevant matters that occurred before or at the time the action began; in some circumstances, a party must obtain the court's permission to amend its complaint.

supplemental complaint. An additional complaint that either corrects a defect in the original complaint or brings to notice relevant matters that occurred after the action began; generally, a party must obtain the court's permission to file a supplemental complaint.

third-party complaint. A complaint filed by the defendant against a third party, alleging that the third party may be liable for some or all of the damages that the plaintiff is trying to recover from the defendant.

well-pleaded complaint. An original or initial pleading that sufficiently sets forth a claim for relief—by including the grounds for the court's jurisdiction, the basis for the relief claimed, and a demand for judgment—so that a defendant may draft an answer that is truly responsive to the issues presented; a well-pleaded complaint must establish a controlling issue of federal law for a federal court to have federal-question jurisdiction over the lawsuit.

completed-contract accounting method. See ACCOUNTING METHOD.

complete diversity. See DIVERSITY OF CITIZENSHIP.

complete integration. See INTEGRATION.

completion bond. See *performance bond* under BOND (2).

complex trust. See TRUST.

complicated larceny. See *mixed larceny* under LARCENY.

complice. *Archaic.* An accomplice or accessory to a crime or immoral behavior.

complicity, *n.* Association or participation in a criminal act; the act or state of being an accomplice. —**complicitous,** *adj.* See ACCOMPLICE.

composite work. In copyright law, a work to which a number of authors have contributed distinguishable parts that are separately protectible; however, the owner of the work—not the author—owns the renewal term, if any. 17 U.S.C. § 304(a).

composition, *n.* **1.** At common law, an agreement between a debtor and creditors for the adjustment or discharge of an obligation for some lesser amount. **2.** The compensation paid as part of such an agreement. — **compose,** *vb.*

compos mentis (kom-pəs-**men**-təs), *adj.* [Latin "master of one's mind"] Of sound mind; having use and control over one's own mental faculties. Cf. NON COMPOS MENTIS.

compound, *vb.* **1.** To put together, combine, or construct. **2.** To compute (interest) on the principal and the accrued interest. **3.** To settle (a matter, esp. a debt) by a money payment, in lieu of other liability; to adjust by agreement. **4.** To agree for consideration not to prosecute (a crime); compounding a felony in this way is itself a felony. **5.** Loosely, to aggravate; to make (a crime, etc.) more serious by further bad conduct.

compound interest. See INTEREST (3).

compound larceny. See *mixed larceny* under LARCENY.

comprehensive general liability policy. See INSURANCE POLICY.

comprehensive insurance. See INSURANCE.

comprehensive nonliteral similarity. See SUBSTANTIAL SIMILARITY.

comprehensive zoning plan. A general plan to control and direct the use and development of a large piece of property. See ZONING.

comprint (**kom**-print). A surreptitious and illegal printing of another bookseller's copy of a work. See INFRINGEMENT.

compromise, *n.* An agreement between two or more persons to settle matters in dispute between them. — **compromise,** *vb.*

compromise verdict. See VERDICT.

comptroller (kən-**trohl**-ər). An officer of a business, private, state, or municipal corporation, who is charged with duties usu. relating to fiscal affairs, including auditing and examining accounts and reporting the financial status periodically. — Also spelled *controller*.

compulsion, *n.* **1.** The act of compelling; the state of being compelled. **2.** An uncontrollable inclination to do something. **3.** Objective necessity; duress. —**compel,** *vb.*—**compulsory, compulsive,** *adj.*

compulsory appearance. See APPEARANCE.

compulsory arbitration. See ARBITRATION.

compulsory counterclaim. See COUNTERCLAIM.

compulsory joinder. See JOINDER.

compulsory process. See PROCESS.

compulsory self-incrimination. See SELF-INCRIMINATION.

compurgation (kom-pər-**gay**-shən), *n. Archaic.* A trial by which a defendant could have 11 witnesses (called *compurgators*) testify that they thought the defendant was telling the truth. —Also termed *wager of law.* —**compurgatory,** *adj.*

Comstock Law. An 1873 federal statute that tightened rules against mailing "obscene, lewd, or lascivious" books or pictures, as well as "any article or thing designed for the prevention of conception or procuring of abortions"; because of its intolerant nature, the law gave rise to an English word roughly equivalent to *prudery*—namely, *comstockery.*

con. *abbr.* **1.** Confidence <con game>. **2.** Convict <ex-con>. **3.** Contra <pros and cons>. **4.** Constitutional <Con. law>.

concealment, *n.* **1.** The act of refraining from disclosure. **2.** The act of removing from sight or notice; hiding. —**conceal,** *vb.*

active concealment. The concealment by words or acts of something that one has a duty to reveal.

fraudulent concealment. The affirmative suppression or hiding, with the intent to deceive or defraud, of a material fact or circumstance that one is legally or morally bound to reveal.

passive concealment. The act of maintaining silence when one has a duty to speak.

conception of invention. See INVENTION.

concerted action. An action that has been planned, arranged, and agreed on by parties acting together to further some scheme or cause, so that all involved are liable for the actions of one. —Also termed *concert of action.*

concert-of-action rule. WHARTON RULE.

concession, *n.* **1.** A government grant for specific privileges. **2.** The voluntary yielding to a demand for the sake of a settlement. **3.** A rebate or abatement. —**concede,** *vb.* —**concessive,** *adj.*

conciliation, *n.* **1.** A settlement of a dispute in an agreeable manner. **2.** A nonbinding arbitration; MEDIATION (1). —**conciliate,** *vb.* —**conciliative, conciliatory,** *adj.* —**conciliator,** *n.*

conclusion, *n.* **1.** The final part of a speech or writing (such as a jury argument or a pleading). **2.** A judgment arrived at by reasoning; an inferential statement. **3.** The closing, settling, or final arranging (as of a treaty or contract). **4.** *Archaic.* An act by which one estops oneself from doing anything inconsistent with it. — **conclude,** *vb.*

conclusional. CONCLUSORY.

conclusionary. CONCLUSORY.

conclusion of fact. A factual deduction drawn from observed or proven facts; an evidentiary inference. Cf. CONCLUSION OF LAW; FINDING OF FACT.

conclusion of law. A judicial deduction made on a showing of certain facts, no further evidence being required; a legal inference. Cf. CONCLUSION OF FACT; FINDING OF FACT; LEGAL CONCLUSION.

conclusive, *adj.* Authoritative; decisive; convincing <her conclusive argument ended the debate>. Cf. CONCLUSORY.

conclusive evidence. See EVIDENCE.

conclusive presumption. See PRESUMPTION.

conclusive proof. See *conclusive evidence* (a) under EVIDENCE.

conclusory (kən-**kloo**-zə-ree), *adj.* Expressing a factual inference without stating the underlying facts on which the inference is based <the plaintiff's allegations were merely conclusory and lacked any supporting evidence>. —Also termed *conclusional; conclusionary.* Cf. CONCLUSIVE.

concomitant, *adj.* Accompanying; incidental <concomitant actions>. — **concomitant,** *n.*

concord. 1. An amicable arrangement between parties, esp. between peoples or nations; a compact or treaty. **2.** *Archaic.* An agreement to compromise and settle an action in trespass. **3.** *Archaic.* An in-court agreement in which a person who acquired land by force acknowledges that the land in question belongs to the complainant. See DEFORCE.

concordat (kən-**kor**-dat). An agreement between a government and a church, esp. the Catholic Church.

concur, *vb.* **1.** To agree; to consent. **2.** In a judicial opinion, to agree with the result of the opinion of another judge, but often for different reasons or through a different line of reasoning. **3.** In Louisiana law, to join with other claimants in presenting a demand against an insolvent estate.

concurrence. 1. Agreement; assent. **2.** A vote cast by a judge in favor of the judgment reached, often on grounds differing from those expressed in the majority opinion explaining the judgment. **3.** A separate written opinion explaining such a vote. —Also termed (in sense 3) *concurring opinion*.

concurrent, *adj*. **1.** Operating at the same time; covering the same matters <concurrent interests>. **2.** Having authority on the same matters <concurrent jurisdiction>.

concurrent cause. See CAUSE (1).

concurrent condition. See CONDITION.

concurrent covenant. See COVENANT (1).

concurrent estate. See ESTATE.

concurrent interest. See *concurrent estate* under ESTATE.

concurrent jurisdiction. See JURISDICTION.

concurrent lease. See LEASE.

concurrent negligence. See NEGLIGENCE.

concurrent power. See POWER.

concurrent resolution. See RESOLUTION.

concurrent sentences. See SENTENCE.

concurrent tortfeasors. See TORTFEASOR.

concurring opinion. See OPINION (1).

condemnation, *n*. **1.** The act of judicially pronouncing someone guilty; conviction. **2.** The determination and declaration that certain property (esp. land) is assigned to public use, subject to reasonable compensation; the exercise of eminent domain by a governmental entity. See EMINENT DOMAIN.

excess condemnation. The taking of private property beyond what is needed for public use.

inverse condemnation. The constructive condemnation of property through the actual condemnation of land near the first property, so that the value or use of that property suffers to such a degree that just compensation must be paid to the owner. —Also termed *condemnation blight*.

quick condemnation. The immediate taking of private property for public use, whereby the estimated reasonable compensation is placed in escrow until the actual amount of compensation can be established.

3. An official pronouncement that a thing (such as a building) is unfit for use or consumption; the act of making such a pronouncement. —**condemn,** *vb*.—**condemnatory,** *adj*.

condemnation money. 1. Damages that a losing party in a lawsuit is condemned to pay. **2.** Damages paid by an expropriator of land to the landowner for taking the property.

condemnee. One whose property is expropriated for public use or damaged by a public-works project.

condemnor. A public or semipublic entity that expropriates private property for public use.

condition, *n*. **1.** A stipulation or prerequisite in a contract, will, or other instrument. **2.** A future and uncertain event on which the existence or extent of an obligation or liability depends.

concurrent condition. A condition that must occur or be performed at the same time as another condition.

condition precedent. A condition that must occur before something else can occur.

condition subsequent. A condition that, if it occurs, will bring something else to an end.

3. A qualification attached to the conveyance of property providing that if a particular event does or does not take place, the estate will be created, enlarged, defeated, or transferred. **4.** A state of being; an essential quality or status. —**condition**, *vb.* —**conditional**, *adj.*

conditional assault. See ASSAULT.

conditional bequest. See BEQUEST.

conditional contraband. See CONTRABAND.

conditional delivery. See DELIVERY.

conditional devise. See DEVISE.

conditional limitation. See LIMITATION.

conditional purpose. **1.** An intention to do something, conditions permitting. **2.** In criminal law, a possible defense against a crime if the conditions make committing the crime impossible (e.g., "I will steal the money if it's there," and the money is not there).

conditional sale. See SALE.

conditional sales contract. See *retail installment contract* under CONTRACT.

conditional sentence. See SENTENCE.

conditional-use permit. SPECIAL-USE PERMIT.

conditional will. See WILL.

conditioning the market. GUN-JUMPING.

condition of employment. A qualification or circumstance required for obtaining or keeping a job.

condition precedent. See CONDITION.

condition subsequent. See CONDITION.

condominium. **1.** A single real-estate unit in a multi-unit development in which a person has both separate ownership of a unit and a common interest, along with the development's other owners, in the common areas. Cf. COOPERATIVE (2). **2.** Joint sovereignty by two or more nations. **3.** A politically dependent territory under such sovereignty.

condonation (kon-də-**nay**-shən), *n.* A victim's implied forgiveness of an offense by treating the offender as if there had been no offense; esp., before the advent of no-fault divorce, a spouse's forgiveness implied by continuing to live normally with the other spouse after that spouse committed an offense that would otherwise be grounds for divorce. —**condone**, *vb.* —**condonable**, *adj.*

conduct, *n.* Personal behavior; mode of action. —**conduct**, *vb.*

assertive conduct. In the law of evidence, nonverbal behavior that is intended to be a statement, such as pointing one's finger to identify a suspect in a police lineup; assertive conduct is a statement under the hearsay rule, and thus it is not admissible (unless a hearsay exception applies). Fed. R. Evid. 801(a)(2). —Also termed *implied assertion*.

disorderly conduct. A misdemeanor consisting of any behavior that tends to disturb the public peace, offend public morals, or undermine safety. See BREACH OF THE PEACE.

nonassertive conduct. In the law of evidence, nonverbal behavior that is not intended to be a statement, such as fainting while being questioned as a suspect by a police officer; nonassertive conduct is not a statement under the hearsay rule, and thus it is admissible (if it is relevant). Fed. R. Evid. 801.

outrageous conduct. Conduct so extreme that it exceeds all reasonable bounds of decency. See EMOTIONAL DISTRESS.

unprofessional conduct. Behavior that is immoral, unethical, or dishonorable, either generally or when judged by the standards of a specific profession.

conduit taxation. See *pass-through taxation* under TAXATION.

confederacy, *n.* **1.** A league for mutual support or joint action; an alliance. **2.** An association of two or more persons for unlawful purposes; CONSPIRACY. **3.** The fact or condition of being an ally or accomplice. — **confederate,** *n.*

confederation. A league or union of states, groups, or peoples, each of which retains its sovereignty but also delegates some rights and powers to a central authority. Cf. FEDERATION.

conferee. MANAGER (2).

confessed judgment. See *confession of judgment* (b) under JUDGMENT.

confession, *n.* A criminal suspect's acknowledgment of guilt, usu. in writing and often including a disclosure of details about the crime. — **confess,** *vb.*—**confessor,** *n.*

implied confession. A confession in which the person does not plead guilty but invokes the mercy of the court and asks for a light sentence.

indirect confession. A confession that is inferred from the defendant's conduct.

interlocking confessions. Confessions by two or more suspects whose statements are substantially the same and consistent concerning the elements of the crime involved; such confessions are admissible in a joint trial.

involuntary confession. A confession induced by police or other authorities by making promises to, coercing, or deceiving the suspect.

judicial confession. A plea of guilty or some other direct manifestation of guilt in court or in a judicial proceeding.

naked confession. A confession unsupported by any evidence that a crime has been committed, and therefore usu. highly suspect.

plenary confession. A complete confession; one that is believed to be conclusive against the person who made it.

confession and avoidance. A plea in which a defendant admits allegations while adding new information that tends to deprive the admitted facts of an adverse legal effect; for example, a plea of contributory negligence (before the advent of comparative negligence) was a confession and avoidance. —Also termed *avoidance.*

confession of judgment. See JUDGMENT.

confidence. 1. Assured expectation; firm trust; faith <the partner has confidence in the associate's work>. **2.** Reliance on another's discretion; a relation of trust <she took her co-worker into her confidence>. **3.** A communication not intended for public disclosure; a confidence revealed by a client to his or her attorney is protected by the attorney-client privilege <a lawyer may not disclose a client's confidences>. Cf. SECRET. — **confide,** *vb.*

confidence game. A means of obtaining money or property whereby a person intentionally misrepresents facts to gain the victim's trust so that the victim will transfer money or property to the person. —Also termed *con game.*

confidential communication. See COMMUNICATION.

confidentiality, *n.* **1.** Secrecy; the state of having the dissemination of certain information restricted. **2.** The relation between lawyer and client or guardian and ward, or between spouses, with regard to the trust that is placed in the one by the other. — **confidential,** *adj.*

confinee. A person held in confinement.

confinement, *n.* The act of imprisoning or restraining someone; the state of being imprisoned or restrained <solitary confinement>. — **confine,** *vb.*

confirmation, *n.* **1.** The act of giving formal approval <Senate confirmation hearings>. **2.** The act of verifying or corroborating; a statement that verifies or corroborates <the journalist sought confirmation of the district attorney's remarks>. **3.** *Archaic.* The act of ratifying a voidable estate <deed of confirmation>. — **confirm,** *vb.*—**confirmatory,** *adj.* Cf. RATIFICATION.

confirming bank. See BANK.

confiscation, *n.* **1.** Seizure of property for the public treasury. **2.** Seizure of property by actual or supposed authority. —**confiscate,** *vb.*— **confiscatory,** *adj.*—**confiscator,** *n.*

conflict of authority. A disparity between two or more courts, usu. courts of last resort, on some point of law.

conflict of interest. 1. A real or seeming incompatibility between one's private interests and one's public or fiduciary duties. **2.** A real or seeming incompatibility between the interests of two of a lawyer's clients, such that the lawyer is disqualified from representing both clients if the dual representation adversely affects either client or if the clients do not consent.

conflict of laws. 1. A difference between the laws of different states or countries in a case in which a party has acquired rights within two or more jurisdictions. **2.** The body of jurisprudence that undertakes to reconcile such differences or to decide what law is to govern in these situations; the principles of choice of law. —Often shortened (in sense 2) to *conflicts.* —Also termed (in international contexts) *private international law.*

conformed copy. See COPY.

conforming use. See USE (1).

conformity hearing. A court-ordered hearing to determine whether the judgment or decree prepared by the prevailing party conforms to the decision of the court.

Confrontation Clause. The Sixth Amendment provision guaranteeing a criminal defendant's right to directly confront an accusing witness and to cross- examine that witness.

con game. CONFIDENCE GAME.

congeries (kon-jə-reez). A collection or aggregation <a congeries of rights>.

conglomerate, *n.* A corporation that owns unrelated enterprises in a wide variety of industries. —**conglomerate,** *vb.* & *adj.*

conglomerate merger. See MERGER.

congress, *n.* **1.** A formal meeting of delegates or representatives. **2.** (*cap.*) The legislative body of the federal government, created under U.S. Const. art. I, § 1 and consisting of the Senate and the House of Representatives. —**congressional,** *adj.*

congressional immunity. See IMMUNITY (1).

conjecture, *n.* A guess; supposition; surmise. —**conjecture,** *vb.*—**conjectural,** *adj.*

conjoint will. See *joint will* under WILL.

conjugal (**kon**-jə-gəl), *adj.* Of or relating to the married state, often with an implied emphasis on sexual relations between spouses <the prisoner was allowed a private bed for conjugal visits>.

conjunctive denial. See DENIAL.

connecting factors. In conflict of laws, legal considerations that serve to determine the choice of law by connecting an action or individual with the state or jurisdiction.

connecting-up doctrine. The rule allowing something to be put into evidence on condition that the party will connect the thing with later evidence to show its relevance to the case.

connivance, *n.* **1.** The act of ignoring a wrongdoer's illegal conduct; esp., a secret or indirect condonation of another's unlawful act. **2.** In divorce actions, a defense that points to the plaintiff's corrupt consent, implied or express, to the action being complained of. —**connive,** *vb.*

conquest. In international law, the retention of territory taken from an enemy in war, and the exercise there of all the powers of sovereignty, with the intention of continuing to exercise those powers permanently; usu. that intention is explained in a proclamation or some other legal document.

consanguinity (kon-san-**gwin**-ə-tee), *n.* The relationship of persons of the same blood or origin. —**consanguineous,** *adj.*

collateral consanguinity. The relationship between persons who have the same ancestor but do not descend or ascend from one another (for example, uncle and nephew, etc.).

lineal consanguinity. The relationship between persons who are directly descended or ascended from one another (for example, mother and daughter, great-grandfather and grandson, etc.).

conscience. 1. The moral sense of right or wrong; esp., a moral sense applied to one's own judgment and actions. **2.** In law, the moral rule that requires justice and honest dealings between people.

conscience of the court. The court's equitable power to decide issues based on notions of fairness and equality.

conscientious objector. A person who for moral or religious reasons is opposed to participating in any war, and who is therefore excused from military conscription but is subject to serving in civil work for the nation's health, safety, or interest.

conscionable, *adj.* Conforming with good conscience; just and reasonable <a conscionable bargain>. —**conscionableness, conscionability,** *n.* Cf. UNCONSCIONABLE.

consciously parallel. In antitrust law, of, relating to, or characterizing the conduct of a party who has knowledge of a competitor's course of action and who makes an independent decision to take the same actions; in some cases this is viewed as evidence of a conspiracy.

conscription. DRAFT (2).

consecutive sentences. See SENTENCE.

consecutive tortfeasors. See TORTFEASOR.

consensual crime. See *victimless crime* under CRIME.

consent, *n.* Agreement, approval, or permission as to some act or purpose, esp. given voluntarily by a competent person; consent is an affirmative defense to assault, battery, and related torts, as well as such torts as defamation, invasion of privacy, conversion, and trespass. —**consent,** *vb.*—**consensual,** *adj.*

implied consent. Consent inferred from one's conduct rather than from one's direct expression.

informed consent. **a.** A person's agreement to allow something to happen, made with full knowledge of the risks involved and the alternatives. **b.** A patient's intelligent choice about treatment, made after a physician discloses whatever information a reasonably prudent physician in the medical community would provide to a patient regarding the risks involved in the proposed treatment.

consent decree. See DECREE.

consent dividend. See DIVIDEND.

consent judgment. See *agreed judgment* under JUDGMENT.

consent jurisdiction. See JURISDICTION.

consent order. See *consent decree* under DECREE.

consent search. See SEARCH.

consequential contempt. See *constructive contempt* under CONTEMPT.

consequential damages. See DAMAGES.

consequential loss. See LOSS.

conservator. **1.** A guardian, protector, or preserver. **2.** A person appointed by the court to manage the estate or affairs of another who is legally incapable of doing so. Cf. COMMITTEE (3).

conservator of the peace. PEACE OFFICER.

consideration, *n.* Something of value (such as an act, a forbearance, or a return promise) received by a promisor from a promisee; consideration, or a substitute such as promissory estoppel, is necessary for a contract to be enforceable.

fair consideration. Consideration that is a fair equivalent of the thing being exchanged.

good consideration. **a.** Consideration that is valid under the law. —Also termed *valuable consideration*; *good and valuable consideration*. **b.** Consideration based on natural love or affection or on moral duty; such consideration is usu. not valid for the enforcement of a contract.

illegal consideration. Consideration that is contrary to the law or prejudicial to the public interest; such consideration is invalid for the enforcement of a contract.

invented consideration. Fictional consideration created by a court to prevent the invalidation of a contract that lacks consideration.

nominal consideration. Consideration that is so low as to bear no relationship to the value of what is being conveyed (e.g., conveying a piece of real estate for $1 or for no money at all); such consideration

can be valid, since courts do not ordinarily examine the adequacy of consideration (although they do often inquire into such issues as fraud and duress). —Also termed *peppercorn.*

past consideration. An act done or a promise given by a promisee before the making of a promise sought to be enforced; past consideration is not consideration for the new promise, since it has not been given in exchange for this promise (although exceptions exist for new promises to pay debts barred by limitations or debts discharged in bankruptcy). Cf. PREEXISTING-DUTY RULE.

consideration, failure of. See FAILURE OF CONSIDERATION.

consideration, want of. See WANT OF CONSIDERATION.

consign, *vb.* **1.** To transfer to another's custody or charge. **2.** To deliver (goods) to a carrier for transmittal to a designated agent. **3.** To give (merchandise or the like) to another to sell, usu. with the understanding that the owner and the seller will share the proceeds in agreed-on proportions.

consignee (kon-si-**nee** *or* kən-**sI**-nee). One to whom goods are consigned.

consignment (kən-**sIn**-mənt). **1.** The act of consigning goods for custody or sale. **2.** A quantity of goods delivered by this act, esp. in a single shipment.

consignment sale. See SALE.

consignor (kon-si-**nor** or kən-**sI**-nər). One who dispatches goods to another on consignment.

consol. See *annuity bond* under BOND (1).

consolidated appeal. See APPEAL.

consolidated financial statement. See FINANCIAL STATEMENT.

consolidated return. See TAX RETURN.

consolidating statute. See STATUTE.

consolidation, *n.* **1.** The act or process of uniting; the state of being united. **2.** In corporate law, the unification of two or more corporations by dissolving the existing ones and creating a single new corporation. Cf. MERGER (7). **3.** In procedure, the court-ordered unification of two or more actions—involving the same parties and issues—into a single action resulting in a single judgment. Cf. JOINDER. —**consolidate,** *vb.*—**consolidatory,** *adj.*

consolidation loan. See LOAN.

consortium (kən-**sor**-sh[ee]əm). **1.** The interests that one spouse is entitled to receive from the other, including company, cooperation, affection, aid, and sexual relations <a claim for loss of consortium>. See LOSS OF CONSORTIUM. **2.** A group of companies that agree to join or associate for an enterprise beyond their individual capabilities or resources <several high-tech businesses formed a consortium to create a new supercomputer>. Pl. **consortiums, consortia.**

conspiracy, *n.* An agreement by two or more persons to commit an unlawful act; in criminal law, conspiracy is a separate offense from the crime that is the object of the conspiracy. —**conspire,** *vb.*—**conspiratorial,** *adj.*—**conspirator,** *n.* Cf. ATTEMPT (2); SOLICITATION (2).

chain conspiracy. A single large conspiracy in which all parties to subconspiracies are interested in the overall scheme and liable for all other parties' acts in furtherance of that scheme.

civil conspiracy. A tortious conspiracy to defraud or cause damage to a person or property.

wheel conspiracy. A conspiracy in which several independent conspiracies are linked by a common member, who is the only party liable for all of the conspiracies. — Also termed *circle conspiracy*; *hub-and-spoke conspiracy*.

constable, *n.* A peace officer responsible for minor judicial duties, such as serving writs and warrants, but with less authority and smaller jurisdiction than a sheriff. —**constabulary,** *adj.*—**constabulary** (body or force), *n.*

constituent, *n.* **1.** A person who gives another the authority to act for him or her; a principal who appoints an agent. **2.** Someone who is represented by a given legislator or other elected official. **3.** One part of something that makes up a whole; an element. —**constituency,** *n.*

constitution. **1.** The fundamental and organic law of a nation or state, establishing the conception, character, and organization of its government, as well as prescribing the extent of its sovereign power and the manner of its exercise. **2.** The written instrument embodying this law.

constitutional, *adj.* **1.** Of or relating to a constitution <constitutional rights>. **2.** Proper under a constitution <constitutional actions>.

constitutional convention. An assembly of state or national delegates who meet to frame, amend, or revise their constitution.

constitutional court. See COURT.

constitutional-fact doctrine. The rule that federal courts are not bound by an administrative agency's factual findings when the facts involve whether the agency has exceeded constitutional limitations on its power, esp. regarding personal rights; the courts are instead charged with making an independent inquiry based on the existing record. Cf. JURISDICTIONAL-FACT DOCTRINE.

constitutionalize, *vb.* **1.** To provide with a constitution <constitutionalize the new government>. **2.** To make constitutional; to bring in line with a constitution <the court plans to constitutionalize the segregated school district>. **3.** To import a constitution into <the dissenter accused the majority of unnecessarily constitutionalizing its decision>.

constitutional law. The body of law deriving from the U.S. Constitution and dealing primarily with governmental powers and civil rights and liberties; constitutional law originated in *Marbury v. Madison*, 5 U.S. (1 Cranch) 137 (1803), which declared the judiciary's power to construe the Constitution.

constitutional right. A right guaranteed by the U.S. Constitution, as interpreted by the federal courts; also, a right guaranteed by some other constitution (such as a state constitution).

constitutional tort. See TORT.

construction, *n.* **1.** The act of building by combining or arranging parts or elements; the thing so built. **2.** The act or process of interpreting or explaining the sense or intention of something (such as a statute, opinion, or instrument). —**construct** (corresponding to sense 1), *vb.* —**construe** (corresponding to sense 2), *vb.*

liberal construction. An interpretation that favors the applicability of a writing to the situation presented and that tends to effectuate the spirit of the writing. —Also termed *equitable construction*; *loose construction.*

strict construction. An interpretation that considers only the literal words of a writing. —Also termed *literal construction.* See STRICT CONSTRUCTIONISM.

construction lien. See *mechanic's lien* under LIEN.

constructive, *adj.* Having an effect in law though not necessarily in fact; courts usu. give something constructive effect for equitable reasons <the court held that the shift supervisor had constructive knowledge of the machine failure even though he did not actually know until two days later>. See LEGAL FICTION.

constructive bailment. See BAILMENT.

constructive breach. See *anticipatory breach* under BREACH OF CONTRACT.

constructive contempt. See CONTEMPT.

constructive delivery. See DELIVERY.

constructive desertion. See DESERTION.

constructive dividend. See DIVIDEND.

constructive eviction. See EVICTION.

constructive fraud. See FRAUD.

constructive intent. See INTENT.

constructive knowledge. See KNOWLEDGE.

constructive loss. See LOSS.

constructive malice. See *implied malice* under MALICE.

constructive notice. See NOTICE.

constructive payment. See PAYMENT.

constructive possession. See POSSESSION.

constructive-receipt doctrine. The rule that gross income under a taxpayer's control before it is actually received (such as accumulated interest income that has not been withdrawn) must be included by the taxpayer in gross income, unless the actual receipt is subject to significant constraints.

constructive service. See SERVICE.

constructive taking. See TAKING.

constructive trust. See TRUST.

consul, *n.* A governmental representative living in a foreign country to oversee commercial and other matters involving the representative's home country and its citizens in that foreign country; because they are not diplomatic agents, consuls are subject to local law and jurisdiction. —**consular,** *adj.*—**consulship,** *n.*

consul general. A high-ranking consul appointed to a strategically important region and often having supervisory powers over other regions or other consuls.

consulate. 1. The office or jurisdiction of a consul <the senator advised the businessman to notify the U.S. consulate in Kuwait before visiting the country>. **2.** The location of a consul's office or residence <the family was staying on the second floor, just above the Turkish consulate>. **3.** Government by consuls <after the French Revolution, the Directory was overthrown and the consulate was created>.

consultation, *n.* **1.** The act of asking the advice or opinion of someone (as a lawyer). **2.** A meeting in which parties consult or confer. —**consult,** *vb.*—**consulting, consultative,** *adj.*

consulting expert. See EXPERT.

consumer. One who buys goods or services with no intention of resale; a user of a commodity.

consumer boycott. See BOYCOTT.

Consumer Credit Code. UNIFORM CONSUMER CREDIT CODE.

Consumer Credit Protection Act. A federal statute that safeguards the consumer in connection with the use of credit by (1) requiring full disclosure of the terms of the loan agreement, including finance charges, (2) restricting the garnishment of wages, and (3) regulating the use of credit cards (15 U.S.C. §§ 1601 et seq.); many states have adopted their own consumer-credit-protection acts. — Also termed *Truth in Lending Act.* Cf. UNIFORM CONSUMER CREDIT CODE.

consumer debt. See DEBT.

consumer goods. See GOODS.

consumer loan. See LOAN.

consumer price index. An index that tracks the price level of goods and services purchased by the average consumer and that is published monthly by the Bureau of Labor Statistics. —Abbr. CPI. —Also termed *cost-of-living index.*

consumer-protection law. A state or federal statute designed to protect consumers against unfair trade and credit practices involving consumer goods, as well as to protect consumers against faulty and dangerous goods.

consummate (**kon[t]-sə-mayt**), *vb.* **1.** To bring to a completion; esp., to make (a marriage) complete by sexual intercourse. **2.** To achieve; fulfill. **3.** To perfect; carry to the highest degree. —**consummate** (**kon[t]-sə-mət**) *adj.*

consummate lien. See LIEN.

containment. In international law, the policy of restricting the ideological and physical expansion of one's enemy; this was the basic philosophy of the U.S. during the Cold War.

contemn, *vb.* To treat (as laws or court orders) with contemptuous disregard. —**contemner, contemnor,** *n.* See CONTEMPT.

contemplation of death. The thought of dying, not necessarily as an imminent danger, but as the compelling reason to transfer property to another. See *gift causa mortis* under GIFT.

contemporaneous-construction doctrine. The rule that an administrative body's interpretation of an ambiguous law is entitled to great deference in determining the law's meaning if the interpretation has been used over a long period.

contemporaneous-objection rule. The doctrine that an objection to the admission of evidence must be made in a specific and timely manner for the question of admissibility to be considered on appeal.

contempt, *n.* **1.** The act or state of despising; the condition of being despised. **2.** Conduct that defies the authority or dignity of a court or legislature; because such conduct interferes with the administration of justice, it is punishable, usu. by fine or imprisonment. CONTUMACY. — Also termed *contempt of court*—**contemptuous,** *adj.*

civil contempt. The failure to obey a court order that was issued for another party's benefit; a civil-contempt proceeding is coercive or remedial in nature.

constructive contempt. Contempt that is committed outside of court, as when a party disobeys a court order. —Also termed *consequential contempt*; *indirect contempt*.

criminal contempt. An act that obstructs justice or attacks the integrity of the court; a criminal-contempt proceeding is punitive in nature.

direct contempt. Contempt that is committed in open court, as when a lawyer insults a judge on the bench.

contempt power. The power of a public institution (as Congress or a court) to punish someone who shows contempt for the decrees, orders, and proceedings of that institution.

contest (kən-**test**), *vb.* **1.** To strive to win or hold; contend <he chose to contest for the prize>. **2.** To litigate or call in question; challenge <they want to contest the will>. **3.** To assert a defense to an adverse claim in a court proceeding <she contests that charge>. —**contest** (**kon**-test), *n.*

contestant. One who contests the validity of a will. —Also termed *objectant*; *caveator*.

context, *n.* **1.** The surrounding text of a word or passage, used to determine the meaning of that word or passage <his remarks were taken out of context>. **2.** Setting or environment <in the context of foreign relations>. —**contextual,** *adj.*

contiguous (kən-**tig**-yə-wəs), *adj.* **1.** Touching at a point or along a boundary; ADJOINING <Texas and Oklahoma are contiguous>. **2.** Near in time or sequence; successive <contiguous thunder and lightning>. —**contiguity,** *n.*

Continental Congress. The first national governmental assembly in the United States, formed in 1774 to protest British treatment of the colonies; the Second Continental Congress, commencing in 1775, adopted the Declaration of Independence and served as the national government until the Articles of Confederation were ratified in 1781.

contingency. **1.** An event that may or may not occur; a possibility. **2.** The condition of being dependent on chance; uncertainty. **3.** CONTINGENT FEE.

contingency fee. CONTINGENT FEE.

contingency reserve. See *contingency fund* under FUND.

contingent, *adj.* **1.** Possible; uncertain; unpredictable <the trust was merely contingent, and the contingency never occurred>. **2.** Dependent on something else; conditional <her acceptance of the position was contingent upon the firm's agreeing to guarantee her husband a position as well>.

contingent annuity. See ANNUITY.

contingent beneficiary. See BENEFICIARY.

contingent claim. See CLAIM (3).

contingent debt. See DEBT.

contingent estate. See ESTATE.

contingent fee. A fee charged for a lawyer's services only if the lawsuit is successful or is favorably settled out of court; contingent fees are usu. calculated as a percentage of the client's recovery (such as 25% of the recovery if the case is settled, and 33% if the case is won at trial). —Also termed *contingency fee*; *contingency*.

reverse contingent fee. A fee in which a defense lawyer's compensation depends in whole or in part on how much money the lawyer saves the client, given the client's potential liability—so that the lower the settlement or judgment, the higher the lawyer's fee; for example, if a corporate client might be liable for up to $2 million, and agrees to pay the lawyer 40% of any settlement or judgment for under $1 million, then a settlement of $800,000 would result in a fee of $80,000 (40% of the $200,000 under the threshold amount of $1 million). — Also termed *negative contingent fee*; *defense contingent fee*.

contingent fund. See FUND.

contingent-interest mortgage. See MORTGAGE.

contingent remainder. See REMAINDER.

continuance, *n.* **1.** The act of keeping up, maintaining, or prolonging <continuance of the formal tradition>. **2.** Duration; time of continuing <the senator's continuance in office>. **3.** In procedure, the adjournment or postponement of a trial or other proceeding until a future date <motion for continuance>. — **continue,** *vb.* Cf. RECESS (1).

continuing breach. See BREACH OF CONTRACT.

continuing judicial education. Continuing legal education for judges, usu. organized and sponsored by a governmentally subsidized body and often involving topics such as judicial writing, efficient decision-making, caseload management, and the like. —Abbr. CJE.

continuing jurisdiction. See JURISDICTION.

continuing-jurisdiction doctrine. In family law, the rule that once a court has acquired jurisdiction over a child-custody or support case, that court continues to have jurisdiction for purposes of modifying orders, notwithstanding the removal of the child to another state.

continuing legal education. 1. The process or system through which lawyers extend their learning beyond their law-school studies, usu. by attending seminars designed to sharpen lawyering skills or to provide updates on legal developments within particular practice areas; in some jurisdictions, lawyers have annual or biennial requirements to devote a given number of hours (usu. 12-15) to continuing legal education. **2.** The enhanced skills or knowledge derived from this process. **3.** The business field in which educational providers supply the demand for legal seminars, books, audio recordings, and videotapes designed for furthering the education of fully licensed lawyers. —Abbr. CLE.

continuing offense. See OFFENSE.

continuing trespass. See TRESPASS.

continuing warranty. See *promissory warranty* under WARRANTY (3).

continuity of business enterprise. A judicial requirement for acquisitive reorganizations whereby the acquiring corporation must continue the target corporation's historical business or must use a significant portion of the target's business assets in a new business.

continuity of interest. 1. A judicial requirement for acquisitive reorganizations whereby a target corporation's shareholders must retain a share in the acquiring corporation. **2.** A judicial requirement for divisive reorganizations whereby a target corporation's shareholders must retain an interest in both the distributing and the controlled corporations.

contort (**kon**-tort), *n.* **1.** (*usu. pl.*) The overlapping domain of contract law and tort law. **2.** A specific wrong that falls within that domain.

contra. *prep.* Against or contrary to; as a citation signal, *contra* denotes that the cited authority supports a contrary view.

contra account. See ACCOUNT.

contraband, *n.* **1.** Illegal or prohibited trade; smuggling. **2.** Goods that are unlawful to import, export, or possess. **—contraband,** *adj.*

absolute contraband. Goods used primarily and ordinarily for warlike purposes, such as arms and ammunition.

conditional contraband. Goods used indifferently for warlike and peaceful purposes, such as coal and food. —Also termed *ancipitis usus.*

contraband per se. Property whose possession is unlawful regardless of how it is used.

derivative contraband. Property whose possession becomes unlawful when it is used in committing an illegal act.

contra bonos mores (kon-trə-**boh**-nohs-**mor**-eez *or* -ayz). [Latin "against good morals"] Offensive to the conscience and to a sense of justice <a contract found to be *contra bonos mores* would be invalid>.

contract, *n.* **1.** An agreement between two or more parties creating obligations that are enforceable or otherwise recognizable at law; the writing that sets forth such an agreement <a contract is valid if valid under the law of the residence of the party wishing to enforce the contract>. **2.** Loosely, an unenforceable agreement between two or more parties to do or not to do a thing or set of things; a compact <when they finally agreed, they had a contract>. **3.** Broadly, any legal duty or set of duties not imposed by the law of tort; esp., a duty created by a decree or declaration of a court <an obligation of record, as a judgment, recognizance, or the like, is included within the term contract>. **4.** A promise or set of promises by a party to a transaction, enforceable or otherwise recognizable at law; the writing expressing that promise or set of promises <when the lessor learned that the rooms were to be used for the delivery of blasphemous lectures, he declined to carry out his contract>. **5.** The division or body of law dealing with agreements and exchange <the general theory of contract>. **6.** The terms of an agreement, or any particular term <there was no express contract about when the money was payable>. **—contract,** *vb.* **—contractual,** *adj.*

adhesion contract. A standard-form contract prepared by one party, to be signed by the party in a weaker position, usu. a consumer, who has little choice about the terms. — Also termed *take-it-or-leave-it con-*

tract; *leonine contract*; *adhesory contract*; *adhesionary contract*.

aleatory contract. A contract in which one party's performance depends on some uncertain event that is beyond the control of the parties involved; most insurance contracts are of this type. —Also termed *hazardous contract*.

alternative contract. A contract in which the performing party may elect to perform one of two or more specified acts to satisfy the obligation.

bilateral contract. A contract in which each party promises a performance, so that each party is an obligor on his or her own promise and an obligee on the other's promise. —Also termed *mutual contract*; *reciprocal contract*.

contract for deed. A conditional sales contract for the sale of real property. —Also termed *installment land contract*; *land sales contract*; *land contract*.

contract for sale. **a.** A contract for the present transfer of property for a price. **b.** A contract to sell goods at a future time. —Also termed (in sense b) *contract to sell*.

contract under seal. A formal contract that requires no consideration and has the seal of the signer attached; modern statutes have mostly eliminated the special effects of a sealed contract. —Also termed *sealed contract*; *special contract*; *specialty contract*; *specialty*.

cost-plus contract. A contract in which payment is on the basis of a fixed fee or a percentage added to the actual cost incurred.

destination contract. A contract between a buyer and seller providing that the risk of loss passes to the buyer once the seller delivers the goods to their destination.

executory contract. A contract that remains wholly unperformed or for which there remains something still to be done on both sides.

gratuitous contract. A contract made for the benefit of a promisee who does not give or promise consideration to the promisor. —Also termed *contract of beneficence*; *contract of benevolence*.

illegal contract. A promise that is prohibited because the performance, formation, or object of the agreement is against the law; technically speaking, an illegal contract is not a contract at all, so the phrase is a misnomer.

immoral contract. A contract that so flagrantly violates societal norms as to be rendered void.

implied contract. **a.** An implied-in-law contract. **b.** An implied-in-fact contract.

implied-in-fact contract. A contract that the parties presumably intended, either by tacit understanding or by the assumption that it existed. —Also termed *contract implied in fact*.

implied-in-law contract. An obligation imposed by law because of the conduct of the parties, because of some special relationship between them, or because one of them would otherwise be unjustly enriched. —Also termed *contract implied in law*; *quasi-contract*. See UNJUST ENRICHMENT.

integrated contract. A contract that expresses the full and complete intent of the parties, who are therefore prohibited from varying or supplementing the contractual terms through parol (extrinsic) evidence. —Also termed *integrated agreement*; *integrated writing*. See INTEGRATION (2).

naked contract. NUDUM PACTUM.

option contract. OPTION (2).

output contract. A contract in which a buyer promises to buy all the goods or services that a seller can supply during a specified period and at a set price. Cf. *requirements contract*.

parol contract. **a.** A contract or modification of a contract that is not in writing or is only partially in writing. —Also termed *oral contract*; *parol agreement*. **b.** At common law, a contract not under seal, although it could be in writing. —Also termed *informal contract*; *simple contract*. See PAROL-EVIDENCE RULE.

precontract. A contract that precludes a party from entering into a comparable agreement with someone else.

requirements contract. A contract in which a seller promises to supply all the goods or services that a buyer needs during a specific period and at a set price, and in which the buyer promises (explicitly or implicitly) to obtain those goods or services exclusively from the seller. Cf. *output contract*.

retail installment contract. A contract for the sale of goods under which the buyer makes periodic payments and the seller retains title to or a security interest in the goods. —Also termed *retail installment contract and security agreement*; *conditional sales contract*. Cf. *chattel mortgage* under MORTGAGE.

severable contract. A contract that includes two or more promises each of which can be enforced separately, so that failure to perform one of the promises does not necessarily put the promisor in breach of the entire contract. —Also termed *divisible contract*. See SEVERABILITY CLAUSE.

special contract. **a.** See *contract under seal*. **b.** A contract with peculiar provisions that are not ordinarily found in contracts relating to the same subject matter.

subcontract. A contract made by a party to another contract for carrying the other contract, or a part of it, out.

take-or-pay contract. A contract requiring the buyer to either purchase and receive a minimum amount of product at a set price ("take") or pay for this minimum without taking immediate delivery ("pay"); these contracts are most often used in the energy and oil-and-gas business.

unilateral contract. A contract in which only one party makes a promise or undertakes a performance.

contract, freedom of. See FREEDOM OF CONTRACT.

contract for deed. See CONTRACT.

contract for sale. See CONTRACT.

contract not to sue. See *covenant not to sue* under COVENANT (1).

contract of beneficence. See *gratuitous contract* under CONTRACT.

contract of benevolence. See *gratuitous contract* under CONTRACT.

contractor. One who is a party to a contract; esp., one who contracts to do work or provide supplies for another.

general contractor. One who contracts for the completion of an entire project, including hiring and paying subcontractors and coordinating all the work. —Also termed *original contractor*; *prime contractor.*

independent contractor. See INDEPENDENT CONTRACTOR.

subcontractor. One who is awarded a portion of an existing contract by a contractor, esp. a general contractor; for example, a contractor who builds homes typically retains subcontractors to perform specialty work such as installing plumbing, laying carpet, making cabinetry, and landscaping—each subcontractor is paid a somewhat lesser sum than the contractor receives for their work.

contract rate. See INTEREST RATE.

Contracts Clause. U.S. Const. art. I, § 10, cl. 1, which prohibits states from impairing private contractual obligations; the Supreme Court generally has interpreted this clause so that states can in fact regulate contractual obligations if such regulation is reasonable and necessary.

contract to sell. See *contract for sale* (b) under CONTRACT.

contract under seal. See CONTRACT.

contra pacem (kon-trə-**pay**-səm *or* -**pah**-chem). [Latin] Against the peace; this term was formerly used in indictments to signify that the alleged offense is against the public peace.

contra proferentem (kon-trə-proh-fər-**en**-təm) [Latin "against the offeror"] The doctrine that, in interpreting documents, ambiguities are to be construed unfavorably to the drafter. —Also spelled *contra proferentes.*

contravene, *vb.* **1.** To violate or infringe; to defy <the soldier contravened the officer's order, and then went AWOL>. **2.** To come into conflict with; to be contrary to <the court held that the regulation contravenes public policy>. —**contravention,** *n.*

contributing to the delinquency of a minor. The offense of an adult's engaging in conduct involving a minor—or in the presence of a minor—likely to result in delinquent conduct; examples include encouraging a minor to shoplift, to lie under oath, or to commit vandalism. —Also termed *contributing to delinquency.* See JUVENILE DELINQUENCY. Cf. IMPAIRING THE MORALS OF A MINOR.

contribution. 1. The right to demand that another who is jointly responsible for a third party's injury supply part of what one is required to compensate the third party. —Also termed *right of contribution.* **2.** The actual payment by a joint tortfeasor of his or her share of what is due. Cf. INDEMNITY.

contributory infringement. See INFRINGEMENT.

contributory negligence. See NEGLIGENCE.

contributory-negligence doctrine. The tort-law principle that completely bars a plaintiff's recovery if the damage suffered is partly the plaintiff's own fault; most states have abolished this doctrine and have adopted instead a comparative- negligence scheme. See NEGLIGENCE. Cf. COMPARATIVE-NEGLIGENCE DOCTRINE.

controlled substance. Any of the drugs whose possession and use are regulated by law, including narcotics, stimulants, and hallucinogens.

controller. COMPTROLLER.

control person. In securities law, a person who has actual control or significant influence over the issuer of securities, such as by directing corporate policy; the control person is subject to many of the same requirements applicable to the sale of securities by the issuer. —Also termed *controlling person*.

control test. IRRESISTIBLE-IMPULSE TEST.

control-your-kid law. PARENTAL-RESPONSIBILITY STATUTE.

controversy. 1. A disagreement or a dispute, esp. in public. **2.** A justiciable dispute in either law or equity. **3.** In constitutional law, a case that requires a definitive determination of the law on the facts alleged, and not merely on assumed potential inva-

sions of rights. See CASE-OR-CONTROVERSY REQUIREMENT.

controvert, *vb.* To dispute or contest; to oppose in argument <during rebuttal, Peck controverted his opponent's points one by one>.

contumacy (kən-**tyoo**-mə-see *or* **kon**-tyə-mə-see), *n.* Willful contempt of court. —**contumacious,** *adj.* See CONTEMPT.

convention. 1. An agreement or compact, esp. one among nations; TREATY <the Geneva Convention>. **2.** An assembly or meeting of members belonging to an organization or having a common objective <an ABA convention>. **3.** A generally accepted rule or practice; usage or custom <the court dispensed with the convention of having counsel approach the bench>. —**conventional,** *adj.*

conventional mortgage. See MORTGAGE.

conventional subrogation. See SUBROGATION.

conversion, *n.* **1.** The act of changing from one form to another; the process of being exchanged.

equitable conversion. The act of treating real property as personal property, or vice versa, in certain circumstances; courts usu. apply the doctrine of equitable conversion in order to recognize the transfer of land when a party dies after the signing of an agreement to sell real property but before the transfer of title.

forced conversion. The conversion of a convertible security, after a call for redemption, when the value of the security that it may be converted to is greater than the amount that will be received if the holder permits the security to be redeemed.

2. In tort law, the wrongful possession or disposition of another's tangible property as if it were one's own. —**convert,** *vb.*

involuntary conversion. The loss or destruction of property through theft, casualty, or condemnation.

conversion price. The contractually specified price per share at which a convertible security can be converted into shares of common stock.

conversion ratio. 1. The number of common shares into which a convertible security may be converted. **2.** The ratio of the face amount of the convertible security to the conversion price.

conversion security. See SECURITY.

convertible arbitrage. See *kind arbitrage* under ARBITRAGE.

convertible bond. See BOND (1).

convertible debenture. See DEBENTURE.

convertible debt. See DEBT.

convertible insurance. See INSURANCE.

convertible security. See SECURITY.

conveyance, *n.* **1.** The transfer of an interest in real property from one living person to another, by means of an instrument such as a deed. **2.** The document (usu. a deed) by which such a transfer occurs. **3.** A means of transport; a vehicle. **4.** In bankruptcy, a transfer of an interest in real or personal property, including an assignment, release, monetary payment, or the creation of a lien or encumbrance. See FRAUDULENT CONVEYANCE; PREFERENTIAL TRANSFER. —**convey,** *vb.*

conveyancer. A lawyer who specializes in real-estate transactions.

conveyancing. The act or business of drafting and preparing legal instruments, esp. those (such as deeds or leases) that transfer an interest in real property.

conveyee. One to whom property is conveyed.

conveyor. One who transfers or delivers title to another.

convict (kon -vikt), *n.* A person who has been found guilty of a crime and is serving a sentence for that crime; a prison inmate.

conviction, *n.* **1.** The act or process of judicially finding someone guilty of a crime; the state of being proved guilty. **2.** The judgment (as by a jury verdict) that a person is guilty of a crime. **3.** A strong belief or opinion. —**convict** (kən-**vikt**), *vb.*

conviction rate. Within a given area or for a given time, the number of convictions (including plea bargains) as a percentage of the total number of prosecutions undertaken.

convoy, *n.* A protective escort, esp. for ships. —**convoy,** *vb.*

Cooley **doctrine.** In constitutional law, the principle that Congress has exclusive power under the Commerce Clause to regulate national commercial matters, and that the states share this power (in the absence of federal preemption) with respect to local matters; the Supreme Court has abandoned the *Cooley* doctrine in favor of a balancing test for Commerce Clause cases. *Cooley v. Board of Wardens*, 53 U.S. (12 How.) 299 (1851).

cooling-off period. 1. During a dispute, a period during which no action of a particular sort may be taken by either side. **2.** A period during which a buyer may cancel a purchase. **3.** An automatic delay in some states between the filing of divorce papers and the divorce hearing. **4.** In securities law, a period (usu. at least 20 days) between the filing of a registration and the effective registration.

cooling time. Time to recover "cool blood" after great excitement, stress, or provocation, so that one is considered able to contemplate, comprehend, and act with reference to the consequences that are likely to follow.

cool blood. In the law of homicide, the finding that the defendant's emotions were not in such an excited state that they interfered with his or her faculties and reason. —Also termed *cool state of blood*. See COLD BLOOD. Cf. HEAT OF PASSION.

cooperative, *n.* **1.** An organization or enterprise (as a store) owned by those who use its services. **2.** A dwelling (as an apartment building) owned or leased by its residents. —Often shortened to *coop; co-op.*

co-opt, *vb.* **1.** To select as a member. **2.** To assimilate; absorb. —**co-optation,** *n.*—**co-optative,** *adj.*

coordinate jurisdiction. See *concurrent jurisdiction* under JURISDICTION.

co-owner, *n.* A person who is in concurrent ownership, possession, and enjoyment of property with one or more others; a tenant in common or a joint tenant. —**co-own,** *vb.*—**co-ownership,** *n.*

cop a plea, *vb. Slang.* (Of a criminal defendant) to plead guilty to a lesser charge in order to avoid standing trial for a more serious offense. See PLEA BARGAIN.

coparcenary (koh-**pahrs**-[ə]n-er-ee), *n.* An estate that arises when two or more persons jointly inherit from one ancestor, the estate being shared equally, in title and right of possession, by all. —Also termed *parcenary.* —**coparcenary,** *adj.*—**coparcener,** *n.*

coplaintiff. One of two or more plaintiffs in the same litigation.

copy, *n.* An imitation or reproduction of an original; in the law of evidence, a copy is admissible to prove the contents of a writing only if the original is unavailable. See BEST-EVIDENCE RULE.

certified copy. A duplicate of an original (usu. official) document, certified as an exact reproduction by the officer responsible for issuing or keeping the original. —Also termed *attested copy; exemplified copy; verified copy; verification.*

conformed copy. An exact copy of a document bearing written explanations of things that were not or could not be copied, such as a note on the document indicating that it was signed by a person whose signature appears on the original.

copyright, *n.* **1.** A property right in an original work of authorship fixed in any tangible medium of expression (such as a literary, musical, artistic, photographic, or film work), giving the holder the exclusive right to reproduce, adapt, distribute, perform, and display the work. **2.** The body of law relating to such works; federal copyright law is governed by the Copyright Act of 1976. 17 U.S.C. §§ 101 et seq. —**copyright,** *vb.*—**copyrighted,** *adj.*

common-law copyright. Before the Copyright Act of 1976, a property right that arose at the time when the work was created, rather than when it was published; today, common-law copyright still applies in a few specific areas not addressed by the federal statute.

Copyright Clause. U.S. Const. art. I, § 8, cl. 8, which secures authors the exclusive rights to their writings for a limited time.

copyright infringement. See INFRINGEMENT.

copyright notice. A notice that a work is copyright-protected, usu. placed in each published copy of the work; since 1989, such notice is not required for a copyright to be valid (although it continues to provide certain procedural advantages).

coram (**kor**-əm). [Latin] (Of a person) before; in the presence of.

coram nobis (**noh**-bəs). [Latin "before us"] Formerly, a writ of error directed to a court for review of its own judgment and predicated on alleged errors of fact. —Also termed *writ of error coram nobis.*

coram non judice (non-**joo**-di-see). [Latin "not before a judge"] **1.** Outside the presence of a judge. **2.** Be-fore a judge who is not the proper one or who cannot take legal cognizance of the matter.

coram vobis (**voh**-bəs). [Latin "before you"] Formerly, a writ of error sent by an appellate court to a trial court for correction of the trial court's error of fact. —Also termed *writ of error coram vobis.*

core proceeding. In bankruptcy law, a proceeding involving claims that substantially affect the debtor-creditor relationship (such as an action to recover a preferential transfer); in such a proceeding, the bankruptcy court, as opposed to the district court, conducts the trial or hearing and enters a final judgment. Cf. RELATED PROCEEDING.

correspondent. 1. A coparty who responds to a petition, such as a petition for writ of certiorari; a co-appellee. **2.** In a divorce suit based on adultery, the person with whom the spouse is accused of having committed adultery. See RESPONDENT.

cornering the market. The act or process of acquiring ownership or control of a large portion of the available supply of a commodity or security, permitting manipulation of the commodity's or security's price.

coroner. 1. A public official whose duty is to investigate the causes and circumstances of any death that occurs suddenly, suspiciously, or violently. See MEDICAL EXAMINER. **2.** Historically, an officer with the responsibility of preserving the sovereign's private property.

coroner's court. See COURT.

corporal punishment. See PUNISHMENT.

corporate acquisition. The take-over of one corporation by another if both parties retain their legal existence after the transaction. Cf. MERGER (7).

corporate charter. See CHARTER (2).

corporate citizenship. Corporate status in the state of incorporation, though a foreign corporation is not a citizen for the purposes of the Privileges and Immunities Clause of the U.S. Constitution.

corporate crime. See CRIME.

corporate distribution. See DISTRIBUTION.

corporate domicile. See DOMICILE (1).

corporate franchise. FRANCHISE (2).

corporate indenture. See INDENTURE.

corporate officer. See OFFICER.

corporate-opportunity doctrine. The rule that a corporation's directors, officers, and employees are precluded from taking personal advantage of any business opportunities that the corporation has an expectancy right or property interest in, or that in fairness should otherwise belong to the corporation; in a partnership, the analogous principle is the *firm-opportunity doctrine.*

corporate purpose. The general scope of the business or other objective for which a corporation was created; a statement of this purpose is commonly required in the articles of incorporation.

corporate raider. A person or business that attempts to take control of a corporation, against its wishes, by buying its stock and replacing its management. —Often shortened to *raider.* —Also termed *hostile bidder; unfriendly suitor.* Cf. WHITE KNIGHT.

corporate seal. See SEAL.

corporate speech. See SPEECH.

corporate veil. The legal assumption that the actions of a corporation are not the actions of its owners, so that the owners are exempt from liability for the corporation's actions. See PIERCING THE CORPORATE VEIL.

corporation, *n.* A statutory entity (usu. a business) having authority under law to act as a single person distinct from the shareholders who make it up and having rights to issue stock and exist indefinitely. —**incorporate,** *vb.*—**corporate,** *adj.* See COMPANY.

C corporation. A corporation whose income is taxed at the corporate level rather than at the shareholder level; any corporation not electing S-corporation tax status under the Internal Revenue Code is a C corporation by default. —Also termed *subchapter-C corporation.* Cf. *S corporation.*

charitable corporation. A nonprofit corporation that is dedicated to benevolent purposes and thus entitled to special tax status under the Internal Revenue Code. —Also termed *eleemosynary corporation.* See CHARITABLE ORGANIZATION.

close corporation. A corporation whose stock is not freely traded and is held by only a few share-holders (often within the same family); the requirements and privileges of close corporations vary by jurisdiction. —Also termed *closely held corporation*; *closed corporation*.

corporation by estoppel. A business that is deemed, by operation of law, to be a corporation because a third party dealt with the business as if it were a corporation, thus preventing the third party from holding an owner or officer of the business individually liable. See ES-TOPPEL.

de facto corporation. An incompletely formed corporation whose exis-tence operates as a defense to per-sonal liability of the owners who in good faith thought they were oper-ating the business as a duly formed corporation.

de jure corporation. A corporation formed in accordance with all ap-plicable laws and recognized as a corporation for liability purposes.

dummy corporation. A corporation whose only function is to hide the principal's identity and to protect the principal from liability.

foreign corporation. A corporation that was created or organized un-der the laws of another state, gov-ernment, or country <in Arizona, a California corporation is said to be a foreign corporation>.

limited-liability corporation. See *lim-ited-liability company* under COM-PANY.

municipal corporation. See MUNICI-PAL CORPORATION.

nonprofit corporation. A corporation organized under special statutes for some purpose other than mak-ing a profit, and therefore afforded special tax treatment. —Also termed *not-for-profit corporation*.

nonstock corporation. A corporation that does not issue shares of stock as evidence of ownership but in-stead is owned by its members in accordance with a charter or agree-ment; examples are mutual insur-ance companies, charitable organi-zations, and private clubs.

parent corporation. A corporation that owns more than 50 percent of the voting shares of, or has an otherwise controlling interest in, another corporation (called a *sub-sidiary corporation*). —Also termed *parent company*.

professional corporation. A corpora-tion that renders a personal service to the public of a type that re-quires a license or legal authoriza-tion, such as architects, accoun-tants, physicians, veterinarians, and the like. —Abbr. P.C.

public corporation. **a.** A corporation whose shares are traded to and among the general public. —Also termed *publicly held corporation*. **b.** A corporation that is created by the state for political purposes and to act as an agency in the adminis-tration of civil government. **c.** A government-owned corporation that engages in a specific govern-mental activity, usu. while remain-ing financially independent; such a corporation is managed by a pub-licly appointed board. —Also termed (in sense c) *government corporation*.

quasi-corporation. An entity that exercises some of the functions of a corporation but that has not been granted corporate status by statute; esp., a public corporation with limited authority and powers (such as a county or school district). Cf. MUNICIPAL CORPORATION.

quasi-public corporation. A for-profit corporation providing a service that the public depends on; an example is an electric company or other utility.

registered corporation. A publicly held corporation that has registered under section 12 of the Securities Exchange Act of 1934 and is therefore subject to the Act's periodic disclosure requirements and proxy regulations.

S corporation. A corporation whose income is taxed at the shareholder level (similar to a partnership's income) rather than at the corporate level; only corporations with a limited number of shareholders can elect S-corporation tax status under Subchapter S of the Internal Revenue Code. —Also termed *subchapter-S corporation.* Cf. *C corporation.*

shell corporation. A corporation that has no active business and usu. exists only in name as a vehicle for another company's business maneuvers.

sister corporation. One of two or more corporations having the same, or substantially the same, owners.

stock corporation. A corporation in which the capital is contributed by the shareholders and divided into shares represented by certificates.

subsidiary corporation. A corporation in which a parent corporation has a controlling share. —Often shortened to *subsidiary.*

target corporation. A corporation over which control is being sought by another party. See TAKEOVER.

thin corporation. A corporation with an excessive amount of debt in its capitalization. See *thin capitalization* under CAPITALIZATION.

corporation by estoppel. See CORPORATION.

corporeal (kor-**por**-ee-əl), *adj.* Having a physical material body; tangible <land and fixtures are corporeal property>. —**corporeality,** *n.* Cf. INCORPOREAL.

corporeal hereditaments. See HEREDITAMENT.

corpus (**kor**-pəs). [Latin "body"] **1.** An abstract collection or body. **2.** The property for which a trustee is responsible; the trust principal. —Also termed *res; trust estate; trust fund; trust property; trust res.* **3.** Principal (as of a fund or estate), as opposed to interest or income. Pl. **corpora.**

corpus delicti (də-**lik**-tee *or* -tI). [Latin "body of the crime"] **1.** The nature of the transgression; ACTUS REUS. **2.** Loosely, the material substance on which a crime has been committed; the physical evidence of a crime, such as the corpse of a murdered person.

corpus delicti rule. The criminal-law doctrine that disallows a conviction based solely on a defendant's extrajudicial confession; the prosecution must establish the *corpus delicti* with corroborating evidence to uphold the conviction.

corpus juris (**juur**-əs). [Latin "body of law"] The law as the sum or collection of laws <*Corpus Juris Secundum*>. —Abbr. C.J.

Corpus Juris Civilis (si-**vil**-əs). The body of the civil law, compiled and codified under the direction of the Roman emperor Justinian in 528-534 A.D.; the collection includes four works—the Institutes, the Digest (or Pandects), the Code, and the Novels. See CIVIL LAW (2).

correction, *n.* **1.** Generally, the act or an instance of making right what is wrong <mark your corrections in red ink>. **2.** A decrease in business activity or market price following and counteracting an increase in such activity or price <the broker advised investors to sell before the inevitable stock-market correction>. **3.** (*usu. pl.*) The punishment and treatment of a criminal offender through a program of imprisonment, parole, and probation <Department of Corrections>. —**correct,** *vb.*—**corrective** (corresponding to senses 1 & 2), **correctional** (corresponding to sense 3), *adj.*

corrective advertising. Advertising that informs consumers that earlier advertisements contained a deceptive claim, and that provides consumers with corrected information; this type of advertising is usu. ordered by the Federal Trade Commission.

correspondence audit. See AUDIT.

correspondent, *n.* **1.** The writer of a letter or letters. **2.** A person employed by the media to report on events. **3.** A securities firm or financial institution that performs services for another in a place or market that the other does not have direct access to. —**correspond,** *vb.*

correspondent bank. See BANK.

corrigendum (kor-ə-**jen**-dəm). [Latin "correction"] An error in a printed work discovered after the work has gone to press. —Also termed *erratum.* Pl. **corrigenda.**

corroborating evidence. See EVIDENCE.

corroboration, *n.* **1.** Confirmation or support by additional evidence or authority <corroboration of the witness's testimony>. **2.** Formal confirmation or ratification <corroboration of the treaty>. —**corroborate,** *vb.*—**corroborative,** *adj.*—**corroborator,** *n.*

corruption in office. See *official misconduct* under MISCONDUCT.

corruption of the blood. A former doctrine, now considered unconstitutional, under which a person loses the ability to inherit or pass property as a result of an attainder or of being declared civilly dead. See ATTAINDER; CIVIL DEATH.

corrupt-motive doctrine. In criminal law, the rule that conspiracy is punishable only if the agreement was entered into with an evil purpose, not merely with an intent to do the illegal act; this doctrine—which originated in *People v. Powell*, 63 N.Y. 88 (1875)—has been rejected by the Model Penal Code and most modern courts. —Also termed *Powell doctrine.*

corrupt-practices act. A federal or state statute that regulates campaign contributions and expenditures as well as their disclosure.

Cosa Nostra. ORGANIZED CRIME (2).

cosign, *vb.* To sign a document along with another person, usu. to assume obligations and to supply credit support to the main obligor. —**cosignature,** *n.*

cosigner. COMAKER.

cost, *n.* **1.** The amount paid or charged for something; price or expenditure. Cf. EXPENSE.

carrying cost. In accounting, the variable cost of carrying one unit of inventory in stock for one year, includes the opportunity cost of the capital invested in the inventory. —Also termed *cost of carrying*.

direct cost. The amount of money for material and labor and variable overhead to produce a product.

distribution cost. Any cost incurred in marketing a product or service, such as advertising, storage, and shipping.

fixed cost. A cost whose value does not fluctuate according to changes in output or business activity; esp., overhead expenses such as rent, salaries, and depreciation. —Also termed *fixed charge*; *fixed expense*.

indirect cost. A cost that is not specific to the production of any specific good or service, but that arises from any production activity in general, such as overhead allocations for general and administrative activities. —Also termed *common cost*.

marginal cost. The additional cost incurred in producing one more unit of output.

net cost. The cost of an item, arrived at by subtracting any financial gain from the total cost.

opportunity cost. The cost of acquiring an asset measured by the value of an alternative investment that is forgone <her opportunity cost of $1000 in equipment was her consequent inability to invest that money in bonds>. —Also termed *implicit cost*.

replacement cost. The cost of acquiring an asset that is as equally useful or productive as an asset currently held.

sunk cost. A cost that has already been incurred and that cannot be recovered.

transaction cost. (*usu. pl.*) A cost connected with the making of a transaction, such as a commission to a broker or the time and effort expended to arrange a deal.

variable cost. The cost that varies in the short run in close relationship with changes in output.

2. (*pl.*) The charges or fees taxed by the court, such as filing fees, jury fees, courthouse fees, and reporter fees. —Also termed *court costs*. **3.** (*pl.*) The expenses of litigation, prosecution, or other legal transaction, esp. those allowed in favor of one party against the other. —Also termed *litigation costs*.

cost accounting method. See ACCOUNTING METHOD.

cost and freight. A term in a quoted sales price indicating that the quoted price includes the cost of the goods and freight charges, but not insurance or other special charges. — Abbr. C.F.; C & F.

cost basis. See BASIS (2).

cost-benefit analysis. An analytical technique that weighs the expense of a proposed decision, holding, or project against the expected advantages, economic or otherwise.

cost, insurance, and freight. A term in a quoted sales price indicating that the quoted price includes the cost of the goods as well as freight and insurance charges. —Abbr. C.I.F. Cf. FREE ALONGSIDE SHIP; FREE ON BOARD.

cost justification. Under the Robinson-Patman Act, an affirmative defense against a charge of price discrimination dependent on the seller's showing that it incurs lower costs in serving those customers who are paying less.

cost of carrying. See *carrying cost* under COST.

cost-of-living clause. A provision (as in a contract or lease) that gives an automatic wage, rent, or benefit increase tied in some way to cost-of-living rises in the economy. See INFLATION.

cost-of-living index. CONSUMER PRICE INDEX.

cost-plus contract. See CONTRACT.

cosurety. One of two or more sureties to the same obligation. See SURETY.

cotenancy. See TENANCY.

cotortfeasor. One who, together with another, has committed a tort. See TORTFEASOR.

council. **1.** A deliberative assembly <the U.N. Security Council>. **2.** An administrative or executive body <a parish council>.

councillor, *n.* A person who serves on a council, esp. at the local level— **councillorship,** *n.*

counsel, *n.* **1.** Advice or assistance <the lawyer's counsel was to petition immediately for a change of immigration status>. **2.** One or more lawyers who represent a client <the client acted on advice of counsel>. —In the singular, also termed *counselor.* Cf. ATTORNEY; LAWYER.

assigned counsel. An attorney appointed by the court to represent an indigent person. —Also termed *court-appointed attorney.*

counsel of record. ATTORNEY OF RECORD.

general counsel. **a.** A lawyer or law firm that represents a client in all or most of the client's legal matters, but that sometimes refers extraordinary matters—such as intellectual-property cases—to a specialist. **b.** The most senior lawyer in a corporation's legal department, usu. also a corporate officer.

independent counsel. An attorney hired to provide an unbiased opinion about a lawsuit or to conduct an impartial investigation; esp., an attorney appointed by a governmental branch or agency to investigate alleged misconduct within that branch or agency. See *special prosecutor* under PROSECUTOR. Cf. *special counsel*.

in-house counsel. One or more lawyers employed full-time by a company. —Also termed *house counsel*.

lead counsel. The more highly ranked lawyer if two or more are retained; the lawyer who manages or controls the case. —Also termed *senior counsel*; *attorney in charge*.

of counsel. **a.** A lawyer employed by a party in a case; esp., one who—although not the principal attorney of record—is employed to assist in the preparation or management of the case or in its presentation on appeal. **b.** A lawyer (often in semi-retirement) who is affiliated with a private law firm, though not as a member, partner, or associate.

special counsel. An attorney employed by the state to assist in a particular case when public interest so requires. —Also termed *special attorney*. Cf. *independent counsel*.

counsel, assistance of. See ASSISTANCE OF COUNSEL.

counsel, right to. See RIGHT TO COUNSEL.

counselor. See COUNSEL (2).

count, *n.* **1.** The part of an indictment charging the suspect with a distinct offense. **2.** In pleading, the plaintiff's statement of a distinct claim.

common count. In a pleading in an action for debt, boilerplate that is not founded on the circumstances of the individual case but is intended to guard against a possible variance and to enable the plaintiff to take advantage of any ground of liability that the proof may disclose.

general count. A count that states the plaintiff's claim without undue particularity.

multiple counts. Several separate causes of action or charged offenses contained in a single pleading or indictment.

special count. A pleading in which the plaintiff's claim is presented with great particularity—usu. employed only when the pleading rules require a welter of detail.

counterclaim, *n.* A defendant's claim in opposition to, or as a setoff against, the plaintiff's claim. —**counterclaim,** *vb.*—**counterclaimant,** *n.* Cf. CROSS-CLAIM.

compulsory counterclaim. A counterclaim that is logically related to the opposing party's claim and arises out of the same subject matter; if a defendant fails to assert a compulsory counterclaim in the original action, that claim may not be brought in a later, separate action (with some exceptions).

permissive counterclaim. A counterclaim that does not arise out of the same subject matter as the opposing party's claim or that involves third parties over which the court does not have jurisdiction; permissive counterclaims may be brought in a later, separate action.

counterfeit, *vb.* To forge, copy, or imitate (something) without a legal right to do so and with the purpose of deceiving or defrauding. —**counterfeit,** *n.*—**counterfeit,** *adj.*

countermand, *n.* An action that has the effect of voiding something previously executed; a revocation. — **countermand,** *vb.*

counteroffer, *n.* In contract law, an offeree's new offer that varies the terms of the original offer and that therefore constitutes a rejection of the original offer. —**counteroffer,** *vb.*—**counterofferor,** *n.* See MIRROR-IMAGE RULE.

countersign, *vb.* To write one's own name next to someone else's in order to verify the other signer's identity. —**countersignature,** *n.*

county. The largest territorial division for local government within a state, generally considered to be a political subdivision and a quasi-corporation.

county commissioner. See COMMISSIONER.

county court. See COURT.

county supervisor. See *county commissioner* under COMMISSIONER.

coup d'état (koo-day-**tah**). [French "stroke of state"] A sudden, usu. violent, government takeover.

coupon (**koo**-pon). An interest or dividend certificate that is attached to another instrument, such as a bond, and that may be detached and separately presented for payment of a definite sum at a specified time.

coupon bond. See BOND (1).

coupon interest rate. See *nominal rate* under INTEREST RATE.

course of business. That which is normally done in managing a trade or business. —Also termed *ordinary course of business*; *regular course of business*.

course of dealing. Prior conduct between parties by which they develop a tacit or explicit understanding that serves as the basis for interpreting their future action with regard to each other. See *trade usage* under USAGE.

course of employment. Events that occur or circumstances that exist as a part of one's employment; esp., the time during which an employee furthers an employer's goals through employer-mandated directives.

court. 1. A governmental body consisting of one or more judges who sit to adjudicate disputes and administer justice <a question of law for the court to decide>. **2.** The judge or judges who sit on such a governmental body <the court asked the parties to approach the bench>. **3.** A legislative assembly <in Massachusetts, the General Court is the legislature>. **4.** The locale for a legal proceeding <an out-of-court statement>. **5.** The building where the judge or judges convene to adjudicate disputes and administer justice <the lawyers agreed to meet at the court at 8:00 a.m.>. —Also termed (in sense 5) *courthouse*.

admiralty court. ADMIRALTY (1).

appellate court. A court with jurisdiction to review decisions of one or more lower courts. —Also termed *appeals court*; *appeal court*; *court of appeals*.

Article III Court. See ARTICLE III COURT.

bankruptcy court. See BANKRUPTCY COURT.

business court. A court that handles exclusively commercial litigation; in the late 20th century, business courts emerged in many states as a way to unclog the general dockets and to dispose of complex commercial cases more efficiently and consistently. —Also termed *commercial division.*

circuit court. A court usu. having jurisdiction over several counties, districts, or states, and holding sessions in all those areas.

civil court. A court with jurisdiction over minor civil or criminal cases, or both. —Abbr. C.C.

commissioner's court. In certain states, a court having jurisdiction over county affairs and often functioning more as a managerial group than as a judicial tribunal.

constitutional court. A court named or described and expressly protected in a constitution <in our federal system, the courts mentioned in Article III are constitutional courts>.

coroner's court. In England, a common-law court that holds an inquisition if there are reasonable grounds to believe that a person died a violent or unnatural death; the court has the power to charge a suspect with murder, manslaughter, or infanticide.

county court. A court with powers and jurisdiction dictated by a state constitution or statute; the county court may govern administrative or judicial matters, depending on the state's legislation. —Abbr. C.C.

court above. A court to which a case is appealed. —Also termed *higher court*; *upper court.*

court a quo. A court from which a case has been removed or appealed.

court below. A trial court or intermediate appellate court from which a case is appealed. —Also termed *lower court.*

court of appeals. **a.** An intermediate appellate court. **b.** In some states, such as New York, the highest appellate court within the jurisdiction. —Also termed (as in California) *court of appeal.*

court of equity. A court that (1) has jurisdiction in equity, (2) administers and decides controversies in accordance with the rules, principles, and precedents of equity, and (3) follows the forms and procedures of chancery.

court of general jurisdiction. A court having unlimited trial jurisdiction in both civil and criminal cases.

court of inquiry. **a.** In English law, a court appointed by the Monarch to ascertain whether it was proper to use extreme measures against someone who has been court-martialed. **b.** Formerly, under American law, an agency created under articles of war and vested with the power to investigate the nature of a transaction or accusation of an officer or soldier. **c.** In some jurisdictions, a procedure that allows a magistrate to examine witnesses in relation to any offense that the magistrate has a good faith suspicion to believe was committed.

court of last resort. The court having the authority to handle the final appeal of a case.

court of record. A court that is required to keep a record of its proceedings and that may fine and imprison for contempt; its records are presumed accurate and cannot be collaterally impeached. See OF RECORD (2).

district court. A trial court having general jurisdiction within its judicial district. —Abbr. D.C.

ecclesiastical court (i-klee-zee-**as**-ti-kəl). **a.** A court that hears mainly religious matters. **b.** In England, a court having jurisdiction over matters concerning the Church of England, the established church, as well as the duties and rights of the people serving it, but whose modern jurisdiction is limited to matters of ecclesiastical discipline and church property. —Also termed *church court*; *court christian*; *spiritual court*.

examining court. A lower court (usu. presided over by a magistrate) that conducts the preliminary investigation in a criminal matter to determine probable cause and to set bail before the grand-jury hearing.

family court. A court having jurisdiction over matters involving divorce, child custody and support, paternity, domestic violence, and other family-law issues. —Also termed *domestic-relations court*; *court of domestic relations*.

federal court. A court created by the U.S. Constitution or by Congress and having both diversity jurisdiction and federal-question jurisdiction.

hot court. A court, esp. an appellate court, that is familiar with the briefing in the case, and therefore with the issues, before oral argument; typically, a hot court directs an oral argument with its questioning, as opposed to listening passively to set presentations of counsel.

inferior court. **a.** Any court that is subordinate to the chief appellate tribunal within a particular judicial system. **b.** A court of special, limited, or statutory jurisdiction, whose record must show the existence of jurisdiction in any given case to give its ruling presumptive validity. —Also termed *lower court*.

insular court. A federal court with jurisdiction over U.S. island territories, such as Puerto Rico.

juvenile court. A court having jurisdiction over cases involving children under a specified age, usu. 18.

kangaroo court. A court, often illegitimately held, in which the principles of law and justice are disregarded or perverted; a sham legal proceeding.

legislative court. A court created by statute, as opposed to one created by a constitution. —Also termed (in federal law) *Article I Court*.

magistrate's court. **a.** A court with jurisdiction over minor criminal offenses; such a court also has the power to bind over for trial persons accused of more serious offenses. —Also termed *police court*. **b.** A court with limited jurisdiction over minor criminal and civil matters.

mayor's court. A municipal court in which the mayor presides as judge, with jurisdiction over minor criminal (and sometimes civil) matters, traffic offenses, and the like.

moot court. See MOOT COURT.

municipal court. A court having jurisdiction (usu. civil and criminal) over cases arising within the municipality in which it sits.

piepowder court. See PIEPOWDER COURT.

prize court. A court having jurisdiction to adjudicate the captures made at sea in time of war. See PRIZE (2).

probate court. A court with the power to declare wills valid or invalid, to oversee the administration of estates, and in some states to appoint guardians and approve the adoption of minors. —Also termed *surrogate court; surrogate's court;* and (in a few states) *orphan's court.* See PROBATE.

small-claims court. A court that informally and expeditiously adjudicates claims that seek damages below a specified monetary amount, usu. a claim to collect a small account or debt.

state court. A court of the state judicial system, as opposed to a federal court.

superior court. **a.** In some states, a trial court of general jurisdiction. **b.** In some states, an intermediate court between the trial court and the chief appellate court.

supreme court. See SUPREME COURT.

territorial court. A U.S. court established in each U.S. territory (such as the Virgin Islands) and serving as both a federal and state court; the court was created under U.S. Const. art. IV, § 3, cl. 2.

trial court. The court of original jurisdiction where all the evidence is first received and considered. — Also termed *court of first instance; instance court.*

court-appointed attorney. See *assigned counsel* under COUNSEL.

court christian. See *ecclesiastical court* under COURT.

court commissioner. See COMMISSIONER.

court costs. COST (2).

courthouse. COURT (5).

court-martial, *n.* An ad hoc military court, convened under governmental authority, for trying and punishing those who violate the Uniform Code of Military Justice, particularly members of the armed forces. —**court-martial,** *vb.*

general court-martial. A proceeding that is presided over by a law officer, usu. with at least five other officers, and that has jurisdiction over all the members of the armed forces.

special court-martial. A proceeding that is presided over by three members to hear noncapital offenses and prescribe a sanction of hard labor, dismissal, or extended confinement.

summary court-martial. A proceeding presided over by a single commissioned officer and jurisdictionally limited in what sanctions it can prescribe.

court of appeals. See COURT.

court of chancery. CHANCERY (1).

Court of Claims. CLAIMS COURT, U.S.

Court of Criminal Appeals. 1. For each armed service, an intermediate appellate court that reviews court-martial decisions; the court was established by the Military Justice Act of 1968. 10 U.S.C. §§ 859 et seq. — Formerly termed *Court of Military Review*. **2.** In some jurisdictions, such as Texas, the highest appellate court that hears criminal cases.

Court of Customs and Patent Appeals. An Article III court created in 1929 to hear appeals from the Customs Court and the Patent Office; this court was abolished in 1982 and was superseded by the U.S. Court of Appeals for the Federal Circuit.

court of domestic relations. See *family court* under COURT.

court of equity. See COURT.

Court of Exchequer (eks-**chek**-ər *or* eks-**chek**-ər). A former English superior court responsible primarily for adjudicating disputes about the collection of public revenue; in 1881, the Court was merged into the Queen's Bench Division. See QUEEN'S BENCH DIVISION.

court of first instance. See *trial court* under COURT.

Court of International Trade. A court with jurisdiction over any civil action against the United States arising from federal laws governing import transactions or the eligibility of workers, firms, and communities for adjustment assistance under the Trade Act of 1974 (19 U.S.C. §§ 2101 et seq.); its exclusive jurisdiction also includes actions to recover customs duties, to recover on a customs bond, and to impose certain civil penalties for fraud or negligence. —Also termed *International Trade Court*.

Court of King's Bench. KING'S BENCH.

Court of Military Appeals. UNITED STATES COURT OF APPEALS FOR THE ARMED FORCES.

Court of Military Review. COURT OF CRIMINAL APPEALS (1).

court of piepowder. PIEPOWDER COURT.

Court of Queen's Bench. QUEEN'S BENCH.

Court of Star Chamber. See STAR CHAMBER, COURT OF.

court order. ORDER (2).

court papers. All documents that a party files with the court, including pleadings, motions, notices, and the like. —Often shortened to *papers*. — Also termed *suit papers*.

court reporter. 1. A person who transcribes by shorthand, stenographically takes down, or electronically records testimony during court proceedings or trial-related proceedings <the deposition could not start until the court reporter arrived>. **2.** REPORTER OF DECISIONS.

court rules. Regulations having the force of law and governing practice and procedure in the various courts, such as the Federal Rules of Civil and Criminal Procedure, the U.S. Supreme Court Rules, and the Federal Rules of Evidence, as well as any local rules that a particular court may promulgate.

covenant, *n.* **1.** A formal agreement or promise, usu. under seal.

concurrent covenant. A covenant that requires performance by one party at the same time as another's performance.

covenant not to sue. A covenant in which a party having a right of action agrees not to assert that right in litigation. —Also termed *contract not to sue.*

independent covenant. A covenant that makes each party independently liable for its promises, regardless of the other party's actions.

negative covenant. A covenant that requires a party to refrain from doing something; esp., in a real-estate financing transaction, the borrower's promise to the lender not to encumber or transfer the real estate as long as the loan remains unpaid.

noncompetition covenant. A contractual provision—typically found in employment, partnership, or sale-of-business agreements—in which one party agrees to refrain from conducting business similar to that of the other party; courts generally uphold these clauses for the duration of the original business relationship, but clauses extending beyond termination must usu. be reasonable as to scope, time, and territory. —Also termed *covenant not to compete; restrictive covenant.*

2. TREATY. **3.** A common-law action to recover damages for breach of a formal agreement or promise. **4.** A promise made in a deed or implied by law; esp., an obligation burdening or favoring a landowner.

covenant against encumbrances. A grantor's promise that the property has no encumbrances; in a special warranty deed, the covenant is limited to encumbrances made by the grantor.

covenant for quiet enjoyment. **a.** A covenant assuring against the consequences of a defective title or any other disturbance of the title. **b.** A covenant assuring that the tenant will not be evicted or disturbed by the grantor or a person having a lien or superior title. —Also termed *covenant of quiet enjoyment.*

covenant for title. A covenant that binds the grantor of land to ensure the completeness, security, and continuance of the title transferred; this covenant usu. includes the covenants for seisin, against encumbrances, for the right to convey, for quiet enjoyment, and of warranty.

covenant of habitability. See *implied warranty of habitability* under WARRANTY (2).

covenant of seisin. A covenant appearing in a warranty deed and stating that the grantor has an estate, or the right to convey an estate, of the quality and size that the grantor purports to convey. — Also termed *covenant of good right to convey; right-to-convey covenant.*

covenant running with the land. A covenant whose benefit or liability concerns the land itself, so that every consecutive grantee is tied to it, neither the land nor the covenant being transferable without the other. —Also termed *real covenant*.

covenant running with the title. A covenant that is specific to the conveyance of title between a particular grantor and a particular grantee.

implied reciprocal covenant. A court's presumption that a promisee has, in return for a promise made respecting land, impliedly made a promise to the promisor respecting other land. —Also termed *implied reciprocal servitude*.

restrictive covenant. **a.** A private agreement, usu. in a deed or lease, that restricts the use and occupancy of real property, esp. by specifying lot size, building lines, architectural styles, and the uses to which the property may be put. — Also termed *equitable easement*; *equitable servitude*. **b.** See *noncompetition covenant* under COVENANT (1).

covenant, *vb.* To promise or undertake in a covenant; to agree formally.

covenantee. The person to whom a promise by covenant is made.

covenant not to compete. See *noncompetition covenant* under COVENANT (1).

covenantor. The person who makes a promise by covenant. —Also spelled *covenanter*.

cover, *n.* The purchase on the open market, by the buyer in a breach-of-contract dispute, of goods to substitute for those promised but never

delivered by the seller; under U.C.C. § 2-712, the buyer can recover from the seller the difference between the cost of the substituted goods and the original contract price. —**cover,** *vb.*

coverage, *n.* Inclusion of a risk under an insurance policy; the risks within the scope of an insurance policy. —**cover,** *vb.*

full coverage. Insurance protection that pays for the full amount of a loss with no subtraction for the amount of a deductible.

coverage opinion. See OPINION (2).

cover-all clause. MOTHER HUBBARD CLAUSE (2).

coverture (kə-vər-chər *or* -tyoor), *n. Archaic.* The condition of being a married woman <under former law, a woman under coverture was allowed to sue only through the personality of her husband>. —**covert** (kəv-ərt), *adj.*

CPA. See *certified public accountant* under ACCOUNTANT.

CPI. *abbr.* CONSUMER PRICE INDEX.

craft union. See UNION.

cramdown, *n.* Court confirmation of a debtor's bankruptcy plan despite the opposition of creditors. —**cram down,** *vb.*

crashworthiness doctrine. In tort law, the rule that liability is imposed on a vehicle manufacturer if design defects cause additional damage in an accident, apart from the direct damage caused by the collision.

creator. SETTLOR (1).

credibility, *n.* The quality that makes something (as a witness or some evidence) worthy of belief. — **credible,** *adj.*

credible witness. See WITNESS.

credit, *n.* **1.** Belief; trust <the jury gave credit to Benson's version>. **2.** One's ability to borrow money; the faith in one's ability to pay debts <a favorable credit rating>. **3.** The time that a seller gives the buyer to make the payment that is due <30 days' credit>. **4.** The availability of funds from either a financial institution or under a letter of credit <the bank extended a line of credit to the customer>. **5.** LETTER OF CREDIT <the bank issued a credit in favor of the exporter>. **6.** A deduction from an amount due; an accounting entry reflecting an addition to revenue or net worth <confirm that the credit was properly applied to my account>. Cf. DEBIT. **7.** TAX CREDIT <the $500 credit reduced his income-tax liability by $500>.

installment credit. A commercial arrangement whereby the buyer will pay in more than one payment and the seller can exact finance charges.

revolving credit. A consumer-credit arrangement that allows the borrower to buy goods or secure loans on a continuing basis as long as the outstanding loans do not exceed a specified limit. —Also termed *open credit*; *revolving charge account.*

credit, *vb.* **1.** To believe <the jury did not credit his testimony>. **2.** To enter (as an amount) on the credit side of an account <her account was credited with $500>.

credit balance. In accounting, the status of an account when the sum of the credit entries exceeds the sum of the debit entries.

credit line. LINE OF CREDIT.

creditor. One to whom a debt is owed; one who gives credit for money or goods.

hypothetical creditor. In bankruptcy, an actual or code-created judicial-lien creditor or bona fide purchaser who claims property through the debtor at the time of the bankruptcy filing, and whose rights and powers the trustee assumes in the Bankruptcy Code's priority scheme.

lien creditor. A creditor whose claim is secured by a lien on a particular piece of the debtor's property.

secured creditor. A creditor who has the right, on the debtor's default, to proceed against collateral and apply it to the payment of the debt. —Also termed *secured party*.

unsecured creditor. A creditor who, upon giving credit, takes no rights against specific property of the debtor.

creditor beneficiary. See BENEFICIARY.

creditor's bill. An equitable suit in which a judgment creditor seeks to reach property that cannot be reached by ordinary legal process. — Also termed *creditor's suit*.

creditors' committee. In bankruptcy, a committee comprising representatives of the creditors in a Chapter 11 proceeding, formed to negotiate the debtor's plan of reorganization.

creditors' meeting. See MEETING.

creditor's suit. CREDITOR'S BILL.

credit-shelter trust. See *bypass trust* under TRUST.

creditworthy, *adj.* (Of a borrower) financially sound enough that a lender will extend credit in the belief that the chances of default are slight; fiscally healthy. —**creditworthiness,** *n.*

creeping tender offer. See TENDER OFFER.

crier. 1. An officer of the court who makes public pronouncements as required by the court. See BAILIFF. **2.** An auctioneer. —Also spelled *cryer*.

crim. con. *abbr.* CRIMINAL CONVERSATION.

crime. An act or omission that the law makes punishable. See OFFENSE.

capital crime. See *capital offense* under OFFENSE.

common-law crime. A crime that is punishable under the common law, rather than by force of statute.

corporate crime. A crime committed either by a corporate body or by its representatives acting on its behalf; examples include price-fixing and consumer fraud.

crime against nature. SODOMY.

crime of omission. An offense that carries as its material component the failure to act.

crime of passion. A crime committed in the heat of an emotionally charged moment, with no opportunity to reflect on what is happening. See HEAT OF PASSION.

crime malum in se. See MALUM IN SE.

crime malum prohibitum. See MALUM PROHIBITUM.

index crime. See *index offense* under OFFENSE.

infamous crime (**in**-fə-məs). **a.** At common law, a crime for which part of the penalty was infamy, so that one who committed it would be declared ineligible to serve on a jury, hold public office, or testify; examples are perjury, treason, and fraud. **b.** A crime punishable by imprisonment in a penitentiary; the Fifth Amendment requires a grand-jury indictment for the prosecution of infamous (or capital) crimes, which include all federal felony offenses. See *indictable offense* under OFFENSE.

organized crime. See ORGANIZED CRIME.

status crime. A type of crime that accuses a person of being in a certain condition or of a specific character, such as vagrancy.

strict-liability crime. A crime that does not require a *mens rea* element, such as speeding or attempting to carry a weapon aboard an aircraft.

vice crime. A crime of immoral conduct, such as gambling, prostitution, or child pornography.

victimless crime. A crime that is considered to have no direct victim, usu. because only consenting adults are involved; examples are possession of drugs, deviant sexual intercourse between consenting adults, and prostitution. —Also termed *consensual crime*.

white-collar crime. See WHITE-COLLAR CRIME.

crimen (**krī**-mən *or* **krī**-). [Latin] **1.** Crime. **2.** An accusation or charge of a crime.

crimen falsi (**fahl**[t]-sī). [Latin "the crime of falsifying"] A crime in the nature of perjury; any other offense that involves some element of deceit or falsification.

crimes against persons. A category of criminal offenses in which the perpetrator uses or threatens to use force; examples include murder, rape, aggravated assault, and robbery. —Also termed *crimes against the person*.

crimes against property. A category of criminal offenses in which the perpetrator seeks to derive an unlawful benefit from—or do damage to—another's property without the use or threat of force; examples include burglary, theft, and arson (even though arson may result in injury or death). —Also termed *property crimes*.

criminal, *adj.* Connected with the administration of penal justice; having the character of a crime. —**criminal,** *n.*

criminal action. See ACTION.

criminal code. A legislative code that defines particular crimes and specifies punishments.

criminal coercion. See COERCION.

criminal contempt. See CONTEMPT.

criminal conversation. *Archaic.* A tort action for adultery, brought by one spouse against a third party who engaged in sexual intercourse with the other spouse. —Abbr. crim. con.

criminal desertion. See DESERTION.

criminal forfeiture. See FORFEITURE.

criminal homicide. See HOMICIDE.

criminal intent. MENS REA.

criminalistics, *n.* The science of crime detection, usu. involving the subjection of physical evidence to ballistic analysis, blood-stain analysis, and other tests that are helpful in determining guilt or innocence. —**criminalist,** *n.* Cf. CRIMINOLOGY.

criminalization, *n.* **1.** The act or an instance of making a previously legal act criminal, usu. by passing a statute. Cf. DECRIMINALIZATION. **2.** The process by which a person develops into a criminal. —**criminalize,** *vb.*

criminal law. The body of law defining criminal offenses, regulating how suspects are investigated, charged, and tried, and establishing punishments for convicted offenders.

criminal libel. See LIBEL.

criminal mischief. MALICIOUS MISCHIEF.

criminal negligence. See NEGLIGENCE.

criminal procedure. The legal rules governing the mechanisms under which crimes are investigated, prosecuted, adjudicated, and punished, as well as the protection of accused persons' constitutional rights. Cf. CIVIL PROCEDURE.

criminal registration. See REGISTRATION (1).

criminal responsibility. See RESPONSIBILITY.

criminal syndicalism. See SYNDICALISM.

criminal trespass. See TRESPASS.

criminate. INCRIMINATE.

criminology, *n.* The study of crime and criminal punishment as social phenomena. —**criminologist,** *n.* Cf. CRIMINALISTICS.

crit. An advocate of critical legal studies. —Also termed *CLSer*; *critter*.

fem-crit. A feminist adherent of critical legal studies.

critical legal studies. (*often cap.*) **1.** A school of thought advancing the idea that the legal system's manipulative nature masks its true purpose, which is to perpetuate the socioeconomic status quo. **2.** The body of work produced by adherents of this school of thought. —Abbr. CLS.

critical race theory. (*often cap.*) **1.** A reform movement within the legal profession, particularly within academia, whose adherents believe that the legal system has disempowered racial minorities; having adopted the term in 1989, critical race theorists observe that, even if the law is couched in neutral language, it cannot be neutral because those who fashioned it had their own subjective perspectives that, once enshrined in law, have disadvantaged minorities and even perpetuated racism. **2.** The body of work produced by adherents of this theory. —Abbr. CRT.

critter. CRIT.

cross-action. CROSS-CLAIM.

cross-appeal. See APPEAL.

cross-claim, *n.* A claim that arises between codefendants or coplaintiffs in a case and that relates to the subject of the original claim or counterclaim. —Also termed *cross-action*. —**cross-claim,** *vb.* —**cross-claimant,** *n.* Cf. COUNTERCLAIM.

cross-collateral. See COLLATERAL.

cross-examination, *n.* The formal questioning of a witness by the party opposed to the party who called the witness to testify; the cross-examiner is typically allowed to ask leading questions but is usu. limited to matters covered on direct examination and to credibility issues. —**cross-examine,** *vb.* Cf. DIRECT EXAMINATION; RECROSS-EXAMINATION.

cross-offer, *n.* In contract law, an offer made to another in ignorance that the offeree has made the same offer to the offeror. —**cross-offer,** *vb.* —**cross-offeror,** *n.*

crown jewel. A company's most valuable asset, esp. as valued at a time when the company is the subject of a hostile takeover; a common antitakeover device is for the target company to sell its crown jewel to a third party so that the company will be less attractive to an unfriendly suitor. See SCORCHED-EARTH DEFENSE.

CRT. *abbr.* CRITICAL RACE THEORY.

cruel and unusual punishment. See PUNISHMENT.

cruelty. The intentional and malicious infliction of mental or physical suffering on a living creature, esp. a human; abusive treatment; outrage.

extreme cruelty. As grounds for divorce, one spouse's physical violence toward the other spouse, or conduct that destroys or severely impairs the other spouse's mental health.

mental cruelty. As grounds for divorce, one spouse's course of conduct that creates such anguish that it endangers the life, person, physical health, or mental health of the other spouse. See EMOTIONAL DISTRESS.

cryer. CRIER.

CSV. *abbr.* CASH SURRENDER VALUE.

c.t.a. See *administration cum testamento annexo* under ADMINISTRATION.

culpa (kəl-pə). [Latin] In civil law, fault, neglect, or negligence. See NEGLIGENCE.

lata culpa. See *gross negligence* under NEGLIGENCE.

levis culpa. See *ordinary negligence* under NEGLIGENCE.

levissima culpa. See *slight negligence* under NEGLIGENCE.

culpable, *adj.* **1.** Guilty; blameworthy. **2.** Involving the breach of a duty. —**culpability,** *n.*

culpable intoxication. See *voluntary intoxication* under INTOXICATION.

cum testamento annexo. See *administration cum testamento annexo* under ADMINISTRATION.

cumulative dividend. See DIVIDEND.

cumulative-effects doctrine. The rule that a transaction affecting interstate commerce in a trivial way may be taken together with other transactions of a similar nature to establish that the combined effect on interstate commerce is far from trivial and can therefore be regulated under the Commerce Clause.

cumulative evidence. See EVIDENCE.

cumulative preferred stock. See STOCK.

cumulative punishment. See PUNISHMENT.

cumulative remedy. See REMEDY.

cumulative sentences. See *consecutive sentences* under SENTENCE.

cumulative stock. See *cumulative preferred stock* under STOCK.

cumulative-to-the-extent-earned dividend. See DIVIDEND.

cumulative voting. See VOTING.

cumulative zoning. See ZONING.

Cur. adv. vult. *abbr.* CURIA ADVISARI VULT.

curative-admissibility doctrine. The rule that ordinarily inadmissible evidence will be allowed if similar evidence has been introduced by the adverse party.

cure, *vb.* To remove legal defects or correct legal errors; for example, curing title involves the removal of defects from title to unmarketable land so that it is now marketable. —**curative,** *adj.*

Curia advisari vult (**kyoor**-ee-ə-ad-və-**ser**-ee-vəlt). [Latin] The court will be advised; the court will consider. —Abbr. *Cur. adv. vult*; *C.A.V.*; *c.a.v.*

curia regis. [Latin] The King's Court.

currency swap. See SWAP.

current asset. See ASSET.

current liabilities. See *short-term debt* under DEBT.

current yield. See YIELD.

curtesy (**kərt**-ə-see). At common law, a husband's right, upon his wife's death, to a life estate in the land that his wife owned during their marriage, assuming a child was born to the couple; this right has been largely abolished. Cf. DOWER.

curtesy consummate. The interest the husband has in his wife's estate after her death.

curtesy initiate. The interest the husband has in his wife's estate after the birth of issue capable of inheriting, and before the death of the wife.

curtilage (**kərt**-[ə-]ləj). The land or yard adjoining a house, usu. within an enclosure; for police searches under the Fourth Amendment, the curtilage is an area protected, in most cases, from warrantless searches. See OPEN-FIELD DOCTRINE. Cf. MESSUAGE.

custodial interrogation. See INTERROGATION.

custodian, *n.* A person or institution that has charge or custody of property, papers, or other valuables; GUARDIAN. —**custodianship,** *n.*

custody, *n.* **1.** The care and control of a thing or person for inspection, preservation, or security.

protective custody. The government's confinement of a person for that person's own security or well-being, such as a witness whose safety is in jeopardy, or an incompetent who may harm others <the state held its key informant in protective custody while the trial was pending>.

2. The care, control, and maintenance of a child awarded by a court to one of the parents in a divorce or separation proceeding.

divided custody. An arrangement by which each parent has custody and full control of and responsibility for the child for part of the year, with reciprocal visitation rights.

joint custody. An arrangement by which both parents share the responsibility for and authority over the child at all times. —Also termed *shared custody.*

sole custody. An arrangement by which one parent has full responsibility to the exclusion of the other.

3. The detention of a person by virtue of lawful process or authority. —**custodial,** *adj.*

custom, *n.* **1.** A practice that by its common adoption and long, unvarying habit has become force of law with respect to the place or subject matter to which it relates. See USAGE. **2.** (*pl.*) Duties imposed on imports or exports. **3.** (*pl.*) The agency or procedure for collecting such duties. —**customary** (corresponding to sense 1), *adj.*

customary, *n.* A record of all the established legal and quasi-legal practices within a community.

customary law. Practices and beliefs that are so vital and intrinsic a part of a social and economic system that they are treated as if they were laws.

customhouse. A building or office, esp. at a port, where duties or customs are collected and where ships are cleared for entering or leaving the country. —Also spelled *customshouse*.

Customs and Patent Appeals, Court of. See COURT OF CUSTOMS AND PATENT APPEALS.

Customs Court, U.S. A court that formerly heard cases involving customs and duties; abolished in 1980, its responsibilities have been taken over by the Court of International Trade. See COURT OF INTERNATIONAL TRADE.

cy pres (sI-**pray** *or* see-). [Law French "as near as"] The equitable doctrine that written instruments should be construed as closely to the parties' intention as possible; courts use *cy pres* esp. in construing charitable gifts when the donor's original charitable purpose cannot be fulfilled. —Also termed *doctrine of approximation*.

D

D.A. *abbr.* DISTRICT ATTORNEY.

dactylography (dak-tə-**log**-rə-fee), *n.* The scientific study of fingerprints as a method of identification. —**dactylographic** (dak-til-ə-**graf**-ik), *adj.*

daily balance. The final daily accounting for a day on which interest is to be accrued or paid.

average daily balance. The average amount of money in an account (such as a bank account or credit-card account) during a given period; this amount serves as the basis for computing interest or a finance charge for the period.

damage, *n.* Loss or injury to person or property <actionable damage resulting from the defendant's negligence>.

damages, *n. pl.* Monetary compensation for loss or injury to person or property <the plaintiff seeks a total of $950,000 in damages from the defendant>. —**damage,** *adj.*

actual damages. An amount awarded to a complainant to compensate for a proven injury or loss; damages that repay actual losses. —Also termed *compensatory damages.*

consequential damages. Losses that do not flow directly and immediately from an injurious act, but that result indirectly from the act.

double damages. Damages that, by statute, are twice the amount that the fact-finder determines is owed, or twice the amount of actual damages awarded; in some cases, double damages are awarded in ad-

dition to actual damages, so the effect is the same as treble damages.

excessive damages. A jury award that grossly exceeds the amount warranted by law based on the facts and circumstances of the case; unreasonable or outrageous damages, which are subject to reduction by remittitur. See REMITTITUR.

expectation damages. Compensation awarded for the loss of what a person reasonably anticipated from a transaction that was not completed. —Also termed *expectancy damages; loss-of-bargain damages; lost-expectation damages.*

future damages. Money awarded to an injured party for an injury's residual or projected effects that reduce the person's ability to function; examples are expected pain and suffering, loss or impairment of earning capacity, and projected medical expenses.

general damages. Damages that the law presumes follow from the type of wrong complained of; general damages do not need to be specifically claimed or proved to have been sustained. —Also termed *direct damages.*

hedonic damages (hi-**don**-ik). Damages that attempt to compensate the loss of the pleasure of being alive; such damages are not allowed in most jurisdictions.

incidental damages. **a.** Losses reasonably associated with or related to actual damages. **b.** A seller's commercially reasonable expenses incurred in stopping delivery or in transporting and caring for goods after a buyer's breach. U.C.C. § 2-

710. **c.** A buyer's expenses reasonably incurred in caring for goods after a seller's breach. U.C.C. § 2-715(1).

liquidated damages. An amount contractually stipulated as a reasonable estimation of actual damages to be recovered by one party if the other party breaches. —Also termed *stipulated damages.* See LIQUIDATED-DAMAGES CLAUSE. Cf. PENALTY (3).

nominal damages. A trifling sum awarded when a legal injury is suffered but when there is no substantial loss or injury to be compensated.

punitive damages. Damages awarded in addition to actual damages when the defendant acted with recklessness, malice, or deceit; such damages, which are intended to punish and thereby deter blameworthy conduct, are generally not recoverable for breach of contract. —Also termed *exemplary damages*; *vindictive damages*; *smart money.*

special damages. Damages that are alleged to have been sustained in the circumstances of a particular wrong; to be awardable, special damages must be specifically claimed and proved.

treble damages. Damages that, by statute, are three times the amount that the fact-finder determines is owed. —Also termed *triple damages.*

damages, mitigation of. See MITIGATION-OF-DAMAGES DOCTRINE.

damnum. [Latin] Damage suffered. See AD DAMNUM.

damnum absque injuria (**dam**-nəm-**ab**-skwee-in-**juur**-ee-ə). [Latin "damage without wrongful act"] Loss or harm for which there is no legal remedy. —Also termed *damnum sine injuria.* Cf. INJURIA ABSQUE DAMNO.

damnum infectum. [Latin] Loss not yet suffered but only apprehended.

damnum sine injuria (**dam**-nəm-**sI**-nee-in-**juur**-ee-ə *or* -**see**-nay-). DAMNUM ABSQUE INJURIA.

D & O liability insurance. See *directors' and officers' liability insurance* under INSURANCE.

dangerous instrumentality. An instrument, substance, or condition so inherently dangerous that it may cause serious bodily injury or death without human use or interference; it may serve as the basis for strict liability. See ATTRACTIVE-NUISANCE DOCTRINE. Cf. DEADLY WEAPON.

dangerous-proximity test. In criminal law, a common-law test for the crime of attempt, focusing on whether the defendant is dangerously close to completing the offense; factors include the gravity of the potential crime, the apprehension of the victim, and the uncertainty of the crime's occurrence. Cf. SUBSTANTIAL-STEP TEST.

date of issue. 1. An arbitrary date fixed as the beginning of a term; EFFECTIVE DATE. **2.** In an insurance policy, the date set forth in the policy itself, rather than the date of actual signing or the delivery date.

date of maturity. The date on which a debt becomes due and payable, as in the case of a promissory note, bond, or other evidence of indebtedness.

date rape. See RAPE.

day in court. 1. The right and opportunity to litigate claims, seek relief, or defend one's rights in a judicial tribunal. **2.** The right to be notified and given an opportunity to appear and to be heard when one's case is called.

day order. See ORDER (4).

days of grace. GRACE PERIOD.

d/b/a. *abbr.* Doing business as <Highland, Inc. d/b/a Burger World>.

d.b.n. See *administration de bonis non* under ADMINISTRATION.

D.C. *abbr.* **1.** DISTRICT OF COLUMBIA. **2.** See *district court* under COURT.

DCF. See *discounted cash flow* under CASH FLOW.

dead asset. See ASSET.

deadbeat. *Slang.* A person who does not pay debts or financial obligations, usu. with the suggestion that the person is also adept or experienced at evading creditors.

dead freight. The amount paid by a shipper to a shipowner for the ship's unused cargo space.

deadhand control. The use of executory interests that vest at some indefinite and remote time in the future to restrict alienability and ensure that property remains in the hands of a particular family or organization; the rule against perpetuities restricts this activity. See MORTMAIN.

dead letter. 1. A law or practice that, although not formally abolished, is no longer used, observed, or enforced. **2.** A piece of mail that can be neither delivered nor returned because it lacks a good address for both the intended recipient and the sender.

deadlock, *n.* **1.** A state of inaction resulting from opposition or lack of compromise. **2.** In corporate law, the blocking of corporate action by one or more factions of shareholders or directors if they disagree about some aspect of corporate policy. —**deadlock,** *vb.*

deadlocked jury. See *hung jury* under JURY.

deadly force. See FORCE.

deadly weapon. Any firearm or other device, instrument, material, or substance that, from the manner it is used or is intended to be used, is calculated or likely to produce death. Cf. DANGEROUS INSTRUMENTALITY.

dead man's statute. A law prohibiting the admission of a decedent's statements as evidence in certain circumstances, as when an opposing party or witness seeks to use those statements to support a claim against a decedent's estate. —Also termed *dead person's statute*.

dead pledge. *Archaic.* MORTGAGE (1).

dealer, *n.* **1.** A person who purchases goods or property for sale to others; a retailer. **2.** A person or firm that buys and sells securities for its own account as a principal, and then sells to a customer. —**deal,** *n.* & *vb.*

death. The ending of life; the cessation of all vital functions and signs.

brain death. The bodily condition of showing no response to external stimuli, no spontaneous movements, no breathing, no reflexes, and a flat reading (usu. for a full day) on a machine that measures the brain's electrical activity. — Also termed *legal death.*

civil death. See CIVIL DEATH.

natural death. Bodily death, as opposed to civil death. —Also termed *mors naturalis.* See NATURAL-DEATH ACT.

presumptive death. Death inferred from proof of the person's long, unexplained absence, usu. after seven years.

simultaneous death. The death of two or more persons in the same mishap in circumstances making it impossible to determine who was the first to die or the last to survive. See SIMULTANEOUS-DEATH ACT; COMMORIENTES.

death, contemplation of. See CONTEMPLATION OF DEATH.

death action. WRONGFUL-DEATH ACTION.

deathbed declaration. See *dying declaration* under DECLARATION (6).

death by misadventure. ACCIDENTAL KILLING.

death case. 1. A criminal case in which the death penalty may be or has been imposed. **2.** WRONGFUL-DEATH ACTION.

death certificate. An official document issued by the Register of Deaths or some other public official verifying that a person has died, with such information as the time of death, the cause of death, and the signature of the attending or examining physician.

death penalty. State-imposed death as punishment for a serious crime. — Also termed *capital punishment.*

death-qualified jury. See JURY.

death row. The area of a prison where those who have been sentenced to death are confined.

death sentence. See SENTENCE.

death statute. A law that protects the interests of a decedent's family and other dependents, who may recover in damages what they would reasonably have received from the decedent if the death had not occurred. Cf. SURVIVAL STATUTE.

death tax. See TAX.

debarment, *n.* The act of precluding from having or doing something; exclusion or hindrance. —**debar,** *vb.*

debauchery (di-**boch**-[ə-]ree), *n.* Excessive indulgence in sensual pleasures; sexual immorality or excesses. —**debauch,** *vb.*

de bene esse (day-ben-ee-**es**-ee), *adv.* [Law Latin "of well-being"] As conditionally allowed for the present; in anticipation of a future need <Willis's deposition was taken *de bene esse*>. —**de bene esse,** *adj.*

debenture. 1. A debt secured only by the debtor's earning power, not by any specific asset; an instrument acknowledging such a debt. **2.** A bond that is backed only by the general credit and financial reputation of the corporate issuer, not by a lien on the corporation's assets. —Also termed *debenture bond; unsecured bond; naked debenture.* Cf. BOND (1).

convertible debenture. A debenture that the holder may change or convert into some other security, such as stock.

sinking-fund debenture. A debenture that is secured by periodic payments into a fund established to retire long-term debt.

subordinate debenture. A debenture that is subject to the prior payment of ordinary debentures and other indebtedness.

3. In England, a company's security for a monetary loan; the security usu. creates a charge on company stock or property. **4.** A customhouse certificate providing for a refund of the duties on imported goods when the importer reexports the goods rather than selling them in the country where they were imported.

debit. 1. A sum charged as due or owing. **2.** In bookkeeping, an entry made on the left side of a ledger or account, noting an increase in assets or a decrease in liabilities. **3.** An account balance showing that something remains owing to the holder of the account. Cf. CREDIT.

de bonis asportatis. See TRESPASS DE BONIS ASPORTATIS.

de bonis non. See *administration de bonis non* under ADMINISTRATION.

debt. 1. The aggregate of all existing claims against a person, entity, or state <the bank denied the loan application after analyzing the applicant's outstanding debt>. **2.** A specific sum of money due by agreement or otherwise <the debt amounted to $2,500>. **3.** A nonmonetary thing that one person owes another, such as goods or services <her debt was to supply him with 20 international first-class tickets on the airline of his choice>. **4.** A common-law writ by which a court adjudicates claims involving fixed sums of money <he brought suit in debt>. —Also termed (in sense 4) *writ of debt.*

antecedent debt. **a.** In contract law, an old debt that may serve as consideration for a new promise if the statute of limitations has run on the old debt. See PREEXISTING-DUTY RULE. **b.** In bankruptcy law, a debtor's prepetition obligation that existed before a debtor's transfer of an interest in property; for a transfer to be preferential, it must be for or on account of an antecedent debt. See PREFERENTIAL TRANSFER.

bad debt. A debt that is uncollectible and that may be deductible for tax purposes.

bonded debt. A business or government debt represented by issued bonds; a debt secured by a bond.

consumer debt. A debt incurred by an individual primarily for a personal, family, or household purpose.

contingent debt. A debt that is not presently fixed but that may become fixed in the future with the occurrence of some event.

convertible debt. A debt whose security may be changed by a creditor into another form of security.

floating debt. Short-term debt that is continuously renewed to finance the ongoing operations of a business or government.

funded debt. **a.** A state or municipal debt to be paid out of an accumulation of money or by future taxation. **b.** Secured long-term corporate debt meant to replace short-term, floating, or unsecured debt.

installment debt. A debt that is to be paid at regular times over a specified period.

judgment debt. A debt that is evidenced by a legal judgment or brought about by successful legal action against the debtor.

liquidated debt. A debt whose amount has been predetermined by agreement of the parties or by operation of law.

liquid debt. A debt that is due immediately and unconditionally.

long-term debt. Generally, a debt that will not come due within the next year.

national debt. See NATIONAL DEBT.

passive debt. A debt that, by agreement between the debtor and creditor, is interest-free.

public debt. A debt owed by a municipal, state, or national government.

secured debt. A debt backed by collateral.

short-term debt. Debts and other liabilities payable within one year. — Also termed *current liabilities.*

unliquidated debt. A debt that has not been reduced to a specific amount, and about which there may be a dispute.

unsecured debt. A debt not supported by collateral or other security.

debt capital. See CAPITAL.

debt-equity ratio. DEBT-TO-EQUITY RATIO.

debt financing. See FINANCING.

debt instrument. A written promise to repay a debt, such as a promissory note, bill, bond, or commercial paper.

debtor. **1.** One who owes an obligation to another, esp. an obligation to pay money. **2.** In bankruptcy, a person who files a voluntary petition or against whom an involuntary petition is filed—Also termed (in sense 2) *bankrupt.*

debtor-in-possession. In bankruptcy law, a Chapter 11 or 12 debtor that continues to operate its business as a fiduciary to the bankruptcy estate; with certain exceptions, the debtor-in-possession has all the rights, powers, and duties of a Chapter 11 trustee. —Abbr. DIP.

debtor rehabilitation. REHABILITATION (3).

debt pooling. An arrangement by which a person's debts are consolidated and adjustments are made with creditors to accept lower monthly payments or to take less money.

debt ratio. A corporation's total long-term and short-term liabilities divided by the firm's total assets; a low debt ratio indicates conservative financing and thus an enhanced ability to borrow in the future. —Also termed *debt-to-total-assets ratio.*

debt retirement. Repayment of debt; RETIREMENT (3).

debt security. See SECURITY.

debt service. **1.** The funds needed to meet a long-term debt's annual interest expenses, principal payments, and sinking-fund contributions. **2.** Payments due on a debt, including interest and principal.

debt-to-equity ratio. A corporation's long-term debt divided by its owners' equity, calculated to assess a firm's capitalization. —Also termed *debt-equity ratio*; *debt-to-net-worth ratio*.

debt-to-total-assets ratio. DEBT RATIO.

decedent (də-**seed**-[ə]nt), *n.* A dead person, esp. one who has died recently. —Also termed *deceased*.

decedent's estate. See ESTATE.

deceit, *n.* **1.** The act of intentionally giving a false impression <the juror's deceit led the lawyer to believe that she was not biased>. **2.** A tort arising from a false representation made knowingly or recklessly with the intent that another person should detrimentally rely on it <the new homeowner sued both the seller and the realtor for deceit after discovering termites>. —**deceive,** *vb.* See FRAUD; MISREPRESENTATION.

deceptive act. As defined by the Federal Trade Commission and most state statutes, conduct that is likely to deceive a consumer acting reasonably in the circumstances. —Also termed *deceptive practice*.

decision, *n.* A judicial determination after consideration of the facts and the law; esp., a ruling, order, or judgment pronounced by a court when considering or disposing of the case. —**decisional,** *adj.* See JUDGMENT; OPINION.

appealable decision. A decree or order that is sufficiently final to re-

ceive appellate review, such as an order granting (but not one denying) summary judgment, or an interlocutory decree or order that is deemed appealable, such as an order denying immunity from liability to a police officer in a civil-rights suit. —Also termed *reviewable issue*. See COLLATERAL-ORDER DOCTRINE.

final decision. See *final judgment* under JUDGMENT.

interlocutory decision. See *interlocutory order* under ORDER.

decisional law. CASELAW.

decision on the merits. See *judgment on the merits* under JUDGMENT.

declarant, *n.* **1.** One who has made a statement <in accordance with the rules of evidence, the statement was offered to prove the declarant's state of mind>. **2.** One who has signed a declaration, esp. one stating an intent to become a U.S. citizen <the declarant grew up in Italy>.

declaration, *n.* **1.** A formal statement, proclamation, or announcement, esp. one embodied in an instrument.

declaration of dividend. A corporation's setting aside of a portion of its net or surplus income for distribution among its shareholders.

declaration of intention. An alien's formal statement of the resolution to become a citizen of the United States and to renounce allegiance to any other government or country.

declaration of trust. **a.** The act by which the person who holds legal title to property or an estate acknowledges that the property is being held in trust for another person or for certain specified purposes. **b.** The instrument that creates a trust. —Also termed (in sense b) *trust deed*; *trust agreement*.

2. In international law, the stipulations within a treaty according to which the parties agree to conduct their actions; TREATY. **3.** In international law, a nation's unilateral pronouncement that affects the rights and duties of other nations.

declaration of war. A nation's announcement that it is commencing war against another nation.

4. A document that governs legal rights to certain types of realty, such as a condominium or a residential subdivision. **5.** A listing of the merchandise that a person intends to bring into the United States; this listing is given to U.S. Customs when one enters the country. **6.** In the law of evidence, an unsworn statement made by someone having knowledge of facts relating to an event in dispute.

declaration against interest. An out-of-court statement that, when made, is against the declarant's welfare; such a statement is admissible under an exception to the hearsay rule. —Also termed *admission against interest*.

dying declaration. A statement that is made by a person who believes he or she is about to die and that relates to the cause or circumstances of the person's imminent death; the statement is admissible in evidence as an exception to the

hearsay rule. —Also termed *deathbed declaration*.

self-serving declaration. An out-of-court statement made by a party to benefit his or her own interest.

7. At common law, the plaintiff's first pleading in a civil action. Cf. PLEA (2). **8.** In a few U.S. jurisdictions, a formal written statement—resembling an affidavit—that attests, under penalty of perjury, to facts known by the declarant. **9.** See *declaratory judgment* under JUDGMENT. —**declare,** *vb.*—**declaratory,** *adj.*

Declaration of Independence. The formal proclamation of July 4, 1776, in the name of the people of the American colonies, asserting their independence from the British Crown and announcing themselves to the world as an independent nation.

declaratory decree. See *declaratory judgment* under JUDGMENT.

declaratory judgment. See JUDGMENT.

declaratory statute. See STATUTE.

declining-balance depreciation method. See DEPRECIATION METHOD.

deconstruction, *n.* In critical legal studies, a method of analyzing legal principles or rules by breaking down the supporting premises to show that these premises might also advance the opposite rule or result. —Also termed *trashing.*—**deconstructionist,** *n.* & *adj.*

decree, *n.* **1.** Traditionally, a judicial decision in a court of equity, admiralty, divorce, or probate—similar to a judgment of a court of law <the

judge's decree in favor of the will's beneficiary>. **2.** Any court order, but esp. one in a matrimonial case <divorce decree>. —**decretal** (di-**kreet**-[ə]ll), *adj.* See JUDGMENT; ORDER (2); DECISION.

consent decree. A court decree that all parties agree to. —Also termed *consent order.*

decree absolute. A ripened decree nisi; a court's decree that has become unconditional because the time specified in a decree nisi has passed. —Also termed *order absolute*; *rule absolute.*

decree nisi (**nee**-see *or* **nis**-ee *or* **nI**-see *or* **nI**-sI). A court's decree that will become absolute unless the adversely affected party shows the court, within a specified time, why it should be set aside. —Also termed *order nisi*; *rule nisi.* See NISI.

deficiency decree. See *deficiency judgment* under JUDGMENT.

final decree. See *final judgment* under JUDGMENT.

interlocutory decree. See *interlocutory judgment* under JUDGMENT.

decriminalization, *n.* The legislative act or process of legalizing an illegal act <many doctors seek the decriminalization of euthanasia>. —**decriminalize,** *vb.* Cf. CRIMINALIZATION (1).

dedication, *n.* In property law, the donation of land or creation of an easement for public use. —**dedicate,** *vb.*—**dedicatory,** *adj.*

deductible, *adj.* Capable of being subtracted, esp. from taxable income. See DEDUCTION (2).

deductible, *n.* **1.** Under an insurance policy, the portion of the loss to be borne by the insured before the insurer becomes liable for payment. **2.** The insurance-policy clause specifying the amount of this portion.

deduction, *n.* **1.** The act or process of subtracting or taking away. **2.** In tax law, an amount subtracted from gross income when calculating adjusted gross income, or from adjusted gross income when calculating taxable income. Cf. EXEMPTION (3); TAX CREDIT.

additional standard deduction. The sum of the additional amounts that a taxpayer is entitled to deduct if he or she turns 65 or becomes blind before the close of the taxable year.

charitable deduction. A deduction for a contribution to a qualified charity or other tax-exempt institution. See CHARITABLE CONTRIBUTION (2); CHARITABLE ORGANIZATION.

itemized deduction. An expense— such as medical payments, home-mortgage interest, or charitable contributions—that can be subtracted from adjusted gross income to determine taxable income.

marital deduction. A federal tax deduction allowed for lifetime and testamentary transfers from one spouse to another. I.R.C. §§ 2056, 2523.

miscellaneous itemized deduction. A deduction other than those allowable in computing adjusted gross income, those enumerated in I.R.C. § 67(b), and personal exemptions; such a deduction is allowed only to an itemizing taxpayer whose total miscellaneous itemized deductions exceed a statutory percentage of adjusted gross income. I.R.C. § 67(b).

standard deduction. A specified dollar amount that a taxpayer can deduct from adjusted gross income, instead of itemizing deductions, to determine taxable income.

3. The act or process of reasoning from the general propositions to a specific application or conclusion. Cf. INDUCTION (2). —**deduct** (corresponding to senses 1 & 2), *vb.* —**deduce** (corresponding to sense 3), *vb.*

deed, *n.* **1.** Something that is done or carried out; an act or action. **2.** At common law, any written instrument that is signed, sealed, and delivered and that conveys some interest in property. **3.** A written instrument by which land is conveyed. —**deed,** *vb.* Cf. CONVEYANCE.

absolute deed. A deed that conveys title without condition or encumbrance. —Also termed *deed absolute.*

administrator's deed. A document that conveys property owned by a person who has died intestate.

bargain-and-sale deed. A deed that conveys property to a buyer for valuable consideration but that lacks any guarantee from the seller about the validity of the title.

deed in fee. A deed conveying the title to land in fee simple, usu. with covenants.

deed in lieu of foreclosure. A deed by which a borrower conveys fee-simple title to a lender in satisfaction of a mortgage debt and as a substitute for foreclosure.

deed of release. A deed that surrenders full title of a property upon payment or performance of specified conditions.

deed of trust. A deed conveying title to real property to a trustee as security until the grantor repays a loan; this type of deed resembles a mortgage. —Also termed *trust deed.*

deed poll. A deed made by and binding on only one party, or on two or more parties having similar interests; it is so called because, traditionally, the parchment was "polled" (that is, shaven) so that it would be even at the top (unlike an indenture). —Also spelled *deed-poll.* Cf. INDENTURE.

grant deed. A deed containing or having implied by law some but not all of the usual covenants of title.

quitclaim deed. A deed that conveys a grantor's complete interest or claim in real property but that neither warrants nor professes that the title is valid. —Often shortened to *quitclaim.* —Also termed *deed without covenants.* Cf. *warranty deed.*

sheriff's deed. A deed that gives ownership rights in property bought at a sheriff's sale.

special warranty deed. **a.** A deed in which the grantor covenants to warrant and defend the title against claims and demands of only the grantor and all persons claiming by and under him or her. **b.** In a few jurisdictions, a quitclaim deed. Cf. *warranty deed.*

statutory deed. A warranty-deed form prescribed by state law and containing certain warranties and covenants even though they are not included in the printed form.

title deed. A deed that evidences a person's legal ownership of a piece of property. See TITLE.

warranty deed. A deed that expressly guarantees the grantor's good, clear title and that contains covenants concerning the quality of title, including warranties of seisin, quiet enjoyment, right to convey, freedom from encumbrances, and defense of title against all claims. —Also termed *general warranty deed; full-covenant-and-warranty deed.* See WARRANTY (1). Cf. *quitclaim deed; special warranty deed.*

wild deed. A recorded deed that is not in the chain of title because a previous instrument connected to the chain of title has not been recorded.

deem, *vb.* **1.** To treat (a thing) as being something it is not, or as having certain qualities that it does not have <the fact was deemed admitted because the party did not respond to the opposing party's request for admission>. **2.** To consider, think, judge, or esteem <she deemed it urgent>.

deep pocket. 1. (*pl.*) Substantial wealth and resources <the plaintiff nonsuited the individuals and targeted the corporation with deep pockets>. **2.** A person or entity with substantial wealth and resources against which a claim may be made or a judgment may be taken <that national insurance company is a favor-

ite deep pocket among plaintiff's lawyers>.

Deep Rock doctrine. In bankruptcy law, the principle by which unfair or inequitable claims presented by controlling shareholders of bankrupt corporations may be subordinated to claims of general or trade creditors.

deface (di-**fays**), *vb.* **1.** To mar or destroy (a written instrument, signature, or inscription) by obliteration, erasure, or superinscription. **2.** To detract from the value of (a coin) by punching, clipping, cutting, or shaving. **3.** To mar or injure (a building, monument, or other structure). —**defacement,** *n.*

de facto (də-**fak**-toh *or* day-), *adj.* **1.** Actual; existing in fact; having effect even though not formally or legally recognized <a de facto contract> **2.** Illegitimate <a de facto government>. Cf. DE JURE.

de facto corporation. See CORPORATION.

de facto dissolution. See DISSOLUTION.

de facto merger. See MERGER.

de facto segregation. See SEGREGATION.

defalcation (dee-fal-**kay**-shən), *n.* **1.** EMBEZZLEMENT. **2.** Loosely, the failure to meet an obligation; a nonfraudulent default. **3.** *Archaic.* A deduction; a setoff. —**defalcate** (di-**fal**-kayt *or* dee-), *vb.*—**defalcator,** *n.*

defamation, *n.* **1.** The act of harming the reputation of another by making a statement to a third person; if the alleged defamation involves a matter of public concern, the plaintiff is constitutionally required to prove both the statement's falsity and the defendant's fault. **2.** A written or oral statement that damages another's reputation. —**defame,** *vb.*—**defamatory,** *adj.* See LIBEL; SLANDER. Cf. DISPARAGEMENT.

default, *n.* The omission or failure to perform a legal or contractual duty, such as the failure to pay a debt when due. —**default,** *vb.*

default judgment. 1. A judgment entered against a defendant who has failed to plead or otherwise defend against the plaintiff's claim or the failure to appear at trial. **2.** A judgment entered as a penalty against a party who does not comply with an order, esp. an order to provide or permit discovery. —Also termed *judgment by default.* See JUDGMENT.

nil-dicit default judgment (nil-**dis**-ət or -**dik**-ət). [Latin "he says nothing"] A judgment for the plaintiff entered after the defendant fails to file a timely answer, often after appearing in the case by filing preliminary motions. —Also termed *nihil-dicit default judgment.*

no-answer default judgment. In Texas, a judgment for the plaintiff entered after the defendant fails both to file an answer and to make an appearance.

post-answer default judgment. In Texas, a judgment for the plaintiff entered after the defendant files an answer but fails to appear at trial.

defeasance (di-**feez**-[ə]n[t]s), *n.* **1.** An annulment or abrogation; VOIDANCE. **2.** The fact or an instance of bringing an estate or status to an end, esp. by conditional limitation. **3.** A condition upon the performance of which a deed or other instrument is defeated or made void; a contractual provision containing such a condition. —**defease,** *vb.*—**defeasible,** *adj.*

defeasance clause. A mortgage provision stating that the conveyance to the mortgagee will be ineffective if the mortgagor pays the debt on time.

defeasible fee simple. See *fee simple defeasible* under FEE SIMPLE.

defeasible remainder. See REMAINDER.

defect, *n.* An imperfection or shortcoming in a part that is essential to the operation or safety of a product. —**defective,** *adj.*

design defect. A product imperfection occurring when the seller or distributor could have reduced or avoided the foreseeable risks of harm by adopting a reasonable alternative design, and when, as a result of not using that alternative, the product is not reasonably safe.

hidden defect. A product imperfection that is not discoverable by reasonable inspection and for which a seller or lessor is generally liable if the flaw causes harm; upon discovering a hidden defect, a purchaser may revoke a prior acceptance. U.C.C. § 2-608(1)(b). —Also termed *latent defect.*

manufacturing defect. An imperfection in a product that departs from its intended design even though all possible care was exercised in its assembly and marketing.

product defect. An imperfection in a product that has a manufacturing defect or design defect, or is faulty because of inadequate instructions or warnings.

defective condition. An unreasonably dangerous state that might well cause physical harm beyond that contemplated by the ordinary user or consumer who purchases the product. See PRODUCTS LIABILITY.

defective pleading. See PLEADING (1).

defective title. See TITLE.

defend, *vb.* **1.** To deny, contest, or oppose (an allegation or claim) <the corporation vigorously defended against the shareholder's lawsuit>. **2.** To represent (someone) as an attorney <the accused retained a well-known lawyer to defend him>.

defendant. A person sued in a civil proceeding or accused in a criminal proceeding. Cf. PLAINTIFF.

defendant in error. *Archaic.* In a case on appeal, the prevailing party in the court below; APPELLEE; RESPONDENT (1).

defense (di-**fens**). **1.** A defendant's statement of a reason why the plaintiff or prosecutor has no valid case against the defendant; esp., a defendant's answer, denial, or plea <her defense was that she was 25 miles from the building at the time of the robbery>.

affirmative defense. A defendant's assertion raising new facts and arguments that, if true, will defeat the plaintiff's or government's claim even if all allegations in the complaint are true; examples of affirmative defenses include duress and contributory negligence (in civil

cases) and insanity and self-defense (in criminal cases).

capacity defense. A defense based on the defendant's inability to be held accountable for his or her actions. See CAPACITY.

collateral defense. In a criminal case, a defense of justification or excuse not involving a rebuttal of the allegation and therefore collateral to the elements the prosecutor must prove in the case. See EXCUSE (2); JUSTIFICATION (2).

equitable defense. A defense formerly available only in a court of equity but now maintainable in a court of law; examples include mistake, fraud, illegality, and failure of consideration.

inconsistent defense. A defense so contrary to another defense that the acceptance of one requires abandonment of the other; for example, a person accused of murder cannot claim both self-defense and the alibi of having been in a different city when the murder took place.

insanity defense. See INSANITY DEFENSE.

issuable defense. In common-law pleading, a plea on the merits setting forth a legal defense. Cf. *issuable plea* under PLEA.

justification defense. See JUSTIFICATION (2).

meritorious defense. **a.** A defense that addresses the substance or essentials of a case rather than dilatory or technical objections. **b.** A defense that appears likely to succeed or has already succeeded.

peremptory defense. A defense that questions the plaintiff's legal right to sue or claims that such a right has been extinguished.

pretermitted defense. A defense that is available to a party but that must be pleaded at the right time or it will be waived.

self-defense. See SELF-DEFENSE.

2. A defendant's method and strategy in opposing the plaintiff or the prosecution; a doctrine giving rise to such a method or strategy <the lawyer advised her client to adopt a passive defense and to avoid taking the stand>.

derivative defense. A defense that rebuts the criminal elements that a prosecutor must establish in order to justify submission of a criminal case to a jury.

dwelling defense. CASTLE DOCTRINE.

empty-chair defense. See EMPTY-CHAIR DEFENSE.

3. One or more defendants in a trial <the defense rests>. **4.** In commercial law, a basis for avoiding liability on a negotiable instrument <the drawer asserted a real defense against the holder in due course>.

personal defense. A defense that can be asserted against only those transferees of an instrument who are not holders in due course; examples include mistake, unconscionability, failure of consideration, and impossibility of performance. —Also termed *limited defense.*

real defense. A defense that is good against every possible claimant, including a holder in due course; ex-

amples include fraud, forgery, incapacity, and suretyship. —Also termed *absolute defense*; *universal defense.*

defense contingent fee. See *reverse contingent fee* under CONTINGENT FEE.

defense of habitation. CASTLE DOCTRINE.

defense of others. A justification defense available if one harms or threatens another when defending a third person. See JUSTIFICATION (2).

defense of property. A justification defense available if one harms or threatens another when defending one's property. See JUSTIFICATION (2).

defensive collateral estoppel. See COLLATERAL ESTOPPEL.

deferment, *n.* The act of delaying; postponement <deferment of a judicial decision>. —**defer,** *vb.*—**deferred,** *adj.*

deferred annuity. See ANNUITY.

deferred compensation. See COMPENSATION.

deferred income. See INCOME.

deferred-payment annuity. See *deferred annuity* under ANNUITY.

deferred stock. See STOCK.

deficiency, *n.* **1.** Generally, a lack, shortage, or insufficiency. **2.** A shortfall in paying taxes; the amount by which the tax properly due exceeds the sum of the amount of tax shown on a taxpayer's return plus amounts previously assessed or collected as a deficiency, minus any credits, refunds, or other payments due the taxpayer. **3.** The amount still owed on a secured debt (such as a mortgage) after the sale of the security fails to yield sufficient proceeds to cover the debt's full amount.

deficiency assessment. See ASSESSMENT.

deficiency decree. See *deficiency judgment* under JUDGMENT.

deficiency dividend. See DIVIDEND.

deficiency judgment. See JUDGMENT.

deficiency letter. An SEC letter to a registrant of a securities offering, detailing the ways in which the registration statement fails to meet SEC requirements. —Also termed *letter of comment*; *letter of comments*.

deficiency notice. NINETY-DAY LETTER.

deficit. **1.** A deficiency or disadvantage; a deficiency in the amount or quality of something.

trade deficit. In economics, the excess of merchandise imports over merchandise exports during a specific period. —Also termed *trade gap*.

2. An excess of expenditures or liabilities over revenues or assets.

definite sentence. See *determinate sentence* under SENTENCE.

deflation, *n.* A decline in the price of goods and services. —**deflate,** *vb.*—**deflationary,** *adj.* Cf. INFLATION.

deforce, *vb.* **1.** To keep (lands) from the true owner by means of force. **2.** To oust another from possession by means of force. **3.** To detain (a creditor's money) unjustly and forcibly. —**deforcement,** *n.*—**deforciant,** *n.*

defraud, *vb.* To cause injury or loss to (a person) by deceit. —**defraudation,** *n.* See FRAUD.

degree. **1.** Generally, a classification or specification <degrees of proof>. **2.** An incremental measure of guilt or negligence; a grade based on the seriousness of an offense <murder in the first degree>. **3.** A step in lineal descent <a cousin of distant degree>. See CONSANGUINITY.

equal degree. A relationship between two or more relatives who are the same number of steps away from a common ancestor.

4. A title conferred on graduates of a school, college, or university <she began studying for the bar exam only one day after receiving her law degree>.

dehors (di-**hor**). [Law French] *Jargon.* Outside of; beyond the scope of <the court cannot consider the document because it is dehors the record>.

de jure (də-**juur**-ee *or* day-**juur**-ay). Existing by right or according to law <de jure segregation during the pre-*Brown* era>. Cf. DE FACTO; DE GRATIA.

de jure corporation. See CORPORATION.

de jure segregation. See SEGREGATION.

del credere (del-**krayd**-ə-ray), *adj.* [Italian] Of belief or trust.

del credere **agent.** See AGENT.

delectus personae (də-**lek**-təs-pər-**soh**-nI *or* -nee). [Latin "choice of the person"] A partner's right to accept or reject candidates proposed as new partners.

delegable duty. See DUTY.

delegate (**del**-i-gət), *n.* One who represents or acts for another or a group of others.

delegatee (del-i-gə-**tee**). An agent or representative to whom a matter is delegated.

delegation, *n.* **1.** The act of entrusting another with authority or empowering another to act as an agent or representative <delegation of contractual duties>. **2.** A group of representatives <a large delegation from Texas>. —**delegate** (**del**-i-gayt) (corresponding to sense 1), *vb.*—**delegable** (corresponding to sense 1), *adj.*

delegation doctrine. In constitutional law, the principle (based on the separation-of-powers concept) limiting Congress's ability to transfer its legislative power to other governmental branches, esp. the executive branch; delegation is permitted only if Congress prescribes an intelligible principle to guide an executive agency in making policy. —Also termed *nondelegation doctrine.* See *legislative veto* under VETO.

deliberate (di-**lib**-[ə]rət), *adj.* **1.** Intentional; premeditated; fully considered. **2.** Unimpulsive; slow in deciding.

deliberate elicitation. In criminal procedure, the purposeful yet covert drawing forth of an incriminating response (usu. not during a formal interrogation) from a suspect whose Sixth Amendment right to counsel has attached (but who has not waived the right to counsel), as by engaging an arrested suspect in conversation on the way to the police station; deliberate elicitation violates the Sixth Amendment. *Massiah v. United States,* 377 U.S. 201 (1964).

deliberate speed, with all. As quickly as the maintenance of law and order and the welfare of the people will allow, esp. with respect to the desegregation of public schools. *Brown v. Board of Educ.,* 347 U.S. 483 (1954).

deliberation, *n.* The act of carefully considering issues and options before making a decision or taking some action; esp., the process by which a jury reaches a verdict, as by analyzing, discussing, and weighing the evidence. —**deliberate** (di-**lib**-ə-rayt), *vb.*

delict (**dee**-likt *or* di-**likt**), *n.* A violation of the law; a tort. —Also termed *delictum.* —**delictual** (di-**lik**-chə-wəl), *adj.*

delinquency, *n.* **1.** A failure or omission; a violation of a law or duty. See JUVENILE DELINQUENCY. **2.** A debt that is overdue in payment. —**delinquent,** *adj.*—**delinquent** (corresponding to sense 1), *n.*

delisting, *n.* The suspension of the privileges of having a security listed on an exchange for failure to meet the requirements of the listing, such as a temporary suspension for failing to file correct forms. —**delist,** *vb.*

deliverance. 1. A jury's verdict. **2.** A judicial opinion or judgment. **3.** *Archaic.* An ecclesiastical court's order directing that a person in custody be released. —Also termed *writ of deliverance.* **4.** *Archaic.* In a replevin action, a writ ordering the redelivery to the owner of goods. —Also termed *writ of second deliverance.* **5.** Such a release (as in sense 3) or redelivery (as in sense 4).

delivery, *n.* The formal act of transferring or conveying something, such as a deed; the thing so transferred or conveyed. —**deliver,** *vb.* Cf. LIVERY.

absolute delivery. A delivery that is complete upon the actual transfer of the instrument from the grantor's possession; such a delivery usu. does not depend on recordation.

actual delivery. The act of giving real and immediate possession to the buyer or the buyer's agent.

conditional delivery. A delivery that passes the thing subject to delivery from the grantor's possession and upon the happening of a specified event.

constructive delivery. An act that amounts to a transfer of title by operation of law when the actual transfer is impractical or impossible; for example, the delivery of a deposit-box key by someone who is ill and immobile amounts to a constructive delivery of the box's contents even though the box may be miles away.

symbolic delivery. The constructive delivery of the subject matter of a sale by the actual delivery of an article that represents the item, that renders access to it possible, or that is the evidence of the purchaser's title to it, such as the key to a warehouse or a bill of lading for goods on shipboard.

delivery bond. See BOND (2).

delivery in escrow. The physical transfer of something to an escrow agent to be held until some condition is met, at which time the agent will release it; an example of such a delivery is a stock buyer's transfer of cash to a bank that will give the seller the cash upon receiving the stock certificates. See ESCROW.

delivery of deed. The placing of a deed in the grantee's hands or within the grantee's control; by this act, the grantor shows an intention that the deed operates immediately as a conveyance.

demand, *n.* **1.** The assertion of a legal right. **2.** A request for payment of a debt or an amount due. **3.** In economics, the intensity of buyer pressure on the availability and cost of a commodity or service.

demand, *vb.* **1.** To claim as one's due; to require; to seek relief. **2.** To summon; to call in court.

demandant. *Archaic.* The plaintiff in a real action (the defendant being called a *tenant*). See *real action* under ACTION.

demand clause. A provision in a note allowing the holder to compel full payment if the maker fails to meet an installment.

demand deposit. See DEPOSIT.

demand draft. See *sight draft* under DRAFT.

demand for relief. PRAYER FOR RELIEF.

demand instrument. An instrument payable on demand, at sight, or on presentation, as opposed to an instrument that is payable at a set future date. —Also termed *demand note.*

demand letter. A letter by which one party explains its legal position in a dispute and requests that the recipient take some action, such as paying money owed, or else risk being sued; under some statutes (esp. consumer-protection laws), a demand letter is a prerequisite for filing a lawsuit.

demand loan. See *call loan* under LOAN.

demand note. See NOTE.

démarche (day-**mahrsh**). [French "gait; walk"] An oral or written diplomatic statement, esp. one containing a demand, offer, protest, threat, or the like. —Also spelled *demarche*.

demeanor. A person's outward bearing or behavior, such as facial expressions, tone of voice, gestures, the hesitation or readiness with which answers are given, and general aura.

demeanor evidence. A witness's behavior on the witness stand as it may affect the fact-finder's weighing of credibility issues.

demesne (di-**meen** *or* di-**mayn**), *n.* [French] **1.** At common law, land held in one's own right, and not through a superior. **2.** Domain; realm. —**demesnial**, *adj.*

de minimis (də-**min**-ə-məs), *adj.* [Latin "of the least"] **1.** Trifling; minimal. **2.** (Of a fact or thing) so insignificant that a court may overlook it in deciding an issue or case. **3.** DE MINIMIS NON CURAT LEX.

de minimis non curat lex (də-**min**-ə-məs-non-**kyoor**-at-**leks**). [Latin] The law does not concern itself with trifles. —Often shortened to *de minimis*.

demise, *n.* **1.** The conveyance of an estate by will or lease; the instrument by which such a conveyance is accomplished <the demise of the land for one year>. **2.** The passing of property by descent or bequest <a testator's demise of $100,000 to charity>. **3.** The death of a person or (figuratively) of a thing <the corporation's untimely demise>. —**demise,** *vb.*

democracy, *n.* Government by the people, either directly or indirectly through representatives. —**democratic,** *adj.* Cf. REPUBLIC.

demonstrative bequest. See BEQUEST.

demonstrative evidence. See EVIDENCE.

demonstrative legacy. See LEGACY.

demur (də-**mər**), *vb.* To file a demurrer; to object to the legal sufficiency of a claim alleged in a pleading without denying the truth of the facts stated. —**demurrant,** *n.* See DEMURRER.

demurrage (də-**mər**-əj). (*usu. pl.*) In maritime law, a liquidated penalty owed by a charterer to a shipowner for the charterer's failure to load or unload cargo by a certain time.

demurrer (də-**mər**-ər). A pleading stating that although the facts alleged in a complaint may be true, they are insufficient for the plaintiff to state a claim for relief and for the defendant to frame an answer; in most jurisdictions, such a pleading is now termed a *motion to dismiss*, but the demurrer is still used in a few states, including California, Nebraska, and Pennsylvania. Cf. DENIAL (1).

general demurrer. An objection pointing out a substantive defect in an opponent's pleading, such as the insufficiency of the claim or the court's lack of subject-matter jurisdiction. —Also termed *general exception.*

speaking demurrer. A demurrer that cannot be sustained because it introduces new facts not contained in the original complaint.

special demurrer. An objection that questions the form of the pleading and states specifically the nature of the objection, such as a violation of the rules of pleading or practice.

demurrer to evidence. A party's objection or exception that the evidence is legally insufficient to make a case.

demutualization, *n.* The process of converting a mutual insurance company (which is owned by its policyholders) to a stock insurance company (which is owned by outside shareholders), usu. as a means of increasing the insurer's capital by allowing the insurer to issue shares; about half the states have demutualization statutes authorizing such a conversion. —**demutualize,** *vb.*

denationalization, *n.* **1.** The act of depriving a person of national rights or status. **2.** The act of returning government ownership and control of an industry or function to private ownership and control. —**denationalize,** *vb.*

denial, *n.* **1.** A defendant's response controverting the facts that a plain-

tiff has alleged in a complaint; a repudiation <the worker's denial that physical contact occurred>. Cf. DEMURRER.

conjunctive denial. A response that controverts all the material facts alleged in a complaint.

disjunctive denial. A response that controverts the truthfulness of two or more allegations of a complaint in the alternative.

general denial. A response that puts in issue all the material assertions of a complaint or petition.

specific denial. A separate response applicable to one or more particular allegations in a complaint.

2. A refusal or rejection <denial of an employment application>. **3.** A deprivation or withholding <denial of due process>. —**deny,** *vb.*

denizen (**den**-ə-zən). **1.** In American law, a person given certain rights in a foreign nation or living habitually in a foreign nation. **2.** In English law, a person who holds a position midway between being an alien and a natural-born or naturalized subject.

denotative fact. See FACT.

denounce, *vb.* **1.** To condemn openly, esp. publicly. **2.** To declare (an act or thing) to be a crime and prescribe a punishment for it. **3.** To accuse or inform against. **4.** To give formal notice to a foreign country of the termination of (a treaty). —**denunciation,** *n.* —**denunciatory, denunciative,** *adj.*

de novo (di-**noh**-voh *or* dee-), *adj.* Anew.

hearing de novo. See HEARING DE NOVO.

trial de novo. See TRIAL DE NOVO.

venire facias de novo. See VENIRE FA-
CIAS.

density zoning. See *cluster zoning*
under ZONING.

deodand (dee-ə-dand). An old English practice of forfeiting to the
Crown the thing (such as an animal)
that has done wrong.

departure, *n.* **1.** A deviation or di-
vergence from a standard rule, regulation, measurement, or course of
conduct. **2.** A variance between a
pleading and a subsequent pleading
or proof. —**depart,** *vb.*

dépeçage (dep-ə-**sahzh**). [French] A
court's application of different state
laws to different issues in a legal
dispute; choice of law on an issue-by-
issue basis.

dependency. 1. A land or territory
geographically distinct from the
country governing it, but belonging
to it and governed by its laws; the
Philippines was formerly a dependency of the U.S. Cf. COMMONWEALTH;
TERRITORY. **2.** A relationship between two persons or things whereby
one is sustained by the other or relies
on the other for support or necessities.

dependency exemption. See EX-
EMPTION.

dependent, *n.* **1.** One who relies on
another for support; one not able to
exist or sustain oneself without the
power or aid of someone else. **2.** In
tax law, a relative, such as a child or
parent, for which a taxpayer may
claim an exemption if the taxpayer
provides more than half of the per-

son's support during the taxable
year. —**dependent,** *adj.*

dependent relative revocation.
The doctrine that regards as mutually dependent the acts of destroying a
will and substituting a new one when
both acts are the result of one plan,
so that, if a testator fails to complete
the substitution, it is presumed that
the testator would have preferred the
old will to take effect; this doctrine
is a specific application of the rule
that the testator's intent governs.

depletion, *n.* An emptying, exhaust-
ing, or wasting of an asset, esp. of a
finite natural resource such as oil. —
deplete, *vb.*—**depletive,** *adj.*

depletion allowance. See ALLOW-
ANCE (2).

deponent, *n.* **1.** One who testifies by
deposition. **2.** A witness who gives
written testimony for later use in
court; AFFIANT. —**depone,** *vb.*

deportation, *n.* The act or an instance of removing a person to another country; esp., the expulsion or
transfer of an alien from a country. —**deport,** *vb.*

depose, *vb.* **1.** To examine (a witness) in a deposition <the defendant's attorney will depose the plaintiff on Tuesday>. **2.** To testify; to
bear witness <the affiant deposes
and states that he is at least 18 years
old>. **3.** To deprive (a sovereign) of
authority <the rebels sought to depose the dictator>.

deposit, *n.* **1.** The act of giving money or other property to another who
promises to preserve it or to use it
and return it in kind; esp., the act of
placing money in a bank for safety

and convenience. **2.** The money or property so given.

demand deposit. A bank deposit that the depositor may withdraw at any time without prior notice to the bank.

time deposit. A bank deposit that is to remain for a specified period or on which notice must be given to the bank before withdrawal.

3. Money placed with a person as earnest money or security for the performance of a contract; the money will be forfeited if the depositor fails to perform. **4.** In copyright law, the placing of two copies of a published work with the Library of Congress within three months of publication; this requirement is independent of copyright registration. —**deposit,** *vb.*—**depositor,** *n.*

depositary. A person or institution that one leaves money or valuables with for safekeeping <a title-insurance officer is the depositary of the funds>. Cf. DEPOSITORY.

deposit box. SAFE-DEPOSIT BOX.

deposit in court. The placing of money or other property that represents a person's potential liability in the court's temporary custody, pending the outcome of a lawsuit. —Also termed *deposit into the registry of the court.*

deposit insurance. See INSURANCE.

deposition (de-pə-zi-shən). **1.** A witness's out-of-court testimony that is reduced to writing (usu. by a court reporter) for later use in court or for discovery purposes. **2.** The session at which such testimony is recorded.

deposition de bene esse (day-ben-ee-es-ee *or* də-ben-ay-**es**-ə). A deposition taken from a witness who will likely be unable to attend a scheduled trial or hearing.

deposition on written questions. A deposition given in response to a prepared set of written questions, as opposed to a typical oral deposition.

oral deposition. A deposition given in response to oral questioning by a lawyer.

depository. A place where one leaves money or valuables for safekeeping <the grade school's depository for used books>. Cf. DEPOSITARY.

depository-transfer check. See CHECK.

Depository Trust Corporation. The principal central clearing agency for securities transactions on the public markets. —Abbr. DTC.

depreciation, *n.* A decline in an asset's value due to use, wear, or obsolescence. —**depreciate,** *vb.*—**depreciable,** *adj.* Cf. APPRECIATION; AMORTIZATION (2).

depreciation method. A set formula used in estimating an asset's use, wear, or obsolescence over the asset's useful life; this method is useful in calculating the allowable annual tax deduction for depreciation. See USEFUL LIFE.

accelerated-depreciation method. A depreciation method that yields larger deductions in the earlier years of an asset's life and smaller deductions in the later years.

declining-balance depreciation method. A method of computing the annual depreciation allowance by multiplying the asset's undepreciated cost each year by a uniform rate that may not exceed double the straight-line rate or 150 percent.

double-declining depreciation method. A depreciation method that spreads over time the initial cost of a capital asset by deducting in each period twice the percentage recognized by the straight-line method and applying that double percentage to the undepreciated balance existing at the start of each period.

replacement-cost depreciation method. A depreciation method that fixes an asset's value by the price of its substitute.

sinking-fund depreciation method. A depreciation method that accounts for the time value of money by setting up a depreciation-reserve account that earns interest, resulting in a gradual yearly increase in the depreciation deduction.

straight-line depreciation method. A depreciation method that writes off the cost or other basis of the asset by deducting the expected salvage value from the initial cost of the capital asset, and dividing the difference by the asset's estimated useful life.

sum-of-the-years'-digits depreciation method. A method of calculating the annual depreciation allowance by multiplying the depreciable cost basis (cost minus salvage value) by a constantly decreasing fraction, which is represented by the remaining years of useful life at the beginning of each year divided by the total number of years of useful life at the time of acquisition.

unit depreciation method. A depreciation method—directly related to the productivity of the asset—that divides the asset's value by the estimated total number of units to be produced, and then multiplies the unit cost by the number of units sold during the year, representing the depreciation expense for the year.

units-of-output depreciation method. A method by which the cost of a depreciable asset, minus salvage value, is allocated to the accounting periods benefited based on output (as miles, hours, number of times used, and the like).

depression. A period of economic stress that persists over an extended period of time, accompanied by poor business conditions and high unemployment. Cf. RECESSION.

deputy, *n.* A person appointed or delegated to act as a substitute for another, esp. for an official. —**deputize,** *vb.*

deregistration, *n.* The point at which an issuer's registration under § 12 of the Securities Exchange Act of 1934 is no longer required due to the decline in the number of holders of the issuer's securities. 15 U.S.C. § 78*l*. —**deregister,** *vb.* Cf. DELISTING.

deregulation, *n.* The reduction of governmental control of business, esp. to permit free markets and competition. —**deregulate,** *vb.*

derelict, *adj.* **1.** Forsaken; abandoned; cast away <derelict property>. **2.** Lacking a sense of duty; in breach of legal or moral obligations <the managers were unquestionably derelict in their duties>.

derelict, *n.* **1.** Personal property abandoned or thrown away by the owner with an intent to no longer claim it, such as a boat deserted or abandoned on the sea by a master or crew. **2.** Land uncovered by receding water from its former bed. **3.** A street person or vagrant; a hobo.

dereliction, *n.* **1.** Abandonment, esp. through neglect or moral wrong. **2.** An increase of land caused by a sea, river, or stream shrinking from its usual water mark. See RELICTION.

derivative, *n.* A volatile financial instrument whose value depends on or is derived from the performance of a secondary source such as an underlying bond, currency, or commodity.

derivative action. 1. A suit by a beneficiary of a fiduciary to enforce a right belonging to the fiduciary; esp., a suit asserted by a shareholder on the corporation's behalf against a third party (usu. a corporate officer) because of the corporation's failure to take some action against the third party. —Also termed *derivative suit*; *shareholder derivative suit*; *stockholder derivative suit*; *representative action*. Cf. DIRECT ACTION (3). **2.** A lawsuit based on injury to another, such as an action for loss of consortium by a husband against a third person for injuries to his wife.

derivative contraband. See CONTRABAND.

derivative defense. See DEFENSE (2).

derivative evidence. See EVIDENCE.

derivative-jurisdiction doctrine. The principle that a case is not properly removable unless it is within the subject-matter jurisdiction of the state court from which it is removed.

derivative liability. See LIABILITY.

derivative suit. DERIVATIVE ACTION.

derivative-use immunity. See *use immunity* under IMMUNITY (3).

derivative work. In copyright law, something produced that is based on a preexisting product, such as a translation, musical arrangement, fictionalization, motion-picture version, abridgment, or any other recast or adapted form, and that only the holder of the copyright on the original form can produce or give permission to another to produce.

derogation (der-ə-**gay**-shən), *n.* **1.** The partial repeal or abrogation of a law by a subsequent act that limits its scope or impairs its utility and force <statutes in derogation of the common law>. **2.** Disparagement; depreciation in value or estimation <some argue that the derogation of family values has caused an increase in crime>. **3.** Detraction, prejudice, or destruction (of a grant or right) <an attorney may be punished for derogation from professional integrity>. —**derogate** (**der**-ə-gayt), *vb.*

descendant. One who follows in lineage, such as a child or grandchild— but not a collateral relative. Cf. ASCENDANT.

descent, *n.* **1.** The acquisition of real property by act of law, as by inheritance; the passing of intestate real property to heirs. Cf. DISTRIBUTION; PURCHASE (2). **2.** The fact or process of originating from a common ancestor. —**descend,** *vb.*

desegregation, *n.* **1.** The abrogation of policies that separate and place races into different institutions and facilities (as public schools). **2.** The state of having had such policies abrogated. —**desegregate,** *vb.* Cf. INTEGRATION (3).

desertion, *n.* The willful and unjustified abandonment of one's duties or obligations, esp. to military service or to one's spouse or family. —**desert,** *vb.*

constructive desertion. One spouse's misconduct that forces the other spouse to leave the marital abode.

criminal desertion. A husband's or wife's willful failure without just cause to provide for the care, protection, or support of a spouse who is in ill health or needy circumstances.

deserts. JUST DESERTS.

design, *n.* **1.** A plan or scheme. **2.** In evidence, purpose or intention combined with a plan. **3.** The pattern or configuration of elements in something, such as a work of art. **4.** In patent law, the drawing or the depiction of an original plan for a novel pattern, model, shape, or configuration that is chiefly decorative or ornamental. —**design,** *vb.*

design defect. See DEFECT.

designedly, *adv.* Willfully; intentionally.

design patent. See PATENT (2).

design review. A process by which a building permit is not issued until the proposed building meets the architectural standards established by land-use regulations. —Also termed *architectural review.*

desist. To stop or leave off. See CEASE-AND-DESIST ORDER.

de son tort (də-son-**tort** *or* -sohn-**tor[t]**). [Law French "by his own wrongdoing"] Wrongful.

executor de son tort. See EXECUTOR.

trustee de son tort. See TRUSTEE.

despoil (di-**spoil**), *vb.* To deprive (a person) of possessions illegally by violence or by clandestine means; to rob. —**despoliation,** *n.*—**despoilment,** *n.*

despot (**des**-pət), *n.* **1.** A ruler with absolute power and authority. **2.** A tyrant. —**despotism** (**des**-pə-tiz-əm), *n.*—**despotic** (di-**spot**-ik), *adj.*

destination contract. See CONTRACT.

destitute, *adj.* Not possessing the necessaries of life; lacking possessions and resources; indigent.

destructibility, *n.* The capability of being destroyed by some action, turn of events, or operation of law. —**destructible,** *adj.*

destructibility of contingent remainders. In property law, the doctrine requiring a future interest to become vested by the time it is to become possessory or else suffer total destruction (the interest then reverting to the grantor).

desuetude (**des**-wə-t[y]ood). **1.** Lack of use; obsolescence through disuse. **2.** The doctrine holding that if a statute or treaty is left unenforced long enough, the courts will no longer regard it as having any legal effect even though it has not been repealed.

detainer. 1. The action of detaining, withholding, or keeping something in one's custody.

forcible detainer. See FORCIBLE DETAINER.

unlawful detainer. The unjustifiable retention of the possession of real property by one whose original entry was lawful, such as a tenant holding over after the termination of the lease despite the landlord's demand for possession.

2. The confinement of a person in custody. **3.** A writ authorizing prison officials to continue holding a prisoner in custody.

détente (day-**tont**). [French] **1.** The relaxation of tensions between two or more parties, esp. nations. **2.** A policy promoting such a relaxation of tensions. **3.** A period during which such tensions are relaxed. Cf. ENTENTE; ALLIANCE.

detention, *n.* The act or fact of holding a person in custody; confinement or compulsory delay. —**detain,** *vb.*

investigative detention. The holding of a suspect without formal arrest during the investigation of the suspect's participation in a crime; detention of this kind is constitutional only if probable cause exists.

pretrial detention. The holding of a defendant before trial on criminal charges either because the established bail could not be posted or because release was denied.

preventive detention. Confinement imposed generally on a criminal defendant who has threatened to escape or has otherwise violated the law while awaiting trial, or on a mentally ill person who may cause harm.

detention hearing. A judicial proceeding to determine the propriety of detaining a person, esp. a juvenile.

determinable, *adj.* **1.** Liable to end upon the happening of a certain contingency; terminable <fee simple determinable>. **2.** Able to be determined or ascertained <the delivery date is determinable because she kept the written invoice>.

determinable fee. See *fee simple determinable* under FEE SIMPLE.

determinate sentence. See SENTENCE.

determination, *n.* **1.** A final decision by a court or administrative agency <the court's determination of the issue>. **2.** The ending or expiration of an estate or interest in property, or of a right, power, or authority <the easement's determination after four years>. —**determine,** *vb.*

determination letter. A document issued by the Internal Revenue Service, in response to a taxpayer's request, giving an opinion about the tax significance of a transaction, such as whether a nonprofit corporation is entitled to tax-exempt status.

deterrence, *n.* The act or process of discouraging certain behavior, particularly by fear; esp., as a goal of criminal law, the prevention of criminal behavior by fear of punishment. —**deter,** *vb.*—**deterrent,** *adj.*

& *n*. Cf. REHABILITATION; RETRIBU-TION (1).

general deterrence. A goal of criminal law generally, or of a specific conviction and sentence, to discourage people from committing crimes in the future.

special deterrence. A goal of a specific conviction and sentence to dissuade the offender from committing crimes in the future.

detinue (det-ən-[y]oo). A common-law action to recover personal property wrongfully taken by another. Cf. REPLEVIN; TROVER.

detour, *n*. In tort law, an employee's minor deviation from the employer's business for personal reasons; a detour falls within the scope of employment, and thus the employer is still vicariously liable for the employee's actions. Cf. FROLIC.

detriment. 1. Any loss or harm suffered by person or property. **2.** In contract law, the relinquishment of some legal right that a promisee would have otherwise been entitled to exercise.

detrimental reliance. See RELIANCE.

devaluation, *n*. The reduction in the value of one currency in relation to another currency. —**devalue,** *vb*. Cf. REVALUATION.

devastavit (dev-ə-**stay**-vət). [Latin "he (or she) has wasted"] A personal representative's failure to administer a decedent's estate promptly and properly, esp. by spending extravagantly or misapplying assets; a personal representative who commits waste in this way becomes personally liable to those having claims on the assets, such as creditors and beneficiaries.

deviance, *n*. The quality or state of departing from established norms, esp. in social customs. —**deviate** (**dee**-vee-ayt), *vb*.—**deviant,** *adj*.—**deviate** (**dee**-vee-ət), *n*.

device. 1. An invention or contrivance; any result of design. **2.** A scheme to trick or deceive; a stratagem or artifice, as in the law relating to fraud or cheating.

devisavit vel non (dev-ə-**zay**-vət-vel-non *or* -**say**-). [Latin "he (or she) devises or not"] *Archaic*. In former practice, an issue sent from an equity or probate court to a court of law to determine the validity of a purported will. See VEL NON.

devise, *n*. **1.** The act of giving property (usu. real property) by will; the provision in a will containing such a gift. **2.** Property (usu. real property) disposed of in a will. **3.** A will disposing of real property. Cf. TESTAMENT (1). —**devise,** *vb*. Cf. BEQUEST; LEGACY.

conditional devise. A devise that depends on some uncertain event occurring, by which it is either to take effect or be defeated.

executory devise. An interest in land—created by a will—that takes effect in the future and that depends on a future contingency.

general devise. A devise that passes the testator's lands without particular enumeration or description of them.

lapsed devise. A devise that fails because of the death of the named recipient before the devisor.

residuary devise. A devise of the remainder of the testator's real property left after the other devises are taken.

specific devise. A devise that passes a particular piece of property.

devisee. A recipient of property (usu. real property) by will.

deviser. One who invents or contrives <the deviser of these patents>.

devisor. One who disposes of property (usu. real property) in a will.

devolution, *n.* The act or an instance of transferring one's rights, duties, or powers to another; the passing of such rights, duties, or powers by transmission or succession <the federal government's devolution of police power to the states>. —**devolve,** *vb.*—**devolutionary,** *adj.*

dictum (dik-təm**).** **1.** A statement of opinion or belief held to be authoritative because of the dignity of the person making it. **2.** A familiar rule; a maxim. **3.** OBITER DICTUM. Pl. **dicta.**

gratis dictum. A statement made by a party, but not obligatorily; a voluntary assertion.

judicial dictum. An opinion by a court on a question that is directly involved, briefed, and argued by counsel, and even passed on by the court, but that is not essential to the decision. Cf. OBITER DICTUM.

simplex dictum. An unproved or dogmatic statement; IPSE DIXIT.

dictum page. See *pinpoint citation* under CITATION.

differential pricing. The setting of the price of the same product or service differently for different customers. See PRICE DISCRIMINATION.

digest, *n.* **1.** An index of reported cases arranged by subject and subdivided by jurisdiction and court, providing brief statements of the facts and the court holdings; the American Digest System, for example, covers the decisions of all American courts of last resort, state and federal, from 1658 to present. **2.** In civil law, a compilation and systematic discussion of the various areas of law; chiefly, the Pandects of Justinian in 50 books. See PANDECT.

dilatory, *adj.* Tending to cause delay <the judge's opinion criticized the lawyer's persistent dilatory tactics>.

dilatory plea. See PLEA.

diligence. See DUE DILIGENCE.

dilution. 1. The act or an instance of diminishing a thing's strength or lessening its value. **2.** In corporate law, the reduction in the monetary value or voting power of stock by increasing the total number of outstanding shares. **3.** In constitutional law, the limitation of the effectiveness of a particular group's vote by legislative reapportionment or political gerrymandering; this type of dilution violates the Equal Protection Clause. —Also termed *vote dilution.* **4.** In trademark law, the use of a trademark by a party who is prohibited from using it—even when there is no competition or likelihood of confusion—because of the concern that the use will impair the trademark's effectiveness by blurring its distinctive character or tarnishing it through unsavory association.

diminished capacity. See CAPACITY (3).

diminished responsibility. See *diminished capacity* under CAPACITY (3).

diminution (dim-ə-n[y]oo-shən), *n.* **1.** The act or process of decreasing, lessening, or taking away. **2.** *Archaic.* The lack of a complete or certified court record sent from a lower court to a superior court. —**diminish** (corresponding to sense 1), *vb.*

diminution-in-value method. A way of calculating damages for breach of contract based on the reduced value in the market price caused by the breach.

DIP. *abbr.* DEBTOR-IN-POSSESSION.

diplomacy, *n.* The art and practice of conducting negotiations between foreign governments to attain mutually satisfactory political relations. —**diplomatic,** *adj.*—**diplomat,** *n.*

diplomatic immunity. See IMMUNITY (1).

direct, *n.* DIRECT EXAMINATION.

direct action. 1. A lawsuit by an insured against his or her own insurance company rather than against the tortfeasor and the tortfeasor's insurer. **2.** A lawsuit by a person claiming against an insured but suing the insurer directly instead of pursuing compensation indirectly through the insured. **3.** A lawsuit to enforce a shareholder's own rights against a corporation. Cf. DERIVATIVE ACTION.

direct attack. A straightforward challenge, for sufficient cause, to annul, reverse, vacate, correct, void, or enjoin a judgment or decree, such as by an appeal, writ of error, bill of review, or injunction. Cf. COLLATERAL ATTACK.

direct cause. See *proximate cause* under CAUSE (1).

direct charge-off accounting method. See ACCOUNTING METHOD.

direct contempt. See CONTEMPT.

direct cost. See COST.

direct damages. See *general damages* under DAMAGES.

directed verdict. See VERDICT.

direct estoppel. COLLATERAL ESTOPPEL.

direct evidence. See EVIDENCE.

direct examination. The first questioning of a witness in a trial or other proceeding, conducted by the party who called the witness to testify. — Often shortened to *direct.* —Also termed *examination-in-chief.* Cf. CROSS-EXAMINATION; REDIRECT EXAMINATION.

direct infringement. See *patent infringement* under INFRINGEMENT.

direct line. See LINE.

direct loss. See LOSS.

director. 1. One who manages, guides, or orders; a chief administrator. **2.** A person appointed or elected to sit on a board that manages the affairs of a corporation or company by electing and exercising control over its officers. See BOARD OF DIRECTORS. Cf. OFFICER.

dummy director. A board member who is a mere figurehead and exercises no real control over the corporation's business.

inside director. A director who is also an employee, officer, or major shareholder of the corporation.

interlocking director. A director who simultaneously serves on the boards of two or more corporations that deal with each other or have allied interests.

outside director. A nonemployee director with little or no direct interest in the corporation. —Also termed *affiliated director*.

provisional director. A director appointed by a court to serve on a close corporation's deadlocked board of directors.

direct order of alienation. In real-property law, the principle that a grantee who assumes the debt on a portion of mortgaged property is required to pay the mortgage debt if the original mortgagor defaults.

directors' and officers' liability insurance. See INSURANCE.

directory requirement. A minor statutory or contractual instruction that is desirable but not absolutely necessary, as opposed to a mandatory requirement; such an instruction is frequently introduced by the word *should* or, less frequently, *shall*.

directory statute. See STATUTE.

directory trust. See *fixed trust* under TRUST.

direct placement. 1. The offering by a company, such as an industrial or utility company, of an entire issue of securities directly to a lender, such as an insurance company or group of investors, instead of involving an underwriter; such an offering is exempt from SEC filing. **2.** PRIVATE PLACEMENT (1).

direct-reduction mortgage. See MORTGAGE.

direct trust. See *express trust* under TRUST.

disability. 1. The lack of ability to perform some function <his disability entitled him to workers'-compensation benefits>.

partial disability. A worker's inability to perform duties that he or she accomplished before an accident, even though the worker can engage in some gainful activity on the job.

permanent disability. A disability that will indefinitely prevent a worker from performing duties accomplished before an accident.

physical disability. An incapacity caused by a physical defect or infirmity, or by bodily imperfection or mental weakness.

temporary disability. A disability that exists until an injured employee is as far restored as the nature of the injury will permit.

total disability. A worker's inability to substantially perform employment-related duties because of physical condition.

2. Incapacity in the eyes of the law <most of a minor's disabilities are removed when the minor turns 18>.

civil disability. The condition of a person who has had a legal right or privilege revoked as a result of a criminal conviction, as when a person's driver's license is revoked after a DWI conviction. Cf. CIVIL DEATH (2).

disability compensation. Payments from public or private funds to a person during a period of disability and incapacity from work, such as social-security or workers'-compensation benefits. —Also termed *disability benefits*.

disability insurance. See INSURANCE.

disablement, *n.* **1.** The action of incapacitating or immobilizing. **2.** The imposition of a legal disability. —**disable,** *vb.*

disabling restraints. Limits on the alienation of property, which are usu. void as being against public policy.

disabling statute. See STATUTE.

disaffirm, *vb.* To repudiate; to revoke consent once given; to disclaim the intention of being bound by an earlier transaction. —**disaffirmation,** *n.*

disaster area. A region officially declared to have suffered a catastrophic emergency, such as a flood or hurricane, and therefore eligible for governmental aid.

disaster loss. See LOSS.

disbarment, *n.* The action of expelling a lawyer from the bar or from the practice of law, usu. because of some disciplinary violation. —**disbar,** *vb.*

disbursement, *n.* The act of paying out money, commonly from a fund or in settlement of a debt or account payable <dividend disbursement>. —**disburse,** *vb.*

discharge, *vb.* **1.** To pay a debt or satisfy some other obligation <Thompson discharged all the debts>. **2.** To release (a debtor) from monetary obligations upon adjudication of bankruptcy <Thompson was discharged from those debts>. **3.** To dismiss (a case) <the court discharged several cases from its docket>. **4.** To cancel or vacate (a court order) <the TRO was then discharged>. **5.** To release (a prisoner) from confinement <the offender was conditionally discharged>. **6.** To relieve (a jury or juror) from further responsibilities in considering a case <the jury was discharged after two weeks of deliberation>. **7.** To fire (an employee) <the employer refused to explain why it discharged the whole department>. **8.** To dismiss a member of the armed services from military service <the sergeant was honorably discharged>. —**discharge,** *n.*

discharge in bankruptcy. The release of a debtor from any further personal liability for prebankruptcy debts; a bankruptcy court's decree releasing a debtor from that liability.

discharging bond. See BOND (2).

disciplinary proceeding. An action brought to reprimand, suspend, or disbar a lawyer for unprofessional, unethical, or illegal conduct.

disciplinary rule. (*usu. cap.*) A mandatory regulation stating the minimum level of professional conduct that a lawyer must sustain to avoid being subject to disciplinary action; these rules are found in the Model Code of Professional Responsibility. —Abbr. DR. Cf. ETHICAL CONSIDERATION.

discipline, *n.* **1.** Punishment intended to correct or instruct; esp., a sanction or penalty imposed on a lawyer after an official finding of misconduct. **2.** Control gained by enforcing compliance or order. **—discipline,** *vb.*—**disciplinary,** *adj.*

disclaimer, *n.* **1.** A renunciation of one's own legal right or claim. **2.** A repudiation of another's legal right or claim. **3.** A writing that contains such a renunciation or repudiation. **—disclaim,** *vb.*

disclaimer of warranty. An oral or written statement intended to limit a seller's liability for defects in the goods sold; in some circumstances, printed words must be specific and conspicuous to be effective.

patent disclaimer. A patent applicant's amendment of a specification in order to relinquish part of the claim to the invention; when part of the invention is not patentable, such a disclaimer can be filed to protect the rest of the patent. See SPECIFICATION (2).

qualified disclaimer. A person's refusal to accept an interest in property in order to avoid having to pay estate and gift taxes; to be effective under federal tax law, the refusal must be in writing and must be received no later than nine months from the time when the interest was created. I.R.C. § 2518.

disclosed principal. See PRINCIPAL (1).

disclosure, *n.* The act or process of making known something that was previously unknown; a revelation of facts <a lawyer's disclosure of a conflict of interest>. **—disclose,** *vb.*—

disclosural, *adj.* See DISCOVERY; INITIAL DISCLOSURE.

discontinuance, *n.* The termination of a lawsuit by the plaintiff; a voluntary dismissal or nonsuit. **—discontinue,** *vb.* See DISMISSAL; NONSUIT.

discount, *n.* **1.** A reduction from the full amount or value of something, esp. a price. **2.** A deduction of interest in advance when one lends money on a note, bill of exchange, or other commercial paper, resulting in its present value. See PRESENT VALUE. **3.** The amount by which a security's market value is below its face value. Cf. PREMIUM (3). **—discount,** *vb.*

discount bond. See BOND (1).

discounted cash flow. See CASH FLOW.

discount market. See MARKET.

discount rate. See INTEREST RATE.

discount share. See *discount stock* under STOCK.

discount stock. See STOCK.

discoverable, *adj.* Subject to pretrial discovery <the defendant's attorney argued that the defendant's income-tax returns were not discoverable during the liability phase of the trial>.

discovered-peril doctrine. LAST-CLEAR-CHANCE DOCTRINE.

discovery, *n.* **1.** The act or process of finding or learning something that was previously unknown <after making the discovery, the inventor immediately applied for a patent>. **2.** Compulsory disclosure by a party to an action, at another party's request, of facts or documents relevant to the action; the primary discovery devices are interrogatories, depositions, requests for admissions, and requests for production <the plaintiff filed a motion to compel discovery>. **3.** The facts or documents disclosed <the new associate spent all her time reviewing discovery>. —**discover,** *vb.*—**discoverable,** *adj.*

postjudgment discovery. Discovery conducted after judgment has been rendered, usu. either to determine the nature of the judgment debtor's assets or to obtain testimony for use in future proceedings. — Also termed *posttrial discovery.*

pretrial discovery. Discovery conducted to reveal facts and develop evidence before trial; modern procedural rules have broadened the scope of pretrial discovery to prevent the parties from surprising each other with new evidence at trial.

discovery abuse. 1. The misuse of the discovery process, esp. by requesting information that is unnecessary, excessive, overbroad, or beyond the scope of permissible disclosure. **2.** The failure to respond adequately to proper discovery requests. —Also termed *abuse of discovery.*

discovery policy. See *claims-made policy* under INSURANCE POLICY.

discovery rule. In civil procedure, the rule that a limitations period does not begin running until the plaintiff discovers (or reasonably should have discovered) the injury giving rise to the claim; the discovery rule usu. applies to injuries that are inherently difficult to detect, such as those resulting from medical malpractice. See STATUTE OF LIMITATIONS. Cf. OCCURRENCE RULE.

discredit, *vb.* To destroy or impair the credibility of (as a witness, a piece of evidence, or a theory); to lessen the degree of trust to be accorded to (a witness or document). — **discredit,** *n.*

discretion. 1. A public official's power or right to act in certain circumstances according to personal judgment and conscience.

judicial discretion. The exercise of judgment by a judge or court based on what is fair under the circumstances and guided by the rules and principles of law; a court's power to act or not act when a litigant cannot demand the act as a matter of right. —Also termed *legal discretion.*

prosecutorial discretion. The varying options available to a prosecutor when prosecuting a criminal case, such as whether to prosecute, which charges to file, whether to bargain a plea, and what sentence to recommend to the court.

2. In criminal law and tort law, the capacity to distinguish between right and wrong, sufficient to render one responsible for one's own actions. **3.** Wise conduct and management; cautious discernment; prudence.

discretion, abuse of. See ABUSE OF DISCRETION.

discretionary, *adj.* (Of an act or duty) involving an exercise of judgment and choice, not an implementation of a hard-and-fast rule; such an act by a court may be overturned only after a showing of abuse of discretion.

discretionary account. An account that allows a broker access to a customer's money to purchase and sell securities or commodities for the customer based on the broker's judgment and without first having to obtain the customer's consent to the purchase or sale.

discretionary order. See ORDER (4).

discretionary review. See REVIEW.

discretionary trust. See TRUST.

discrimination, *n.* **1.** The effect of a statute or established practice that confers privileges on a certain class or that denies privileges to another class because of race, age, sex, nationality, religion, or handicap. **2.** Differential treatment; esp., a failure to treat all persons equally when no reasonable distinction can be found between those favored and those not favored.

invidious discrimination. Discrimination that is offensive or objectionable, esp. because it involves prejudice or stereotyping.

reverse discrimination. Preferential treatment of minorities, usu. through affirmative-action programs, in a way that adversely affects members of a majority group. See AFFIRMATIVE ACTION.

3. The effect of state laws that favor local interests over out-of-state interests unless they are narrowly tailored to achieve an important state interest. —**discriminate,** *vb.*— **discriminatory,** *adj.*

discriminatee. A person unlawfully discriminated against.

discriminatory tariff. See TARIFF.

disenfranchise. DISFRANCHISE.

disenfranchisement.   DISFRAN-CHISEMENT.

disentailment   (dis-en-**tayl**-mənt), *n.* The act or process by which a tenant in tail bars the entail on an estate and converts it into a fee simple, thereby nullifying the rights of any later claimant to the fee tail. — **disentail,** *vb.*

disfranchise, *vb.* To deprive (a person) of the right to exercise a franchise or privilege, esp. to vote. —Also termed *disenfranchise.*

disfranchisement. 1. The act of depriving a member of a corporation of a right, as by expulsion. **2.** The act of taking away the right to vote in public elections from a citizen or class of citizens. —Also termed *disenfranchisement.*

disgorgement, *n.* The act of giving up something (such as profits illegally obtained) on demand or by legal compulsion. —**disgorge,** *vb.*

disguised dividend. See *informal dividend* under DIVIDEND.

disherison (dis-**her**-ə-zən) The act of disinheriting; the state of being disinherited. —Also termed *disinherison.* See DISINHERITANCE.

dishonor, *vb.* **1.** To refuse to accept or pay (a negotiable instrument) when properly presented. See NOTICE OF DISHONOR. **2.** To deface or defile (the flag). —**dishonor,** *n.*

disinheritance, *n.* **1.** The act by which an owner of an estate deprives a would-be heir of the expectancy to inherit the estate. **2.** The state of being disinherited. —**disinherit,** *vb.*

disinterested, *adj.* Free from bias, prejudice, or partiality; not having a pecuniary interest <a disinterested witness>. —**disinterest,** *n.*

disintermediation. The process of bank depositors' withdrawing their funds to put them into investments that pay higher returns when the free-market interest rates exceed the regulated interest ceiling for time deposits.

disinvestment, *n.* **1.** The consumption of capital. **2.** The withdrawal of investments, esp. on political grounds. —Also termed (in sense 2) *divestment.* —**disinvest,** *vb.*

disjoinder. The undoing of the joinder of parties or claims. See JOINDER. Cf. MISJOINDER; NONJOINDER.

disjunctive denial. See DENIAL.

dismissal, *n.* **1.** Termination of an action or claim without further hearing, and esp. without trial of the issues involved.

dismissal for want of prosecution. A court's dismissal of a lawsuit because the plaintiff has failed to pursue the case diligently toward completion. —Also termed *dismissal for failure to prosecute.*

dismissal without prejudice. A dismissal that does not bar the plaintiff from refiling the lawsuit within the applicable limitations period.

dismissal with prejudice. A dismissal, usu. after an adjudication on the merits, barring any subsequent action on the same claim.

involuntary dismissal. A court's dismissal of a lawsuit because the plaintiff failed to prosecute or failed to comply with a procedural rule or court order. Fed. R. Civ. P. 41(b).

voluntary dismissal. A plaintiff's dismissal of a lawsuit at the plaintiff's own request or by stipulation of all the parties. Fed. R. Civ. P. 41(a).

2. A release or discharge from employment. —**dismiss,** *vb.*

disorderly conduct. See CONDUCT.

disorderly house. 1. A dwelling where persons carry on activities that are a nuisance to the neighborhood. **2.** A dwelling where persons conduct criminal or immoral activities; examples are brothels and gambling houses. —Also termed *bawdy house.*

disparagement (di-**spar**-ij-mənt), *n.* A false statement that discredits or detracts from the reputation of another's property, product, or business; to recover in tort for disparagement, the plaintiff must prove that the statement resulted in specific pecuniary loss. —Also termed *injurious falsehood.* —More narrowly termed *slander of title; trade libel.* —**disparage,** *vb.* Cf. DEFAMATION.

disparate impact (dis-pə-rət). The adverse effect of a facially neutral practice (esp. an employment practice) that nonetheless discriminates against persons because of their race, sex, national origin, age, or disability and that is not justified by business necessity; discriminatory intent is irrelevant in a disparate-impact claim. —Also termed *adverse impact.*

disparate treatment. The practice, esp. in employment decisions, of intentionally dealing with persons differently because of their race, sex, national origin, age, or disability; to succeed on a disparate-treatment claim, the plaintiff must prove that the defendant acted with discriminatory intent or motive.

dispensation. An exemption from a law, duty, or penalty; permission to do something forbidden.

display right. A copyright holder's exclusive right to show or exhibit a copy of the protected work publicly, whether directly or by technological means; for example, this right makes it illegal for a copyrighted work to be transmitted without permission over the Internet.

disposable income. See INCOME.

disposition, *n.* **1.** The act of transferring something to another's care or possession, esp. by deed or will; the giving up of property <a testamentary disposition of all the assets>. **2.** A final settlement or determination <the court's disposition of the case without trial>. **3.** Temperament or character; personal makeup <a surly disposition>. —**dispose,** *vb.*—**dispositive,** *adj.*

dispossession, *n.* Deprivation of or eviction from possession of property; ouster. —**dispossess,** *vb.*

dispossess proceeding. A summary procedure initiated by a landlord to oust a defaulting tenant and regain possession of the premises. See FORCIBLE ENTRY AND DETAINER.

disputable presumption. See *rebuttable presumption* under PRESUMPTION.

dispute, *n.* A conflict or controversy, esp. one that has given rise to a particular lawsuit. —**dispute,** *vb.*

disqualification, *n.* **1.** Something that makes one ineligible; esp., a bias or conflict of interest that pre-

vents a judge or juror from impartially hearing a case. **2.** The act of making ineligible; the fact or condition of being ineligible. —**disqualify,** *vb.* Cf. RECUSAL.

disregarding the corporate entity. PIERCING THE CORPORATE VEIL.

disseisin (dis-[s]eez-[ə]n), *n.* The act of wrongfully depriving someone of the freehold possession of property; DISPOSSESSION. —**disseise,** *vb.*

dissent, *n.* **1.** A difference of opinion, esp. among judges. **2.** See *dissenting opinion* under OPINION (1). **3.** A withholding of assent or approval. —**dissent,** *vb.*

dissent and appraisal, right of. APPRAISAL REMEDY.

dissenters' right. APPRAISAL REMEDY.

dissenting opinion. See OPINION (1).

dissolution, *n.* **1.** The act of bringing to an end; termination. **2.** The cancellation or abrogation of a contract by the parties, with the effect of annulling the contract's binding force and restoring the parties to their original rights. See RESCISSION. **3.** The termination of a corporation's legal existence by expiration of its charter, by legislative act, by bankruptcy, or by other means; the event immediately preceding the liquidation or winding-up process. —**dissolve,** *vb.*

de facto dissolution. The termination and liquidation of a corporation's business, esp. because of an inability to pay its debts.

involuntary dissolution. The termination of a corporation administratively (as by the state for failure to file reports or pay taxes), judicially (as by the attorney general for abuse of corporate authority, management deadlock, or failure to pay creditors), or by filing bankruptcy.

voluntary dissolution. A corporation's termination initiated by the board of directors and approved by the shareholders.

4. In partnership law, the termination of a previously existing partnership upon the occurrence of some specified event, such as a partner's withdrawal from the partnership or some other reason named in the partnership agreement.

dissolution bond. See *discharging bond* under BOND (2).

dissolution of marriage. DIVORCE.

distinctiveness, *n.* The quality of a trademarked word, symbol, or device that identifies the goods of a particular merchant and distinguishes them from the goods of others. —**distinctive,** *adj.*

distinguish, *vb.* **1.** To note a significant difference in (a case) so as to minimize the precedential effect of the earlier of two cases being considered <the lawyer distinguished the cited case from the case at bar>. **2.** To make a distinction <the court distinguished between willful and reckless conduct>. —**distinction,** *n.*

distrain, *vb.* **1.** To force (a person, usu. a tenant), by the seizure and detention of property, to perform an obligation (such as paying overdue rent). **2.** To seize (goods) by distress, a legal remedy entitling the rightful owner to recover property wrongfully taken. —**distraint,** *n.*

distress, *n.* **1.** The seizure of another's property to secure the performance of a duty, such as the payment of overdue rent. **2.** The legal remedy authorizing such a seizure; the procedure by which the seizure is carried out. **3.** The property seized. — Also termed *distraint.*

distressed goods. See GOODS.

distressed property. See PROPERTY.

distress sale. See SALE.

distress warrant. See WARRANT (1).

distributee, *n.* An heir, esp. one who takes intestate personal property.

distribution, *n.* **1.** At common law, the passing of intestate personal property to a decedent's heirs. Cf. DESCENT (1). **2.** The act or process of apportioning or giving out. —**distribute,** *vb.*

corporate distribution. A corporation's direct or indirect transfer of money or other property, or incurring of indebtedness to or for the benefit of its shareholders, such as a dividend payment out of current or past earnings, a declaration, a purchase, a redemption, or other acquisition of shares.

liquidating distribution. A distribution of trade or business assets by a dissolving corporation or partnership.

partnership distribution. A partnership's payment of cash or property to a partner out of current earnings or as an advance against future earnings, or a payment of the partners' capital in the event of the partners' liquidation.

probate distribution. The judicially supervised apportionment and division—after payment of the debts and charges—of the remainder of an intestate estate among those legally entitled to share in the estate.

secondary distribution. **a.** The public sale of a large block of previously issued stock that is held by a corporation or investor. —Also termed *secondary offering.* See OFFERING. **b.** The sale of a large block of stock after the close of the exchange.

trust distribution. The cash or other property paid or credited to the beneficiaries of a trust.

distribution cost. See COST.

distribution in kind. A transfer of property in its original state, such as a distribution of land instead of a sale of land followed by a distribution of the proceeds.

distribution right. A copyright holder's exclusive right to sell, lease, or otherwise transfer copies of the protected work to the public. See FIRST-SALE DOCTRINE.

distributive deviation. A trustee's transfer of principal to income beneficiaries when the income is inadequate to carry out the settlor's scheme of distribution, and without the permission of the remainderman who owns a future interest in the principal; this practice is usu. considered impermissible except when life income beneficiaries need the money to buy necessaries.

distributive finding. A jury's decision partly in favor of one party and partly in favor of the other.

distributive share. 1. The share a given heir receives from the legal distribution of an intestate estate. **2.** The portion (as determined in the partnership agreement) of a partnership's income, gain, loss, or deduction that is passed through to a partner and reported on the partner's tax return. **3.** The share of assets or liabilities that a partner or partner's estate acquires after the partnership is dissolved.

distributor. A wholesaler, jobber, or other manufacturer or supplier that sells chiefly to retailers and commercial users.

district. A territorial area into which a country, state, county, municipality, or other political subdivision is divided for judicial, political, electoral, or administrative purposes.

assessment district. In taxation, a usu. municipal subdivision in which separate assessments of taxable property are made.

land district. A federally created state or territorial division containing a U.S. land office that manages the disposition of the district's public lands.

metropolitan district. A special district, embracing parts of or entire cities and towns in a metropolitan area, created by a state to provide unified administration of one or more common services, such as water supply or public transportation.

district attorney. A state official appointed or elected to represent the state in criminal cases in a particular judicial district; PROSECUTOR (1). —Abbr. D.A. —Also termed *public prosecutor; state's attorney; prosecuting* *attorney.* Cf. UNITED STATES ATTOR-NEY.

district court. See COURT.

district judge. See JUDGE.

districting. The act of drawing lines or establishing boundaries between geographic areas for the purpose of creating voting districts. See APPOR-TIONMENT; GERRYMANDERING.

District of Columbia. The seat of the U.S. Government, situated on the Potomac River between Maryland and Virginia; though neither a state nor a territory, it is constitutionally subject to the exclusive jurisdiction of Congress. —Abbr. D.C.

disturbance, *n.* **1.** An act causing annoyance or disquiet, or interfering with a person's pursuit of a lawful occupation or the peace and order of a neighborhood, community, or meeting. **2.** At common law, a wrong done to an incorporeal hereditament by hindering the owner's enjoyment of it. —**disturb,** *vb.*

disturbance of the peace. BREACH OF THE PEACE.

disturbing the peace. BREACH OF THE PEACE.

diversification, *n.* **1.** A company's movement into a broader range of products, usu. by buying firms already serving the market or by expanding existing operations <the soft-drink company's diversification into the potato-chip market has increased its profits>. **2.** The act of investing in a wide range of companies to reduce the risk if one sector of the market suffers losses <the prudent investor's diversification of the

portfolio among 12 companies>. —**diversify,** *vb.*

diversion, *n.* **1.** A deviation or alteration from the natural course of things; esp., the unauthorized alteration of a watercourse to the prejudice of a lower riparian, or the unauthorized use of funds. **2.** A distraction or pastime. —**divert,** *vb.*

diversion program. A program that refers certain criminal defendants before trial to community programs on job training, education, and the like, which if successfully completed may lead to the dismissal of the charges. —Also termed *pretrial diversion; pretrial intervention.*

diversity, *n.* DIVERSITY OF CITIZENSHIP.

diversity, *adj.* See *diversity jurisdiction* under JURISDICTION.

diversity jurisdiction. See JURISDICTION.

diversity of citizenship. The basis for granting to federal courts jurisdiction over cases between citizens of different states, or between a citizen of a state and an alien, subject to the minimum jurisdictional amount of $50,000. 28 U.S.C. § 1332. —Often shortened to *diversity.* See *diversity jurisdiction* under JURISDICTION.

complete diversity. In a multiparty case, diversity between both sides to the lawsuit—that is, all plaintiffs having different citizenship from all defendants (but not necessarily all plaintiffs or all defendants having diversity among themselves); complete diversity must exist in order for a federal court to assert diversity jurisdiction over the matter. *Strawbridge v. Curtiss*, 7 U.S. (3 Cranch) 267 (1806).

manufactured diversity. Improper or collusively created diversity of citizenship for the sole or primary purpose of obtaining federal jurisdiction; manufactured diversity is prohibited by 28 U.S.C. § 1359.

divestiture (dI-**ves**-tə-chuur), *n.* **1.** The loss or surrender of an asset or interest. **2.** A court order to a party to dispose of assets or property. **3.** In antitrust law, a court order to a defendant to rid itself of property, securities, or other assets to prevent a monopoly or restraint of trade. —**divest,** *vb.*

divestment, *n.* **1.** In property law, the cutting short of an interest in property before its normal termination. **2.** The complete or partial loss of an interest in an asset, such as land or stock. **3.** DISINVESTMENT (2). —**divest,** *vb.*

divided court. An appellate court whose opinion or decision in a particular case is not unanimous.

divided custody. See CUSTODY (2).

dividend. A portion of a company's earnings or profits distributed pro rata to its shareholders.

asset dividend. A dividend paid in the form of property, usu. the company's product, rather than in cash or stock. —Also termed *property dividend.*

cash dividend. A dividend paid to shareholders in the form of money.

consent dividend. A dividend that is not actually paid to the shareholders, but that is taxed to the shareholders and increases the basis in

their stock investment; a corporation declares a consent dividend to avoid or reduce an accumulated-earnings or personal-holding-company penalty tax.

constructive dividend. A taxable benefit derived by a shareholder from the corporation even though the benefit was not designated a dividend; examples include excessive compensation, bargain purchases of corporate property, or shareholder use of corporate property.

cumulative dividend. A dividend—usu. on preferred shares—that must be paid in full before common shareholders may receive any dividend; if the corporation passes a dividend in a particular year or period, it is carried over to the next year or period and must be paid before the common shareholders receive any payment. Cf. *noncumulative dividend.*

cumulative-to-the-extent-earned dividend. A cumulative dividend that supplies the holder with priority in that year only.

deficiency dividend. A dividend paid to reduce or avoid personal-holding-company tax in a prior year.

extraordinary dividend. An irregular dividend that is not derived from profits arising out of the ordinary course of business but that is declared because of unusually large income or an unexpected increment in capital assets due to fortuitous conditions. —Also termed *extra dividend*; *nonrecurring dividend*; *special dividend.*

informal dividend. A payment of salary, rent, interest, or the like to a shareholder as a substitute for a dividend. —Also termed *disguised dividend*.

liquidation dividend. A dividend paid to a dissolving corporation's shareholders, usu. from the capital of the corporation, upon the decision to suspend all or part of its business operations. —Also termed *liquidating dividend*.

nimble dividend. A dividend paid out of current earnings when there is a deficit in the account from which dividends may be paid; some state statutes prohibit nimble dividends.

noncumulative dividend. A dividend that does not accrue for the benefit of a preferred shareholder if there is a passed dividend in a particular year or period. Cf. *cumulative dividend*.

passed dividend. A dividend not paid when due by a company that has a history of paying regular dividends.

preferred dividend. A dividend paid to preferred shareholders who are generally paid a fixed amount and who take priority over common shareholders.

scrip dividend. A dividend paid in certificates entitling the holder to ownership of capital stock to be issued in the future; this type of dividend usu. signals that the corporation's cash flow is poor. —Also termed *liability dividend*.

stock dividend. A dividend paid in stock expressed as a percentage of the number of shares already held by a shareholder.

year-end dividend. An extra dividend paid at the end of the fiscal year

depending on the amount of the profits.

dividend date. The date on which a corporation distributes dividends to record owners of stock shares. Cf. EX-DIVIDEND DATE; RECORD DATE.

dividend-payout ratio. A profitability ratio based on annual dividends per share divided by earnings per share.

dividend preference. The right of a holder of preferred shares to receive a dividend before the company pays dividends to holders of common shares. See *preferred stock* under STOCK.

dividend-reinvestment plan. A company-sponsored program that enables common shareholders to reinvest their dividends plus supplementary cash into shares of the firm's common stock.

dividend yield. The current annual dividend divided by the market price per share.

divisible contract. See *severable contract* under CONTRACT.

divisible divorce. See DIVORCE.

divisible offense. See OFFENSE.

division of fees. See FEE-SPLITTING.

division of powers. The allocation of power between the national government and the states; under the Tenth Amendment, powers not delegated to the national government are reserved to the states or to the people, but today the Tenth Amendment provides only a limited check on Congress's power to regulate the states. Cf. SEPARATION OF POWERS.

divorce. The legal dissolution of a marriage by a court. —Also termed *dissolution of marriage.* Cf. ANNULMENT.

divisible divorce. A divorce whereby the marriage itself is dissolved but the issues incident to the divorce, such as alimony, child custody, and visitation, are reserved until a later proceeding; this type of divorce can be granted when the court has subject-matter jurisdiction but lacks personal jurisdiction over the defendant-spouse. —Also termed *bifurcated divorce.*

divorce a mensa et thoro (ah-**men**-sə-et-**thor**-oh). [Latin "(divorce) from board and bed"] A partial or qualified divorce by which the parties are separated and forbidden to live or cohabit together, without affecting the marriage itself; this type of divorce was the forerunner of modern judicial separation.

divorce a vinculo matrimonii (ah-**vin[g]**-kyə-loh-mat-rə-**moh**-nee-I). [Latin "(divorce) from the chains of marriage"] A total divorce of husband and wife, dissolving the marriage tie and releasing the parties wholly from their matrimonial obligations.

ex parte divorce. A divorce proceeding in which only one spouse participates or appears in court.

foreign divorce. A divorce obtained outside the state or country in which one of the spouses resides.

limited divorce. **a.** A divorce with no provision that one spouse must provide financial support to the other. **b.** Loosely, a legal separation.

mail-order divorce. A divorce obtained by parties who are not physically present or domiciled in the jurisdiction purporting to grant the divorce; such a divorce is not recognized in the U.S. because of the absence of the usual bases for jurisdiction.

Mexican divorce. A divorce obtained in Mexico by mail order or by the appearance of one spouse who does not have a Mexican domicile; neither type is recognized in the U.S.

migratory divorce. A divorce obtained by a spouse who moves to, or temporarily resides in, another state or country to get the divorce.

no-fault divorce. A divorce in which the parties are not required to prove fault or grounds beyond a showing of the irretrievable breakdown of the marriage or irreconcilable differences; the system of no-fault divorce was adopted in the U.S. during the late 1960s and the 1970s.

DJIA. *abbr.* DOW JONES INDUSTRIAL AVERAGE.

DNA identification. An analysis of deoxyribonucleic acid (DNA) resulting in the identification of an individual's patterned chemical structure of genetic information in order to identify the source of a biological specimen, such as blood, tissue, or hair. —Also termed *DNA fingerprinting.* Cf. HLA TEST.

docket, *n.* **1.** A formal record in which a judge or court clerk briefly notes all the proceedings and filings in a court case <review the docket to determine the filing date>. —Also termed *judicial record.*

appearance docket. A list of the parties and lawyers participating in an action, together with a brief abstract of the successive steps in the action.

judgment docket. A book that a court clerk keeps for the entry or recordation of judgments, giving official notice of existing judgment liens to interested parties; in many courts, it is called the *civil docket* or *criminal docket.* —Also termed *judgment book*; *judgment file*; *judgment record*; *judgment roll.*

2. A schedule of pending cases <the case is third on Monday's trial docket>. —Also termed *court calendar*; *cause list.* **3.** DOCKET CALL <the agreed judgment was signed at an uncontested docket on May 9>. **4.** A written abstract that provides specific information (usu. about something attached), esp. a label <check the docket to determine the goods' destination and value>. —**docket,** *vb.*

docket call. A court session in which attorneys (and sometimes parties) appear to announce readiness for trial, announce settlements, present proposed orders, and the like. — Often shortened to *docket.*

docket fee. See FEE.

dock receipt. An interim certificate issued by a maritime shipping company for the delivery of goods at the dock and entitling the designated person to receive a bill of lading. — Also termed *dock warrant.* See DOCUMENT OF TITLE.

doctor-patient privilege. See PRIVILEGE.

doctrine of approximation. CY PRES.

doctrine of equivalents. In patent law, the doctrine providing that if two devices perform the same work in a substantially similar manner and accomplish nearly the same result, they are considered identical, regardless of differences in name, form, or shape. —Also termed *equivalents doctrine.*

reverse doctrine of equivalents. The doctrine preventing infringement liability when the invention is substantially described by the claims of another's patent but performs the same or similar function in a substantially different way.

doctrine of incontrovertible physical facts. PHYSICAL-FACTS RULE.

doctrine of necessaries. *Archaic.* The common-law rule holding a husband or father liable to one who sells goods to his wife or child if the goods are required for their sustenance or support. See NECESSARIES.

doctrine of preclusion of inconsistent positions. See *judicial estoppel* under ESTOPPEL.

doctrine of the conclusiveness of the judgment. See *judicial estoppel* under ESTOPPEL.

doctrine of worthier title. See WORTHIER-TITLE DOCTRINE.

document, *n.* **1.** Something tangible on which words, symbols, or marks are recorded. **2.** (*pl.*) The deeds, agreements, title papers, letters, receipts, and other written instruments used to prove a fact. **3.** Within the meaning of the best-evidence rule, a physical embodiment of information or ideas, such as a letter, contract, receipt, account book, blueprint, or

X-ray plate; esp., the originals of such embodiments.

document, *vb.* **1.** To support with records, instruments, or other evidentiary authorities <document the chain of custody>. **2.** To record; to create a written record of <document a file>.

documentary draft. See DRAFT.

documentary evidence. See EVIDENCE.

documentary stamp tax. See *stamp tax* under TAX.

document of title. A written description, identification, or declaration of goods authorizing the holder (usu. a bailee) to receive, hold, and dispose of the document and the goods it covers; documents of title, such as bills of lading, warehouse receipts, and delivery orders, are governed by Article 7 of the U.C.C. See BAILMENT.

negotiable document of title. A document of title that actually stands for the goods it covers, so that any transfer of the goods requires a surrender of the document. U.C.C. 7-104(1).

nonnegotiable document of title. A document of title that merely serves as evidence of the goods it covers. U.C.C. 7-104(2).

D'Oench Duhme **doctrine.** The rule that estops a borrower from asserting claims or defenses against a federal successor to a failed financial institution—if those claims or defenses are based on side or secret agreements or representations—unless the agreement or representation has been (1) put into writing, (2) execut-

ed by the financial institution and borrower when the loan was issued, (3) approved by the financial institution's board of directors or loan committee, and (4) made a permanent part of the financial institution's records. *D'Oench, Duhme & Co. v. FDIC*, 315 U.S. 447 (1942) (now partially codified at 12 U.S.C. § 1823(e), and otherwise of questionable standing in light of *O'Melveny & Myers v. FDIC*, 114 S.Ct. 2048 (1994)).

dogma. A strongly held, authoritative opinion or tenet; a formally stated and proclaimed doctrine of faith. Pl. **dogmas, dogmata.**

DOJ. *abbr.* Department of Justice.

dollar-averaging. The investment practice of purchasing a fixed dollar amount of a given security at regular intervals.

dolus (**doh**-ləs). [Latin "device; artifice"] **1.** Fraud, deceit. **2.** Intentional aggression; willful injury. —Also termed *dolus malus*.

domain (doh-**mayn**), *n.* **1.** The territory over which sovereignty is exercised <the 19th-century domains of the British Empire>. **2.** An estate in land <the family domain is more than 6,000 acres>. **3.** The complete and absolute ownership of land <his domain over this land has now been settled>. See EMINENT DOMAIN; PUBLIC DOMAIN.

Dombrowski **doctrine.** The rule entitling a person to a federal-court injunction to prevent prosecution under a broad or vague state statute that affects rights guaranteed by the First Amendment. *Dombrowski v. Pfister*, 380 U.S. 479 (1965).

Domesday Book (**doomz**-day). The census or survey, ordered by William the Conqueror and substantially completed in 1086, of England's land-holdings, buildings, people, and livestock.

domestic, *adj.* **1.** Of or relating to one's own country <domestic affairs>. **2.** Of or relating to one's own jurisdiction <in Alaska, a domestic corporation is an Alaskan one>. **3.** Of or relating to the family or the household <a domestic dispute>.

domestic judgment. See JUDGMENT.

domestic-relations court. See *family court* under COURT.

domicile (**dom**-ə-sIl *or* -səl *or* **doh**-mi-), *n.* **1.** A person's true, fixed, and permanent home and principal establishment, to which that person intends to return and remain even though he or she may for a time reside elsewhere. —Also termed *permanent abode.* **2.** The residence of a person or corporation for legal purposes. —**domicile, domiciliate,** *vb.*—**domiciliary,** *adj.*—**domiciliary,** *n.* Cf. RESIDENCE.

after-acquired domicile. A domicile established after the facts relevant to an issue arose; an after-acquired domicile cannot be used to establish jurisdiction or choice of law.

commercial domicile. **a.** A domicile acquired by a nonresident corporation conducting enough managerial activities to permit taxation of the corporation's property or activities located outside the bounds of the taxing state. **b.** A domicile acquired by a person or company freely re-

siding or carrying on business in enemy territory or enemy-occupied territory. —Also termed *quasi-domicile.*

corporate domicile. The place considered by law as the center of corporate affairs and as the place where the corporation's functions are discharged; the legal home of a corporation, usu. its state of incorporation.

domicile of choice. **a.** A domicile established by physical presence at a dwelling coupled with the intention to make it home. **b.** The domicile a person chooses after reaching majority or being emancipated.

domicile of origin. The domicile of a person at birth, derived from the custodial parent or imposed by law. —Also termed *natural domicile.*

foreign domicile. A domicile established by a citizen or subject of one sovereignty within the territory of another.

matrimonial domicile. The place where a husband and wife have established a home in which they live as a married couple. —Also termed *matrimonial home.*

domiciliary administration. See ADMINISTRATION.

dominant estate. See ESTATE.

dominant tenant. The person who holds a dominant estate and therefore benefits from an easement. Cf. SERVIENT TENANT.

dominant tenement. See *dominant estate* under ESTATE.

dominion. 1. Control; possession <dominion over the car>. **2.** Sovereignty <dominion over the nation>.

donate, *vb.* To give (property or money) without receiving consideration for the transfer. **—donation,** *n.*—**donative** (**doh**-nə-tiv), *adj.*

donatio (doh-**nay**-shee-oh *or* -**nah**-tee-oh). [Latin] A gift.

donatio causa mortis. See *gift causa mortis* under GIFT.

donatio inter vivos. See *inter vivos gift* under GIFT.

donatio mortis causa. See *gift causa mortis* under GIFT.

donee. One to whom a gift is made.

donee beneficiary. See BENEFICIARY.

donor. 1. One who gives something without receiving consideration for the transfer. **2.** SETTLOR (1).

door-closing statute. A state law that may close local courts to plaintiffs unless they meet specified conditions; esp., a statute requiring foreign corporations to "qualify" before doing business in the state, including registering with the secretary of state, paying a fee or tax, and appointing an agent to receive service of process.

dormant, *adj.* Inactive; suspended; latent <a dormant judgment>. — **dormancy,** *n.*

Dormant Commerce Clause. See COMMERCE CLAUSE.

dormant execution. See EXECUTION.

dormant judgment. See JUDGMENT.

dormant partner. See *silent partner* under PARTNER.

DOT. *abbr.* Department of Transportation.

double damages. See DAMAGES.

double-declining depreciation method. See DEPRECIATION METHOD.

double hearsay. See HEARSAY.

double indemnity. See INDEMNITY.

double jeopardy. The fact of being prosecuted twice for substantially the same offense; double jeopardy is prohibited by the Fifth Amendment. Cf. FORMER JEOPARDY.

double taxation. See TAXATION.

double wills. See *mutual wills* under WILL.

doubt, reasonable. See REASONABLE DOUBT.

doubtful title. See TITLE.

Dow. DOW JONES INDUSTRIAL AVERAGE.

dowager (**dow**-ə-jər). A widow holding property or title—esp. a life estate in real property—received from her deceased husband.

dower. At common law, the right of a wife, upon her husband's death, to a life estate in one-third of the land that he owned, of which she cannot (with few exceptions) be deprived by any transfer made by him; although most states have abolished dower, many of the jurisdictions retaining the concept have expanded the wife's share from one-third to a full interest. Cf. CURTESY.

consummate dower. A wife's interest in her deceased husband's estate up to the time when that interest is legally assigned to her.

inchoate dower. A wife's interest in her husband's estate while both are living.

Dow Jones Industrial Average. A stock-market-performance indicator that consists of the price movements in the stocks of 30 leading industrial companies in the United States. — Abbr. DJIA. —Often shortened to *Dow*. —Also termed *Dow Jones Average.*

down payment. See PAYMENT.

downstream merger. See MERGER.

dowry. *Archaic.* The money, goods, or property that a woman brings to her husband in marriage. —Also termed *maritagium.*

DR. *abbr.* DISCIPLINARY RULE.

Draconian (drə-**koh**-nee-ən *or* dra- *or* dray-), *adj.* (Of a law) harsh; severe; this term derives from the name *Draco*, the ancient Athenian lawgiver. —Also termed *draconic.*

draft, *n.* **1.** An unconditional written order signed by one person (the *drawer*) directing another person (the *drawee* or *payor*) to pay a certain sum of money on demand or at a definite time to a third person (the *payee*) or to bearer; a check is the most common example of a draft <a draft in the amount of $500>. —Also termed *bill of exchange.* Cf. NOTE (1).

bank draft. A draft drawn by one financial institution on another.

documentary draft. A payment demand conditioned on the presentation of a document, such as a document of title, invoice, certificate, or notice of default.

export draft. A draft drawn by a domestic seller on a foreign buyer, directing the buyer to pay the trade amount to the seller or the seller's bank.

foreign draft. A draft drawn in one country but payable in another. — Also termed *international bill of exchange.*

share draft. An instrument used to withdraw funds from a credit union.

sight draft. A draft that is payable on the bearer's demand or on proper presentment to the drawer. —Also termed *demand draft.*

time draft. A draft that contains a specified payment date. U.C.C. § 3-108.

2. The compulsory enlistment of persons into military service <his illness disqualified him from the draft>. —Also termed *conscription.* **3.** An initial or preliminary version <the second draft of the contract>. —**draft,** *vb.*

drafter. A person who draws or frames a legal document, such as a will, contract, or legislative bill. — Also termed *draftsman.*

drafting. The practice, technique, or skill involved in preparing legal documents—such as statutes, rules, regulations, contracts, and wills—that set forth the rights, duties, liabilities, and entitlements of persons and legal entities.

dragnet clause. MOTHER HUBBARD CLAUSE (1).

dram-shop liability. **1.** A statutory claim to recover limited damages from a commercial seller of alcoholic beverages for a person's injuries caused by a customer's intoxication. **2.** Any common-law claim recognized against a commercial seller of alcoholic beverages.

draw, *vb.* **1.** To create and sign (a draft) <draw a check to purchase goods>. **2.** To prepare or frame (a legal document) <a poorly drawn will>. **3.** To take out (money) from a bank, treasury, or depository <she then drew $6,000 from her account>. **4.** To select (a jury) <the lawyers then began voir dire and had soon drawn a jury>.

drawee. The person or entity that a draft is directed to and that is requested to pay the amount stated on it; the drawee is usu. a bank that is directed to pay a sum of money on an instrument. —Also termed *payor.*

drawee bank. See *payor bank* under BANK.

drawer. One who directs a person or entity, usu. a bank, to pay a sum of money stated in an instrument—for example, a person who writes a check; the maker of a note or draft. See MAKER.

driving under the influence. The offense of operating a motor vehicle in a physically or mentally impaired condition after consuming alcohol or drugs; generally, this is a lesser offense than driving while intoxicated—in Mississippi the maximum penalty for a first-time offender is a $1,000 fine, 48 hours in jail, and 10 days of community service—but in a few jurisdictions the two are synonymous. —Abbr. DUI. —Also termed (in N.Y.) *driving while ability-impaired* (DWAI). Cf. DRIVING WHILE INTOXICATED.

driving while ability-impaired. DRIVING UNDER THE INFLUENCE.

driving while intoxicated. The offense of operating a motor vehicle in a physically or mentally impaired condition after consuming enough to raise one's blood alcohol content above the statutory limit (usu. 0.1%), or after consuming drugs; penalties vary widely, the maximum penalty in Missouri and Louisiana, for example, being a $500 fine and six months in jail, whereas the penalties in New York range from $500 to $5,000 in fines and up to four years in jail. — Abbr. DWI. Cf. DRIVING UNDER THE INFLUENCE.

DRM. *abbr.* See *direct-reduction mortgage* under MORTGAGE.

droit (dr[w]ah *or* droyt). [French "right"] **1.** A legal right or claim. **2.** The whole body of law.

drug, *n.* **1.** A substance intended for use in the diagnosis, cure, treatment, or prevention of disease. **2.** A natural or synthetic substance that alters one's perception or consciousness. — **drug,** *vb.* See CONTROLLED SUBSTANCE.

addictive drug. Any natural or synthetic drug that causes periodic or chronic intoxication by its repeated consumption.

drunkometer. BREATHALYZER.

dry-hole clause. A provision in an oil-and-gas lease specifying what a lessee must do to maintain the lease for the remainder of the primary term after drilling an unproductive well.

dry trust. See *passive trust* under TRUST.

DTC. *abbr.* DEPOSITORY TRUST CORPORATION.

dual-capacity doctrine. The principle that makes an employer—who is normally shielded from tort liability by workers'-compensation laws—liable in tort to an employee if the employer and employee stand in a secondary relationship that confers independent obligations on the employer. Cf. DUAL-PURPOSE DOCTRINE.

dual citizenship. 1. A person's status as a citizen of two countries, as when the person is born in the U.S. to parents who are citizens of another country, or one country still recognizes a person as a citizen even though that person has acquired citizenship in another country. **2.** The status of U.S. citizens who are citizens of both the United States and the state in which they reside.

dual distributor. A firm that sells goods simultaneously to buyers on two different levels of the distribution chain; esp., a manufacturer who sells directly to both wholesalers and retailers.

dual listing. See LISTING (2).

dual-purpose doctrine. The principle that an employer is liable for an employee's injury that occurs during a business trip even though the trip also serves a personal purpose. Cf. DUAL-CAPACITY DOCTRINE.

duces tecum (doo-səs-**tee**-kəm *or* -**tay**-kəm). [Latin] Bring with you. See *subpoena duces tecum* under SUBPOENA.

due, *adj.* **1.** Just, proper, regular, and reasonable <due care> <due notice>. **2.** Immediately enforceable

<payment is due on delivery>. **3.** Owing or payable; constituting a debt <the tax refund is due from the IRS>.

due-bill. IOU.

due care. See *reasonable care* under CARE.

due course, payment in. See PAYMENT IN DUE COURSE.

due-course holder. HOLDER IN DUE COURSE.

due diligence. 1. The care and attention required by the circumstances to satisfy a legal requirement or to discharge an obligation. —Also termed *reasonable diligence.* **2.** In corporate and securities law, a prospective buyer's or broker's investigation and analysis of a target company or of newly issued securities; a failure to exercise due diligence may sometimes result in liability, as when a broker recommends a security without first investigating it adequately.

due notice. See NOTICE.

due-on-encumbrance clause. A mortgage provision giving the lender the option to accelerate the debt if the borrower further mortgages the real estate without the lender's consent.

due-on-sale clause. A mortgage provision that gives the lender the option to accelerate the debt if the borrower transfers or conveys any part of the mortgaged real estate to someone without the lender's consent.

due process. The conduct of legal proceedings according to the rules and principles established in the systems of jurisprudence for the protection and enforcement of private rights, including notice and the right to a fair hearing before a tribunal with the power to decide the case. — Also termed *due process of law*.

economic substantive due process. The doctrine that certain social policies, such as the freedom of contract or the right to enjoy property without interference by government regulation, exist in the Due Process Clause of the Fourteenth Amendment, particularly in the words "liberty" and "property."

procedural due process. The minimal requirements of notice and a hearing guaranteed by the Due Process Clauses of the Fifth and Fourteenth Amendments, if the deprivation of a significant life, liberty, or property interest will occur.

substantive due process. The doctrine that the Due Process Clauses of the Fifth and Fourteenth Amendments require legislation to be fair and reasonable in content and to further a legitimate governmental objective.

Due Process Clause. The constitutional provision that prohibits the government from unfairly or arbitrarily depriving a person of life, liberty, or property; there are two Due Process Clauses in the U.S. Constitution, one in the Fifth Amendment applying to the federal government, and one in the Fourteenth Amendment applying to the states. Cf. EQUAL PROTECTION CLAUSE.

DUI. *abbr.* DRIVING UNDER THE INFLUENCE.

dummy, *n.* **1.** A party who participates in a transaction only to help achieve a legal goal but who really has no interest in the transaction. **2.** One who purchases property and holds legal title for another.

dummy, *adj.* Sham; make-believe; pretend <dummy corporation>.

dummy corporation. See CORPORATION.

dummy director. See DIRECTOR.

dummy shareholder. See SHAREHOLDER.

dumping. **1.** The act of selling a large quantity of goods at less than fair value. **2.** Selling goods abroad at less than the market price at home. See ANTIDUMPING LAW. **3.** The disposal of waste matter into the environment.

dun, *vb.* To demand payment from (a delinquent debtor) <his creditors are dunning him daily>. **—dun,** *n.*

duplicate (**doo**-pli-kət), *n.* **1.** A reproduction of an original document having the same particulars and effect of the original. **2.** A new original, made to replace an instrument that is lost or destroyed. —Also termed (in sense 2) *duplicate original*. **—duplicate** (**doo**-pli-kayt), *vb.*—**duplicate** (**doo**-pli-kət), *adj.*

duplicity (doo-**plis**-ət-ee), *n.* **1.** Deceitfulness; double-dealing. **2.** The pleading of two or more matters in one plea; double pleading. **—duplicitous,** *adj.*

durable goods. See GOODS.

durable power of attorney. See POWER OF ATTORNEY.

durables. See *durable goods* under GOODS.

durational-residency requirement. The requirement that one be a state resident for a certain time, such as one year, as a precondition to the exercise of a specified right or privilege; when applied to voting, this requirement has been held to be an unconstitutional denial of equal protection because it burdens the exercise of the franchise and impairs the fundamental personal right of travel.

duress. **1.** Strictly, the physical confinement of a person or the detention of a contracting party's property. **2.** Broadly, the threat of such confinement or detention, or other threat of harm, used to compel another to do something against his or her will or judgment; duress is a recognized defense to a crime, contractual breach, or tort. See COERCION; EXTORTION.

economic duress. An unlawful coercion to perform by threatening financial injury at a time when one cannot exercise free will. —Also termed *business compulsion.*

Durham rule. In criminal law, a test for the insanity defense, holding that a defendant is not criminally responsible for an act that was the product of mental disease or defect (*Durham v. United States*, 214 F.2d 862 (D.C.Cir.1954)); formerly used in New Hampshire and the District of Columbia, the *Durham* rule has been criticized as being too broad and is no longer accepted in any American jurisdictions. —Also termed *product test.* Cf. MCNAGHTEN RULES.

duty. **1.** A legal disadvantage that is owed or due to another and that needs to be satisfied; for every duty somebody else has a corresponding right.

delegable duty. An obligation that may be transferred to another to perform. See ASSIGNMENT.

legal duty. An obligation arising by contract or by operation of law <the legal duty of parents to support their children>.

nondelegable duty. **a.** In contract law, a duty that cannot be delegated by a contracting party to a third party; if the duty is transferred, the other contracting party can refuse to accept performance by the third party and not breach the contract. **b.** In tort law, a duty that may be delegated to an independent contractor by a principal, who retains primary (as opposed to vicarious) responsibility if the duty is not properly performed; for example, a landlord's duty to maintain common areas, though delegated to a service contractor, remains the landlord's responsibility if someone is injured by the maintenance.

preexisting duty. An obligation that one is already legally bound to perform. See PREEXISTING-DUTY RULE.

2. Any action, performance, task, or observance required by a person in an official or fiduciary capacity. **3.** In tort law, a legal relationship arising from a standard of care, the violation of which subjects the actor to liability. **4.** A tax imposed on a commodity or transaction, esp. on imports; a duty in this sense is imposed on things, not persons.

duty of tonnage. A charge imposed on a commercial vessel for entering, remaining in, or leaving a port.

duty to act. The obligation to take some action to prevent harm to another, and for the failure of which one may be liable depending on the relationship of the parties and the circumstances.

duty-to-defend clause. A liability-insurance provision obligating the insurer to take over the defense of any lawsuit brought by a third party against the insured on a claim that falls within the policy's coverage.

duty to mitigate. See MITIGATION-OF-DAMAGES DOCTRINE.

DWAI. *abbr.* Driving while ability-impaired. See DRIVING UNDER THE INFLUENCE.

dwelling defense. CASTLE DOCTRINE.

dwelling-house. 1. The house or other structure in which a person lives; a residence or abode. **2.** In real-property law, the house and all buildings attached to or connected with the house. **3.** In criminal law, a building, a part of a building, a tent, a mobile home, or other enclosed space that is used or intended for use as a human habitation. —Also termed *dwelling*.

DWI. *abbr.* DRIVING WHILE INTOXICATED.

dying declaration. See DECLARATION (6).

dynamite charge. ALLEN CHARGE.

dynamite instruction. ALLEN CHARGE.

E

E & O insurance. See *errors-and-omissions insurance* under INSURANCE.

earned income. See INCOME.

earned-income credit. See TAX CREDIT.

earned premium. See PREMIUM.

earned surplus. See *retained earnings* under EARNINGS.

earnest, *n.* A nominal payment or token act done beforehand as a pledge or a sign of good faith, esp. as the partial purchase price of property sold; though legally unnecessary, an earnest may help the parties come to an agreement.

earnest money. A deposit paid by a buyer both to hold a seller to a deal and to show good faith, and ordinarily forfeited if the buyer defaults; although an *earnest* has traditionally been a nominal sum (such as a nickel or a dollar) used in the sale of goods, *earnest money* is not a mere token in the real-estate context: it may amount to many thousands of dollars, or more. Cf. BINDER (2).

earning capacity. One's ability or power to earn money given one's physical or mental capabilities; earning capacity is one element considered when measuring the damages recoverable in a personal-injury lawsuit. —Also termed *earning power*.

earnings. Revenue gained from one's labor or services or from the investment of capital. See INCOME. Cf. PROFIT.

lost earnings. Wages or salary that could have been earned if death or a disabling injury had not occurred; lost earnings are typically awarded as damages to a plaintiff in a workers'-compensation claim or a wrongful-death suit. —Also termed *future earnings.* Cf. LOST EARNING CAPACITY.

retained earnings. A corporation's accumulated income after dividends have been distributed. —Also termed *earned surplus*; *undistributed profit.*

surplus earnings. The excess of corporate assets over liabilities.

earnings per share. The value of a common-stock share, determined by dividing a corporation's annual net income by the number of common-stock shares outstanding throughout the year. —Abbr. EPS.

fully diluted earnings per share. The value of a common-stock share if all convertible securities had been transferred to common equity and all stock options had been exercised.

earnings-price ratio. See *earnings yield* under YIELD.

earnings report. INCOME STATEMENT.

earnings yield. See YIELD.

earnout agreement. An agreement for the sale of a business whereby the buyer first pays an amount up front, and the final purchase price is later determined by the business's future profits; usu. the seller helps manage the business for a period after the sale. —Sometimes shortened to *earnout.*

earwitness. A witness who testifies about something that he or she heard but did not see.

easement. A legal or equitable right acquired by the owner of one piece of land (the *dominant estate*) to use another's land (the *servient estate*) for a special purpose, such as to drive through it to reach a road; unlike a lease or license, an easement lasts forever, but it does not give the owner a right to sell or improve the land.

access easement. The right to use another's land to get to a nearby road; the access easement is perhaps the most common type of easement of necessity. —Also termed *easement of access.*

affirmative easement. An easement that forces the owner of the servient estate to permit certain actions by the easement holder, such as discharging water on the servient estate. —Also termed *positive easement.* Cf. *negative easement.*

apparent easement. A visually evident easement, such as a paved trail.

avigational easement. An easement permitting free aircraft flights over the land in question. —Also termed *avigation easement; flight easement.*

easement appurtenant. An easement created to benefit another tract of land, the use of which is incident to the ownership of the land. —Also termed *appurtenant easement; appendant easement; pure easement; easement proper.* Cf. *easement in gross.*

easement by estoppel. A court-ordered easement created from a voluntary servitude because a person, believing the servitude to be permanent, acted in reasonable reliance on the mistaken belief.

easement by necessity. An easement created by operation of law because it is indispensable to the use of nearby property, such as an easement connecting a parcel of land to a road. —Also termed *easement of necessity.*

easement in gross. An easement benefiting a particular person and not a particular piece of land; the beneficiary need not, and usu. does not, own any land adjoining the servient estate. Cf. *easement appurtenant.*

equitable easement. **a.** An implied easement created by equity when adjacent lands derive from a common source, usu. to allow implied privileges to continue. **b.** See *restrictive covenant* (a) under COVENANT (4).

implied easement. An easement created by law when an owner of two parcels of land uses one parcel to benefit the other to such a degree that, upon the sale of the benefited parcel, the purchaser could reasonably expect the use to be included in the sale. —Also termed *easement by implication.*

light-and-air easement. A negative easement preventing an adjoining landowner from constructing a building that would obstruct light or air.

negative easement. An easement that prohibits the owner of the servient estate from doing something, such as building an obstruction. Cf. *affirmative easement.*

prescriptive easement. An easement created from an open, adverse, and continuous use over a statutory period. —Also termed *easement by prescription; adverse easement.*

public easement. An easement for the benefit of an entire community, such as the right to pass down a street.

quasi-easement. **a.** An easement-like right occurring when both tracts of land are owned by the same person; a quasi-easement may become a true easement if the landowner sells one of the tracts. **b.** An obligation or license that relates to land but that is not a true easement, such as a landowner's obligation to keep the fence between two properties in good repair.

reciprocal negative easement. An easement created when a landowner sells part of the land and restricts the buyer's use of that part, and, in turn, that same restriction is placed on the part kept by the landowner; such an easement usu. arises when the original landowner intends a common scheme of development for the lands.

reserved easement. An easement created by the grantor of real property to benefit the grantor's retained property and to burden the granted property.

EAT. *abbr.* Earnings after taxes.

eavesdropping. The act of secretly listening to the private conversation of others without their consent. Cf. BUGGING.

EBIT. *abbr.* Earnings before interest and taxes.

EC. *abbr.* **1.** ETHICAL CONSIDERATION. **2.** European Community. See EUROPEAN UNION.

ecclesiastical (i-klee-zee-**as**-ti-kəl), *adj.* Of or relating to the church, esp. as an institution.

ecclesiastical court. See COURT.

ecclesiastical law. 1. The body of law administered by the ecclesiastical courts. **2.** The law governing the doctrine and discipline of an established church. See CANON LAW.

ECJ. *abbr.* EUROPEAN COURT OF JUSTICE.

economic duress. See DURESS.

economic-harm rule. ECONOMIC-LOSS RULE.

economic indicator. A statistical measure of a market area used to describe the state of the economy or predict its direction.

lagging economic indicator. An economic indicator that tends to respond to the direction of the economy, such as new-home sales.

leading economic indicator. An economic indicator that tends to predict the future direction of the economy, such as interest rates.

economic life. The duration of an asset's profitability, usu. shorter than its physical life.

economic-loss rule. In tort law, the principle that a plaintiff cannot recover damages for purely monetary harm—as opposed to physical injury or property damage—caused by the defendant unless a special relationship exists between the parties, such as an attorney-client relationship. — Also termed *economic-harm rule.*

economic-realities test. 1. The principle requiring a court to examine the totality of a commercial situation, rather than just the documents. **2.** The principle that, for a person to be considered an employee, an employer must have the practical ability to control that person's actions.

economic rent. 1. The return gained from an economic resource (such as a worker or land) above the minimum cost of keeping the resource in service. **2.** Rent that yields a fair return on capital and expenses.

economic substantive due process. See DUE PROCESS.

economy of scale. (*usu. pl.*) A decline in the per-unit cost of a product resulting from increased output, usu. due to increased production facilities; savings resulting from the greater efficiency of large-scale processes.

ECU. *abbr.* EUROPEAN CURRENCY UNIT.

E.D. *abbr.* Eastern District, in reference to U.S. judicial districts.

edict (ee-dikt), *n.* A formal decree, demand, or proclamation issued by the sovereign of a country; in countries where edicts are issued, they are the equivalent of statutes. —**edictal,** *adj.*

editorial privilege. See *journalist's privilege* (b) under PRIVILEGE.

educational expense. See EXPENSE.

EEC. *abbr.* European Economic Community. See EUROPEAN UNION.

EEOC. *abbr.* EQUAL EMPLOYMENT OPPORTUNITY COMMISSION.

effect, *vb.* To bring about; to make happen <the improper notice did not effect a timely appeal>.

effective assistance of counsel. See ASSISTANCE OF COUNSEL.

effective cause. See *immediate cause* under CAUSE (1).

effective date. The date on which a law, contract, insurance policy, or other such instrument becomes enforceable or otherwise takes effect, rather than the date it was signed or circulated.

effective rate. See INTEREST RATE.

effects, *n. pl.* Movable property; goods <personal effects>.

effects doctrine. AFFECTS DOCTRINE.

efficient breach. See BREACH OF CONTRACT.

efficient-breach theory. In contract law, the view that a party should be allowed to breach a contract and pay damages, if that would be economically efficient, rather than be forced to perform under the contract; this relatively modern theory stems from the law-and-economics movement. See BREACH OF CONTRACT.

efficient cause. See *proximate cause* under CAUSE (1).

efficient intervening cause. See *intervening cause* under CAUSE (1).

effluxion of time (e-**flək**-shən). In real-estate law, the expiration of a lease term resulting from the passage of time rather than from a specific action or event. —Also termed *efflux of time.*

e.g. *abbr.* [Latin *exempli gratia*] For example <an intentional tort, e.g., battery or false imprisonment>. Cf. I.E.

eggshell-skull rule. In tort law, the principle that a defendant is liable for a plaintiff's unforeseeable and uncommon reactions to the defendant's negligent or intentional act; under this rule, for example, if one person negligently scrapes another who turns out to be a hemophiliac, the negligent defendant is liable for the full extent of the plaintiff's injuries even though the accident was a minor one. —Also termed *eggshell-plaintiff rule*; *thin-skull rule*; *special-sensitivity rule*.

egress (ee-gres). **1.** The act of going out or leaving. **2.** The right or ability to leave; a way of exit. Cf. INGRESS.

Eighteenth Amendment. The constitutional amendment, ratified in 1919 and repealed by the Twenty-First Amendment in 1933, that prohibited the manufacture, sale, and transportation of alcoholic beverages.

Eighth Amendment. The constitutional amendment, ratified in 1791, prohibiting excessive bail, excessive fines, and cruel and unusual punishment.

8-K. An SEC form that a registered corporation is required to file if a specified event occurs between the due dates for regular SEC filings such as the 10-K. —Also termed *Form 8-K*. Cf. 10-K.

eiusdem generis. EJUSDEM GENERIS.

ejection, *n.* An expulsion by action of law or by physical force or the threat of it. —**eject,** *vb.*—**ejector,** *n.* See OUSTER.

ejectment. 1. The ejection of an owner or occupier from property. **2.** A legal action by which a person wrongfully ejected from property seeks to recover possession and damages. Cf. EVICTION.

ejusdem generis (ee-**joos**-dəm-**jen**-ə-ris *or* -**yoos**-). [Law Latin *eiusdem generis* "of the same genus"] A canon of construction holding that when a general word or phrase follows an enumeration of specific persons or things, the general word or phrase will be construed as applying only to persons or things of the class within which the specific types fall; for example, in the phrase *horses, cattle, sheep, pigs, goats, or any other barnyard animal*, the general language *or any other barnyard animal*—despite its seeming breadth—would probably be held as applying only to four-legged, hoofed mammals (and thus would exclude chickens). —Also termed *Lord Tenterden's rule*. Cf. INCLUSIO UNIUS EST EXCLUSIO ALTERIUS; NOSCITUR A SOCIIS.

elder law. The legal specialty concerned with the issues faced by older individuals, such as age discrimination, housing alternatives, health care, and social security.

election, *n.* **1.** The exercise of a choice; esp., the act of choosing from among several possible rights or remedies in a way that precludes the use of other rights or remedies <the taxpayers' election to file jointly instead of separately>. **2.** The process of selecting a person to occupy a position or office, usu. a public office <the

Republicans fared surprisingly well in the 1994 congressional election>.

general election. An election that occurs at a regular time each year.

primary election. A preliminary election in which a political party's registered voters nominate the candidate who will run in the general election. —Often shortened to *primary.*

special election. An election that occurs in an interim between general elections, usu. to fill a sudden vacancy in office.

3. An obligation imposed on a party to choose between alternative rights or claims, so that the party is entitled to enjoy only one <the widower was put to an election between inheriting his intestate share of his deceased wife's estate and taking under her will>. See RIGHT OF ELECTION. —**elect,** *vb.*—**elective,** *adj.*

election of remedies. 1. A claimant's act of choosing between two or more concurrent but inconsistent remedies based on a single set of facts. **2.** The affirmative defense barring a litigant from pursuing a remedy inconsistent with another remedy already pursued, when that other remedy has given the litigant an advantage over, or has damaged, the opposing party; this doctrine has largely fallen into disrepute and is now rarely applied.

elective franchise. FRANCHISE (1).

elective share. In probate law, the share that a surviving spouse might choose when exercising the legal option of either taking under the will or taking under statute. See RIGHT OF ELECTION.

elector. 1. A member of the electoral college chosen to elect the president and the vice-president. **2.** A voter. **3.** One who chooses between alternative rights or claims.

electoral college. The body of electors chosen from each state to formally elect the president and vice-president by casting votes based on the popular vote.

eleemosynary (el-ə-**mos**-ə-ner-ee), *adj.* Of, relating to, or assisted by charity; not-for-profit <an eleemosynary institution>.

eleemosynary corporation. See *charitable corporation* under CORPORATION.

eleemosynary defense. See *charitable immunity* under IMMUNITY (2).

Eleventh Amendment. The constitutional amendment, ratified in 1795, prohibiting federal courts from hearing actions between a state and a person who is not a citizen of that state.

elisor (ə-**lI**-zər). A person appointed by a court to assemble a jury, serve a writ, or perform other duties of the sheriff or coroner in case either is disqualified. —Also spelled *eslisor.*

emancipate, *vb.* **1.** To set free from legal, social, or political restraint. **2.** To release (a child) from the control and support of a parent or guardian. —**emancipation,** *n.*—**emancipative, emancipatory,** *adj.*—**emancipator,** *n.*

emancipated minor. See MINOR.

embargo, *n.* **1.** A government's wartime or peacetime detention of an offending nation's private ships found in the ports of the aggrieved nation <the President called off the embargo of Iraq's ships after the war ended>. **2.** A nation's detention of its own ships in its own ports <the embargo of all U.S. ships traveling to Iraq remained in effect until hostilities subsided>. **3.** The conscription of private property for federal use, such as to transport troops <the Army's embargo of the company jet to fly General White to Washington>. **4.** A temporary prohibition on disclosure <the embargo on the press release expired at 10:00 a.m.>. —**embargo,** *vb.*

embassy. 1. The building in which a diplomatic body is located; esp., the residence of the ambassador. **2.** A body of diplomatic representatives headed by an ambassador. **3.** The mission, business, and function of an ambassador. Cf. LEGATION.

embezzlement, *n.* The fraudulent taking of personal property with which one has been entrusted, esp. as a fiduciary; the criminal intent for embezzlement—unlike larceny and false pretenses—arises after taking possession (not before or during the taking). —Also termed *defalcation*; *peculation*. —**embezzle,** *vb.* See LARCENY; FALSE PRETENSES.

emblements (**em**-bli-mənts). **1.** The growing crop annually produced by labor and not by accident; emblements are considered personal property that the executor or administrator of a deceased tenant may harvest and take regardless of who may have since occupied the land. **2.** The tenant's right to harvest and take away such crops after the tenancy has ended.

embossed seal. See NOTARY SEAL.

embracery (im-**brays**-[ə-]ree), *n.* The common-law offense of attempting to corrupt or instruct a jury to reach a particular conclusion by means other than presenting evidence or argument in court, as by bribing or threatening jurors. —Also termed *jury-tampering.* —**embracer, embraceor,** *n.* Cf. JURY-FIXING; JURY-PACKING.

Emergency Court of Appeals. A temporary court, first established during World War II, whose purpose is to review wage- and price-control matters.

emergency doctrine. 1. A legal principle exempting a person from the ordinary standard of reasonable care if that person acted instinctively to meet a sudden and urgent need for aid. —Also termed *imminent-peril doctrine*; *sudden-emergency doctrine*; *sudden-peril doctrine.* **2.** A legal principle that implies consent to medical treatment in a dire situation when neither the patient nor a responsible party can consent but a reasonable person would do so. —Also termed *emergency-treatment doctrine.* Cf. GOOD SAMARITAN DOCTRINE; RESCUE DOCTRINE.

emigration, *n.* The act of departing or exiting from one country in the hope of settling in another. —**emigrate,** *vb.*—**emigrant, émigré, emigré** (**em**-i-gray), *n.* Cf. IMMIGRATION.

eminent domain. The power of a governmental entity to convert privately owned property, esp. land, to public use, subject to reasonable compensation for the taking. See CONDEMNATION (2); EXPROPRIATION; TAKING (2).

emissary. One sent on a special mission as another's agent or representative, esp. to promote a cause or to gain information.

emit, *vb.* **1.** To give off or discharge into the air <emit light>. **2.** To issue with authority <emit a new series of currency>. **—emission,** *n.*

emolument (i-**mol**-yə-mənt), *n.* (*usu. pl.*) Any advantage, profit, or gain received as a result of one's employment or one's holding of office.

emotional distress. Pain or suffering affecting the mind, often (but not necessarily) as a result of physical injury; emotional distress can be either recoverable as damages or actionable as a ground for divorce. — Also termed *mental distress*; *mental anguish*. See *mental cruelty* under CRUELTY.

intentional infliction of emotional distress. The tortious offense of intentionally or recklessly causing another severe emotional distress through one's extreme or outrageous acts; in a few jurisdictions, a physical manifestation of the mental suffering, such as a miscarriage, is required. —Also termed (in some states) *outrage.*

negligent infliction of emotional distress. The tortious offense of causing another severe emotional distress through one's negligent conduct; most courts will allow a plaintiff to recover damages for emotional distress if the defendant's conduct results in physical contact with the plaintiff, or, if no contact occurs, the plaintiff is in the zone of danger.

empanel, *vb.* To swear (a jury) to try an issue or case. —Also spelled *impanel.* —**empanelment, empaneling,** *n.*

emphasis added. A citation signal indicating that the writer quoting another's words has italicized or otherwise emphasized some of them. — Also termed *emphasis supplied.*

emphyteusis (em-fi-t[y]oo-səs), *n.* [Latin "implanting"] In civil law, a nonowner's right to use land in perpetuity, subject to forfeiture for nonpayment of a fixed rent. ***—emphyteutic,*** *adj.*

empirical (im-**pir**-i-kəl), *adj.* Of, relating to, or based on experience, experiment, or observation. —Also termed *empiric.*

employee. One who works for another under an express or implied contract. —Formerly also termed *servant.* Cf. AGENT; INDEPENDENT CONTRACTOR.

borrowed employee. An employee whose services are, with the employee's consent, lent to another employer who temporarily assumes control over the employee's work; the borrowing employer bears vicarious liability for the employee's acts under the doctrine of *respondeat superior.* —Also termed *borrowed servant*; *loaned employee*; *loaned servant*; *employee pro hac vice.*

Employee Retirement Income Security Act. A federal statute that regulates private pensions and established the Pension Benefit Guaranty Corporation. 29 U.S.C. §§ 1001 et seq. —Abbr. ERISA.

employee stock option. See *stock option* (b) under OPTION.

employee-stock-ownership plan. A profit-sharing plan designed primarily to give an employee retirement benefits and a stake in the company, but also used to allow employees to purchase their employer company if it is closing. —Abbr. ESOP.

employer. One who controls and directs a worker under an express or implied contract and who pays the worker's salary or wages. —Formerly also termed *master*. Cf. PRINCIPAL (1).

employers' liability. WORKERS' COMPENSATION.

employers'-liability insurance. See INSURANCE.

employment, *n.* **1.** The act of employing; the state of being employed. **2.** Work for which one has been hired and is being paid by an employer. —**employ,** *vb.*

casual employment. Work that is occasional, irregular, or for a limited, temporary purpose.

employment at will. An employee-employer relationship that usu. is undertaken without a contract and that may be severed at any time by either party without cause.

permanent employment. Work that, under a contract, is to continue indefinitely until either party wishes to terminate it for some good reason.

seasonal employment. An occupation possible only during limited parts of the year, such as a summer-camp counselor or a baseball-park vendor.

emptor. [Latin] Buyer. See *caveat emptor* under CAVEAT.

empty-chair defense. A trial tactic in a multiparty case whereby one defendant attempts to put all the fault on a defendant who settled before trial.

empty-chair doctrine. ADVERSE-INTEREST RULE.

enablement requirement. In patent law, the rule that the specification portion of a patent application must describe the invention so that a person with ordinary skill in the art could make and use the invention without experimenting unduly. Cf. ENABLING SOURCE.

enabling act. See *enabling statute* under STATUTE.

enabling source. A document that defeats the patentability of an invention because the information provided made it possible—before the patent application was filed—for a person skilled in the art to make the invention. Cf. ENABLEMENT REQUIREMENT.

enabling statute. See STATUTE.

enacting clause. The part of a statute stating the legislative authority by which it is made and stating when the statute takes effect.

enactment, *n.* **1.** The action or process of making into law <enactment of a legislative bill>. **2.** A statute <a recent enactment>. —**enact,** *vb.*—**enactor,** *n.*

en banc (on-**bonk** *or* en-**bank**). [French "on the bench"] **1.** *adj.* Of or referring to a session in which the full membership of the court participates <en banc proceeding>. **2.** *adv.* With full membership; as a complete body <the court heard the case en banc>. —Also spelled *in banc*; *in bank*.

enbancworthy, *adj. Slang.* Worthy of being considered en banc <the Fifth Circuit concluded that two of the four issues are truly enbancwor­thy>. —**enbancworthiness,** *n.*

en bloc (on-**blok**). [French] As a whole; as a unit.

encroachment, *n.* An infringement of another's rights or intrusion on another's property <the court remedied the encroachment by order­ing the defendant to cut down the tree limb hanging over the plaintiff's yard>. —Formerly also spelled *incroachment.* —**encroach,** *vb.* See TRESPASS.

encumbrance, *n.* A claim or liability that is attached to property and that may lessen its value, such as a lien or mortgage; an encumbrance cannot defeat the transfer of possession, but it remains after the property is transferred. —Also spelled *incumbrance.* —**encumber,** *vb.*

encumbrancer. One having a legal claim, such as a lien or mortgage, against property.

endangerment, reckless. RECKLESS ENDANGERMENT.

endless-chain scheme. PYRAMID SCHEME.

endnote. A note that, instead of appearing at the bottom of the page (as a footnote does), appears at the end of the book, chapter, or paper.

endorsed bond. See *guaranteed bond* under BOND (1).

endorsee. INDORSEE.

endorsement, *n.* **1.** INDORSEMENT. **2.** An amendment to an insurance policy; a rider. —**endorse,** *vb.*

endorser. INDORSER.

endowment, *n.* **1.** The assigning or giving of dower to a woman. See DOWER. **2.** A gift of money or property to an institution for a specific purpose, esp. one in which the principal is kept intact indefinitely and only the income from that principal is used. —**endow,** *vb.*

end position. One's legal and financial position upon the signing of a contract, including the choices now available, such as renewal and renegotiation.

enemy alien. See ALIEN.

enfeoff (in-**feef** *or* in-**fef**), *vb.* To put (a person) in legal possession of a freehold interest. —Formerly spelled *infeoff.* —Also termed *feoff; infeudate.*

enfeoffment (in-**feef**-mənt *or* in-**fef**-), *n.* **1.** At common law, the act or process of transferring possession and ownership of an estate in land. —Also termed *infeudation.* **2.** The property or estate so transferred. **3.** The instrument or deed by which one obtains such property or estate. —Also spelled *infeoffment.* —Also termed *feoffment.*

enfranchise, *vb.* **1.** To grant voting rights or other rights of citizenship. **2.** To set free, as from slavery. —**enfranchisement,** *n.*

engagement, *n.* **1.** A contract or agreement involving mutual prom ises. **2.** An agreement to marry; the period after which a couple has agreed to marry but before they do so. —**engage,** *vb.*

***England* procedure.** A procedure by which—after a federal court has referred a case back to state court under the *Pullman* abstention, and the state court has adjudicated the state-court issues—a litigant may return to federal court to have his or her federal claims adjudicated. *England v. Louisiana State Bd. of Medical Examiners*, 375 U.S. 411 (1964). See *Pullman abstention* under AB-STENTION.

English rule. The requirement that the losing litigant must pay the winner's costs and attorney's fees. —Also termed *loser-pays rule.* Cf. AMERICAN RULE.

engross, *vb.* **1.** To prepare a copy of (a legal document, as a deed) for execution. **2.** To prepare a copy of (a bill or mandate) before a final legislative vote. **3.** To buy large quantities of (a stock or commodity) in order to corner the market and control the price. —Formerly also spelled *ingross.* Cf. ENROLL.

engrossed bill. See BILL (3).

enjoin, *vb.* **1.** To legally prohibit or restrain by injunction <the company was enjoined from selling its stock>. **2.** To prescribe, mandate, or strongly encourage <the graduating class was enjoined to uphold the highest professional standards>. —**enjoinment** (corresponding to sense 1), *n.*—**enjoinder** (corresponding to sense 2), *n.*

enjoinable, *adj.* Capable of being prohibited by injunction <an enjoinable nuisance>.

enjoyment, *n.* **1.** Possession and use, esp. of rights or property. **2.** The exercise of a right. —**enjoy,** *vb.*

adverse enjoyment. The possession or use of an easement under a claim of right against the owner of the property out of which the easement derives.

quiet enjoyment. The possession of real property with the assurance that the possession will not be disturbed by superior title. See *covenant for quiet enjoyment* under COVENANT (4).

enlarge, *vb.* **1.** To increase in size or extend in scope or duration <the court enlarged the time allotted for closing statements>. **2.** To free from custody or imprisonment <at common law, an action for escape lay when a prisoner was wrongly enlarged>. —**enlargement,** *n.*

enlargement of time. A usu. court-ordered extension of the time allowed to perform an action, esp. a procedural one.

enlistment, *n.* Voluntary entry into a branch of the armed services. —**enlist,** *vb.*

en masse (on-**mas** *or* -**mahs**). [French] In a mass; in a large group all at once; all together.

Enoch Arden law. A statute granting a divorce or exempting from liability a person who remarries when his or her spouse has been absent without explanation for a specified number of years, usu. seven. —Also spelled *Enoc Arden law*. See *presumptive death* under DEATH.

enroll, *vb.* **1.** To register or transcribe (a legal document, as a deed) into an official record on execution. —Formerly also spelled *inroll*. **2.** To prepare (a bill passed by the legislature) for the executive's signature. —**enrollment,** *n.* Cf. ENGROSS.

enrolled bill. See BILL (3).

enrolled-bill rule. The conclusive presumption that a statute, once formalized, appears precisely as the legislature intended, thereby preventing any challenge to the drafting of the bill.

en route (on-**root** *or* en-**root**). [French] On the way; in the course of transportation.

entail, *vb.* **1.** To make necessary; to involve <responding to this onerous discovery will entail countless hours of work>. **2.** To limit the inheritance of (an estate) to only the owner's issue or class of issue, so that none of the heirs can transfer the estate <the grantor entailed the property through a so-called "tail female">. See FEE TAIL. —**entailment** (corresponding to sense 1), *n.*—**entail** (corresponding to sense 2), *n.*

entailed estate. FEE TAIL.

entente (ahn-**tahnt**). [French "intent, understanding"] **1.** In international law, an understanding that two or more nations have for carrying out a common policy or course of action; an *entente* is looser than an alliance but stronger than the nations' merely having good relations. **2.** The member nations of such an understanding. Cf. ALLIANCE; DÉTENTE.

enter, *vb.* **1.** To go on land to take possession <Tornquist then entered on the land>. **2.** To become a party to <they entered into an agreement>. **3.** To place before the court <the corporation duly entered an appearance>. —**entry,** *n.*

enterprise liability. See LIABILITY.

entertain, *vb.* To give judicial consideration to <the court then entertained motions for continuance>.

entire-controversy doctrine. The rule that a party to a lawsuit must assert against an opponent all claims and defenses that are related to the underlying controversy.

entireties, tenancy by the. See *tenancy by the entireties* under TENANCY.

entitle, *vb.* **1.** To grant a legal right to or qualify for. **2.** In ecclesiastical law, to ordain as a minister. —Formerly also spelled *intitle*.

entitlement. An absolute right to a usu. monetary benefit, such as social security, granted immediately upon meeting a legal requirement.

entity assumption. The assumption that a business is a unit separate from its owners or from other firms.

entrapment, *n.* A law-enforcement officer's inducement of a person to commit a crime, for the purpose of bringing a criminal prosecution against that person. —**entrap,** *vb.*

entrust, *vb.* To give (a person) the responsibility for something, usu. after establishing a confidential relationship. —**entrustment,** *n.* See NEGLIGENT ENTRUSTMENT.

entry, *n.* **1.** Generally, the right, privilege, or act of entering. **2.** An item written in a record; a notation. **3.** In procedure, the placement of anything before the court or in the court record. **4.** In copyright law, the title of a written work that has been deposited with the Register of Copyrights to secure protection. **5.** In immigration law, any coming of an alien into the U.S. **6.** In criminal law, the unlawful coming into a building to commit a crime. **7.** In customs law, the coming in of imported goods to a customhouse. **—enter,** *vb.*

entry of judgment. The ministerial recording of a court's final decision, usu. by noting it in a judgment book or civil docket. Cf. RENDITION OF JUDGMENT.

enumerate (i-n[y]oo-mə-rayt), *vb.* To count off or designate one by one; to list. **—enumeration,** *n.*

enumerated power. See POWER.

enunciate (i-nən-see-ayt), *vb.* **1.** To state publicly; to announce or proclaim <the court enunciated a new doctrine yesterday>. **2.** To articulate or pronounce <enunciate your syllables more clearly when you speak>. **—enunciation,** *n.*—**enunciable,** *adj.*—**enunciator,** *n.*

enure. INURE.

en ventre sa mere (on-**von**-trə-sah-mer). [Law French "in utero"] *Jargon.* (Of a fetus) in the mother's womb <child *en ventre sa mere*>.— Also spelled *in ventre sa mere.*

en vie (on-**vee**). [Law French "in life"] Alive.

environmental-impact statement. A federally required report that accompanies a proposal for a program or law and details the likely effects on the environment.

Environmental Protection Agency. A federal agency created in 1970 to coordinate governmental action to protect the environment. —Abbr. EPA.

envoy (**en**-voy *or* **ahn**-). **1.** A high-ranking diplomat sent to a foreign country to execute a special mission or to serve as a permanent diplomatic representative. —Also termed *envoy extraordinary.* **2.** A messenger or representative.

eo instante (ee-oh-in-**stan**-tə). [Latin] At that very instant.

eo ipso. [Latin] By that very act.

eo nomine (ee-oh-**nom**-ə-nee). [Latin] By that name; in that name <interest *eo nomine*>.

EPA. *abbr.* ENVIRONMENTAL PROTECTION AGENCY.

E pluribus unum (ee-**pluur**-ə-bəs-[**y]oo**-nəm). [Latin "one out of many"] The motto on the official seal of the United States.

EPS. *abbr.* EARNINGS PER SHARE.

epoch (**ep**-ək), *n.* **1.** The date of an important occurrence that marks a set of new conditions. **2.** A period of history. **—epochal,** *adj.*

Equal Access to Justice Act. A federal statute enacted in 1980 to allow the prevailing party in certain actions against the government to recover attorney's or expert-witness fees. Pub. L. 96-481, title II, 94 Stat. 2325 (codified as amended in scattered sections of 5, 15, 28, and 42 U.S.C.).

equal degree. See DEGREE.

equal-dignities rule. In agency law, the doctrine that all acts requiring a writing signed by the principal can be performed by the agent only if there is a writing that sets forth the agent's authority; this rule is an adjunct to the statute of frauds in circumstances in which one or more of the signatories to a contract acted through an agent.

Equal Employment Opportunity Commission. A federal agency created under the Civil Rights Act of 1964 to end discriminatory employment practices and to promote non-discriminatory employment programs. —Abbr. EEOC.

equality of states. The doctrine that all fully independent nations are equal in the eye of international law; this doctrine does not, of course, mean that all nations are equal in power or influence, but merely that, as nations, they all have the same legal rights.

equalization, *n.* **1.** The raising or lowering of assessed values to achieve conformity. **2.** In tax law, the adjustment of an assessment or tax to create a rate uniform with another. —**equalize,** *vb.*

equalization board. The local governmental agency responsible for equalizing taxes between districts to ensure an equitable distribution of the tax burden.

equal-opportunity employment practice. An employer's method of hiring without regard to race, color, religion, sex, or national origin.

equal protection. 1. A constitutional requirement guaranteeing that similarly situated persons will receive the same constitutional rights. —Also termed *equal protection of the laws*. **2.** In tax law, a rule providing that persons will receive different classifications based only on actual and relevant differences, and that any disparate treatment will not be arbitrary.

Equal Protection Clause. The Fourteenth Amendment provision requiring that persons under like circumstances be given the same constitutional rights. Cf. DUE PROCESS CLAUSE.

Equal Rights Amendment. A failed constitutional amendment that, if it had been ratified, would have prohibited sex-based discrimination; Congress passed the Amendment in 1972, but it failed in 1982, having been ratified by only 35 of the required 38 states. —Abbr. ERA.

equitable adoption. See *adoption by estoppel* under ADOPTION (1).

equitable construction. See *liberal construction* under CONSTRUCTION.

equitable conversion. See CONVERSION (1).

equitable defense. See DEFENSE (1).

equitable distribution. In family law, the usu. equal division, after a divorce, of property accumulated by the spouses during marriage; equitable distribution is applied in 40 states.

equitable easement. See EASEMENT.

equitable estate. See ESTATE.

equitable life tenant. See LIFE TENANT.

equitable owner. See OWNER.

equitable remedy. See REMEDY.

equitable right to setoff. The right to cancel cross-demands, usu. used by a bank to take from a customer's deposit accounts the amount equal to the customer's debts that have matured and that are owed to that bank.

equitable servitude. See *restrictive covenant* under COVENANT (4).

equitable title. See TITLE.

equitable waste. See WASTE.

equity, *n.* **1.** Fairness; impartiality; evenhanded dealing <she did not feel that the company had dealt with her in equity>. **2.** The body of principles constituting what is fair and right; natural law <the concept of "inalienable rights" reflects the influence of equity on the Declaration of Independence>. **3.** The recourse to principles of justice to correct or supplement the law as applied to particular circumstances <the judge decided the case by equity because the statute did not fully address the issue>. **4.** The system of law or body of principles originating in the English Court of Chancery and superseding the common and statute law (together called "law" in the narrower sense) when the two conflict <in appealing to the equity of the court, she was appealing to the "King's conscience">. **5.** A right, interest, or remedy recognizable by a court of equity <there was no formal contract formation, so they sued for breach in equity>. **6.** The right to decide matters in equity; equity jurisdiction <the court decided that the wrong was egregious enough to ignore the statute of limitations and decide the case in equity>. **7.** The amount by which the value of a property or an interest in property exceeds secured claims or liens <thanks to the real-estate boom, the mortgaged house still had high equity>. **8.** An ownership interest in property, esp. in a business <the founders gave her equity in the business in return for all her help>. See OWNERS' EQUITY. **9.** A share in a publicly traded company <he did not want to cash in his equity>. —**equitable,** *adj.*

equity accounting method. See ACCOUNTING METHOD.

equity capital. See CAPITAL.

equity financing. See FINANCING.

equity insolvency. See INSOLVENCY.

equity jurisdiction. See JURISDICTION.

equity kicker. EQUITY PARTICIPATION.

equity loan. See *home equity loan* under LOAN.

equity of redemption. See REDEMPTION (4).

equity participation. The inclusion of a lender in the equity ownership of a project as a condition of the lender's granting a loan. —Also termed *equity kicker.*

equity ratio. 1. The percentage relationship between a purchaser's equity value (esp. the amount of a down payment) and the property value. **2.** The measure of a shareholder's equity divided by total equity.

equity security. See SECURITY.

equity term. The period during which a court tries only equity cases.

equivalents doctrine. DOCTRINE OF EQUIVALENTS.

equivocality. RES IPSA LOQUITUR (2).

ERA. *abbr.* EQUAL RIGHTS AMENDMENT.

erasure of record. EXPUNGEMENT OF RECORD.

ergo (e[ə]r-goh *or* ər-). [Latin] Therefore; thus.

Erie **doctrine.** A doctrine, established by the U.S. Supreme Court, recognizing that because rights created by state law should be decided under state law rather than federal law, a federal action not involving a congressional or constitutional issue will be decided according to the law of the state in which the federal court sits. *Erie v. Tompkins*, 304 U.S. 64 (1938).

Erie/Klaxon **doctrine.** KLAXON DOCTRINE.

ERISA (ee-**ris**-ə *or* ə-**ris**-ə). *abbr.* EMPLOYEE RETIREMENT INCOME SECURITY ACT.

eristic (i-**ris**-tik *or* ee-), *adj.* Of or pertaining to controversy or disputation. —Also termed *eristical*.

ermine (ər-min *or* -mən). The station of a judge; judgeship—named after the fur trimmings (made from the coats of weasels called "ermine") adorning official robes of English judges.

errant, *adj.* **1.** Fallible; incorrect; straying from what is proper <an errant judicial holding>. **2.** Traveling <a knight errant>.

erratum (ə-**rah**-təm). [Latin "error"] CORRIGENDUM. Pl. **errata.**

error, *n.* **1.** A mistake of law or of fact in a court's judgment, opinion, or order <the appellant sought a reversal based on the trial court's error in admitting the evidence seized without a search warrant>. **2.** An appeal <proceedings in error>. — **err** (ər *or* e[ə]r), *vb.*—**erroneous,** *adj.*

clerical error. An error resulting from a minor mistake or inadvertence, esp. in writing or copying something on the record, and not from judicial reasoning or determination; a court can correct a clerical error at any time, even after judgment has been entered.

harmless error. An error that does not affect a party's substantive rights or the case's outcome; a harmless error is not grounds for reversal. —Also termed *technical error.*

plain error. An error so obvious and substantial that failure to correct it would infringe a party's due-process rights and damage the integrity of the judicial process; a plain error can be reversed even if the party did not properly object. — Also termed *fundamental error.*

reversible error. An error that affects a party's substantive rights or the case's outcome, and thus is grounds for reversal if the party properly objected. —Also termed *prejudicial error; harmful error.*

errors, assignment of. See ASSIGNMENT OF ERRORS.

errors-and-omissions insurance. See INSURANCE.

escalator clause. A contractual provision that increases or decreases the contract price according to changing market conditions, such as higher or lower taxes or operating costs. —Also termed *escalation clause*; *fluctuating clause*.

escape, *n.* **1.** An unlawful departure from legal custody without the use of force. **2.** At common law, a criminal offense committed by a peace officer who allows a prisoner to unlawfully depart from legal custody. —**escape,** *vb.*

escape clause. A contractual provision that allows a party to avoid performance under specified conditions.

escheat, *n.* **1.** Reversion of property (esp. real property) to the state upon the death of the intestate owner without heirs. **2.** Property that has so reverted. —**escheat,** *vb.*

Escobedo rule. The principle that a statement by an unindicted, targeted suspect in police custody is inadmissible at trial unless the police warn the suspect of the right to remain silent and provide an opportunity for the suspect to consult with retained counsel; a precursor to the rule established in *Miranda v. Arizona. Escobedo v. Illinois*, 378 U.S. 478 (1964).

escrow, *n.* **1.** A legal document or property delivered by a promisor to a third party to be held by the third party for a given amount of time or until the occurrence of a condition, at which time the third party is to hand over the document or property to the promisee <the agent received the escrow two weeks before the closing date>. **2.** An account held in trust or as security <the earnest money is in escrow>. —Also termed *escrow account*; *impound account*;

reserve account. See *escrow account* under ACCOUNT. **3.** The holder of such document, property, or deposit <the attorney performed the function of escrow>. —Also termed *escrow agent.* **4.** The general arrangement under which a legal document or property is delivered to a third person until the occurrence of a condition <creating an escrow>. —**escrow,** *vb.*

escrow account. See ACCOUNT.

escrow agent. The third-party depositary of an escrow; ESCROW (3). —Also termed *escrow holder*; *escrowee.*

escrow agreement. The instructions given to the third-party depositary of an escrow.

escrowee. ESCROW AGENT.

eslisor. ELISOR.

ESOP (ee-sop). *abbr.* EMPLOYEE-STOCK-OWNERSHIP PLAN.

espionage (es-pee-ə-nahzh). The practice of using spies to collect information about what another government or company is doing or plans to do.

Esquire. A mild honorific title commonly appended after the name of a lawyer. —*Abbr.* Esq.

essence, of the. See OF THE ESSENCE.

Establishment Clause. The constitutional provision (U.S. Const. amend. I) prohibiting the government from creating a church or favoring a particular religion. Cf. FREE EXERCISE CLAUSE.

estate. 1. All that a person owns, including both heritable and movable property. **2.** The degree, quantity, or nature of a person's rights in property, esp. in land. See TENANCY.

absolute estate. A full and complete estate that cannot be defeated.

ancestral estate. An estate that is acquired by descent or by operation of law with no other consideration than that of blood.

bankruptcy estate. See BANKRUPTCY ESTATE.

concurrent estate. Ownership or possession of property by two or more persons at the same time, such as a tenancy in common or a joint tenancy. —Also termed *concurrent interest.*

contingent estate. **a.** An estate that depends for its effect on an event that may or may not happen. **b.** An estate that is conditioned on the existence of a person who answers the description of the taker but who cannot be ascertained until the termination of a preceding or particular estate.

decedent's estate. The real and personal property that a person possesses at the time of death and that descends to the heirs subject to the payment of debts and claims.

dominant estate. An estate benefiting from an easement. —Also termed *dominant tenement.* Cf. *servient estate.*

equitable estate. An estate recognized in equity, such as a trust beneficiary's interest. See EQUITY.

estate at sufferance. See *tenancy at sufferance* under TENANCY.

estate at will. See *tenancy at will* under TENANCY.

estate by curtesy. An estate owned by a wife to which the husband is entitled upon her death. See CURTESY.

estate by the entireties. See *tenancy by the entireties* under TENANCY.

estate for years. See *tenancy for a term* under TENANCY.

estate in reversion. REVERSION.

estate on limitation. An estate that automatically reverts back to the grantor according to a provision, usu. regarding the passage of a determined time period, designated by words like "during," "while," and "so long as."

estate tail. FEE TAIL.

freehold estate. FREEHOLD.

future estate. FUTURE INTEREST.

gross estate. The total value of a decedent's property subject to federal estate and gift taxes.

leasehold estate. LEASEHOLD.

legal estate. An interest enforced in law rather than in equity.

life estate. An estate held only for the duration of a specified person's life, usu. the possessor's; most life estates—created, for example, by a grant "to Jane for life"—are beneficial interests under trusts, the corpus being personal property, not real property. —Also termed *estate for life; life tenancy.*

life estate pur autre vie. A life estate for which the measuring life is someone other than the life tenant. —Also spelled *life estate per autre vie*.

net estate. The portion of an estate—specifically, gross estate minus legal deductions—subject to state and federal estate taxes.

periodic estate. See *periodic tenancy* under TENANCY.

real estate. See *real property* under PROPERTY.

servient estate. An estate burdened by an easement. —Also termed *servient tenement*. Cf. *dominant estate*.

vested estate. An estate with a present right of enjoyment or a present fixed right of future enjoyment.

estate freeze. An estate-planning maneuver whereby a closely-held-business owner exchanges common stock for dividend-paying preferred stock and gives the common stock to his or her children, thus guaranteeing a pension and avoiding estate tax.

estate tax. See TAX.

estimated tax. See TAX.

estimated useful life. See USEFUL LIFE.

Estin **doctrine.** In family law, the principle that, although full faith and credit is given to a divorce decree to terminate a marriage, a spousal-support provision may not be recognized unless the court entering the order had jurisdiction over both spouses. *Estin v. Estin*, 334 U.S. 541 (1948).

estop (e-**stop**), *vb.* To stop, bar, hinder, or preclude.

estoppel (e-**stop**-əl). **1.** A legally imposed bar resulting from one's own conduct and precluding any denial or assertion regarding a fact. **2.** A doctrine that prevents a person from adopting an inconsistent position, attitude, or action if it will result in injury to another. **3.** An affirmative defense alleging good-faith reliance on a misleading representation and an injury or detrimental change in position resulting from that reliance. Cf. WAIVER (1).

collateral estoppel. See COLLATERAL ESTOPPEL.

equitable estoppel. **a.** See *promissory estoppel.* **b.** See *estoppel in pais.*

estoppel by contract. A bar against denying a term, fact, or performance arising from a contract that one has entered.

estoppel by judgment. COLLATERAL ESTOPPEL.

estoppel by silence. Estoppel that arises when a party is under a duty to speak but fails to do so.

estoppel in pais (in-**pays** *or* -**pay**). A defensive doctrine preventing one party from taking unfair advantage of another when, through false language or conduct, the person to be estopped has induced another person to act in a certain way, with the result that the other person has been injured in some way. — Also termed *equitable estoppel*.

judicial estoppel. Estoppel that prevents a party from contradicting its previous declarations during the same or a subsequent proceeding if the change in position would adversely affect the proceeding. — Also termed *doctrine of preclusion of inconsistent positions*; *doctrine of the conclusiveness of the judgment*.

promissory estoppel. The principle that a promise made without consideration becomes binding if (1) the promisor intends, or should reasonably expect, the promise to induce reliance, (2) a party actually relies on the promise, and (3) non-enforcement of the promise will cause detrimental injury or injustice. —Also termed *equitable estoppel.*

prosecution-history estoppel. See PROSECUTION-HISTORY ESTOPPEL.

quasi-estoppel. An equitable doctrine preventing one from repudiating an act or assertion if it would harm another who relied on the act or assertion.

et al. (ed-**ahl**). *abbr.* [Latin *et alii*] And others; used only of persons <the office of Thomas Webb et al.>.

etc. *abbr.* ET CETERA.

et cetera (et-**sed**-ə-rə). [Latin "and others"] And other things; usu. used to denote additional, unspecified items in a series. —Abbr. etc.

ethical, *adj.* **1.** Of or relating to moral obligations that one person owes another; esp., in law, of or relating to legal ethics <the ethical rules regarding confidences>. See LEGAL ETHICS. **2.** In conformity with moral norms or standards of professional conduct <the judge's recusal was a perfectly ethical act>.

ethical absolutism. MORAL ABSOLUTISM.

ethical consideration. (*usu. cap.*) An aspirational goal or principle on which a lawyer can rely for guidance in matters of professional conduct; a lawyer's violation of these considerations (which are contained in the Model Code of Professional Responsibility) does not necessarily subject the lawyer to discipline. —Abbr. EC. Cf. DISCIPLINARY RULE.

ethical relativism. MORAL RELATIVISM.

ethics. See LEGAL ETHICS.

et seq. (et-**sek**). *abbr.* [Latin *et sequentes* "the following ones"] The following page or pages <11 U.S.C. §§ 101 et seq.>.

et ux. (ed-**əks**). *abbr.* [Latin *et uxor*] *Archaic.* And his wife <conveyed the land to Donald Baird et ux.>.

EU. *abbr.* EUROPEAN UNION.

Euclidean zoning. See ZONING.

Eurobond. An international bond issued in a country other than the one in whose currency the bond is denominated.

Eurodollar. A U.S. dollar deposited in a foreign bank and used in the European money markets.

European Community. See EUROPEAN UNION.

European currency unit. A monetary unit whose value is calculated as a weighted average of currencies from ten member-nations of the European Union; it is the accounting unit used in all intermember transactions and many private transactions in the EU. —Abbr. ECU; ecu.

European Economic Community. See EUROPEAN UNION.

European Union. An association—formed as the *European Economic Community* (EEC) by the Treaty of Rome in 1957 and later renamed the

European Community (EC)—of European nations with the purpose of achieving full economic unity (and eventual political union) by agreeing to eliminate barriers to the free movement of capital, goods, and labor among the member-nations; the *European Community* became the *European Union* when the Maastricht Treaty on European Union took effect in November 1993, and currently Austria, Belgium, Denmark, Finland, France, Germany, Great Britain, Greece, Ireland, Italy, Luxembourg, Netherlands, Portugal, Spain, and Sweden have full membership privileges. —Abbr. EU.

euthanasia (yoo-thə-**nay**-zhə), *n.* The mercy-killing of another for the purpose of ending the other's intolerable and incurable suffering; euthanasia is usu. regarded by the law as second-degree murder, manslaughter, or criminally negligent homicide. —Also termed *mercy-killing.* — **euthanize, euthanatize** (yoo-**tha**-nə-tIz), *vb.*

active euthanasia. Euthanasia performed by a facilitator (usu. a physician) who not only provides the means of death but also carries out the final death-causing act. Cf. *assisted suicide* under SUICIDE.

involuntary euthanasia. Euthanasia of a competent, nonconsenting person.

nonvoluntary euthanasia. Euthanasia of an incompetent, thus nonconsenting, person.

passive euthanasia. The act of allowing a terminally ill person to die by either withholding or withdrawing life-sustaining support such as a respirator or feeding tube.

voluntary euthanasia. Euthanasia performed with the terminally ill person's consent.

evaluative fact. See FACT.

evasion. See TAX EVASION.

evasive answer. A response that neither directly admits nor denies a question; in pleading, this is considered a failure to answer. Fed. R. Civ. P. 37(3).

even date. *Jargon.* The same date.

even lot. See *round lot* under LOT (3).

evict, *vb.* **1.** To expel (a person, esp. a tenant), from real property, usu. by legal process. **2.** *Archaic.* To recover (property or title) from a person by legal process. —**evictor,** *n.*

eviction. The act or process of legally dispossessing a person of land or rental property. Cf. EJECTMENT.

actual eviction. A physical expulsion of a person from land or rental property.

constructive eviction. **a.** A landlord's act of making premises unfit for occupancy, often with the result that the tenant is compelled to leave. **b.** The inability of a land purchaser to obtain possession because of paramount outstanding title; such an eviction usu. constitutes a breach of the covenants of warranty and quiet enjoyment.

partial eviction. An eviction, either constructive or actual, from a portion of a tenant's premises.

retaliatory eviction. An eviction—often illegal—commenced in response to a tenant's complaints or involvement in activities with which the landlord does not agree.

evidence, *n.* **1.** A perceptible thing that tends to establish or disprove a fact, including testimony, documents, and other tangible objects <the bloody glove is the key piece of evidence for the prosecution>. **2.** The collective mass of things, esp. testimony and exhibits, that are presented before a tribunal in a given dispute <the evidence will show that the defendant breached the contract>. **3.** The body of law regulating the burden of proof, admissibility, relevance, and the weight and sufficiency of what should be admitted into the record of legal proceedings <according to the rules of evidence, leading questions are impermissible during direct examination in most cases>. —**evidence,** *vb.*—**evidentiary,** *adj.*

admissible evidence. Evidence that is relevant and of such a character (i.e., not overly prejudicial or based on hearsay) that the court should receive it. —Also termed *competent evidence.*

best evidence. Evidence of the highest quality available, as measured by the nature of the case rather than the thing being offered as evidence. —Also termed *primary evidence.* See BEST-EVIDENCE RULE. Cf. *secondary evidence.*

character evidence. Evidence regarding someone's personality traits; evidence of a person's moral standing in a community, based on reputation.

circumstantial evidence. Evidence based on inference and not on personal knowledge or observation. —

Also termed *indirect evidence.* Cf. *direct evidence* (a).

clear and convincing evidence. Evidence indicating that the thing to be proved is highly probable or reasonably certain; this is a greater burden than preponderance of the evidence, the standard applied in most civil cases, and less than evidence beyond a reasonable doubt, the norm for criminal trials. —Also termed *clear and convincing proof.*

competent evidence. **a.** See *admissible evidence.* **b.** See *relevant evidence.*

conclusive evidence. **a.** Evidence so strong as to overbear any other evidence to the contrary. —Also termed *conclusive proof.* **b.** Evidence that, though not irrebuttable, so preponderates as to oblige a fact-finder to come to a certain conclusion.

corroborating evidence. Evidence that strengthens or confirms existing evidence.

cumulative evidence. Additional evidence that supports a fact established by existing evidence.

demonstrative evidence. Physical evidence that one can see and inspect, such as a model or photograph. — Also termed *real evidence*; *tangible evidence*; *autoptic evidence.* Cf. *testimonial evidence.*

derivative evidence. Evidence that is spawned from illegally obtained evidence and is therefore inadmissible because of the primary taint. See EXCLUSIONARY RULE; FRUIT-OF-THE-POISONOUS-TREE DOCTRINE.

direct evidence. **a.** Evidence that is based on personal knowledge or observation and that, if true, proves a fact without inference or presumption. Cf. *circumstantial evidence.* **b.** See *original evidence.*

documentary evidence. Evidence supplied by a writing or other document, which must be authenticated before the evidence is admissible.

exculpatory evidence. Evidence tending to establish a criminal defendant's innocence; the prosecution has a duty to disclose exculpatory evidence in its possession or control when the evidence may be material to the outcome of the case.

expert evidence. Evidence about a scientific, technical, or professional issue given by a person qualified to testify because of familiarity with the subject or special training in the field. —Also termed *expert testimony.*

extrinsic evidence. **a.** Evidence relating to a contract but not appearing on the face of the contract because it comes from other sources, such as statements between the parties or the circumstances surrounding the agreement; such evidence is usu. not admissible to contradict or add to the terms of an unambiguous document. —Also termed *extraneous evidence*; *parol evidence*; *evidence aliunde.* **b.** Evidence that is not legitimately before the court.

fabricated evidence. False or deceitful evidence that is unlawfully created after the relevant event, usu. in an attempt to avoid liability.

forensic evidence. Evidence determined by scientific means, esp. relating to ballistics or medicine.

habit evidence. Evidence of one's regular response to a repeated specific situation.

hearsay evidence. HEARSAY.

illegally obtained evidence. Evidence obtained by violating a statute or a person's Fourth Amendment guarantee against unreasonable searches.

immaterial evidence. **a.** Evidence lacking in probative value. **b.** Evidence offered to prove a matter not in issue.

incompetent evidence. Evidence that is for any reason inadmissible.

incriminating evidence. Evidence tending to establish guilt or from which a court can infer guilt.

inculpatory evidence. Evidence showing or tending to show one's involvement in a crime.

material evidence. Evidence having some logical connection with the consequential facts. Cf. *relevant evidence.*

mathematical evidence. Loosely, evidence that establishes its conclusions with absolute certainty.

moral evidence. Loosely, evidence that depends on a belief, rather than complete and absolute proof; testimony as opposed to demonstrative evidence.

newly discovered evidence. Evidence existing at the time of trial but then unknown to a party who, upon later discovering it, may assert it as grounds for a new trial.

opinion evidence. A witness's belief, thought, or inference about a disputed fact, usu. admissible only when the witness is an expert. See OPINION (3).

original evidence. A witness's statement that he or she perceived a fact in issue by one of the five senses, or that he or she was in a particular physical or mental state. —Also termed *direct evidence*. Cf. HEARSAY.

parol evidence. **a.** Evidence given orally. **b.** See *extrinsic evidence* (a). See PAROL-EVIDENCE RULE.

presumptive evidence. Evidence deemed true and sufficient unless discredited by other evidence.

prima facie evidence. Evidence that will support a fact or sustain a judgment unless contradictory evidence is produced.

rebuttal evidence. Evidence offered to disprove or contradict the evidence presented by an opposing party.

relevant evidence. Evidence tending to prove or disprove a matter in issue; relevant evidence is both probative and material and is admissible unless excluded by a specific statute or rule. —Also termed *competent evidence*. Fed. R. Evid. 401, 402. Cf. *material evidence*.

reputation evidence. Evidence of what one is thought by others to be; reputation evidence may be introduced as proof of character when character is in issue or is used circumstantially. Fed. R. Evid. 405(a). —Also termed *reputational evidence*.

secondary evidence. Evidence that is inferior to the primary or best evidence and that becomes admissible when the primary or best evidence is lost or inaccessible; examples include a copy of a lost instrument or testimony regarding the contents of a lost document. Cf. *best evidence*.

secondhand evidence. HEARSAY.

substantial evidence. Evidence that a reasonable mind might accept as adequate to support a conclusion; evidence beyond a scintilla. See SUBSTANTIAL-EVIDENCE RULE.

substantive evidence. Evidence offered to support a fact in issue, as opposed to impeachment or corroborating evidence.

tainted evidence. Evidence that is inadmissible because it was directly or indirectly obtained by illegal means. See FRUIT-OF-THE-POISONOUS-TREE DOCTRINE.

testimonial evidence. Evidence elicited from a witness. Cf. *demonstrative evidence*.

traditionary evidence. Evidence derived from a deceased person's former statements or reputation; such evidence is admissible to prove ancestry, ancient boundaries, or similar facts, usu. when no living witnesses are available to testify.

evince, *vb.* To show, indicate, or reveal <in abstaining from the vote, Hariden evinced misgivings about the nomination>.

ex. 1. Former <ex-wife>. **2.** Without <ex rights>. **3.** From <*ex cathedra*>. **4.** *abbr.* Exhibit <Ex. 4>. **5.**

abbr. Example <this is but one ex. of several that might be cited>.

exaction, *n.* The wrongful demand of a reward or fee for an official service performed in the normal course of duty. —**exact,** *vb.*

ex aequo et bono (eks-**e**-kwo-et-**boh**-no). [Latin] According to what is just and good; a decision-maker who is authorized to decide *ex aequo et bono* is not bound by legal rules but may take account of what is just and fair.

examination. See DIRECT EXAMINATION; CROSS-EXAMINATION.

examination-in-chief. DIRECT EXAMINATION.

examination on the voir dire. VOIR DIRE.

examiner. 1. One authorized to conduct an examination or appointed by the court to take testimony. See MASTER (2). **2.** A patent officer responsible for determining the patentability of inventions submitted to the patent office.

examining board. An appointed group of public officials responsible for conducting the tests required by those applying for occupational and professional licenses.

examining court. See COURT.

examining trial. PRELIMINARY HEARING.

ex ante (eks-**an**-tee). [Latin] Based on assumption and prediction; subjective; prospective. Cf. EX POST.

ex bonis (eks-**boh**-nəs). [Latin] In civil law, of or referring to goods or property.

ex cathedra (eks-kə-**thee**-drə *or* eks-**ka**-thə-drə). [Latin "from the chair"] **1.** *adj.* Authoritative. **2.** *adv.* Authoritatively.

exceptio (ek-**sep**-sh[ee]oh). [Latin] **1.** Generally, an exception, plea, or objection. **2.** In civil law, a defendant's plea admitting the claim, but alleging that new facts exist that negate the complaint. **3.** A defense to a complaint that is justly brought but that unjustly accuses the particular defendant named.

exception, *n.* **1.** A formal objection to a court's ruling by a party who wants to preserve the objection for appeal; in federal courts and most state courts, an *exception* has been superseded by an *objection* <the prosecutor stated her exception to the court's ruling disallowing the witness's testimony>. **2.** Something that is excluded from a rule's operation <employers with less than five employees are an exception to the rule>. —**except,** *vb.*—**exceptor,** *n.*

excess clause. An insurance-policy provision that limits the insured's liability to the amount exceeding available coverage. Cf. *excess insurance* under INSURANCE.

excess condemnation. See CONDEMNATION.

excess insurance. See INSURANCE.

excessive bail. See BAIL.

excessive damages. See DAMAGES.

excessive force. See FORCE.

excessive punishment. See PUNISHMENT.

excessive verdict. See VERDICT.

exchange, *n.* **1.** The act of transferring interests, each in consideration for the other. **2.** In commercial law, the payment of a debt using a bill of exchange or credit rather than money. **3.** An organization that brings together buyers and sellers of securities, commodities, and the like, such as the New York Stock Exchange or the Chicago Board of Trade. See SECURITIES EXCHANGE. —**exchange,** *vb.*

exchange broker. One who negotiates money or merchandise matters for others.

exchange rate. The price of converting one country's money into another country's money. See FOREIGN EXCHANGE.

exchange ratio. The amount of shares that an acquiring company must give for each share of an acquired company.

Exchequer, Court of. See COURT OF EXCHEQUER.

excise tax. See TAX.

excited utterance. A statement about a startling event made under the stress and excitement of the event; an excited utterance can be admissible as a hearsay exception. Fed. R. Evid. 803(2). Cf. PRESENT SENSE IMPRESSION.

exclusion, *n.* **1.** In tax law, an item of income excluded from gross income. **2.** In the law of evidence, a trial judge's determination that a fact-trier may not consider a certain item of evidence. **3.** An insurance-policy provision that excepts certain events or conditions from coverage. —**exclude,** *vb.*—**exclusionary,** *adj.*

exclusionary hearing. A pretrial hearing conducted to review and determine the admissibility of alleged illegally obtained evidence.

exclusionary rule. In criminal procedure, the rule providing that illegally obtained evidence is not admissible in court, often with the exception that it is admissible when the evidence was obtained in the good-faith belief that its obtainment was legal <in accordance with the exclusionary rule, the court did not admit the drugs into evidence because they were obtained during a warrantless search of the defendant's home>.

exclusionary zoning. See ZONING.

exclusive agency. See AGENCY (1).

exclusive-agency listing. See LISTING (1).

exclusive authorization-to-sell listing. See *exclusive-agency listing* under LISTING (1).

exclusive-dealing arrangement. An agreement requiring a buyer to purchase all needed goods from one seller. —Also termed *exclusive dealing.* Cf. *requirements contract* under CONTRACT.

exclusive franchise. See *exclusive agency* under AGENCY (1).

exclusive jurisdiction. See JURISDICTION.

exclusive license. See LICENSE.

exclusive possession. See POSSESSION.

exclusive use. See USE (1).

ex contractu (eks-kən-**trak**-too). [Latin "from a contract"] *Jargon.*

Arising from a contract <action *ex contractu*>. Cf. EX DELICTO.

exculpate (**ek**-skəl-payt), *vb*. To free from blame or accusation. —**exculpation**, *n*.—**exculpatory**, *adj*. Cf. EXONERATE (1).

exculpatory clause. A contractual provision relieving a party from any liability resulting from a negligent or wrongful act.

exculpatory evidence. See EVIDENCE.

ex curia (eks-**kyoor**-ee-ə). [Latin] Out of court; away from the court.

excusable, *adj*. Of an illegal act or omission that, because of certain circumstances, will not be punished <excusable neglect>.

excusable homicide. See HOMICIDE.

excuse (eks-**kyoos**), *n*. **1.** A reason that justifies an act or omission or relieves one of a duty. **2.** In criminal law, a defense that arises because the defendant is not blameworthy for having acted in a way that would otherwise be criminal; traditionally, the following defenses were excuses: duress, entrapment, infancy, insanity, and involuntary intoxication. Cf. JUSTIFICATION (2). —**excuse** (eks-**kyooz**), *vb*.—**excusatory** (eks-**kyooz**-ə-tor-ee) *adj*.

ex-date. EX-DIVIDEND DATE.

ex delicto (eks-də-**lik**-toh). [Latin "from a tort"] *Jargon*. Arising from a tort <action *ex delicto*>. Cf. IN DELICTO; EX CONTRACTU.

ex dividend. Without dividend <the shares were traded ex dividend>.

ex-dividend date. The date on or after which the buyer of a security does not acquire the right to receive a recently declared dividend. —Also termed *ex-date*. Cf. DIVIDEND DATE.

execute, *vb*. **1.** To perform or complete (a contract or duty). **2.** *Jargon*. To make (a legal document) valid by signing; to bring (a legal document) into its final, legally enforceable form. **3.** To put to death, esp. by legal sentence.

executed remainder. See *vested remainder* under REMAINDER.

execution, *n*. **1.** The act of carrying out or putting into effect (as an action or an order) <execution of the court's decree>. **2.** Validation of a written instrument, such as a contract or will, by fulfilling the necessary legal requirements <delivery of the goods completed the contract's execution>. **3.** Judicial enforcement of a money judgment, usu. by seizing and selling the judgment debtor's property <even if the plaintiff receives a judgment against the foreign debtor, execution is unlikely>. **4.** A court order directing a sheriff or other officer to enforce a judgment, usu. by seizing and selling the judgment debtor's property <the court issued the execution authorizing seizure of the car>. —Also termed (in sense 4) *writ of execution*; *judgment execution*; *general execution*.

alias execution. A second execution issued to enforce a judgment not fully satisfied by the original writ.

dormant execution. An execution authorizing an officer to seize and hold property rather than sell it, until further notice.

junior execution. An execution that is subordinate to another execution issued from an earlier judgment against the same debtor.

special execution. An execution authorizing a judgment to be satisfied from specified property.

5. In criminal law, the carrying out of a death sentence <the Supreme Court stayed the execution>. —**execute,** *vb.*

execution clause. The part of a deed containing the date, seal (if required), and signatures of the grantor, grantor's spouse, and witnesses.

executioner. One who puts another to death in satisfaction of a death sentence.

execution lien. See LIEN.

execution-proof. JUDGMENT-PROOF.

execution sale. See SALE.

executive, *n.* **1.** The branch of government responsible for effecting and enforcing laws; the person or persons who constitute this branch. Cf. LEGISLATURE; JUDICIARY (1).

chief executive. The head of the executive branch of a government, such as the President of the United States.

2. A corporate officer at the upper levels of management. —**executive,** *adj.*

executive agreement. An international agreement entered into by the executive branch, without the need for approval by the Senate, and usu. involving routine diplomatic matters. Cf. TREATY.

executive clemency. CLEMENCY.

executive immunity. See IMMUNITY (1).

executive order. An order issued by or on behalf of the President regarding a constitutional provision, law, or treaty.

executive pardon. PARDON.

executive privilege. See PRIVILEGE.

executor, *n.* **1.** (ek-sǝ-kyoo-tǝr) One who performs or carries some act. **2.** (ig-**zek**-yǝ-tǝr) One who is appointed by a testator, usu. in the will, to administer the testator's estate. Cf. ADMINISTRATOR (1).

executor de son tort. A person who, without legal authority, takes on the responsibility to act as an executor or administrator of a decedent's property, usu. to the detriment of the estate's beneficiaries or creditors.

independent executor. An executor who, unlike an ordinary executor, can administer the estate with very little supervision by the probate court; only a few states—mostly in the West and Southwest—allow testators to designate independent executors.

special executor. An executor whose power is limited to a portion of the decedent's estate.

substituted executor. An executor appointed to act in the place of an executor who cannot or will not perform the required duties.

3. (ig-**zek**-yǝ-tǝr) In patent law, one who represents a legally incapacitated inventor. —**executorship,** *n.*—**executorial,** *adj.*

executory, *adj.* **1.** Taking full effect at a future time <executory judgment>. **2.** To be performed at a future time; yet to be completed <executory contract>.

executory accord. ACCORD (2).

executory bequest. See BEQUEST.

executory contract. See CONTRACT.

executory devise. See DEVISE.

executory interest. A future interest, held by a third person, that either cuts off another's interest or begins after the natural termination of a preceding estate. Cf. REMAINDER.

executory limitation. See LIMITATION.

executory remainder. See *contingent remainder* under REMAINDER.

executrix (ig-**zek**-yə-triks). *Archaic.* A female executor. See EXECUTOR.

exemplar (ig-**zem**-plahr), *n.* An ideal or typical example; a standard specimen <handwriting exemplars>.

exemplary, *adj.* **1.** Serving as an ideal example; commendable <exemplary behavior>. **2.** Serving as a warning; admonitory <exemplary damages>.

exemplary damages. See *punitive damages* under DAMAGES.

exemplification, *n.* An official transcript of a public record, authenticated as a true copy for use as evidence. —**exemplify,** *vb.*

exemplified copy. See *certified copy* under COPY.

exempt, *adj.* Free or released from a duty or liability to which others are held <persons exempt from military service> <property exempt from sequestration>. —**exempt,** *vb.*

exempt income. See INCOME.

exemption. 1. Freedom from a duty, liability, or other requirement. See IMMUNITY. **2.** A privilege given to a judgment debtor by law, allowing the debtor to retain certain property without liability. **3.** In taxation, an amount allowed as a deduction from adjusted gross income, used to determine taxable income. Cf. DEDUCTION (2).

dependency exemption. An exemption granted to an individual taxpayer for each dependent whose gross income is less than the exemption amount and for each child who is either less than 19 years old or a student less than 24 years old.

personal exemption. An amount allowed as a deduction from an individual taxpayer's adjusted gross income.

exemption equivalent. The maximum value of assets one can transfer to another before incurring federal gift and estate tax.

exempt property. A debtor's holdings and possessions that, by law, a creditor cannot attach to satisfy a debt; all the property that creditors may lawfully reach is known as *nonexempt property*.

exempt security. See SECURITY.

exercise, *vb.* **1.** To make use of; to put into action <exercise the right to vote>. **2.** To implement the terms of; to execute <exercise the option to buy the commodities>. —**exercise,** *n.*

exercise price. See *strike price* under PRICE.

exercise value. The value to the optionholder of using an option.

ex facie (eks-**fay**-shee *or* -shə). [Latin "from the face"] Apparently; evidently; facially.

ex gratia (eks-**grahd**-ee-ah *or* -**gray**-sh[ee]-ə). [Latin] As a favor; not legally necessary.

exhaustion of remedies. The doctrine that, if an administrative remedy is provided by statute, a claimant must seek relief first from the administrative body before judicial relief is available; the doctrine maintains comity between the courts and administrative agencies. —Also termed *exhaustion of administrative remedies.*

exhaustion of state remedies. The doctrine that an available state remedy must be exhausted in certain types of cases before a party can gain access to federal court; for example, a state prisoner must exhaust all state remedies before a federal court will hear a petition for habeas corpus.

exhibit, *n.* **1.** A document, record, or other tangible object formally introduced as evidence in court. **2.** A document attached to and made part of a pleading, motion, contract, or other instrument.

exhibitionism, *n.* The indecent display of one's body. —**exhibitionist,** *adj.* & *n.*

ex hypothesi (eks-hI-**poth**-ə-sI). [Latin] Hypothetically; by hypothesis; on the assumption.

exigency (**ek**-sə-jən-see *or* eg-**zi**-jən-see), *n.* A demand for immediate action or performance arising from a circumstance or condition <exigency of a bond> <exigency of a writ>. —**exigent,** *adj.*

exigent circumstances. See CIRCUMSTANCE.

exile, *vb.* To expel from a country; to banish. —**exile,** *n.*

Ex-Im Bank. See EXPORT-IMPORT BANK.

exit, *n.* **1.** The way out. See EGRESS. **2.** In a docket entry, an issuance of something (as a writ or process); for example, "exit attachment" denotes that a writ of attachment has been issued in the case. —**exit,** *vb.*

ex lege (eks-**lay**-gay). [Latin] By virtue of law; as a matter of law <property forfeited *ex lege*>.

ex maleficio (eks-mahl-ə-**fik**-ee-oh *or* -mal-ə-**fish**-[i-]oh), *adv.* [Latin] By malfeasance.

ex maleficio, adj. [Latin] Tortious.

ex officio (**eks**-ə-**fish**-ee-oh). [Latin] By virtue of the office; by virtue of the authority implied by office.

ex officio **justice.** A judge who serves on a commission or board only because the law requires the presence of a judge rather than because the judge was selected for the position.

ex officio **service.** A service that the law imposes on an official by virtue of the office held, such as a local sheriff's duty to perform marriage ceremonies.

exonerate, *vb.* **1.** To free one from responsibility <exonerate from the

payment of the debt>. Cf. EXCUL-PATE. **2.** To free from encumbrances <exonerate the property from the mortgage lien>. —**exoneration,** *n.* —**exonerative,** *adj.*

exordium. INTRODUCTORY CLAUSE.

ex parte (eks-**pahr**-tee *or* -tay). [Latin "from the part"] **1.** *adv.* On or from one party only, usu. without notice to or argument from the adverse party <the judge conducted the hearing ex parte>. **2.** *adj.* Done or issued by or for one party only <an ex parte injunction>.

ex parte divorce. See DIVORCE.

ex parte proceeding. See PROCEEDING.

expatriate (ek-**spay**-tree-ayt), *vb.* **1.** To leave one's home country to live elsewhere. **2.** To banish (a person); to exile. —**expatriation,** *n.*—**expatriate** (ek-**spay**-tree-ət), *n.*

expectancy, *n.* **1.** In property law, an estate with a reversion, a remainder, or an executory interest. **2.** In wills and trusts, the possibility that an heir apparent, heir presumptive, or a presumptive next-of-kin will acquire property by devolution on intestacy, and the possibility that a presumptive legatee or devisee will acquire property by will. **3.** In insurance law, the probable number of years in one's life. See LIFE EXPECTANCY. —**expectant,** *adj.*

expectancy damages. See *expectation damages* under DAMAGES.

expectancy table. ACTUARIAL TABLE.

expectant heir. See HEIR.

expectation damages. See DAMAGES.

expense, *n.* An expenditure of money, time, labor, or resources to accomplish a result. —**expense,** *vb.* Cf. COST (1).

accrued expense. An expense incurred but not yet paid.

educational expense. For tax purposes, a deductible expense incurred either to maintain or to improve an existing job skill or to meet a legally imposed job requirement.

fixed expense. See *fixed cost* under COST.

operating expense. An expense incurred in running a business and producing output.

organizational expense. An expense incurred while setting up a corporation or other entity.

out-of-pocket expense. An expense that one has to pay from one's own funds.

prepaid expense. An expense (such as rent, interest, or insurance) that is paid before the due date.

expense stop. A lease provision establishing the maximum expenses to be paid by the landlord, beyond which the tenant must bear all remaining expenses.

experimental use. See USE (1).

expert, *n.* A person who, through education or experience, has developed knowledge of a particular subject, so that he or she may form an opinion that one without such knowledge could not provide. —**expertise,** *n.*

consulting expert. An expert who is retained by a party but who is not expected to be called as a witness at trial; such an expert's opinions are generally exempt from discovery. Fed. R. Civ. P. 26(b)(4)(B).

impartial expert. An expert who is appointed by the court in order to present an unbiased opinion.

testifying expert. An expert who is identified by a party as a potential witness at trial; such an expert's opinions are subject to discovery. Fed. R. Civ. P. 26(b)(4)(A).

expert evidence. See EVIDENCE.

expert testimony. See *expert evidence* under EVIDENCE.

expert witness. See WITNESS.

expiration date. The date on which an offer, option, or the like ceases to exist.

exploitation, *n.* The act of taking unjust advantage of another for one's own benefit. —**exploit,** *vb.*—**exploitative,** *adj.*

exploration manager. LAND MANAGER.

export, *n.* **1.** A product or service created in one country and transported to another. **2.** The process of transporting products or services to another country. —**export,** *vb.*—**exportation,** *n.*

Export Clause. IMPORT-EXPORT CLAUSE.

export draft. See DRAFT.

Export-Import Bank. A federal agency, established in 1934, that encourages trade with foreign countries by financing exports and imports with funds borrowed from the U.S. Treasury. —Abbr. Ex-Im Bank.

export letter of credit. See LETTER OF CREDIT.

ex post. [Latin] Based on knowledge and fact; objective; retrospective. Cf. EX ANTE.

ex post facto (eks-pohst-**fak**-toh). [Latin] After the fact.

ex post facto **law.** A law passed after an action in order to retroactively change the legal treatment of the action to the disadvantage of the actor; *ex post facto* criminal laws are unconstitutional.

express, *adj.* Clearly and unmistakably communicated; directly stated.

express assumpsit. See *special assumpsit* under ASSUMPSIT.

express authority. See AUTHORITY.

expression, freedom of. See FREEDOM OF EXPRESSION.

expressio unius est exclusio alterius. INCLUSIO UNIUS EST EXCLUSIO ALTERIUS.

express malice. See MALICE.

express power. See *enumerated power* under POWER.

express repeal. See REPEAL.

express trust. See TRUST.

express warranty. See WARRANTY (2).

expropriation, *n.* A governmental taking or modification of an individual's property rights, esp. by eminent domain; CONDEMNATION (2). —**expropriate,** *vb.*—**expropriator,** *n.* Cf. APPROPRIATION.

expulsion, *n.* An ejectment or banishment, either through depriving one of a benefit or by forcibly evicting one. —**expulsive,** *adj.*

expunge (ek-**spənj**), *vb.* To erase or destroy <the trustee wrongfully expunged the creditor's claim against the debtor>. —**expungement, expunction,** *n.*

expungement of record. The removal of convictions (esp. for first offenses) from a person's criminal record. —Also termed *erasure of record.*

ex rel. *abbr.* [Latin *ex relatione*] On the relation or information of; a suit *ex rel.* is typically brought by the government upon the application of a private party (called a *relator*) who is interested in the matter. See RELATOR (1).

ex rights. Without rights; esp. describes a stock whose holder does not have the privilege to purchase shares of a new stock issue at a reduced price.

ex-rights date. The date on which a share of common stock no longer offers privilege subscription rights.

ex ship. Of or referring to a shipment of goods for which the liability passes to the buyer once the goods leave the ship.

ex tempore (eks-**tem**-pə-ree), *adv.* [Latin] By lapse of time; equivalent to the anglicized word *extemporaneously.*

extended first mortgage. See *wraparound mortgage* under MORTGAGE.

extension, *n.* The continuation of the same contract for a specified period. —**extend,** *vb.* Cf. RENEWAL.

extenuating circumstances. See *mitigating circumstances* under CIRCUMSTANCE.

extenuation (ek-sten-yə-**way**-shən), *n.* The fact of rendering a crime or tort less severe; the act that does so. —**extenuate,** *vb.*

extern. CLERK (4).

externality. (*usu. pl.*) A social or monetary consequence or side-effect of one's economic activity, causing another to benefit without paying or to suffer without compensation. — Also termed *spillover; neighborhood effect.*

negative externality. An externality that is detrimental to another; for example, water pollution created by a nearby factory.

positive externality. An externality that benefits another; for example, the advantage received by a neighborhood when a homeowner attractively landscapes the property.

external sovereignty. See SOVEREIGNTY.

exterritorial. EXTRATERRITORIAL.

exterritoriality. EXTRATERRITORIALITY.

extinguishment, *n.* The cessation or cancellation of some right or interest; for example, the extinguishment of a legacy occurs when the item bequeathed no longer exists or no longer belongs to the testator's estate. —**extinguish,** *vb.*

extortion, *n.* **1.** The act or practice of obtaining something or compelling some action by illegal means, such as by force or coercion. **2.** The offense committed by a public official who illegally obtains property under the color of office. —**extort,** *vb.*—**extortionate,** *adj.*

extortionate credit transaction. LOANSHARKING.

extradite, *vb.* **1.** To surrender or deliver (a fugitive) to another jurisdiction. **2.** To obtain the surrender of (a fugitive) from another jurisdiction.

extradition. The surrender of an alleged criminal by one state or nation to another having jurisdiction over the crime charged.

extra dividend. See *extraordinary dividend* under DIVIDEND.

extrajudicial, adj. **1.** Out-of-court. **2.** Outside the judicial process.

extrajudicial admission. See ADMISSION.

extrajudicial oath. See OATH.

extrajudicial remedy. See REMEDY.

extrajudicial statement. Any utterance made outside of court; it is usu. treated as hearsay under the rules of evidence.

extralegal, *adj.* Beyond the province of law.

extraneous evidence. See *extrinsic evidence* (a) under EVIDENCE.

extraneous offense. See OFFENSE.

extraordinary circumstances. See CIRCUMSTANCE.

extraordinary dividend. See DIVIDEND.

extraordinary hazard. See HAZARD (1).

extraordinary majority. See *supermajority* under MAJORITY.

extraordinary remedy. See REMEDY.

extraordinary session. See *special session* under SESSION.

extraordinary writ. See WRIT.

extrapolate (ek-**strap**-ə-layt), *vb.* To estimate an unknown number from outside the range of known numbers; to deduce an unknown legal principle from a known case. —**extrapolation,** *n.*—**extrapolative, extrapolatory,** *adj.*—**extrapolator,** *n.*

extra session. See *special session* under SESSION.

extraterritorial, *adj.* Beyond the geographic limits of a particular jurisdiction. —Also termed *exterritorial.*

extraterritoriality. The freedom of diplomats, foreign ministers, and royalty from the jurisdiction of the country in which they temporarily reside. —Also termed *exterritoriality.* See *diplomatic immunity* under IMMUNITY (1).

extraterritorial jurisdiction. See JURISDICTION.

extra vires (ek-strə-**veer**-eez *or* -**vI**-reez). ULTRA VIRES.

extreme cruelty. See CRUELTY.

extrinsic, *adj.* From outside sources.

extrinsic ambiguity. See *latent ambiguity* under AMBIGUITY.

extrinsic evidence. See EVIDENCE.

extrinsic fraud. See FRAUD.

eyewitness. One who personally observes an event.

F

F. *abbr.* The first series of the Federal Reporter, which includes federal cases (trial and appellate) decided from 1880 to 1924.

F.2d. *abbr.* The second series of the Federal Reporter, which includes federal appellate cases decided from 1924 to 1993.

F.3d. *abbr.* The third series of the Federal Reporter, which includes federal appellate cases decided from 1993.

fabricated evidence. See EVIDENCE.

face, *n.* **1.** The surface of anything, esp. the front, upper, or outer part <the face of a clock>. **2.** The inscribed side of a document, instrument, or judgment <although the contract appeared valid on its face, the seller did not have the legal capacity to enter into it>. —**facial,** *adj.*

face interest rate. See *nominal rate* under INTEREST RATE.

face value. PAR VALUE.

facial, *adj.* Complete; as a whole.

facilitation, *n.* The act or an instance of aiding or helping; esp., in criminal law, the act of making it easier for another person to commit a crime. —**facilitate,** *vb.*—**facilitator,** *n.*

facility-of-payment clause. An insurance-policy provision allowing the appointment of a person to receive payment from the insurer on the beneficiary's behalf.

facsimile (fak-**sim**-ə-lee). **1.** An exact copy. **2.** FAX.

fact. 1. An event, occurrence, or circumstance <discoverable facts>. **2.** An evil deed; a crime <accessory after the fact>.

adjudicative fact. A fact that concerns the parties to a judicial or administrative proceeding and that helps the court or agency determine how the law applies to those parties; for example, adjudicative facts include those that the jury weighs in a jury trial. Cf. *legislative fact.*

denotative fact. A fact relevant to the use of a nonlegal term in a legal rule.

evaluative fact. A fact used to assess some action as being reasonable or negligent.

inferential fact. A fact established by conclusions drawn from other evidence rather than from direct testimony or evidence; a fact drawn by inference from one or more primary facts.

judicial fact. A fact taken by the court as proved without hearing evidence. See JUDICIAL NOTICE.

jurisdictional facts. Facts that must exist before a court can properly hear a particular case. See JURISDICTIONAL-FACT DOCTRINE.

legal fact. A fact that triggers a particular legal consequence.

legislative fact. A fact that explains a particular law's rationality and that helps a court or agency determine the law's content; legislative facts ordinarily do not pertain to the specific parties in the proceeding. Cf. *adjudicative fact.*

material fact. A fact that is significant or essential to the issue or matter at hand.

primary fact. A fact dependent on what a witness saw or perceived.

probative fact. A fact in evidence used to prove an ultimate fact.

relative fact. A fact incidental to another fact; a minor fact.

ultimate fact. A fact essential to the claim or the defense.

fact-finder. One or more persons—such as a jury in a jury trial or an administrative-law judge in a hearing—who hear testimony and review evidence to make the ultimate ruling about a factual issue such as whether certain events took place. —Also termed *finder of fact* and (in a judicial proceeding) *fact-trier* or *trier of fact.* See FINDING OF FACT.

facto. See DE FACTO; IPSO FACTO.

factor, *n.* **1.** An agent or cause that contributes to a particular result <punishment appears to be a factor in the court's decision>. **2.** A broker, consignee, or commission agent <a factor was employed to sell goods for the company>.

factor's act. A statute protecting a buyer of goods from a factor or agent by creating the presumption that the agent was acting on the owner's behalf and with the owner's approval.

fact pleading. See *code pleading* under PLEADING (2).

fact question. QUESTION OF FACT.

fact-trier. FACT-FINDER.

factual impossibility. See IMPOSSIBILITY.

factual presumption. See *presumption of fact* under PRESUMPTION.

factum (fak-təm**).** [Latin] **1.** A person's physical presence in a new domicile. **2.** Due execution of a will. **3.** A fact or statement of facts. **4.** An act or deed. See *fraud in the factum* under FRAUD.

failure of consideration. A situation whereby a contract's basis or inducement ceases to exist or becomes worthless. See CONSIDERATION. Cf. WANT OF CONSIDERATION.

failure of issue. The fact of dying without children, esp. if they would have inherited the decedent's estate. See ISSUE (3).

fair comment. In defamation law, a statement based on the writer's or speaker's honest opinion about a matter of public concern; fair comment is a defense to a libel or slander action.

fair consideration. See CONSIDERATION.

fair market value. The price at which a seller is ready and willing to sell and a buyer is ready and willing to buy on the open market and in an arm's-length transaction; the point at which supply and demand intersect. —Abbr. FMV. —Also termed *actual value; actual cash value; actual market value; cash value; clear market value; just value; market value.*

fairness doctrine. A federal law, based on an FCC rule, requiring the broadcast media to provide a reasonable opportunity for the discussion of conflicting views on issues of public importance; Congress repealed the fairness doctrine in 1987.

fair notice. FAIR WARNING.

fair-trade agreement. A commercial agreement providing that a seller will sell all of a producer's goods for at least a specified minimum price; this type of agreement was valid until Congress passed the Consumer Goods Pricing Act in 1975, which abolished state statutes that permitted such agreements. 15 U.S.C. §§ 1, 45.

fair trial. A trial conducted by an impartial and disinterested tribunal in an orderly manner; esp., a criminal trial in which the defendant's constitutional and legal rights are safeguarded.

fair use. In copyright law, reasonable and limited use of a copyrighted work without the author's permission, such as quoting from a book in a book review; fair use is a defense to an infringement claim, depending on the following statutory factors: (1) the purpose and character of the use, (2) the nature of the copyrighted work, (3) the amount of the work used, and (4) the economic impact of the use. 17 U.S.C. § 107.

fair-value accounting method. See ACCOUNTING METHOD.

fair-value legislation. A statute requiring a deficiency judgment to be measured by the difference between the mortgage debt and the fair value of the foreclosed real estate.

fair warning. In criminal law, the requirement that a criminal statute define an offense with enough precision so that a reasonable person can know what conduct is prohibited and so that a reasonably skilled lawyer can predict what conduct falls within the statute's scope. —Also termed *fair notice.*

fair wear and tear. WEAR AND TEAR.

false arrest. See ARREST.

false check. See *bad check* under CHECK.

false conflict. In conflict of laws, a situation resembling but not embodying an actual conflict because the potentially applicable laws do not differ, because the laws' underlying policies have the same objective, or because one of the laws is not meant to apply to the case before the court.

false imprisonment. A confinement or restraint of a person to a bounded area without justification or consent; false imprisonment is a common-law misdemeanor and a tort.

false light. In an invasion-of-privacy action, a plaintiff's allegation that the defendant attributed to the plaintiff views that he or she does not hold and placed the plaintiff before the public in a highly offensive and untrue manner; if the matter at issue is in the public interest, the plaintiff must prove the defendant's malice. See INVASION OF PRIVACY.

false oath. PERJURY.

false plea. See *sham pleading* under PLEADING (1).

false pretenses. The common-law crime of knowingly obtaining title to another's personal property by means of a misrepresentation of fact and with intent to defraud. Cf. *larce-*

ny by trick under LARCENY; EMBEZZLEMENT.

false representation. MISREPRESENTATION.

false return. 1. A process server's or other court official's misrepresentation that process was served, that some other action was taken, or that something is true. **2.** See TAX RETURN.

false swearing. PERJURY.

false verdict. See VERDICT.

***falsus in uno* doctrine** (**fol**-səs-in-**yoo**-noh). [Latin *falsus in uno, falsus in omnibus* "false in one thing, false in everything"] The principle that if the jury believes that a witness's testimony on a material issue is intentionally deceitful, the jury may disregard all of that witness's testimony.

family, the. ORGANIZED CRIME (2).

family allowance. See ALLOWANCE (1).

family-automobile doctrine. FAMILY-PURPOSE RULE.

family court. See COURT.

family-farmer bankruptcy. See CHAPTER 12.

family law. The body of law dealing with marriage, divorce, adoption, child custody and support, and other domestic-relations issues.

family-partnership rules. Laws designed to prevent the shifting of income among partners, esp. family members, who may not be dealing at arm's length.

family-purpose rule. In tort law, the doctrine holding a vehicle's owner liable for injuries or damage caused by a family member negligently driving the vehicle; many states have abolished this doctrine. —Also termed *family-automobile doctrine*. Cf. GUEST STATUTE.

Fannie Mae. FEDERAL NATIONAL MORTGAGE ASSOCIATION.

Farmers Home Administration. A division of the U.S. Department of Agriculture that makes mortgage loans to farmers, provides home-mortgage insurance, and funds public-works programs in rural areas and small towns. —Abbr. FHA; FmHA.

F.A.S. *abbr.* FREE ALONGSIDE SHIP.

FASB (**faz**-bee). *abbr.* FINANCIAL ACCOUNTING STANDARDS BOARD.

fatal, *adj.* **1.** Of or relating to death <the decision had fatal consequences>. **2.** Providing grounds for legal invalidity <a fatal defect in the contract>.

fatal error. See ERROR.

fatal variance. See VARIANCE (1).

fault. An error or defect of judgment or of conduct; any deviation from prudence or duty resulting from inattention, incapacity, perversity, bad faith, or mismanagement. See NEGLIGENCE.

***Fauntleroy* doctrine.** The principle that a state must give full faith and credit to another state's judgment, if the other state had proper jurisdiction, even though the judgment is based on a claim that is illegal in the state in which enforcement is sought. *Fauntleroy v. Lum*, 210 U.S. 230 (1908).

favored beneficiary. In wills and estates, a beneficiary who receives more willed property than others having equal claims to the property, raising a prima facie presumption of the beneficiary's undue influence over the testator. See UNDUE INFLUENCE.

favored-nation clause. MOST-FAVORED-NATION CLAUSE.

fax, *n.* **1.** A method of transmitting over telephone lines an exact copy of a printing. **2.** A machine used for such transmission. —Also termed *telecopier*. **3.** The communication sent or received by such a machine. —Also termed *facsimile*; (in senses 1 & 3) *facsimile transmission*. —**fax,** *vb.*

FBI. *abbr.* FEDERAL BUREAU OF INVESTIGATION.

F. Cas. *abbr.* Federal Cases, a series of reported cases (1789-1880) predating the Federal Reporter.

FCC. *abbr.* FEDERAL COMMUNICATIONS COMMISSION.

FDA. *abbr.* FOOD AND DRUG ADMINISTRATION.

FDIC. *abbr.* FEDERAL DEPOSIT INSURANCE CORPORATION.

fealty (fee[ə]l-tee). *Archaic.* In feudal law, the allegiance that a tenant or vassal owes to a lord.

feasance (feez-ən[t]s), *n.* The doing or execution of an act, condition, or obligation. —**feasor,** *n.* Cf. MALFEASANCE; MISFEASANCE; NONFEASANCE.

featherbedding. A union practice designed to increase employment and guarantee job security by requiring employers to hire or retain more employees than are needed; featherbedding is restricted by federal law.

Fed. *abbr.* **1.** FEDERAL. **2.** FEDERAL RESERVE SYSTEM.

federal, *adj.* Of or relating to the national government of the United States.

Federal Bureau of Investigation. A division of the U.S. Department of Justice charged with investigating all violations of federal laws except those specifically assigned to another federal agency. —Abbr. FBI.

federal common law. The body of decisional law developed by federal courts adjudicating federal questions and other matters of federal concern, such as the law applying to disputes between two states.

Federal Communications Commission. The federal agency that regulates interstate and foreign communications by radio, television, telephone, and telegraph, and oversees radio and television broadcasting standards, cable-television operations, two-way radio operators, and satellite communications. —Abbr. FCC.

federal court. See COURT.

Federal Deposit Insurance Corporation. An independent governmental agency that insures bank deposits up to a statutory amount per depositor at each participating bank; the insurance fund is financed by a small fee paid by the participating banks. —Abbr. FDIC.

Federal Employers' Liability Act. A workers'-compensation law that provides death and disability benefits for employees of railroads engaged in interstate and foreign commerce. 45 U.S.C. §§ 51 et seq. —Abbr. FELA.

Federal Home Loan Mortgage Corporation. A corporation that purchases both conventional and federally insured first mortgages from members of the Federal Reserve System and other approved banks; it is under the Federal Home Loan Bank Board. —Abbr. FHLMC. —Also termed *Freddie Mac*.

Federal Housing Administration. The HUD division that encourages mortgage lending by insuring mortgage loans made by approved lenders on homes meeting the agency's standards. —Abbr. FHA.

Federal Insurance Contributions Act. The federal act imposing the social-security tax on employers and employees. 26 U.S.C. §§ 3101 et seq. —Abbr. FICA.

federalism. The relationship and distribution of power between the individual states and the national government. See OUR FEDERALISM.

Federalist Society. A national association of lawyers, law students, and other persons committed to expressing and promoting their conservative and libertarian viewpoints on political and social matters; the group is based in Washington, D.C. Cf. NATIONAL LAWYERS GUILD.

federal magistrate. See UNITED STATES MAGISTRATE JUDGE.

Federal National Mortgage Association. A corporation that is chartered by the U.S. Government but is privately owned and managed, and that provides a secondary mortgage market for the purchase and sale of mortgages guaranteed by the Veterans Administration and those insured under the Federal Housing Administration. —Abbr. FNMA. —Also termed *Fannie Mae*.

federal preemption. PREEMPTION (5).

federal question. A legal issue involving the interpretation and application of the U.S. Constitution, an act of Congress, or a treaty; jurisdiction over federal questions rests with the federal courts. 28 U.S.C. § 1331.

federal-question jurisdiction. See JURISDICTION.

Federal Register. A daily publication in which U.S. administrative agencies publish their rules and regulations, including proposed rules and regulations for public comment.

Federal Reserve System. A network of twelve central banks supervised by the Board of Governors, who are appointed by the President and confirmed by Congress and who set the reserve requirements for the member banks, review the discount-rate actions of the regional Federal Reserve banks, and set ceilings on the interest rates that member banks may pay. —Abbr. Fed.

Federal Rules of Appellate Procedure. The rules governing appeals to the U.S. courts of appeals from lower courts, some federal-agency proceedings, and applications for writs. —Abbr. FRAP.

Federal Rules of Bankruptcy Procedure. The rules governing proceedings instituted under the Bankruptcy Code.

Federal Rules of Civil Procedure. The rules governing civil actions in the U.S. district courts and before U.S. Magistrates. —Abbr. FRCP.

Federal Rules of Criminal Procedure. The rules governing criminal proceedings in the U.S. District Courts and before U.S. Magistrates.

Federal Rules of Evidence. The rules governing the admissibility of evidence at trials in federal courts and before U.S. Magistrates. —Abbr. FRE.

Federal Savings and Loan Insurance Corporation. A federal agency created in 1934 to insure deposits in savings-and-loan associations and savings banks; when this agency became insolvent in 1989, its assets and liabilities were transferred to an insurance fund managed by the FDIC. —Abbr. FSLIC. Cf. RESOLUTION TRUST CORPORATION.

Federal Tort Claims Act. A statute that limits federal sovereign immunity and allows recovery in federal court for tort damages caused by federal employees, but only if the law of the state where the injury occurred would hold a private person liable for the injury. 28 U.S.C. §§ 2671 et seq.

Federal Trade Commission. The independent regulatory agency created in 1914 to enforce the antitrust laws and other prohibitions against false, deceptive, and unfair advertising or trade practices. —Abbr. FTC.

federal transfer. The federal district court's right to move a civil action filed in its court to any other district or division where the plaintiff could have brought the action originally. 28 U.S.C. § 1404(a). See CHANGE OF VENUE.

federation. A league or union of states, groups, or peoples arranged with a strong central authority and no regional sovereignties, though the individual states, groups, or peoples may retain rights of varying degrees. Cf. CONFEDERATION.

fee. 1. A charge for labor or services, esp. professional services.

attorney's fees. See ATTORNEY'S FEES.

contingent fee. See CONTINGENT FEE.

docket fee. A fee charged by a court for filing a claim.

2. An inheritable interest in land, constituting maximal legal ownership; esp., a fee simple absolute. See FEE SIMPLE.

feemail. *Slang.* **1.** An attorney's fee extorted by intimidation, threats, or pressure. **2.** The act or process of extorting such a fee. Cf. GREENMAIL; BLACKMAIL.

fee simple. An interest in land that, being the broadest property interest allowed by law, endures until the current holder dies without heirs; esp., a fee simple absolute.

fee simple absolute. An estate of indefinite or potentially infinite duration (e.g., "to Albert and his heirs").

fee simple conditional. An estate restricted to some specified heirs, exclusive of others (e.g., "to Albert and his female heirs"); the fee simple conditional is obsolete except in Iowa, Oregon, and South Carolina.

fee simple defeasible. An estate that ends either because there are no more heirs of the person to whom it is granted or because a special limitation, condition subsequent, or executory limitation takes effect before the line of heirs runs out. — Also termed *qualified fee*.

fee simple determinable. An estate that will automatically end and revert to the grantor if some specified event ever occurs (e.g., "to Albert and his heirs while the property is used for charitable purposes"); the future interest retained by the grantor is called a *possibility of reverter*. —Also termed *determinable fee*; *qualified fee*; *fee simple subject to common-law limitation*; *fee simple subject to special limitation*; *fee simple subject to special interest*.

fee simple subject to a condition subsequent. An estate subject to the grantor's power to end the estate if some specified event happens (e.g., "to Albert and his heirs, upon condition that no alcohol is sold on the premises"); the future interest retained by the grantor is called a *power of termination* (or a *right of entry*). —Also termed *fee simple on a condition subsequent*; *fee simple subject to a power of termination*; *fee simple upon condition*.

fee simple subject to an executory limitation. A fee simple defeasible that is subject to divestment in favor of someone other than the grantor if a specified event happens (e.g., "to Albert and his heirs, but if the property is ever used as a parking lot, then to Bob"). —Also termed *fee simple subject to an executory interest*.

fee-splitting. 1. The division of attorney's fees between the lawyer who handles a matter and the lawyer who referred the matter; some states consider this practice unethical. **2.** The division of attorney's fees between two or more lawyers who represent a client jointly but are not in the same firm; an attorney is prohibited from splitting a fee with a nonlawyer.

fee statement. A lawyer's bill for services either already rendered or to be rendered, usu. including itemized expenses.

fee tail. An estate that is inheritable only by specified descendants of the original grantee, and that endures until its current holder dies without issue (e.g., "to Albert and the heirs of his body"); most jurisdictions—except Delaware, Maine, Massachusetts, and Rhode Island—have abolished the fee tail. —Also termed *entailed estate*; *estate tail*; *tenancy in tail*. See ENTAIL (2).

FELA (**fee-**lə). *abbr.* FEDERAL EMPLOYERS' LIABILITY ACT.

fellow-servant rule. A common-law doctrine holding that an employer is not liable for an employee's injuries caused by a negligent coworker; this doctrine has generally been abrogated by workers'-compensation statutes.

felonious assault. See *assault with a deadly weapon* under ASSAULT.

felony, *n.* A serious crime usu. punishable by imprisonment for more than one year or by death; examples include murder, rape, arson, and burglary. —Also termed *major crime*. — **felonious** (fə-**loh-**nee-əs), *adj.*—**felon,** *n.* Cf. MISDEMEANOR.

felony-murder rule. The doctrine holding that any death resulting from the commission or attempted commission of a felony is murder;

most states restrict this rule to inherently dangerous felonies such as rape, arson, robbery, or burglary.

fem-crit. See CRIT.

feme covert (fem-**kəv**-ərt). [Law French] *Archaic.* A married woman. See COVERTURE.

feme sole (fem-**sohl**). [Law French] *Archaic.* **1.** An unmarried woman. **2.** A married woman handling the affairs of her separate estate.

fence, *n.* **1.** A person who receives stolen goods. **2.** A place where stolen goods are sold. See RECEIVING STOLEN PROPERTY.

feoff (fef *or* feef), *vb.* ENFEOFF.

feoffee (fef-**ee** *or* feef-**ee**). The transferee of an estate in fee simple.

feoffment (fef-**mənt** *or* feef-**mənt**). ENFEOFFMENT.

feoffor (fef-**or** *or* feef-**or**). The transferor of an estate in fee simple.

ferae naturae (fe-rI-nə-**tuu**-rI). [Latin "of a wild nature"] **1.** *adj.* (Of animals) wild; untamed. **2.** *n.* Wild animals. See RULE OF CAPTURE.

fertile-octogenarian rule. The legal fiction, assumed under the rule against perpetuities, that a woman can become pregnant as long as she is alive.

feticide. The act or an instance of killing a fetus, usu. by assaulting and battering the mother; an intentionally induced miscarriage. Cf. INFANTICIDE (1).

feudalism (**fyoo**-d[ə]l-iz-[ə]m). A landholding system, particularly applying to medieval Europe, in which all are bound by the obligation of service and defense.

FHA. *abbr.* **1.** FARMERS HOME ADMINISTRATION. **2.** FEDERAL HOUSING ADMINISTRATION.

FHLMC. *abbr.* FEDERAL HOME LOAN MORTGAGE CORPORATION.

fiat (**fee**-aht). [Latin "let it be done"] **1.** An order or decree, esp. an arbitrary one <judicial fiat>. **2.** A decree rendered by a court, esp. one relating to a routine matter such as scheduling <the court requires all motions to contain a fiat—to be filled in by the court—fixing the hearing date>.

FICA (**fIk**-ə). *abbr.* FEDERAL INSURANCE CONTRIBUTIONS ACT.

fiction, legal. See LEGAL FICTION.

fidelity bond. See BOND (2).

fidelity guaranty insurance. See *fidelity insurance* under INSURANCE.

fidelity insurance. See INSURANCE.

fiduciary (fi-**d[y]oo**-shee-er-ee), *n.* **1.** One who owes to another the duties of good faith, trust, confidence, and candor <the corporate officer is a fiduciary to the shareholders>. **2.** One who must exercise a high standard of care in managing another's money or property <the beneficiary sued the fiduciary for investing in speculative securities>. — **fiduciary,** *adj.*

fiduciary relationship. A relationship requiring the highest duty of care and arising between parties usu. in one of four situations: (1) when one person places trust in the faithful integrity of another, who as a result gains superiority or influence over the first, (2) when one person assumes control and responsibility over another, (3) when one person has a duty to act for or give advice to another on matters falling within the scope of the relationship, or (4) when there is a specific relationship that has traditionally been recognized as involving fiduciary duties, as with a lawyer and a client or a stockbroker and a customer.

fiduciary-shield doctrine. In corporate law, the principle that a corporate officer's act cannot provide the basis for jurisdiction over the officer in his or her individual capacity.

field audit. See AUDIT.

Field Code. The New York Code of Procedure of 1848, which was the first comprehensive Anglo-American code of civil procedure and served as a model for the Federal Rules of Civil Procedure. See *code pleading* under PLEADING (2).

field sobriety test. See SOBRIETY TEST.

fieri facias (fī-ər-I-**fays**[h]-[ee-]əs *or* fee-er-ee-**fahk**-ee-ahs). [Latin "that you cause to be done"] A writ of execution that directs a marshal or sheriff to seize and sell a defendant's property to satisfy a money judgment. —Abbr. *fi. fa.* or *Fi. Fa.*

FIFO (**fī**-foh). *abbr.* FIRST-IN, FIRST-OUT.

Fifteenth Amendment. The constitutional amendment, ratified in 1870, guaranteeing all citizens the right to vote regardless of race, color, or prior condition of slavery.

Fifth Amendment. The constitutional amendment, ratified with the Bill of Rights in 1791, providing that a person cannot be (1) required to answer for a capital or otherwise infamous offense unless a grand jury issues an indictment or presentment, (2) subjected to double jeopardy, (3) compelled to testify against himself or herself, (4) deprived of life, liberty, or property without due process of law, and (5) deprived of private property for public use without just compensation.

Fifth Amendment, pleading the. See PLEADING THE FIFTH.

fighting words. Inflammatory speech that is not protected by the First Amendment's free-speech guarantee because it might incite a violent response.

file, *n.* **1.** A court's complete and official record of a case <the law clerk went to the courthouse to verify that the motion is in the file>. **2.** A lawyer's complete record of a case <the paralegal stored the file in three drawers in her office>. **3.** A portion or section of a lawyer's case record <the janitor found the correspondence file behind the copy machine>. **4.** A case <Jonah was assigned the Watson file after Amy left the firm>.

file, *vb.* **1.** To deliver a legal document to the court clerk or record custodian for placement into the official record <Tuesday is the deadline for filing a reply brief> <they perfected the security interest by filing>. **2.** To commence a lawsuit <the seller threatened to file against the buyer>. **3.** To record or deposit something in an organized retention system or container for preservation and future reference <please file my notes under the heading "research">.

file wrapper. PROSECUTION HISTORY.

file-wrapper estoppel. PROSECUTION-HISTORY ESTOPPEL.

filiation (fil-ee-**ay**-shən). **1.** The fact or condition of being a son or daughter; relationship of a child to a parent. **2.** Judicial determination of paternity. See PATERNITY SUIT.

filibuster, *n.* The use of dilatory tactics, esp. prolonged and often irrelevant speechmaking, in an attempt to obstruct legislative action; the filibuster is common in the U.S. Senate, where the right to debate is unlimited. —**filibuster,** *vb.*

final argument. CLOSING ARGUMENT.

final decision. See *final judgment* under JUDGMENT.

final decree. See *final judgment* under JUDGMENT.

final judgment. See JUDGMENT.

final order. See ORDER (2).

final settlement. See SETTLEMENT.

finance charge. An additional payment, usu. in the form of interest, paid by a retail buyer for the privilege of purchasing goods or services in installments.

finance lease. See LEASE.

Financial Accounting Standards Board. The independent body of accountants responsible for establishing and interpreting generally accepted accounting principles. —Abbr. FASB.

financial institution. A business, organization, or other entity that manages money, credit, or capital, such as a bank, credit union, savings-and-loan association, securities broker or dealer, pawnbroker, or investment company.

financial intermediary. A financial entity—usu. a commercial bank—that advances the transfer of funds between borrowers and lenders, buyers and sellers, and investors and savers.

financial-responsibility act. A state statute requiring owners of motor vehicles to produce proof of insurance or other financial accountability as a condition to acquiring a license and registration.

financial statement. A balance sheet, income statement, or annual report that summarizes an individual's or organization's financial condition on a certain date or for a specified period by analyzing its assets and liabilities. Cf. FINANCING STATEMENT.

consolidated financial statement. The financial report of a company and all its subsidiaries combined, usu. without intercompany transactions.

financing, *n.* **1.** The act or process of raising or providing funds. **2.** Funds that are raised or provided. —**finance,** *vb.*

asset-based financing. A method of funding in which lenders and investors look principally to the cash flow from a particular asset for the return on their investment.

debt financing. Raising funds by issuing bonds or notes or by borrowing from a financial institution to acquire working capital or to retire short-term indebtedness.

equity financing. The raising of corporate capital by issuing securities rather than taking out loans or selling bonds; the capital so raised.

gap financing. Interim financing used to fund the difference between a current loan and a loan for a greater amount to be received in the future. See *bridge loan* under LOAN.

interim financing. A short-term loan secured to cover certain major expenditures, such as construction costs, until permanent financing is obtained.

internal financing. A method of funding a project or investment using funds generated through the company's operations rather than from stock issues or bank loans.

link financing. The process of depositing funds in another's bank account to aid in obtaining a loan.

permanent financing. A long-term loan obtained to repay an interim loan, such as a mortgage loan that is used to repay a construction loan.

financing statement. A document filed properly in the public records to notify third parties, usu. prospective buyers and lenders, of a secured party's security interest in goods. Cf. FINANCIAL STATEMENT.

finder. An intermediary who brings together parties for a business opportunity, such as two companies for a merger, a borrower and a financial institution, or an issuer and an underwriter of securities.

finder of fact. FACT-FINDER.

finder's fee. The amount charged by a person who brings together parties for a business opportunity.

finding of fact. A determination by a judge, jury, or administrative agency of a fact supported by the evidence presented at the trial or hearing <he agreed with the jury's finding of fact that the driver did not stop before proceeding into the intersection>. — Often shortened to *finding.* Cf. CONCLUSION OF FACT; CONCLUSION OF LAW.

fine, *n.* **1.** *Archaic.* An amicable final agreement or compromise of a fictitious or actual suit to determine the true possessor of land; formerly used as a form of conveyance. **2.** *Archaic.* A fee paid by a tenant to the landlord upon transfer of the tenant's rights to another. —Also termed *fine for alienation.* **3.** A fee paid by a tenant to the landlord at the commencement of the tenancy in order to reduce the rent payments. **4.** A pecuniary criminal punishment or civil penalty payable to the public treasury. —**fine,** *vb.*

firebug. INCENDIARY (1).

fire insurance. See INSURANCE.

firm, *n.* **1.** The title under which one or more persons carry on business jointly. **2.** The association by which persons are united for business purposes; esp., a partnership. See LAW FIRM.

firm-commitment underwriting. See UNDERWRITING.

firm offer. See *irrevocable offer* under OFFER.

firm-opportunity doctrine. See CORPORATE-OPPORTUNITY DOCTRINE.

First Amendment. The constitutional amendment, ratified with the Bill of Rights in 1791, guaranteeing the freedoms of speech, religion, press, and assembly and the right to petition the government for the redress of grievances.

first chair, *n.* A lawyer who acts as the lead attorney in court for a given case <despite having worked at the firm for six years, the associate had yet to be first chair in a jury trial>. —**first chair,** *vb.*

first-degree murder. See MURDER.

first devisee. The first intended recipient of an estate devised by will.

firsthand knowledge. See *personal knowledge* under KNOWLEDGE.

first impression, case of. See CASE (1).

first-in, first-out. An accounting method that assumes that goods are sold in the order in which they were purchased—that is, the oldest items are sold first. —Abbr. FIFO. Cf. LAST-IN, FIRST-OUT; NEXT-IN, FIRST-OUT.

first instance, court of. See *trial court* under COURT.

first lien. See LIEN.

first magistrate. MAGISTRATE (1).

first mortgage. See MORTGAGE.

first offender. See OFFENDER.

first option to buy. RIGHT OF PRE-EMPTION.

first-party insurance. See INSURANCE.

first refusal, right of. See RIGHT OF FIRST REFUSAL.

first-sale doctrine. In copyright law, the rule that a copyright owner, after conveying the title to a particular copy of the protected work, loses the exclusive right to sell that copy and therefore cannot interfere with subsequent sales or distributions by the new owner.

fisc (fisk). The public treasury.

fiscal (**fis**-kəl), *adj.* **1.** Of or relating to financial matters <fiscal year>. **2.** Of or relating to public finances or taxation <the city's sound fiscal policy>.

fiscal year. An accounting period of 12 consecutive months; a fiscal year is often different from the calendar year, esp. for tax purposes <the company's fiscal year is October 1 to September 30>.

fishing expedition. An attempt, through broad discovery requests, to elicit reams of information from another party in hopes that something relevant might turn up; esp., such an attempt that exceeds the scope of discovery as allowed by procedural rules.

fitness for a particular purpose. See *implied warranty of fitness for a particular purpose* under WARRANTY (2).

fixation, *n.* In copyright law, the process or result of recording a work of authorship in tangible form so that it can be copyrighted under federal law; fixation occurs, for instance, when a live television broadcast is transmitted and simultaneously recorded on videotape. —**fixed,** *adj.*

fixed annuity. See ANNUITY.

fixed asset. See *capital asset* (a) under ASSET.

fixed capital. See CAPITAL.

fixed charge. See *fixed cost* under COST.

fixed cost. See COST.

fixed expense. See *fixed cost* under COST.

fixed income. See INCOME.

fixed-rate mortgage. See MORTGAGE.

fixed sentence. See *determinate sentence* under SENTENCE.

fixed trust. See TRUST.

fixing a jury. JURY-FIXING.

fixture. Personal property that has been attached to land or a building and that is regarded as an irremovable part of the real property; an example is a fireplace built into a home. Cf. IMPROVEMENT.

trade fixture. Removable personal property that a tenant attaches to leased property for business purposes, such as a display counter; despite its name, a trade fixture is not usu. treated as a fixture—that is, as irremovable.

fixture filing. The act or an instance of recording, in public real-estate records, a security interest in personal property that is intended to become a fixture.

flag of truce. A white flag used as a signal when one belligerent wishes to communicate with the other in the field; the bearers of such a flag may not be fired on, injured, or taken

prisoner, as long as they carry out their mission in good faith.

flash-of-genius rule. In patent law, the now-defunct rule that a device is not patentable if it was invented as the result of trial and error rather than as a "flash of creative genius"; the rule, which takes its name from language in *Cuno Eng'g Corp. v. Automatic Devices Corp.*, 314 U.S. 84, 91 (1941), was legislatively overturned in 1952. 35 U.S.C. § 103.

flat sentence. See *determinate sentence* under SENTENCE.

flat tax. See TAX.

flexible-rate mortgage. See *adjustable-rate mortgage* under MORTGAGE.

flight. The act or an instance of fleeing, esp. to evade arrest or prosecution <the judge denied bail because the defendant is a flight risk>.

flight easement. See *avigational easement* under EASEMENT.

flip, *vb. Slang.* **1.** To buy and then immediately resell securities or real estate in an attempt to turn a profit. **2.** To refinance consumer loans. **3.** To turn state's evidence.

flip mortgage. See MORTGAGE.

float, *n.* **1.** The sum of money represented by outstanding or uncollected checks. **2.** The delay between a transaction (as by check or on credit) and the withdrawal of funds to cover the transaction. **3.** The amount of a corporation's shares that are available for trading on the securities market.

float, *vb.* **1.** (Of a currency) to attain an exchange-market value solely on the basis of supply and demand <allowed the dollar to float>. **2.** To issue (a security) for sale on the market <PDQ Corp. floated a new series of preferred shares>. **3.** To arrange or negotiate (a loan) <the bank floated a car loan to Alice despite her poor credit history>.

floater insurance. See INSURANCE.

floating capital. See CAPITAL.

floating charge. See *floating lien* under LIEN.

floating debt. See DEBT.

floating lien. See LIEN.

floating policy. See INSURANCE POLICY.

floating rate. See INTEREST RATE.

floating zoning. See ZONING.

floor. 1. A legislature's central meeting place where the members sit and conduct business, as distinguished from the galleries, corridors, or lobbies <the floor of the Texas Senate>. **2.** The trading area where stocks and commodities are bought and sold on exchanges <the broker placed his buy order with the trader on the floor of the NYSE>. **3.** The lowest limit <the floor for that position is $25,000 per year>.

floor-plan financing. A loan that is secured by merchandise and paid off as the goods are sold; usu. such a loan is given by a manufacturer to a retailer or other dealer (as a car dealer).

floor price. See PRICE.

flotsam (flot-səm). Goods that float on the water's surface after being abandoned at sea. Cf. JETSAM; LAGAN.

fluctuating clause. ESCALATOR CLAUSE.

FmHA. *abbr.* FARMERS HOME ADMINISTRATION.

FNMA. *abbr.* FEDERAL NATIONAL MORTGAGE ASSOCIATION.

F.O.B. *abbr.* FREE ON BOARD.

FOIA (foi-ə). *abbr.* FREEDOM OF INFORMATION ACT.

foiable (foi-ə-bəl), *adj. Slang.* (Of documents) subject to disclosure under the Freedom of Information Act (FOIA).

Food and Drug Administration. The federal agency within the Department of Health and Human Services established to determine safety and quality standards for foods, drugs, medical devices, cosmetics, and other household products. — Abbr. FDA.

forbearance, *n.* **1.** The act of refraining from enforcing a legal right, obligation, or debt. **2.** The act of tolerating or abstaining. —**forbear,** *vb.*

force, *n.* Power, violence, or pressure directed against a person or thing. —**force,** *vb.*

deadly force. Violent action known to create a substantial risk of causing death or serious bodily harm; a person may use deadly force in self-defense only if retaliating against another's deadly force.

excessive force. Force beyond that which is reasonable or necessary under the circumstances.

reasonable force. Force that is not excessive and that is appropriate for protecting oneself or one's property; the use of reasonable force will not render a person criminally or tortiously liable.

unlawful force. Action constituting an offense or actionable tort directed against a person without that person's consent.

forced conversion. See CONVERSION (1).

forced heir. See HEIR.

forced sale. See SALE.

force majeure (fors-mə-**zhoor** or -mah-**zhər**). [Law French "a superior force"] An event or effect that can be neither anticipated nor controlled; the term includes both acts of nature (such as floods or hurricanes) and acts of people (such as riots, strikes, or wars). —Also termed *force majesture*; *vis major*. Cf. ACT OF GOD.

forcible detainer. 1. The wrongful retention of possession of property by one originally in lawful possession, usu. with threats or actual use of violence. **2.** FORCIBLE ENTRY AND DETAINER.

forcible entry. At common law, the act or an instance of violently and unlawfully taking possession of lands and tenements against the will of those entitled to possession.

forcible entry and detainer. A quick and simple legal proceeding for regaining possession of real property from someone who has wrongfully taken, or refused to surrender, possession. —Also termed *forcible detainer*.

foreclosure, *n.* A legal proceeding for the termination of a mortgagor's interest in property, instituted by the lender either to gain title or to force a sale in order to satisfy all or part of the unpaid debt secured by the property. —**foreclose,** *vb.*

judicial foreclosure. A costly and time-consuming foreclosure method by which the mortgaged property is sold through a court proceeding requiring many standard legal steps such as the filing of a complaint, service of process, notice, and a hearing; judicial foreclosure is available in all jurisdictions and is the exclusive or most common method of foreclosure in at least 40 percent of the states.

nonjudicial foreclosure. **a.** See *power-of-sale foreclosure.* **b.** A foreclosure method that does not require court involvement.

power-of-sale foreclosure. A foreclosure process by which, according to the mortgage instrument and a state statute, the mortgaged property is sold at a nonjudicial public sale by a public official, the mortgagee, or a trustee, without the stringent notice requirements, burdens, or delays of a judicial foreclosure; power-of-sale foreclosure is authorized and used in over 30 states. —Also termed *nonjudicial foreclosure*; *statutory foreclosure.*

strict foreclosure. A rare procedure that gives the mortgagee title to the mortgaged property—without first conducting a sale—after a defaulting mortgagor fails to pay the mortgage debt within a court-specified period; the use of strict foreclosure is limited to special situations except in those few states that permit this remedy in all foreclosure proceedings.

foreclosure sale. See SALE.

foreign, *adj.* **1.** Of or relating to another country <foreign affairs>. **2.** Of or relating to another jurisdiction <the Arizona court gave full faith and credit to the foreign judgment from Mississippi>. —**foreigner,** *n.*

foreign agent. See AGENT.

foreign corporation. See CORPORATION.

foreign divorce. See DIVORCE.

foreign domicile. See DOMICILE.

foreign-earned-income exclusion. The Internal Revenue Code provision that excludes from taxation income earned outside of the United States; the taxpayer must elect between this exclusion and the foreign tax credit. I.R.C. § 911(a) and (b). See *foreign tax credit* under TAX CREDIT.

foreign exchange. 1. The process of making international monetary transactions; esp., the conversion of one currency to that of a different country. **2.** Foreign currency or negotiable instruments payable in foreign currency, such as traveler's checks.

foreign immunity. See IMMUNITY (1).

foreign judgment. See JUDGMENT.

foreign jurisdiction. See JURISDICTION.

foreign jury. See JURY.

foreign tax credit. See TAX CREDIT.

foreign trade zone. FREE-TRADE ZONE.

foreman. See *presiding juror* under JUROR.

forensic (fə-**ren**[t]-zik), *adj.* **1.** Used in or suitable to courts of law or public debate <forensic psychiatry>. **2.** Rhetorical; argumentative <he praised Spence's considerable forensic skills>.

forensic evidence. See EVIDENCE.

forensic medicine. The branch of medicine that establishes or interprets evidence involving scientific or technical facts, such as ballistics. — Also termed *medical jurisprudence*.

forensics (fə-**ren**[t]-ziks). **1.** The art of argumentative discourse. **2.** The branch of law enforcement dealing with legal evidence relating to firearms and ballistics.

foreperson. See *presiding juror* under JUROR.

foreseeability, *n.* The capacity to be reasonably anticipated; foreseeability, along with actual causation, is an element of proximate cause in tort law. —**foreseeable,** *adj.*

forfeiture (**for**-fi-chər), *n.* **1.** The divestiture of property without compensation. **2.** The act or process of losing a right, privilege, or property because of a crime, breach of obligation, or neglect of duty. **3.** Something (esp. money or property) lost or confiscated by this process; a penalty. —**forfeit,** *vb.*

criminal forfeiture. The governmental taking of property due to its, or its owner's, involvement in a crime, such as the impounding of a private motorboat used for smuggling drugs.

forgery, *n.* **1.** The act of fraudulently making a false document or altering a real one so that it may be used as if it were genuine <the contract was void because of the seller's for-

gery>. **2.** A false or altered document made to look genuine by someone with the intent to deceive <he was not the true property owner because the deed of trust was a forgery>. — **forge,** *vb.*

Form 8-K. See 8-K.

Form 10-K. See 10-K.

Form 10-Q. See 10-Q.

formal party. See *nominal party* under PARTY.

forma pauperis. See IN FORMA PAUPERIS.

formbook. A book that contains sample legal documents.

former jeopardy. The fact of having previously been prosecuted for the same offense; a defendant enters a plea of former jeopardy to inform the court that he or she should not be prosecuted again. Cf. DOUBLE JEOPARDY.

form of action. The common-law legal and procedural device associated with a particular writ, each of which had specific forms of process, pleading, trial, and judgment; the 11 common-law forms of action were trespass, trespass on the case, trover, ejectment, detinue, replevin, debt, covenant, account, special assumpsit, and general assumpsit.

Form S-1. See S-1.

formula instruction. See JURY INSTRUCTION.

fornication, *n.* Voluntary sexual intercourse between two unmarried persons; fornication is a crime in some states, such as Virginia. —**fornicate,** *vb.* Cf. ADULTERY.

forswearing, *n.* **1.** The act of repudiating or renouncing. **2.** PERJURY. —**forswear,** *vb.*

forthcoming bond. See *delivery bond* under BOND (2).

forthwith, *adv.* **1.** Immediately; without delay. **2.** Directly; within a reasonable time under the circumstances.

forum. 1. A court or other judicial body; a place of jurisdiction. **2.** A public place devoted to assembly or debate. Pl. **forums; fora.**

forum non conveniens (for-əm-non-kən-**veen**-ee-enz). [Latin "an inconvenient court"] In civil procedure, the doctrine that an inappropriate forum—even though competent under the law—may be divested of jurisdiction if, for the convenience of the litigants and the witnesses, it appears that the action should be instituted in another forum in which the action might originally have been brought. —Also termed *forum inconveniens.*

forum-selection clause. A contractual provision in which the parties establish the venue (such as the country, state, or court) for any litigation between them arising under the contract. Cf. *choice-of-law clause* under CHOICE OF LAW.

forum-shopping. The practice of choosing the most favorable jurisdiction or court in which a claim might be heard; a plaintiff might engage in forum-shopping, for example, by filing suit in a jurisdiction with a reputation for high jury awards.

forward contract. An agreement, usu. between financial institutions or a financial institution and its client, to buy or sell a particular nonstandardized asset at a fixed price on a future date; unlike a futures contract, a forward contract is not traded on a formal exchange. —Also termed *forward agreement*. Cf. FUTURES CONTRACT.

forward triangular merger. See *triangular merger* under MERGER.

foundation. 1. The basis on which something is supported; esp., evidence or testimony that establishes the admissibility of other evidence <laying the foundation>. **2.** A fund established for charitable, educational, religious, research, or other benevolent purposes; an endowment <the foundation for the arts>.

four, rule of. See RULE OF FOUR.

four-corners rule. 1. The principle that a document's meaning is to be gathered from the entire document and not from its isolated parts. **2.** The principle that no extraneous evidence should be considered when interpreting the meaning of an unambiguous document. Cf. PAROL-EVIDENCE RULE.

Fourteenth Amendment. The constitutional amendment, ratified in 1868, whose primary provisions forbid states from denying due process and equal protection and from abridging the privileges and immunities of U.S. citizenship; the amendment also gives Congress the power to enforce these provisions, leading to such legislation as the Civil Rights Acts.

Fourth Amendment. The constitutional amendment, ratified with the Bill of Rights in 1791, prohibiting unreasonable searches and seizures

and the issuance of warrants without probable cause.

four-unities test. In property law, the test for determining whether a joint tenancy has been established; the four unities are interest, possession, time, and title. See *joint tenancy* under TENANCY; UNITY (2).

fragmented literal similarity. See SUBSTANTIAL SIMILARITY.

frame, *vb.* **1.** To plan, shape, or construct; esp., to draft or otherwise draw up (a document). **2.** To incriminate (an innocent person) with false or fabricated evidence. —**framable, frameable,** *adj.*

franchise, *n.* **1.** The right to vote. — Also termed *elective franchise.* **2.** The right conferred by the government to engage in a certain business or to exercise corporate powers. —Also termed *corporate franchise.* **3.** The sole right granted by the owner of a trademark or tradename to engage in business or to sell a good or service in a certain area. **4.** The business or territory controlled by the person or entity that has been granted such a right.

franchise, *vb.* To grant (to another) the sole right of engaging in a certain business or in a business with a particular trademark in a certain area.

franchisee. One who is granted a franchise.

franchiser. One who grants a franchise. —Also spelled *franchisor.*

franchise tax. See TAX.

frank, *n.* **1.** A signature, stamp, or mark affixed to mail as a substitute for postage. **2.** The privilege of sending mail free of charge, accorded to members of Congress and other federal officials. —Also termed (in sense 2) *franking privilege.* —**frank,** *vb.*

FRAP. *abbr.* FEDERAL RULES OF APPELLATE PROCEDURE.

fraud, *n.* **1.** A knowing misrepresentation of the truth or concealment of a material fact to induce another to act to his or her injury. **2.** A misrepresentation made recklessly without belief in its truth to induce another person to act. **3.** A tort arising from a knowing misrepresentation, concealment of material fact, or reckless misrepresentation made to induce another to act to his or her detriment. **4.** Unconscionable dealing; esp., in contract law, the unconscientious use of the power arising out of the parties' relative positions and resulting in an unconscionable bargain. —**fraudulent,** *adj.*

actual fraud. A concealment or false representation through a statement or conduct that causes injury to another. —Also termed *fraud in fact*; *positive fraud.*

constructive fraud. **a.** Unintentional deception or misrepresentation that causes injury to another. — Also termed *legal fraud*; *fraud in contemplation of law.* **b.** See *fraud in law.*

extrinsic fraud. **a.** Deception that is collateral to the issues being considered in the case. —Also termed *collateral fraud.* **b.** Deception that prevents a person from knowing about or asserting certain rights.

fraud in law. Fraud that is presumed under the circumstances, as when a debtor transfers assets and thereby impairs creditors' efforts to collect sums due. —Also termed *constructive fraud.*

fraud in the factum. Fraud occurring when a legal instrument as actually executed differs from the one intended for execution by the person who executes it, or when the instrument may have had no legal existence; compared to fraud in the inducement, fraud in the factum occurs only rarely, as when a blind person signs a mortgage when misleadingly told that it's just a letter. —Also termed *fraud in the execution*; *fraud in the making.*

fraud in the inducement. Fraud occurring when misrepresentations lead another to enter into a transaction with a false impression of the risks, duties, or obligations involved.

intrinsic fraud. Deception that pertains to an issue involved in an original action, such as perjury.

promissory fraud. A promise to perform made at a time when the promisor had no intention of performing the promise. —Also termed *common-law fraud.*

fraud, badge of. See BADGE OF FRAUD.

fraudfeasor. One who has committed fraud.

fraud in contemplation of law. See *constructive fraud* under FRAUD.

fraud in fact. See *actual fraud* under FRAUD.

fraud in law. See FRAUD.

fraud in the execution. See *fraud in the factum* under FRAUD.

fraud in the factum. See FRAUD.

fraud in the inducement. See FRAUD.

fraud in the making. See *fraud in the factum* under FRAUD.

fraud on creditors. FRAUDULENT CONVEYANCE (1).

fraud-on-the-market principle. In securities law, the doctrine that a plaintiff may presumptively establish reliance on a misstatement or omission concerning a security's market price—without proving actual knowledge of the fraudulent statement or omission—if the plaintiff's injury is caused by the purchase or sale at the deceptive price; this doctrine recognizes that the market price of an issuer's stock reflects all available public information and that the market cannot adjust for deceptive or manipulative conduct. —Also termed *fraud-on-the-market theory*.

frauds, statute of. See STATUTE OF FRAUDS.

fraudulent concealment. See CONCEALMENT.

fraudulent conveyance. 1. The transfer of property for little or no consideration, made for the purpose of hindering or delaying a creditor by putting the property beyond the creditor's reach. —Also termed *fraud on creditors*. **2.** In bankruptcy law, a prebankruptcy transfer or obligation made or incurred by a debtor for little or no consideration or with the actual intent to hinder, delay, or defraud a creditor; a bankruptcy trustee may recover such a conveyance from the transferee if the requirements described in 11 U.S.C. § 548 are met. —Also termed *fraudulent*

transfer. Cf. PREFERENTIAL TRANSFER.

fraudulent inducement. See *fraud in the inducement* under FRAUD.

fraudulent joinder. See JOINDER.

fraudulent misrepresentation. See MISREPRESENTATION.

FRCP. *abbr.* FEDERAL RULES OF CIVIL PROCEDURE.

FRE. *abbr.* FEDERAL RULES OF EVIDENCE.

Freddie Mac. FEDERAL HOME LOAN MORTGAGE CORPORATION.

free agency, *n.* A professional athlete's ability to negotiate an employment contract with any team in the league; free agency is usu. granted to veteran players who have been in the league for a certain number of years. —**free agent,** *n.* Cf. RESERVE CLAUSE.

free alongside ship. A mercantile term designating that the seller is responsible for delivering the goods to the dock and for paying the costs of delivery. —Abbr. F.A.S. Cf. FREE ON BOARD; COST, INSURANCE, AND FREIGHT.

free and clear. Unencumbered by any liens; marketable <free-and-clear title>.

freedom of assembly. RIGHT OF ASSEMBLY.

freedom of association. The First Amendment right to join with others in a common undertaking that would be lawful if pursued individually; the government may not prohibit outsiders from joining an association, but the insiders do not necessarily have a right to exclude others. Cf. RIGHT OF ASSEMBLY.

freedom of contract. A judicial concept that contracts are based on mutual agreement and free choice, and thus should not be hampered by external control such as governmental interference. —Also termed *liberty of contract*.

freedom of expression. The freedom of speech, press, assembly, or religion as guaranteed by the First Amendment.

Freedom of Information Act. The federal statute that establishes the guidelines for the public disclosure of documents and materials created and held by federal agencies. 5 U.S.C. § 552. —Abbr. FOIA.

freedom of petition. RIGHT TO PETITION.

freedom of religion. The right to believe in any form of religion, to practice or exercise one's religious belief, and to be free from unreasonable governmental interference in one's religion, as guaranteed by the First Amendment.

freedom of speech. The right to express one's thoughts and opinions without unreasonable governmental restriction, as guaranteed by the First Amendment. —Also termed *liberty of speech*.

freedom of the press. The right to print and publish materials without governmental intervention, as guaranteed by the First Amendment. —Also termed *liberty of the press*.

Free Exercise Clause. The constitutional provision (U.S. Const. amend. I) prohibiting the government from interfering in people's religious practices or forms of worship. Cf. ESTABLISHMENT CLAUSE.

freehold, *n.* **1.** A possessory estate held in fee simple, in fee tail, or for term of life. **2.** The tenure by which such an estate is held. —Also termed *freehold estate*; *freehold interest*. Cf. LEASEHOLD.

free market. See *open market* under MARKET.

free on board. A mercantile term denoting that the seller is responsible for delivering goods to a designated place. —Abbr. F.O.B. Cf. FREE ALONGSIDE SHIP; COST, INSURANCE, AND FREIGHT.

F.O.B. destination. A mercantile term denoting that the seller is required to pay the freight charges as far as the buyer's named designation.

F.O.B. shipping. A mercantile term denoting that the seller is required to bear the risk of placing the goods on a carrier.

free port. FREE-TRADE ZONE.

free rider. One who obtains an economic benefit without paying for it, usu. at another's expense.

free-trade zone. An area within a country where foreign merchandise may enter duty-free until it enters the country's market or is exported. —Also termed *foreign trade zone*; *free port*.

freeze-out. In corporate law, the process, usu. in a closely held corporation, by which the majority shareholders or the board of directors reduces or eliminates the power of minority shareholders in an effort to persuade them to liquidate their investment on terms favorable to the controlling shareholders.

freeze-out merger. See *cash merger* under MERGER.

freight. 1. Goods transported by water or by land. **2.** The price or compensation paid to a carrier for transporting goods.

freight absorption. ABSORPTION (5).

fresh-complaint rule. The theory that the credibility of a sexual-assault victim is bolstered if the victim reports the assault soon after it occurs; most courts no longer recognize this theory.

fresh pursuit. 1. The right of a police officer to cross jurisdictional lines in order to make a warrantless search of or to arrest a fleeing suspect. **2.** The right of a person to use reasonable force to retake property that has just been taken. —Also termed *hot pursuit*.

fresh start. In bankruptcy law, the favorable financial status obtained by a debtor who receives a release from personal liability on prepetition debts or who reorganizes debt obligations through the confirmation and completion of a bankruptcy plan.

friendly suit. A lawsuit in which all the parties have agreed beforehand to allow a court to resolve the issues involved; friendly suits are often filed by settling parties who wish to have a judgment entered.

friendly suitor. WHITE KNIGHT.

friendly takeover. See TAKEOVER.

friend of the court. AMICUS CURIAE.

fringe benefit. See BENEFIT.

frisk, *n.* A pat-down search of a suspect by police to discover something (such as a concealed weapon). —Also termed *pat-down*.

frivolous suit. A lawsuit having no legal basis, often filed to harass the defendant.

FRM. See *fixed-rate mortgage* under MORTGAGE.

frolic, *n.* In tort law, an employee's significant deviation from the employer's business for personal reasons; a frolic is outside the scope of employment, and thus the employer is not vicariously liable for the employee's actions. Cf. DETOUR.

frontage assessment. A municipal fee charged to a property owner for local improvements that abut a street or highway, such as sidewalks, pavements, or sewage lines.

front-end money. SEED MONEY.

front wages. See WAGE.

frozen asset. See ASSET.

fructus industriales (**fruuk**-təs-in-dəs-tree-**ah**-ləs). [Latin "industrial fruits"] Annual crops produced by labor, such as wheat, corn, and potatoes; *fructus industriales* are not considered part of the real property. See EMBLEMENTS.

fructus naturales (**fruuk**-təs-nah-chuur-**ah**-ləs *or* -nahd-ə-**rah**-lays). [Latin "natural fruits"] Perennial plants, such as trees, shrubs, and grasses; *fructus naturales* are considered part of the real property.

fruit-and-the-tree doctrine. In tax law, the rule that an individual who earns income cannot assign that income to another person in order to avoid taxation.

fruit-of-the-poisonous-tree doctrine. In criminal procedure, the rule that evidence derived from an illegal search, arrest, or interrogation is inadmissible because the evidence (the "fruit") was tainted by the illegality (the "poisonous tree"); under this doctrine, for example, a murder weapon is inadmissible if the map showing its location and used to find it was seized during an illegal search. See EXCLUSIONARY RULE; ATTENUATION DOCTRINE; INDEPENDENT-SOURCE RULE; INEVITABLE-DISCOVERY RULE.

fruits of a crime. The material objects acquired by the means and in consequence of the commission of a crime.

frustration, *n.* **1.** Something that prevents or hinders the attainment of a goal, such as contractual performance.

commercial frustration. In contract law, an excuse for a party's nonperformance due to some unforeseeable and uncontrollable circumstance.

temporary frustration. In contract law, an occurrence that prevents performance and legally suspends the duty to perform for the duration of the event; if the burden or circumstance is substantially different after the event, then the duty may be discharged.

2. In contract law, the doctrine that, if the entire performance of a contract becomes fundamentally changed without any fault by either party, the contract is considered dissolved. —Also termed *frustration of purpose.* —**frustrate,** *vb.* Cf. IMPOSSIBILITY (4); IMPRACTICABILITY.

FSLIC. *abbr.* FEDERAL SAVINGS AND LOAN INSURANCE CORPORATION.

F.Supp. *abbr.* Federal Supplement, a series of reported cases, including federal district-court cases from 1932 to the present.

FTC. *abbr.* FEDERAL TRADE COMMISSION.

fugitive. 1. A person who flees or escapes from something; a refugee. **2.** A criminal suspect who flees, evades, or escapes arrest, prosecution, or imprisonment, esp. by fleeing from the jurisdiction or by hiding. —Also termed (in sense 2) *fugitive from justice.*

full-covenant-and-warranty deed. See *warranty deed* under DEED.

full coverage. See COVERAGE.

full faith and credit. A state's enforcement of another jurisdiction's laws or judicial decisions.

Full Faith And Credit Clause. U.S. Const. art IV, § 1, which requires states to recognize and enforce the legislative acts, public records, and judicial decisions of other states.

full pardon. See *absolute pardon* under PARDON.

full partner. See *general partner* under PARTNER.

full-service lease. See LEASE.

fully diluted earnings per share. See EARNINGS PER SHARE.

functionality. A shape, configuration, design, or color that is so superior to available alternatives that competition would be hindered by giving the first user exclusive trademark rights.

aesthetic functionality. In trademark law, a doctrine that denies protection to the design of a product or its container when the design is necessary to enable the product to function as intended.

functus officio (**fəng[k]**-təs-ə-**fish**-ee-oh). [Latin "having performed his or her office"] (Of an officer) without further authority or legal competence because the duties and functions of the original commission have been fully accomplished.

fund, *n.* **1.** A sum of money or other liquid assets set apart for a specific purpose <a fund reserved for unanticipated expenses>.

contingent fund. **a.** A fund created by a municipality for expenses that will necessarily arise during the year but that cannot be appropriately classified under any of the specific purposes for which taxes are collected. **b.** A fund set apart by a business to pay unknown costs that may arise in the future. —Also termed *contingency reserve.*

fund in court. **a.** Contested money deposited with the court. See INTERPLEADER. **b.** Money deposited to pay a contingent liability.

revolving fund. A fund whose moneys are continually expended and then replenished, such as a petty-cash fund.

sinking fund. See SINKING FUND.

trust fund. See TRUST FUND.

2. (*usu. pl.*) Money or other assets, such as stocks, bonds, or working capital, available to pay debts, expenses, and the like <Sue invested her funds in her sister's business>. **3.** MUTUAL FUND <a diverse portfolio of funds>.

fund, *vb.* **1.** To provide money to (an individual, entity, or venture), esp. to finance a particular project. **2.** To utilize resources in a manner that produces interest. **3.** To convert (a debt) into a long-term debt that bears interest at a fixed rate.

fundamental error. See *plain error* under ERROR.

fundamental interest. FUNDAMENTAL RIGHT.

fundamental law. The basic, organic law that establishes the governing principles of a nation or state; esp., CONSTITUTIONAL LAW. —Also termed *organic law.* Cf. NATURAL LAW.

fundamental right. 1. A right derived from natural or fundamental law. **2.** In constitutional law, a right that triggers strict scrutiny of a law to determine whether the law violates the Due Process Clause or the Equal Protection Clause; fundamental rights, as enunciated by the Supreme Court, include the right to vote, the right to interstate travel, and the various rights of privacy (such as marriage and contraception rights). —Also termed *fundamental interest.* See STRICT SCRUTINY. Cf. SUSPECT CLASSIFICATION.

fundamental term. A contractual provision that specifies an essential purpose of the contract, so that a breach of the provision through inadequate performance makes the performance not only defective but essentially different from what had been promised.

funded debt. See DEBT.

fungible (fən-jə-bəl), *adj.* Regarded as commercially interchangeable with other property of the same kind <corn and wheat are each a type of fungible goods, whereas unique property such as land is not fungible>. — **fungible,** *n.*

further assurance. See ASSURANCE.

furlough (fər-loh). **1.** A leave of absence from military or employment duty. **2.** A brief release from prison. See STUDY RELEASE.

future-acquired property. AFTERACQUIRED PROPERTY (1).

future advances. Money secured by an original security agreement even though it is lent after the security interest has attached.

future damages. See DAMAGES.

future earnings. See *lost earnings* under EARNINGS.

future interest. A property interest in which the privilege of possession or of enjoyment is future and not present; a future interest can exist in either the grantor (as with a reversion) or the grantee (as with a remainder or executory interest). — Also termed *future estate.*

futures, *n. pl.* **1.** Standardized assets (such as commodities, stocks, or foreign currencies) bought or sold for future acceptance or delivery. **2.** FUTURES CONTRACT.

futures contract. An agreement to buy or sell a standardized asset (such as a commodity, stock, or foreign currency) at a fixed price at a future time, usu. during a particular time of a month; futures contracts are traded on organized exchanges such as the Chicago Board of Trade or the Chicago Mercantile Exchange. —Often shortened to *futures.* —Also termed *futures agreement.* Cf. FORWARD CONTRACT; OPTION.

G

GAAP (gap). *abbr.* GENERALLY AC-CEPTED ACCOUNTING PRINCIPLES.

GAAS (gas). *abbr.* GENERALLY AC-CEPTED AUDITING STANDARDS.

gage (gayj). A pledge, pawn, or other thing deposited as security for perfor-mance.

gag order. 1. A judge's order direct-ing parties, attorneys, witnesses, or journalists to refrain from publicly discussing the facts of a case; when directed to the press, such an order is generally unconstitutional under the First Amendment. **2.** A judge's order that an unruly defendant be bound and gagged during trial to prevent further interruptions.

gain, *n.* **1.** An increase in amount, degree, or value. **2.** Excess of receipts over expenditures or of sale price over cost. See PROFIT. **3.** In tax law, the excess of the amount realized from a sale or other disposition of property over the property's adjusted value. See CAPITAL GAIN.

gambling policy. See *wager policy* under INSURANCE POLICY.

ganancial (gə-**nan**-shəl), *adj.* Of, re-lating to, or consisting of community property <a spouse's ganancial rights>. See COMMUNITY PROPER-TY.

GAO. *abbr.* GENERAL ACCOUNTING OFFICE.

gap-filler. In contract law, a U.C.C. provision that supplies a contractual term that the parties failed to include in the contract; for example, if the contract does not contain a sales price, U.C.C. § 2-305(1) establishes the price as being a reasonable one at the time of delivery.

gap financing. See FINANCING.

garnishee, *n.* A person or institu-tion (such as a bank) that is indebted to or is bailee for another whose property has been subjected to gar-nishment. —Also termed *garnishee-defendant* (as opposed to the "princi-pal defendant," i.e., the primary debtor).

garnisher. A creditor who initiates a garnishment action in order to reach the debtor's property that is thought to be held or owed by a third party (the *garnishee*). —Also spelled *gar-nishor*.

garnishment, *n.* **1.** A judicial pro-ceeding in which a creditor (or poten-tial creditor) asks the court to order a third party who is indebted to or is bailee for the debtor to turn over to the creditor any of the debtor's prop-erty (such as wages or bank ac-counts) held by that third party; a plaintiff initiates a garnishment ac-tion as a means of either prejudg-ment seizure or postjudgment collec-tion. **2.** The judicial order by which such a turnover is effected. —**gar-nish, garnishee,** *vb.*—**garnishable,** *adj.* Cf. ATTACHMENT (1); SEQUES-TRATION (1).

garnishment lien. See LIEN.

garnishor. GARNISHER.

GATT (gat). *abbr.* GENERAL AGREE-MENT ON TARIFFS AND TRADE.

g.b.h. See *grievous bodily harm* un-der HARM.

General Accounting Office. The federal agency that provides legal and accounting assistance to Congress, audits and investigates federal programs, and settles claims against the United States. —Abbr. GAO.

general agency. See AGENCY (1).

General Agreement on Tariffs and Trade. A multiparty international agreement—signed originally in 1948—that promotes international trade by lowering import duties and providing equal access to markets; over 100 nations are parties to the agreement. —Abbr. GATT.

general appearance. See APPEARANCE.

general assignment. See ASSIGNMENT.

general assumpsit. See ASSUMPSIT.

general average. See AVERAGE.

general benefit. See BENEFIT.

general bequest. See BEQUEST.

general challenge. See *challenge for cause* under CHALLENGE (2).

general contractor. See CONTRACTOR.

general counsel. See COUNSEL.

general count. See COUNT.

general court-martial. See COURT-MARTIAL.

general damages. See DAMAGES.

general demurrer. See DEMURRER.

general denial. See DENIAL.

general deterrence. See DETERRENCE.

general devise. See DEVISE.

general election. See ELECTION.

general exception. See *general demurrer* under DEMURRER.

general execution. EXECUTION (4).

general indorsement. See *blank indorsement* under INDORSEMENT.

general intent. See INTENT.

general issue. See ISSUE (1).

general jurisdiction. See JURISDICTION.

general jurisprudence. See JURISPRUDENCE.

general legacy. See LEGACY.

general legislation. See LEGISLATION.

general liability policy. See *comprehensive general liability policy* under INSURANCE POLICY.

general lien. See LIEN.

general listing. See *open listing* under LISTING (1).

generally accepted accounting principles. The conventions, rules, and procedures issued by the Financial Accounting Standards Board for use by accountants in preparing financial statements. —Abbr. GAAP. —Also termed *generally accepted accountancy principles*.

generally accepted auditing standards. The guidelines issued by the American Institute of Certified Public Accountants establishing an auditor's professional qualities and the criteria for the auditor's examination and required reports. —Abbr. GAAS.

general pardon. AMNESTY.

general partner. See PARTNER.

general partnership. See PARTNERSHIP.

general power of appointment. See POWER OF APPOINTMENT.

general retainer. See RETAINER.

general statute. See STATUTE.

general strike. See STRIKE.

general term. See TERM.

general traverse. See TRAVERSE.

general verdict. See VERDICT.

general warranty. See WARRANTY (1).

general warranty deed. See *warranty deed* under DEED.

General Welfare Clause. U.S. Const. art. I, § 8, cl. 1, which empowers Congress to levy taxes and pay debts in order to provide for the country's general welfare; the Supreme Court has broadly interpreted this clause to allow Congress to create, for example, the social-security system. —Also termed *Welfare Clause.*

genericide (jə-ner-ə-sId). In trademark law, the loss or cancellation of a trademark that no longer distinguishes the owner's goods from others' goods; genericide may be imminent for any trademark that becomes such a household name that the consuming public begins to think of the mark not as a brand name but as a synonym for the product itself.

generic name. In trademark law, a term that describes something generally without designating the thing's source or creator, such as the words "car" or "sink"; generic names cannot be protected as trademarks. —Also termed *generic term*; *generic mark*; *common descriptive name.*

Geneva Convention. An international agreement establishing the proper treatment of prisoners of war and of persons injured or killed in battle; drafted in 1864, the Convention has since been adopted in revised form by most nations.

gentlemen's agreement. An unenforceable and usu. oral agreement that depends merely on the good faith of the parties.

genuine issue of material fact. In the law of summary judgments, a triable, substantial, or real question of fact supported by substantial evidence; an issue of this kind precludes entry of summary judgment.

geographic market. See MARKET.

gerrymandering (jer-ee-man-də-ring), *n.* **1.** The practice of arranging electoral divisions to give one political party an unfair advantage by diluting the opposition's voting strength. —Also termed *political gerrymandering.* **2.** The practice of dividing a geographical or jurisdictional area into political units to give some group a special advantage. —Also termed *jurisdictional gerrymandering.* —**gerrymander,** *vb.* Cf. REAPPORTIONMENT.

gift, *n.* **1.** The act of voluntarily transferring property to another without compensation. **2.** A thing so transferred. —**gift,** *vb.*

anatomical gift. A testamentary donation of a bodily organ or organs, esp. for transplant or for medical research.

class gift. A gift to a group of persons, uncertain in number at the time of the gift but to be ascertained at a future time, who are all to take in definite proportions, the share of each being dependent on the ultimate number in the group.

gift causa mortis. A gift made in contemplation of the donor's imminent death. —Also termed *donatio causa mortis*; *donatio mortis causa*; *transfer in contemplation of death*. See CONTEMPLATION OF DEATH.

inter vivos gift. A gift made within the donor's lifetime. —Also termed *lifetime gift*.

prenuptial gift. A gift of property from one spouse to another before marriage; in community-property states, such gifts are often made to preserve the property's classification as separate property.

testamentary gift. A gift made by will.

gift over. A transfer of property to take effect after the termination of an intermediate estate, such as a life estate <to Sue for life, with gift over to Don in fee>.

Gifts to Minors Act. UNIFORM TRANSFERS TO MINORS ACT.

gift tax. See TAX.

gilt-edged, *adj.* (Of a security) having the highest rating for safety of investment; being an exceptionally safe investment.

Ginnie Mae. GOVERNMENT NATIONAL MORTGAGE ASSOCIATION.

gist (jist). **1.** The ground or essence (of a legal action) <the gist of the crime>. **2.** The main point <she skimmed the brief to get the gist of it>.

gloss, *n.* **1.** A note inserted between the lines or in the margin of a text to explain a difficult or obscure word in the text <this edition of Shakespeare's works is bolstered by its many glosses on Elizabethan English>. **2.** A collection of explanations; a glossary <the hornbook's copious gloss>. **3.** Pronouncements considered collectively, usu. by courts; interpretation <the statute and its judicial gloss>.

glossators (**glo**-say-tərz *or* -sə-tərz) (*usu. cap.*) A group of Italian jurisconsults who, from the 11th to the 13th centuries, were primarily responsible for the revival of the study of Roman law; they originally worked by glossing (that is, explaining in the margin) difficult or unclear passages, and gradually their writings blossomed into full-blown commentaries and discussions. See POST-GLOSSATORS.

GMI. *abbr.* GUILTY BUT MENTALLY ILL.

GNMA. *abbr.* GOVERNMENT NATIONAL MORTGAGE ASSOCIATION.

GNP. *abbr.* GROSS NATIONAL PRODUCT.

go hence without day. *Jargon.* (Of a defendant to a lawsuit) to be finished with legal proceedings without any further settings on the court's calendar; thus, a defendant who "goes hence without day" succeeds in getting a case finally resolved, usu. by dismissal. Cf. SINE DIE.

going-and-coming rule. 1. The principle that torts committed by an employee while driving to and from work are generally outside the scope of employment. **2.** The principle that denies workers'-compensation benefits to an employee injured while commuting to or from work.

going concern. A commercial enterprise, esp. a partnership, actively engaging in business with the expectation of indefinite continuance.

going private. The process by which a publicly owned company limits ownership by purchasing all outstanding publicly held shares or by merging with or selling its assets to another corporation; through this process, the company attains private status. —Also termed *management buyout*.

going public. 1. The process by which a company sells stock to the investing public for the first time, after registering under the applicable securities laws. **2.** The process by which a company embarks on a plan to sell stock in this way.

going short. An investor's selling of a borrowed stock or commodity and repaying the lender with the identical property purchased at a lower price. See *short sale* under SALE.

golden parachute. An employment-contract provision that grants an upper-level executive lucrative severance benefits—including long-term salary guarantees or bonuses—if control of the company changes hands (as by a merger).

golden rule. The principle that, in construing written instruments, a court should adhere to the grammatical and ordinary sense of the words unless that adherence would lead to some manifest absurdity. Cf. MISCHIEF RULE; PLAIN-MEANING RULE.

golden-rule argument. A jury argument in which a lawyer asks the jurors to reach a verdict by imagining themselves or someone they care about in the place of the injured plaintiff or crime victim; because they combine pity with self-interest in a prejudicial way, golden-rule arguments are widely condemned and are considered improper in most states.

good and valuable consideration. See *good consideration* (a) under CONSIDERATION.

good behavior. 1. A standard by which judges are considered fit to continue their tenure. **2.** Orderly conduct, which in the context of penal law allows a prisoner to reduce the amount of time in prison. Cf. GOOD TIME.

good cause. See CAUSE (2).

good consideration. See CONSIDERATION.

good faith, *n.* A state of mind denoting: (1) honesty or lawfulness of belief or purpose, (2) faithfulness to one's duty or obligation, (3) observance of reasonable commercial standards of fair dealing in a given trade or business, or (4) absence of intent to defraud or to seek unconscionable advantage. —Also termed *bona fides*. Cf. BAD FAITH.

good-faith purchaser. See *bona fide purchaser* under PURCHASER.

goods. 1. Tangible or movable personal property <goods and services>. **2.** Things that have value, whether tangible or not <the importance of social goods varies from society to society>. **3.** Items of merchandise; supplies; raw materials; finished products <the sale of goods is governed by the U.C.C.>.

capital goods. Goods used for the production of other goods or services, such as equipment and machinery.

consumer goods. Goods bought or used primarily for personal, family, or household purposes, and not for resale or for producing other goods. U.C.C. § 9-109(1).

distressed goods. Merchandise sold at unusually low prices or at a loss.

durable goods. Consumer goods that are designed to be used repeatedly over a long period, such as automobiles or personal computers. —Also termed *durables*.

noncomforming goods. In commercial law, goods that fail to meet contractual specifications, allowing the buyer to reject the tender of the goods or to revoke their acceptance. U.C.C. §§ 2-601,-608. See PERFECT-TENDER RULE.

prize goods. Goods captured at sea during wartime.

Good Samaritan doctrine. In tort law, the principle that a person who aids another in imminent danger will not be charged with contributory negligence unless the rescuer worsens the position of the person in distress. Cf. EMERGENCY DOCTRINE; RESCUE DOCTRINE.

Good Samaritan statute. A law that requires a person to come to the aid of another who is exposed to grave physical harm, if there is no danger of risk of injury to the rescuer.

good time. The credit awarded to a prisoner for good conduct, which can reduce the duration of the prisoner's sentence. Cf. GOOD BEHAVIOR.

good title. See TITLE.

goodwill. A business's reputation, patronage, and other intangible assets that are considered when appraising the business, esp. for purchase.

goose case. WHITEHORSE CASE.

governmental-function theory. In constitutional law, a principle by which private action is characterized as state action, for due-process and equal-protection purposes, when a private party is exercising a public function; under this theory, for example, a political party (which is a private entity) cannot exclude voters from primary elections on the basis of race. —Also termed *public-function rationale*.

governmental immunity. See *sovereign immunity* under IMMUNITY (1).

governmental instrumentality. A constitutionally or legislatively created agency that is immune from taxation.

government corporation. See *public corporation* (c) under CORPORATION.

Government National Mortgage Association. A federally owned corporation that purchases, on the secondary market, residential mortgages originated by local lenders and that issues federally insured securities backed by such mortgages. —Abbr. GNMA. —Also termed *Ginnie Mae*.

government security. See SECURITY.

grab law. The various means of debt collection involving remedies outside the scope of federal bankruptcy law, such as attachment and garnishment; aggressive collection practices.

grace period. 1. A gratuitous but sometimes legally imposed extension of time to comply with some requirement, such as the short period beyond the premium's due date (usu. 30 or 31 days) during which an insurance policy stays in effect and payment may be made to keep the policy in good standing. **2.** In commercial law, a certain number of days (usu. three) given to the maker or acceptor of a bill, draft, or note to make a payment after the time specified in the paper has expired. **3.** In consumer law, a certain number of days (usu. three) within which a consumer may rescind a transaction that occurred at his or her house. —Also termed *days of grace*; *grace days*.

graded offense. See OFFENSE.

graduated lease. See LEASE.

graduated-payment mortgage. See MORTGAGE.

graduated tax. See *progressive tax* under TAX.

graft, *n.* **1.** The act of taking advantage of a position of trust to gain money or property dishonestly; esp., a public official's fraudulent acquisition of public funds. **2.** Money or property gained illegally or unfairly.

grandfather, *vb.* To cover (a person) with the benefits of a grandfather clause <the statute sets the drinking age at 21 but grandfathers those who are 18 or older on the statute's effective date>.

grandfather clause. 1. A clause in the constitutions of some southern American states exempting from suffrage restrictions the descendants of men who voted before the Civil War. **2.** A statutory or regulatory clause that exempts a class of persons or transactions because of circumstances existing before the clause takes effect.

grand jury. A body of (often 23) people who are chosen to sit permanently for at least a month—and sometimes a year—and who, in ex parte proceedings, decide whether indictments should be issued; if the grand jury decides that evidence is strong enough to hold a suspect for trial, it returns a bill of indictment (a *true bill*) charging the suspect with a specific crime. —Also termed *accusing jury*; *presenting jury*; *jury of indictment*. —**grand juror,** *n.* Cf. *petit jury* under JURY.

investigative grand jury. A grand jury whose primary function is to examine possible crimes and develop evidence not currently available to the prosecution.

screening grand jury. A grand jury whose primary function is to decide whether to issue an indictment.

grand larceny. See LARCENY.

grant, *n.* **1.** The formal transfer of real property. **2.** The document by which such a transfer is effected; DEED. **3.** The property so transferred.

grant, *vb.* **1.** To give or confer, with or without compensation <the father granted the car to his son>. **2.** To formally transfer (real property) by deed or other writing <grant Black-acre in fee simple>. **3.** To permit (a right, favor, or privilege) <grant the reporter access to the oval office>. **4.** To approve, warrant, or order (a request, motion, or the like) <the court granted the continuance>.

grant deed. See DEED.

grantee. One to whom property is conveyed.

grantee-grantor index. See INDEX.

grant-in-aid. A sum of money given by a governmental agency to a person or institution for a specific purpose; esp., federal funding for a state public program.

grantor. 1. One who conveys property to another. **2.** SETTLOR (1).

grantor-grantee index. See INDEX.

grantor trust. See TRUST.

gratis (**grat**-is *or* **grayd**-), *adj*. Free; without compensation.

gratis dictum. See DICTUM.

gratuitous (grə-**t[y]oo**-ə-təs), *adj*. **1.** Done or performed without obligation to do so; given without consideration <gratuitous promise>. **2.** Done unnecessarily <gratuitous obscenities>. —**gratuity,** *n*.

gratuitous bailment. See BAILMENT.

gratuitous contract. See CONTRACT.

gravamen (grə-**vay**-mən). The point or essence of a claim, grievance, or complaint.

graymail. The practice of a criminal defendant threatening to reveal classified information during the trial in the hope of forcing the government to drop the criminal charge.

gray market. See MARKET.

gray mule case. WHITEHORSE CASE.

great care. See CARE.

Great Writ. HABEAS CORPUS.

green card. A registration card evidencing a resident alien's status as a permanent U.S. resident.

green-card marriage. See *sham marriage* under MARRIAGE (1).

greenmail. 1. An unfriendly suitor's act of buying enough stock in a company to threaten a hostile takeover, and of then agreeing to sell the stock back to the corporation at an inflated price. **2.** The money paid for stock in the corporation's buy-back. Cf. BLACKMAIL; FEEMAIL.

Green River ordinance. A local licensing law that protects residents from unwanted peddlers and salespersons, typically by prohibiting door-to-door solicitations without prior consent; the ordinance takes its name from Green River, Wyoming, which enacted the first such law in the early 20th century before others came into vogue during the 1930s and 1940s throughout the U.S.

grievance, *n*. **1.** An injury, injustice, or wrong that gives ground for a complaint <a petition for a redress of grievances>. **2.** The complaint itself <the client filed a grievance with the state-bar committee>. —**grievable,** *adj*.—**grievant,** *n*.

grievous bodily harm. See HARM.

gross, easement in. See *easement in gross* under EASEMENT.

gross average. See *general average* under AVERAGE.

gross charter. See CHARTER (3).

gross earnings. See *gross income* under INCOME.

gross estate. See ESTATE.

gross income. See INCOME.

gross lease. See LEASE.

gross national product. The market value of all goods and services produced in a country within a year, used to measure a country's economic development and wealth. —Abbr. GNP.

gross negligence. See NEGLI-GENCE.

gross profit. See PROFIT.

ground lease. See LEASE.

ground rent. See RENT.

ground-rent lease. See *ground lease* under LEASE.

group annuity. See ANNUITY.

grouping-of-contacts theory. CEN-TER-OF-GRAVITY DOCTRINE.

group insurance. See INSURANCE.

group libel. See LIBEL.

group litigation. A set of lawsuits on behalf of or against numerous persons recognized as one litigating entity, such as a civil-rights group.

growth fund. See MUTUAL FUND.

growth management. In land-use planning, the regulation of a community's rate of growth through ordinances that restrict the issuance of residential building permits. See ZONING.

guarantee, *n.* **1.** The act of giving security; the assurance that a contract or legal act will be duly carried out. **2.** Something given or existing as security, as to fulfill a future engagement or a condition subsequent. —Also spelled *guaranty.* — **guarantee,** *vb.*

guarantee clause. 1. A provision in a contract, deed, or mortgage by which one person promises to pay the obligation of another. **2.** (*cap.*) U.S. Const. art. IV, § 4, under which the federal government ensures for the states both a republican form of government and protection from invasion or domestic violence.

guaranteed bond. See BOND (1).

guarantor. One who makes a guaranty or gives security for a debt.

guaranty, *n.* **1.** A promise to answer for the debt of another, usu. in finance and banking contexts. **2.** GUARANTEE.

guaranty insurance. See INSUR-ANCE.

guaranty letter of credit. See *standby letter of credit* under LETTER OF CREDIT.

guardhouse lawyer. JAILHOUSE LAWYER.

guardian, *n.* One who has the legal authority and duty to care for another's person or property, esp. because of the other's incapacity or disability; a guardian may be appointed either for all purposes or for specific purposes. —Also termed *custodian.* — **guardianship,** *n.*

guardian ad litem (gahr-dee-ən-ad-**li**-təm). A guardian, usu. a lawyer, appointed by the court to appear in a lawsuit on behalf of an incompetent or minor defendant. —Also termed *special guardian*. Cf. NEXT FRIEND.

guest. **1.** A person who is entertained or to whom hospitality is extended. **2.** A person who pays for services at an establishment, esp. a hotel or restaurant. **3.** A nonpaying passenger in a motor vehicle.

business guest. In tort law, an invitee. See INVITEE.

social guest. In tort law, a licensee. See LICENSEE (2).

guest statute. A law that bars a nonpaying passenger in a noncommercial vehicle from suing the host-driver for damages resulting from the driver's ordinary negligence; though once common, guest statutes remain valid in only a few states. —Also termed *automobile guest statute*. Cf. FAMILY-PURPOSE RULE.

guilty, *adj.* **1.** Having committed a crime; responsible for a crime <the suspect admitted that he was guilty of the alleged charges>. **2.** Justly chargeable with a crime <the jury found the defendant guilty>. **3.** Responsible for a civil wrong, such as a tort or breach of contract <guilty of fraudulent misrepresentation>.

guilty but mentally ill. A form of verdict in a criminal case whereby the defendant raises an insanity defense that is rejected by the jury, which nevertheless recommends treatment because the defendant is mentally ill. —Abbr. GMI. See INSANITY DEFENSE.

guilty verdict. See VERDICT.

gun-jumping. *Slang.* The act of unlawfully soliciting the public's purchase of securities before the SEC approves a registration statement. — Also termed *conditioning the market*. See REGISTRATION STATEMENT.

H

habeas corpus (hay-bee-əs-**kor**-pəs). [Latin "you should have the body"] A writ employed to bring a person before a court, most frequently to ensure that the party's imprisonment is not illegal. —Usu. short for *habeas corpus ad subjiciendum.* —Sometimes shortened to *habeas.* —Also termed *writ of habeas corpus*; *Great Writ.*

habeas corpus ad faciendum et recipiendum (ad-fay-shee-**en**-dəm-et-rə-sip-ee-**en**-dəm). [Latin "you should have the body to do and receive"] *Archaic.* A writ used in civil cases to remove the case, and also the body of the defendant, from an inferior court to a superior court. —Also termed *habeas corpus cum causa.* See CERTIORARI.

habeas corpus ad prosequendum (ad-pro-sə-**kwen**-dəm). [Latin "you should have the body to prosecute"] *Archaic.* A writ used in criminal cases to bring before a court a prisoner to be tried on charges other than those for which the prisoner is currently being confined.

habeas corpus ad respondendum (ad-rə-spon-**den**-dəm). [Latin "you should have the body to respond"] *Archaic.* A writ used in civil cases to remove a person from one court's custody into that of another court, in which the person may then be sued.

habeas corpus ad subjiciendum (ad-səb-jis[h]-ee-**en**-dəm). [Latin "you should have the body to submit to"] A writ directed to someone detaining another person and commanding that the detainee be brought to court.

habeas corpus ad testificandum (ad-tes-tə-fə-**kan**-dəm). [Latin "you should have the body to testify"] *Archaic.* A writ used in civil and criminal cases to bring a prisoner to court to testify.

habendum clause (hə-**ben**-dəm). **1.** The part of a deed that defines the extent of the interest being granted and any conditions affecting the grant; the introductory words to the clause are ordinarily *to have and to hold.* —Also termed *to-have-and-to-hold clause.* **2.** An oil-and-gas lease provision that defines the lease's primary term and that usu. extends the lease for a secondary term of indefinite duration as long as oil, gas, or other minerals are being produced.

habit evidence. See EVIDENCE.

habitability. The condition of a building in which inhabitants can live free of serious defects that might harm health and safety <lack of running water adversely affects the apartment's habitability>.

habitability, implied warranty of. See *implied warranty of habitability* under WARRANTY (2).

habitual criminal. RECIDIVIST.

habitual offender. RECIDIVIST.

had-not test. BUT-FOR TEST.

haeres (**hay**-reez). [Medieval Latin] An heir. —Also spelled *heres.* Pl. *haeredes* (hay-**ray**-deez) or (corresponding to *heres*) *heredes.*

Hague Convention. One of a number of international conventions that address different legal issues and attempt to standardize procedures between nations.

Hague Convention on the Civil Aspects of International Child Abduction. An international convention that seeks to counteract child-snatching by the noncustodial parent.

Hague Convention on the Service Abroad of Judicial and Extrajudicial Documents. An international convention that dictates the formal and usu. complicated procedures for effecting service of process in a foreign country; over 30 countries are parties to the convention, including the U.S., which became a signatory on February 10, 1969.

Hague Convention on the Taking of Evidence Abroad in Civil or Commercial Matters. An international convention that provides the formal procedures for obtaining evidence in a foreign country, such as taking a deposition abroad.

haircut reorganization. See REORGANIZATION.

halfway house. A transitional housing facility designed to rehabilitate persons who have recently left a prison or medical-care facility, or who otherwise need help in adjusting to a normal life. —Also termed *residential community treatment center*.

Hand formula. A balancing test for determining whether conduct has created an unreasonable risk of harm, first formulated by Judge Learned Hand in *United States v. Carroll Towing Co.*, 159 F.2d 169 (2d Cir.1947); under this test, an actor is negligent if the burden of taking adequate precautions against the harm is outweighed by both the probability that harm will result from the conduct and the gravity of that harm.

hanged, drawn, and quartered. An ancient sentence for high treason, consisting of the prisoner's being hanged by the neck (but not until dead), disemboweled, beheaded, and then divided into four pieces to be at the king's disposal; the sentence was abolished in England in 1870. See TREASON.

hanging judge. See JUDGE.

harassment (**har**-is-mənt *or* hə-**ras**-). Words, conduct, or action directed at a specific person, that annoys, alarms, or causes substantial emotional distress in that person and serves no legitimate purpose; harassment is actionable in some circumstances, such as when a creditor uses threatening or abusive tactics to collect a debt. —**harass,** *vb.* See SEXUAL HARASSMENT.

harboring. The act of affording lodging, shelter, or refuge to a person, esp. a criminal or illegal alien.

hard case. A lawsuit involving equities that tempt a judge to stretch or even disregard a principle of law at issue—hence the expression, "Hard cases make bad law."

hard dollars. 1. Cash proceeds given to a seller. **2.** The part of an equity investment that is not deductible in the first year. Cf. SOFT DOLLARS.

harm, *n.* Injury, loss, or detriment.

bodily harm. Physical pain, illness, or impairment of the body.

grievous bodily harm. In criminal and tort law, serious physical impairment of the human body; typically, the fact-finder must decide in any given case whether the injury meets this general standard. — Abbr. g.b.h.

physical harm. Any physical impairment of land, chattels, or the human body.

harmful error. See *reversible error* under ERROR.

harmless error. See ERROR.

hate speech. Communication that carries no meaning other than the expression of hatred for some group, such as a particular race, esp. in circumstances in which the communication is likely to provoke violence. Cf. *group libel* under LIBEL.

hazard, *n.* **1.** Danger; peril.

extraordinary hazard. In workers'-compensation law, an unusual occupational danger that is increased by the acts of employees other than the injured worker.

2. The risk or probability of loss or injury, esp. a loss or injury covered by an insurance policy.

moral hazard. The risk that an insured will destroy property or allow it to be destroyed (usu. by burning) in order to collect the insurance proceeds; the insured's potential interest, if any, in the burning of the property.

hazardous contract. See *aleatory contract* under CONTRACT.

H.B. *abbr.* HOUSE BILL.

HDC. *abbr.* HOLDER IN DUE COURSE.

headnote. A case summary that appears before the printed judicial opinion in a law report, addresses a point of law, and usu. includes the relevant facts bearing on that point of law. — Also termed *syllabus; synopsis.*

head of household. 1. The primary income-provider within a family. **2.** For income-tax purposes, an unmarried or separated person (other than a surviving spouse) who provides a home for dependents for more than one-half of the taxable year.

head-start injunction. An injunction prohibiting the defendant from using a trade secret for a period equal to the time between the date of the secret's theft and the date when the secret became public, since that period equals the "head start" that the defendant unfairly obtained over the rest of the industry.

health-maintenance organization. A group of participating health-care providers that furnish medical services to enrolled members of a group health- insurance plan. — Abbr. HMO. Cf. PREFERRED-PROVIDER ORGANIZATION.

hearing. 1. A judicial session, usu. open to the public, held for the purpose of deciding issues of fact or of law, sometimes with witnesses testifying <the court held a hearing on the admissibility of DNA evidence in the murder case>. **2.** In administrative law, any setting in which an affected individual presents arguments to an agency decision-maker <hearing on zoning variations>. **3.** In legislative process, any proceeding in which legislators or their designees receive testimony about legislation that might be enacted <the shooting victim spoke at the Senate's

hearing on gun control>. See PRELIMINARY HEARING.

hearing de novo. 1. A reviewing court's suspension of a lower court's findings and determination of the issue as though for the first time. **2.** A new hearing of a matter, conducted as if the original hearing had not taken place.

hearing examiner. ADMINISTRATIVE-LAW JUDGE.

hearing officer. ADMINISTRATIVE-LAW JUDGE.

hearsay. 1. Traditionally, testimony that is given by a witness who relates not what he or she knows personally, but what others have said, and that is therefore dependent on the credibility of someone other than the witness; such testimony is generally inadmissible under the rules of evidence. **2.** In federal law, a statement (either a verbal assertion or nonverbal assertive conduct), other than one made by the declarant while testifying at the trial or hearing, offered in evidence to prove the truth of the matter asserted. Fed. R. Evid. 801(c). —Also termed *hearsay evidence*; *secondhand evidence*.

double hearsay. A hearsay statement that contains further hearsay statements within it, none of which is admissible unless exceptions to the rule against hearsay can be applied to each level <the witness's testimony that Amy told John that she ran the red light is double hearsay>. Fed. R. Evid. 805. —Also termed *multiple hearsay*; *hearsay within hearsay*.

hearsay rule. The rule that hearsay is not admissible except as provided otherwise by the rules of evidence, by court rules, or by statute, the chief reasons for which are that out-of-court statements amounting to hearsay are not made under oath and are not subject to cross-examination (Fed. R. Evid. 802); Rule 803 of the Federal Rules of Evidence provides 24 explicit exceptions to the hearsay rule, regardless of whether the out-of-court declarant is available to testify, and Rule 804 provides 5 more exceptions for situations in which the declarant is unavailable to testify.

heartbalm statute. A state law that abolishes the rights of action for alienation of affections, breach of promise to marry, criminal conversation, and seduction of a person over the legal age of consent.

heat of passion. Rage, terror, or furious hatred suddenly aroused by some immediate provocation, usu. another person's words or actions; at common law, this could serve, in a murder defense, as mitigating circumstances that would reduce the charge to manslaughter. —Also termed *sudden heat of passion*; *hot blood*. Cf. COLD BLOOD; COOL BLOOD.

hedge, *vb.* To make advance arrangements to safeguard oneself from loss on an investment, speculation, or bet, as when a buyer of commodities insures against unfavorable price changes by buying in advance at a fixed rate for later delivery. — **hedging,** *n.*

hedge fund. A specialized investment group—usu. organized as a limited partnership or offshore investment company—that offers the possibility of high returns through risky techniques such as selling short or buying derivatives; most hedge funds are not registered with the SEC and are therefore restricted in marketing their services to the public.

hedonic damages. See DAMAGES.

hegemony (hi-**jem**-ə-nee), *n.* **1.** Influence, authority, or supremacy over others <the hegemony of capitalism>. **2.** The leadership or predominant authority of one state of a confederacy or union over the others; political domination <the former Soviet Union's hegemony over Eastern Europe>. —**hegemonic** (hej-ə-**mahn**-ik), *adj.*

heightened scrutiny. INTERMEDIATE SCRUTINY.

heir. **1.** A person who, under the laws of intestacy, is entitled to receive an intestate decedent's property, esp. real property. —Also termed *legal heir*; *heir at law*; *lawful heir*; *heir general.* **2.** One who inherits real or personal property, whether by will or by intestate succession.

and his heirs. A term of art formerly required to create a fee simple absolute in transferring real property by will <A conveys Blackacre to B and his heirs>.

collateral heir. One who is neither a descendant nor an ancestor of the decedent, but whose kinship is through a collateral line, such as a brother, sister, uncle, aunt, nephew, niece, or cousin. Cf. *lineal heir.*

expectant heir. An heir who has a reversionary or remainder interest in property, or a chance of succeeding to it. See REVERSION; REMAINDER. Cf. *prospective heir.*

forced heir. A person whom the testator or donor cannot disinherit because the law reserves part of the estate for that person.

heir apparent. An heir who is certain to inherit unless he or she dies first or is excluded by a valid will. —Also termed *apparent heir.* Cf. *heir presumptive.*

heir by devise. One to whom lands are given by will.

heir presumptive. An heir who will inherit if the potential intestate dies immediately, but who may be excluded if another more closely related heir is born. —Also termed *presumptive heir.* Cf. *heir apparent.*

heirs and assigns. A term of art formerly required to create a fee simple <A conveys Blackacre to B and his heirs and assigns>.

heirs of the body. A term of art formerly required to create a fee tail <A conveys Blackacre to B and the heirs of his body>. —Also termed *bodily heirs.*

known heir. An heir who is present to claim an inheritance, the extent of which depends on there being no closer relative.

laughing heir. An heir distant enough to feel no grief when a relative dies and leaves a windfall to the heir.

lineal heir. One who is either an ancestor or a descendant of the decedent, such as a parent or child. Cf. *collateral heir.*

pretermitted heir. A child or spouse who has been omitted from a will, as when a testator makes a will naming his or her two children and then, sometime after, has two more children who are not mentioned in the will; most states have so-called "pretermitted-heir statutes" under which an omitted child or spouse receives the same share of the estate as if the testator had died intestate, unless the omission was intentional. —Also termed (more specifically) *pretermitted child*; *pretermitted spouse*. See PRETERMITTED-HEIR STATUTE.

prospective heir. An heir who may inherit but may be excluded; an heir apparent or an heir presumptive. Cf. *expectant heir*.

henceforth, *adv. Jargon.* From now on <the newly enacted rule shall be applied henceforth>.

hereafter, *adv. Jargon.* **1.** From now on; henceforth <because of the highway construction, she will hereafter take the bus to work>. **2.** At some future time <the court will hereafter issue a ruling on the gun's admissibility>. **3.** Loosely, HEREINAFTER <the exhibits hereafter referred to as Exhibit A and Exhibit B>.

hereby, *adv. Jargon.* By this document; by these very words <I hereby declare my intention to run for public office>.

heredes. See HAERES.

hereditament (hə-**red**-i-tə-mənt *or* her-ə-**did**-ə-mənt). **1.** Any property that can be inherited; anything that passes by intestacy. **2.** Real property; land.

corporeal hereditaments. Tangible items of property, such as land, buildings, or fixtures.

incorporeal hereditaments. Intangible rights in land, such as easements.

hereditary succession. INTESTATE SUCCESSION.

herein, *adv. Jargon.* In this thing (such as a document, section, or matter) <the appellant's due-process arguments stated herein should convince the court to reverse the case>.

hereinafter, *adv. Jargon.* Later in this document <the buyer agrees to purchase the property described hereinafter>. —Also loosely termed *hereafter*.

hereof, *adv. Jargon.* Of this thing (such as a provision or document) <before we agree to the promissory note's repayment terms, let's discuss the effects hereof>.

heres. HAERES.

hereto, *adv. Jargon.* To this document <the exhibits are attached hereto>.

heretofore, *adv. Jargon.* Up to now; before this time <a question that has not heretofore been decided>.

hereunder, *adv. Jargon.* **1.** Later in this document <review the provisions hereunder before signing the consent form>. **2.** In accordance with this document <the tenant breached the lease because she failed to give the landlord notice hereunder>.

herewith, *adv. Jargon.* With or in this document <enclosed herewith are three copies>.

heritable (**her**-ət-ə-bəl), *adj.* Capable of passing by inheritance <a heritable estate>.

hermeneutics (hər-mə-**n[y]oot**-iks), *n.* The art of interpreting texts, esp. important to advocates of critical legal studies. —**hermeneutical, hermeneutic,** *adj.*

heuristic ([h]yuu-**ris**-tik), *adj.* Of or relating to a method of learning or problem-solving by using trial-and-error and other experimental techniques <heuristic discovery methods>.

HEW. *abbr.* The Department of Health, Education, and Welfare, a former agency of the U.S. Government created in 1953; when the Department of Education was created in 1979, the name HEW was changed to the Department of Health and Human Services (HHS).

Heydon's case, rule in. MISCHIEF RULE.

HHS. *abbr.* The Department of Health and Human Services, a federal agency that administers health, welfare, and income-security policies and programs, the largest of which is social security.

HIDC. *abbr.* HOLDER IN DUE COURSE.

hidden asset. See ASSET.

hidden defect. See DEFECT.

hidden tax. See TAX.

higher court. See *court above* under COURT.

highest and best use. See USE (1).

highest degree of care. See CARE.

high seas. The seas or oceans apart from territorial waters and therefore beyond the jurisdiction of any country; under international law, the high seas usu. begin three miles from the coast. —Also termed *open seas.*

high treason. TREASON.

hijack, *vb.* **1.** To commandeer (a vehicle or airplane), esp. at gunpoint. **2.** To steal or rob from (a vehicle or airplane in transit).

hired gun. 1. An expert witness who testifies favorably for the party paying his or her fee, often because of that financial relationship rather than because of the facts. **2.** *Slang.* A lawyer who stops at nothing to accomplish the client's goals, regardless of moral consequences.

hire-purchase agreement. LEASE-PURCHASE AGREEMENT.

hit-and-run statute. A law requiring a motorist involved in an accident to remain at the scene and to give certain information to the police and others involved.

hitherto, *adv. Jargon.* Until now; heretofore.

HLA test. *abbr.* A human-leukocyte-antigen test that uses a tissue-typing process to determine the probability of fatherhood. See PATERNITY TEST. Cf. DNA IDENTIFICATION.

HMO. *abbr.* HEALTH-MAINTENANCE ORGANIZATION.

hoard, *vb.* To acquire and hold (goods) beyond one's reasonable needs, usu. because of an actual or anticipated shortage or price increase <hoarding food and medical supplies during wartime>.

hodgepodge. 1. HOTCHPOT (1). **2.** An unorganized mixture.

holder. 1. A person who has legal possession of a negotiable instrument and is entitled to receive payment on it. **2.** A person with legal possession of a document of title or an investment security. **3.** A person who possesses or uses property.

holder for value. A person who has given value in exchange for a negotiable instrument; under the U.C.C, examples of "giving value" include acquiring a security interest in the instrument or accepting the instrument in payment of an antecedent claim. U.C.C. 3-303(a).

holder in due course. A person who in good faith has given value for a negotiable instrument that is complete and regular on its face, is not overdue, and, to the possessor's knowledge, has not been dishonored; under U.C.C. § 3-305, a holder in due course takes the instrument free of all claims and personal defenses, but subject to real defenses. —Abbr. HDC; HIDC. —Also termed *due-course holder*.

hold harmless, *vb.* To absolve (another party) from any responsibility for damage or other liability arising from the transaction; INDEMNIFY. — Also termed *save harmless*.

hold-harmless agreement. A contract in which one party agrees to indemnify the other. —Also termed *save-harmless agreement*. See INDEMNITY.

holding, *n.* **1.** A determination of a matter of law that is pivotal to a judicial decision; a principle drawn from such a decision. Cf. OBITER DICTUM. **2.** A ruling on evidence or other questions presented at trial. **3.** (*usu. pl.*) Property (esp. land) owned by a person. **4.** In feudal law, tenure.

holding cell. JAIL.

holding charge. A criminal charge of some minor offense filed to keep the accused in custody while prosecutors take time to build a bigger case and prepare more serious charges.

holding company. See COMPANY.

holding over. *Jargon.* A tenant's action in continuing to occupy the leased premises after the lease term has expired; holding over creates a tenancy at sufferance, with the tenant being referred to as a *holdover*. See *tenancy at sufferance* under TENANCY.

holding zone. In zoning law, a temporary low-density zone, used only until the community decides how to rezone the area. See ZONING.

hold order. A notation in a prisoner's file stating that another jurisdiction has charges pending against the prisoner and instructing prison officials to alert authorities in that other jurisdiction instead of releasing the prisoner.

hold out, *vb.* To represent oneself or another as having a certain legal status, such as an agent or partner with authority to enter into transactions <they held themselves out as husband and wife>.

holdover tenancy. See *tenancy at sufferance* under TENANCY.

holograph. See *holographic will* under WILL.

holographic will. See WILL.

homage (**hom**-ij). In feudal times, a ceremony that a new tenant performed for his lord to acknowledge the tenure.

home equity loan. See LOAN.

home-port doctrine. In maritime law, the rule mandating that a vessel engaged in interstate and foreign commerce is taxable only at its home port, usu. where the vessel is registered.

home rule. A state legislative provision or action allocating a measure of autonomy to a local government, conditional on its acceptance of terms. Cf. LOCAL OPTION.

homestead. 1. The house, outbuildings, and land forming a person's or family's residence <Scarlett's homestead was called "Tara">. **2.** The land owned and occupied by one or more persons, usu. a husband and wife, as their home, as long as the land does not exceed in area or value the limits fixed by law; in some states, a homestead is exempt from forced sale for collection of a debt <an exemption for homestead and personal effects>.

homestead law. A statute exempting a homestead from execution or judicial sale for debt, unless all owners, usu. a husband and wife, have jointly mortgaged the property or otherwise subjected it to creditors' claims.

homicide (**ho**-mə-sīd *or* **hoh**-). The killing of one person by another.

criminal homicide. **a.** Homicide prohibited and punishable by law, such as murder or manslaughter. **b.** The act of purposely, knowingly, recklessly, or negligently causing the death of another human being. Model Penal Code § 210.1.

excusable homicide. **a.** Homicide resulting from a person's lawful act, committed without intention to harm another. **b.** See *justifiable homicide* (a).

homicide by misadventure. ACCIDENTAL KILLING.

justifiable homicide. **a.** The killing of another in self-defense when danger of death or serious bodily injury to the killer exists. —Also termed *excusable homicide.* See SELF-DEFENSE. **b.** A killing mandated or permitted by the law, such as execution for a capital crime or killing to prevent a crime or a criminal's escape.

negligent homicide. Homicide resulting from the careless performance of a legal or illegal act in which the danger of death is apparent; the killing of a human being by criminal negligence. See *criminal negligence* under NEGLIGENCE.

reckless homicide. The unlawful killing of another person as a result of conscious indifference toward that person's life. Cf. MANSLAUGHTER.

vehicular homicide. The killing of another person by one's unlawful or negligent operation of a motor vehicle.

homologate (hoh-**mol**-ə-gayt), *vb.* To approve or confirm officially <the court homologated the sale>. —**homologation,** *n.*

Hon. *abbr.* HONORABLE.

honor, *vb.* **1.** To accept or pay (a negotiable instrument) when presented. **2.** To recognize, salute, or praise.

Honorable. A title of respect given to judges, members of the U.S. Congress, ambassadors, and the like <The Honorable Ruth Bader Ginsburg>. —*Abbr.* Hon.

honorary trust. See TRUST.

horizontal integration. See *horizontal merger* under MERGER.

horizontal merger. See MERGER.

horizontal price-fixing. See PRICE-FIXING.

horizontal privity. See PRIVITY.

horizontal restraint. See RESTRAINT OF TRADE.

horizontal union. See *craft union* under UNION.

hornbook. **1.** A book explaining the basics of a given subject. **2.** A textbook containing the rudimentary principles of an area of law. Cf. CASEBOOK.

hornbook law. BLACKLETTER LAW.

hors (or). [French] **1.** Out or out of. **2.** Outside or outside of.

horse case. WHITEHORSE CASE.

horseshedding, *n.* The instruction of a witness favorable to one's case (esp. a client) about the proper method of responding to questions while testifying. —Also termed *woodshedding.* —**horseshed,** *vb.* Cf. SANDPAPERING.

hostile bidder. CORPORATE RAIDER.

hostile possession. See POSSESSION.

hostile takeover. See TAKEOVER.

hostile witness. See WITNESS.

hot blood. HEAT OF PASSION.

hotchpot, *n.* **1.** The blending of properties to secure equality of division, esp. as practiced in cases in which an intestate's property is to be distributed. —Also termed *hotchpotch*; *hodgepodge.* **2.** In community-property states, the property that falls within the community estate.

hot court. See COURT.

hot issue. See ISSUE (2).

hot pursuit. FRESH PURSUIT.

hot stock. See *hot issue* under ISSUE (2).

house. **1.** A home, dwelling, or residence. **2.** A branch of a legislature or a quorum of such a branch; esp., the lower chamber of a bicameral legislature. **3.** HOUSE OF REPRESENTATIVES.

house arrest. The confinement of a person who is accused or convicted of a crime to his or her home usu. by attaching an electronically monitored bracelet to the criminal offender; most house-arrest programs require the offender to work and permit leaving the home only for reasons such as work, medical needs, or community-service obligations.

House Bill. A legislative bill in the process of going through a house of representatives before being enacted as a statute. —Abbr. H.B. See BILL (3).

houseburning. The common-law misdemeanor of intentionally burning one's own house that is within city limits or that is close enough to other houses that they might be in danger of catching fire (although no actual damage to them results). Cf. ARSON.

house counsel. See *in-house counsel* under COUNSEL.

House of Commons. The lower chamber of the British parliament.

House of Delegates. The body vested with the control and administration of the American Bar Association.

House of Lords. The upper chamber of the British parliament, the ten-member judicial committee of which serves as the final court of appeal in most civil cases. —Also termed *Lords*.

House of Representatives. 1. The lower chamber of the U.S. Congress, composed of 435 members—apportioned among the states on the basis of population—who are elected to two-year terms. **2.** The lower house of a state legislature. —Abbr. H.R. — Often shortened to *House*.

howsoever. *Jargon.* In whatever way; however.

H.R. *abbr.* HOUSE OF REPRESENTATIVES.

hub-and-spoke conspiracy. See *wheel conspiracy* under CONSPIRACY.

HUD. *abbr.* The Department of Housing and Urban Development, a federal agency responsible for programs and policies that address the country's housing needs and that develop and improve neighborhoods.

hue and cry. *Archaic.* **1.** The public uproar that, at common law, a citizen was expected to initiate after discovering a crime. **2.** The pursuit of a felon accompanying such an uproar. **3.** A written proclamation for the capture of a felon.

humanitarian doctrine. LAST-CLEAR-CHANCE DOCTRINE.

hung jury. See JURY.

husband-wife privilege. See *marital privilege* under PRIVILEGE.

husbandman. *Archaic.* A farmer.

husband-wife immunity. See IMMUNITY (2).

hybrid class action. See CLASS ACTION.

hypothecation (hI-poth-ə-**kay**-shən), *n.* The act or an instance of pledging something as security without delivery of title or possession. — **hypothecate** (hI-**poth**-ə-kayt), *vb.*— **hypothecator** (hI-poth-ə-**kayt**-er), *n.*

hypothetical creditor. See CREDITOR.

hypothetical question. A trial device that solicits an expert witness's opinion based on assumptions treated as facts established by evidence.

I

ibid (**ib**-id). *abbr.* [Latin *ibidem*] In the same place; this abbreviation, used in citations (mostly outside law), denotes that the reference is to a work cited immediately before, and that the cited matter appears on the same page of the same book (unless a different page is specified). —Also termed *ib*. Cf. ID.

ICC. *abbr.* INTERSTATE COMMERCE COMMISSION.

ICJ. *abbr.* INTERNATIONAL COURT OF JUSTICE.

id (id). *abbr.* [Latin *idem*] The same; *id.* is used in a legal citation to refer to the cited authority immediately preceding <*id.* at 55>. Cf. IBID.

idem sonans (I-dəm-**soh**-nahnz *or* -nanz), *adj.* [Latin] (Of words or names) sounding the same, regardless of spelling <the names Jon and John are *idem sonans*>.

idem sonans, n. [Latin] A legal doctrine preventing a variant spelling of a name in a document from voiding the document if the misspelling is pronounced the same way as the true spelling.

identity. 1. In the law of evidence, the authenticity of a person or thing. **2.** The identical nature of two or more things; esp., in patent law, the sameness of the construction and results of inventions, or of the visual appearance of designs.

identity of interests. In civil procedure, a relationship between two parties who are so close that suing one serves as notice to the other, so that the other may be joined in the suit. Fed. R. Civ. P. 15(c)(3).

identity of parties. In civil procedure, a relationship between two parties who are so close that a judgment against one prevents action against the other because of res judicata.

i.e. *abbr.* [Latin *id est*] That is <the federal government's highest judicial body, i.e., the Supreme Court>. Cf. E.G.

IFP. *abbr.* IN FORMA PAUPERIS.

IFP affidavit. See *poverty affidavit* under AFFIDAVIT.

ignorantia juris neminem excusat (ig-nə-**ran**-shee-ə-**juur**-is-**nem**-i-nəm-ek-**skyoo**-zat *or* ig-nə-**rahn**-tee-ə-). [Latin] The legal maxim that one's lack of knowledge about a legal requirement or prohibition is never an excuse to a criminal charge; in English, the idea is commonly rendered *ignorance of the law excuses no one*. —Often shortened to *ignorantia juris*. —Also termed *ignorantia juris non excusat* (ignorance of the law is no excuse); *ignorantia legis non excusat*.

ignore. 1. To refuse to notice or recognize. **2.** (Of a grand jury) to reject (an indictment) as groundless; to no-bill (a charge).

illegal alien. See ALIEN.

illegal consideration. See CONSIDERATION.

illegal contract. See CONTRACT.

illegal entry. 1. In criminal law, the unlawful act of going into a building with the intent to commit a crime; in some jurisdictions, illegal entry is a lesser included offense of burglary. **2.** In immigration law, the unauthorized entrance of an alien into the U.S. by arriving at the wrong time or place, by evading inspection, or by fraud. See ENTRY.

illegality, *n.* **1.** An act that is not authorized by law. **2.** The state or condition of being unlawful; the affirmative defense of illegality must be expressly set forth in the response to the opponent's pleading. Fed. R. Civ. P. 8(c). —**illegal,** *adj.*

illegally obtained evidence. See EVIDENCE.

illegal rate of interest. See INTEREST RATE.

illegal search. See *unreasonable search* under SEARCH.

illegitimacy. The condition or state of one born outside a lawful marriage. —Also termed *bastardy*.

illegitimate. 1. (Of a child) born out of wedlock <illegitimate son>. **2.** Against the law; unlawful <illegitimate contract for the sale of contraband>. **3.** Improper <illegitimate conduct>. **4.** Incorrectly inferred <illegitimate conclusions>.

illicit (i[l]-**lis**-ət), *adj.* Illegal, esp. in reference to sexual relations.

illicit cohabitation. See COHABITATION.

illicit relations. Any type of illegal sexual intercourse. —Also termed *illicit connection*.

Illinois land trust. See *land trust* under TRUST.

illiquid asset. See *frozen asset* (a) under ASSET.

illusory (i-**loos**-[ə-]ree), *adj.* Deceptive; based on a false impression.

illusory promise. See PROMISE.

IMF. *abbr.* INTERNATIONAL MONETARY FUND.

immaterial, *adj.* Lacking any logical connection with the consequential facts; unimportant. —**immateriality,** *n.* Cf. IRRELEVANT.

immaterial breach. See *partial breach* under BREACH.

immaterial evidence. See EVIDENCE.

immaterial variance. See VARIANCE (1).

immediate, *adj.* **1.** Made or performed without delay <an immediate acceptance>. **2.** Not separated by other persons or things <her immediate neighbor>. **3.** Having a direct impact; without an intervening agency <the immediate cause of the accident>. —**immediacy, immediateness,** *n.*

immediate cause. See CAUSE (1).

immemorial, *adj.* Beyond memory or record; very old. See TIME IMMEMORIAL.

immigration, *n.* The act of entering a country with the intention of settling there permanently. —**immigrate,** *vb.*—**immigrant,** *n.* Cf. EMIGRATION.

Immigration and Nationality Act. A comprehensive federal law regulating immigration, naturalization, and the exclusion of aliens. 8 U.S.C. §§ 1101 et seq. —Also termed *Nationality Act*.

Immigration and Naturalization Service. A U.S. Department of Justice agency that administers the Immigration and Nationality Act and operates the U.S. Border Patrol. — Abbr. INS.

Immigration Appeals Board. The highest administrative tribunal in U.S. immigration law, charged with administering and interpreting immigration law and hearing appeals from the Immigration and Naturalization Service.

imminent-peril doctrine. EMERGENCY DOCTRINE (1).

immoral contract. See CONTRACT.

immovable, *n.* (*usu. pl.*) Property that cannot move itself or be moved by another; an object so firmly attached to land that it is regarded as part of the land. —**immovable,** *adj.* See FIXTURE. Cf. MOVABLE.

immunity. 1. Any exemption from a duty, liability, or service of process; esp., such an exemption granted to a public official.

congressional immunity. Either of two special immunities given to members of Congress: (1) the privilege from arrest while attending a session of the body to which the member belongs, excluding arrests for treason, breach of the peace, or a felony, or (2) the privilege from arrest or questioning for any presentation or debate entered into during a legislative session. U.S. Const. art. I, § 6, cl. 1. See SPEECH AND DEBATE CLAUSE.

diplomatic immunity. The general exemption of diplomatic ministers from the operation of local law, the exception being if they are actually plotting against the security of the nation to which they are accredited, in which event they may be arrested and sent out of the country; their families share in this exemption to a great, though ill-defined, degree.

executive immunity. **a.** The absolute immunity of the U.S. President or a state governor from civil damages for actions that are within the scope of his or her official responsibilities while in office. **b.** The qualified immunity from civil claims against lesser executive officials, who are liable only for clearly established responsibilities about which a reasonable person would know. Cf. *executive privilege* under PRIVILEGE.

foreign immunity. The immunity of a foreign sovereign, its agents, or its instrumentalities from litigation in U.S. courts.

intergovernmental immunity. See INTERGOVERNMENTAL-IMMUNITY DOCTRINE.

judicial immunity. The immunity of a judge from civil liability arising from the performance of judicial duties.

legislative immunity. The immunity of a legislator from civil liability arising from the performance of legislative duties. See *congressional immunity*.

qualified immunity. Immunity from civil liability for public officials who are performing discretionary functions, as long as their conduct does not violate clearly established constitutional or statutory rights.

sovereign immunity. **a.** A government's immunity from being sued in its own courts without its consent; Congress has waived much of the federal government's sovereign immunity. See FEDERAL TORT CLAIMS ACT. **b.** A state's immunity from being sued in federal court by the state's own citizens. —Also termed *governmental immunity*.

2. In tort law, a doctrine providing a complete defense to a tort action; unlike a privilege, immunity does not negate the tort, and it must be raised affirmatively or it will be waived. Cf. PRIVILEGE (2).

charitable immunity. Immunity of charitable organizations from tort liability; this immunity has been eliminated or restricted in most states. —Also termed *eleemosynary defense*.

husband-wife immunity. Immunity of one spouse from a tort action by the other spouse for personal injury; this immunity has been abolished in most states. —Also termed *interspousal immunity*.

parent-child immunity. Immunity of parents from tort actions by their children for personal injury; this immunity has been retained by most states but is not applied in intentional-tort cases or in auto-accident cases covered by insurance.

3. In criminal law, freedom from prosecution granted by the government in exchange for the person's testimony; by granting immunity, the government can compel testimony—despite the Fifth Amendment privilege against self-incrimination—because that testimony can no longer incriminate the witness.

testimonial immunity. Immunity from the use of the compelled testi-mony against the witness; the fruits of such testimony, however, are generally admissible against the witness.

transactional immunity. Immunity from prosecution for any event or transaction described in the compelled testimony; this is the broadest form of immunity.

use immunity. Immunity from the use of the compelled testimony (or any information derived from that testimony) in a future prosecution against the witness; after granting use immunity, the government can still prosecute if it shows that its evidence comes from a legitimate independent source. —Also termed *use/derivative-use immunity.*

impact rule. In tort law, the common-law requirement that physical contact must have occurred to allow damages for negligent infliction of emotional distress; this rule has been abandoned in most jurisdictions. —Also termed *physical-impact rule.*

impaired capital. See CAPITAL.

impairing the morals of a minor. The offense of an adult's engaging in sex-related acts, short of intercourse, with a minor; examples of this conduct are fondling, taking obscene photographs, and showing pornographic materials. Cf. CONTRIBUT-ING TO THE DELINQUENCY OF A MINOR.

impairment, *n.* The fact or state of being damaged, weakened, or diminished <impairment of collateral>. — **impair,** *vb.*

impanel. EMPANEL.

imparl, *vb. Archaic.* To obtain leave of court to adjourn proceedings so that the parties can try to settle the case. —**imparlance,** *n.*

impartial, *adj.* Unbiased; disinterested.

impartial expert. See EXPERT.

impartial jury. See JURY.

impartible, *adj.* Indivisible <an impartible estate>.

impeach, *vb.* **1.** To accuse (a public official) of a crime in office by presenting a written charge called "articles of impeachment"; esp., to conduct a criminal proceeding against (a public official), initiated by the U.S. House of Representatives for the purpose of removing the official from office on a two- thirds vote of the U.S. Senate <President Nixon resigned to avoid being impeached>. **2.** To discredit the veracity of (a witness) <the lawyer hoped her star witness wouldn't be impeached on cross-examination>. **3.** To challenge the accuracy or authenticity of (a document) <the handwriting expert impeached the holographic will>. —**impeachment,** *n.*

impediment. A hindrance or obstruction; esp., some fact (such as legal minority) that bars a marriage if known but that does not void the marriage if discovered after the ceremony.

imperfect justification. See JUSTIFICATION.

imperfect self-defense. See SELF-DEFENSE.

imperfect statute. See STATUTE.

impertinent matter. In pleading, a matter that is not relevant to the action or defense; a federal court may strike an impertinent matter from a pleading. Fed. R. Civ. P. 12(f). Cf. SCANDALOUS MATTER.

impleader, *n.* A procedure by which a third party is brought into a lawsuit, esp. through a defendant's third-party action. Fed. R. Civ. P. 14. —Also termed *third-party practice; vouching-in.* —**implead,** *vb.* Cf. INTERPLEADER; INTERVENTION (1).

implicate, *vb.* **1.** To show (a person) to be involved in (a crime, misfeasance, etc.) <when he turned state's evidence, he implicated three other suspects>. **2.** To be involved or affected <three judges were implicated in the bribery>. —**implication,** *n.*

implicit cost. See *opportunity cost* under COST.

implied admission. See ADMISSION.

implied assertion. See *assertive conduct* under CONDUCT.

implied assumption. See ASSUMPTION (2).

implied authority. See AUTHORITY.

implied confession. See CONFESSION.

implied consent. See CONSENT.

implied contract. See CONTRACT.

implied easement. See EASEMENT.

implied in fact. Inferable from the facts of the case.

implied-in-fact contract. See CONTRACT.

implied in law. Imposed by operation of law and not because of any inferences that can be drawn about the facts of the case.

implied-in-law contract. See CONTRACT.

implied malice. See MALICE.

implied notice. See NOTICE.

implied power. See POWER.

implied reciprocal covenant. See COVENANT (4).

implied reciprocal servitude. See *implied reciprocal covenant* under COVENANT (4).

implied repeal. See REPEAL.

implied-reservation-of-water doctrine. A legal doctrine permitting the federal government to use and control, for public purposes, water appurtenant to federal lands. See EMINENT DOMAIN.

implied trust. See *resulting trust* under TRUST.

implied warranty. See WARRANTY (2).

implied warranty of fitness for a particular purpose. See WARRANTY (2).

implied warranty of habitability. See WARRANTY (2).

implied warranty of merchantability. See WARRANTY (2).

imply, *vb.* **1.** To express or involve indirectly; to suggest <the opinion implies that the court has adopted a stricter standard for upholding punitive-damages awards>. **2.** (Of a court) to impute or impose on equitable or legal grounds <the court implied a contract between the parties>. **3.** To read into (a document) <citing grounds of fairness, the court

implied a condition that the parties had not expressed>. —**implication,** *n.*

import, *n.* **1.** A product or service brought into a country from a foreign country where it originated <imports declined in the third quarter>. **2.** The process of bringing foreign goods or services into a country <the import of products affects the domestic economy in significant ways>. **3.** Something implied; meaning <the court must decide the import of that obscure provision>. **4.** Importance <time will tell the relative import of Judge Posner's decisions in American law>.

imported litigation. One or more lawsuits brought in a state that has no interest in the dispute.

Import-Export Clause. U.S. Const. art. I, § 10, cl. 2, which prohibits states from taxing imports or exports; the Supreme Court has liberally interpreted this clause, allowing states to effectively tax imports as long as the tax does not discriminate in favor of domestic goods. — Also termed *Export Clause*.

import letter of credit. See LETTER OF CREDIT.

impossibility. 1. The fact or condition of not being able to occur, exist, or be done. **2.** A thing or circumstance that cannot occur, exist, or be done. **3.** In contract law, a fact excusing performance because: (1) the subject or means of performance has deteriorated, has been destroyed, or is no longer available, (2) the method of delivery or payment has failed, (3) a law now prevents performance, or (4) death or illness prevents performance. **4.** The doctrine by which such a fact excuses contractual performance. Cf. FRUSTRATION; IMPRACTICABILITY. **5.** In criminal law, a fact or circumstance preventing the commission of a crime; impossibility can be a defense to a charge of attempt.

factual impossibility. Impossibility due to the fact that the crime cannot be actually or physically accomplished (such as trying to pick an empty pocket); factual impossibility is not a defense to attempt. —Also termed *physical impossibility.*

legal impossibility. Impossibility due to the fact that what the defendant intended to do is not prohibited by law (such as trying to hunt game while erroneously believing that hunting season has not begun); legal impossibility is traditionally a defense to attempt.

impost. A tax or duty, esp. a customs duty <the impost was assessed when the ship reached the mainland>.

impostor. One who pretends to be someone else in order to deceive others, esp. to receive the benefits of a negotiable instrument. —Also spelled *imposter.*

impostor rule. In commercial law, the principle that an impostor's indorsement of a negotiable instrument is not a forgery, and that the drawer or maker who issues the instrument is negligent and therefore liable to the holder for payment. U.C.C. § 3-404.

impotence (**im**-pə-təns). A man's inability to achieve an erection and therefore to have sex; because an

impotent husband cannot consummate a marriage, impotence is often cited as grounds for annulment or divorce. —Also termed *impotency.*

impound, *vb.* **1.** To place something (as a car or other personal property) in the custody of the police or the court, often with the understanding that it will be returned intact at the end of the action. **2.** To take and retain possession of (as a forged document to be produced as evidence in a criminal trial) in preparation for a prosecution.

impound account. See ACCOUNT.

impoundment. 1. The action of impounding; the state of being impounded. See IMPOUND. **2.** In constitutional law, the President's confiscation of funds appropriated by Congress; although not authorized by the Constitution, the impoundment power has effectively given the executive branch a line-item veto over legislative spending.

impracticability (im-prak-ti-kə-**bil**-ə-tee). **1.** A fact that excuses a party from performing an act, esp. a contractual duty, because (though possible) it would cause extreme and unreasonable difficulty. **2.** The doctrine by which such a fact excuses performance. Cf. FRUSTRATION; IMPOSSIBILITY (4).

commercial impracticability. In contract law, the occurrence of a contingency whose nonoccurrence was an assumption in the contract, as a result of which one party cannot perform.

impressment (im-**pres**-mənt), *n.* **1.** The act of forcibly taking (something) for public service. **2.** A court's imposition of a constructive trust on equitable grounds. See *constructive trust* under TRUST. **3.** *Archaic.* The method by which armed forces were formerly recruited, when so-called press-gangs seized men off the streets and forced them to join the army or navy. —**impress,** *vb.*

imprest money (**im**-prest). A payment made to soldiers or sailors upon enlistment or impressment.

imprimatur (im-**prim**-ə-tər *or* -pri-**mah**-dər). [Latin "let it be printed"] **1.** A license required to publish a book; once required in England, the imprimatur is now encountered only rarely in countries that censor the press. **2.** A general grant of approval; commendatory license or sanction.

imprisonment, *n.* The act of confining a person, esp. in a prison; the state of being confined. —**imprison,** *vb.* See FALSE IMPRISONMENT.

improper, *adj.* **1.** Incorrect; unsuitable; irregular. **2.** Fraudulent or otherwise wrongful.

improve, *vb.* **1.** To increase the value or enhance the appearance of something. **2.** To develop (land), whether or not the development enhances or lessens the value of the land.

improved value. In real-estate appraisal, the land value plus the value of any improvements.

improvement. An addition to real property, whether permanent or not; esp., one that increases its value or utility or that enhances its appearance. Cf. FIXTURE.

improvident (im-**prah**-və-dənt), *adj.* **1.** Lacking foresight and care in

the management of property. **2.** Of or relating to a judgment arrived at by using misleading information or a mistaken assumption. —**improvidence,** *n.*

impugn (im-**pyoon**), *vb.* To challenge or call into question (a person's character, the truth of a statement, etc.). —**impugnment,** *n.*

impunity (im-**pyoo**-nə-tee). An exemption or protection from punishment <because she was a foreign diplomat, she was able to disregard the parking tickets with impunity>. See IMMUNITY.

impute (im-**pyoot**), *vb.* To ascribe or attribute; to regard (usu. something undesirable) as being done, caused, or possessed by <the court imputed malice to the defamatory statement>. —**imputation,** *n.*

imputed income. See INCOME.

imputed interest. See INTEREST (3).

imputed knowledge. See KNOWLEDGE.

imputed negligence. See NEGLIGENCE.

inadequate remedy at law. A remedy (such as money damages) that does not sufficiently correct the wrong, as a result of which an injunction may be available to the disadvantaged party. See IRREPARABLE-INJURY RULE.

inadmissible, *adj.* (Of a thing) not allowable or worthy of being admitted; esp., of or relating to evidence that is impermissible before the factfinder.

inalienable, *adj.* Not transferable or assignable <inalienable property interests>.

inalienable right. See RIGHT.

in arrears. Behind in the discharging of a debt or other obligation.

inauguration (i-naw-gyə-**ray**-shən), *n.* **1.** A formal ceremony inducting someone into office. **2.** A formal ceremony introducing something into public use. **3.** The formal commencement of a period of time or course of action. —**inaugurate,** *vb.*—**inauguratory,** *adj.*—**inaugurator,** *vb.*

in banc. EN BANC.

in bank. EN BANC.

in being. Existing in life; in property law, this includes unborn children <life in being plus 21 years>. See LIFE IN BEING.

in blank. (Of an indorsement) not restricted to a particular indorsee. See *blank indorsement* under INDORSEMENT.

Inc. *abbr.* Incorporated.

in cahoots. See CAHOOTS.

in camera. 1. In the judge's private chambers. —Also termed *in chambers*. **2.** In the courtroom with all spectators excluded. **3.** (Of a judicial action) taken when court is not in session.

in camera inspection. A trial judge's private consideration of evidence.

incapacitation, *n.* **1.** The action of disabling or depriving of legal capacity. **2.** The state of being disabled or lacking legal capacity. —**incapacitate,** *vb.*

incapacity. 1. Lack of physical or mental capabilities. **2.** Lack of ability to have certain legal consequences attach to one's actions; for example, a five-year-old has an incapacity to make a binding contract. See DISABILITY. Cf. INCOMPETENCY.

in capita. Individually. See PER CAPITA.

incarceration, *n.* The act or process of confining someone; IMPRISONMENT. —**incarcerate,** *vb.*—**incarcerator,** *n.*

incendiary (in-**sen**-dee-er-ee), *n.* **1.** One who deliberately and unlawfully sets fire to property. —Also termed *arsonist; firebug.* **2.** An instrument (such as a bomb) or chemical agent designed to start fires. —**incendiary,** *adj.*

incentive stock option. See *stock option* (b) under OPTION.

incest, *n.* Sexual relations between family members or close relatives, including children related by adoption. —**incestuous,** *adj.*

in chambers. IN CAMERA (1).

in chief. *Jargon.* **1.** Principal, as opposed to collateral or incidental. **2.** Denoting the part of a trial or testimony in which the main body of evidence is presented. See CASE-IN-CHIEF.

inchmaree clause (**inch**-mə-ree). In maritime law, an insurance-policy provision that protects against risks not caused by nature, such as sailors' negligence or latent defects in machinery.

inchoate (in-**koh**-ət), *adj.* Partially completed or imperfectly formed;

just begun. —**inchoateness,** *n.* Cf. CHOATE.

inchoate crime. See *inchoate offense* under OFFENSE.

inchoate dower. See DOWER.

inchoate interest. In property law, an interest that has not yet vested.

inchoate lien. See LIEN.

inchoate offense. See OFFENSE.

inchoate right. 1. A right that has not fully developed, matured, or vested. **2.** In patent law, an inventor's right that has not yet matured into property because the patent application is pending.

incident, *adj.* Connected with (something else) but usu. able to exist independently; naturally dependent or attaching <the easement is incident to one's ownership of the land>. —**incident,** *n.*

incidental, *adj.* Subordinate to something of greater importance; having a minor role <the FAA determined that the wind played only an incidental part in the plane crash>.

incidental admission. See ADMISSION.

incidental authority. See AUTHORITY.

incidental beneficiary. See BENEFICIARY.

incidental damages. See DAMAGES.

incidental use. See USE (1).

incident power. See POWER.

incitement, *n.* **1.** The act or an instance of provoking, urging on, or stirring up. **2.** In criminal law, the act of persuading another to commit a crime; SOLICITATION (2). —**incite,** *vb.* —**inciteful,** *adj.*

included offense. See *lesser included offense* under OFFENSE.

inclusio unius est exclusio alterius (in-**kloo**-zee-oh-**oon**-ee-əs-est-ek-**skloo**-zee-oh-ahl-**ter**-ee-əs). [Latin] A canon of construction holding that to express or include one thing implies the exclusion of the other, or of the alternative; for example, the rule that "each citizen is entitled to vote" implies that noncitizens are not entitled to vote. —Also termed *expressio unius est exclusio alterius.* Cf. EJUSDEM GENERIS; NOSCITUR A SOCIIS.

incognito (in-kog-**nee**-toh), *adj.* Without one's name or identity becoming known <she flew incognito to France>.

income. The money or other form of payment that one receives, usu. periodically, from employment, business, investments, royalties, gifts, and the like. See EARNINGS. Cf. PROFIT.

accrued income. Money earned but not yet received.

adjusted gross income. Gross income minus allowable deductions specified in the tax code.

aggregate income. The total income of a husband and wife who file a joint tax return.

blocked income. Money earned by a foreign taxpayer but not subject to U.S. taxation because the foreign country prohibits changing the income into dollars.

deferred income. Money received at a time later than when it was earned, such as a check received in

December for commissions earned in November.

disposable income. Income that may be spent or invested after payment of taxes or other obligations.

earned income. Money derived from one's own labor or active participation; earnings from services. Cf. *unearned income.*

exempt income. Income that is not subject to income tax.

fixed income. Money received at a constant rate, such as payments from a pension or annuity.

gross income. Total income from all sources before deductions, exemptions, or other tax reductions.

imputed income. The benefit one receives from the use of one's own property, the performance of one's services, or the consumption of self-produced goods and services; imputed income is excluded from gross income for tax purposes.

net income. Total income from all sources after calculating deductions, exemptions, and other tax reductions; income tax is computed from net income.

net operating income. Income earned from running a business, calculated by subtracting operating costs from total earnings.

nonoperating income. Business income derived from investments rather than operations.

ordinary income. **a.** For business-tax purposes, earnings from the normal operations or activities of a business. **b.** For individual income-tax purposes, income that is de-

rived from sources such as wages, commissions, interest, and the like.

passive income. Income derived from a business activity over which the earner does not have immediate control, such as copyright royalties.

real income. Income adjusted to allow for inflation or deflation so that it reflects true purchasing power.

split income. An equal division between spouses of earnings reported on a joint tax return, allowing for equal tax treatment in community-property and common-law states.

taxable income. Gross income minus all allowable deductions and exemptions; taxable income is multiplied by the applicable tax rate to compute one's tax liability.

unearned income. **a.** Earnings from investments rather than labor. — Also termed *investment income.* **b.** Income received but not yet earned; income paid in advance. Cf. *earned income.*

unrelated business income. Taxable income generated by a tax-exempt organization from a trade or business unrelated to its exempt purpose or activity.

income-basis method. A method of computing the rate of return on a security using the interest and price paid rather than the face value.

income fund. See MUTUAL FUND.

income-shifting. The practice of transferring income to a taxpayer who is subject to a lower rate, such as a child, to reduce tax liability. See *kiddie tax* under TAX.

income statement. A statement of all the revenues, expenses, gains, and losses that a business incurred during a period of time. —Also termed *statement of income*; *profit-and-loss statement*; *earnings report*. Cf. BALANCE SHEET.

income tax. See TAX.

income-tax return. TAX RETURN.

income-tax withholding. See WITHHOLDING.

income yield. CAPITALIZATION RATE.

in common. Shared equally with others, without division into separate ownership parts. See *tenancy in common* under TENANCY.

incommunicado (in-kə-myoo-ni-**kah**-doh). [Spanish] **1.** Without any means of communication. **2.** (Of a prisoner) having the right to communicate only with designated people.

incompetence, *n.* **1.** The state or fact of being unable or unqualified to do something <the dispute was over her alleged incompetence as a legal assistant>. **2.** INCOMPETENCY <the court held that the affidavit was inadmissible because of the affiant's incompetence>. —**incompetent,** *adj.*

incompetency, *n.* Lack of legal ability in some respect, esp. to stand trial or to testify <once the defense lawyer established her client's incompetency, the client did not have to stand trial>. —Also termed *incompetence*. —**incompetent,** *adj.* Cf. INCAPACITY.

incompetent evidence. See EVIDENCE.

inconsistent defense. See DEFENSE (1).

inconsistent statement. See PRIOR INCONSISTENT STATEMENT.

incontestability clause. An insurance-policy provision (esp. found in a life-insurance policy) that prevents the insurer, after a specified period (usu. one or two years), from disputing the policy's validity on the basis of fraud or mistake. —Also termed *noncontestability clause*; *incontestable clause*. Cf. NO-CONTEST CLAUSE.

incorporation, *n.* **1.** The formation of a legal corporation. See ARTICLES OF INCORPORATION. **2.** In constitutional law, the process of applying the provisions of the Bill of Rights to the states by interpreting the Fourteenth Amendment's Due Process Clause as encompassing those provisions; in a variety of opinions since 1897, the Supreme Court has incorporated all of the Bill of Rights except the following provisions: (1) the Second Amendment right to bear arms, (2) the Third Amendment prohibition of quartering soldiers, (3) the Fifth Amendment right to grand-jury indictment, (4) the Seventh Amendment right to a jury trial in civil cases, and (5) the Eighth Amendment prohibition of excessive bail and fines.

selective incorporation. Incorporation of certain provisions of the Bill of Rights; Justice Benjamin Cardozo, who served from 1932 to 1938, first espoused this approach.

total incorporation. Incorporation of all of the Bill of Rights; Justice Hugo Black, who served from 1937 to 1971, first advocated this approach.

3. INCORPORATION BY REFERENCE. —**incorporate,** *vb.*—**incorporator,** *n.*

incorporation by reference. A method of making a secondary document part of a primary document by including in the primary document a statement that the secondary document should be treated as if it were contained within the primary one. — Often shortened to *incorporation*.

incorporeal (in-kor-**por**-ee-əl), *adj.* Having a conceptual existence but no physical existence; intangible <copyrights and patents are incorporeal property>. —**incorporeality,** *n.* Cf. CORPOREAL.

incorporeal hereditaments. See HEREDITAMENT.

incorrigible (in-**kor**-ə-jə-bəl), *adj.* Incapable of being reformed; delinquent.

increase, *n.* **1.** The extent of growth or enlargement. **2.** *Archaic.* The produce of land or the offspring of humans or animals. —**increase,** *vb.*

increment (**in**[g]-krə-mənt). A unit of increase in quantity or value. — **incremental,** *adj.*

incremental cash flow. See CASH FLOW.

increscitur (in-**kres**-[s]i-tər). ADDITUR.

incriminate, *vb.* **1.** To charge (someone) with a crime <the state incriminated the murder suspect>. **2.** To indicate (one's or another's) involvement in the commission of a crime or other wrongdoing <the defendant incriminated an accomplice>. —**incrimination,** *n.*—**incriminatory,** *adj.*—Also termed *criminate*. See SELF-INCRIMINATION.

incriminating circumstance. A situation or fact showing either that a crime was committed or that a particular person committed it.

incriminating evidence. See EVIDENCE.

incroachment. ENCROACHMENT.

inculpate (**in**-kəl-payt), *vb.* **1.** To accuse. **2.** To implicate in a crime or other wrongdoing; INCRIMINATE. — **inculpation,** *n.*—**inculpatory** (in-**kəl**-pə-tor-ee), *adj.*

inculpatory evidence. See EVIDENCE.

incumbent, *n.* One who holds an official post, esp. a political one. — **incumbency,** *n.*—**incumbent,** *adj.*

incumbrance. ENCUMBRANCE.

incur, *vb.* To suffer or bring on oneself (a liability or expense). —**incurrence,** *n.*—**incurrable,** *adj.*

in custodia legis (in-kəs-**toh**-dee-ə-**lay**-gəs *or* -**lee**-jəs). [Latin] In the custody of the law <the debtor's automobile was *in custodia legis* after being seized by the sheriff>.

indebitatus assumpsit. See *general assumpsit* under ASSUMPSIT.

indebtedness (in-**de**-təd-nəs). **1.** The quality or state of owing money. **2.** Something owed; a debt.

indecency, *n.* The quality or state of being offensive, esp. in a vulgar or sexual way; unlike obscene material, indecent speech is protected under the First Amendment. —**indecent,** *adj.* Cf. OBSCENITY.

indecent assault. See *sexual assault* (b) under ASSAULT.

indecent exposure. An offensive display of one's body in public, esp. of the genitals.

indecent liberties. Improper, although not necessarily sexual, behavior toward a child.

indefeasible (in-də-**feez**-ə-bəl), *adj.* (Of a claim or right) that cannot be defeated, revoked, or lost <an indefeasible estate>.

indefeasible remainder. See REMAINDER.

indefeasibly vested remainder. See *indefeasible remainder* under REMAINDER.

indefinite sentence. See *indeterminate sentence* under SENTENCE.

in delicto (in-də-**lik**-toh). [Latin] *Jargon.* In fault. Cf. EX DELICTO.

indemnification. 1. The action of compensating for loss or damage sustained. **2.** The compensation so made.

indemnifier. INDEMNITOR.

indemnify, *vb.* **1.** To reimburse a loss that someone has suffered because of another's act or default. **2.** To promise to reimburse such a loss. **3.** To give security against such a loss.

indemnitee. One who receives indemnity from another.

indemnitor. One who indemnifies another. —Also termed *indemnifier*.

indemnity (in-**dem**-nə-tee), *n.* **1.** A duty to make good any loss, damage, or liability another has incurred. **2.** The right of an injured party to claim reimbursement for its loss, damage, or liability from a person who has such a duty. **3.** Reimbursement or compensation for loss, damage, or liability. —**indemnificatory, indemnitory,** *adj.* Cf. CONTRIBUTION.

double indemnity. The payment of twice the basic benefit in the event of a specified loss, esp. as in an insurance contract requiring the insurer to pay twice the policy's face amount in the case of accidental death.

indemnity insurance. See *first-party insurance* under INSURANCE.

indemnity principle. In insurance law, the doctrine that an insurance policy should not confer a benefit greater in value than the loss suffered by the insured.

indenture, *n.* **1.** A formal written instrument made by two or more persons with different interests, traditionally having the edges serrated, or indented, in a zigzag fashion to reduce the possibility of forgery and to distinguish it from a deed poll. Cf. *deed poll* under DEED. **2.** A deed or elaborate contract signed by two or more parties.

corporate indenture. A document containing the terms and conditions governing the issuance of debt securities, such as bonds or debentures.

trust indenture. A document containing the terms and conditions governing a trustee's conduct and the trust beneficiaries' rights. —Also termed *indenture of trust*.

independence. A nation's right to manage all its affairs, whether external or internal, without control from other nations.

independent agency. See AGENCY (3).

independent agent. See AGENT.

independent audit. See AUDIT.

independent contractor. One who is hired to complete a specific project but who is left free to do the assigned work and to choose the method for accomplishing it; unlike an employee, an independent contractor does not, upon committing a wrong while carrying out the work, create vicarious liability for an employer who did not authorize the wrongful act. Cf. EMPLOYEE.

independent counsel. See COUNSEL.

independent covenant. See COVENANT (1).

independent executor. See EXECUTOR.

independent intervening cause. See *intervening cause* under CAUSE (1).

independent-source rule. In criminal procedure, the rule providing—as an exception to the fruit-of-the-poisonous-tree doctrine—that evidence obtained by illegal means may nonetheless be admissible if such evidence is also obtained by legal means unrelated to the original illegal conduct. See FRUIT-OF-THE-POISONOUS-TREE DOCTRINE. Cf. INEVITABLE-DISCOVERY RULE.

independent union. See UNION.

indestructible trust. See TRUST.

indeterminate conditional release. A type of release from prison granted upon the fulfillment of certain conditions; the release remains revocable if additional conditions are breached.

indeterminate sentence. See SENTENCE.

index, *n.* **1.** An alphabetized listing of the contents of a single book or document, or of a series of volumes, usu. found at the end of the book, document, or series <index of authorities>.

grantee-grantor index. An index, usu. kept in the county recorder's office, alphabetically listing by grantee the volume and page number of the grantee's recorded property transactions.

grantor-grantee index. An index, usu. kept in the county recorder's office, alphabetically listing by grantor the volume and page number of the grantor's recorded property transactions.

tract index. An index, usu. kept in the county recorder's office, listing by location of the property the volume and page number of the recorded property transactions in the county.

2. A number, usu. expressed in the form of a percentage or ratio, that indicates or measures a series of observations, esp. those involving a market or the economy <cost-of-living index>.

index crime. See *index offense* under OFFENSE.

index fund. See MUTUAL FUND.

indexing. The practice or method of adjusting the value of wages, pension benefits, insurance, or other types of payments to account for inflation. — Also termed *indexation*.

index offense. See OFFENSE.

Indian Claims Commission. A federal agency—dissolved in 1978—that adjudicated claims brought by an American Indian, a tribe, or other identifiable group of Indians against the United States; the U.S. Claims Court currently hears such claims.

Indian country. The land within the borders of all Indian reservations, the land occupied by an Indian community (whether or not located within a recognized reservation), and any land held in trust by the United States but beneficially owned by an Indian or tribe.

Indian land. Land owned by the United States but held in trust for and used by American Indians. — Also termed *Indian tribal property*.

Indian reservation. An area that the federal government has designated for use by an American Indian tribe, where the tribe generally settles and establishes a tribal government.

Indian Territory. A former U.S. territory—bordered on the north by Kansas, on the east by Arkansas and Missouri, on the south by Texas, and on the west and north by Oklahoma—to which the Cherokee, Choctaw, Chickasaw, Creek, and Seminole tribes were forcibly removed between 1830 and 1843; in the late 19th century, most parts of this territory were ceded to the U.S., and in 1907 the greater part of it became the State of Oklahoma.

Indian title. A right of occupancy that the federal government grants to an American Indian tribe based on its immemorial possession of the area. —Also termed *aboriginal title*.

Indian tribal property. INDIAN LAND.

indicia (in-**dish**-[ee-]ə), *n. pl.* Signs; indications <the purchase receipts are indicia of ownership>.

indictable offense (in-**dI**-tə-bəl-ə-fen[t]s). See OFFENSE.

indictee. A person charged with a crime.

indictment (in-**dIt**-mənt), *n.* **1.** The formal written accusation of a crime, affirmed by a grand jury and presented to a court for commencement of criminal proceedings against the accused. **2.** The act or process of preparing or bringing forward such a formal written accusation. —**indict,** *vb.* Cf. INFORMATION; PRESENTMENT (2).

indictor. A person who indicts another.

in diem (in-**dee**-əm *or* -**dI**-əm). [Latin] For a day. Cf. PER DIEM.

indigent (**in**-di-jənt), *n.* A poor person. —**indigency, indigence,** *n.*— **indigent,** *adj.* See PAUPER.

indigent defendant. A person who is too poor to hire a lawyer and who, upon indictment, becomes eligible to receive a court-appointed attorney and a waiver of court costs. See IN FORMA PAUPERIS.

indignity. In family law, a ground for divorce consisting in one spouse's pattern of behavior calculated to humiliate the other.

indirect attack. COLLATERAL ATTACK.

indirect confession. See CONFESSION.

indirect contempt. See *constructive contempt* under CONTEMPT.

indirect cost. See COST.

indirect evidence. See *circumstantial evidence* under EVIDENCE.

indirect-purchaser doctrine. In antitrust law, the doctrine holding that in litigation for price discrimination, the court will ignore sham middle parties in determining whether different prices were paid by different customers for the same good; thus, if the seller sells to A for $10, and sells to B for $10, who then sells to C for $15, the court will ignore B and compare the pricing between A and C.

indispensable-element test. In criminal law, a common-law test for the crime of attempt, based on whether the defendant acquires control over the thing that is essential to the crime; under this test, for example, a person commits attempted murder once he buys a gun to shoot the intended victim. Cf. SUBSTANTIAL-STEP TEST.

indispensable party. See PARTY.

individual proprietorship. SOLE PROPRIETORSHIP.

individual retirement account. In tax law, a savings account in which a person can deposit up to a specified amount of income each year ($2,000 under current law) with the deposits being tax-deductible for that year; the deposits, along with any interest earned, are not taxed until the money is withdrawn when the person re-tires (or, with certain penalties, before retirement). —Abbr. IRA.

indorsee (in-dor-**see**). One to whom a negotiable instrument is transferred by indorsement. —Also spelled *endorsee*.

indorsement, *n.* **1.** The act of signing one's name on the back of a negotiable instrument in order to transfer it to someone else (esp. in return for the cash or credit value indicated on its face). **2.** The signature itself. —Also spelled *endorsement.* —**indorse,** *vb.*

blank indorsement. An indorsement that names no specific payee, thus making the instrument payable to bearer and negotiable by delivery only. U.C.C. § 3-204(2). —Also termed *indorsement in blank; general indorsement.*

irregular indorsement. An indorsement made by a person who signs outside the chain of title and who therefore is not a holder or transferor of the instrument. —Also termed *anomalous indorsement.*

qualified indorsement. An indorsement that limits the signer's liability if the instrument is dishonored; typically, a qualified indorsement is made by adding to the signature the words "without recourse." U.C.C. § 3-415(b). See WITHOUT RECOURSE.

restrictive indorsement. An indorsement that makes the instrument no longer transferable or negotiable; typically, a restrictive indorsement is made by adding to the signature the words "for deposit only." U.C.C. § 3-205.

special indorsement. An indorsement that specifies a person to whom the instrument is payable or to whom the goods named by the document should be delivered. U.C.C. § 3-204(1). —Also termed *indorsement in full.*

indorser. One who transfers a negotiable instrument by indorsement. —Also spelled *endorser.*

inducement, *n.* **1.** The act or process of enticing or persuading another to take a certain course of action. See *fraud in the inducement* under FRAUD. **2.** In contract law, the benefit or advantage that causes the promisor to enter into the contract. **3.** In criminal law, the motive for committing a crime. **4.** In defamation law, the plaintiff's allegation of extrinsic facts that gave a defamatory meaning to a statement that is not defamatory on its face. Cf. INNUENDO (2); COLLOQUIUM. —**induce,** *vb.*

induction. 1. The act or process of initiating <when did the induction of this practice take place? >. **2.** The act or process of reasoning from specific instances to general propositions <after looking at several examples, the group reasoned by induction that it is a very poor practice to begin a new paragraph by abruptly bringing up a new case>. Cf. DEDUCTION (3).

industrial relations. All dealings and relationships between an employer and its employees, including collective bargaining, safety, and benefits.

industrial union. See UNION.

industry-wide liability. See *enterprise liability* under LIABILITY.

ineffective assistance of counsel. See ASSISTANCE OF COUNSEL.

inescapable peril. A danger that one cannot avoid without another's help. See LAST-CLEAR-CHANCE DOCTRINE.

in esse (in-**es**-ee). [Latin "in being"] In actual existence; IN BEING <the court was concerned only with the rights of the children *in esse*>. Cf. IN POSSE.

in evidence. Having been admitted into evidence <the photograph was already in evidence when the defense first raised an objection to it>.

inevitable-discovery rule. In criminal procedure, the rule providing—as an exception to the fruit-of-the-poisonous-tree doctrine—that evidence obtained by illegal means may nonetheless be admissible if the prosecution can show that the evidence would eventually have been legally obtained anyway. See FRUIT-OF-THE-POISONOUS-TREE DOCTRINE. Cf. INDEPENDENT-SOURCE RULE.

in extremis (in-ek-**stree**-məs). [Latin "in extremity"] **1.** In extreme circumstances. **2.** Near the point of death; on one's deathbed.

infamous crime. See CRIME.

infamous punishment. See PUNISHMENT.

infamy (**in**-fə-mee), *n.* **1.** Disgraceful repute. **2.** The loss of reputation or position resulting from a person's being convicted of an infamous crime. —**infamous** (**in**-fə-məs), *adj.* See *infamous crime* under CRIME.

infancy. MINORITY (1).

infant, *n.* **1.** A newborn baby. **2.** MINOR.

infanticide (in-**fant**-ə-sId). **1.** The act of killing a newborn child; in archaic usage, the word referred also to the killing of an unborn child. Cf. FETICIDE. **2.** The practice of killing newborn children. **3.** One who kills a newborn child.

infect, *vb.* **1.** To contaminate <the virus infected the entire network>. **2.** To taint with crime <in some cities, housing projects become infected as soon as they are built>. **3.** To involve (a ship or cargo) in the seizure to which contraband, being only a part of the cargo, is liable <claiming that the single package of marijuana had infected the ship, the Coast Guard seized the entire vessel>. —**infection,** *n.*—**infectious,** *adj.*

in feodo simpliciter (in-fee-**oh**-doh-sim-**pli**-sə-tər). [Law Latin] In fee simple. See FEE SIMPLE.

infeoff. ENFEOFF.

infeoffment. ENFEOFFMENT.

inference (in-f[ə-]rən[t]s), *n.* **1.** A conclusion reached by considering other facts and deducing a logical consequence from them. **2.** The process by which such a conclusion is reached. —**infer,** *vb.*—**inferential,** *adj.*—**inferrer,** *n.*

inferential fact. See FACT.

inferior court. See COURT.

inferred authority. See *incidental authority* under AUTHORITY.

infeudation (in-fyoo-**day**-shən), *n.* Under the feudal system of landholding, the process of giving a person legal possession of land; ENFEOFFMENT (1). —**infeudate,** *vb.* Cf. SUBINFEUDATION.

in fine (in-**fIn**-ee *or* in-**fIn**), *adv.* [Latin] **1.** In short; in summary. **2.** At the end (of a book, chapter, section, etc.).

infirmity, *n.* Physical weakness caused by age or disease; esp., in insurance law, an applicant's ill health that is poor enough to deter an insurance company from insuring the applicant. —**infirm,** *adj.*

in flagrante delicto (in-flə-**grahn**-tee-də-**lik**-toh *or* -**gran**-). [Latin "while the crime is ablaze"] In the very act of committing a crime or other wrong; red-handed <the sheriff caught them *in flagrante delicto*>.

inflation, *n.* A general increase in prices coinciding with a fall in the real value of money. —**inflationary,** *adj.* Cf. DEFLATION.

infliction of emotional distress. See EMOTIONAL DISTRESS.

informal contract. See *parol contract* (b) under CONTRACT.

informal dividend. See DIVIDEND.

informal marriage. See *common-law marriage* under MARRIAGE (1).

informal proceeding. See PROCEEDING.

informant. One who informs against another; esp., one who confidentially supplies information to the police about a crime, sometimes in exchange for a reward. —Also termed *informer*.

in forma pauperis (in-for-mə-**paw**-pər-əs). [Latin "in the manner of a pauper"] In the manner of an indigent who has permission to disregard filing fees and court costs <when suing, a poor person is generally enti-

tled to proceed *in forma pauperis>*. —Abbr. IFP.

in forma pauperis **affidavit.** See *poverty affidavit* under AFFIDAVIT.

information. A formal criminal charge filed by a prosecutor without the aid of the grand jury; the information is used for the prosecution of misdemeanors in almost all states, many of which allow its use for felony prosecutions as well. Cf. INDICTMENT.

information and belief, on. *Jargon.* (Of an allegation or assertion) based on secondhand information that the declarant believes to be true.

information return. See TAX RETURN.

informed consent. See CONSENT.

informed intermediary. See INTERMEDIARY.

informer. INFORMANT.

informer's privilege. The government's right to refuse to disclose an informant's identity.

in foro conscientiae (in-for-oh-kon-shee-**en**-shee-ee *or* I), [Latin "in the forum of conscience"] Privately or morally rather than legally <this moral problem cannot be dealt with by this court, but only *in foro conscientiae>*.

infra (**in**-frə). [Latin "below"] Later in this text; *infra* is used as a citational signal to refer to a subsequently cited authority. Cf. SUPRA.

infraction, *n.* A violation, usu. of a rule, statute, or local ordinance and usu. not punishable by incarceration. —**infract,** *vb.*

infrastructure. The underlying framework of a system; esp., public services and facilities (such as highways, schools, bridges, sewers, and water systems) needed to support commerce as well as economic and residential development.

infringement, *n.* Violation of another's right or privilege, esp. of an intellectual-property right (such as a patent, copyright, or trademark). —**infringe,** *vb.* Cf. PLAGIARISM.

contributory infringement. The act or fact of intentionally helping an unauthorized person to make, sell, or use protected intellectual property.

copyright infringement. Unauthorized exercise of the rights reserved exclusively for the copyright owner.

innocent infringement. In copyright law, infringement by unintentionally or unconsciously borrowing from a protected work.

patent infringement. The unauthorized making, using, or selling of an invention protected by a patent; the test for infringement is whether the allegedly infringing device performs substantially the same function to obtain substantially the same overall result as the patented product. —Also termed *direct infringement*; *literal infringement*.

trademark infringement. Unauthorized use or imitation of an insignia used to identify another company's product or service. See LIKELIHOOD-OF-CONFUSION TEST.

vicarious infringement. In copyright law, infringement by controlling or supervising an infringing performance, with the potential for profiting from that performance; for example, a concert theater can be vicariously liable for the infringing performance of a hired band.

in futuro (in-fyoo-**tyoor**-oh), *adv.* [Latin] In the future. Cf. IN PRAESENTI.

in genere (in-**jen**-ər-ee). [Latin "in kind"] Belonging to the same class, but not identical.

ingress. 1. The act of entering. **2.** The right or ability to enter; access. Cf. EGRESS.

in gross. Undivided; still in one large mass. See *easement in gross* under EASEMENT.

ingross. ENGROSS.

in hac parte (in-hak-**pahr**-tee). [Latin] On this part or side.

in haec verba (in-hayk-**vər**-bə *or* -heek-). [Latin] In these same words; verbatim.

inherently dangerous. Requiring special precautions at all times to avoid injury; dangerous per se. See DANGEROUS INSTRUMENTALITY.

inherent power. See POWER.

inherent right. See *inalienable right* under RIGHT.

inherit, *vb.* **1.** To receive (property) from an ancestor under the laws of intestate succession upon the ancestor's death. **2.** To receive (property) as a bequest or devise. —**inheritance,** *n.*—**inheritable, heritable,** *adj.*—**inheritor,** *n.*

inheritance tax. See TAX.

in-house counsel. See COUNSEL.

inhuman treatment. In family law, physical or mental cruelty so severe

that it endangers life or health; inhuman treatment is usu. grounds for divorce. See CRUELTY.

in infinitum (in-in-fə-**nI**-təm). [Latin "in infinity"] To infinity; used in reference to a line of succession that is indefinite.

in initio (in-i-**nish**-ee-oh). [Latin "in the beginning"] At the beginning or outset. Cf. AB INITIO.

in invitum (in-in-**vI**-təm). *Jargon.* Against an unwilling person <the nonparty appealed after being compelled to participate in proceedings that were *in invitum*>.

initial disclosure. In federal practice, the requirement that parties must make available to each other the following information without first receiving a discovery request: (1) the name, address, and telephone number of individuals likely to have relevant, discoverable information, (2) a copy or description of all relevant documents, data compilations, and tangible items in the party's possession, custody, or control, (3) a damages computation, and (4) any relevant insurance agreements. Fed. R. Civ. P. 26(a)(1)(A-D).

initial margin requirement. See MARGIN REQUIREMENT.

initial public offering. See OFFERING.

initiative. An electoral process by which a percentage of voters can propose legislation and compel a vote on it by the legislature or by the full electorate; recognized in some state constitutions, the initiative is one of the few methods of direct democracy in an otherwise representative system. Cf. REFERENDUM.

injunction, *n.* A court order commanding or preventing an action. — **enjoin,** *vb.*—**injunctive,** *adj.*

mandatory injunction. An injunction that orders an affirmative act or mandates a specified course of conduct. Cf. *prohibitory injunction.*

permanent injunction. An injunction granted after a final hearing on the merits; despite its name, a permanent injunction does not necessarily last forever. —Also termed *perpetual injunction.*

preliminary injunction. A temporary injunction issued before or during trial to prevent an irreparable injury from occurring before the court has a chance to decide the case; a preliminary injunction will be issued only after the defendant receives notice and an opportunity to be heard. —Also termed *interlocutory injunction; temporary injunction.* Cf. TEMPORARY RESTRAINING ORDER.

preventive injunction. An injunction designed to prevent a loss or injury in the future. Cf. *reparative injunction.*

prohibitory injunction. An injunction that forbids or restrains an act. Cf. *mandatory injunction.*

quia-timet injunction (**kwee**-ə-**tim**-it *or* -**teem**-it). [Latin "because he fears"] An injunction granted to prevent an action that has been threatened but has not yet violated the plaintiff's rights. See QUIA TIMET.

reparative injunction (ri-**pair**-ə-tiv). An injunction requiring the defendant to restore the plaintiff to the position he or she was in before

the defendant committed the wrong. Cf. *preventive injunction.*

in jure (in-**juur**-ee). [Latin "in law"] According to the law.

injuria (in-**juur**-ee-ə). [Latin] Injury.

injuria absque damno (in-**juur**-ee-ə-ab-skwee-**dam**-noh). [Latin "injury without damage"] A legal wrong that will not sustain a lawsuit because no harm resulted from it. —Also termed *injuria sine damno.* Cf. DAMNUM ABSQUE INJURIA.

injurious falsehood. DISPARAGEMENT.

injury, *n.* **1.** The violation of another's legal right, for which the law provides a remedy; a wrong or injustice. **2.** Harm or damage. —**injure,** *vb.*—**injurious,** *adj.*

bodily injury. Physical damage to a person's body. —Also termed *physical injury.* Cf. *grievous bodily harm* under HARM.

civil injury. Physical harm or property damage caused by the breach of a contract or by a criminal offense redressable through a civil action.

compensable injury. In workers'-compensation law, an injury caused by an accident arising from the employment and in the course of the employee's work, and for which the employee is statutorily entitled to receive compensation.

irreparable injury (i-**rep**-[ə-]rə-bəl). An injury that cannot be adequately measured or compensated by money and is therefore often considered remediable by injunction. See IRREPARABLE-INJURY RULE.

malicious injury. **a.** An injury resulting from a willful act committed with knowledge that it is likely to injure another or with reckless disregard of the consequences. **b.** MALICIOUS MISCHIEF.

personal injury. **a.** In a tort action for negligence, any harm caused to a person, such as a broken bone, a cut, or a bruise; bodily injury. **b.** Any invasion of personal rights, including mental suffering and false imprisonment. **c.** In workers'-compensation law, any harm (including a worsened preexisting condition) that arises in the scope of employment.

scheduled injury. A partially disabling injury for which a predetermined amount of compensation is allowed under a workers'-compensation statute.

injustice. 1. An unjust state of affairs; unfairness. **2.** An unjust act.

in kind, *adv.* With another (article or commodity) that is of the same type or quality, instead of cash <he made a repayment in kind>. —**in-kind,** *adj.*

inland revenue. See INTERNAL REVENUE.

inland waters. Waterways that are within or partially within land, such as rivers and bays. —Also termed *internal waters.*

in-law, *n.* A relative by marriage.

in limine (in-**lim**-ə-nee), *adv.* [Latin "at the outset"] Preliminarily; presented before or during trial <motion in limine>. See MOTION IN LIMINE.

in loco parentis (in-**loh**-koh-pə-**ren**-təs), *adv.* [Latin "in the place of a parent"] Acting as a temporary guardian of a child.

in loco parentis, *n.* Supervision of a young adult by an administrative body such as a university.

inmate. 1. A person confined in a prison, hospital, or other institution. **2.** *Archaic.* A person living inside a place; one who lives with others in a dwelling.

innocent agent. In criminal law, a person whose action on behalf of a principal is unlawful but does not merit prosecution because he or she had no knowledge of the principal's illegal purpose.

innocent infringement. See INFRINGEMENT.

innocent junior user. In trademark law, a party who, without any actual or constructive knowledge, uses a trademark that has been previously used in a geographically distant market, and who may continue to use the trademark in a limited geographic area.

innocent misrepresentation. See MISREPRESENTATION.

innocent passage. In maritime law, the right of foreign ships to pass through a country's territorial waters, esp. those connecting two open seas.

innocent purchaser. See *bona fide purchaser* under PURCHASER.

innocent trespass. See TRESPASS.

Inn of Court. 1. Any of four autonomous institutions in which English barristers must join to receive their training and to which they remain a member for life: The Honourable Societies of Lincoln's Inn, the Middle Temple, the Inner Temple, and Gray's Inn; these powerful bodies examine candidates for the Bar, "call" them to the Bar, and award the degree of barrister. **2.** (*pl.*) In the U.S., an organization (formally named the *American Inns of Court Foundation*) with over 100 local chapters whose members include judges, law professors, law students, and attorneys; through monthly meetings, the chapters emphasize practice skills, professionalism, and ethics, and provide mentors to train students and young lawyers in the finer points of good legal practice.

innuendo (in-yə-**wen**-doh). [Latin "by hinting"] **1.** An oblique remark or indirect suggestion, usu. of a derogatory nature. **2.** In defamation law, the plaintiff's explanation of a statement's defamatory meaning when that meaning is not apparent from the statement's face; for example, the innuendo of the statement "David burned down his house" can be shown by pleading that the statement was understood to mean that David was defrauding his insurance company (the fact that he had insured his house is pleaded and proved by *inducement*). Cf. INDUCEMENT (4); COLLOQUIUM. **3.** An explanatory word or passage inserted parenthetically into a legal document.

in pais (in-**pays** *or* -**pay**). [Law French "in the country"] Outside court or legal proceedings. See *estoppel in pais* under ESTOPPEL.

in pari causa (in-**pahr**-ee-**koz**-ə), *adv.* [Latin "in an equal case"] In a case affecting two parties equally or in which they have equal rights <*in pari causa*, the possessor ordinarily defeats the nonpossessory claimant>.

in pari delicto (in-**pahr**-ee-də-**lik**-toh), *adv.* [Latin "in equal fault"] Equally at fault <courts usually deny relief when parties have made an illegal agreement and both stand *in pari delicto*>.

in pari materia (in-**pahr**-ee-mə-**teer**-[i-]yə). [Latin "in the same matter"] **1.** *adj.* Relating to the same matter or subject; in statutory interpretation, the common maxim is that statutes *in pari materia* are to be construed together <there is nothing in the way of other laws *in pari materia* by which to flesh out this statute>. **2.** *adv.* Loosely, in conjunction with <the Maryland constitutional provision is construed *in pari materia* with the Fourth Amendment>.

in perpetuity (in-pər-pə-t[y]oo-ə-tee). Forever. See PERPETUITY.

in personam (in-pər-**soh**-nəm), *adj.* [Latin "against a person"] Involving or determining the personal rights and interests of the parties. —**in personam**, *adv.* See *action in personam* under ACTION. Cf. IN REM.

in personam jurisdiction. See *personal jurisdiction* under JURISDICTION.

in point. ON POINT.

in posse (in-**paw**-see). [Latin] Not currently existing, but ready to come into existence under certain conditions in the future; potential <the will contemplated both living children and children *in posse*>. Cf. IN ESSE.

in praesenti (in-prI-**zen**-tI). [Latin] At present; right now. Cf. IN FUTU-RO.

in propria persona (in-**proh**-pree-ah-pər-**soh**-nə). [Latin "in one's own person"] PRO SE.

inquest. 1. An inquiry by a coroner or medical examiner, sometimes with the aid of a jury, into the manner of death of anyone who has been murdered or found dead under suspicious circumstances, or who has died in prison. —Also termed *inquisition after death.* **2.** A judicial inquiry into a certain matter by a jury empaneled for that purpose. **3.** The finding of such a specially empaneled jury. Cf. INQUISITION.

inquest jury. See JURY.

inquiry notice. See NOTICE.

inquisition. 1. A judicial inquiry, esp. in a derogatory sense. **2.** A persistent, grueling examination conducted without regard for the examinee's dignity or civil liberties. Cf. INQUEST.

inquisition after death. INQUEST (1).

inquisitorial system. A system of proof-taking used in civil law, whereby the judge conducts the trial, determines what questions to ask, and defines the scope and the extent of the inquiry; this system prevails in most of continental Europe, in Japan, and in Central and South America. Cf. ADVERSARY SYSTEM.

in re (in-ray *or* -ree). [Latin "in the matter of"] (Of a judicial proceeding) not formally including adverse parties, but rather concerning something (such as an estate); the term is often used in case citations, esp. in uncontested proceedings <In re Butler's Estate>. —Also termed *matter of* <Matter of Butler's Estate>.

in rem, *adj.* [Latin "against a thing"] Involving or determining the status of a thing, and therefore the rights of persons generally with respect to that thing. —**in rem,** *adv.* See *action in rem* under ACTION. Cf. IN PERSONAM.

quasi in rem. [Latin "as if against a thing"] Involving or determining the rights of a person having an interest in property located within the court's jurisdiction. See *action quasi in rem* under ACTION.

in rem jurisdiction. See JURISDICTION.

inroll. ENROLL (1).

INS. *abbr.* IMMIGRATION AND NATURALIZATION SERVICE.

insanity, *n.* Any mental disorder severe enough that it prevents one from having legal capacity and excuses one from criminal or civil responsibility; insanity is a legal, not a medical, standard. —Also termed *legal insanity.* —**insane,** *adj.*

temporary insanity. Insanity that exists only at the time of a criminal act.

insanity defense. In criminal law, an affirmative defense alleging that a mental disorder caused the accused to commit the crime; unlike other defenses, a successful insanity defense results not in acquittal but instead in a special guilty verdict ("not guilty by reason of insanity") that usu. leads to the defendant's commitment to a mental institution. —Also

termed *insanity plea*. See MCNAGHT-
EN RULES; SUBSTANTIAL-CAPACITY
TEST; IRRESISTIBLE-IMPULSE TEST;
DURHAM RULE.

inscription, *n.* **1.** The act of entering a fact or name on a list, register,
or other record. **2.** An entry so recorded. **3.** In civil law, an agreement
whereby an accuser must, if the accusation is false, receive the same punishment that the accused would have
been given if he or she had been
found guilty. —**inscribe,** *vb.*—**in-
scriptive,** *adj.*

insecurity clause. A loan-agreement provision that allows the creditor to demand immediate and full
payment of the loan balance if the
creditor has reason to believe that
the debtor is about to default, such
as if the debtor suddenly loses a significant source of income. Cf. ACCEL-
ERATION CLAUSE.

inside director. See DIRECTOR.

inside information. Information
about a company's financial situation
obtained from a source within the
corporation rather than from a public
or published source. —Also termed
insider information.

insider. 1. In securities law, one
who has knowledge of material facts
not available to the general public
and who therefore has a duty to disclose the information before making
transactions in reliance on it.

temporary insider. A person or firm
that receives inside information in
the course of performing professional duties for the issuer of the
shares; usu. that person or firm is
subject to the same proscriptions
as any other insider.

2. One who controls a corporation,
such as an officer or director, or one
who owns 10% or more of the corporation's stock. **3.** In bankruptcy, an
entity or person who is so closely
related to a debtor that any deal between them will not be considered an
arm's-length transaction and will be
subject to close scrutiny.

insider information. INSIDE IN-
FORMATION.

insider trading. In securities law,
illegally transacting in a corporation's stock to take advantage of
one's knowledge of secret information, usu. acquired through a confidential relationship with the corporation. —Also termed *insider dealing.*

in solido (in-**sol**-ə-doh *or* -so-**lee**-
doh). [Latin "as a whole"] (Of an
obligation) creating joint and several
liability; the term is used in civil-law
jurisdictions such as Louisiana. Cf.
SOLIDARY.

insolvency, *n.* The inability to pay
debts as they mature. —**insolvent,**
adj. & *n.* See BANKRUPTCY (2).

balance-sheet insolvency. Insolvency
created when the debtor's liabilities exceed its assets; under some
state laws, balance-sheet insolvency prevents a corporation from
making distributions to its shareholders.

equity insolvency. Insolvency created
when the debtor cannot meet its
obligations as they come due in the
ordinary course of business; under
most state laws, equity insolvency
prevents a corporation from making distributions to its shareholders.

insolvency proceeding. *Archaic.* A bankruptcy proceeding to either liquidate or rehabilitate one's estate. See BANKRUPTCY (1).

in specie (in-**spee**-s[h]ee[-ee]). [Latin "in kind"] In the same or like form; IN KIND <the partners were prepared to return the borrowed items *in specie*>.

inspection right. The legal entitlement in certain circumstances to examine articles or documents, such as a consumer's right to inspect goods before paying for them.

Inspector General. One of several federal officials charged with supervising a particular agency's audits or investigations.

installment, *n.* One of several portions of a debt that is repaid periodically.

installment accounting method. See ACCOUNTING METHOD.

installment credit. See CREDIT.

installment debt. See DEBT.

installment land contract. See *contract for deed* under CONTRACT.

installment loan. See LOAN.

installment note. See NOTE.

installment plan. See *installment sale* under SALE.

installment sale. See SALE.

instance, *n.* **1.** An example or occurrence <there were 55 instances of reported spousal abuse in this small community last year>. **2.** The act of instituting legal proceedings <court of first instance>. **3.** Urgent solicitation or insistence <she applied for the job at the instance of her friend>.

instance, *vb.* To illustrate by example; to cite <counsel instanced three cases for the court to consider>.

instance court. See *trial court* under COURT.

instant, *adj. Jargon.* This; the present (case, judgment, order, etc.); now being discussed <the instant order is not appealable>.

instanter (in-**stan**-tər), *adv. Jargon.* Instantly; at once <the defendant was ordered to file its motion instanter>.

in statu quo. [Latin "in the state in which"] In the same condition as previously. —Also termed *in statu quo ante.* Cf. STATUS QUO.

instinct, *adj.* Imbued or charged <the contract is instinct with an obligation of good faith>.

in stirpes (in-**stər**-peez). See PER STIRPES.

institute, *n.* **1.** A legal treatise or commentary, such as Coke's *Institutes* in four volumes (published in 1628). **2.** (*cap. & pl.*) An elementary treatise on Roman law in four books; this treatise is one of the four component parts of the *Corpus Juris Civilis.* See CORPUS JURIS CIVILIS. **3.** In civil law, a person named in a will as heir, but with the direction that he or she must pass the estate on to some other specified person (called the *substitute*).

institute, *vb.* To begin or start; commence <institute legal proceedings against the manufacturer>.

institutional investor. One who trades in large volumes of securities, usu. by investing other people's money into large, managed funds such as pension plans. See MUTUAL FUND.

institutional lender. A business, esp. a bank, that routinely loans money to the general public.

institutional litigant. An organized group that brings lawsuits not for the purpose of merely winning an individual suit but rather to bring about a change in the law or to defend an existing law.

instructed verdict. See *directed verdict* under VERDICT.

instrument. A formal legal document that entails rights, duties, entitlements, and liabilities, such as a contract, will, promissory note, or share certificate. See NEGOTIABLE INSTRUMENT.

instrumentality rule. In corporate law, the principle that a corporation's existence will be disregarded if that corporation is controlled to such an extent by another corporation that it is actually a mere subsidiary.

insufficient funds. NOT SUFFICIENT FUNDS.

insular court. See COURT.

insurable, *adj.* Able to be insured <an insurable risk>. —**insurability,** *n.*

insurable interest. The financial or legal interest that an insured must have in the person, object, or activity covered by an insurance policy; if the policy does not have an insurable interest as its basis, it will usu. be considered a form of wagering and therefore held to be unenforceable. See *wager policy* under INSURANCE POLICY.

insurable value. The worth of the subject of an insurance contract to the insured or the beneficiary, usu. expressed as a monetary amount.

insurance (in-**shuur**-əns), *n.* **1.** An agreement by which one party (the *insurer*) commits to do something of value for another party (the *insured*) upon the occurrence of some specified contingency; esp., a contract whereby the insurer, in exchange for a paid premium, agrees to indemnify or guarantee the insured against a loss caused by a specified event or risk. **2.** The sum for which something (as a person or property) is covered by such an agreement. —**insure,** *vb.*

accident insurance. An agreement to indemnify against expense, loss of time, suffering, or death resulting from accidents. Cf. *casualty insurance.*

all-risk insurance. Insurance that covers every kind of loss except those specifically excluded.

automobile insurance. An agreement to indemnify against one or more kinds of loss associated with the use of an automobile, including damage to a vehicle or liability for personal injuries.

business-interruption insurance. An agreement to protect against one or more kinds of loss from interruption of an ongoing business, such as loss of profits while the business is shut down to repair fire damage.

casualty insurance. An agreement to indemnify against losses resulting from a broad group of causes such as legal liability, theft, accident, property damage, and workers' compensation; the meaning of casualty insurance has become blurred because of the rapid increase in different types of insurance coverage. Cf. *accident insurance*.

coinsurance. **a.** Insurance provided jointly by two or more insurers. **b.** Property insurance that requires the insured to bear a portion of the risk of partial or total destruction of the property if the property is not covered up to a certain percentage of its full value.

commercial insurance. An indemnity agreement in the form of a deed or bond to protect against a loss caused by a party's breach of contract.

comprehensive insurance. Insurance that combines coverage against many kinds of losses that may also be insured separately; this is commonly used, for example, in automobile-insurance policies.

convertible insurance. Insurance that can be changed to another form without further evidence of insurability, usu. referring to a term-life-insurance policy that can be changed to permanent insurance without a medical examination.

deposit insurance. A federally sponsored indemnification program to protect depositors against the loss of their money, up to a specified maximum, if the bank or savings-and-loan association closes.

directors' and officers' liability insurance. An agreement to indemnify corporate directors and officers against judgments, settlements, and fines arising from negligence

suits, shareholder actions, and other business-related suits. —Often shortened to *D & O liability insurance*; *D & O insurance*.

disability insurance. Coverage purchased to protect a person financially during periods of incapacity from working.

employers'-liability insurance. An agreement to indemnify an employer against an employee claim not covered under the workers'-compensation system.

errors-and-omissions insurance. An agreement to indemnity for loss sustained because of a mistake or oversight by the insured—though not for loss due to intentional wrongdoing; for example, lawyers often carry this insurance as part of their malpractice coverage to protect them in suits for damages resulting from inadvertent mistakes (such as missing a procedural deadline). —Often shortened to *E & O insurance*.

excess insurance. An agreement to indemnify against any loss that exceeds the amount of coverage under another policy. Cf. EXCESS CLAUSE.

fidelity insurance. An agreement to indemnify an employer against a loss arising from the lack of integrity or honesty of an employee or of a person holding a position of trust, such as a loss from embezzlement. —Also termed *fidelity guaranty insurance*.

fire insurance. An agreement to indemnify against property damage caused by fire, wind, rain, or other similar disasters; property damage resulting from a fire that is deliberately caused by the insured is not covered.

first-party insurance. A policy that applies to oneself or one's own property, such as life insurance, health insurance, and disability insurance. —Also termed *indemnity insurance.*

floater insurance. An agreement to indemnify against a loss sustained to moveable property, wherever its location within the territorial limit set by the policy.

group insurance. A form of insurance offered to a member of a group, such as the employees of a business, so long as that person remains a member of the group.

guaranty insurance. An agreement to cover a loss resulting from another's default, insolvency, or specified misconduct.

key-person life insurance. A type of life insurance purchased by a business to protect it against any loss caused by the death of an important officer or employee.

liability insurance. An agreement to cover a loss resulting from one's liability to a third party, such as a loss incurred by a driver who injures a pedestrian; the insured has a claim under the policy once the insured's liability to a third party has been fixed. —Also termed *third-party insurance.*

life insurance. An agreement between an insurance company and the policyholder to pay a specified amount to a designated beneficiary on the insured's death. —Also termed (in England) *assurance.*

Lloyd's insurance. See LLOYD'S INSURANCE.

malpractice insurance. An agreement to indemnify professionals, such as doctors or lawyers, against negligence claims.

manual-rating insurance. A type of insurance whereby the premium is set using a book that classifies certain risks on a general basis, rather than evaluating each individual case.

marine insurance. An agreement to indemnify against injury to a ship, cargo, or profits involved in a certain voyage or for a fixed time period.

mortgage insurance. An agreement to provide money for mortgage payments if the insured dies or becomes disabled.

mutual insurance. A system of insurance (esp. life insurance) whereby the policyholders become members of the insurance company, each paying premiums into a common fund from which each can claim in the event of a loss.

no-fault auto insurance. An agreement to indemnify against claims for personal injury and property damage, regardless of who caused the accident.

overinsurance. An indemnification that, through the purchase of one or more policies, exceeds the value of the property insured.

participating insurance. A type of insurance that is issued by a mutual company and allows a policyholder to receive dividends.

reciprocal insurance. A system whereby several individuals or businesses act through an agent to underwrite one another's risks, making each insured an insurer of the other members of the group. — Also termed *interinsurance.*

reinsurance. Insurance of all or part of one insurer's risk by a second insurer, who accepts the risk in exchange for a percentage of the original premium. —Also termed *reassurance.*

retirement-income insurance. An agreement whereby the insurance company agrees to pay the value of the policy if the insured dies before a certain age and an annuity if the insured survives beyond a certain age.

self-insurance. A plan under which a business sets aside money to cover any losses.

term life insurance. Life insurance that covers the insured for only a specified period. Cf. *whole life insurance.*

title insurance. An agreement to indemnify against damage or loss arising from a defect in title to real property, usu. issued to the buyer of the property by the title company that conducted the title search.

underinsurance. An agreement to indemnify against property damage up to a certain amount but for less than the property's full value.

whole life insurance. Life insurance that covers the insured for his or her entire life, during which the insured pays fixed premiums, accumulates savings from an invested portion of the premiums, and re-ceives a guaranteed benefit upon death. —Also termed *ordinary life insurance; straight life insurance.* Cf. *term life insurance.*

insurance adjuster. One who determines the value of the loss to the insured and settles the claim against the insurer. See ADJUSTER.

insurance agent. One authorized by an insurance company to sell its insurance policies. —Also termed (in property insurance) *recording agent.*

insurance broker. One who sells insurance policies without an exclusive affiliation with a particular insurance company.

insurance commissioner. A public official who supervises the insurance business conducted in a state.

insurance company. A corporation or association that issues insurance policies.

insurance policy. A contract for insurance; a document detailing such a contract. —Often shortened to *policy.* —Also termed *policy of insurance.*

blanket policy. An agreement to indemnify all property, regardless of location.

claims-made policy. An agreement to indemnify against all claims made during a particular period, regardless of when the incidents that gave rise to the claims occurred. — Also termed *discovery policy.*

comprehensive general liability policy. An insurance policy, usu. obtained by a business, that covers those damages that the insured becomes legally obligated to pay to a third party because of bodily injury or property damage; this type of third-party insurance first became popular in the 1940s. —Often shortened to *CGL policy*; *general liability policy*. —Also termed *commercial general liability policy*.

floating policy. A supplemental insurance policy covering property that frequently changes in quantity or location, such as jewelry.

master policy. An insurance policy that covers those under a group-insurance plan. See *group insurance* under INSURANCE.

nonmedical policy. An insurance policy that is issued without a prior medical examination of the applicant.

occurrence policy. An agreement to indemnify for any act that occurs during a specific period, regardless of when the claim is made.

standard policy. An insurance policy providing insurance that is recommended or required by state law, usu. regulated by an administrative agency.

umbrella policy. An insurance policy providing supplemental insurance that exceeds the basic or usual limits of liability.

unvalued policy. An insurance policy that does not provide for property valuation until a loss occurs.

wager policy. An insurance policy issued to a person who has no insurable interest in the person or property covered by the policy; wager policies are illegal in many states. —Also termed *gambling policy*. See INSURABLE INTEREST.

insurance pool. A group of several insurers who, in order to spread the risk, combine and share premiums and losses.

insurance premium. PREMIUM (1).

insurance underwriter. INSURER.

insured, *n.* One who is covered or protected by an insurance policy. —Also termed *assured*.

additional insured. A party covered by an insurance policy but not specifically named in the policy.

named insured. A party designated in an insurance policy as the one covered by the policy.

insurer. One who agrees, under an insurance policy, to assume the risk of another's loss and to compensate for that loss. —Also termed *underwriter*; *insurance underwriter*; *carrier*; *assurer* (for life insurance).

insurgent, *n.* A person who, for political purposes, engages in armed hostility against an established government. —**insurgency,** *n.*—**insurgent,** *adj.*

insurrection. A violent revolt against an oppressive authority, usu. a government.

in tail. See TAIL.

intake day. The day on which new cases are assigned to the courts.

intangible asset. See ASSET.

intangible property. See PROPERTY.

integrated agreement. See *integrated contract* under CONTRACT.

integrated bar. See BAR ASSOCIATION.

integrated contract. See CONTRACT.

integrated writing. See *integrated contract* under CONTRACT.

integration. 1. The process of making whole or combining into one. 2. In contract law, the process of expressing the parties' intent in a way that does not allow either party to later contradict that expression. See PAROL-EVIDENCE RULE.

complete integration. The fact or state of fully expressing the intent of the parties.

partial integration. The fact or state of not fully expressing the parties' intent, so that the contract can be changed by the admission of parol (extrinsic) evidence.

3. The incorporation of different races into existing institutions (such as public schools) for the purpose of reversing the historical effects of racial discrimination. Cf. DESEGREGATION. 4. In antitrust law, a firm's performance of a function that it could have purchased on the open market; a firm can achieve integration by entering a new market on its own, by acquiring a firm that operates in a secondary market, or by entering into a contract with a firm that operates in a secondary market. —Also termed *vertical integration.* See *vertical merger* under MERGER. 5. In securities law, the requirement that all offerings of securities over a given period are to be considered a single offering for purposes of determining an exemption from registration.

integration clause. MERGER CLAUSE.

intellectual property. 1. A category of intangible rights comprising primarily copyright, trademark, and patent law. 2. A copyrightable work, a protectible trademark, or a patentable invention in which one has such intangible rights.

intend, *vb.* 1. To desire that a consequence will follow from one's conduct; to have as one's purpose <he intended to hurt her>. 2. To contemplate that the consequences of one's act will necessarily or probably follow from the act, whether or not those consequences are desired for their own sake <although she didn't purposely defraud the company, her conduct suggests that she intended to do so>. 3. To signify or mean <what did the parties intend by that choice of words? >.

intended beneficiary. See BENEFICIARY.

intended-use doctrine. In products liability, the rule imposing a duty on a manufacturer to consider the marketing scheme of a product and its intended use in order to develop a product that is reasonably safe.

intendment. 1. The sense in which the law understands something <the intendments of a contract are that the contract is legally enforceable>. —Also termed *intendment of law.* 2. A decision-maker's inference about the true meaning or intention of a legal instrument <there is no need for intendment, the court reasoned, when the text of the statute is clear>.

common intendment. The natural or common meaning in legal interpretation.

intent. The state of mind accompanying an act, esp. a forbidden act. Cf. MOTIVE.

constructive intent. The state of mind presumed by law to be actual intent when the acts leading to the result could have reasonably been expected to cause that result.

general intent. The state of mind required for the commission of certain common-law crimes not requiring a specific intent or imposing strict liability; general intent usu. takes the form of recklessness (involving actual awareness of a risk and the culpable taking of that risk) or negligence (involving blameworthy inadvertence).

original intent. The mental state of the drafters or enactors of the U.S. Constitution, a statute, or some other document.

specific intent. The intent to accomplish the precise act with which one has been charged; at common law, the specific-intent crimes were robbery, assault, larceny, burglary, forgery, false pretenses, embezzlement, attempt, solicitation, and conspiracy.

transferred intent. See TRANSFERRED-INTENT DOCTRINE.

intention, *n.* The willingness to bring about something that one plans or foresees; the state of being set to do something. —**intentional,** *adj.*

intentional infliction of emotional distress. See EMOTIONAL DISTRESS.

intentional manslaughter. See *voluntary manslaughter* under MANSLAUGHTER.

intentional tort. See TORT.

inter alia (in-tər-**ah**-lee-ə *or* -**ay**-lee-ə), *adv.* [Latin] Among other things.

inter alios (in-tər-**ah**-lee-ohs *or* -**ay**-lee-ohs), *adv.* [Latin] Among other persons.

intercourse. 1. Dealings or communications, esp. between businesses, governmental entities, or the like. **2.** Physical sexual contact, esp. involving the penetration of the vagina by the penis.

interdict (**in**-tər-dikt), *n.* In civil law, an injunction or other prohibitory decree.

interdict (in-tər-**dikt**), *vb.* To forbid or restrain. —**interdiction,** *n.*

interesse termini (in-tər-**es**-ee-**tər**-mi-nI). [Latin "an interest in a term"] *Archaic.* A lessee's interest in real property before taking possession of the property; a lessee's right of entry.

interest, *n.* **1.** Advantage or profit, esp. of a financial nature <conflict of interest>. **2.** A legal share in something <right, title, and interest>.

future interest. See FUTURE INTEREST.

possessory interest. See POSSESSORY INTEREST.

terminable interest. See TERMINABLE INTEREST.

3. The cost paid to a lender in return for use of borrowed money <the components of a monthly mortgage payment are principal, interest, insurance, and taxes>. See USURY.

accrued interest. Interest that is earned but not yet paid, such as interest that accrues on real estate and that will be paid when the property is sold if, in the meantime, the rental income does not cover the mortgage payments.

compound interest. Interest paid on both the principal and the previously accumulated interest. Cf. *simple interest.*

imputed interest. An interest charge that the IRS automatically attributes to a lender regardless of whether the lender actually charged the interest to the borrower—common esp. with loans between family members.

prepaid interest. Interest paid before it is earned.

simple interest. Interest paid on the principal only and not on accumulated interest. Cf. *compound interest.*

interest-free loan. See LOAN.

Interest on Lawyers' Trust Accounts. A program that allows a lawyer or law firm to deposit a client's retained funds into an interest-bearing account that designates the interest payments to charitable, law-related purposes, such as providing legal aid to the poor; all states except Indiana have either a voluntary or mandatory IOLTA program. —Abbr. IOLTA.

interest-only mortgage. See MORTGAGE.

interest rate. The percentage that a borrower of money must pay to the lender in return for the use of the money, usu. expressed as a percentage of the principal over a one-year period. —Often shortened to *rate.* — Also termed *rate of interest.*

annual percentage rate. The actual cost of borrowing money, expressed in the form of an annualized interest rate. —Abbr. APR.

contract rate. The interest rate printed on the face of a bond certificate.

discount rate. **a.** The interest rate at which member banks may borrow from the Federal Reserve; this rate controls the supply of money available to banks for lending. Cf. *rediscount rate.* **b.** The percentage of a commercial paper's face value paid by a holder who sells the instrument to a financial institution. **c.** The interest rate used in calculating discounted present value.

effective rate. The actual annual interest rate, which incorporates compounding when calculating interest, rather than the stated rate or coupon rate.

floating rate. A varying interest charge that is tied to a financial index such as the prime rate.

illegal rate. An interest charge higher than what is allowed by law. See USURY.

legal rate. **a.** The interest rate imposed as a matter of law when none is provided for contractually. **b.** The maximum interest rate, set by statute, that may be charged on loans. See USURY.

lock rate. A mortgage-application interest rate that is established and guaranteed for a specified period. —Also termed *locked-in rate.*

nominal rate. The interest rate stated in a loan agreement or on a bond, with no adjustment made for inflation. —Also termed *coupon rate; face rate; stated rate.*

prime rate. The lowest interest rate that a commercial bank charges for short-term loans to its most creditworthy borrowers, usu. large corporations; this rate, which can vary slightly from bank to bank, often dictates other interest rates for various personal and commercial loans. —Often shortened to *prime.* —Also termed *prime lending rate.*

real rate. An interest rate that has been adjusted for inflation over time.

rediscount rate. The interest rate at which member banks may borrow from the Federal Reserve on loans secured by commercial paper that has already been resold by the banks. Cf. *discount rate* (a).

variable rate. An interest rate that fluctuates according to the current market rate.

interest-rate swap. An agreement to swap interest-payment obligations, commonly used to adjust one's risk exposure, to speculate on interest-rate changes, or to convert an instrument or obligation from a fixed to a floating rate or vice versa.

interest unity. See *unity of interest* under UNITY.

interference, *n.* **1.** The act of intermeddling in others' affairs, esp. in such a way as to hamper the actions of other persons or things. **2.** In patent and trademark law, a proceeding to determine the priority of invention between two applicants, who are referred to as the *senior party* (the one who filed earlier) and the *junior party* (the one who filed later). —**interfere,** *vb.*

interference with a business relationship. See TORTIOUS INTERFERENCE WITH PROSPECTIVE ADVANTAGE.

interference with a contractual relationship. See TORTIOUS INTERFERENCE WITH CONTRACTUAL RELATIONS.

intergovernmental-immunity doctrine. In constitutional law, the principle that both the federal government and the states are independent sovereigns, and that neither sovereign may intrude on the other within certain political spheres. Cf. PREEMPTION.

interim financing. See FINANCING.

interim-occupancy agreement. A contract regulating an arrangement (called a leaseback) whereby the seller rents back property from the buyer. See LEASEBACK.

interim order. See *interlocutory order* under ORDER (2).

interim receipt. The written acknowledgment of a premium paid on an insurance policy that is pending final approval.

interim statement. In accounting, a periodic financial report issued during the fiscal year (usu. quarterly) that indicates the company's current performance; the SEC requires the company to register such a statement if it is distributed to the company's shareholders. —Also termed *interim report.*

interinsurance. See *reciprocal insurance* under INSURANCE.

interlineation (in-tər-lin-ee-**ay**-shən), *n.* **1.** The act of writing something between the lines of an earlier writing. **2.** Something written between the lines of an earlier writing. —**interline,** *vb.* Cf. INTERPOLATION.

interlocking confessions. See CONFESSION.

interlocking director. See DIRECTOR.

interlocutory (in-tər-**lok**-[y]ə-tor-ee), *adj.* (Of an order, judgment, appeal, etc.) temporary; not final in the determination of an action.

interlocutory appeal. See APPEAL.

interlocutory decision. See *interlocutory order* under ORDER (2).

interlocutory decree. See *interlocutory judgment* under JUDGMENT.

interlocutory injunction. See *preliminary injunction* under INJUNCTION.

interlocutory judgment. See JUDGMENT.

interlocutory order. See ORDER (2).

interloper, *n.* **1.** One who interferes without justification. **2.** One who trades illegally. —**interlope,** *vb.*

intermeddler. See OFFICIOUS INTERMEDDLER.

intermediary (in-tər-**mee**-dee-er-ee), *n.* A mediator; go-between; third-party negotiator. —**intermediate** (in-tər-**me**-dee-ayt), *vb.* Cf. FINDER.

informed intermediary. In products-liability law, a person who is in the chain of distribution from the manufacturer to the consumer and who knows the risks of the product. —Also termed *learned intermediary.*

intermediate scrutiny. In constitutional law, the standard applied to quasi-suspect classifications (laws based on gender or legitimacy) under equal-protection analysis; quasi-suspect classifications must be substantially related to the achievement of important governmental objectives. —Also termed *heightened scrutiny.* Cf. STRICT SCRUTINY; RATIONAL-BASIS TEST.

intern, *n.* An advanced student or recent graduate who is apprenticing to gain practical experience before entering a specific profession. —**intern,** *vb.* —**internship,** *n.* See CLERK (4).

internal audit. See AUDIT.

internal financing. See FINANCING.

internal law. LOCAL LAW (3).

internal rate of return. See RATE OF RETURN.

internal revenue. Governmental revenue derived from domestic taxes rather than from customs or foreign sources. —Also termed (outside the U.S.) *inland revenue.*

Internal Revenue Code. Title 26 of the U.S. Code, containing all current federal tax laws. —Abbr. I.R.C.

Internal Revenue Service. The branch of the U.S. Treasury Department responsible for enforcing the

Internal Revenue Code and providing taxpayer education. —Abbr. I.R.S.

internal sovereignty. See SOVEREIGNTY.

internal waters. INLAND WATERS.

international agreement. A treaty or other contract between different countries, such as GATT or NAFTA. See GENERAL AGREEMENT ON TARIFFS AND TRADE; NORTH AMERICAN FREE TRADE AGREEMENT.

International Bank for Reconstruction and Development. WORLD BANK.

international bill of exchange. See *foreign draft* under DRAFT.

International Court of Justice. The 15-member United Nations tribunal that sits primarily at the Hague, Netherlands, to adjudicate disputes between countries that voluntarily submit cases for a decision; appeal from the Court lies only with the U.N. Security Council. —Abbr. ICJ. —Also termed *World Court*.

International Criminal Police Organization. An international law-enforcement group founded in 1923 and headquartered in Paris, France; the organization gathers and distributes information on international criminals to its 100 or so member nations. —Abbr. Interpol.

international law. The legal principles governing the relationships between nations; more modernly, the law of international relations, embracing not only nations but also such participants as international organizations, multinational corporations, nongovernmental organizations, and even individuals (such as those who invoke their human rights or commit war crimes). —Also termed *public international law*; *law of nations*; *law of nature and nations*; *jus gentium*; *jus gentium publicum*; *interstate law*; *law between states* (the word *state*, in the latter two phrases, being equivalent to nation or country).

private international law. International conflict of laws; legal scholars frequently lament the name "private international law" because it misleadingly suggests a body of law somehow parallel to (public) international law, when in fact it is merely a part of each legal system's private law. —Also termed *international private law*; *jus gentium privatum*. See CONFLICT OF LAWS (2).

International Monetary Fund. A United Nations agency established to stabilize international exchange rates and promote balanced trade. —Abbr. IMF.

International Trade Court. COURT OF INTERNATIONAL TRADE.

internecine (in-tər-**ne**-sin *or* -**nee**-sin *or* in-**tər**-nə-seen), *adj.* **1.** Mutually deadly; destructive of both parties <an internecine civil war>. **2.** Loosely, of or relating to conflict within a group <internecine faculty politics>.

internment, *n.* The government-ordered detention of people suspected of disloyalty to the government, such as the confinement of Japanese Americans during World War II. — **intern,** *vb.*

inter partes (in-tər-**pahr**-teez), *adv.* [Latin "between parties"] Between two or more parties; with two or more parties in a transaction. —*inter partes*, *adj.*

interplead, *vb.* **1.** (Of a claimant) to assert one's own claim regarding property or an issue already before the court. **2.** (Of a stakeholder) to institute an interpleader action, usu. by depositing disputed property into the court's registry to abide the court's decision about who is entitled to the property.

interpleader, *n.* A suit to determine a matter of claim or right to property held by a usu. disinterested third party (called a *stakeholder*) who is in doubt about which claimant should have the property, and who therefore deposits the property with the court while the interested parties litigate over ownership; typically, a stakeholder initiates an interpleader both to determine which claimant should receive delivery or payment and to avoid multiple liability. Fed. R. Civ. P. 22. See STAKEHOLDER (2). Cf. IMPLEADER; INTERVENTION (1).

Interpol (**in**-tər-pohl). *abbr.* INTERNATIONAL CRIMINAL POLICE ORGANIZATION.

interpolation (in-tər-pə-**lay**-shən), *n.* The act of inserting words, often extraneous or false ones, into a document to change the meaning. —**interpolate**, *vb.* —**interpolative**, *adj.* —**interpolator**, *n.* Cf. INTERLINEATION.

interposition, *n.* **1.** The act of submitting something (such as a pleading or motion) as a defense to an opponent's claim. **2.** *Archaic.* The action of a state, in the exercise of its sovereignty, rejecting a federal mandate that it believes is unconstitutional or overreaching; the Supreme Court has declared that interposition is an illegal defiance of constitutional authority. —**interpose**, *vb.*

interpretation, *n.* **1.** The process of determining what something means. **2.** The understanding one has about the meaning of something. **3.** A translation, esp. oral, from one tongue to another. —**interpret**, *vb.* —**interpretative, interpretive**, *adj.* See CONSTRUCTION (2).

interpreter. One who translates, esp. orally, from one tongue to another; esp., one who is sworn at a trial to accurately translate the testimony of a foreign or deaf witness.

interpretative rule. In administrative law, the requirement that an administrative agency clarify and explain the statutory regulations under which it operates. —Also termed *interpretive rule.*

interpretivism. The doctrine of constitutional interpretation holding that judges must confine themselves to norms or values expressly stated or implied in the language of the Constitution; Justices Hugo Black and Antonin Scalia are examples of the so-called interpretivists. Cf. NONINTERPRETIVISM.

interrogatee. One who is interrogated.

interrogation, *n.* The formal or systematic questioning of a person; esp., intensive questioning by the police, usu. of a person arrested for or suspected of committing a crime. —**interrogate**, *vb.* —**interrogative**, *adj.*

custodial interrogation. Intense questioning by the police of a person they have detained.

investigatory interrogation. Routine, nonaccusatory questioning by the police of a person who is not in custody.

interrogator. One who interrogates another.

interrogatory (in-tə-**rah**-gə-tor-ee). *n.* Any one of a numbered list of written questions submitted in a legal context, usu. to an opposing party in a lawsuit as part of discovery.

special interrogatory. A written question submitted to a jury whose answer is a required part of the verdict. Fed. R. Civ. P. 49(b). —Also termed *special issue.*

in terrorem (in-te-**ro**-rəm *or* in-**ter**-ər-əm), *adv.* [Latin "into a state of terror"] By way of threat; as a warning <the demand letter was sent *in terrorem,* as the client has no intention of actually suing>. —*in terrorem,* *adj.*

in terrorem **clause.** A documentary provision designed to threaten one into an action or inaction; esp., a testamentary provision that threatens to dispossess any beneficiaries who challenge the terms of the will. See NO-CONTEST CLAUSE.

inter se (in-tər-**say**). [Latin "between or among themselves"] (Of a right or duty) owed between the parties rather than to others. —Also termed *inter sese.*

interspousal, *adj.* Between husband and wife.

interspousal immunity. See *husband-wife immunity* under IMMUNITY (2).

interstate, *adj.* Between two or more states or residents of different states.

interstate agreement. An agreement between states. Cf. *interstate compact* under COMPACT.

interstate commerce. See COMMERCE.

Interstate Commerce Commission. The now-defunct federal agency established by the Interstate Commerce Act in 1887 to regulate surface transportation between states by certifying carriers and pipelines and by monitoring quality and pricing; in December 1995, when Congress eliminated this agency, the Surface Transportation Board (STB)—a three-member board that is a division of the Department of Transportation—assumed the agency's duties. —Abbr. ICC.

interstate compact. See COMPACT.

interstate law. 1. INTERNATIONAL LAW. **2.** The rules and principles used to determine controversies between residents of different states.

intersubjective zap. In critical legal studies, a so-called spontaneous moment of shared intuition. —Also termed *zap.*

intervening act. See *intervening cause* under CAUSE (1).

intervening cause. See CAUSE (1).

intervenor. One who voluntarily enters a pending lawsuit because of a direct interest in its subject matter. —Also spelled *intervener.*

intervention, *n.* **1.** The act of entering into a lawsuit by a third party who, despite not being named a party to the action, has an interest in the outcome; the intervenor sometimes joins the plaintiff in claiming what is sought, sometimes joins the defendant in resisting what is sought, and sometimes takes a position adverse to both the plaintiff and the defendant. Cf. IMPLEADER; INTERPLEADER. **2.** The legal procedure by which such a third party is allowed to become a party to the litigation. **3.** One nation's interference by force or threat of force in another nation's internal affairs, or in questions arising between other nations. —**intervene,** *vb.*

inter vivos (in-tər-**vI**-vohs *or* -vee-vohs), *adj.* [Latin "between the living"] Of or relating to property conveyed not by will or in contemplation of an imminent death, but during the conveyor's lifetime. —*inter vivos,* *adv.*

inter vivos gift. See GIFT.

inter vivos trust. See TRUST.

intestacy (in-**tes**-tə-see). The state or condition of a person's having died without a valid will. Cf. TESTACY.

intestate (in-**tes**-tayt), *adj.* **1.** Of or relating to a person who has died without a valid will <having revoked her will without making a new one, she was intestate when she died>. **2.** Of or relating to the property owned by a person who died without a valid will <an intestate estate>. **3.** Of or relating to intestacy <a spouse's intestate share>. Cf. TESTATE.

intestate, *n.* One who has died without a valid will. Cf. TESTATOR.

intestate law. The relevant statute governing succession to estates of those who die without a valid will.

intestate succession. The method used to distribute property owned by a person who died without a valid will. —Also termed *hereditary succession.* Cf. TESTATE SUCCESSION.

intimidation, *n.* Unlawful coercion; extortion. —**intimidate,** *vb.*—**intimidatory,** *adj.*—**intimidator,** *n.*

intitle. ENTITLE.

in toto (in-**toh**-toh). [Latin "in the whole"] Completely; as a whole <the company rejected the offer *in toto*>.

intoxication, *n.* A diminished ability to act with full mental and physical capabilities because of alcohol or drug consumption; drunkenness. —**intoxicate,** *vb.*

involuntary intoxication. The ingestion of alcohol or drugs against one's will or without one's knowledge; involuntary intoxication is an affirmative defense to criminal and negligence charges.

public intoxication. The appearance of one who is under the influence of drugs or alcohol in a place open to the general public; in most American jurisdictions, public intoxication is considered a misdemeanor and, in some states, alcoholism is a defense if the offender agrees to attend a treatment program.

voluntary intoxication. A willing ingestion of alcohol or drugs to the point of impairment done with the knowledge that one's physical and mental capabilities would be impaired; voluntary intoxication is not a defense to general-intent crimes, but may be admitted to refute the existence of a particular state of mind in specific-intent crimes. —Also termed *culpable intoxication*; *self-induced intoxication*.

intoxilyzer. BREATHALYZER.

intoximeter. BREATHALYZER.

intra. [Latin "in"] Within.

intragovernmental, *adj.* Within a government; between a single government's departments or officials.

in transitu (in-tran[t]-sə-too). [Latin "in transit; on the journey"] *Archaic.* Being conveyed from one place to another.

intrastate commerce. See COMMERCE.

intra vires (in-trə-veer-eez *or* -vI-reez), *adj.* [Latin "within the powers (of)"] Of or referring to an action taken within a corporation's or person's scope of authority <calling a shareholders' meeting is an *intra vires* function of the board of directors>. —**intra vires,** *adv.* Cf. ULTRA VIRES.

intrinsic, *adj.* Internal; relating to the essential nature of something.

intrinsic ambiguity. See *patent ambiguity* under AMBIGUITY.

intrinsic fraud. See FRAUD.

introduce into evidence. To have a fact or object admitted into the trial record, allowing it to be considered in the jury's or the court's decision.

introductory clause. The first paragraph of a contract, which typically begins with words such as "This Agreement is made on [date] between [parties' names]."—Also termed *commencement*; *exordium*.

intrusion, *n.* **1.** A person's entering without permission. Cf. TRESPASS. **2.** In an action for invasion of privacy, a highly offensive invasion of another person's seclusion or private life. —**intrude,** *vb.*—**intrusive,** *adj.*—**intruder,** *n.*

inure (i-n[y]oor), *vb.* **1.** To take effect; to come into use <the settlement proceeds must inure to the benefit of the widow and children>. **2.** To make accustomed to something unpleasant; to habituate <abused children become inured to violence>. —Also spelled *enure.*—**inurement,** *n.*

in utero (in-yoo-tə-roh). [Latin "in the uterus"] In the womb; during gestation.

invalid (in-val-id), *adj.* **1.** Not legally binding <an invalid contract>. **2.** Without basis in fact <invalid allegations>.

invalid (in-və-lid), *n.* One who, because of serious illness or other disability, lacks the physical or mental capability of managing one's day-to-day life.

invalid will. See WILL.

invasion of privacy. An unjustified exploitation of one's personality or intrusion into one's personal activity, actionable under tort law and sometimes under constitutional law; the four types of invasion of privacy in tort are: (1) an appropriation, for one's benefit, of another's name or likeness, (2) an offensive, intentional interference with a person's seclusion or private affairs, (3) the public disclosure, of an objectionable nature, of private information about another, and (4) the use of publicity to place another in a false light in the public eye. See RIGHT OF PRIVACY.

inveigle (in-**vay**-gəl), *vb.* To lure or entice through deceit or insincerity <she blamed her friend for inveigling her into the investment>. —**inveiglement,** *n.*

invented consideration. See CONSIDERATION.

invention, *n.* **1.** A patentable device or process created through independent experimentation; a newly discovered art or operation. **2.** The act or process by which such a discovery was made. —**invent,** *vb.*—**inventor,** *n.*

    conception of invention. The formation in the inventor's mind of a definite and permanent idea of a complete invention that is thereafter applied in practice; courts usu. consider conception when determining priority of invention.

    priority of invention. The determination that one among several patent applications, for substantially the same invention, should receive the patent when the Patent and Trademark Office has declared interference; this determination depends on the date of conception, the date of reduction to practice, and diligence.

inventory, *n.* **1.** A detailed list of assets <make an inventory of the estate>. **2.** In accounting, the portion of a financial statement reflecting the value of a business's raw materials, works-in-progress, and fin-

ished products <the company's reported inventory was suspiciously low>. **3.** Raw materials or goods in stock <the dealership held a sale to clear out its October inventory>. —**inventory,** *vb.*

inventory search. See SEARCH.

inventory-turnover ratio. In accounting, the result of dividing the cost of goods by the average inventory; this calculation is used to determine the effectiveness of the company's inventory-management policy.

in ventre sa mere. EN VENTRE SA MERE.

inverse condemnation. See CONDEMNATION.

inverse floater. See *inverse-floating-rate note* under NOTE.

inverse-floating-rate note. See NOTE.

inverse-order-of-alienation doctrine. The principle that if one has not collected on the mortgage or lien on a property sold off in successive parcels, one may collect first from the parcel still held by the original owner, then from the parcel sold last, then next to last, and so on until the amount is satisfied. —Also termed *rule of marshaling liens.*

inverse zoning. See ZONING.

invest, *vb.* **1.** To supply with authority or power <the U.S. Constitution invests the President with the power to conduct foreign policy>. **2.** To apply (money) for profit <Jillson invested her entire savings in the mutual fund>. **3.** To make an outlay (of money) for profit <Baird invested in stocks>. —**investment,** *n.*—**investor,** *n.*

investigative detention. See DETENTION.

investigative grand jury. See GRAND JURY.

investigatory interrogation. See INTERROGATION.

investigatory stop. A brief, nonintrusive detention by police, often including preliminary questioning and perhaps a weapons frisk, resulting from a reasonable suspicion of criminal activity.

investment banker. A person or institution that underwrites, sells, or assists in raising capital for businesses, esp. for new issues of stocks and bonds; a trader at an investment bank. See *investment bank* under BANK.

investment company. See COMPANY.

investment-grade rating. Any of the top four symbols (AAA, AA, A, or BAA) given to a bond after an appraisal of its quality by a securities-evaluation agency such as Moody's; the rating indicates whether the bond is a worthwhile risk.

investment income. See *unearned income* (a) under INCOME.

investment trust. See *investment company* under COMPANY.

invidious discrimination (in-vid-ee-əs-dis-krim-ə-**nay**-shən). See DISCRIMINATION.

in vinculis (in-**ving**-k[y]ə-ləs). [Latin "in chains"] In actual custody.

inviolable (in-**vI**-ə-lə-bəl), *adj.* Safe from violation; secure; incapable of being violated. —**inviolability,** *n.*

invisible. In accounting, not reported in a financial statement <invisible earnings>.

invitation, *n.* In negligence law, the enticement of others to enter, remain on, or use property or its structures. —**invite,** *vb.*

invitation to negotiate. A solicitation for one or more offers, usu. as a preliminary step to forming a contract. —Also termed *invitation to bid*; *invitation to treat*; *solicitation for bids*; *preliminary letter*. Cf. OFFER.

invitee (in-vI-**tee**). One who has permission to enter or use another's premises, either as a business visitor or as a member of the public to whom the premises are held open; the occupier has a duty to inspect the premises and to warn the invitee of nonobvious dangerous conditions. —Also termed *business guest*. Cf. LICENSEE (2); TRESPASSER.

invoice, *n.* An itemized list of goods or services furnished by a seller to a buyer, usu. specifying the price and terms of sale; a bill of costs. —**invoice,** *vb.*

involuntary, *adj.* Not resulting from a free and unrestrained choice; not subject to control by the will. —**involuntariness,** *n.*

involuntary bailment. See BAILMENT.

involuntary bankruptcy. See BANKRUPTCY.

involuntary confession. See CONFESSION.

involuntary conversion. See CONVERSION (2).

involuntary dismissal. See DISMISSAL.

involuntary dissolution. See DIS-SOLUTION.

involuntary euthanasia. See EU-THANASIA.

involuntary intoxication. See IN-TOXICATION.

involuntary manslaughter. See MANSLAUGHTER.

involuntary trust. See *constructive trust* under TRUST.

in witness whereof. The tradition-al beginning of the concluding clause (termed the *testimonium clause*) of a will or deed. See TESTIMONIUM CLAUSE.

IOLTA (I-**ohl**-tə). *abbr.* INTEREST ON LAWYERS' TRUST ACCOUNTS.

IOU (I-oh-**yoo**). A memorandum ac-knowledging a debt; the debt itself— the abbreviation is short for "I owe you."—Also termed *due-bill*.

IPO. See *initial public offering* under OFFERING.

ipse dixit (ip-see-**dik**-sət). [Latin "he himself said it" or "she herself said it"] Something asserted but not proved <his testimony that she was a liar was nothing more than an *ipse dixit*>.

ipsissima verba (ip-**sis**-ə-mə-**vər**-bə). [Latin "the very (same) words"] The exact words used by somebody being quoted <on its face, the *ipsissi-ma verba* of the statute supports the plaintiff's position on the ownership issue>.

ipso facto (ip-soh-**fak**-toh). [Latin "by the fact itself"] By the very na-ture of the situation <if 25 percent of all contractual litigation is caused by faulty drafting, then, *ipso facto*,

the profession needs to improve its drafting skills>.

ipso jure (ip-soh-**juur**-ee). [Latin "by the law itself"] By the operation of the law itself <despite the parties' actions, the property will revert to the state, *ipso jure*, on May 1st>.

IRA. *abbr.* INDIVIDUAL RETIRE-MENT ACCOUNT.

IRAC (I-rak). A mnemonic acronym used mostly by law students and their writing instructors, esp. as a method of answering essay questions on law exams; the acronym is com-monly said to stand for either (1) issue, rule, application, conclusion; or (2) issue, rule, analysis, conclu-sion.

I.R.C. *abbr.* INTERNAL REVENUE CODE.

iron-safe clause. A provision in a fire-insurance policy requiring the in-sured to preserve the books and in-ventory records of a business in a fireproof safe.

IRR. See *internal rate of return* un-der RATE OF RETURN.

irrebuttable presumption. See *conclusive presumption* under PRE-SUMPTION.

irreconcilable differences. Persis-tent and unresolvable disagreements between spouses; these differences may be vaguely cited as grounds for no-fault divorce.

irrefragable (i-**ref**-rə-gə-bəl *or* ir-i-**frag**-ə-bəl), *adj.* Unanswerable; not to be controverted; impossible to re-fute <the defense feebly responded to the prosecution's irrefragable ar-guments>.

irregular indorsement. See IN-DORSEMENT.

irrelevant, *adj.* Not tending to prove or disprove a matter in issue; inapplicable. —**irrelevance,** *n.* Cf. IMMATERIAL.

irreparable injury. See INJURY.

irreparable-injury rule. In the law of remedies, the doctrine holding that equitable relief (such as an injunction) is available only when no adequate legal remedy (such as monetary damages) exists; this rule has become nearly obsolete. —Also termed *adequacy test.*

irresistible-impulse test. In criminal law, a test for the insanity defense, holding that a person is not criminally responsible for an act when mental disease prevented the person from controlling his or her conduct; the few jurisdictions that have adopted this test have combined it with the *McNaghten* rules. —Also termed *control test; volitional test.* Cf. MCNAGHTEN RULES.

irrevocable (i-**rev**-ə-kə-bəl), *adj.* Unalterable; committed beyond recall. —**irrevocability,** *n.*

irrevocable offer. See OFFER.

irrevocable trust. See TRUST.

I.R.S. *abbr.* INTERNAL REVENUE SERVICE.

ISO. *abbr.* Incentive stock option. See *stock option* (b) under OPTION.

isolated sale. See SALE.

issuable, *adj.* Capable of being issued <an issuable writ>. **2.** Open to dispute or contention <an issuable argument>. **3.** Possible as an out-come <an award as high as $5 million is issuable in this case>.

issuable defense. See DEFENSE (1).

issuable plea. See PLEA.

issue, *n.* **1.** A material point in dispute.

general issue. **a.** A plea (often a general denial) by which a party denies the truth of every material allegation in an opposing party's pleading. **b.** The issue arising from such a plea.

issue of fact. A point maintained by one party and controverted by another.

issue of law. A point on which the evidence is undisputed, the outcome depending on the court's interpretation of the law.

special issue. **a.** At common law, an issue arising from pleading by specific allegations; special issues are no longer used in most jurisdictions. **b.** See *special interrogatory* under INTERROGATORY.

ultimate issue. A point that is sufficient either in itself or in connection with other points to resolve the entire case.

2. In securities law, a class or series of bonds or stocks that are simultaneously offered for sale. See OFFERING.

hot issue. A security that, after its initial public offering, is resold in the open market at a substantially higher price. —Also termed *hot stock.*

new issue. A stock or bond sold by a corporation for the first time, often to raise working capital. See BLUE-SKY LAW.

shelf issue. An issue of securities that were previously registered but not released at the time of registration; the shares so issued.

3. In wills and trusts, lineal descendants; offspring. **4.** In commercial transactions, the first delivery of a negotiable instrument by its maker or holder, or the first delivery of a document by its creator.

issue preclusion. COLLATERAL ESTOPPEL.

issuer. A person or entity (such as a corporation or bank) that distributes securities or other negotiable instruments for circulation.

item. 1. A piece of a whole, not necessarily separated. **2.** In commercial transactions, a negotiable or nonnegotiable writing for the payment of money. U.C.C. 4-104(a)(9). **3.** In drafting, a subpart of text that is the next smaller unit than a subparagraph; in federal drafting, for example, "(4)" is the item in the following citation: Rule 19(a)(1)(B)(4). —Also termed (in sense 3) *clause*.

itemized deduction. See DEDUCTION.

item veto. See *line-item veto* under VETO.

itinerate (I-**tin**-ə-rayt), *vb.* (Of a judge) to travel on a circuit for the purpose of holding court. —**itineration,** *n.*—**itinerant,** *adj.* & *n.* See CIRCUIT.

ius ([i-]yoos). [Latin "right; law"] JUS.

J

J. *abbr.* JUDGE; JUSTICE. Pl. **JJ.**

JAG. *abbr.* JUDGE ADVOCATE GENERAL.

jail, *n.* A place where persons awaiting trial or those convicted of misdemeanors are confined. —Also termed *holding cell*; *lockup*. —**jail,** *vb.* Cf. PRISON.

jail delivery. 1. An escape by several prisoners from a jail. **2.** *Archaic.* A procedure by which all prisoners at a given jail are tried for the offenses that they are accused of having committed.

jailhouse lawyer. A prison inmate who seeks release through legal procedures or who gives legal advice to other inmates. —Also termed *guardhouse lawyer.*

Jane Doe. See JOHN DOE.

J.D. *abbr.* JURIS DOCTOR.

Jencks material. A prosecution witness's written or recorded pretrial statement that a criminal defendant, upon filing a motion after the witness has testified, is entitled to acquire for preparing to cross-examine the witness; the defense may use a statement of this kind in court solely for impeachment purposes. *Jencks v. United States*, 353 U.S. 657 (1957); Jencks Act, 18 U.S.C. § 3500. Cf. BRADY MATERIAL.

jeopardy. The risk of conviction and punishment that a criminal defendant faces at trial; jeopardy attaches in a jury trial when the jury is empaneled, and in a bench trial when the first witness is sworn. See DOUBLE JEOPARDY.

jeopardy assessment. See ASSESSMENT.

jetsam. Goods that, after being abandoned at sea, sink and remain underwater. Cf. FLOTSAM; LAGAN.

Jim Crow law. A law enacted or purposely interpreted to discriminate against blacks, such as a law requiring separate restrooms for blacks and whites; Jim Crow laws are now unconstitutional under the Fourteenth Amendment.

JJ. *abbr.* Judges or justices.

JNOV. *abbr.* Judgment *non obstante veredicto.* See *judgment notwithstanding the verdict* under JUDGMENT.

jobber, *n.* **1.** One who buys from a manufacturer and sells to a retailer; a wholesaler or middleman. **2.** A middleman in the exchange of securities among brokers. —Also termed *stockjobber.* **3.** One who works by the job; a contractor. —**job,** *vb.*

John Doe. A fictitious name used in legal documents and proceedings to designate a person whose identity is unknown, to protect a person's known identity, or to indicate that a true defendant does not exist. —For a female, the term is *Jane Doe.*

John Doe summons. See SUMMONS.

joinder, *n.* The uniting of parties or claims in a single lawsuit. —**join,** *vb.* Cf. CONSOLIDATION (3).

collusive joinder. Joinder of a defendant, usu. a nonresident, in order to have a case removed to federal court. See *manufactured diversity* under DIVERSITY OF CITIZENSHIP.

compulsory joinder. The necessary joinder of a party if either of the following is true: (1) in that party's absence, those already involved in the lawsuit cannot receive complete relief; or (2) the absence of such a party, claiming an interest in the subject of an action, might either impair the protection of that interest or leave some other party subject to multiple or inconsistent obligations. Fed. R. Civ. P. 19(a). —Also termed *mandatory joinder*.

fraudulent joinder. The bad-faith joinder of a party, usu. a resident of the state, in order to prevent removal of a case to federal court.

permissive joinder. The optional joinder of parties if (1) their claims or the claims asserted against them are asserted jointly, severally, or in respect of the same transaction or occurrence, and (2) any legal or factual question common to all of them will arise. Fed. R. Civ. P. 20.

joinder in demurrer. In common-law pleading, the plaintiff's acceptance of the defendant's issue of law.

joinder in issue. JOINDER OF ISSUE (2).

joinder in pleading. In common-law pleading, one party's acceptance of the opposing party's proposed issue and mode of trial.

joinder of error. A written denial of the errors alleged in an assignment of errors in a criminal case.

joinder of issue. 1. The submission of an issue jointly for decision. **2.** The acceptance or adoption of a disputed point as the basis of argument in a controversy. —Also termed *joinder in issue*. **3.** The taking up of the opposite side of a case, or of the contrary view on a question.

joinder of remedies. The joinder of alternative claims, such as breach of contract and quantum meruit, or of one claim with another prospective claim, such as a creditor's claim against a debtor to recover on a loan and the creditor's claim against a third party to set aside the transfer of the loan's collateral.

joint, *adj.* **1.** (Of a thing) common to or shared by two or more persons or entities <joint bank account>. **2.** (Of a person or entity) combined, united, or sharing with another <joint heirs>.

joint adventure. JOINT VENTURE.

joint and several, *adj.* (Of liability, responsibility, etc.) apportionable either among two or more parties or to only one or a few select members of the group, at the adversary's discretion; together and in separation.

joint and several liability. See LIABILITY.

joint annuity. See ANNUITY.

joint authors. In copyright law, two or more authors who collaborate in producing a copyrightable work, each author intending to merge his or her respective contributions into a single work, and each being able to exploit the work as desired while remaining accountable for a pro rata share of the profits to the coauthor or coauthors.

joint custody. See CUSTODY (2).

joint defendant. CODEFENDANT.

joint-defense privilege. See PRIVILEGE.

joint enterprise. 1. In criminal law, an undertaking by two or more persons who set out to commit an offense they have conspired to commit. See CONSPIRACY. **2.** In negligence law, an undertaking by two or more persons with an equal right to direct and benefit from the endeavor, as a result of which one participant's negligence may be imputed to the others. —Also termed (in senses 1 and 2) *common enterprise*. **3.** JOINT VENTURE.

joint liability. See LIABILITY.

joint resolution. See RESOLUTION.

joint return. See TAX RETURN.

joint session. See SESSION.

joint-stock association. See *joint-stock company* under COMPANY.

joint-stock company. See COMPANY.

joint tenancy. See TENANCY.

joint tortfeasors. See TORTFEASOR.

jointure (**join**-chər). A widow's freehold life estate in land, made in lieu of dower; a settlement under which a wife receives such an estate. See DOWER.

joint venture. A business undertaking by two or more persons engaged in a single defined project, the necessary elements being: (1) an express or implied agreement; (2) a common purpose the group intends to carry out; (3) shared profits and losses; and (4) each member's equal voice in controlling the project. —Also termed *joint adventure*; *joint enterprise*. Cf. PARTNERSHIP; STRATEGIC ALLIANCE.

joint will. See WILL.

joker. 1. An ambiguous clause inserted in a legislative bill to render it inoperative or uncertain in some respect without arousing opposition at the time of passage. **2.** A rider or amendment that is extraneous to the subject of the bill.

Jones Act. A federal maritime-law statute that allows a seaman injured during the course of employment to recover damages for the injuries in a negligence action against the employer; if a seaman dies from such injuries, the seaman's personal representative may maintain an action against the employer. 46 U.S.C. § 688.

journalist's privilege. See PRIVILEGE.

journal of notarial acts. The notary public's sequential record of notarial transactions, usu. a bound book listing the date, time, and type of each official act, the type of instrument acknowledged or verified before the notary, the signature of each person whose signature is notarized, the type of information used to verify the identity of parties whose signatures are notarized, and the fee charged; required by law in most states, this journal provides a record that may be used as evidence in court. —Also termed *notarial record*; *notarial register*; *notary record book*; *sequential journal*.

joyriding, *n.* The illegal driving of someone else's automobile without permission, but with no intent to deprive the owner of it permanently. — **joy-ride,** *vb.*—**joyrider,** *n.*

J.P. *abbr.* JUSTICE OF THE PEACE.

judge, *n.* A presiding officer of a court. —Abbr. J. (and, in plural, JJ.).

chief judge. The senior or principal judge of an appellate court, usu. the highest appellate court in a jurisdiction. —Abbr. C.J.

circuit judge. A federal judge who sits on a U.S. Court of Appeals. —Abbr. C.J.

district judge. A judge in a federal or state judicial district.

hanging judge. A judge who is esp. harsh with defendants accused of capital crimes, and sometimes corruptly so.

lay judge. A judge who is not a lawyer.

presiding judge. A judge in charge of a particular court or judicial district; esp., the senior active judge on a three-member panel that hears and decides cases. —Abbr. P.J.

senior judge. **a.** The judge who has served for the longest time on a given court. **b.** A federal judge who qualifies for senior status and chooses this status over retirement.

visiting judge. A judge appointed by the presiding judge of an administrative region to sit temporarily on a given court, usu. in the regular judge's absence. —Also termed *temporary judge*; *judge pro tempore*.

judge advocate. 1. A legal adviser on a military commander's staff. **2.** Any officer in the Judge Advocate General's Corps or in a department of a U.S. military branch.

Judge Advocate General. The senior legal officer and chief legal adviser of the Army, Navy, or Air Force. —Abbr. JAG.

judge-made law. 1. The law established by judicial precedent rather than by statute. See COMMON LAW (1). **2.** The law that results when judges construe statutes contrary to legislative intent. See JUDICIAL ACTIVISM.

judge *pro tempore* (proh-**tem**-pə-ree). See *visiting judge* under JUDGE.

judge's chambers. See CHAMBER.

judgment. A court's final determination of the rights and obligations of the parties in a case. Cf. RULING; OPINION (1).

accumulative judgment. A second or additional judgment against a person who has already been convicted, the execution of which is postponed until the completion of any prior sentences.

agreed judgment. A parties' settlement that becomes a court judgment when the judge sanctions it. —Also termed *consent judgment*.

alternative judgment. A determination that gives the losing party or parties options for satisfying it.

cognovit judgment. A debtor's confession of judgment; judgment entered in accordance with a cognovit. See *confession of judgment*; COGNOVIT.

confession of judgment. **a.** A defendant's agreeing to a judgment instead of entering a plea or after withdrawing a plea. **b.** The judgment entered when the defendant so agrees; esp., judgment taken against a debtor by the creditor, based on the debtor's written consent. —Also termed *confessed judgment*; *cognovit judgment*. See COGNOVIT.

declaratory judgment. A binding adjudication that establishes the rights and other legal relations of the parties without providing for or ordering enforcement; declaratory judgments are often sought, for example, by insurance companies in determining whether a policy covers a given insured or peril. —Also termed *declaratory decree*; *declaration*.

default judgment. See DEFAULT JUDGMENT.

deficiency judgment. A judgment against a debtor for the unpaid balance of the debt if a foreclosure sale or a sale of repossessed personal property fails to yield the full amount of the debt due. —Also termed *deficiency decree*.

domestic judgment. A judgment rendered by the courts of the state or country where the judgment or its effect is at issue.

dormant judgment. A judgment that has not been executed or enforced within the statutory time limit; as a result, any judgment lien may have been lost and execution cannot be issued unless the judgment creditor first revives the judgment. See REVIVAL (1).

final judgment. A court's last action that settles the rights of the parties and disposes of all issues in controversy, except for the award of costs (and, sometimes, attor-

ney's fees) and enforcement of the judgment. —Also termed *final decision*; *final decree*.

foreign judgment. A judgment rendered by the courts of a state or country different from that where the judgment or its effect is at issue.

interlocutory judgment. An intermediate judgment that determines a preliminary or subordinate point or plea but does not finally decide the case. —Also termed *interlocutory decree*.

judgment as a matter of law. A judgment rendered during a jury trial—either before or after the jury's verdict—against a party on a given issue when there is no legally sufficient basis for a jury to find for that party on that issue; in federal practice, the term *judgment as a matter of law* has replaced both the directed verdict and the judgment notwithstanding the verdict. Fed. R. Civ. P. 50. Cf. SUMMARY JUDGMENT.

judgment by default. DEFAULT JUDGMENT.

judgment in rem. A judgment that determines the status or condition of property and that operates directly on the property itself.

judgment in retraxit (ri-**trak**-sit). A judgment entered after a plaintiff withdraws the claim, often upon settling with the defendant; such a judgment bars the plaintiff from relitigating the claim. —Also termed *judgment of retraxit*. See RETRAXIT.

judgment notwithstanding the verdict. A judgment entered for one party even though a jury verdict has been rendered for the opposite party. —Also termed *judgment non obstante veredicto*. —Abbr. JNOV. See *judgment as a matter of law*.

judgment of conviction. The written record of a criminal judgment, consisting of the plea, the verdict or findings, the adjudication, and the sentence. Fed. R. Crim. P. 32(d)(1).

judgment of dismissal. A final determination of a case without a trial on its merits. See DISMISSAL.

judgment of nolle prosequi. A judgment entered against a plaintiff who, after appearance but before judgment on the merits, has decided to abandon prosecution of the lawsuit. See NOLLE PROSEQUI.

judgment of repleader. REPLEADER.

judgment on the merits. A judgment based on the evidence rather than on technical or procedural grounds. —Also termed *decision on the merits*.

judgment on the pleadings. A judgment based solely on the allegations and information contained in the pleadings, and not on any outside matters. Fed. R. Civ. P. 12(c). Cf. SUMMARY JUDGMENT.

judgment on the verdict. A judgment for the party receiving a favorable jury verdict.

judgment quasi in rem (**kwah**-zee *or* **kway**-zI). A judgment based on the court's jurisdiction over the defendant's interest in property rather than on its jurisdiction over the defendant itself or the property itself.

personal judgment. **a.** A judgment that imposes personal liability on a defendant and that may therefore be satisfied out of any of the defendant's property within judicial reach. **b.** A judgment resulting from an action in which a court has personal jurisdiction over the parties. **c.** A judgment against a person as distinguished from a judgment against a thing, right, or status. —Also termed *judgment in personam*; *judgment inter partes*.

summary judgment. See SUMMARY JUDGMENT.

take-nothing judgment. A judgment for the defendant providing that the plaintiff recover nothing in damages or other relief. —Also termed (in some states) *no cause of action*.

judgment book. See *judgment docket* under DOCKET.

judgment creditor. A person who has won a money judgment that has not yet been satisfied.

judgment debt. See DEBT.

judgment debtor. A person against whom a money judgment has been entered but not yet satisfied.

judgment docket. See DOCKET.

judgment execution. EXECUTION (4).

judgment file. See *judgment docket* under DOCKET.

judgment in personam. See *personal judgment* under JUDGMENT.

judgment in rem. See JUDGMENT.

judgment in retraxit. See JUDGMENT.

judgment *inter partes*. See *personal judgment* under JUDGMENT.

judgment lien. See LIEN.

judgment *non obstante veredicto*. See *judgment notwithstanding the verdict* under JUDGMENT.

judgment notwithstanding the verdict. See JUDGMENT.

judgment-proof, *adj.* (Of an actual or potential judgment debtor) unable to satisfy a judgment for money damages because the person is insolvent, does not own enough property within the court's jurisdiction to satisfy the judgment, or claims the benefit of statutorily exempt wages and property. —Also termed *execution-proof*.

judgment quasi in rem. See JUDGMENT.

judgment record. See *judgment docket* under DOCKET.

judgment roll. See *judgment docket* under DOCKET.

judgment sale. See *execution sale* under SALE.

judicature (**jood**-i-kə-chər). **1.** A judge's office, function, or authority. **2.** JUDICIARY (3). **3.** The action of judging or of administering justice through duly constituted courts.

judicial (joo-**di**-shəl), *adj.* **1.** Of, relating to, or by the court <judicial duty>. **2.** In court <the witness's judicial confession>. **3.** Legal <the Attorney General took no judicial action>. **4.** Of or relating to a judgment <an award of judicial interest at the legal rate>. Cf. JUDICIOUS.

judicial activism, *n.* A philosophy of judicial decision-making whereby judges allow their personal views about public policy, among other factors, to guide their decisions, usu. with the suggestion that adherents of this philosophy tend to find constitutional violations and are willing to ignore precedent. —**judicial activist,** *n.* Cf. JUDICIAL RESTRAINT.

judicial admission. See ADMISSION.

judicial bond. See BOND (2).

judicial cognizance. JUDICIAL NOTICE.

judicial comity. See COMITY.

judicial confession. See CONFESSION.

judicial council. A regularly assembled group of judges whose mission is to increase the efficiency and effectiveness of the courts on which they sit; esp., a semiannual assembly of a federal circuit's judges called by the circuit's chief judge. 28 U.S.C. § 332.

judicial dictum. See DICTUM.

judicial discretion. See DISCRETION.

judicial estoppel. See ESTOPPEL.

judicial fact. See FACT.

judicial foreclosure. See FORECLOSURE.

judicial immunity. See IMMUNITY (1).

judicial knowledge. JUDICIAL NOTICE.

judicial notice. A court's acceptance, for purposes of convenience and without requiring a party's proof, of a well-known and indisputable fact; the court's power to accept such a fact <the trial court took judicial notice of the fact that water

freezes at 32 degrees Fahrenheit>. Fed R. Evid. 201. —Also termed *judicial cognizance*; *judicial knowledge*.

judicial opinion. OPINION (1).

judicial order. ORDER (2).

judicial power. See POWER.

judicial proceeding. See PROCEEDING.

judicial process. PROCESS.

judicial question. A question proper for determination by the courts, as opposed to moot questions or those properly decided by the executive or legislative branch. Cf. POLITICAL QUESTION.

judicial record. DOCKET (1).

judicial restraint. A philosophy of judicial decision-making whereby judges avoid indulging their personal beliefs about the public good and instead try merely to interpret the law as legislated and according to precedent. —Also termed *judicial self-restraint*. Cf. JUDICIAL ACTIVISM.

judicial review. 1. A court's power to review the actions of other branches or levels of government; esp., the courts' power to invalidate legislative and executive actions as being unconstitutional. 2. A court's review of a lower court's or an administrative body's factual or legal findings.

judicial sale. See SALE.

judicial separation. SEPARATION (1).

judiciary (joo-**di**-shee-er-ee), *n.* **1.** The branch of government responsible for interpreting the laws and administering justice. Cf. EXECUTIVE (1); LEGISLATURE. **2.** A system of courts. **3.** A body of judges. —Also

termed (in sense 3) *judicature*. —**judiciary,** *adj.*

judicious, *adj.* Well-considered; discreet; wisely circumspect <the court's judicious application of the rules of evidence>. —**judiciousness,** *n.* Cf. JUDICIAL.

jump bail, *vb.* (Of an accused) to fail to appear in court at the appointed time, even after posting a bail bond and promising to appear. —Also termed *skip bail*. See BAIL-JUMPING.

jump citation. See *pinpoint citation* under CITATION.

junior execution. See EXECUTION.

junior lien. See LIEN.

junior mortgage. See MORTGAGE.

junior partner. See PARTNER.

junk bond. See BOND (1).

jura, n. pl. See JUS.

jural (**juur**-əl), *adj.* **1.** Of or relating to law or jurisprudence; legal <jural and equitable rules>. **2.** Of or pertaining to rights and obligations <jural relations>.

jural cause. See *proximate cause* under CAUSE (1).

jurat (**juur**-at). **1.** [Latin *jurare* "to swear"] A certification added to an affidavit or deposition stating when and before what authority the affidavit or deposition was made; a jurat typically says "Subscribed and sworn to before me this ___ day of [month], [year]," and the officer (usu. a notary public) thereby certifies three things: (1) that the person signing the document did so in the officer's presence, (2) that the signer appeared before the officer on the date indicated, and (3) that the officer administered an oath or affirmation to the signer, who swore to or affirmed the contents of the document. Cf. VERIFICATION.

witness jurat. A subscribing witness's acknowledgment certificate; even though this certificate is technically an acknowledgment and not a true jurat, the phrase *witness jurat* is commonly used. See ACKNOWLEDGMENT.

2. [Latin *juratus* "one sworn"] In France and the Channel Islands, a municipal officer or magistrate.

jure (**juur**-ee). [Latin] **1.** By right or in right. **2.** By law. See DE JURE.

juridical (juu-**rid**-ə-kəl), *adj.* **1.** Of or relating to judicial proceedings or to the administration of justice. **2.** Of or relating to law; legal.

jurimetrics (juur-i-**me**-triks), *n.* The social science that attempts to measure those aspects of law or justice that are of an empirical nature. — **jurimetrician** (juur-i-me-**trish**-ən), *n.*

jurisconsult (**juur**-əs-**kon**-səlt). One who is learned in the law, esp. in civil or international law; JURIST.

jurisdiction, *n.* **1.** A government's general power to exercise authority over all persons and things within its territory <New Jersey's jurisdiction>. **2.** A court's power to decide a case or issue a decree <the constitutional grant of federal-question jurisdiction>. **3.** A geographic area within which political or judicial authority may be exercised <the accused fled to another jurisdiction>. **4.** A political or judicial subdivision within such an area <other jurisdictions have de-

cided the issue differently>. —**jurisdictional,** *adj.* Cf. VENUE.

ancillary jurisdiction. Jurisdiction over a matter auxiliary to an actionable claim pending before the court; federal courts assume such jurisdiction for purposes of convenience to the parties, although the reach of the jurisdiction may extend beyond the constitutional or congressional grant, and it usu. involves subsequent claims joined by defendants <a federal court's ancillary jurisdiction over a defendant's claim against a nondiverse third party>. Cf. *pendent jurisdiction.*

appellate jurisdiction. The power of a court to review and revise a lower court's decision; for example, U.S. Const. art. III, § 2 vests appellate jurisdiction in the Supreme Court, while 28 U.S.C. §§ 1291-1295 grant appellate jurisdiction to lower federal courts of appeals. Cf. *original jurisdiction.*

concurrent jurisdiction. **a.** Jurisdiction exercised simultaneously by more than one court over the same subject matter and within the same territory, the litigant having the initial discretion of choosing the court that will adjudicate the matter. **b.** Jurisdiction shared by two or more states over the physical boundaries (esp. rivers or other bodies of water) between them. — Also termed *coordinate jurisdiction*; *overlapping jurisdiction.* Cf. *exclusive jurisdiction.*

consent jurisdiction. Jurisdiction that parties have agreed to, either by agreement, by contract, or by general appearance; parties may not, by agreement, confer subject-matter jurisdiction on a federal court that would not otherwise have it.

continuing jurisdiction. A court's power to retain jurisdiction over a matter after entering a judgment, allowing the court to modify its previous rulings or orders. See CONTINUING-JURISDICTION DOCTRINE.

diversity jurisdiction. The exercise of federal-court authority over cases involving parties from different states and amounts in controversy greater than $50,000. 28 U.S.C. § 1332. —Often shortened (as an adjective) to *diversity* <a diversity case>. See DIVERSITY OF CITIZENSHIP; AMOUNT IN CONTROVERSY.

equity jurisdiction. At common law, the power to hear a certain class of civil actions according to the procedure of the court of chancery, and to resolve them according to equitable rules.

exclusive jurisdiction. A court's power to adjudicate an action or class of actions to the exclusion of all other courts <federal district courts have exclusive jurisdiction over actions brought under the Securities Exchange Act>. Cf. *concurrent jurisdiction.*

extraterritorial jurisdiction. A court's ability to exercise power beyond the territorial limits of its region. See LONG-ARM STATUTE.

federal-question jurisdiction. The exercise of federal-court power over claims arising under the U.S. Constitution, an act of Congress, or a treaty. 28 U.S.C. § 1331.

foreign jurisdiction. **a.** The powers of a court of a sister state or foreign country. **b.** Extraterritorial process, such as long-arm service of process.

general jurisdiction. **a.** A court's authority to hear a wide range of cases, civil or criminal, that arise within its geographic area. **b.** A court's authority to hear all claims against a defendant, at the place of the defendant's domicile or the place of service, without any showing that a connection exists between the claim and the forum state. Cf. *limited jurisdiction*; *specific jurisdiction.*

in rem jurisdiction. The power of a court to adjudicate the rights to a given piece of property, including the power to seize and hold it. — Also termed *jurisdiction in rem.* See IN REM. Cf. *personal jurisdiction.*

limited jurisdiction. Jurisdiction that is confined to a particular type of case or that may be exercised only under statutory limits and prescriptions. —Also termed *special jurisdiction.* Cf. *general jurisdiction.*

original jurisdiction. The power of a court to hear and decide a matter before any other court can review the matter. Cf. *appellate jurisdiction.*

pendent jurisdiction. Jurisdiction exercised by federal courts over state-law claims that are closely related to the federal claims at bar, on grounds that the state-law claims are so intertwined with the federal claims that they are best adjudicated together <a federal court's pen-

dent jurisdiction over a state-law claim for breach of contract in a federal-question case>. Cf. *ancillary jurisdiction*.

pendent-party jurisdiction. Federal-court jurisdiction over a claim by or against an additional party who is not ordinarily subject to the federal court's jurisdiction; since 1990, this has been an allowable type of supplemental jurisdiction.

personal jurisdiction. A court's power to bring persons into its adjudicative process; jurisdiction over a defendant's personal rights, rather than merely over property interests. —Also termed *in personam jurisdiction*; *jurisdiction in personam*; *jurisdiction of the person*; *jurisdiction over the person*. See IN PERSONAM. Cf. *in rem jurisdiction*.

plenary jurisdiction. A court's full and absolute power over the subject matter and parties in a case.

quasi-in-rem jurisdiction. Jurisdiction over a person but based on that person's interest in property located within the court's territory. —Also termed *jurisdiction quasi in rem*. See *quasi in rem* under IN REM.

specific jurisdiction. Jurisdiction that stems from the defendant's having certain minimum contacts with the forum state so that the court may hear a case whose issues arise from those minimum contacts. Cf. *general jurisdiction*.

subject-matter jurisdiction. Jurisdiction over the nature of the case and the type of relief sought; the extent to which a court can claim to affect the conduct of persons or the status of things. —Also termed *jurisdiction of the subject matter*.

supplemental jurisdiction. Jurisdiction over claims that are part of the same case or controversy as other claims over which the court has original jurisdiction; since 1990, federal district courts have supplemental jurisdiction over both ancillary and pendent claims. 28 U.S.C. § 1367. See *ancillary jurisdiction*; *pendent jurisdiction*.

territorial jurisdiction. **a.** Jurisdiction that is based on the cases arising in or the persons residing within a defined territory. **b.** Territory over which a government, a court, or one of their subdivisions has jurisdiction.

transient jurisdiction. Personal jurisdiction over a defendant who is served with process while in the forum state only temporarily (such as during travel).

jurisdictional amount. AMOUNT IN CONTROVERSY.

jurisdictional-fact doctrine. In federal administrative law, the principle that if evidence is presented challenging the factual findings that triggered an agency's action, then a court will review the facts to determine whether the agency had authority to act in the first place; this doctrine is generally no longer applied. Cf. CONSTITUTIONAL-FACT DOCTRINE.

jurisdictional facts. See FACT.

jurisdictional gerrymandering. GERRYMANDERING (2).

jurisdictional limits. The physical boundaries or the constitutional or statutory limits within which a court's authority may be exercised.

jurisdictional plea. See PLEA (2).

jurisdiction clause. 1. At law, a statement in a pleading that justifies the court's jurisdiction of the case. — Also termed *jurisdictional statement.* 2. In equity practice, the part of the bill intended to show that the court has jurisdiction, usu. by averring that the act complained of is unjust and injurious to the complainant and that adequate relief is unavailable outside equitable channels.

jurisdiction in personam. See *personal jurisdiction* under JURISDICTION.

jurisdiction in rem. See *in rem jurisdiction* under JURISDICTION.

jurisdiction of the person. See *personal jurisdiction* under JURISDICTION.

jurisdiction of the subject matter. See *subject-matter jurisdiction* under JURISDICTION.

jurisdiction over the person. See *personal jurisdiction* under JURISDICTION.

jurisdiction quasi in rem. See *quasi-in-rem jurisdiction* under JURISDICTION.

Juris Doctor (juur-is-**dok**-tər). Doctor of law—the law degree most commonly conferred by American law schools. —Abbr. J.D. Cf. MASTER OF LAWS; LL.B.; LL.D.

jurisprudence, *n.* 1. Knowledge of or practical skill in the law. 2. The philosophy or science of law; legal theory or study.

analytical jurisprudence. A method of legal study that examines law purely in its existing structure, without resort to its history, and that denies the law any validity unless it derives from or is sanctioned by a determinate sovereign.

comparative jurisprudence. The scholarly study of the similarities and differences between the legal systems of different jurisdictions, such as between civil-law and common-law countries. —Also termed *comparative law.* Cf. INTERNATIONAL LAW.

general jurisprudence. The scholarly study of the law, legal theory, and legal systems generally.

particular jurisprudence. The scholarly study of the legal system within a particular jurisdiction.

sociological jurisprudence. A philosophical approach to law stressing the actual social effects of legal institutions, doctrines, and practices; this influential approach was started by Roscoe Pound in 1906 and became a precursor to legal realism. See LEGAL REALISM.

3. A system, body, or division of law. 4. CASELAW. —**jurisprudential,** *adj.*—**jurisprudent, jurisprude,** *n.*

jurist. One who has thorough knowledge of the law; esp., a judge or an eminent legal scholar. —Also termed *legist.*

juristic, *adj.* 1. Of or relating to a jurist <juristic literature>. 2. Of or relating to law <a corporation is a typical example of a juristic person>.

juror. A person serving on a jury panel.

presiding juror. The juror who chairs the jury during deliberations and speaks for the jury in court by announcing the verdict; the presiding juror is usu. elected by the jury at the start of deliberations. —Also termed *foreman*; *foreperson*.

tales-juror. TALESMAN.

jury, *n.* A group of persons selected according to law and given the power to decide questions of fact and return a verdict in the case submitted to them.

advisory jury. A jury empaneled to hear a case when the parties have no right to a jury trial; the judge may accept or reject the advisory jury's verdict.

blue-ribbon jury. A jury consisting of jurors who are the most highly educated on a given panel, sometimes used in complex civil cases (usu. by stipulation of the parties) and sometimes also for grand juries (esp. those investigating governmental corruption); an even more elite group of jurors, involving specialists in a technical field, is called a *blue-blue-ribbon jury.*

death-qualified jury. A jury that is fit to decide cases involving the death penalty because the jurors have no absolute ideological bias against capital punishment.

foreign jury. A jury obtained from a jurisdiction other than that in which the case is brought.

grand jury. See GRAND JURY.

hung jury. A jury that cannot reach a verdict by the required voting margin. —Also termed *deadlocked jury.*

impartial jury. A jury that has no opinion about the case at the start of the trial and that bases its verdict on competent legal evidence.

inquest jury. A jury summoned from a particular district to appear before a sheriff, coroner, or other ministerial officer and inquire about the facts concerning a death. See INQUEST.

jury of indictment. GRAND JURY.

jury of the vicinage. At common law, a jury from the county where the crime occurred. See VICINAGE.

petit jury. A jury (usu. consisting of 12 persons) summoned, empaneled, and participating in the trial of a specific case. —Also termed *petty jury*; *trial jury*; *common jury*; *traverse jury.* Cf. GRAND JURY.

shadow jury. A group of mock jurors paid to observe a trial and report their reactions to a jury consultant hired by one of the litigants; the shadow jurors, who are matched as closely as possible to the real jurors, provide counsel with information about the jury's likely reactions to the trial. —Also termed *phantom jury.*

special jury. **a.** A jury chosen from a panel that is drawn specifically for that case; such a jury is usu. empaneled at a party's request in an unusually important or complicated case. —Also termed *struck jury.* See STRIKING A JURY. **b.** At common law, a jury composed of persons above the rank of ordinary freeholders, usu. summoned to try more important questions than those heard by ordinary juries.

jury challenge. CHALLENGE (2).

jury charge. 1. JURY INSTRUCTION. **2.** A set of jury instructions. —Often shortened to *charge*.

jury-fixing. The act or an instance of illegally procuring the cooperation of one or more jurors who actually influence the outcome of the trial. — Also termed *fixing a jury*. Cf. EMBRACERY; JURY-PACKING.

jury instruction. (*usu. pl.*) A direction or guideline that a judge gives a jury concerning the law of the case. —Also termed *jury charge*.

additional instruction. A jury charge, beyond the original instructions, that is usu. in response to the jury's question about the evidence or some point of law.

cautionary instruction. **a.** A judge's instruction that jurors disregard certain evidence or consider it for specific purposes only. **b.** A judge's instruction for the jury not to be influenced by outside factors and not to talk to anyone about the case while the trial is in progress.

formula instruction. A jury charge intended to be the complete statement of the law on which the jury may base its verdict.

mandatory instruction. An instruction requiring a jury to find for one party and against the other if the jury determines that, based on a preponderance of the evidence, a given set of facts exists. —Also termed *binding instruction*.

ostrich instruction. In a criminal case, an instruction stating that a defendant can be found to have acted knowingly if he or she deliberately avoided acquiring actual knowledge.

peremptory instruction. A court's explicit direction that a jury must obey, such as an instruction to return a verdict for a particular party. See *directed verdict* under VERDICT.

single-juror instruction. In a civil case, an instruction stating that if any juror is not reasonably satisfied with the plaintiff's evidence, then the jury cannot render a verdict against the defendant.

special instruction. An instruction on some particular point or question involved in the case, usu. in response to counsel's request for such an instruction.

jury nullification. A jury's knowing and deliberate rejection of the evidence or refusal to apply the law either because the jury wants to send a message about some social issue that is larger than the case itself or because the result dictated by law is contrary to the jury's sense of justice, morality, or fairness.

jury of indictment. GRAND JURY.

jury of the vicinage. See JURY.

jury-packing. The act or an instance of contriving to have a jury composed of persons who are predisposed toward one side or the other. Cf. EMBRACERY; JURY-FIXING.

jury panel. VENIRE (1).

jury process. 1. The procedure by which jurors are summoned and their attendance is enforced. **2.** The papers served on or mailed to potential jurors to compel their attendance.

jury question. 1. An issue of fact that a jury decides. See QUESTION OF FACT. **2.** A special question that a court may ask a jury that will deliver a special verdict. See *special interrogatory* under INTERROGATORY.

jury sequestration. See SEQUESTRATION (7).

jury summation. CLOSING ARGUMENT.

jury-tampering. EMBRACERY.

jury trial. See TRIAL.

jury wheel. A physical device or electronic system used for storing and randomly selecting names or identifying numbers of potential jurors.

jus (jəs *or* joos *or* yoos), *n.* [Latin] **1.** A legal right, rule, or principle. **2.** Law. —Also spelled *ius* (yoos *or* yəs). Pl. *jura.* Cf. LEX.

jus accrescendi (jəs-ak-rə-**sen**-dee *or* -**shen**- *or* -dI). [Latin] The right of survivorship that a joint tenant enjoys. See *joint tenancy* under TENANCY.

jus civile (jəs-**si**-və-lee). [Latin] CIVIL LAW (2).

jus cogens (jəs-**koh**-jens). [Latin "cogent law"] A mandatory norm of general international law from which no two or more nations may exempt themselves or release one another.

jus disponendi (jəs-dis-pə-**nen**-dee *or* -dI). [Latin] The right to dispose of property.

jus gentium (jəs-**jen**-tee-əm *or* -**gen**-). [Latin "law of nations"] INTERNATIONAL LAW.

jus naturale (jəs-nah-chuur-**ahl** *or* -nahd-ə-**rah**-lay). [Latin] NATURAL LAW.

jus sanguinis (jəs-**sang**-gwə-nəs). [Latin "right of blood"] The rule (prevailing in most nations) that a child's citizenship is determined by its parents' citizenship.

jus scriptum (jəs-**skrip**-təm). [Latin] WRITTEN LAW.

jus soli (jəs-**soh**-lee). [Latin "right of the soil"] The American rule that a child's citizenship can be determined by its place of birth.

just, *adj.* Legally right; lawful; equitable.

just cause. See *good cause* under CAUSE (2).

just compensation. See COMPENSATION.

just deserts (di-**zərts**). What one really deserves; esp., the punishment that a person deserves for having committed a crime. —Also termed *deserts.*

jus tertii (jəs-**tər**-shee-I *or* -shee-ee). [Latin] A third party's right.

justice. 1. The fair and proper administration of laws. **2.** A judge, usu. an appellate judge. —Abbr. J. (and, in plural, JJ.).

associate justice. An appellate-court justice other than the chief justice.

chief justice. The presiding, senior, or principal justice of an appellate court, usu. the highest appellate court in a jurisdiction and esp. the

United States Supreme Court. —Abbr. C.J.

justice of the peace. A low-ranking magistrate having jurisdiction over minor criminal offenses and civil disputes, and authority to perform routine civil matters (such as administering oaths or performing marriages). —Abbr. J.P. Cf. MAGISTRATE.

justiciability (jəs-tish-[ee-]ə-**bil**-ə-tee), *n.* The suitability of a dispute for court review. —**justiciable** (jəs-**tish**-[ee-]ə-bəl), *adj.* See MOOTNESS DOCTRINE; RIPENESS. Cf. STANDING.

justifiable homicide. See HOMICIDE.

justification, *n.* **1.** A lawful or sufficient reason for one's acts or omissions. **2.** In criminal and tort law, a defense that arises when the defendant has acted in a way that the law does not seek to prevent; traditionally, the following defenses were justifications: consent, self-defense, defense of others, defense of property, necessity (choice of evils), the use of force to make an arrest, and the use of force by public authority. —Also termed (in sense 2) *justification defense.* Cf. EXCUSE (2). —**justify,** *vb.* —

justificatory (jəs-**ti**-fi-kə-tor-ee), *adj.*

imperfect justification. A reason or cause that is insufficient to completely justify a defendant's behavior but that can be used to mitigate criminal punishment.

just value. FAIR MARKET VALUE.

juvenile (**joo**-və-nəl *or* -nIl), *n.* A person who has not reached the age (usu. 18) at which one should be treated as an adult by the criminal-justice system; MINOR. —**juvenile,** *adj.*—**juvenility,** *n.*

juvenile court. See COURT.

juvenile delinquency. Antisocial behavior by a minor; esp., behavior that would be criminally punishable if the actor were an adult, but instead is usu. punished by special laws pertaining only to minors.

juvenile delinquent. A minor guilty of criminal behavior, which is usu. punished by special laws not pertaining to adults. —Also termed *juvenile offender; youthful offender.* See OFFENDER.

juzgado (hoos-**gah**-doh). [Spanish "court"] The judiciary; the judges who concur in a decision.

K

K. *abbr.* Contract.

Kaldor-Hicks efficiency. WEALTH MAXIMIZATION.

kangaroo court. See COURT.

K.B. *abbr.* KING'S BENCH.

K.C. *abbr.* KING'S COUNSEL.

Keogh plan (**kee**-oh). A tax-deferred retirement program developed for the self-employed. —Also termed *self-employed retirement plan*. See INDIVIDUAL RETIREMENT ACCOUNT.

key-number system. A legal-research indexing system developed by West Publishing Company to catalogue American caselaw with headnotes; in this system, a number designates a point of law, allowing a researcher to find all reported cases addressing a particular point by referring to its number.

key-person life insurance. See INSURANCE.

kickback, *n.* A return of a portion of a monetary sum received, esp. as a result of coercion or a secret agreement <the contractor paid the city official a five-percent kickback on the government contract>. —Also termed *payoff*. Cf. BRIBERY.

kicker. An extra charge or penalty, esp. a charge added to a loan in addition to interest.

kick-out clause. A contractual provision allowing a party to end or modify the contract if a specified event occurs <under the kick-out clause, the company could refuse to sell the land if it were unable to

complete its acquisition of the new headquarters>.

kiddie tax. See TAX.

kidnapping, *n.* The act or an instance of taking or carrying away a person without consent, by force or fraud, and without lawful excuse—and often with a demand for ransom (which, in most jurisdictions, aggravates the offense). —**kidnap,** *vb.*

child-kidnapping. The kidnapping of a baby or child, often without the element of force or fraud (such as when someone walks off with another's baby stroller). —Also termed *child-stealing*; *baby-snatching*.

killing by misadventure. ACCIDENTAL KILLING.

kin, *n.* **1.** A relative by blood or marriage, though usu. by blood only. **2.** One's relatives; family.

kind arbitrage. See ARBITRAGE.

kindred, *n.* **1.** Relationship between people by blood or descent. —Also termed *kinship*. **2.** One's relatives.

King's Bench. Historically, the highest common-law court in England, so called during the reign of a king; in 1873, the court's jurisdiction was transferred to the Queen's Bench Division of the High Court of Justice. —Abbr. K.B. —Also termed *Court of King's Bench*. Cf. QUEEN'S BENCH; QUEEN'S BENCH DIVISION.

King's Counsel. An elite, senior-level barrister appointed to serve as counsel to the king. —Abbr. K.C. Cf. QUEEN'S COUNSEL.

kinship. KINDRED (1).

kitchen cabinet. See CABINET.

kiting. CHECK-KITING.

***Klaxon* doctrine.** In conflict of laws, the rule that a federal court sitting in diversity must apply the choice-of-law rules of the state in which it sits; this doctrine essentially extends the *Erie* doctrine to choice-of-law issues. *Klaxon Co. v. Stentor Elec. Mfg. Co.*, 313 U.S. 487 (1941). —Also termed *Erie/Klaxon doctrine*. See ERIE DOCTRINE.

knock-and-announce rule. In criminal procedure, the requirement that the police knock at the door and announce their identity, authority, and purpose before entering a residence to execute an arrest or search warrant.

knock-for-knock agreement. An arrangement between insurers whereby each will pay the claim of its insured without claiming against the other party's insurance.

knock-off. A product manufactured to resemble another product and usu. offered at a significantly lower price.

know all men by these presents. *Jargon.* Take note; this archaic form of address was traditionally used to begin certain legal documents such as bonds and powers of attorney, but in modern drafting style the phrase is generally considered deadwood.

know-how. The information, practical knowledge, techniques, and skill required to achieve some practical end, esp. in industry or technology; know-how is considered intangible property in which rights may be bought and sold.

knowledge. An awareness or understanding of a fact or condition. Cf. NOTICE.

actual knowledge. The express awareness of a fact gained through direct information or through a reasonably diligent inquiry based on available information.

constructive knowledge. Knowledge imputed to a person who, through the exercise of reasonable care or because of position or skill, should have been aware of the fact <the purchaser had constructive knowledge of any prior lien on the property because it was a matter of public record>.

imputed knowledge. An understanding attributed to a person who had a duty to learn the facts, whether or not that person actually knew them <the court ruled that the president had imputed knowledge of the company's fraudulent accounting practices>.

personal knowledge. Knowledge that a person acquires directly through his or her own senses, as opposed to learning from some other person or source. —Also termed *firsthand knowledge*.

known heir. See HEIR.

L

L. *abbr.* **1.** LAW (5). **2.** LORD (1). **3.** LOCUS. **4.** Latin.

label, *n.* **1.** An informative logo, title, or similar marking affixed to a manufactured product. **2.** Any writing appended to a larger writing, such as a codicil. **3.** A narrow slip of paper or parchment attached to a deed or writ in order to hold an appended seal.

labor, *n.* **1.** Work; exertion <Douglas enjoyed the fruits of his labor during retirement>. **2.** Laborers considered as a political element <a dispute between management and labor concerning insurance benefits>.

labor contract. An agreement between an employer and a union governing working conditions, wages, benefits, and grievances. —Also termed *labor agreement.*

labor dispute. A controversy between employers and employees concerning terms, tenure, hours, wages, benefits, or conditions of employment, or concerning the association or representation of those who negotiate or seek to negotiate terms and conditions of employment.

Labor-Management Relations Act. A federal statute, enacted in 1947, that regulates certain union activities, permits suits against unions for proscribed acts, prohibits certain strikes and boycotts, and provides steps for settling strikes involving national emergencies. 29 U.S.C. §§ 141 et seq. —Also termed *Taft-Hartley Act.* See NATIONAL LABOR RELATIONS BOARD.

labor organization. UNION.

labor union. UNION.

laches (lach-iz). [Law French "remissness; slackness"] **1.** Unreasonable delay or negligence in pursuing a right or claim, esp. an equitable one; laches can be asserted as a defense in order to prevent the claimant from obtaining relief. **2.** The equitable doctrine by which courts deny relief to a claimant who has unreasonably delayed or been negligent in asserting the claim. Cf. LIMITATION (3).

lack of prosecution. WANT OF PROSECUTION.

lading, bill of. See BILL OF LADING.

laesae majestatis. LESE MAJESTY.

lagan. Goods that are abandoned at sea but attached to a buoy so that they may be recovered. Cf. FLOTSAM; JETSAM.

lagging economic indicator. See ECONOMIC INDICATOR.

laissez-faire (le-say-**fe[ə]r**), *n.* [French "to let (people) do (as they choose)"] **1.** Governmental abstention from interference in economic or commercial affairs. **2.** The doctrine favoring such abstention. —**laissez-faire,** *adj.*

lame duck. An elected official serving out a term after someone else has been elected as a successor.

lame-duck session. See SESSION.

land, *n.* **1.** An immovable and indestructible three-dimensional area consisting of a portion of the earth's surface plus the space above and below the surface, and including everything growing or constructed on it. **2.** An estate or interest in real property.

land agent. LAND MANAGER.

land certificate. A document expressing a governmental obligation entitling a person to a certain amount of land by following legal steps; it contains an official description of the land, as well as the name and address of the person receiving the entitlement, and is prima facie evidence of the truth of matters contained in it. —Also termed *land warrant*.

land contract. See *contract for deed* under CONTRACT.

land district. See DISTRICT.

land grant. A donation of public land to an individual, a corporation, or a subordinate government.

landholder. One who holds or owns land.

land lease. See *ground lease* under LEASE.

landlocked, *adj.* Surrounded by land, often with the suggestion that there is little or no means of ingress or egress <the owner of the land-locked property purchased an access easement from the adjoining land-owner>.

landlord. 1. At common law, the feudal lord who retained the fee of the land. 2. One who owns or holds real property and leases it to others. —Also termed (in sense 2) *lessor*.

absentee landlord. A landlord who does not live on the leased premises—and usu. who lives far away.

landlord's lien. See LIEN.

land manager. In oil-and-gas law, a person who, usu. on behalf of an oil company, contracts with landowners for the mineral rights to their land. —Also termed *exploration manager*; *land agent*; *landman*.

landmark. 1. A feature of land (such as a monument or marker) that demarcates the boundary of the land <according to the 1991 survey, the crooked oak tree is the correct landmark at the property's northeast corner>. 2. A historically significant building or site <the schoolhouse built in 1898 is the county's most famous landmark>. See MONUMENT.

landmark decision. A judicial decision that significantly changes existing law; examples are *Brown v. Board of Education*, 347 U.S. 483 (1954) (holding that segregation in public schools violates the Equal Protection Clause), and *Palsgraf v. Long Island R.R.*, 162 N.E. 99 (N.Y.1928) (establishing the doctrine that a defendant's duty in a negligence action is limited to plaintiffs within the apparent zone of danger—that is, plaintiffs to whom damage could be reasonably foreseen). —Also termed *landmark case*. See LEADING CASE.

land office. A government office in which sales of public land are registered.

landowner. One who owns land.

land patent. See PATENT (1).

land-poor, *adj.* (Of a person) owning a substantial amount of unprofitable or encumbered land, but lacking the funds to improve or maintain the land or to pay off the charges due on it.

land sales contract. See *contract for deed* under CONTRACT.

land scrip. A negotiable instrument entitling the holder, usu. a person or company engaged in public service, to possess specified areas of public land.

lands, tenements, and hereditaments. Real property—traditionally used in wills, deeds, and other instruments.

land-tenant. TERRE-TENANT.

land trust. See TRUST.

land-use planning. The deliberate, careful development of real estate through methods such as zoning, environmental-impact studies, and the like.

land warrant. LAND CERTIFICATE.

Lanham Act. The federal trademark statute, enacted in 1946, which provides for a national system of trademark registration and protects the owner of a federally registered mark against the use of similar marks if any confusion might result; the Lanham Act's scope is independent of and concurrent with state common law. 15 U.S.C. §§ 1051 et seq.

lapse, *n.* **1.** The termination of a right or privilege because of neglect to exercise it within some time limit or because a contingency has not occurred. **2.** In the law of wills, the failure of a testamentary gift, esp. when the beneficiary dies before the testator dies. See ANTILAPSE STATUTE. Cf. ADEMPTION.

lapse, *vb.* **1.** (Of an estate or right) to pass away or revert to someone else because conditions have not been fulfilled or because a person entitled to possession has failed in some duty.

2. (Of a devise or grant) to become void.

lapsed devise. See DEVISE.

lapsed legacy. See LEGACY.

lapse statute. ANTILAPSE STATUTE.

larcenable, *adj.* Subject to larceny <because it cannot be carried away, real estate is not larcenable>.

larcenous, *adj.* Of, relating to, or tainted with larceny; thievish.

larceny, *n.* The unlawful taking and carrying away of someone else's personal property with the intent to deprive the owner of it permanently; common-law larceny has been broadened by some statutes to include embezzlement and false pretenses, all three of which are often subsumed under the statutory crime of "theft."—**larcenist,** *n.*

grand larceny. Larceny of property valued at more than a statutory cut-off amount, usu. $100. Cf. *petit larceny.*

larceny by trick. Larceny in which the taker misleads the rightful possessor, by misrepresentation of fact, into giving up possession of (but not title to) the goods. —Also termed *larceny by trick and deception*; *larceny by fraud and deception.* Cf. FALSE PRETENSES.

larceny from the person. Larceny in which the goods are taken directly from the person, but without violence or intimidation, the victim usu. being unaware of the taking; pickpocketing is a typical example. Cf. ROBBERY.

mixed larceny. **a.** Larceny accompanied by aggravation or violence to the person. **b.** Larceny involving a taking from a house. —Also termed *compound larceny*; *complicated larceny*.

petit larceny. Larceny of property worth less than a statutory cut-off amount, usu. $100. —Also termed *petty larceny.* Cf. *grand larceny*.

last antecedent, rule of the. See RULE OF THE LAST ANTECEDENT.

last-clear-chance doctrine. In tort law, the rule that a plaintiff who is contributorily negligent may nonetheless recover from the defendant if the defendant had the last opportunity to prevent the injury but failed to use reasonable care to do so (in other words, if the defendant's negligence is later in time than the plaintiff's); this doctrine allows the plaintiff to rebut the contributory-negligence defense in the few jurisdictions where contributory negligence completely bars recovery. —Also termed *discovered-peril doctrine*; *humanitarian doctrine*.

last-in, first-out. An accounting method that assumes that the most recent purchases are sold or used first, matching current costs against current revenues. —Abbr. LIFO. Cf. FIRST-IN, FIRST-OUT; NEXT-IN, FIRST-OUT.

last-proximate-act test. In criminal law, a common-law test for the crime of attempt, based on whether the defendant does the final act necessary to commit an offense (such as pulling the trigger of a gun, not merely aiming it); this test has been rejected by most courts as being too forgiving. Cf. SUBSTANTIAL-STEP TEST.

last will and testament. A person's final will. See WILL.

latent (**lay**-tənt), *adj.* Concealed; dormant <a latent defect>. Cf. PATENT.

latent ambiguity. See AMBIGUITY.

latent defect. See *hidden defect* under DEFECT.

lateral support. See SUPPORT.

laughing heir. See HEIR.

laundering, *n.* The federal crime of transferring illegally obtained money through legitimate persons or accounts so that its original source cannot be traced. 18 U.S.C. § 1956. — Also termed *money-laundering*. — **launder,** *vb.*

laundry list. *Slang.* A statutory enumeration of items <Texas's consumer-protection law contains a laundry list of deceptive trade practices>.

law. 1. The regime that orders human activities and relations through systematic application of the force of politically organized society, or through social pressure, backed by force, in such a society; the legal system <respect and obey the law>. **2.** The aggregate of legislation and accepted legal principles; the body of authoritative grounds of judicial and administrative action <the law of the land>. **3.** The set of rules or principles dealing with a specific area of a legal system <copyright law>. **4.** The judicial and administrative process; legal action and proceedings <when settlement negotiations failed, they submitted their dispute to the law>. **5.** A statute <Congress passed a law>. —Abbr. L. **6.** COM-

MON LAW <law but not equity>. **7.** The legal profession <she spent her entire career in law>.

law and economics. (*often cap.*) **1.** A discipline advocating the economic analysis of the law, whereby legal rules are subjected to a cost-benefit analysis in order to determine whether a change from one legal rule to another will increase or decrease allocative efficiency and social wealth; originally developed as an approach to antitrust policy, law and economics is today used by its proponents to explain and interpret a variety of legal subjects. **2.** The field or movement in which scholars devote themselves to this discipline. **3.** The body of work produced by these scholars.

law and literature. (*often cap.*) **1.** Traditionally, the study of how lawyers and legal institutions are depicted in literature; esp., the examination of law-related fiction as sociological evidence of how a given culture, at a given time, views law. —Also termed *law in literature.* **2.** More modernly, the application of literary theory to legal texts, focusing esp. on lawyers' rhetoric, logic, and style, as well as legal syntax and semantics. —Also termed *law as literature.* **3.** The field or movement in which scholars devote themselves to this study or application. **4.** The body of work produced by these scholars.

law between states. INTERNATIONAL LAW.

law clerk. CLERK (4).

law day. 1. *Archaic.* The yearly or twice-yearly meeting of one of the early common-law courts. **2.** *Archaic.* The day appointed for the debtor to discharge a mortgage or else forfeit the property to the mortgagee. **3.** (*cap.*) A day on which American schools, public assemblies, and courts draw attention to the importance of law in modern society; since 1958, the ABA has sponsored Law Day on May 1 of each year.

law firm. An association of lawyers who practice law together, usu. sharing clients and profits, in a business traditionally organized as a partnership but often today as either a professional corporation or a limited-liability company; many law firms have a hierarchical structure in which the partners (or shareholders) supervise junior lawyers known as "associates," who are usu. employed on a track to partnership.

lawful, *adj.* Not contrary to law; permitted by law <the police officer conducted a lawful search of the premises>. See LEGAL.

lawful age. AGE OF CAPACITY.

lawful cause. See *good cause* under CAUSE (2).

lawful heir. HEIR (1).

lawgiver. A legislator, esp. one who promulgates an entire code of laws.

lawmaker. LEGISLATOR.

law merchant. A system of customary law that developed in Europe during the Middle Ages and regulated the dealings of mariners and merchants in all the commercial countries of the world until the 17th century; many of the law merchant's principles came to be incorporated into the common law, which in turn formed the basis of the Uniform Commercial Code. —Also termed *commercial law*; *lex mercatoria*.

lawnote. NOTE (2).

law of capture. RULE OF CAPTURE.

law of nations. INTERNATIONAL LAW.

law of nature. NATURAL LAW.

law of nature and nations. INTERNATIONAL LAW.

law of the case. 1. The doctrine holding that a decision rendered in a former appeal of a case is held to be binding in a subsequent appeal. **2.** An earlier decision giving rise to the application of this doctrine. Cf. RES JUDICATA; STARE DECISIS.

law of the land. 1. The law in effect in a country and applicable to all members of the community, whether resulting from legislative enactments or judicial pronouncements. **2.** Due process of law. See DUE PROCESS. — Also termed *lex terrae*; *ley de terre*.

law of the sea. The body of international law governing how nations use and control the sea and its resources. Cf. MARITIME LAW.

law review. 1. A journal containing scholarly articles, essays, and other commentary on legal topics by professors, judges, and practitioners; law reviews are usu. published at law schools and edited by law students <law reviews are often grossly overburdened with substantive footnotes>. **2.** The editorial board of such a journal <she made law review>.

law school. An institution for formal legal education and training; graduates who complete the standard program, usu. three years in length,

receive a Juris Doctor (or, formerly, a Bachelor of Laws).

accredited law school. A law school approved by the state and the Association of American Law Schools, or by the state and the American Bar Association; in all states except California, only graduates of an accredited law school may take the bar examination.

lawsuit. SUIT.

lawyer, *n.* One who is licensed to practice law. Cf. ATTORNEY; COUNSEL. —**lawyerly, lawyerlike,** *adj.*

lawyer, *vb.* **1.** To practice as a lawyer <Butch spends his days and nights lawyering, with little time for recreation>. **2.** To supply with lawyers <the United States is a well-lawyered country>. —**lawyering** (corresponding to sense 1), *n.*

lay, *adj.* **1.** Not ecclesiastical; nonclerical. **2.** Not expert, esp. with reference to law or medicine; nonprofessional.

lay judge. See JUDGE.

lay witness. See WITNESS.

LBO. See *leveraged buyout* under BUYOUT.

L.C. *abbr.* **1.** LETTER OF CREDIT. **2.** LETTER OF CREDENCE. —Also spelled L/C.

lead counsel. See COUNSEL.

leading case. 1. A judicial decision that first definitively settled an important legal rule or principle and that has since been often and consistently followed; an example is *Miranda v. Arizona*, 384 U.S. 436 (1966) (creating the exclusionary rule for evidence improperly obtained from a suspect being interrogated while in police custody). Cf. LAND-MARK DECISION. **2.** An important, often the most important, judicial precedent on a particular legal issue. **3.** Loosely, a reported case that is cited as the dispositive authority on an issue being litigated. —Also termed (in sense 3) *ruling case*.

leading economic indicator. See ECONOMIC INDICATOR.

leading-object rule. MAIN-PUR-POSE RULE.

leading question. A question that suggests the answer to the person being interrogated; esp., a question that may be answered by a mere "yes" or "no."—Also termed *categorical question*.

learned intermediary. See *informed intermediary* under INTER-MEDIARY.

lease, *n.* **1.** A temporary conveyance of the right to use and occupy real property, usu. in exchange for rent; the lease term can be for life, for a fixed period, or for a period terminable at will—but always for less time than the lessor has a right to. **2.** Such a conveyance plus all covenants attached to it. **3.** The written instrument memorializing such a conveyance and its covenants. **4.** The piece of real property so conveyed. **5.** A temporary conveyance of personal property in exchange for consideration.

concurrent lease. A lease that begins before a previous lease ends, entitling the new lessee to all rents that accrue on the previous lease after the new lease begins, as well as to appropriate remedies against the holding tenant.

finance lease. A lease in which a supplier agrees to deliver goods to the lessor according to the lessee's specification; in effect, a finance lease operates as a secured transaction. U.C.C. § 2A-103(1)(g).

full-service lease. A lease in which the lessor agrees to pay all maintenance expenses, insurance premiums, and property taxes.

graduated lease. A lease providing that rent will vary depending on future contingencies, such as operating expenses or gross income.

gross lease. A lease in which the lessee pays a flat amount for rent, out of which the lessor pays all the expenses (such as gas, water, and electricity).

ground lease. A long-term (usu. 99-year) lease of land only; such a lease typically involves commercial property, and any improvements built by the lessee usu. revert to the lessor. —Also termed *ground-rent lease*; *land lease.*

leveraged lease. A lease that serves as collateral for the loan under which the lessor acquired the leased asset, and that provides the lender's only recourse for nonpayment of the debt. —Also termed *third-party equity lease*; *tax lease.*

master lease. A lease that controls subsequent leases or subleases.

mineral lease. A lease in which the lessee acquires the right to explore for and extract oil, gas, or other minerals, the rent usu. being based on the amount or value of the minerals withdrawn.

mining lease. A lease of a mine or mining claim, to be worked by the lessee, usu. under conditions on the amount and type of work to be done; the lessor is compensated in the form of either fixed rent or royalties based on the amount of ore mined.

month-to-month lease. A tenancy with no written contract; rent is paid monthly, and usu. one month's notice is required to terminate the tenancy. See *periodic tenancy* under TENANCY.

net lease. A lease that requires the lessee to pay rent plus property expenses (such as taxes and insurance).

percentage lease. A lease in which the rent is based on a percentage of gross (or net) sales or profits, with a stipulated minimum rent.

sandwich lease. A lease in which the lessee subleases the property to a third party, esp. for more rent than that under the original lease.

sublease. See SUBLEASE.

top lease. A lease granted on property already subject to a mineral lease, and taking effect only if the existing lease expires or terminates.

lease, *vb.* **1.** To grant the temporary possession and use of (land, buildings, rooms, movable property, etc.) to another in return for rent or other consideration <the city leased the stadium to the football team>. **2.** To take a lease of; to hold by a lease <Carol leased the townhouse from her uncle>.

leaseback, *n.* The sale of property on the understanding, or with the express option, that the seller may lease the property from the buyer immediately upon the sale. —Also termed *sale and leaseback*.

leasehold, *n.* A tenant's possessory estate in land or premises, the four types being the tenancy for years, the periodic tenancy, the tenancy at will, and the tenancy at sufferance; although a leasehold has some of the characteristics of real property, it has historically been classified as a chattel real. —Also termed *leasehold estate*; *leasehold interest*. See TENANCY. Cf. FREEHOLD.

leasehold mortgage. See MORTGAGE.

lease-lend. LEND-LEASE.

lease-purchase agreement. A rent-to-own purchase plan under which the buyer takes possession of the goods with the first payment and ownership with the final payment. —Also termed *lease-to-purchase agreement*; *hire-purchase agreement*.

leave, *vb.* **1.** To give by will; to bequeath or devise <she left her ranch to her stepson>. **2.** To willfully depart with the intent not to return <he left Texas and became a resident of Massachusetts>.

leave of court. Judicial permission to follow a nonroutine procedure <the defense sought leave of court to allow the defendant to exit the courtroom when the autopsy photographs are shown>. —Often shortened to *leave.*

ledger (le-jər). A book or series of books used for recording financial transactions in the form of debits and credits.

legacy (leg-ə-see), *n*. A gift by will, esp. of personal property and often of money. —**legate,** *vb*. Cf. BEQUEST; DEVISE.

accumulative legacy. **a.** Another legacy given to a legatee by a different will. **b.** See *additional legacy.*

additional legacy. Another legacy given to a legatee by the same will (or in a codicil to the same will) that gave the first legacy. —Also termed *accumulative legacy.*

alternate legacy. A legacy by which the testator gives the legatee one of two or more items without designating which to take.

demonstrative legacy. A legacy paid from a particular source if that source has enough money; if it does not, the remaining amount of the legacy is taken from the estate's general assets.

general legacy. A gift of personal property that the testator intends to come from the general assets of the estate, payable in money or items indistinguishable from each other, such as shares of stock.

lapsed legacy. A legacy to a legatee who dies either before the testator dies or before the legacy is payable; it falls into the residual estate unless the jurisdiction has an antilapse statute. See ANTILAPSE STATUTE.

residuary legacy. A gift of the estate remaining after the satisfaction of all claims and all specific, general, and demonstrative legacies.

specific legacy. A testamentary gift of property that can be distinguished from the other property forming the testator's estate. —Also termed *special legacy.*

legal, *adj.* **1.** Of or relating to law; falling within the province of law <pro bono legal services>. **2.** Established, required, or permitted by law; LAWFUL <it's legal to carry a concealed handgun in some states>.

legal-acumen doctrine. The principle that if a defect in, or the invalidity of, a claim of land cannot be discovered without legal expertise, then equity may be invoked to remove the cloud created by the defect or invalidity.

legal age. AGE OF CAPACITY.

legal aid. Free or inexpensive legal services provided to those who cannot afford private counsel; legal aid is usu. administered locally by a specially established organization. See LEGAL SERVICES CORPORATION.

legal asset. See ASSET.

legal assistant. 1. PARALEGAL. **2.** A legal secretary.

legal capital. See CAPITAL.

legal cause. See *proximate cause* under CAUSE (1).

legal centralism. The theory suggesting that state-constructed legal entities form the center of legal life and control lesser normative systems that define appropriate behavior and social relationships, such as the family or business networks. —Also termed *legal centrism*; *legocentrism.*

legal-certainty test. In civil procedure, a test designed to establish whether the jurisdictional amount has been met; the amount claimed in the complaint will control unless there is a "legal certainty" that the claim is actually less than the minimum amount necessary to establish jurisdiction. See AMOUNT IN CONTROVERSY.

Legal Code. CODE (2).

legal conclusion. A statement that expresses a legal duty or result but omits the facts creating or supporting the duty or result. Cf. CONCLUSION OF LAW.

legal death. 1. See *brain death* under DEATH. **2.** CIVIL DEATH.

legal description. A formal description of real property, including a description of any part subject to an easement or reservation, complete enough that a particular piece of land can be located and identified; the description can be made by a government survey, metes and bounds, or lot numbers of a recorded plat.

legal discretion. See *judicial discretion* under DISCRETION.

legal duty. See DUTY.

legal entity. A body, other than a natural person, that can function legally, sue or be sued, and make decisions through agents; a typical example is a corporation.

legalese (lee-gə-leez). The complicated language used by lawyers, esp. in legal documents <the partner scolded her associate about the rampant legalese in the draft sublease>. See PLAIN-LANGUAGE MOVEMENT.

legal estate. See ESTATE.

legal ethics. 1. The customs of the legal profession, involving the moral duties that its members owe one an-

other, their clients, and the courts. **2.** The study or observance of those duties. **3.** The written regulations governing those duties. See MODEL RULES OF PROFESSIONAL CONDUCT.

legal fact. See FACT.

legal fiction. An assumption that something is true even though it may be untrue, made esp. in judicial reasoning to alter the operation of a legal rule; the constructive trust is an example of a legal fiction.

legal formalism, *n.* The theory that law is a set of rules and principles independent of other political and social institutions; legal formalism was espoused by such scholars as Christopher Columbus Langdell and Lon Fuller. —**legal formalist,** *n.* Cf. LEGAL REALISM.

legal fraud. See *constructive fraud* (a) under FRAUD.

legal heir. HEIR (1).

legal holiday. A day designated by law as being exempt from court proceedings, service of process, and the like; legal holidays vary from state to state. —Also termed *nonjudicial day*.

legal impossibility. See IMPOSSIBILITY.

legal insanity. INSANITY.

legalism, *n.* **1.** Formalism carried almost to the point of meaninglessness; an inclination to exalt the importance of law or formulated rules in any area of action. **2.** A mode of expression characteristic of lawyers; a jargonistic phrase characteristic of lawyers, such as "pursuant to."—**legalistic** (corresponding to senses 1 & 2), *adj.*—**legalist** (corresponding to sense 1), *n.*

legality. 1. Strict adherence to law, prescription, or doctrine; the quality of being legal. **2.** The principle that a person may not be prosecuted under a criminal law that has not been previously published. —Also termed (in sense 2) *principle of legality*.

legalize, *vb.* **1.** To make lawful; to authorize or justify by legal sanction <the bill to legalize marijuana never made it to the Senate floor>. **2.** To imbue with the spirit of the law; to make legalistic <legalized conceptions of religion>. —**legalization,** *n.*

legalized nuisance. See NUISANCE.

legal life tenant. See LIFE TENANT.

legal malice. See *implied malice* under MALICE.

legal malpractice. See MALPRACTICE.

legal maxim. MAXIM.

legal memory. The period during which a legal right or custom can be determined or established; traditionally, common-law legal memory began in the year 1189. Cf. TIME IMMEMORIAL.

legal order. 1. Traditionally, a set of regulations governing a society and those responsible for enforcing them. **2.** From a modern perspective, such regulations and officials plus the processes involved in creating, interpreting, and applying the regulations.

legal owner. See OWNER.

legal person. A natural or artificial person possessing legal rights and duties.

legal positivism, *n.* The theory that legal rules are valid only because they are enacted by an existing political authority, not because they are grounded in morality or in natural law; legal positivism has been espoused by such scholars as H.L.A. Hart. —**legal positivist,** *n.* See POSITIVE LAW. Cf. LOGICAL POSITIVISM.

legal presumption. See *presumption of law* under PRESUMPTION.

legal proceeding. Any proceeding authorized by law and instituted in a court or tribunal to acquire a right or to enforce a remedy.

legal process. PROCESS.

legal question. QUESTION OF LAW.

legal rate of interest. See *legal rate* under INTEREST RATE.

legal realism, *n.* The theory that law is based not on formal rules or principles, but instead on judicial decisions that should derive from social interests and public policy; American legal realism—which flourished in the early 20th century—was espoused by such scholars as John Chipman Gray, Oliver Wendell Holmes, and Karl Llewellyn. —**legal realist,** *n.* Cf. LEGAL FORMALISM.

legal representative. See *personal representative* under REPRESENTATIVE.

legal reserve. See RESERVE.

legal separation. SEPARATION (1).

Legal Services Corporation. A corporation established by the Legal Services Corporation Act of 1974 (42 U.S.C. § 2996) to provide legal assistance to clients who cannot afford legal services.

legal signature. SIGNATURE.

legal subrogation. See SUBROGA-TION.

legal tender. The money (bills and coins) approved in a country for the payment of debts, the purchase of goods, and other exchanges for value. See TENDER (3).

legal title. See TITLE.

legatee (leg-ə-**tee**). **1.** One who is named in a will to take personal property; one who has received a legacy or bequest. **2.** Loosely, one to whom a devise of real property is given.

legation (le-**gay**-shən). **1.** The act of sending diplomats to another country; a diplomatic mission. **2.** A body of diplomats in a foreign country. **3.** The official residence of a diplomatic minister in a foreign country. Cf. EM-BASSY.

legator (le-**gay**-tər). One who bequeaths a legacy; TESTATOR.

leges, *n. pl.* See LEX.

legislate, *vb.* **1.** To make or enact laws <the role of our lawmakers is to legislate, not to adjudicate>. **2.** To bring (something) into or out of existence by making laws; to attempt to control (something) by legislation <virtually every attempt to legislate morality has failed>.

legislation. 1. The process of making or enacting a positive law in written form, according to some type of formal procedure, by a branch of government constituted to perform this process. **2.** The law so enacted; the whole body of enacted laws.

general legislation. Legislation that applies to the community at large.

local and special legislation. Legislation that affects only a specific geographic area or a particular class of persons; such legislation is unconstitutional if it arbitrarily or capriciously distinguishes between members of the same class. —Also termed *class legislation.*

pork-barrel legislation. Legislation that favors a particular local district by allocating funds or resources to projects (such as the construction of a highway or a post office) of economic value to the district and of political advantage to the district's legislator.

subordinate legislation. REGULATION (2).

3. Loosely, a proposed law being considered by a legislature.

legislative, *adj.* Of or relating to lawmaking or to the power to enact laws.

legislative council. A state agency that studies legislative problems and plans legislative strategy between regular legislative sessions.

legislative counsel. A person or group charged with helping legislators fulfill their legislative duties, as by performing research, drafting bills, and the like.

legislative court. See COURT.

legislative fact. See FACT.

legislative history. The background and events leading to the enactment of a statute, including committee reports, hearings, and floor debates; legislative history is usu. recorded so that it can later be used to aid in interpreting the statute.

legislative immunity. See IMMUNITY (1).

legislative law. STATUTORY LAW.

legislative rule. A rule that an administrative agency issues under statutory authority and that has the force and effect of law.

legislative veto. See VETO.

legislator, *n.* One who makes laws within a given jurisdiction; a member of a legislative body. —**legislatorial,** *adj.*

legislature. The branch of government responsible for making statutory laws; the federal government and most states have bicameral legislatures, usu. consisting of a House of Representatives and a Senate. Cf. EXECUTIVE (1); JUDICIARY (1).

legist (lee-jist). **1.** One learned or skilled in the law; a lawyer. **2.** JURIST.

legitimacy. **1.** Lawfulness. **2.** The status of a person born within a lawful marriage or acquiring that status by later action of the parents. Cf. ILLEGITIMACY.

legitimate, *adj.* **1.** Complying with the law; lawful <a legitimate business>. **2.** Born of legally married parents <a legitimate child>. **3.** Genuine; valid <a legitimate complaint>. —**legitimacy,** *n.*

legitimation, *n.* **1.** The act of making something lawful; authorization. **2.** The act or process of authoritatively declaring a person legitimate. —**legitimate,** *vb.*

legocentrism. LEGAL CENTRALISM.

lemon law. **1.** A statute designed to protect consumers who buy sub-standard automobiles, usu. by requiring the manufacturer or dealer either to replace the vehicle or to refund the full purchase price; almost all states have lemon laws in effect. — Also termed *lemon protection.* **2.** More broadly, a statute designed to protect consumers who buy any products of inferior quality. —Also termed (in sense 2) *quality-of-products legislation.*

lend, *vb.* **1.** To allow the temporary use of (something), sometimes in exchange for compensation, on condition that the thing or its equivalent be returned. **2.** To provide (money) temporarily on condition of repayment, usu. with interest. —Also termed *loan.*

lend-lease. A mutually beneficial exchange made between friendly parties; esp., an arrangement made in 1941, under the Lend-Lease Act, whereby U.S. destroyers were lent to Great Britain in exchange for Britain's leasing of land to the U.S. for military bases. —Also termed *lease-lend.*

lenity (le-nə-tee). The quality or condition of being lenient; mercy or clemency. See RULE OF LENITY.

leonine contract (lee-ə-nIn). See *adhesion contract* under CONTRACT.

lese majesty (layz-ma-jə-stee *or* lez-). **1.** A crime against the state, esp. against the ruler. **2.** An attack on a custom or traditional belief. — Also spelled *lèse-majesté.* —Also termed *laesae majestatis.*

lessee (le-see). One who has a possessory interest in real or personal property under a lease; TENANT.

lesser included offense. See OFFENSE.

lessor (le-**sor** *or* le-sor). One who conveys real or personal property by lease; LANDLORD.

let, *vb.* **1.** To allow or permit <the court, refusing to issue an injunction, let the nuisance continue>. **2.** To offer (property) for lease; to rent out <the hospital let office space to several doctors>. **3.** To award (a contract), esp. after bids have been submitted <the federal agency let the project to the lowest bidder>.

letter. 1. A written communication—usu. one that is enclosed in an envelope, sealed, stamped, and delivered <please review the letter from opposing counsel>. **2.** (*usu. pl.*) A written instrument containing or affirming a grant of some power or right <letters testamentary>. **3.** Strict or literal meaning <the letter of the law>. Cf. SPIRIT.

letter of attorney. POWER OF ATTORNEY (1).

letter of attornment. A grantor's letter to a tenant, stating that the leased property has been sold and directing the tenant to pay rent to the new owner. See ATTORNMENT (1).

letter of comment. DEFICIENCY LETTER.

letter of credence. A document that accredits a diplomat to the government of the country to which he or she is sent. —Abbr. L.C.; L/C. —Also termed *letters of credence.*

letter of credit. An instrument under which the issuer (usu. a bank), at a customer's request, agrees to honor a draft or other demand for payment made by a third party (the *beneficiary*), as long as the draft or demand complies with specified conditions, and regardless of whether any underlying agreement between the customer and the beneficiary is satisfied; letters of credit are governed by Article 5 of the U.C.C. —Abbr. L.C.; L/C. —Often shortened to *credit.* — Also termed *circular letter of credit; circular note; bill of credit.*

commercial letter of credit. A letter of credit used as a method of payment in a sale of goods (esp. in international transactions), with the buyer being the issuer's customer and the seller being the beneficiary, so that the seller can obtain payment directly from the issuer instead of from the buyer.

export letter of credit. A commercial letter of credit issued by a foreign bank, at a foreign buyer's request, in favor of a domestic exporter.

import letter of credit. A commercial letter of credit issued by a domestic bank, at an importer's request, in favor of a foreign seller.

standby letter of credit. A letter of credit used to guarantee either a monetary or a nonmonetary obligation (such as the performance of construction work), whereby the issuer agrees to pay the beneficiary if the customer defaults on its obligation. —Also termed *guaranty letter of credit.*

letter of intent. A written statement detailing the preliminary understanding of parties who plan to enter into a contract or some other agreement; a letter of intent is not meant to be binding and does not hinder the parties from bargaining with a third party. —Also termed *memorandum of intent.* Cf. *precontract* under CONTRACT.

letter of recall. 1. A document sent from one nation's executive to that of another, informing the latter that a minister sent by the former has been summoned back to his or her own country. **2.** A manufacturer's letter to a buyer of a particular product, requesting that it be brought back to the dealer for repair or replacement.

letter of request. A document issued by one court to a foreign court, requesting that the foreign court (1) take evidence from a specific person within the foreign jurisdiction or effect service of process on an individual or corporation within the foreign jurisdiction and (2) return the testimony or proof of service to the requesting court for use in a pending case. Pl. **letters of request.** —Also termed *letters rogatory*; *letter rogatory*; *rogatory letter*; *requisitory letter.*

letter ruling. A written statement issued by the I.R.S. to an inquiring taxpayer, explaining the tax implications of a particular transaction.

letters. See LETTER (2).

letters close. LETTERS SECRET.

letter security. See *restricted security* under SECURITY.

letters of administration. A formal document issued by a probate court in order to appoint the administrator of an estate. See ADMINISTRATION (3). Cf. LETTERS TESTAMENTARY.

letters of administration c.t.a. Letters of administration appointing an administrator *cum testamento annexo* (with the will annexed) either because the will does not name an executor or because the named executor does not qualify. See *administration cum testamento annexo* under ADMINISTRATION.

letters of administration d.b.n. Letters of administration appointing an administrator *de bonis non* (concerning goods not yet administered) because the named executor failed to complete the estate's probate. See *administration de bonis non* under ADMINISTRATION.

letters of credence. LETTER OF CREDENCE.

letters of guardianship. A document issued by a court appointing a guardian to care for a minor's or an incapacitated adult's well-being, property, and affairs; it defines the scope of the guardian's rights and duties, including the extent of control over the ward's education and medical issues. See GUARDIAN.

letters of marque (mahrk). A license authorizing a private citizen to engage in reprisal against citizens or vessels of another nation; Congress has the exclusive power to grant letters of marque (U.S. Const. art. I, § 8, cl. 11), but it has not done so since the 19th century. —Also termed *letters of marque and reprisal.*

letters patent. 1. *Archaic.* A document granting some right or privilege, issued under governmental seal but open to public inspection. Cf. LETTERS SECRET. **2.** A governmental grant of the exclusive right to use an invention or design. See PATENT (2).

letters rogatory. LETTER OF REQUEST.

letters secret. *Archaic.* A governmental document that is issued to a private person, closed and sealed, and thus not made available for public inspection. —Also termed *letters close.* Cf. LETTERS PATENT (1).

letters testamentary. The instrument by which a probate court approves the appointment of an executor under a will and authorizes the executor to administer the estate. Cf. LETTERS OF ADMINISTRATION.

letter stock. See *restricted security* under SECURITY.

lettre de cachet (le-trə-də-ka-**shay**). [French "letter with a seal"] A warrant issued for the imprisonment of a person without trial.

levari facias (li-**var**-I-**fay**-shee-əs *or* -**var**-ee-). [Latin "cause to be levied"] *Archaic.* A writ ordering a sheriff to seize a person's goods and income from lands until a judgment debt is satisfied.

levée en masse. LEVY EN MASSE.

leverage, *n.* **1.** Positional advantage; effectiveness. **2.** The use of credit or borrowed funds (such as buying on margin) to improve one's speculative ability and to increase an investment's rate of return. **3.** The advantage obtained from using credit or borrowed funds rather than equity capital. **4.** The ratio between a corporation's debt and its equity capital. **5.** The effect of this ratio on common-stock prices.

leverage, *vb.* **1.** To provide (a borrower or investor) with credit or funds to improve speculative ability

and to achieve a high rate of return. **2.** To supplement (available capital) with credit or outside funds.

leveraged buyout. See BUYOUT.

leveraged lease. See LEASE.

leveraged recapitalization. See RECAPITALIZATION.

leverage ratio. The ratio of the amount of a firm's debt to the value of the firm's assets.

leveraging up. See *leveraged recapitalization* under RECAPITALIZATION.

levy (**le**-vee), *n.* **1.** The imposition of a fine or tax; the fine or tax so imposed. **2.** The enlistment of soldiers into the military; the soldiers so enlisted. **3.** The legally sanctioned seizure and sale of property; the money obtained from such a sale. — Also termed (in sense 3) *levy of execution.*

levy, *vb.* **1.** To impose or assess (a fine or a tax) by legal authority <levy a tax on gasoline>. **2.** To enlist for service in the military <the troops were quickly levied>. **3.** To declare or wage (a war) <the rival clans levied war against each other>. **4.** To take or seize property in execution of a judgment <the judgment creditor may levy on the debtor's assets>.

levy en masse. A large conscription or mobilization of troops, esp. in response to a threatened invasion. — Also spelled *levée en masse; levy in mass.*

levy of execution. LEVY (3).

lewd and lascivious cohabitation. See *illicit cohabitation* under COHABITATION.

lewdness. Gross, wanton, and public indecency that is outlawed by many state statutes; an act that the actor knows will likely be observed by someone who will be affronted or alarmed by it. Model Penal Code § 251.1. Cf. INDECENT EXPOSURE; OBSCENITY.

lex (leks). [Latin "law"] **1.** In civil law, a legislative bill. **2.** A collection of uncodified laws within a jurisdiction. **3.** A system or body of laws, written or unwritten, that are peculiar to a jurisdiction or to a field of human activity. **4.** Positive law, as opposed to natural law. Pl. *leges* (**lay**-gays). Cf. JUS.

lex actus (leks-**ak**-təs). [Law Latin] The law of the place where an act was committed, esp. where a document is executed. —Also termed *lex loci actus.*

lex delicti. LEX LOCI DELICTI.

lex domicilii (leks-do-mə-**sil**-ee-I). [Latin] **1.** The law of the country where a person is domiciled. **2.** The determination of a person's rights by establishing where, in law, that person is domiciled.

lex fori (leks-**for**-I). [Latin] The law of the forum; the law of the jurisdiction where the case is pending <the *lex fori* governs whether the death penalty is a possible punishment for a first-degree-murder conviction>. Cf. LEX LOCI (1).

Lexis (**lek**-səs). An on-line computer service that provides access to databases of legal information, including federal and state caselaw, statutes, and secondary materials. Cf. WEST-LAW.

lex loci (leks-**loh**-sI). [Latin] **1.** The law of the place; local law. Cf. LEX FORI. **2.** LEX LOCI CONTRACTUS.

lex loci actus (leks-**loh**-sI-ak-təs). [Latin] LEX ACTUS.

lex loci celebrationis (leks-**loh**-sI-sel-ə-bray-shee-**oh**-nəs). [Latin] The law of the place where a legal ceremony, such as a marriage or an execution of a contract, was performed.

lex loci contractus (leks-**loh**-sI-kən-**trak**-təs). [Latin] The law of the place where the contract was executed; *lex loci contractus* is often the proper law by which to decide contractual disputes. —Often shortened to *lex loci.*

lex loci delicti (leks-**loh**-sI-də-**lik**-tI). [Latin] The law of the place where the tort was committed. —Often shortened to *lex delicti.* —Also termed *lex loci delictus; place-of-wrong rule; place-of-wrong law.*

lex loci rei sitae (leks-**loh**-sI-ree-I-sI-dI). [Latin] LEX SITUS.

lex mercatoria (leks-mər-kə-**tor**-ee-ə). [Latin] LAW MERCHANT.

lex situs (leks-sI-dəs). [Law Latin] The law of the place where property is located. —Also termed *lex loci rei sitae.*

lex terrae. [Law Latin] LAW OF THE LAND.

ley de terre. [Law French] LAW OF THE LAND.

L.F. *abbr.* Law French. —Also written *law French.*

liability, *n.* **1.** The quality or state of being legally obligated or responsible <subject to both civil and criminal liability>. —Also termed *respon-*

sibility. **2.** A pecuniary obligation; DEBT <assets and liabilities>. **3.** A duty or burden <military service was a liability he wasn't prepared to undertake>. —**liable,** *adj.*

derivative liability. Liability for a wrong that a person other than the one wronged has a right to redress; examples include liability to a widow in a wrongful-death action and liability to a corporation in a shareholder's derivative suit.

enterprise liability. Liability imposed on each member of an industry responsible for manufacturing a harmful or defective product, allotted by each manufacturer's market share of the industry. —Also termed *industry-wide liability.*

joint and several liability. Liability that may be apportioned either among two or more parties or to only one or a few select members of the group, at the adversary's discretion; thus, each liable party is individually responsible for the entire obligation, but a paying party has rights of contribution and indemnity against nonpaying parties. —Also termed (in civil-law jurisdictions) *solidary liability.*

joint liability. Liability shared by two or more parties.

limited liability. Liability restricted by statute or contract; esp., the liability of a company's owners for nothing more than the capital they have invested in the business.

personal liability. Liability for which one is personally accountable and for which a wronged party can look to one's personal assets for satisfaction.

premises liability. See PREMISES LIABILITY.

primary liability. Liability for which one is directly responsible, as opposed to secondary liability.

products liability. See PRODUCTS LIABILITY.

secondary liability. Liability that does not arise unless the primarily liable party fails to honor its obligation.

several liability. Liability that is separate and distinct from another's liability, so that the plaintiff may bring a separate action against one defendant without joining the other liable parties.

strict liability. Liability that does not depend on actual negligence or intent to harm, but that is based on the breach of an absolute duty to make something safe; strict liability most often applies either to ultrahazardous activities or in products-liability cases. —Also termed *absolute liability*; *liability without fault.*

vicarious liability. Liability that a supervisory party (such as an employer) bears for the actionable conduct of a subordinate or associate (such as an employee) because of the relationship between the two. See RESPONDEAT SUPERIOR.

liability dividend. See *scrip dividend* under DIVIDEND.

liability insurance. See INSURANCE.

liability limit. The maximum coverage that an insurance company has provided in an insurance policy. —Also termed *limit of liability.*

liability without fault. See *strict liability* under LIABILITY.

libel (lī-bəl), *n.* **1.** A defamatory statement expressed in a permanent medium, esp. writing but also pictures, signs, or electronic broadcasts; libel is classified as both a crime and a tort but is no longer prosecuted as a crime. **2.** The act of making such a statement. **3.** The complaint or initial pleading in an admiralty or ecclesiastical case. —**libelous,** *adj.* See DEFAMATION. Cf. SLANDER.

criminal libel. At common law, libel for which the author may be criminally responsible, such as seditious libel; because of constitutional protections of free speech, libel is no longer criminally prosecuted.

group libel. Libel that defames a class of persons, esp. because of their race, sex, national origin, religious belief, or the like; civil liability for group libel is rare because the plaintiff must prove that the statement applied particularly to him or her. Cf. HATE SPEECH.

libel per quod. **a.** Libel that is actionable only on allegation and proof of special damages; most jurisdictions do not recognize libel per quod, holding instead that general damages from libel are presumed. **b.** Libel in which the defamatory meaning is not apparent from the statement on its face but rather must be proved from extrinsic circumstances. See INNUENDO (2).

libel per se. **a.** Libel that is actionable in itself, requiring no proof of special damages; most jurisdictions do not distinguish between libel per se and libel per quod, holding instead that general damages from libel

are presumed. **b.** Libel that is defamatory on its face, such as the statement "Frank is a thief."

seditious libel. Libel made with the intent of inciting sedition; like other forms of criminal libel, seditious libel is no longer prosecuted. See SEDITION.

trade libel. See TRADE LIBEL.

libel, *vb.* **1.** To defame (someone) in a permanent medium, esp. in writing. **2.** To institute a suit in admiralty or ecclesiastical court.

libelant. **1.** The party who institutes a suit in admiralty or ecclesiastical court by filing a libel. **2.** LIBELER. — Also spelled *libellant.*

libelee. The party against whom a libel has been filed in admiralty or ecclesiastical court. —Also spelled *libellee.*

libeler. One who publishes a written defamatory statement. —Also spelled *libeller.* —Also termed *libelant.*

liberty. **1.** Freedom from arbitrary or undue governmental restraint <give me liberty or give me death>. **2.** A right, privilege, or immunity enjoyed by prescription or by grant <the liberties protected by the Constitution>.

liberty interest. An interest protected by the due-process clauses of state and federal constitutions. See FUNDAMENTAL RIGHT (2).

liberty of contract. FREEDOM OF CONTRACT.

liberty of speech. FREEDOM OF SPEECH.

liberty of the press. FREEDOM OF THE PRESS.

license, *n.* **1.** A revocable permission to commit some act that would otherwise be unlawful. **2.** The certificate or document evidencing such permission. —**license,** *vb.*

exclusive license. A license that gives the licensee the exclusive right to perform the licensed act and that prohibits the licensor from granting that right to anyone else; esp., such a license of a copyright, patent, or trademark right.

licensee. 1. One to whom a license is granted. **2.** One who has permission to enter or use another's premises, but only for his or her own purposes and not for the occupier's benefit (such as a social guest); the occupier has a duty to warn the licensee of any dangerous conditions known to the occupier but unknown to the licensee. Cf. INVITEE; TRESPASSER.

bare licensee. A licensee whose presence on the premises the occupier tolerates but does not necessarily approve, such as one who takes a shortcut across another's land. — Also termed *naked licensee.*

licenser. One who grants a license to another. —Also spelled *licensor.*

licentiate (lI-**sen**(t)-shee-ət). One who has obtained a license or authoritative permission to exercise some function, esp. to practice a profession <a licentiate in law should be held to high ethical standards>.

lie, *vb.* **1.** To tell an untruth; to speak or write falsely <she lied on the witness stand>. **2.** To have foundation in the law; to be legally supportable, sustainable, or proper <in such a situation, an action lies in

tort>. **3.** To exist; to reside <final appeal lies with the Superior Court>.

lie detector. POLYGRAPH.

lien (leen *or* **lee**-ən *or* lin), *n.* A legal right or interest that a creditor has in another's property, lasting usu. until a debt or duty that it secures is satisfied; typically, the creditor does not take possession of the property on which the lien has been obtained. —**lien,** *vb.*—**lienable, liened,** *adj.* Cf. PLEDGE.

architect's lien. A statutory lien on real property in favor of an architect who has drawn the plans for and supervised the construction of improvements on the property.

attachment lien. A lien on property seized by prejudgment attachment; such a lien is initially inchoate but becomes final and perfected upon entry of a judgment for the attaching creditor and relates back to the date when the lien first arose. — Also termed *lien of attachment.* See ATTACHMENT.

attorney's lien. The right of an attorney to hold or retain a client's money or property (a *retaining lien*) or to encumber money payable to the client in the court's possession (a *charging lien*) until the attorney's fees have been properly determined and paid.

charging lien. An attorney's lien on a judgment that a client has obtained with the attorney's help.

choate lien. A lien in which the lienholder, the property, and the monetary amount are established so that the lien is perfected and nothing else needs to be done to make it enforceable.

consummate lien. A judgment lien arising after the denial of a motion for a new trial. Cf. *inchoate lien.*

execution lien. A lien on property seized by a levy of execution; such a lien gives the execution creditor priority over subsequent transferees of the property and over prior unrecorded conveyances of interests in the property. See EXECUTION.

first lien. A lien that takes priority over all other charges or encumbrances on the same property and that must be satisfied before other charges may share in proceeds from the property's sale.

floating lien. A lien that continues to exist even when the collateral changes in character, classification, or location; floating liens also extend to after-acquired property. — Also termed *floating charge.*

garnishment lien. A lien on a debtor's property held by a garnishee; such a lien attaches in favor of the garnishing creditor when a garnishment summons is served and also impounds any credits the garnishee owes the debtor so that they must be paid to the garnishing creditor. —Also termed *lien of garnishment.* See GARNISHMENT.

general lien. A lien on property securing a debt that does not relate specifically to that property. Cf. *particular lien.*

inchoate lien. A judgment lien that may be defeated if the judgment is vacated or a motion for new trial is granted.

judgment lien. A lien imposed on a judgment debtor's nonexempt property; such a lien gives the judgment creditor the right to attach the judgment debtor's property. —Also termed *lien of judgment.* See EXEMPT PROPERTY.

junior lien. A lien that is subordinate to other liens on the same property.

landlord's lien. **a.** At common law, a lien that gave a landlord the right to seize a tenant's property and sell it publicly in satisfaction of overdue rent. See DISTRESS. **b.** Generally, a statutory lien on a tenant's personal property located at the leased premises in favor of a landlord who receives preferred-creditor status with regard to that property; usu. such a lien secures the payment of overdue rent or compensation for damage to the premises.

maritime lien. A lien on a vessel, given to secure the claim of a creditor who provided maritime services to the vessel or who suffered an injury as a result of the vessel's use.

mechanic's lien. A statutory lien that secures payment for labor or materials supplied in improving, repairing, or maintaining real or personal property, such as a building, an automobile, or the like. —Also termed *construction lien* (with respect to labor) or *materialman's lien* (with respect to materials).

particular lien. A lien on a specific piece of property for some charge or claim connected to that property. —Also termed *special lien.* Cf. *general lien.*

possessory lien. A lien allowing the creditor to retain possession of the encumbered property until the debt is satisfied. See PLEDGE.

prior lien. A lien that is superior to other liens on the same property because it was perfected first. — Also termed *priority lien.*

second lien. A lien that is next in rank after a first lien on the same property and therefore is next entitled to satisfaction out of the proceeds from the property's sale.

senior lien. A lien that has priority over other liens on the same property.

statutory lien. A lien arising solely by force of statute, not by agreement of the parties; an example is a federal tax lien.

vendor's lien. **a.** A lien, equal to the unpaid portion of the purchase price, retained by a seller of real property. **b.** A lien held by a seller of goods, who retains possession of the goods until the buyer pays in full.

warehouser's lien. A lien covering storage charges for goods stored with a bailee. —Also termed *warehouseman's lien.*

lien creditor. See CREDITOR.

lienee (lee-nee *or* lin-ee). One whose property is subject to a lien.

lienholder. A person having or owning a lien. —Also termed *lienor.*

lienor. LIENHOLDER.

lien-stripping. In bankruptcy law, the practice of splitting a mortgagee's secured claim into secured and unsecured components and reducing that claim to the market value of the debtor's residence, thereby allowing the debtor to modify the terms of the mortgage and reduce the amount of the debt; the U.S. Supreme Court has prohibited lien-stripping in all Chapter 7 cases (*Nobelman v. American Savs. Bank,* 508 U.S. 324 (1993)) and in Chapter 13 cases involving a debtor's principal residence (*Dewsnup v. Timm,* 502 U.S. 410 (1992)), and the Bankruptcy Reform Act of 1994 modified the Bankruptcy Code to prohibit lien-stripping in Chapter 11 cases involving an individual's principal residence.

lien theory. In real-property law, the idea that a mortgage resembles a lien, so that the mortgagee acquires only a lien on the property and the mortgagor retains both legal and equitable title unless a valid foreclosure occurs; most American states—commonly called *lien states, lien jurisdictions,* or *lien-theory jurisdictions*— have adopted this theory. Cf. TITLE THEORY.

life annuity. See ANNUITY.

life-care contract. An agreement in which one party is assured of care and maintenance for life in exchange for a transfer of property to the other party.

life estate. See ESTATE.

life estate pur autre vie. See ESTATE.

life expectancy. 1. The period for which a person of a given age and sex is expected to live, according to actuarial tables. **2.** The period for which a given person is expected to live, taking into account such individualized characteristics as heredity, past and present diseases, and other relevant medical data. See ACTUARIAL TABLE; LIFE TABLE.

life in being. Under the rule against perpetuities, anyone alive when a future interest is created, whether or not the person has an interest in the estate. Cf. MEASURING LIFE.

life insurance. See INSURANCE.

life-insurance trust. See TRUST.

life interest. An interest in real or personal property measured by the duration of the holder's or another named person's life. See *life estate* under ESTATE.

life-owner. LIFE TENANT.

life sentence. See SENTENCE.

life-sustaining procedure. A medical procedure that uses mechanical or artificial means to sustain, restore, or substitute for a vital function and that serves only or primarily to postpone death.

life table. An actuarial table that gives the probable proportions of people who will live to different ages. Cf. ACTUARIAL TABLE.

life tenancy. See *life estate* under ESTATE.

life tenant. One who holds a life estate. —Also termed *life-owner*. See TENANT.

equitable life tenant. A life tenant not automatically entitled to possession but who makes an election allowed by law to a person of that status—such as a spouse—and to whom a court will normally grant possession if security or an undertaking is given.

legal life tenant. A life tenant who is automatically entitled to possession by virtue of a legal estate.

lifetime gift. See *inter vivos gift* under GIFT.

LIFO (lI-foh). *abbr.* LAST-IN, FIRST-OUT.

light-and-air easement. See EASEMENT.

like-kind exchange. An exchange of trade, business, or investment property (except inventory, stocks, and bonds) for other trade, business, or investment property; such an exchange is not taxable unless cash or other property is received. I.R.C. § 1031.

likelihood-of-confusion test. In trademark law, the test for infringement, based on the probability that a substantial number of ordinarily prudent buyers will be misled or confused about the source of a product when its trademark allegedly infringes on that of an earlier product.

limine. See IN LIMINE.

limitation. 1. The act of limiting; the state of being limited. **2.** A restriction. **3.** A statutory period after which a lawsuit or prosecution cannot be brought in court. —Also termed *limitations period; limitation period.* See STATUTE OF LIMITATIONS. Cf. LACHES. **4.** In property law, the restriction of the extent of an estate; the creation by deed or devise of a lesser estate out of a fee simple.

conditional limitation. **a.** See *executory limitation.* **b.** A lease provision that automatically terminates the lease if a specified event occurs, such as if the lessee defaults.

executory limitation. A restriction that, upon the happening of a specified event, causes an estate to automatically end and revest in a third party. —Also termed *conditional limitation.* See *fee simple subject to an executory limitation* under FEE SIMPLE.

limitation over. An additional estate created or contemplated in a conveyance, to be enjoyed after the first estate expires or is exhausted; for example, "to A for life, remainder to B."

special limitation. A restriction that, upon the happening of a specified event, causes an estate to end automatically and revert to the grantor. See *fee simple determinable* under FEE SIMPLE.

limitation, words of. See WORDS OF LIMITATION.

limitation-of-remedies clause. A contractual provision that restricts the remedies available to the parties in the event of breach; under the U.C.C., such a clause is valid unless it fails of its essential purpose or (with respect to limiting consequential damages) it is unconscionable. U.C.C. § 2-719. Cf. LIQUIDATED-DAMAGES CLAUSE; PENALTY CLAUSE.

limitations, statute of. See STATUTE OF LIMITATIONS.

limitations period. LIMITATION (3).

limited appeal. See APPEAL.

limited appearance. See *special appearance* under APPEARANCE.

limited company. See COMPANY.

limited defense. See *personal defense* under DEFENSE (4).

limited divorce. See DIVORCE.

limited jurisdiction. See JURISDICTION.

limited liability. See LIABILITY.

limited-liability company. See COMPANY.

limited-liability corporation. See *limited-liability company* under COMPANY.

limited-liability partnership. See PARTNERSHIP.

limited partner. See PARTNER.

limited partnership. See PARTNERSHIP.

limited partnership association. PARTNERSHIP ASSOCIATION.

limited power of appointment. See POWER OF APPOINTMENT.

limited warranty. See WARRANTY (2).

limit of liability. LIABILITY LIMIT.

limit order. See ORDER (4).

line, *n.* **1.** A demarcation, border, or limit <the line between right and wrong>. **2.** A person's occupation or business <what line of business is Watson in?>. **3.** The ancestry of a person; lineage <the Fergusons originally came from a long line of wheat farmers>.

collateral line. Persons who descend from the same common ancestor but not from one another, such as sisters or cousins.

direct line. Persons who descend from the same common ancestor and from each other, such as grandparents, parents, children, and so on.

maternal line. A person's ancestry or relationship with another traced through the mother.

paternal line. A person's ancestry or relationship with another traced through the father.

lineage (**lin**-ee-əj). Ancestry and progeny; family, ascending or descending.

lineal (**lin**-ee-əl), *adj.* Derived from or relating to common ancestors, esp. in a direct line; hereditary. Cf. COLLATERAL (2), *adj.*

lineal consanguinity. See CONSANGUINITY.

lineal heir. See HEIR.

line-item veto. See VETO.

line of credit. The maximum amount of credit extended to a borrower by a given lender. —Also termed *credit line.*

line of title. CHAIN OF TITLE.

lines and corners. METES AND BOUNDS.

lineup. A police identification procedure by which a criminal suspect and other physically similar persons are exhibited before the victim or a witness to determine whether the suspect can be identified as the criminal. Cf. SHOW-UP.

link financing. See FINANCING.

liquid, *adj.* **1.** (Of assets) capable of being readily converted into cash. **2.** (Of persons or entities) possessing assets that are readily convertible into cash. —**liquidity,** *n.*

liquid asset. See *current asset* under ASSET.

liquidated amount. A figure readily computed, based on the agreement's terms.

liquidated claim. See CLAIM (2).

liquidated damages. See DAMAGES.

liquidated-damages clause. A contractual provision that determines in advance the measure of damages to be assessed if a party defaults; traditionally, courts will uphold such a clause unless the agreed-upon sum is deemed a penalty for one of the following reasons: (1) the sum grossly exceeds the probable damages on breach, (2) the same sum is made payable for any variety of different breaches (some major, some minor), or (3) a mere delay in payment has been listed among the events of default. Cf. LIMITATION-OF-REMEDIES CLAUSE.

liquidated debt. See DEBT.

liquidating distribution. See DISTRIBUTION.

liquidating partner. See PARTNER.

liquidating trust. See TRUST.

liquidation, *n.* **1.** The act of determining by agreement or by litigation the exact amount of something (as a debt or damages) that before was uncertain. **2.** The act of settling a debt by payment or other satisfaction. **3.** The act of converting assets into cash, esp. for the purpose of settling debts. **4.** In bankruptcy law, the process—under Chapter 7 of the Bankruptcy Code—of collecting a debtor's nonexempt property, converting that property to cash, and distributing the cash to the various creditors; upon liquidation, the debtor hopes to obtain a discharge, which releases the debtor from any further personal liability for prebankruptcy debts. Cf. REHABILITATION (3). — **liquidate,** *vb.*—**liquidator,** *n.*

liquidation dividend. See DIVIDEND.

liquidation preference. See PREFERENCE.

liquidation price. See PRICE.

liquidation value. 1. The value of an asset or business that is sold outside the ordinary course of business. **2.** See *liquidation price* under PRICE.

liquid debt. See DEBT.

liquidity ratio. The comparison of a corporation's assets that are held in cash or liquid form to the amount of its current liabilities, indicating the ability to pay current debts as they come due.

lis (lis *or* lees). [Latin] A piece of litigation; a controversy or dispute.

lis alibi pendens (lis-**al**-ə-bI-**pen**-dənz). [Latin] A lawsuit pending elsewhere.

lis pendens (lis-**pen**-dənz). [Latin "a pending lawsuit"] **1.** A pending litigation. **2.** The jurisdiction, power, or control acquired by a court over property during the pendency of a legal action. **3.** A notice required in some jurisdictions to warn all persons that certain property is the subject matter of litigation, and that any interests acquired during the pendency of the suit are subject to the outcome of the litigation. —Also termed (in sense 3) *notice of lis pen-*

dens; *notice of pendency*. Cf. PENDENTE LITE.

listed security. See SECURITY.

listed stock. See *listed security* under SECURITY.

listing. 1. In real estate, an agreement between a property owner and an agent, whereby the agent agrees to try to secure a buyer or tenant for a specific property at a certain price and terms in return for a fee or commission.

exclusive-agency listing. A listing providing that one agent has the right to be the only person, other than the owner, to sell the property during a specified period. —Also termed *exclusive authorization-to-sell listing.*

multiple listing. A listing providing that the agent will allow other agents to try to sell the property; under this agreement, the original agent gives the selling agent a percentage of the commission or some other stipulated amount.

open listing. A listing that allows selling rights to be given to more than one agent at a time, obligates the owner to pay a commission when a specified broker makes a sale, and reserves the owner's right to personally sell the property without paying a commission. — Also termed *nonexclusive listing*; *general listing*; *simple listing.*

2. In securities trading, the contract between a firm and a stock exchange by which the trading of the firm's securities on the exchange is handled. See *listed security* under SECURITY.

LISTING 386

dual listing. The listing of a security on more than one exchange.

3. In taxation, the creation of a schedule or inventory of a person's taxable property; the official list so created.

listing agent. The real-estate broker's representative who obtains a listing agreement with the owner. Cf. SELLING AGENT.

list of creditors. A schedule that gives the names and addresses of creditors along with amounts owed them; such a list is required in bankruptcy proceedings.

lite pendente (**II**-tee-pen-**den**-tee). [Latin] PENDENTE LITE.

literacy test. A test of one's ability to read and write, formerly required in some states as a condition for registering to vote; Congress banned this use of literacy tests in 1975.

literal canon. STRICT CONSTRUCTIONISM.

literal construction. See *strict construction* under CONSTRUCTION.

literal infringement. See *patent infringement* under INFRINGEMENT.

literal rule. STRICT CONSTRUCTIONISM.

literary property. 1. The physical property in which an intellectual production is embodied, such as a book, screenplay, or lecture. **2.** An owner's exclusive right to possess, use, and dispose of such a production. See COPYRIGHT; INTELLECTUAL PROPERTY.

literary work. A work, other than an audiovisual work, that is expressed in words, numbers, or other symbols, regardless of the medium in which it is embodied. 17 U.S.C. § 101.

litigable (**lid**-i-gə-bəl), *adj.* Able to be contested or disputed in court <litigable claims>. —**litigability,** *n.*

litigant. A party to a lawsuit.

litigation, *n.* **1.** The process of carrying on a lawsuit <the attorney advised his client to make a generous settlement offer in order to avoid litigation>. **2.** A lawsuit itself <several litigations pending before the court>. —**litigate,** *vb.*—**litigatory, litigational,** *adj.*

litigation costs. See COST (3).

litigator. 1. *Archaic.* A party to a lawsuit; a litigant. **2.** A trial lawyer, esp. one who handles mostly pretrial matters such as discovery requests.

litigious (li-**tij**-əs), *adj.* **1.** Fond of legal disputes; contentious <our litigious society>. **2.** *Archaic.* Of or relating to the subject of a lawsuit <the litigious property>. **3.** *Archaic.* Of or relating to lawsuits; litigatory <they couldn't settle the litigious dispute>. —**litigiousness, litigiosity** (lə-tij-ee-**os**-ə-tee), *n.*

littoral (**li**-tə-rəl), *adj.* Of or relating to the coast or shore of an ocean, sea, or lake <the littoral right to limit others' consumption of the water>. Cf. RIPARIAN.

livery (**liv**-[ə-]ree). The delivery of the possession of real property. Cf. DELIVERY.

livery of seisin. At common law, the ceremony by which a grantor conveyed land to a grantee; livery of seisin involved either of the following: (1) going on the land and having the grantor symbolically deliver possession of the land to the grantee by handing over a twig, a clod, or a piece of turf (called *livery in deed*), or (2) going within sight of the land and having the grantor tell the grantee that possession was being given, followed by the grantee's entering the land (called *livery in law*). See SEISIN.

lives in being. See LIFE IN BEING.

living separate and apart. The status of spouses who reside in different places and have no intention of resuming marital relations; this is a basis for no-fault divorce in many states if the spouses have lived apart for a statutory period.

living trust. See *inter vivos trust* under TRUST.

living will. An instrument, signed with the formalities necessary for a will, by which a person states the intention to refuse medical treatment and to release healthcare providers from all liability if the person becomes both terminally ill and unable to communicate such a refusal. Cf. ADVANCE DIRECTIVE.

L.J. *abbr.* **1.** Law Judge. **2.** Law Journal. **3.** Lord Justice.

L.L. *abbr.* Law Latin.

L. Lat. *abbr.* Law Latin.

LL.B. *abbr.* Bachelor of Laws—formerly, the law degree ordinarily conferred by American law schools. Cf. JURIS DOCTOR.

L.L.C. See *limited-liability company* under COMPANY.

LL.D. *abbr.* Doctor of Laws—commonly an honorary law degree.

LL.J. *abbr.* Lords justices.

LL.M. *abbr.* MASTER OF LAWS.

L.L.P. See *limited-liability partnership* under PARTNERSHIP.

Lloyd's. LLOYD'S OF LONDON (1).

Lloyd's association. LLOYD'S UNDERWRITERS.

Lloyd's insurance. Insurance provided by insurers as individuals, not as a corporation; the insurers' liability is several but not joint.

Lloyd's of London. 1. A voluntary association of merchants, shipowners, underwriters, and brokers that does not write policies but that issues a notice of an endeavor to members who may individually underwrite a policy by assuming shares of the total risk of insuring a client; the names of the bound underwriters and the attorney-in-fact appear on the policy. —Also termed *Lloyd's*; *London Lloyd's*. **2.** A London insurance mart where individual underwriters gather to quote rates and write insurance on a wide variety of risks.

Lloyd's underwriters. Any unincorporated association of underwriters who, under a common name, engage in the insurance business through an attorney-in-fact having authority to obligate the underwriters severally, within specified limits, on insurance contracts that the attorney makes or issues in the common name. —Also termed *Lloyd's association*; *American Lloyd's*.

load, *n.* An amount added to a security's price or to an insurance premium in order to cover sales commission and expenses <the mutual fund

had a high front- end load>. —Also termed *sales load*.

load fund. See MUTUAL FUND.

loan, *n.* **1.** An act of lending; a grant of something for temporary use <thank you for the loan of your dress>. **2.** A thing lent for the borrower's temporary use; esp., a sum of money lent at interest <Trent paid off his student loans in February>.

accommodation loan. A loan made without receiving any consideration in return. See ACCOMMODATION.

amortized loan. A loan calling for periodic payments that are applied first to interest and then to principal, as provided by the terms of the note. See AMORTIZATION (1).

back-to-back loan. A loan arrangement by which two firms lend each other funds denominated in different currencies for a specified period.

bridge loan. A short-term loan that is used to cover costs until more permanent financing is arranged.

call loan. A loan for which the lender can demand payment at any time, usu. with 24 hours' notice, because there is no fixed maturity date. — Also termed *broker call loan*; *demand loan*. Cf. *term loan*.

commercial loan. Generally, a loan for 30 to 90 days that a financial institution gives to a business.

consolidation loan. A loan whose proceeds are used to pay off other individual loans, thereby creating a more manageable debt.

consumer loan. A loan that is given to an individual for family, household, personal, or agricultural purposes and that is generally governed by truth-in- lending statutes and regulations.

home equity loan. A line of bank credit given to a homeowner, using as collateral the homeowner's equity in the home. —Often shortened to *equity loan*. See EQUITY (7).

installment loan. A loan that is to be repaid in usu. equal portions over a specified time period.

interest-free loan. Money loaned to a borrower at no charge or, under the Internal Revenue Code, with a charge that is lower than the market rate. I.R.C. § 7872. —Also termed (in the I.R.C.) *below-market loan*.

nonperforming loan. An outstanding loan that is not being repaid.

nonrecourse loan. A secured loan that allows the lender to attach only the collateral, not the borrower's personal assets, if the loan is not repaid.

participation loan. A loan issued by two or more lenders. See LOAN PARTICIPATION.

recourse loan. A loan that allows the lender, if the borrower defaults, not only to attach the collateral but also to seek judgment against the borrower's (or guarantor's) personal assets.

revolver loan. A single loan that a debtor takes out in lieu of several lines of credit or other loans from various creditors, and that is subject to review and approval at certain intervals; a revolver loan is usu. taken out in an attempt to resolve problems with creditors. Cf. *revolving credit* under CREDIT.

secured loan. A loan that is secured by property or securities. —Also termed *collateral loan*.

signature loan. An unsecured loan based solely on the borrower's promise or signature; to obtain such a loan, the borrower must usu. be highly creditworthy.

term loan. A loan with a specified due date, usu. of more than one year; such a loan typically cannot be repaid before maturity without incurring a penalty. —Also termed *time loan.* Cf. *call loan.*

loan, *vb.* LEND.

loan-amortization schedule. A schedule that divides each loan payment into an interest component and a principal component; typically, the interest component begins as the largest part of each payment and declines over time. See AMORTIZATION (1).

loan certificate. A certificate that a clearinghouse issues to a borrowing bank in an amount equal to a specified percentage of the value of the borrowing bank's collateral on deposit with the clearinghouse's loan committee.

loan commitment. A lender's binding promise to a borrower to lend a specified amount of money at a certain interest rate, usu. within a specified time period and for a specified purpose (such as buying real estate). See MORTGAGE COMMITMENT.

loaned employee. See *borrowed employee* under EMPLOYEE.

loaned servant. See *borrowed employee* under EMPLOYEE.

loan for consumption. An agreement by which a lender delivers a given quantity of goods to a borrower who consumes them and who is obligated to return not those very goods, but goods of the same quantity, type, and quality.

loan for exchange. A contract by which a lender delivers personal property to a borrower who agrees to return similar property, usu. without compensation for its use.

loan for use. An agreement by which a lender delivers an asset to a borrower who is to use it according to its normal function or according to the agreement, and who must return it when finished using it; no interest is charged.

loan participation. The coming together of multiple lenders to issue a large loan (called a *participation loan*) to one borrower, thereby reducing each lender's individual risk.

loan ratio. LOAN-TO-VALUE RATIO.

loan-receipt agreement. In tort law, a settlement agreement by which the defendant lends money to the plaintiff interest-free, the plaintiff not being obligated to repay the loan unless he or she recovers money from other tortfeasors responsible for the same injury.

loansharking, *n.* The practice of lending money at excessive and esp. usurious rates, and threatening or using extortion to enforce repayment. —Also termed *extortionate credit transaction.* —**loan shark,** *n.*

loan-to-value ratio. The ratio, usu. expressed as a percentage, between the amount of a mortgage loan and the value of the property pledged as security for the mortgage; for example, an $80,000 loan on property worth $100,000 results in a loan-to-value ratio of 80%—which is usu. the highest ratio lenders will agree to without requiring the debtor to buy mortgage insurance. —Often shortened to *LTV ratio.* —Also termed *loan ratio.*

loan value. The maximum amount that can be safely lent on property or life insurance without damaging the lender's right to protection if the borrower defaults.

lobby, *vb.* **1.** To talk with a legislator, often in a luxurious setting, in an attempt to influence his or her vote <she routinely lobbies for tort reform in the state legislature>. **2.** To support or oppose (a measure) by working to influence a legislator's vote <the organization lobbied the bill through the Senate>. **3.** To try to influence (a decision-maker) <the lumber industry lobbied Senator Packwood at Skamania Lodge, in southern Washington>. —**lobbying,** *n.*—**lobbyist,** *n.*

local action. See ACTION.

local agent. See AGENT.

local and special legislation. See LEGISLATION.

local government. A governing body at a lower level than the state government, such as one carrying out political and legal affairs at the city or county level.

local law. 1. A law that relates to or operates in a particular locality instead of the entire state. **2.** A law that applies only to particular persons or things rather than the entire class of persons or things. **3.** The law of a state having jurisdiction, as opposed to the law of a foreign state. —Also termed *internal law.* **4.** The body of standards, principles, and rules—excluding rules concerning the conflict of laws—that the courts of a state apply.

local option. An option that allows a municipality or other governmental unit to determine a particular course of action without the specific approval of state officials. —Also termed *local veto.* Cf. HOME RULE.

local rule. 1. A rule based on the physical conditions of a state and the character, customs, and beliefs of its people. **2.** A rule by which an individual court supplements the procedural rules applying generally to all courts within the jurisdiction; examples of local rules are a rule requiring extra copies of motions to be filed with the court, or a rule prohibiting the reading of newspapers in the courtroom.

local veto. LOCAL OPTION.

local union. See UNION.

location. 1. A specific place or position where a person or thing is. **2.** The act or process of locating. **3.** In real-estate law, the designation of the boundaries of a particular piece of land, either on the record or on the land itself. **4.** In mining law, the act of appropriating a mining claim; the claim so appropriated. See MINING CLAIM.

Lochnerize (lok-nər-Iz), *vb.* To examine and strike down economic legislation under the guise of enforcing the Due Process Clause, esp. in the manner of the U.S. Supreme Court during the early 20th century; the term takes its name from the infamous decision in *Lochner v. New York*, 198 U.S. 45 (1905), in which the Court invalidated New York's maximum-hours law for bakers. — **Lochnerization,** *n.*

lockbox. 1. A secure box, such as a post-office box, strongbox, or safe-deposit box. **2.** A facility offered by a financial institution for quickly collecting and consolidating checks and other funds from a party's customers.

lockdown. The temporary confinement of prisoners in their cells during a state of heightened alert caused by an escape, riot, or other emergency.

locked-in rate. See *lock rate* under INTEREST RATE.

lockout. 1. An employer's withholding of work and closing of a business because of a labor dispute. **2.** Loosely, an employee's refusal to work because the employer unreasonably refuses to abide by an expired employment contract while a new one is being negotiated. Cf. STRIKE.

lock rate. See INTEREST RATE.

lockup, *n.* **1.** JAIL. **2.** *Jargon.* In corporate law, a defensive measure that allows a friendly suitor to purchase securities—or an entire division—when a hostile takeover is threatened.

loco parentis. See IN LOCO PARENTIS.

locus (loh-kəs). [Latin "place"] The place where or position at which something is done or exists. —Abbr. L. See SITUS.

locus contractus (loh-kəs-kən-trak-təs). [Latin "place of the contract"] The place where a contract is made. Cf. LEX LOCI CONTRACTUS.

locus delicti (loh-kəs-də-**lik**-tI). [Latin "place of the wrong"] The place where an offense is committed; the place where the last event necessary to making the actor liable occurs. Cf. LEX LOCI DELICTI.

locus in quo (loh-kəs-in-**kwoh**). [Latin "place in which"] The place where something is alleged to have been done.

locus poenitentiae (loh-kəs-pen-i-**ten**-shee-I). [Latin "place of penitence"] A point at which it is not too late for a person to change his or her legal position; the possibility of withdrawing from a contemplated course of action, esp. a wrong, before being committed to it.

locus sigilli (loh-kəs-sə-**ji**-lI). See L.S.

locus standi (loh-kəs-**stan**-dee *or* -dI). [Latin "place of standing"] The right to bring an action or to be heard in a given forum; STANDING.

lodestar. 1. A guiding star; an inspiration or model. **2.** *Jargon.* A reasonable amount of attorney's fees in a given case, usu. calculated by multiplying a reasonable number of hours worked by the prevailing hourly rate in the community for similar work, and often considering such additional factors as the degree of skill and difficulty involved in the case, the degree of its urgency, its novelty, and the like; most statutes that authorize an award of attorney's fees use the lodestar method for computing the award.

logical positivism. A philosophical system or movement involving formal verification of empirical questions. Cf. LEGAL POSITIVISM.

logrolling, *n.* **1.** The exchanging of political favors; esp., the trading of votes among legislators to gain support of measures that are beneficial to each legislator's constituency. **2.** The legislative practice of including several propositions in one measure or proposed constitutional amendment so that the legislature or voters will pass all of them, even though these propositions might not have passed if they had been submitted separately; many state constitutions have single-subject provisions that prohibit this practice. —**logroll,** *vb.*

loitering, *n.* The criminal offense of remaining in a certain place (such as a public street) for no apparent reason; loitering statutes are generally held to be unconstitutionally vague. —**loiter,** *vb.* Cf. VAGRANCY.

London Lloyd's. LLOYD'S OF LONDON.

long-arm statute. A statute providing for the maintenance of jurisdiction over nonresident defendants who have had contacts with the territory where the statute is in effect; most state long-arm statutes extend this jurisdiction to its constitutional limits.

long-term debt. See DEBT.

long-term security. See SECURITY.

look-and-feel protection. Copyright protection of the images generated or revealed when one activates a computer program.

lookout, *n.* A careful, vigilant watching <the motorist's statutory duty of proper lookout>.

loophole. An ambiguity, omission, or exception (as in a statute or other legal document) that provides a means of avoiding a rule without violating its literal requirements; esp., a tax-code provision that allows a taxpayer to legally avoid or reduce income taxes.

loopification, *n.* In critical legal studies, the collapse of a legal distinction resulting when the two ends of a continuum become so similar that they become indistinguishable <it may be impossible to distinguish "public" from "private" because of loopification>. —**loopify,** *vb.*

loose construction. See *liberal construction* under CONSTRUCTION.

lord. 1. A title of honor or nobility belonging properly to a baron but applied also to anyone who attains the rank of a peer. —Abbr. L. **2.** (*cap. & pl.*) HOUSE OF LORDS. **3.** A property owner whose land is in a tenant's possession; LANDLORD (1).

Lord Campbell's Act. 1. The 1846 English statute that created a wrongful-death claim for the relatives of a decedent when the decedent would have had a claim if he or she had been merely injured and not killed. **2.** An American state's wrongful-death statute patterned after the original English act.

Lord Langdale's Act. WILLS ACT (2).

Lord Mansfield's rule. The principle that neither spouse may testify about whether the husband had access to the wife at the time of a child's conception; in effect, this rule—which has been abandoned by many states—made it impossible to bastardize a child born during a marriage.

Lord Tenterden's rule. EJUSDEM GENERIS.

loser-pays rule. ENGLISH RULE.

loss. 1. The failure to keep possession (of something); the thing so lost. **2.** A decrease in value; the amount by which a thing's original cost exceeds its subsequent selling price. **3.** The amount of financial detriment caused by an insured person's death or an insured property's damage, for which the insurer becomes liable.

actual loss. A loss resulting from the real and substantial destruction of insured property.

capital loss. The loss realized upon selling or exchanging a capital asset.

casualty loss. For tax purposes, the total or partial destruction of an asset resulting from an unexpected or unusual event, such as an automobile accident or a tornado.

consequential loss. A loss arising from the results of damage rather than from the damage itself. Cf. *direct loss.*

constructive loss. A loss resulting from injuries that, while not destroying the property, render it worthless to the insured or prevent its restoration except at a cost exceeding its value.

direct loss. A loss that results immediately and proximately from an event. Cf. *consequential loss.*

disaster loss. A casualty loss sustained in a geographic area that the President designates as a disaster area; it may be treated as having occurred during the previous tax year so that a victim may receive immediate tax benefits.

net loss. The excess of all expenses and losses over all revenues and gains.

net operating loss. The excess of operating expenses over revenues, which amount can be deducted from gross income if other deductions do not exceed gross income. —Abbr. NOL.

ordinary loss. In tax law, a loss incurred from the sale or exchange of an item that is used in a trade or business.

out-of-pocket loss. The difference between the value of what the buyer paid and the market value of what was received in return; in breach-of-contract cases, out-of-pocket loss is used to measure restitution damages.

paper loss. A loss that is realized only by selling something (such as a security) that has decreased in market value. —Also termed *unrealized loss.*

passive loss. A loss, with limited tax deductibility, from an activity in which the taxpayer does not materially participate, a rental activity, or a tax-shelter activity.

pecuniary loss. A loss of money or of something having monetary value.

salvage loss. **a.** Generally, a loss that presumptively would have been a total loss if certain services had not been rendered. **b.** In marine underwriting, the difference between the salvage value, less the charges, and the original value of the insured property.

loss carryback. See CARRYBACK.

loss carryover. See CARRYOVER.

loss leader. A good or commodity sold at a very low price, usu. below cost, to attract customers to buy other items. See BAIT AND SWITCH.

loss-of-bargain damages. See *expectation damages* under DAMAGES.

loss-of-bargain rule. The doctrine that damages for breach of a contract should put the injured party in the position it would have been in if both parties had performed their contractual duties.

loss of consortium. A loss of the interests that one spouse is entitled to receive from the other, including companionship, cooperation, affection, aid, and sexual relations; such a loss can be recoverable as damages in a personal-injury or wrongful-death action.

loss-payable clause. An insurance-policy provision that authorizes payment of proceeds to someone other than the named insured, esp. to someone with a security interest in the insured property; typically, a loss-payable clause either designates the person as a beneficiary of the

proceeds or assigns to the person a claim against the insurer, but the clause usu. does not treat the person as an additional insured. See MORTGAGE CLAUSE.

loss payee. A person or entity named in an insurance policy (under a loss-payable clause) to be paid if the insured property suffers a loss.

loss ratio. 1. In insurance, the ratio between premiums paid and losses incurred during a given period. **2.** In finance, a bank's loan losses compared to its loan assets; a business's receivable losses compared to its receivables.

loss reserve. The portion of a company's (esp. an insurer's) assets set aside for paying probable losses, or losses incurred but not yet paid.

lost earning capacity. A person's diminished earning power resulting from an injury; this impairment is recoverable as an element of damages in a tort action. Cf. *lost earnings* under EARNINGS.

lost earnings. See EARNINGS.

lost-expectation damages. See *expectation damages* under DAMAGES.

lost profits. A measure of damages that allows a seller to collect the profit that would have been made on the sale if the buyer had not breached. U.C.C. § 2-708(2).

lost property. See PROPERTY.

lost-volume seller. A seller of goods who, after a buyer has breached a sales contract, resells the goods to a different buyer who would have bought identical goods from the seller's inventory even if the original buyer had not breached; such a seller is entitled to lost profits, rather than contract price less market price, as damages from the original buyer's breach. U.C.C. § 2-708(2).

lost will. See WILL.

lot. 1. A tract of land, esp. one having specific boundaries or being used for a given purpose.

minimum lot. A lot that has the least amount of square footage allowed by local zoning laws.

nonconforming lot. A previously lawful lot that now violates newly adopted, revised, or amended zoning ordinances.

2. A parcel or article that is the subject of a separate sale or delivery, whether or not it is sufficient to perform the contract. U.C.C. § 2-105(5). **3.** In the securities and commodities market, a specified number of shares or a specific quantity of a commodity designated for trading.

odd lot. An amount of stocks or bonds that is less than a round lot.

round lot. The established unit of trading for stocks and bonds; a round lot of stock is usu. 100 shares, and a round lot of bonds is usu. $1000 or $5000 par value. — Also termed *even lot.*

lot line. A land boundary that separates one tract from another <from the street to the alley, the lot line is 150 feet>.

lottery. A method of raising revenues, esp. state-government revenues, by selling tickets and giving prizes (usu. large cash prizes) to those who hold tickets bearing winning numbers that are drawn at random. —Also termed *lotto.*

lower chamber. See CHAMBER.

lower court. 1. See *court below* under COURT. **2.** See *inferior court* under COURT.

lower-of-cost-or-market method. A means of inventory-costing that sets the inventory value at acquisition cost or market cost, whichever is lower.

lowest responsible bidder. A bidder who has the lowest price conforming to the contract specifications and who is financially able and competent to complete the work, as shown by the bidder's prior performance.

loyalty oath. See *oath of allegiance* under OATH.

L.P. See *limited partnership* under PARTNERSHIP.

L.R. *abbr.* Law Reports.

L.S. *abbr.* [Latin *locus sigilli* "the place of the seal"] The traditional letters appearing on many notarial certificates to indicate where the notary public's embossed seal should be placed; if a rubber-stamp seal is used, it should be placed near but not over this abbreviation. See NOTARY SEAL.

Ltd. *abbr.* Limited—used in company names to indicate limited liability.

LTV ratio. LOAN-TO-VALUE RATIO.

lucrative bailment. See *bailment for hire* under BAILMENT.

lucri causa (loo-kree-kaw-zə). [Latin] For the sake of gain; *lucri causa* was formerly an essential element of larceny, but today the thief's intent to deprive the owner of property is generally sufficient. See LARCENY.

lumping sale. See SALE.

lump-sum alimony. See *alimony in gross* under ALIMONY.

lump-sum payment. See PAYMENT.

luxury tax. See TAX.

lynch, *vb.* To hang (a person) by mob action without legal authority.

lynch law. The administration of summary punishment, esp. death, for an alleged crime, without legal authority.

lying in wait. Hiding for the purpose of ambushing a person expected to arrive at the scene; in murder cases, lying in wait can demonstrate the defendant's premeditation.

M

M1. A measure of the money supply including cash, checking accounts, and travelers' checks.

M2. A measure of the money supply including M1 items, plus savings and time deposits, money-market accounts, and overnight-repurchase agreements.

M3. A measure of the money supply including M2 items, plus large time deposits and money-market funds held by institutions.

MACRS. *abbr.* MODIFIED ACCELERATED COST-RECOVERY SYSTEM.

Mafia. ORGANIZED CRIME.

magisterial precinct. A county subdivision that defines the territorial jurisdiction of a magistrate, constable, or justice of the peace. —Also termed *magisterial district*.

magistracy (**maj**-ə-strə-see). **1.** The office, district, or power of a magistrate. **2.** A body of magistrates.

magistrate (**maj**-ə-strayt), *n.* **1.** The highest ranking official in a government, such as the king in a monarchy, the president in a republic, or the governor in a state. —Also termed *chief magistrate; first magistrate*. **2.** A local official who possesses whatever power is specified in the appointment or statutory grant of authority. **3.** A judicial officer with strictly limited jurisdiction and authority, often on the local level and often restricted to criminal cases. Cf. JUSTICE OF THE PEACE. —**magisterial** (maj-ə-**stir**-ee-əl), *adj.*

committing magistrate. An inferior judicial officer who has the authority to conduct a preliminary criminal hearing and release the defendant for lack of evidence, send him or her to jail to await trial, or, in some jurisdictions, release him or her on bail. See *examining court* under COURT.

police magistrate. An inferior judicial officer who has jurisdiction of minor criminal offenses, breaches of police regulations, and similar violations.

U.S. Magistrate. UNITED STATES MAGISTRATE JUDGE.

Magistrate Judge, U.S. See UNITED STATES MAGISTRATE JUDGE.

magistrate's court. See COURT.

Magna Carta. [Latin "great charter"] The English charter that King John granted to the barons in 1215 and that Henry III and Edward I later confirmed; the Magna Carta is generally regarded as one of the great common-law documents and as the foundation of constitutional liberties. —Also spelled *Magna Charta*.

Magnuson-Moss Warranty Act. A federal statute requiring that a written warranty of a consumer product fully and conspicuously disclose, in plain language, the terms and conditions of the warranty, including whether the warranty is full or limited, according to standards given in the statute. 15 U.S.C. §§ 2301 et seq.

mail, *n.* **1.** An item that has been properly addressed, stamped with postage, and deposited for delivery in the postal system. **2.** An official system for delivering such items; the postal system.

certified mail. Mail for which the sender requests proof of delivery in the form of a receipt signed by the addressee; if this receipt is returned to the sender, the service is called *certified mail—return receipt requested.*

registered mail. Mail that the U.S. Post Office records at the time of mailing and at each point on its route so as to guarantee safe delivery.

mailbox rule. In contract law, the rule that an acceptance becomes effective—and binds the offeror—once it is properly mailed; the mailbox rule does not apply, however, if the offer states that an acceptance is not effective until received.

mail-order divorce. See DIVORCE.

maim, *n. Archaic.* The type of injury required for the commission of mayhem. —**maim,** *vb.* See MAYHEM.

main opinion. See *majority opinion* under OPINION (1).

main-purpose rule. In contract law, the doctrine holding that if the main purpose behind a promise to guarantee another's debt is the promisor's own benefit, then the statute of frauds does not apply and the promise does not have to be in writing. —Also termed *main-purpose doctrine*; *leading-object rule.*

maintenance, *n.* **1.** The care and work put into property to keep it operating and productive; general repair and upkeep. **2.** ALIMONY. **3.** Assistance in prosecuting or defending a lawsuit given to a litigant by someone who has no bona fide interest in the case; meddling in someone else's litigation. Cf. CHAMPERTY. —**maintainor** (corresponding to sense 3), *n.*

maintenance and cure. In maritime law, compensation given to a sailor who gets sick or is injured while working on a vessel.

maintenance assessment. See ASSESSMENT.

maintenance call. See CALL.

maintenance fee. See *maintenance assessment* under ASSESSMENT.

maintenance margin requirement. See MARGIN REQUIREMENT.

major, *n.* ADULT.

major-and-minor fault rule. MAJOR-MINOR FAULT RULE.

major crime. FELONY.

majority. 1. The status of one who has attained the age of majority (usu. 18). See AGE OF MAJORITY. Cf. MINORITY (1). **2.** A number that is more than half of a total; a group of more than 50 percent <the candidate received 50.4 percent of the votes— barely a majority>. Cf. PLURALITY; MINORITY (2).

absolute majority. A majority of all those who are entitled to vote in a particular election, whether or not they actually cast a ballot. See QUORUM.

simple majority. A majority of those who actually vote in a particular election.

supermajority. A majority substantially greater than 50 percent; such a majority is needed for certain extraordinary actions, such as ratification of a constitutional amendment or of a fundamental corporate change. —Also termed *extraordinary majority*.

majority-consent procedure. In corporate law, a statutory provision allowing shareholders to avoid a shareholders' meeting and to act instead by written consent of the holders of a majority of shares; Delaware and a few other states have enacted such procedures.

majority opinion. See OPINION (1).

majority rule. 1. A political principle that a majority of a group has the power to make decisions that are binding on that group; it is governance by the majority of those who actually participate, regardless of the number entitled to participate. **2.** In corporate law, the common-law principle that a director or officer owes no fiduciary duty to a shareholder with respect to stock transactions; the principle has been restricted by both federal insider-trading rules and state-law doctrines. Cf. SPECIAL-FACTS RULE.

majority shareholder. See SHARE-HOLDER.

majority voting. See VOTING.

major-minor fault rule. In maritime law, the principle that if the fault of one vessel in a collision is uncontradicted and sufficient to account for the accident, then the other vessel is presumed not to have been at fault and therefore not to have contributed to the accident. —Also termed *major-and-minor fault rule*.

maker. 1. One who frames, promulgates, or ordains (as in *lawmaker*). **2.** A person who makes a promise in a promissory note by signing it. See NOTE (1). Cf. COMAKER. **3.** DRAWER.

mala fides (**mal**-ə-**fī**-deez), *n.* BAD FAITH.

malapportionment, *n.* The improper or unconstitutional apportionment of legislative districts. —**malapportion,** *vb.* See APPORTIONMENT; GERRYMANDERING.

malconduct in office. See *official misconduct* under MISCONDUCT.

malefaction (mal-ə-**fak**-shən), *n.* [Latin *malefacere* "to do evil"] *Archaic.* An evil deed; offense; crime. —**malefactory,** *adj.*—**malefactor,** *n.*

malfeasance (mal-**feez**-[ə]n[t]s), *n.* A wrongful or unlawful act; esp., wrongdoing or misconduct by a public official. —**malfeasant,** *adj.*—**malfeasor,** *n.* Cf. MISFEASANCE; NONFEASANCE.

malice, *n.* **1.** The intent, without justification or excuse, to commit a wrongful act. **2.** Reckless disregard of the law or of a person's legal rights. **3.** Ill will; wickedness of heart—this sense is most typical in nonlegal contexts. —**malicious,** *adj.*

actual malice. The deliberate intent to commit an injury, as evidenced by external circumstances. —Also termed *express malice; malice in fact.* Cf. *implied malice.*

express malice. **a.** In criminal law, the intent to kill or seriously injure arising from a deliberate, rational mind. **b.** See *actual malice.* **c.** In defamation law, the bad-faith publication of defamatory material.

implied malice. Malice inferred from a person's conduct. —Also termed *constructive malice; legal malice; malice in law.* Cf. *actual malice.*

particular malice. Malice that is directed at a particular person. — Also termed *special malice.*

universal malice. The state of mind of a person who determines to take life on slight provocation, without knowing or caring who may be the victim.

malice aforethought. The requisite mental state for common-law murder, encompassing any one of the following: (1) the intent to kill, (2) the intent to inflict grievous bodily harm, (3) extremely reckless indifference to the value of human life (the so-called "abandoned and malignant heart"), or (4) the intent to commit a felony (which leads to culpability under the felony-murder rule). —Also termed *premeditated malice*; *preconceived malice.*

malice in fact. See *actual malice* under MALICE.

malice in law. See *implied malice* under MALICE.

malicious abuse of process. The improper and tortious use of a legitimately issued court process to obtain a result that is either unlawful or beyond the process's scope. —Often shortened to *abuse of process.* Cf. MALICIOUS PROSECUTION.

malicious arrest. See ARREST.

malicious injury. See INJURY.

malicious mischief. The common-law misdemeanor of intentionally destroying or damaging another's property. —Also termed *malicious mischief and trespass*; *malicious injury*; *malicious trespass*; *maliciously damaging the property of another*, and (in the Model Penal Code) *criminal mischief.*

malicious prosecution. The institution of criminal or civil proceedings for an improper purpose and without probable cause; once the prosecution has been terminated in his or her favor, the accused may sue for tort damages. —Also termed (in the context of civil proceedings) *malicious use of process.* Cf. MALICIOUS ABUSE OF PROCESS.

malicious trespass. MALICIOUS MISCHIEF.

malicious use of process. See MALICIOUS PROSECUTION.

Mallory **rule.** MCNABB-MALLORY RULE.

malpractice. Negligence or incompetence on the part of a professional; an instance of this.

legal malpractice. A lawyer's failure to render professional services with the skill, prudence, and diligence that an ordinary and reasonable lawyer would use under similar circumstances. —Also termed *attorney malpractice.*

medical malpractice. A tort that arises when a doctor violates the standard of care owed to a patient and the patient is injured as a result. —Often shortened to *med. mal.*

malpractice insurance. See INSURANCE.

malum (mal-əm), *adj.* [Latin] Wrong; evil.

malum in se (ma-ləm-in-say), *n.* [Latin "evil in itself"] A crime or an act that is inherently immoral, such as murder, arson, or rape. Pl. *mala*

in se.—malum in se, *adj.* Cf. MA-
LUM PROHIBITUM.

malum prohibitum (ma-ləm-proh-
hib-i-təm), *n.* [Latin "prohibited
evil"] An act that is a crime merely
because it is prohibited by statute,
although the act itself is not necessarily immoral; misdemeanors such
as jaywalking and running a stop-
light are *mala prohibita,* as are most
securities-law violations. Pl. *mala
prohibita.—malum prohibitum,*
adj. Cf. MALUM IN SE.

management buyout. See BUYOUT.

manager. **1.** A person who administers or supervises the affairs of a
business, office, or other organization. **2.** A legislator appointed by either legislative house to serve on a
conference committee, esp. a joint
committee that tries to reconcile differences in a bill passed by both
houses in different versions. —Also
termed *conferee.* **3.** A representative
appointed by the House to prosecute
impeachments before the Senate.

managing agent. See AGENT.

M & A. *abbr.* Mergers and acquisi-
tions. See MERGER.

mandamus (man-**day**-məs), *n.* [Lat-
in "we command"] A writ issued by a
superior court to compel a lower
court or a government officer to perform mandatory or purely ministerial
duties correctly. —Also termed *writ
of mandamus.* Pl. **mandamuses.** —
mandamus, *vb.*

mandatary (**man**-də-ter-ee), *n.* **1.** A
person to whom a mandate is given.
2. An agent, esp. one who acts gratuitously. —Also termed (in Roman
law) *mandatarius.* —**mandatary,**
adj.

mandate, *n.* **1.** An order from an
appellate court directing a lower
court to take a specified action. **2.** A
judicial command directed to an officer of the court to enforce a court
order. **3.** In politics, the electorate's
overwhelming show of approval for a
given political platform. **4.** In civil
law, a written command given by a
principal to an agent. **5.** In civil law,
a commission by which one person
(the *mandator*) requests someone
(the *mandatary*) to perform some
service gratuitously, the commission
becoming effective when the mandatary agrees. —Also termed *manda-
tum.* **6.** *Archaic.* In international law,
an authority given by the League of
Nations to certain governments to
take over the administration and development of certain territories. Cf.
TRUSTEESHIP (2). —**mandate,** *vb.*—
mandatory, *adj.*

mandator. **1.** A person who delegates the performance of a mandate
to another. **2.** In civil law, the person
who employs a mandatary.

mandatory injunction. See IN-
JUNCTION.

mandatory instruction. See JURY
INSTRUCTION.

mandatory joinder. See *compulsory joinder* under JOINDER.

mandatory penalty. See *mandatory
sentence* under SENTENCE.

mandatory presumption. See *conclusive presumption* under PRESUMP-
TION.

mandatory punishment. See *mandatory sentence* under SENTENCE.

mandatory sentence. See SEN-
TENCE.

mandatory statute. See STATUTE.

mandatum. MANDATE (5).

manifest, *n.* A document listing the cargo or passengers carried on a ship, plane, or other vehicle.

manifest necessity. In criminal procedure, a sudden and overwhelming emergency, beyond the court's and parties' control, that makes conducting a trial or reaching a fair result impossible and that therefore authorizes the granting of a mistrial; the termination of a trial for manifest necessity precludes the defendant from successfully raising a plea of former jeopardy.

manifesto. A written statement publicly declaring the issuer's principles, policies, or intentions; esp., a formal document explaining why a state or nation declared war or took some other significant international action.

manipulation. In securities law, the illegal practice of raising or lowering a security's price by creating the appearance of active trading; manipulation is prohibited by Section 10(b) of the Securities Exchange Act of 1934. 15 U.S.C. § 78j.

manslaughter, *n.* The unlawful killing of a human being without malice aforethought. —**manslaughter,** *vb.* Cf. MURDER.

involuntary manslaughter. Homicide in which there is no intention to kill or do grievous bodily harm, but that is committed with criminal negligence or during the commission of an unlawful act (i.e., a misdemeanor or a felony not included within the felony-murder rule).

voluntary manslaughter. An act of murder reduced to manslaughter because of extenuating circumstances such as adequate provocation—arousing the "heat of passion"—or diminished capacity. — Also termed *intentional manslaughter.*

manual-rating insurance. See INSURANCE.

manufactured diversity. See DIVERSITY OF CITIZENSHIP.

manufacturing defect. See DEFECT.

march-in rights. In patent law, the government's right to step in and grant a new license or revoke an existing license if the owner of a federally funded invention (or the owner's licensee) has not adequately developed or applied the invention within a reasonable time. 35 U.S.C. § 203.

margin, *n.* **1.** A boundary or edge. **2.** A measure or degree of difference. **3.** PROFIT MARGIN. **4.** The difference between a loan's face value and the market value of the collateral that secures the loan. **5.** Cash or collateral paid to a securities broker by an investor to protect the broker against losses from securities bought on credit. **6.** The amount of an investor's equity in securities bought on credit through the broker. —**margin,** *vb.*— **marginal, margined,** *adj.*

marginable security. See SECURITY.

margin account. See ACCOUNT.

marginal cost. See COST.

marginal revenue. See REVENUE.

marginal tax rate. See TAX RATE.

margin call. See CALL.

margined security. See SECURITY.

margin requirement. In securities transactions, the percentage of the purchase price that a buyer must deposit with a broker to buy a security on margin.

initial margin requirement. The minimum percentage of the purchase price that a buyer must deposit with a broker; the Federal Reserve Board establishes minimum margin requirements in order to prevent excessive speculation and price volatility.

maintenance margin requirement. The minimum equity that a buyer must keep in a margin account, expressed as a percentage of the account value.

margin transaction. A securities or commodities transaction made through a broker on a margin account. —Also termed *buying on margin*. See MARGIN (5).

marine insurance. See INSURANCE.

marine interest. MARITIME INTEREST.

mariner's will. See *soldier's will* under WILL.

maritagium. DOWER.

marital agreement. Any agreement between spouses concerning the division and ownership of marital property; esp., a premarital contract or separation agreement that is primarily concerned with dividing marital property in the event of divorce. — Also termed *marriage settlement*; *property settlement*. See PRENUPTIAL AGREEMENT; POSTNUPTIAL AGREEMENT.

marital-communications privilege. See *marital privilege* (a) under PRIVILEGE.

marital deduction. See DEDUCTION.

marital privilege. See PRIVILEGE.

marital property. See PROPERTY.

marital rape. See RAPE.

maritime (mar-i-tIm *or* **mer-**), *adj.* **1.** Connected with or situated near the ocean. **2.** Of or relating to sea navigation or commerce.

maritime court. ADMIRALTY (1).

maritime interest. Interest charged on a loan secured by a sea vessel or its cargo, or both; because of the lender's considerable risk, the interest rate may be extraordinarily high. —Also termed *marine interest*.

maritime law. The body of law governing marine commerce and navigation, the transportation at sea of persons and property, and marine affairs in general. —Also termed *admiralty*; *admiralty law*. Cf. LAW OF THE SEA.

maritime lien. See LIEN.

maritime tort. See TORT.

mark, *n.* **1.** TRADEMARK (1). **2.** SERVICEMARK.

market, *n.* **1.** A place of commercial activity in which goods or services are bought and sold <the farmers' market>. **2.** A geographic area or demographic segment considered as a place of demand for a particular good or service <the foreign market for microchips>. **3.** The opportunity for buying and selling goods or services;

the extent of economic demand <a slow job market for lawyers>. **4.** A securities or commodities exchange <the stock market closed early because of the blizzard>. **5.** The business of such an exchange; the enterprise of buying and selling securities or commodities <the stock market is approaching an all-time high>. **6.** The price at which the buyer and seller of a security or commodity agree <the market for oil is 16 dollars per barrel>.

bear market. A securities market characterized by falling prices over a prolonged period.

black market. An illegal market for goods that are controlled or prohibited by the government, such as the underground market for prescription drugs.

bull market. A securities market characterized by rising prices over a prolonged period.

buyer's market. A market in which supply exceeds demand, resulting in lowered prices.

capital market. A securities market in which stock and bonds with long-term maturities are traded.

common market. An economic association formed by several nations to reduce trade barriers among them; esp. (usu. cap.), EUROPEAN UNION.

discount market. The portion of the money market in which banks and other financial institutions trade commercial paper.

geographic market. In antitrust law, the part of a relevant market that identifies the physical area in which a firm might compete; if a

firm can raise prices or cut production without causing a quick influx of supply to the area from outside sources, that firm is operating in a distinct geographic market.

gray market. A market in which legal but perhaps unethical methods are used in order to avoid a manufacturer's distribution chain and thereby sell goods (esp. imported goods) at prices lower than those intended by the manufacturer.

market overt. An open, legally regulated public market where buyers, with some exceptions, acquire good title to products regardless of any defects in the seller's title.

money market. The financial market for dealing in short-term negotiable instruments such as commercial paper, certificates of deposit, banker's acceptances, and U.S. Treasury securities.

open market. A market with no competitive restrictions on price or availability of products. —Also termed *free market.*

over-the-counter market. The market for securities that are not traded on an organized exchange; over-the-counter (OTC) trading usu. occurs through telephone or computer negotiations between buyers and sellers, and many of the more actively traded OTC stocks are listed on NASDAQ.

primary market. The market for goods or services that are newly available for buying and selling; esp., the securities market in which new securities are issued by corporations in order to raise capital. —Also termed *original market.*

product market. In antitrust law, the part of a relevant market that applies to a firm's particular product by identifying all reasonable substitutes for the product and by determining whether these substitutes limit the firm's ability to affect prices.

relevant market. In antitrust law, a market that is capable of being monopolized—that is, a market in which a firm can raise prices above the competitive level without losing so many sales that the price increase would be unprofitable; the relevant market includes both the *product market* and the *geographic market.*

secondary market. The market for goods or services that have previously been available for buying and selling; esp., the securities market in which previously issued securities are traded among investors. — Also termed *aftermarket.*

seller's market. A market in which demand exceeds supply, resulting in raised prices.

thin market. A market in which the number of bids or offerings are relatively few.

marketable, *adj.* Of commercially acceptable quality; fit for sale and in demand by buyers. —Also termed *merchantable.* —**marketability,** *n.*

marketable security. See SECURITY.

marketable title. See TITLE.

marketable-title act. A state statute providing that good title to land can be established by searching the public records only back to a speci-

fied time (such as 40 years ago). See *marketable title* under TITLE.

market-making, *n.* The practice of establishing prices for over-the-counter securities by reporting bid-and-asked quotations; a broker-dealer engaged in this practice, which is regulated by both the NASD and the SEC, buys and sells securities as a principal for its own account, and thus accepts two-way bids (both to buy and to sell). —**market-maker,** *n.* See BID AND ASKED.

market order. See ORDER (4).

market overt. See MARKET.

marketplace of ideas. A forum in which expressions of opinion can freely compete for acceptance without governmental restraint; although Justice Oliver Wendell Holmes was the first jurist to discuss the concept as a metaphor for explaining freedom of speech, the phrase *marketplace of ideas* dates in American caselaw from 1954.

market portfolio. See PORTFOLIO.

market power. The ability to reduce output and raise prices above the competitive level—specifically, above marginal cost—for a sustained period, and to make a profit by doing so; in antitrust law, a large amount of market power constitutes monopoly power. See MONOPOLIZATION. Cf. MARKET SHARE.

market price. See PRICE.

market share. The percentage of the market for a product that a firm supplies, usu. calculated by dividing the firm's output by the total market output; in antitrust law, market share is used to measure a firm's market power, and if the share is high enough—generally 70 percent or more—then the firm may be guilty of monopolization. See MONOPOLIZA-TION. Cf. MARKET POWER.

market value. FAIR MARKET VALUE.

markup, *n.* **1.** An amount added to an item's cost to determine its selling price. See PROFIT MARGIN. **2.** A session of a U.S. Congressional committee during which a bill is revised and put into final form before it is reported to the appropriate house.

marque (mahrk). *Archaic.* Reprisal. See LETTERS OF MARQUE.

marriage, *n.* **1.** The legal union of a man and woman as husband and wife.

common-law marriage. A marriage that takes legal effect, without license or ceremony, when a couple live together as husband and wife, intend to be married, and hold themselves out to others as a married couple; common-law marriages are permitted in 14 states and in the District of Columbia. — Also termed *informal marriage.*

marriage of convenience. A marriage contracted for social or financial advantages rather than out of mutual love.

plural marriage. A marriage in which one spouse is already married to someone else; a bigamous or polygamous union.

putative marriage. A marriage in which the husband and wife believe in good faith that they are married, but for some technical reason are not formally married (such as when the ceremonial official was not capable of performing a marriage); putative marriages are usu. treated as valid and do not need to be formalized.

sham marriage. A marriage in which a U.S. citizen marries a foreign citizen for the sole purpose of allowing the foreign citizen to become a permanent U.S. resident; sham marriages are illegal if made with the intent to circumvent immigration law. —Also termed *green-card marriage.*

voidable marriage. A marriage that is initially invalid but that remains in effect unless terminated by court order; for example, a marriage is voidable if either party is underage or otherwise legally incompetent, or if one party used fraud, duress, or force to induce the other party to enter the marriage.

void marriage. A marriage that is invalid from its inception, that cannot be made valid, and that can be terminated by either party without obtaining a divorce or annulment; for example, a marriage is void if the parties are too closely related or if either party is already married.

2. The act or ceremony uniting a husband and wife; a wedding.

ceremonial marriage. A wedding that follows all the statutory requirements and that has been solemnized before a religious or civil official.

civil marriage. A wedding ceremony conducted by a governmental official, such as a judge, or by some other authorized person—as distinguished from one solemnized by a member of the clergy.

proxy marriage. A wedding in which someone stands in for an absent bride or groom, such as when one party is stationed overseas in the military; proxy marriages are prohibited in most states.

marriage article. A premarital stipulation between spouses who intend to incorporate the stipulation in a postnuptial agreement.

marriage broker. One who arranges a marriage in exchange for consideration; such a person may be subject to criminal liability for public-policy reasons.

marriage ceremony. The religious or civil proceeding that solemnizes a marriage. —Also termed *wedding*.

marriage certificate. A document that is executed by the religious or civil official presiding at a marriage ceremony and filed with a public authority (usu. the county clerk) as evidence of the marriage.

marriage license. A document, issued by a public authority, that grants a couple permission to get legally married; most states require the couple to take blood tests before obtaining the license.

marriage of convenience. See MARRIAGE (1).

marriage settlement. MARITAL AGREEMENT.

marshal, *n.* **1.** A law-enforcement officer with duties similar to those of a sheriff. **2.** A judicial officer who provides court security, executes process, and performs other tasks for the court. —**marshalship,** *n.*

United States Marshal. A federal official who carries out the orders of a federal court; U.S. Marshals are members of the executive branch of government.

marshal, *vb.* To arrange or rank in order <the brief effectively marshaled the appellant's arguments>.

marshaling assets, rule of. See RULE OF MARSHALING ASSETS.

martial law (**mahr**-shəl). A body of rules applied on grounds of necessity by a country's rulers when the civil government has failed or appears as if it might fail to function; the military assumes control and enforces these rules purportedly until civil processes and courts can be restored to their lawful places. Cf. MILITARY LAW.

Mary Carter agreement. A contract by which one codefendant settles with the plaintiff and obtains a release, along with a provision granting that codefendant a portion of any recovery the plaintiff may receive from one or more other defendants; such an agreement is void as against public policy in some states but valid in others if disclosed to the jury. *Booth v. Mary Carter Paint Co.*, 202 So.2d 8 (Fla. Dist. Ct.App.1967).

masking, *n.* In critical legal studies, the act or an instance of concealing something's true nature <being a crit, she contends that the legal system is merely an elaborate masking of social injustices>. —**mask,** *vb.*

Massachusetts trust. See *business trust* under TRUST.

mass tort. See TORT.

master, *n.* **1.** *Archaic.* One who has personal authority over another's services; EMPLOYER <the law of master and servant>. **2.** A parajudicial officer (such as a referee, an auditor, an examiner, or an assessor) specially appointed to help a court with its proceedings; among the functions a master may perform are taking testimony, computing interest, valuing annuities, investigating encumbrances on land titles, and the like—virtually always with a written report to the court <in some states, a master will preside over uncontested divorces>. Fed. R. Civ. P. 53.

special master. A master appointed to assist the court with a particular matter or case.

standing master. A master appointed to assist the court on an ongoing basis.

master agreement. In labor law, an agreement between a union and industry leaders, the terms of which serve as a model for agreements between the union and individual companies within the industry.

master lease. See LEASE.

master limited partnership. See PARTNERSHIP.

Master of Laws. A law degree conferred on those completing graduate-level legal study. —Abbr. LL.M. Cf. JURIS DOCTOR.

master plan. In land-use law, a municipal plan for housing, industry, and recreation facilities, including the projected environmental impact. See PLANNED-UNIT DEVELOPMENT.

master policy. See INSURANCE POLICY.

master-servant rule. RESPONDEAT SUPERIOR.

material, *adj.* **1.** Of or relating to matter; physical <material goods>. **2.** Having some logical connection with the consequential facts <material evidence>. **3.** Significant; essential <material alteration of the document>. —**materiality,** *n.* Cf. RELEVANT.

material allegation. See ALLEGATION.

material breach. See BREACH OF CONTRACT.

material evidence. See EVIDENCE.

material fact. See FACT.

materialman's lien. See *mechanic's lien* under LIEN.

material representation. See REPRESENTATION.

material witness. See WITNESS.

maternal, *adj.* Of, relating to, or coming from one's mother <maternal property>. Cf. PATERNAL.

maternal line. See LINE.

mathematical evidence. See EVIDENCE.

matricide (**ma-trə-sId**), *n.* **1.** The act of killing one's own mother. **2.** One who kills his or her mother. —**matricidal,** *adj.*

matrimonial action. See ACTION.

matrimonial cohabitation. See COHABITATION.

matrimonial domicile. See DOMICILE.

matrimonial home. See *matrimonial domicile* under DOMICILE.

matrimonial res. The marriage state. See RES.

matrimony, *n.* The act or state of being married; MARRIAGE. —**matrimonial,** *adj.*

matter, *n.* **1.** A subject under consideration, esp. involving a dispute or litigation; CASE (1) <this is the only matter on the court's docket today>. **2.** Something that is to be tried or proved; an allegation forming the basis of a claim or defense <the matters raised in the plaintiff's complaint are not actionable under state law>.

matter of fact. A matter involving a judicial inquiry about the truth of alleged facts.

matter of law. A matter involving a judicial inquiry about the correctness of legal procedure.

matter of record. A matter that has been entered on judicial or other public records and therefore can be proved by producing those records.

new matter. A matter not previously raised by either party in the pleadings, usu. involving new issues with new facts to be proved.

special matter. In common-law pleading, out-of-the-ordinary evidence that a defendant is allowed to enter, after notice to the plaintiff, under a plea of the general issue.

matter of. See IN RE.

mature, *vb.* (Of a debt or obligation) to become due <the bond matures in ten years>. —**maturity,** *n.*—**mature,** *adj.*

matured claim. See CLAIM (2).

maturity date. See DATE OF MATURITY.

maturity value. The amount that is due and payable on an obligation's maturity date.

maugre (**maw**-gər), *prep. Archaic.* Despite <the witness may testify maugre counsel's objection>.

maxim (**mak**-sim). A traditional legal principle that has been frozen into a concise expression; examples are "possession is nine-tenths of the law" and *caveat emptor* ("let the buyer beware"). —Also termed *legal maxim.*

mayhem, *n.* **1.** The crime of maliciously injuring a person's body, esp. so as to impair or destroy the victim's capacity for self-defense; modern statutes usu. treat this as a form of aggravated battery. See BATTERY. **2.** Violent destruction. **3.** Rowdy confusion or disruption. —**maim** (corresponding to sense 1), *vb.*

may it please the court. The standard introductory phrase that lawyers use when presenting oral argument to an appellate court.

mayor, *n.* An official who is elected or appointed as the chief executive of a city, town, or other municipality. —**mayoral,** *adj.*—**mayoralty, mayorship,** *n.*

mayor's court. See COURT.

MBE. See *Multistate Bar Examination* under BAR EXAMINATION.

MBO. See *management buyout* under BUYOUT.

McNabb-Mallory **rule.** In criminal procedure, the rule that a confession is inadmissible if obtained during an unreasonably long detention period between arrest and a preliminary hearing; because of the broader protections afforded under the *Miranda* rule, the *McNabb-Mallory* rule is rarely applied in modern cases. —Often shortened to *Mallory rule*. *McNabb v. United States*, 318 U.S. 332 (1943); *Mallory v. United States*, 354 U.S. 449 (1957).

McNaghten rules (mik-**nawt**-[ə]n). In criminal law, a test for the insanity defense, holding that a person is not criminally responsible for an act when a mental disability prevented the person from knowing either (1) the nature and quality of the act, or (2) whether the act was right or wrong; the federal courts and most states have adopted this test in some form. *McNaghten's Case*, 8 Eng.Rep. 718, 10 Cl. & Fin. 200 (1843). —Also spelled *McNaughten rules*; *M'Naghten rules*; *M'Naughten rules*. —Also termed *right-and-wrong test*. Cf. SUBSTANTIAL-CAPACITY TEST; IRRESISTIBLE-IMPULSE TEST; DURHAM RULE.

M.D. *abbr.* **1.** Middle District, in reference to U.S. judicial districts. **2.** Doctor of medicine.

MDL. *abbr.* MULTIDISTRICT LITIGATION.

mean reserve. See RESERVE.

measuring life. Under the rule against perpetuities, the last to die of the beneficiaries who were alive at the testator's death and who usu. hold a preceding interest; a measuring life is used to determine whether an interest will vest within the perpetuities period. Cf. LIFE IN BEING.

mechanic's lien. See LIEN.

mediation, *n.* **1.** A method of dispute resolution involving a neutral third party who tries to help the disputing parties reach a mutually agreeable solution but whose decision is not binding. Cf. ARBITRATION. **2.** In international law, a neutral nation's interference in the controversies of others to maintain international stability. —**mediate,** *vb.*—**mediatory,** *adj.*—**mediator,** *n.*

Medicaid. A government program that provides medical aid to those who cannot afford private medical services; Medicaid is jointly funded by the federal and state governments.

medical directive. ADVANCE DIRECTIVE.

medical examiner. A public official who investigates deaths, conducts autopsies, and helps the state prosecute homicide cases; medical examiners have replaced coroners in many states.

medical jurisprudence. FORENSIC MEDICINE.

medical malpractice. See MALPRACTICE.

Medicare. A federal program—established under the Social Security Act—that provides health insurance for the elderly and the disabled.

medicolegal, *adj.* Involving the application of medical science to law <the coroner's medicolegal functions>. See FORENSIC MEDICINE.

med. mal. See *medical malpractice* under MALPRACTICE.

meeting, *n.* An assembly of persons, esp. to discuss and act on matters in which they have a common interest. —**meet,** *vb.*

annual meeting. In corporate law, a yearly meeting of shareholders for the purpose of electing directors and conducting other routine business; the time and place of such a meeting are usu. specified in the corporation's articles or bylaws. — Also termed *regular meeting*; *stated meeting.*

creditors' meeting. In bankruptcy law, the first meeting of a debtor's creditors and equity security holders, presided over by the U.S. Trustee and at which a bankruptcy trustee may be elected and the debtor may be examined under oath. 11 U.S.C. § 341. —Also termed *341 meeting.*

organizational meeting. In corporate law, a meeting of the directors named in a new corporation's articles of incorporation, called so that the directors can adopt bylaws, elect officers, and conduct other initial business.

special meeting. In corporate law, a meeting called by the board of directors, an officer, or a group of shareholders for some extraordinary purpose, such as to vote on a merger or takeover. —Also termed *called meeting.*

meeting-competition defense. In antitrust law, a defense to a charge of price discrimination whereby the defendant shows that the lower price was a good-faith attempt to match what it believed to be a competitor's equally low offer.

meeting of the minds. In contract law, actual assent by both parties to

the formation of a contract; this was required under the traditional subjective theory of assent, but modern contract doctrine requires only objective manifestations of assent. See MUTUAL ASSENT.

member bank. See BANK.

member firm. In securities and commodities trading, a brokerage firm with at least one director, officer, or general partner who is a member of an organized securities exchange. —Also termed (if organized as a corporation) *member corporation.*

memorandum. 1. An informal written note or record outlining the terms of a transaction or contract <the memorandum indicated the developer's intent to buy the property at its appraised value>; to satisfy the statute of frauds, a memorandum (though it can be written in any form) must (1) identify the parties to the contract, (2) indicate the contract's subject matter, (3) contain the contract's essential terms, and (4) contain the signature of the party against whom enforcement is sought. —Also termed *memorial.* See STATUTE OF FRAUDS. **2.** An informal written communication used esp. in offices <the firm sent a memorandum reminding all its lawyers to turn in their timesheets>. —Often shortened to *memo.* **3.** A party's written statement of its legal arguments presented to the court, usu. in the form of a brief <memorandum of law>. Pl. **memoranda, memorandums.**

memorandum check. See CHECK.

memorandum decision. See *memorandum opinion* under OPINION (1).

memorandum of intent. LETTER OF INTENT.

memorandum opinion. See OPINION (1).

memorandum sale. See SALE.

memorial, *n.* **1.** An abstract of a legal record, esp. a deed; MEMORANDUM (1). **2.** A written statement of facts presented to a legislature or executive as a petition.

menacing, *n.* In some jurisdictions (esp. those that have defined assault to include battery), common-law assault. See ASSAULT.

mens rea (menz-**ray**[-ə] *or* -**ree**-ə). [Law Latin "guilty mind"] The state of mind that the prosecution, to secure a conviction, must prove that a defendant had when committing a crime; criminal intent or recklessness <the *mens rea* for theft is the intent to deprive the rightful owner of the property>. —Also termed *mental element*; *criminal intent.* Cf. ACTUS REUS.

mental anguish. EMOTIONAL DISTRESS.

mental capacity. CAPACITY (3).

mental cruelty. See CRUELTY.

mental distress. EMOTIONAL DISTRESS.

mental element. MENS REA.

mercantile (mər-kən-teel *or* -til *or* -tIl), *adj.* Of or relating to merchants or trading; commercial <the mercantile system>.

mercantile law. COMMERCIAL LAW (1).

merchandise. Goods that are bought and sold in business; commercial wares.

merchant. One whose business is buying and selling goods for profit; esp., a person or entity that holds itself out as having expertise peculiar to the goods in which it deals, and is therefore held by the law to a higher standard than a consumer or other nonmerchant is held.

merchantable (mər-chənt-ə-bəl), *adj.* MARKETABLE. —**merchantability,** *n.* See *implied warranty of merchantability* under WARRANTY (2).

merchantable title. See *marketable title* under TITLE.

mercy. Compassionate treatment, as of criminal offenders or of those in distress; esp., imprisonment, rather than death, imposed as punishment for capital murder. See CLEMENCY.

mercy-killing. EUTHANASIA.

mere-evidence rule. In criminal procedure, the obsolete rule that a search warrant allows seizure of the instrumentalities of the crime (such as a murder weapon) or the fruits of the crime (such as stolen goods), but does not permit the seizure of items that have evidentiary value only (such as incriminating documents); the Supreme Court has abolished this rule, and today warrants may be issued to search for and seize all evidence of a crime. *Warden v. Hayden,* 387 U.S. 294 (1967); Fed. R. Crim. P. 41(b).

meretricious (mer-ə-**tri**-shəs), *adj.* **1.** Involving prostitution; of an unlawful sexual nature <a meretricious encounter>. **2.** (Of a romantic relationship) involving either two people of the same sex or lack of capacity on the part of one party <a meretricious marriage>. **3.** Superficially attractive but fake nonetheless; alluring by false show <meretricious advertising claims>.

mergee. A participant in a corporate merger.

merger. 1. Generally, the act or an instance of combining or uniting. **2.** In contract law, the substitution of a superior form of contract for an inferior form, as when a written contract supersedes all oral agreements and prior understandings. **3.** In property law, the absorption of a lesser estate into a greater estate when both become the same person's property. **4.** In criminal law, the absorption of a lesser included offense into a more serious offense when a person is charged with both crimes, so that the person is not subject to double jeopardy; for example, a defendant cannot be convicted of both attempt (or solicitation) and the completed crime—though merger does not apply to conspiracy and the completed crime. **5.** In civil procedure, the effect of a judgment for the plaintiff, which absorbs any claim that was the subject of the lawsuit into the judgment, so that the plaintiff's rights are confined to enforcing the judgment. Cf. BAR (5). **6.** The joining of the procedural aspects of law and equity. **7.** The absorption of one company (esp. a corporation) that ceases to exist into another that retains its own name and identity and acquires the assets and liabilities of the former; corporate mergers must conform to statutory formalities and usu. must be approved by a supermajority of

shareholders. Cf. AMALGAMATION; CONSOLIDATION (2).

bust-up merger. A merger in which the acquiring corporation sells off lines of business owned by the target corporation in order to repay the loans used in the acquisition.

cash merger. A merger in which certain shareholders must accept cash for their shares while other shareholders receive shares in the continuing enterprise. —Also termed *cash-out merger; freeze-out merger.*

conglomerate merger. A merger between unrelated businesses that are neither competitors nor customers or suppliers of each other.

de facto merger. A transaction that has the economic effect of a statutory merger but that is cast in the form of an acquisition of assets or voting stock; although such a transaction does not meet the statutory requirements for a merger, a court will generally treat it as a statutory merger.

downstream merger. A merger of a parent corporation into its subsidiary.

horizontal merger. A merger between two or more businesses that are on the same market level because they manufacture similar products in the same geographic region. — Also termed *horizontal integration.*

reverse triangular merger. A merger in which the acquiring corporation's subsidiary is absorbed into the target corporation, which becomes a new subsidiary of the acquiring corporation. —Also termed *reverse subsidiary merger.*

short-form merger. A merger that is less expensive and time-consuming than an ordinary statutory merger, usu. permitted when a subsidiary merges into a parent that already owns most of the subsidiary's shares; such a merger is generally accomplished when the parent adopts a merger resolution, mails a copy of the plan to the subsidiary's record shareholders, and files the executed articles of merger with the secretary of state, who issues a certificate of merger.

stock merger. A merger involving one company's purchase of another company's capital stock.

triangular merger. A merger in which the target corporation is absorbed into the acquiring corporation's subsidiary, with the target's shareholders receiving stock in the parent corporation. —Also termed *subsidiary merger; forward triangular merger.*

upstream merger. A merger of a subsidiary corporation into its parent.

vertical merger. A merger between businesses occupying different levels of operation for the same product, such as between a manufacturer and a retailer.

merger clause. A contractual provision stating that the contract represents the parties' complete and final agreement and supersedes all informal understandings and oral agreements relating to the subject matter of the contract. —Also termed *integration clause; zipper clause.* See INTEGRATION (2); PAROL-EVIDENCE RULE.

meritorious defense. See DEFENSE (1).

merit regulation. Under state bluesky laws, the practice of requiring securities offerings not only to have a full and adequate disclosure but also to be substantively fair, just, and equitable.

merits. The elements or grounds of a claim or defense; the substantive considerations to be taken into account in deciding a case, as opposed to extraneous or technical points, esp. of procedure <trial on the merits>.

merit system. The practice of hiring and promoting government employees on the basis of competence rather than political favoritism. Cf. SPOILS SYSTEM.

mesne (meen), *adj.* Occupying a middle position; intermediate or intervening <the mesne encumbrance has priority over the third mortgage, but is subordinate to the first mortgage>.

mesne lord. A feudal lord who holds an estate as tenant of a superior lord while being a lord over his own tenants. See LORD (3).

mesne process. See PROCESS.

mesne profits. See PROFIT.

messuage (**mes**-wij). A dwelling house together with the curtilage, including any outbuildings. See CURTILAGE.

metalaw (**met**-ə-law). A hypothetical set of legal principles based on the rules of existing legal systems and designed to provide a framework of agreement for these different systems.

metes and bounds. The territorial limits of real property as measured by distances and angles from designated landmarks and in relation to adjoining properties; metes and bounds are usu. described in deeds and surveys to establish the boundary lines of land. —Also termed *butts and bounds*; *lines and corners*.

metropolitan district. See DISTRICT.

Mexican divorce. See DIVORCE.

middleman. An intermediary or agent between two parties; esp., a dealer (such as a wholesaler) who buys from producers and sells to retailers or consumers.

migratory divorce. See DIVORCE.

military board. A group of persons appointed to act as a fact-finding agency or as an advisory body to the appointing military authority.

military commission. A court, usu. composed of both civilians and military officers, that is modeled after a court-martial and that tries and decides cases concerning martial-law violations. See COURT-MARTIAL.

military court. A court that has jurisdiction over members of the armed forces and that enforces the Code of Military Justice. See CODE OF MILITARY JUSTICE.

military court of inquiry. A military court that has special and limited jurisdiction and that is convened to investigate specific matters and, traditionally, to determine whether further procedures are warranted. 10 U.S.C. § 935.

military government. Government exercised by a military commander under the direction of the executive or sovereign, either externally during a foreign war or internally during a civil war; it supersedes all local law. See MARTIAL LAW.

military jurisdiction. The three types of governmental power given the military by the U.S. Constitution—specifically, jurisdiction under military law, jurisdiction under military government, and jurisdiction under martial law.

military law. The branch of law governing military discipline and other rules regarding service in the armed forces. —Also termed *military justice*. Cf. MARTIAL LAW.

military offense. An offense, such as desertion, that lies within the jurisdiction of a military court. See COURT-MARTIAL.

militate, *vb.* To exert a strong influence <the evidence of police impropriety militates against a conviction>. Cf. MITIGATE.

militia (mə-**lish**-ə). A body of citizens armed and trained, esp. by a state, for military service apart from the regular armed forces; the Constitution recognizes the people's right to form a "well-regulated militia" but also grants Congress the power to activate, organize, and govern the militia. U.S. Const. amend. II; U.S. Const. art. I, § 8, cl. 15-16.

mind and memory. A testator's mental capacity to make a will <she argued that her uncle was not of sound mind and memory when executing the will because he had Alzheimer's disease>. See CAPACITY.

mineral lease. See LEASE.

mineral right. The right to search for, develop, and remove minerals from land or to receive a royalty based on the production of minerals; such a right is usu. granted by a mineral lease. —Also termed *mineral interest*. See SUBSURFACE RIGHT. Cf. SURFACE RIGHT.

minimal contacts. MINIMUM CONTACTS.

mini-maxi, *n.* An underwriting arrangement for a securities transaction, whereby a broker is required to sell the minimum number of securities on an all-or-none basis and the balance on a best-efforts basis. See UNDERWRITING (2).

minimum contacts. A nonresident defendant's forum-state connections, such as business activity or actions foreseeably leading to business activity, that are substantial enough to bring the defendant within the forum-state court's personal jurisdiction without offending traditional notions of fair play and substantial justice. *International Shoe Co. v. Washington*, 326 U.S. 310 (1945). — Also termed *minimal contacts*.

minimum-fee schedule. A list of the lowest fees that a lawyer may charge according to the state bar association; the courts have held that these schedules violate antitrust laws.

minimum lot. See LOT (1).

minimum-royalty clause. In patent law, a royalty-agreement provision that prescribes a fixed payment by the licensee to the patent owner, regardless of whether the invention is used or not.

minimum tax. See *alternative minimum tax* under TAX.

minimum wage. See WAGE.

mining claim. A parcel of land that contains precious metal in its soil or rock and that is appropriated by a person according to established rules and customs known as the process of *location*. See LOCATION (4). Cf. PLACER CLAIM.

mining lease. See LEASE.

minister, *n.* **1.** A person acting under another's authority; an agent. **2.** A prominent government officer appointed to manage an executive or administrative department. **3.** A diplomatic representative, esp. one ranking below an ambassador. **4.** A person authorized by a Christian church to perform religious functions.

ministerial, *adj.* Of or relating to an act that involves obedience to instructions or laws instead of discretion, judgment, or skill <the court clerk's ministerial duties include recording judgments on the docket>.

minitrial. A private, voluntary, and informal form of dispute resolution in which each party's attorney presents its case to a neutral third party and to the opponent's representatives, who have settlement authority; the third party may render an advisory opinion on the anticipated outcome of litigation.

minor, *n.* A person who has not reached full legal age; a child or juvenile. —Also termed *infant*.

emancipated minor. A minor who is self-supporting and independent of parental control, usu. as a result of a court order terminating parental rights.

minor crime. MISDEMEANOR.

minority. 1. The state or condition of being under legal age. —Also termed *infancy; nonage.* Cf. MAJORITY (1). **2.** A group having fewer than a controlling number of votes. Cf. MAJORITY (2). **3.** A group that is different in some respect (such as race or religious belief) from the majority and that is sometimes treated differently as a result; a member of such a group.

minority opinion. See *dissenting opinion* under OPINION (1).

minority shareholder. See SHAREHOLDER.

minute book. 1. A book in which a court clerk enters memoranda of court proceedings. **2.** A record of all subjects discussed and actions authorized at a corporate board of directors' or shareholders' meeting. — Also termed *minutes book.*

Miranda hearing. A pretrial proceeding that is held to determine whether the *Miranda* rule has been followed and thus whether the prosecutor may introduce the defendant's custodial statements into evidence.

Miranda rule. The requirement that, before any custodial interrogation, a person must be informed of the right to remain silent so as to avoid self-incrimination and the right to have a private or court-appointed attorney present; if the giving of these warnings (commonly called *Miranda warnings*) or a waiver of the named rights is not demonstrated at trial, any evidence obtained in the interrogation cannot be used against the defendant. *Miranda v. Arizona*, 384 U.S. 436 (1966).

Mirandize (mə-**ran**-dīz). *Slang.* To read (an arrestee) rights under the *Miranda* rule <the defendant was arrested, Mirandized, and interrogated>.

mirror-image rule. In contract law, the common-law principle requiring an acceptance's terms to correspond exactly with the offer's terms in order for a contract to be formed; in modern commercial contexts, the mirror-image rule has been replaced by U.C.C. § 2-207, which allows parties to enforce their agreement despite minor discrepancies between the offer and the acceptance. See BATTLE OF THE FORMS.

misadventure. 1. A mishap or misfortune. **2.** Homicide committed accidentally by a person doing a lawful act and having no intent to injure; ACCIDENTAL KILLING.

misapplication, *n.* The improper or illegal use of funds or property lawfully held. —**misapply,** *vb.*

misappropriation, *n.* The act or an instance of applying another's property or money dishonestly to one's own use. —**misappropriate,** *vb.* See EMBEZZLEMENT.

misappropriation theory. In federal securities law, the idea that any employee who trades shares on information not publicly known, and in violation of rules imposed by or duties owed to the employer, is in violation of the prohibition against insider trading.

misbehavior in office. See *official misconduct* under MISCONDUCT.

misbranding, *n.* The act or an instance of labeling one's product falsely or in a misleading way; misbranding is prohibited by federal and state statutes. —**misbrand,** *vb.*

miscegenation (mi-se-jə-**nay**-shən). *Archaic.* A marriage between persons of different races—formerly considered illegal in some jurisdictions.

miscellaneous itemized deduction. See DEDUCTION.

mischarge. An erroneous jury instruction that may be grounds for reversing a verdict. —Also termed *misdirection.*

mischief (**mis**-chəf). **1.** A condition in which a person suffers a wrong or is under some hardship, esp. one that a statute seeks to remove or for which equity provides a remedy <this legislation seeks to eliminate the mischief of racially restrictive deed covenants>. **2.** Injury or damage caused by a specific person or thing <the vandals were convicted of criminal mischief>.

mischief rule. In statutory construction, the principle that a judge should interpret an ambiguous statute so that it curtails the mischief that it was intended to address. —Also termed *rule in Heydon's case.* Cf. GOLDEN RULE; PLAIN-MEANING RULE.

misconduct. 1. A dereliction of duty; unlawful or improper behavior.

official misconduct. A public officer's corrupt violation of his or her duties by malfeasance, misfeasance, or nonfeasance. —Also termed *misconduct in office; misbehavior in office; malconduct in office; misdemeanor in office; corruption in office; official corruption.*

wanton misconduct. An act, or a failure to act when there is a duty to do so, in reckless disregard of another's rights, coupled with the knowledge that injury will probably result. —Also termed *wanton and reckless misconduct.*

2. An attorney's dishonesty or attempt to persuade a court or jury by using deceptive or reprehensible methods.

misdemeanant (mis-də-**mee**-nənt). One who has been convicted of a misdemeanor.

misdemeanor (mis-də-**mee**-nər). A crime that is less serious than a felony and is usu. punishable by fine, penalty, forfeiture, or confinement in a place other than prison. —Also termed *minor crime.* Cf. FELONY.

misdemeanor in office. See *official misconduct* under MISCONDUCT.

misdemeanor-manslaughter rule. The principle that a death occurring during the commission of a misdemeanor (or sometimes a nondangerous felony) is involuntary manslaughter; many states and the Model Penal Code have abolished this rule. Cf. FELONY-MURDER RULE.

misdescription. 1. A contractual error or falsity that deceives, injures, or materially misleads one of the contracting parties. **2.** A bailee's inaccurate identification, in a document of title, of goods received from the bailor. See BAILMENT.

misdirection. MISCHARGE.

misfeasance (mis-**feez**-[ə]n[t]s), *n.*
1. A lawful act performed in a
wrongful manner. **2.** More broadly, a
transgression or trespass; MALFEA-
SANCE. —**misfeasant,** *adj.*—**mis-
feasor,** *n.* Cf. NONFEASANCE.

misjoinder. The improper uniting of
parties or claims in a single lawsuit.
See JOINDER. Cf. DISJOINDER; NON-
JOINDER.

mislaid property. See PROPERTY.

misnomer (**mis**-noh-mər *or* mis-
noh-mər). A mistake in naming a
person, place, or thing, esp. in a legal
instrument; in federal pleading—as
well as in most states—misnomer of
a party can be corrected by an
amendment, which will relate back to
the date of the original pleading. Fed.
R. Civ. P. 15(c)(3).

misprision (mis-**pri**-zhən *or* -zee-
ən). **1.** Concealment of treason or
felony by one not participating in the
crime. —Also termed *misprision of
treason/felony.* **2.** Seditious conduct
against the government. **3.** An official's failure to perform duties of
public office. **4.** Misunderstanding;
mistake.

misprisor (mis-**prIz**-ər). One who
commits misprision of felony.

misrecital. An incorrect statement
of a factual matter in a contract,
deed, pleading, or other instrument.

misrepresentation, *n.* **1.** The act of
making a false or misleading statement about something, usu. with the
intent to deceive. **2.** The statement
so made. —Also termed *false representation.* —**misrepresent,** *vb.*

fraudulent misrepresentation. A false
statement known to be false and

intended to induce a party to detrimentally rely on it.

innocent misrepresentation. A false
statement not known to be false.

negligent misrepresentation. A careless or inadvertent false statement.

mistake, *n.* A misunderstanding of
the meaning or implication of something; an error or inadvertence arising from such a misunderstanding.
Cf. FRUSTRATION.

mistake of fact. **a.** An unconscious
ignorance or forgetfulness of a past
or present fact that is material to a
transaction. **b.** A belief in the existence of a past or present fact that
has not existed or does not exist
and that is material to a transaction.

mistake of law. An erroneous conclusion about the legal effect of
known, true facts.

mutual mistake. **a.** A misunderstanding in which each party misappre-
hends the other's intent. —Also
termed *bilateral mistake.* **b.** A misunderstanding in which the parties
share the same misapprehension of
material fact. —More correctly
termed (in sense b) *common mistake.*

unilateral mistake. A mistake by only
one party to an agreement.

mistrial. **1.** A trial that ends without a determination on the merits
because of some procedural error or
serious misconduct during the proceedings. **2.** A trial that ends incon-
clusively because the jury cannot
agree on a verdict.

misuse, *n.* **1.** In a products-liability
action, a manufacturer's defense al-

leging that the plaintiff used the product in an unintended or unforeseeable manner. **2.** In patent law, the use of a patent either to improperly extend the granted monopoly to non-patented goods or to violate antitrust laws.

mitigate, *vb.* To make less severe or intense <the fired employee mitigated her damages for wrongful termination by accepting a new job>. — **mitigation,** *n.*—**mitigatory,** *adj.* Cf. MILITATE.

mitigating circumstances. See CIRCUMSTANCE.

mitigation-of-damages doctrine. The principle requiring a plaintiff, after an injury or breach of contract, to use ordinary care to alleviate the effects of the injury or breach; if the defendant can show that the plaintiff failed to do so, the plaintiff's damages may be reduced. —Also termed *avoidable-consequences doctrine.*

mittimus (mid-ə-məs). A court order or warrant directing a jailer to detain a person until ordered otherwise. Pl. **mittimuses.**

mixed action. See ACTION.

mixed larceny. See LARCENY.

mixed nuisance. See NUISANCE.

mixed property. See PROPERTY.

mixed question of law and fact. A question that combines a question of law for the judge with a question of fact for the jury.

MLA. *abbr.* MOTION FOR LEAVE TO APPEAL.

M'Naghten rules. MCNAGHTEN RULES.

M'Naughten rules. MCNAGHTEN RULES.

M.O. *abbr.* MODUS OPERANDI.

mob, the. ORGANIZED CRIME (2).

mock trial. A fictitious trial organized to allow law students, or sometimes lawyers, to practice the techniques of trial advocacy. Cf. MOOT COURT.

model act. A statute drafted by the National Conference of Commissioners on Uniform State Laws and proposed as guideline legislation for the states to borrow from or adapt to suit their individual needs; example of model acts include the Model Employment Termination Act and the Model Punitive Damages Act. Cf. UNIFORM ACT.

Model Code of Professional Responsibility. A set of ethical guidelines for lawyers, organized in the form of canons, disciplinary rules, and ethical considerations; published by the ABA in 1969, this code has been replaced in most states by the Model Rules of Professional Conduct.

Model Penal Code. A proposed criminal code drafted by the American Law Institute and used as the basis for criminal-law revision by many states. —Abbr. MPC.

Model Rules of Professional Conduct. A set of ethical guidelines for lawyers, organized in the form of 52 rules—some mandatory, some discretionary—together with explanatory comments; published by the ABA in 1983, these rules have generally replaced the Model Code of Professional Responsibility and have been adopted as law by many states.

modified accelerated cost-recovery system. An accounting method used to determine the income-tax deduction for depreciation of tangible property; this system replaced and significantly changed the original accelerated cost-recovery system in 1986. —Abbr. MACRS. Cf. ACCELERATED COST-RECOVERY SYSTEM.

modus (**moh**-dəs). [Latin "mode"] In criminal pleading, the part of a charging instrument describing the manner in which an offense was committed.

modus operandi (**moh**-dəs-op-ə-**ran**-dee *or* -dI). A method of operating or a manner of procedure; esp., a pattern of criminal behavior so distinctive that investigators attribute it to the work of the same person <staging a fight at the train station was part of the pickpocket's modus operandi>. —Abbr. M.O. Pl. **modi operandi.**

moiety (**moy**-ə-tee). **1.** A half. **2.** Loosely, a portion less than half; a small segment. **3.** In American customs law, a payment made to an informant who assists in the seizure of contraband.

money had and received, action for. At common law, an action by which the plaintiff could recover money paid to the defendant, the money usu. being recoverable because (1) the money had been paid under mistake or compulsion, or (2) the consideration had wholly failed. Cf. MONEY PAID, ACTION FOR.

money-laundering. LAUNDERING.

money market. See MARKET.

money-market account. An interest-bearing account at a bank or other financial institution; such an account usu. pays interest competitive with money-market funds but allows a limited number of transactions per month. See *money market* under MARKET.

money paid, action for. At common law, an action by which the plaintiff could recover money paid to a third party—not to the defendant—in circumstances in which the defendant had benefited. Cf. MONEY HAD AND RECEIVED, ACTION FOR.

money supply. The total amount of money in circulation in the economy. See M1; M2; M3.

monition (mə-**nish**-ən), *n.* **1.** Generally, a warning or caution; ADMONITION. **2.** In admiralty and civil-law contexts, a summons to appear and answer in court as a defendant or to contempt charges. **3.** In ecclesiastical law, a formal notice from a bishop demanding that an offense within the clergy be corrected. —**monish** (**mo**-nish), *vb.*—**monitory,** *adj.*

monogamy (mə-**nog**-ə-mee), *n.* **1.** The custom prevalent in most modern cultures restricting a person to one spouse only. **2.** The fact of being married to only one spouse. —**monogamous,** *adj.*—**monogamist,** *n.* Cf. BIGAMY; POLYGAMY.

monopolization, *n.* The act or process of obtaining a monopoly; in federal antitrust law, monopolization is an offense with two elements: (1) the possession of monopoly power—that is, the power to fix prices and exclude competitors—within the relevant market, and (2) the willful acquisition or maintenance of that power, as distinguished from growth or development as a consequence of a superior product, business acumen, or historical accident. *United States v. Grinnell Corp.*, 384 U.S. 563 (1966). —**monopolize,** *vb.*—**monopolistic,** *adj.*—**monopolist,** *n.*

monopoly, *n.* **1.** Control or advantage obtained by one supplier or producer over the commercial market within a given region. **2.** The market condition existing when only one economic entity produces a particular product or provides a particular service; the term is now commonly applied also to situations that approach but do not strictly meet this definition.

bilateral monopoly. A hypothetical market condition in which there is only one buyer and one seller, resulting in transactional delays because either party can hold out for a better deal without fearing that the other party will turn to a third party.

3. In patent law, the exclusive right to make, use, and sell an invention.

monopsony (mə-**nop**-sə-nee), *n.* A market situation in which one buyer controls the market. —**monopsonistic,** *adj.*

Monroe Doctrine. The principle that the United States will allow no intervention or domination by any non-American nation in the Western hemisphere; this principle, which has some recognition in international law (though not as a formal doctrine), was first announced by President James Monroe in 1823.

month-to-month lease. See LEASE.

month-to-month tenancy. See *periodic tenancy* under TENANCY.

monument, *n.* **1.** A written document or record, esp. a legal one. **2.** Any natural or artificial object that is fixed permanently in land and referred to in a legal description of the land. —**monumental,** *adj.*

moot, *adj.* **1.** *Archaic.* Open to argument; debatable <one-L's are required to practice delivering oral arguments before a moot court>. **2.** Having no practical significance; hypothetical or academic <the question on appeal became moot once the parties settled their case>. —**mootness,** *n.*

moot, *vb.* **1.** *Archaic.* To raise or bring forward (a point or question) for discussion. **2.** To render (a question) moot or of no practical significance.

moot court. A fictitious court held usu. in law schools to argue moot or hypothetical cases, esp. at the appellate level. Cf. MOCK TRIAL.

mootness doctrine. The principle that American courts will not decide moot cases—that is, cases in which there is no longer any actual controversy. Cf. RIPENESS.

moral absolutism. The view that people's actions can properly be seen as right or wrong regardless of the situation or the consequences. —Also termed *ethical absolutism; objective ethics.* Cf. MORAL RELATIVISM.

moral evidence. See EVIDENCE.

moral hazard. See HAZARD (2).

moral obligation. A duty that is based only on one's conscience and that is not legally enforceable; in contract law, moral obligation may support a promise in the absence of traditional consideration, but only if the promisor has previously received some actual benefit from the promisee.

moral relativism. The view that there are no absolute or constant standards of right and wrong. —Also termed *ethical relativism*; *subjective ethics*. Cf. MORAL ABSOLUTISM.

moral turpitude. Conduct that is contrary to justice, honesty, or good morals; in the area of professional responsibility, offenses involving moral turpitude—such as fraud or breach of trust—are traditionally considered to reflect adversely on one's fitness to practice law.

moratorium (mor-ə-**tor**-ee-əm). **1.** An authorization permitting a debtor to temporarily suspend repayment of the debt; the period of this delay. **2.** A delay or suspension of an activity. Pl. **moratoria.**

mors naturalis. See *natural death* under DEATH.

mortality table. ACTUARIAL TABLE.

mortgage (**mor**-gij), *n.* **1.** A pledge of property (esp. real property) to a creditor as security for the performance of an obligation (esp. a debt involving the property), the pledge being extinguished once the obligation is satisfied. **2.** An instrument (such as a deed or contract) specifying the terms of such a pledge. **3.** Loosely, the loan on which such a pledge is based. —**mortgage,** *vb.*

adjustable-rate mortgage. A mortgage in which the lender can periodically adjust the mortgage's interest rate in accordance with fluctuations in some external market in-

dex. —Abbr. ARM. —Also termed *variable-rate mortgage*; *flexible-rate mortgage.*

amortized mortgage. A mortgage in which the mortgagor pays the interest as well as a portion of the principal in the periodic payment; at maturity, the periodic payments will have completely repaid the loan. —Also termed *self-liquidating mortgage.* See AMORTIZATION.

balloon-payment mortgage. A mortgage requiring periodic payments for a specified time and a lump-sum payment of the outstanding balance at maturity.

blanket mortgage. A mortgage covering two or more properties that are pledged to support a debt.

chattel mortgage. A mortgage that covers the installment purchase of goods, whereby the seller transfers title to the buyer but retains a lien securing the unpaid balance; chattel mortgages have generally been replaced by security agreements, which are governed by Article 9 of the U.C.C. Cf. *retail installment contract* under CONTRACT.

closed mortgage. A mortgage that cannot be paid in full before maturity without the lender's consent.

closed-end mortgage. A mortgage that does not permit either prepayment or additional borrowing against the collateral. Cf. *open-end mortgage.*

contingent-interest mortgage. A mortgage whose interest rate is directly related to the economic performance of the pledged property.

conventional mortgage. A mortgage, not backed by government insurance, by which the borrower transfers a lien or title to the lending bank or other financial institution; these mortgages, which feature a fixed periodic payment of principal and interest throughout the mortgage term, are typically used for home financing.

direct-reduction mortgage. An amortized mortgage in which the principal and interest payments are paid at the same time—usu. monthly in equal amounts—with interest being computed on the remaining balance. —Abbr. DRM.

first mortgage. A mortgage that is senior to all other mortgages on the same property.

fixed-rate mortgage. A mortgage with an interest rate that remains the same over the life of the mortgage regardless of market conditions. — Abbr. FRM.

flip mortgage. A graduated-payment mortgage allowing the borrower to place all or some of the down payment in a savings account and to use the principal and interest to supplement lower mortgage payments in the loan's early years.

graduated-payment mortgage. A mortgage whose initial payments are lower than its later payments, which typically increase as the borrower's income increases over time.

interest-only mortgage. A balloon-payment mortgage on which the borrower must at first make only interest payments, but must make a lump-sum payment of the full principal at maturity. —Also termed *standing mortgage*; *straight-term mortgage*.

junior mortgage. A mortgage that is subordinate to another mortgage on the same property.

leasehold mortgage. A mortgage secured by a lessee's leasehold interest.

open-end mortgage. A mortgage that allows the mortgagor to borrow additional funds against the same property. Cf. *closed-end mortgage*.

participation mortgage. **a.** A mortgage that permits the lender to receive profits of the venture in addition to the normal interest payments. **b.** A mortgage held by more than one lender.

price-level-adjusted mortgage. A mortgage with a fixed interest rate but the principal balance of which is adjusted to reflect inflation. — Abbr. PLAM.

purchase-money mortgage. A mortgage that a buyer gives the seller, when the property is conveyed, to secure the unpaid balance of the purchase price. —Abbr. PMM. See SECURITY AGREEMENT.

reverse annuity mortgage. A mortgage in which the lender disburses money over a long time period to provide regular income to the borrower, and in which the loan is repaid in a lump sum when the borrower dies or when the property is sold. —Abbr. RAM.

second mortgage. A mortgage that is junior to a first mortgage on the same property, but that is senior to any subsequent mortgages.

senior mortgage. A mortgage having priority over other mortgages on the same property.

shared-equity mortgage. A mortgage in which the lender shares in the profits from the property's resale; usu. the lender must first purchase a portion of the property's equity by providing a portion of the down payment.

submortgage. A mortgage used as security by someone who has rights to that mortgage only as a security; a loan to a mortgagee who puts up the mortgage as collateral or security for the loan.

wraparound mortgage. A second mortgage issued when a lender assumes the payments on the borrower's low-interest first mortgage (usu. issued through a different lender) and lends additional funds; such a mortgage covers both the outstanding balance of the first mortgage and the additional funds loaned. —Also termed *all-inclusive mortgage*; *extended first mortgage*.

zero-rate mortgage. A mortgage with a large down payment but no interest payments, with the balance paid in equal installments.

mortgage bond. See BOND (1).

mortgage certificate. A document evidencing part ownership of a mortgage.

mortgage clause. An insurance-policy provision that protects the rights of a mortgagee when the insured property is secured by a mortgage; such a clause usu. provides that any insurance proceeds must be allocated between the named insured and the mortgagee "as their interests may

appear."—Also termed *mortgagee clause.* See LOSS-PAYABLE CLAUSE.

open mortgage clause. A mortgage clause that does not protect the mortgagee if the insured mortgagor does something to invalidate the policy (such as committing fraud). —Also termed *simple mortgage clause*.

standard mortgage clause. A mortgage clause that protects the mortgagee's interest even if the insured mortgagor does something to invalidate the policy; in effect, this clause creates a separate contract between the insurer and the mortgagee. —Also termed *union mortgage clause*.

mortgage commitment. A lender's written agreement with a borrower stating the terms on which it will lend money for the purchase of specified real property, usu. with a time limitation.

mortgage company. A company that makes and closes mortgage loans and then sells or assigns them to investors.

mortgage-contingency clause. A real-estate-sale provision that conditions the buyer's performance on obtaining a mortgage loan.

mortgagee (mor-gə-**jee**). One to whom property is mortgaged; the mortgage-creditor, or the lender. — Also termed *mortgage-holder*.

mortgagee clause. MORTGAGE CLAUSE.

mortgagee policy. In real-estate law, a title-insurance policy that covers only the mortgagee's title and not the owner's title. Cf. OWNER'S POLICY.

mortgage-holder. MORTGAGEE.

mortgage note. See NOTE.

mortgage point. POINT (2).

mortgaging out. *Slang.* The act of purchasing property by securing 100-percent financing of the purchase price.

mortgagor (mor-gə-**jor**). One who mortgages property; the mortgage-debtor, or the borrower. —Also spelled *mortgager*.

mortis causa. See *gift causa mortis* under GIFT.

mortmain (**mort**-mayn). [French "deadhand"] The condition of lands or tenements held inalienably by an ecclesiastical or other corporation. See DEADHAND CONTROL.

most-favored-nation clause. 1. A clause in an agreement between two nations providing that each will treat the other as well as it treats any nation that is given preferential treatment. **2.** By extension, such a clause in any contract, but esp. an oil-and-gas contract. —Often shortened to *favored-nation clause.* —Also termed *most-favored-nations clause*.

most-favored-tenant clause. A commercial-lease provision ensuring that the tenant will be given any negotiating concessions given to other tenants.

most suitable use. See *highest and best use* under USE (1).

Mother Hubbard clause. 1. A clause stating that a mortgage secures all the debts that the mortgagor may at any time owe to the mort-

gagee. —Also termed *anaconda clause*; *dragnet clause*. **2.** In oil-and-gas law, a provision in an oil-and-gas lease or a mineral or royalty deed conveying small strips of land or irregularly shaped acreage outside the area described in the lease or deed; such a provision is usu. included to override any inaccuracies in the description of the land. —Also termed *cover-all clause*. **3.** A court's written declaration that any relief not expressly granted in a specific ruling or judgment is denied.

motion. 1. A written or oral application requesting a court to make a specified ruling or order. **2.** A proposal made under formal parliamentary procedure.

motion for leave to appeal. A request for an appellate court to review an interlocutory order that meets the standards of the collateral-order doctrine. —Abbr. MLA. See COLLATERAL-ORDER DOCTRINE.

motion for more definite statement. A request for the court to order an opponent to amend a vague or ambiguous pleading to which the party cannot reasonably be required to respond. Fed. R. Civ. P. 12(e).

motion for new trial. A post-judgment request that the court vacate the judgment and order a new trial for any of various reasons, such as insufficient evidence, newly discovered evidence, or jury misconduct; in many jurisdictions, this motion is required before a party can file an appeal.

motion for summary judgment. A request that the court enter judgment without a trial because there is no genuine issue of material fact to be decided by a fact-trier; the movant claims an entitlement to prevail as a matter of law. —Also termed *summary-judgment motion*; *motion for summary disposition*. See SUMMARY JUDGMENT.

motion in limine (**lim**-i-nee). A pretrial request that certain inadmissible evidence not be referred to or offered before the jury; typically, a party makes this motion when it believes that mere mention of the evidence during trial would be highly prejudicial and could not be remedied by an instruction to disregard.

motion to strike. 1. In pleading, a request that either insufficient defenses or immaterial, redundant, impertinent, or scandalous statements be deleted from an opponent's pleading. Fed. R. Civ. P. 12(f). **2.** In evidence, a request that inadmissible evidence be deleted from the record.

motion to suppress. A request that the court prohibit the introduction of illegally obtained evidence at a criminal trial.

motion to transfer venue. A request that the court transfer the case to another district or county, usu. because the original venue is improper or because of local prejudice. See VENUE; CHANGE OF VENUE.

motive. Something, esp. willful desire, that causes one to act. Cf. INTENT.

movable, *n.* (*usu. pl.*) Property that can be moved or displaced, such as personal goods. —**movable,** *adj.* Cf. IMMOVABLE.

movant (**moo**-vənt). One who makes a motion to the court.

move, *vb.* **1.** To make an application to (a court) for a ruling, order, or some other judicial action <the appellant moved the court for a new trial>. **2.** To propose under formal parliamentary procedure <the senator moved that a vote be taken>.

moving papers. The papers that constitute or support a motion in court proceedings.

MPC. *abbr.* MODEL PENAL CODE.

MSJ. *abbr.* MOTION FOR SUMMARY JUDGMENT.

mulct (məlkt), *n.* A fine or penalty.

mulct, *vb.* **1.** To punish by a fine. **2.** To deprive or divest of, esp. fraudulently.

multidistrict litigation. In federal procedure, the temporary transfer of civil actions pending in different districts and involving common fact questions to a single district for purposes of coordinated pretrial proceedings, after which the actions are returned to their original districts for trial; multidistrict litigation—which usu. is initiated only for complex actions such as antitrust or securities cases—is governed by a special judicial panel composed of seven circuit and district judges appointed by the Chief Justice of the U.S. Supreme Court. —Abbr. MDL. 28 U.S.C. § 1407.

multifarious (məl-tə-**fer**-ee-əs), *adj.* **1.** (Of a single pleading) improperly joining distinct matters or causes of action, and thereby confounding them. **2.** Improperly joining parties in a lawsuit. **3.** Diverse; many and various. —**multifariousness,** *n.*

multilateral, *adj.* Involving more than two parties <a multilateral agreement>.

multilevel-distribution program. PYRAMID SCHEME.

multiple access. See ACCESS.

multiple counts. See COUNT.

multiple hearsay. See *double hearsay* under HEARSAY.

multiple listing. See LISTING (1).

multiple offense. See OFFENSE.

multiple sentences. See SENTENCE.

multiplicity (məl-tə-**plis**-ə-tee), *n.* In criminal procedure, the charging of the same offense in several counts of the indictment or information; multiplicity violates constitutional protections against double jeopardy. —**multiplicitous,** *adj.*

multiplicity of actions. The existence of two or more lawsuits litigating the same issue against the same defendant. —Also termed *multiplicity of suits*; *multiplicity of proceedings*.

Multistate Bar Examination. See BAR EXAMINATION.

multital (**məl**-ti-təl). *Archaic.* IN REM.

muni, *n.* See *municipal bond* under BOND (1).

municipal, *adj.* **1.** Of or relating to a city, town, or local governmental unit. **2.** Of or relating to the internal government of a state or nation (as contrasted with *international*).

municipal, *n.* See *municipal bond* under BOND (1).

municipal bond. See BOND (1).

municipal corporation. A city, town, or other local political entity formed by charter from the state and having the authority to self-govern and to administer the state's local affairs. —Also termed *municipality*. Cf. *quasi-corporation* under CORPORATION.

municipal court. See COURT.

municipality. 1. MUNICIPAL CORPORATION. **2.** The governing body of a municipal corporation.

municipal law. 1. The internal law of a nation, as opposed to international law. **2.** The ordinances and other laws applicable specifically within a city, town, or other local governmental entity.

muniment (**myoo**-nə-mənt). A document (such as a deed or charter) evidencing the rights or privileges of a person, family, or corporation.

muniment of title. Documentary evidence of title, such as a deed or a judgment regarding the ownership of property. —Also termed *common assurance*. See CHAIN OF TITLE.

murder, *n.* The unlawful killing of a human being with malice aforethought; at common law, the crime of murder was not subdivided, but many state statutes have adopted the degree structure outlined below (though the Model Penal Code has not). —**murder,** *vb.*—**murderous,** *adj.* See MALICE AFORETHOUGHT. Cf. MANSLAUGHTER.

first-degree murder. Murder that is willful, deliberate, or premeditated, or that is committed during the course of another serious felony (often limited to rape, kidnapping, robbery, burglary, or arson). —Also termed *murder one*.

second-degree murder. Murder that is not aggravated by any of the elements of first-degree murder. — Also termed *murder two*.

mutation, *n.* A significant and basic alteration; esp., in property law, the alteration of a thing's status, such as from separate property to community property. —**mutate,** *vb.*—**mutational,** *adj.*

mutilation, *n.* **1.** The act or an instance of rendering a document legally ineffective by subtracting or altering—but not completely destroying—an essential part through cutting, tearing, burning, or erasure. **2.** In criminal law, to cut off or permanently incapacitate another's limb. See MAYHEM. —**mutilate,** *vb.*—**mutilator,** *n.*

mutiny (**myoo**-t[ə]n-ee), *n.* An insubordination or insurrection of armed forces, esp. sailors, against the authority of their commanders. — **mutinous,** *adj.*

mutual, *adj.* Directed by each toward the other or others; reciprocal <mutual and bargained-for exchange>. —**mutuality,** *n.*

mutual assent. Agreement by both parties to a contract, usu. in the form of offer and acceptance; in modern contract law, mutual assent is determined by an objective standard—that is, by the apparent intention of the parties as manifested by their actions. Cf. MEETING OF THE MINDS.

mutual contract. See *bilateral contract* under CONTRACT.

mutual fund. 1. An investment company that invests its shareholders' money in a usu. diversified selection of securities. —Often shortened to *fund*. **2.** Loosely, a share in such a company.

closed-end fund. A mutual fund having a fixed number of shares that are traded on a major securities exchange or an over-the-counter market.

growth fund. A mutual fund that typically invests in well-established companies whose earnings are expected to increase; growth funds usu. pay small dividends but offer the potential for large share-price increases.

income fund. A mutual fund that typically invests in securities that consistently produce a steady income, such as bonds or dividend-paying stocks.

index fund. A mutual fund that invests in companies constituting a specific market index, such as the Standard & Poor's 500-stock average of large companies.

load fund. A mutual fund that charges a commission, usu. ranging from 2 to 8 percent, either when shares are purchased (a *front-end load*) or when they are redeemed (a *back-end load*).

no-load fund. A mutual fund that does not charge any sales commission (although it may charge fees to cover operating costs).

open-end fund. A mutual fund that continually offers new shares and buys back existing shares on demand; an open-end fund will continue to grow as more shareholders invest because it does not have a fixed number of shares outstanding.

mutual insurance. See INSURANCE.

mutual insurance company. An insurer whose policyholders are its owners, as opposed to a stock insurance company owned by outside shareholders.

mutuality of obligation. The fact of both parties to a contract having agreed to be bound in some way. —

Also termed *mutuality of contract*. See MUTUAL ASSENT.

mutuality of remedy. The availability of a remedy, esp. equitable relief, to both parties to a transaction, usu. required before either party can be granted specific performance. See SPECIFIC PERFORMANCE.

mutual mistake. See MISTAKE.

mutual rescission. RESCISSION (2).

mutual savings bank. See BANK.

mutual wills. See WILL.

N

NAFTA (**naf**-tə). *abbr.* NORTH AMERICAN FREE TRADE AGREEMENT.

naked, *adj.* (Of a legal act or instrument) lacking confirmation or validation <naked ownership of property>.

naked authority. See AUTHORITY.

naked bailment. See *gratuitous bailment* under BAILMENT.

naked confession. See CONFESSION.

naked contract. NUDUM PACTUM.

naked debenture. DEBENTURE (2).

naked licensee. See *bare licensee* under LICENSEE.

naked option. See OPTION.

naked power. See POWER.

naked promise. See PROMISE.

named insured. See INSURED.

named plaintiff. See *class representative* under REPRESENTATIVE.

name partner. See PARTNER.

nanny tax. See TAX.

Napoleonic Code. 1. (*usu. pl.*) The codification of French law commissioned by Napoleon in the 19th century, including the *Code civil* (1804), the *Code de procédure civil* (1806), the *Code de commerce* (1807), the *Code pénal* (1810), and the *Code d'instruction crimenelle* (1811). —Also termed *Code Napoléon*. 2. Loosely, CIVIL CODE (2).

narcotic, *n.* 1. An addictive drug, esp. an opiate, that dulls the senses and induces sleep. 2. (*usu. pl.*) A drug that is controlled or prohibited by law. —**narcotic,** *adj.*

NASD. *abbr.* NATIONAL ASSOCIATION OF SECURITIES DEALERS.

NASDAQ (**naz**-dak). *abbr.* NATIONAL ASSOCIATION OF SECURITIES DEALERS AUTOMATED QUOTATION SYSTEM.

nation, *n.* 1. A large group of people having a common origin, language, and tradition and usu. constituting a political entity. —Also termed *nationality*. 2. A community of people inhabiting a defined territory and organized under an independent government; a sovereign political state. —**national,** *adj.* Cf. STATE.

National Association of Securities Dealers. A group of brokers and dealers empowered by the SEC to regulate the over-the-counter securities market. —Abbr. NASD.

National Association of Securities Dealers Automated Quotation System. A computerized system for recording transactions and displaying price quotations for a group of actively traded securities on the over-the-counter market. —Abbr. NASDAQ.

national bank. See BANK.

National Conference of Commissioners on Uniform State Laws. An organization that drafts and proposes statutes for adoption by individual states, with the goal of making the laws on various subjects uniform among the states; founded in 1892 and composed of representatives from all 50 states, the Conference has drafted more than 200 uniform laws, including the Uniform Commercial Code. —Abbr. NCCUSL. —

Also termed *Uniform Law Commissioners*. See UNIFORM ACT; MODEL ACT.

national debt. The total financial obligation of the federal government, including such instruments as Treasury bills, notes, and bonds, as well as foreign debt.

nationality. NATION (1).

Nationality Act. IMMIGRATION AND NATIONALITY ACT.

nationalize, *vb.* **1.** To bring (an industry) under governmental control or ownership. **2.** To give (a person) the status of a citizen; NATURALIZE. —**nationalization,** *n.*

National Labor Relations Board. A federal agency (created by the National Labor Relations Act) that regulates employer-employee relations by establishing collective bargaining, conducting union elections, and prohibiting unfair labor practices. 29 U.S.C. § 153. —Abbr. NLRB.

National Lawyers Guild. An association of lawyers, law students, and legal workers dedicated to promoting a left-wing political and social agenda; founded in 1937, it now comprises some 4,000 members. Cf. FEDERALIST SOCIETY.

national-security privilege. See *state-secrets privilege* under PRIVILEGE.

national-treatment clause. A provision contained in some treaties, usu. commercial ones, according foreigners the same rights in certain respects as those accorded to nationals.

natural-born citizen. See CITIZEN.

natural death. See DEATH.

natural-death act. A statute that allows a person to issue a written directive instructing a physician to withhold life-sustaining procedures if the person is terminally ill. Cf. RIGHT-TO-DIE LAW.

natural domicile. See *domicile of origin* under DOMICILE.

naturalize, *vb.* To grant citizenship to (a foreign-born person) under statutory authority. —**naturalization,** *n.*

naturalized citizen. See CITIZEN.

natural law. A philosophical system of legal principles purportedly deriving from a universalized conception of human nature or divine justice rather than from legislative or judicial action. —Also termed *law of nature*; *jus naturale.* Cf. FUNDAMENTAL LAW; POSITIVE LAW.

natural person. See PERSON.

natural right. See RIGHT.

NAV. *abbr.* NET ASSET VALUE.

navigable water. Any body of water that is usable for commerce or travel; under the Commerce Clause, Congress has broad jurisdiction over all navigable waters in the U.S.

N.B. *abbr.* [Latin *nota bene*] Note well; take notice—used in documents to call attention to something important.

NCCUSL (nə-k[y]oo-səl). *abbr.* NATIONAL CONFERENCE OF COMMISSIONERS ON UNIFORM STATE LAWS.

N.D. *abbr.* Northern District, in reference to U.S. judicial districts.

necessaries. 1. Things that are indispensable to living <an infant's necessaries include food, shelter, and

clothing>. **2.** Things that are essential to maintaining the lifestyle to which one is accustomed <a multi-millionaire's necessaries may include a chauffeured limousine and a private chef>.

necessarily included offense. See *lesser included offense* under OFFENSE.

Necessary and Proper Clause. The constitutional provision permitting Congress to make laws "necessary and proper" for the execution of its enumerated powers (U.S. Const. art. I, § 8, cl. 18); the Supreme Court has broadly interpreted this clause to grant Congress the implied power to enact any law reasonably designed to achieve an express constitutional power. *McCulloch v. Maryland*, 17 U.S. (4 Wheat.) 316 (1819).

necessary party. See PARTY.

necessity. 1. In criminal law, a justification defense for a person who acts in an emergency that he or she did not create and who commits a harm that is less severe than the harm that would have occurred but for the person's actions; for example, a mountain climber can assert necessity as a defense to theft if, while lost in a blizzard, he takes food and blankets from another's cabin. —Also termed *choice of evils*. **2.** In tort law, a privilege that may relieve a person from liability if that person, having no alternative, harms another's property in order to protect life or health, and liability for trespass or conversion might otherwise arise.

private necessity. In tort law, a necessity that involves only the defendant's personal interest and thus provides only a limited privilege; for example, if the defendant injures the plaintiff's dock by keeping a boat moored to the dock during a hurricane, the defendant can assert private necessity but must compensate the plaintiff for the dock's damage.

public necessity. In tort law, a necessity that involves the public interest and thus completely excuses the defendant's liability; for example, if the defendant destroys the plaintiff's house to stop the spread of a fire that threatens the town, the defendant can assert public necessity.

ne exeat (nee-**ek**-see-ət). [Latin "let him or her not go out"] A writ ordering the person to whom it is addressed not to leave the jurisdiction of the court or the state; *ne exeat* writs—no longer widely used—are usu. issued to ensure the satisfaction of a claim against the defendant.

negative amortization. See AMORTIZATION.

negative averment. See AVERMENT.

negative cash flow. See CASH FLOW.

negative contingent fee. See *reverse contingent fee* under CONTINGENT FEE.

negative covenant. See COVENANT (1).

negative easement. See EASEMENT.

negative externality. See EXTERNALITY.

negative pregnant. A denial implying its affirmative opposite by seeming to deny only a qualification of the allegation and not the allegation itself; an example is the statement, "I didn't steal the money last Tuesday," the implication being that the theft might have happened on another day. —Also termed *negative pregnant with an affirmative.*

negative prescription. PRESCRIPTION (2).

neglect, *n.* The omission of proper attention to a person or thing, whether inadvertent, negligent, or willful; the act or condition of disregarding. —**neglect,** *vb.*—**neglectful,** *adj.*

neglected child. See CHILD.

negligence, *n.* **1.** The failure to exercise the standard of care that a reasonably prudent person would have exercised in the same situation. **2.** A tort grounded in this failure, usu. expressed in terms of the following elements: duty, breach of duty, causation, and damages. —**negligent,** *adj.*

collateral negligence. An independent contractor's negligence, for which the employer is generally not liable. See COLLATERAL-NEGLIGENCE DOCTRINE.

comparative negligence. A plaintiff's own negligence that proportionally reduces the damages recoverable by the plaintiff. —Also termed *comparative fault.* See COMPARATIVE-NEGLIGENCE DOCTRINE.

concurrent negligence. The negligence of two or more parties acting independently but causing the same damage.

contributory negligence. A plaintiff's own negligence that played a part in causing the plaintiff's injury and that is significant enough (in a few jurisdictions) to bar the plaintiff from recovering damages; in most jurisdictions, this defense has been superseded by comparative negligence. See CONTRIBUTORY-NEGLIGENCE DOCTRINE.

criminal negligence. Gross negligence so extreme that it is punishable as a crime; for example, involuntary manslaughter or other negligent homicide can be based on criminal negligence, as when an extremely careless automobile driver kills someone.

gross negligence. A conscious, voluntary act or omission in reckless disregard of a legal duty and of the consequences to another party, who may typically recover exemplary damages. —Also termed *reckless negligence*; *wanton negligence*; *willful negligence.*

imputed negligence. Negligence resulting from a party's special relationship with another party who is originally negligent—so that, for example, a parent might be held responsible for some acts of a child; negligence of one person charged to another.

negligence per se. Negligence as a matter of law, so that breach of the duty is not a jury question; negligence per se usu. arises from a statutory violation.

slight negligence. The failure to exercise the great care of an extraordinarily prudent person, resulting in liability in special circumstances (esp. those involving bailments or carriers) in which lack of ordinary care would not result in liability.

negligent entrustment. The act of leaving a dangerous article (such as a gun or car) with a person who the lender knows or should know is likely to use it in an unreasonably risky manner.

negligent homicide. See HOMICIDE.

negligent infliction of emotional distress. See EMOTIONAL DISTRESS.

negligent misrepresentation. See MISREPRESENTATION.

negotiable document of title. See DOCUMENT OF TITLE.

negotiable instrument. A written instrument that (1) is signed by the maker or drawer, (2) includes an unconditional promise or order to pay a specified sum of money, (3) is payable on demand or at a definite time, and (4) is payable to order or to bearer. U.C.C. § 3-104(a).

negotiable order of withdrawal. A negotiable instrument (such as a check) payable on demand and issued against funds deposited with a financial institution. —Abbr. N.O.W.

negotiation, *n.* **1.** (*usu. pl.*) Dealings conducted between two or more parties for the purpose of reaching an understanding. **2.** The transfer of an instrument by delivery or indorsement whereby the transferee takes it for value, in good faith, and without notice of conflicting title claims or defenses. —**negotiate,** *vb.*—**negotiable,** *adj.*—**negotiability,** *n.* See HOLDER IN DUE COURSE.

n.e.i. *abbr.* NON EST INVENTUS.

neighborhood effect. EXTERNALITY.

nepotism (**nep**-ə-tiz-əm), *n.* Bestowal of official favors (esp. in hiring) on one's relatives. —**nepotistic,** *adj.*

net asset value. The market value of a share in a mutual fund, computed by deducting total liabilities from total assets and dividing the difference by the number of outstanding shares. —Abbr. NAV. —Also termed *asset value.* See MUTUAL FUND.

net cash flow. See CASH FLOW.

net cost. See COST.

net estate. See ESTATE.

net income. See INCOME.

net lease. See LEASE.

net loss. See LOSS.

net operating income. See INCOME.

net operating loss. See LOSS.

net present value. See PRESENT VALUE.

net profit. See PROFIT.

net worth. A measure of one's wealth, usu. calculated as the excess of total assets over total liabilities.

neutrality, *n.* The condition of a nation that in time of war takes no part in the dispute but continues peaceful dealings with the belligerents. —**neutral,** *adj.*

neutrality law. An act that prohibits a nation from militarily aiding either of two or more belligerent powers with which the nation is at peace.

neutral principles. In constitutional law, rules grounded in law, as opposed to rules based on personal interests or beliefs.

new issue. See ISSUE (2).

newly discovered evidence. See EVIDENCE.

new matter. See MATTER.

new ruling. In criminal procedure, a Supreme Court ruling not dictated by precedent existing when the defendant's conviction became final and thus not applicable retroactively to habeas cases; for example, when the Court in *Ford v. Wainwright* (477 U.S. 399 (1986)) ruled that the Eighth Amendment prohibits execution of insane prisoners, this new ruling was nonretroactive because it departed so widely from prior doctrine. *Teague v. Lane*, 489 U.S. 288 (1989). See HABEAS CORPUS.

newsman's privilege. See *journalist's privilege* (a) under PRIVILEGE.

New York Stock Exchange. An unincorporated association of member firms that handle the purchase and sale of securities both for themselves and for customers; this exchange, the dominant one in the U.S., trades in only large companies having at least one million outstanding shares. —Abbr. NYSE.

next friend. A person who appears in a lawsuit on behalf of an incompetent or minor plaintiff, but who is not a party to the lawsuit and is not appointed as a guardian. —Also termed *prochein ami*. Cf. GUARDIAN AD LITEM.

next-in, first-out. A method of inventory valuation (but not a generally accepted accounting principle) whereby the cost of goods is based on their replacement cost rather than their actual cost. —Abbr. NIFO. Cf.

FIRST-IN, FIRST-OUT; LAST-IN, FIRST-OUT.

next of kin. 1. The person or persons most closely related by blood to a decedent. **2.** The person or persons entitled to inherit personal property from a decedent who has not left a will. See HEIR.

nexus. A connection or link, often a causal one <cigarette packages must inform consumers of the nexus between smoking and lung cancer>. Pl. **nexuses; nexus**.

NGO. *abbr.* NONGOVERNMENTAL ORGANIZATION.

NGRI. See *not guilty by reason of insanity* under NOT GUILTY.

NIFO (**nI**-foh). *abbr.* NEXT-IN, FIRST-OUT.

nihil. NIHIL EST.

nihil-dicit **default judgment.** See *nil-dicit default judgment* under DEFAULT JUDGMENT.

nihil est (**nee**-əl-est *or* **nI**-[h]il-est). [Latin "there is nothing"] A form of return by a sheriff or constable who was unable to serve a writ because nothing was found to levy on. —Often shortened to *nihil*. Cf. NULLA BONA.

nihil habet (**nee**-əl-**ha**-bət *or* **nI**-[h]il-**hay**-bət). [Latin "he has nothing"] A form of return by a sheriff or constable who was unable to serve a *scire facias* or other writ on the defendant. See SCIRE FACIAS.

nil debet (nil-**deb**-ət). [Latin "he owes nothing"] The archaic pleading form of the general denial in debt actions on a simple contract.

nil-dicit default judgment. See DEFAULT JUDGMENT.

nimble dividend. See DIVIDEND.

Nineteenth Amendment. The constitutional amendment, ratified in 1920, providing that a citizen's right to vote cannot be denied or abridged by the U.S. or any state on the basis of sex.

ninety-day letter. Statutory notice of a tax deficiency sent by the IRS to a taxpayer; during the 90 days after receiving the notice, the taxpayer must pay the taxes (and, if desired, seek a refund) or challenge the deficiency in Tax Court. I.R.C. §§ 6212, 6213. —Also termed *notice of deficiency*; *deficiency notice*.

Ninth Amendment. The constitutional amendment, ratified with the Bill of Rights in 1791, providing that rights listed in the Constitution must not be construed in a way that denies or disparages unlisted rights, which are retained by the people.

nisi (**nee**-see *or* **nis**-ee *or* **nI**-see *or* **nI-sI**). [Latin "unless"] (Of a court's ex parte ruling or grant of relief) having validity unless the adversely affected party appears and shows cause why it should be withdrawn <a decree *nisi*>. See *decree nisi* under DECREE.

nisi prius (-**prI**-əs). [Latin "unless before then"] A civil trial court in which issues are tried before the jury, as opposed to an appellate court; the term is obsolete in the U.S. except in New York and Oklahoma.

nitroglycerine charge. ALLEN CHARGE.

N.L. *abbr.* NON LIQUET.

NLRB. *abbr.* NATIONAL LABOR RELATIONS BOARD.

no-action clause. A liability-insurance policy provision that prevents the insured from recovering under the policy until a lawsuit against the insured results in a judgment or settlement.

no-action letter. A letter from a lawyer for a governmental agency stating that, if the facts are as represented in a person's request for an agency ruling, the lawyer will advise the agency not to take action against the person; typically, such a letter is requested from the SEC by an issuer of securities with respect to financing or marketing techniques.

no-answer default judgment. See DEFAULT JUDGMENT.

no bill, *n.* A grand jury's statement that insufficient evidence exists for an indictment on a criminal charge <the grand jury returned a no bill instead of the indictment the prosecutors expected>. —**no-bill,** *vb.* <the grand jury no-billed three of the charges>. Cf. TRUE BILL.

no-bonus clause. In property law, a lease provision that takes effect upon governmental condemnation, limiting the lessee's damages to the value of any improvements to the property and preventing the lessee from recovering the difference between the lease's fixed rent and the property's market rental value. See CONDEMNATION (2).

no contest. A criminal defendant's plea that, while not admitting guilt, the defendant will not contest the charge; this plea is often preferable to a guilty plea, which can be used against the defendant in a subsequent civil lawsuit. —Also termed *nolo contendere*; *non vult contendere*.

no-contest clause. A testamentary provision stating that a named beneficiary forfeits any gift granted by the will if he or she challenges the will. Cf. INCONTESTABILITY CLAUSE.

Noerr-Pennington **doctrine.** The principle that the First Amendment shields from liability (esp. under antitrust laws) companies that join together to lobby the government; the doctrine derives from a line of Supreme Court cases beginning with *Eastern R.R. Presidents Conference v. Noerr Motor Freight, Inc.*, 365 U.S. 127 (1961), and *United Mine Workers v. Pennington*, 381 U.S. 657 (1965).

no-eyewitness rule. In tort law, the largely defunct principle holding that if no direct evidence shows what a dead person did to avoid an accident, the jury may infer that the person acted with ordinary care for his or her own safety; in jurisdictions where the rule persists, plaintiffs in survival or wrongful-death actions can assert it to counter a defense of contributory negligence.

no-fault auto insurance. See INSURANCE.

no-fault divorce. See DIVORCE.

NOL. See *net operating loss* under LOSS.

nolens volens (**noh**-lenz-**voh**-lenz). [Latin] Willingly or unwillingly <the school district is subject *nolens volens* to the court's desegregation order>.

nolle prosequi (**nol**-ee-**pros**-ə-kwI), *n.* [Latin "not to wish to prosecute"] **1.** The legal notice that a lawsuit has been abandoned. **2.** A docket entry showing that the plaintiff or the prosecution has abandoned the action. —Often shortened to *nolle*.

nolle prosequi, *vb.* To abandon (a suit or prosecution); to have (a case) dismissed by a nolle prosequi <the state nolle prosequied the charges against Johnson>. —Often shortened to *nolle pros*; *nol-pros*; *nol-pro*.

no-load fund. See MUTUAL FUND.

nolo contendere (**noh**-loh-kən-**ten**-də-ree). [Latin "I do not wish to contend"] NO CONTEST. —Often shortened to *nolo*.

nominal asset. See ASSET.

nominal consideration. See CONSIDERATION.

nominal damages. See DAMAGES.

nominal partner. See PARTNER.

nominal party. See PARTY.

nominal-payee rule. In commercial law, the rule that validates any person's indorsement of an instrument (such as a check) when the instrument's drawer intended for the payee to have no interest in the instrument. U.C.C. § 3-404(b).

nominal rate. See INTEREST RATE.

nominal trust. See *passive trust* under TRUST.

nominal value. PAR VALUE.

nominal yield. See YIELD.

nominate, *vb.* **1.** To propose (a person) for election or appointment <Steven nominated Jane for president>. **2.** To name or designate (a person) for a position <the testator nominated an executor, who later withdrew because he couldn't perform his duties>. —**nomination,** *n.*

nominee. 1. A person who is proposed for office. **2.** A person designated to act in place of another, usu. in a very limited way. **3.** A party who holds bare legal title for the benefit of others or who receives and distributes funds for the benefit of others.

nonaccess. In family law, absence of opportunity for sexual intercourse; nonaccess is often used as a defense by the alleged father in paternity cases.

nonacquiescence (non-ak-wee-**es**-[ə]n[t]s). In administrative law, an agency's policy of declining to be bound by lower-court precedent that is contrary to the agency's interpretation of its organic statute, but only until the Supreme Court has ruled on the issue.

nonage (**non**-ij). MINORITY (1).

nonapparent easement. See *discontinuous easement* under EASEMENT.

nonassertive conduct. See CONDUCT.

nonassessable stock. See STOCK.

non assumpsit. [Latin "he did not undertake"] The archaic pleading form of a general denial in an action of assumpsit. See ASSUMPSIT.

noncallable security. See SECURITY.

noncancelability clause. An insurance-policy provision that prevents the insurer from canceling the policy after an insured's loss, as long as the premium has been paid.

non cepit (non-**kay**-pit *or* -**see**-pət). [Latin "he did not take"] *Archaic.* A general denial in a replevin action. See REPLEVIN.

noncompetition covenant. See COVENANT (1).

non compos mentis (non-kom-pəs-**men**-təs), *adj.* [Latin "not master of one's mind"] **1.** Insane. **2.** Incompetent. Cf. COMPOS MENTIS.

nonconforming goods. See GOODS.

nonconforming lot. See LOT (1).

nonconforming use. See USE (1).

nonconsent. 1. Lack of voluntary agreement. **2.** In the law of rape, the refusal to engage in sexual intercourse—usu. interpreted by courts as requiring some type of physical resistance. See CONSENT.

nonconstitutional, *adj.* Of or relating to some legal basis or principle other than those of the U.S. Constitution or a state constitution <the appellate court refused—on nonconstitutional procedural grounds—to hear the defendant's argument about cruel and unusual punishment>. Cf. UNCONSTITUTIONAL.

noncontestability clause. INCONTESTABILITY CLAUSE.

noncontinuous easement. See *discontinuous easement* under EASEMENT.

noncontribution clause. A fire-insurance-policy provision stating that only the interests of the property owner and the first mortgagee are protected under the policy.

non culpabilis (non-kəl-**pay**-bə-ləs). [Latin] Not guilty. —Abbr. *non cul.*

noncumulative dividend. See DIVIDEND.

noncumulative preferred stock. See STOCK.

noncumulative voting. See VOTING.

noncustodial sentence. See SENTENCE.

nondelegable duty. See DUTY.

nondelegation doctrine. DELEGATION DOCTRINE.

non detinet (non-**det**-ə-nət). [Latin "he does not detain"] The archaic pleading form of a general denial in a detinue action. See DETINUE.

nondiscretionary trust. See *fixed trust* under TRUST.

non est factum (non-est-**fak**-təm). [Latin "it is not my deed"] The archaic pleading form denying the execution of an instrument sued on.

non est inventus (non-est-in-**ven**-təs). [Latin "he is not found"] A statement on a sheriff's return of process, noting that the defendant is not to be found in the sheriff's jurisdiction. —Abbr. *n.e.i.*

nonexclusive listing. See *open listing* under LISTING (1).

nonexempt property. See EXEMPT PROPERTY.

nonfeasance (non-**feez**-[ə]n[t]s), *n.* The failure to act when a duty to act existed. —**nonfeasant,** *adj.*—**nonfeasor,** *n.* Cf. MALFEASANCE; MISFEASANCE.

nongovernmental organization. In international law, any scientific, professional, business, or public-interest organization that is neither af-filiated with nor under the direction of a government; examples of these organizations, which are often granted consultative status with the U.N., include OPEC, Greenpeace, and the Red Cross. —Abbr. NGO.

noninterpretivism, *n.* The doctrine of constitutional interpretation holding that judges are not confined to the Constitution's text or preratification history but may instead look to evolving social norms and values as the basis for constitutional judgments; Justices William Douglas and William Brennan are commonly cited exponents of this view. —**noninterpretivist,** *n.* Cf. INTERPRETIVISM.

nonintervention will. See WILL.

nonissuable plea. See PLEA.

nonjoinder. The failure to bring a person who is a necessary party into a lawsuit. See JOINDER. Cf. MISJOINDER; DISJOINDER.

nonjudicial day. LEGAL HOLIDAY.

nonjudicial foreclosure. See FORECLOSURE.

nonjury trial. See *bench trial* under TRIAL.

nonlapse statute. ANTILAPSE STATUTE.

non liquet (non-**li**-kwet). [Latin "it is not clear"] **1.** In some legal systems (such as early Roman law), the principle that a decision-maker may be relieved of the necessity of deciding a dispute if the applicable law is unclear. **2.** A tribunal's nondecision resulting from the unclarity of the law applicable to the dispute at hand; in modern usage, the phrase appears almost always in passages stating what a court must not do: tribunals are routinely disallowed from declaring a *non liquet*. —Abbr. N.L.

nonmedical policy. See INSURANCE POLICY.

nonmovant. A litigating party other than the one that has filed a motion currently under consideration <the court, in ruling on the plaintiff's motion for summary judgment, properly resolved all doubts in the nonmovant's favor>.

nonnegotiable document of title. See DOCUMENT OF TITLE.

non obstante veredicto (non-əb-**stahn**-tee-ver-ə-**dik**-toh).   [Latin] Notwithstanding the verdict. —Abbr. n.o.v.; NOV. See *judgment notwithstanding the verdict* under JUDGMENT.

nonobviousness. 1. In patent law, the fact that an invention is not obvious to a person with ordinary skill in the relevant prior art or trade. **2.** The requirement that this fact must be demonstrated for an invention to be patentable; nonobviousness can be demonstrated by evidence of prior art or other objective evidence, such as commercial success or professional approval. 35 U.S.C. § 103. Cf. NOVELTY.

nonoperating income. See INCOME.

nonparticipating   preferred stock. See STOCK.

nonperformance. Failure to discharge an obligation (esp. a contractual one). Cf. PERFORMANCE.

nonperforming loan. See LOAN.

nonpersonal action. See ACTION.

nonprobate, *adj.* **1.** Of or relating to some method of estate disposition apart from wills <nonprobate administration>. **2.** Of or relating to the property so disposed <nonprobate assets>.

nonprofit corporation. See CORPORATION.

non prosequitur (non-proh-**sek**-wəd-ər). [Latin "he does not prosecute"]   The judgment rendered against a plaintiff who has not pursued the case. —Often shortened to *non pros*.

nonpublic forum. In constitutional law, public property that is not designated or traditionally considered an arena for public communication, such as a jail or a military base; the government's means of regulating a nonpublic forum need only be reasonable and viewpoint-neutral to be constitutional. Cf. PUBLIC FORUM.

nonrecognition provision. In tax law, a statutory rule that allows all or part of a realized gain or a loss not to be recognized for tax purposes; usu. this type of provision only postpones the recognition of the gain or loss. See RECOGNITION (3).

nonrecourse loan. See LOAN.

nonrecurring dividend. See *extraordinary dividend* under DIVIDEND.

nonrefund annuity. See ANNUITY.

nonresident, *n.* One who does not live within the jurisdiction in question. —**nonresident,** *adj.*

nonresident alien. See ALIEN.

nonresident-motorist statute. A state law governing the liabilities and obligations of nonresidents who use the state's highways.

non sequitur (non-**sek**-wəd-ər). [Latin "it does not follow"] **1.** An inference or conclusion not logically following from the premises. **2.** A remark or response not logically following from what was previously said.

nonshareholder constituency. A group of nonstockholders, such as employees or the public, who have an interest in the business of the corporation, and whose interest may be legally considered, in addition to shareholders' interests, by the corporation when making major policy decisions. —Also termed *alternative constituency*.

nonstock corporation. See CORPORATION.

non sui juris (non-soo-ee-**juur**-əs), *adj.* [Latin "not of one's own right"] Lacking legal age or capacity. Cf. SUI JURIS.

nonsuit, *n.* **1.** A plaintiff's voluntary dismissal of a case or of a defendant. **2.** A court's dismissal of a case or of a defendant because the plaintiff has failed to make out a legal case or to bring forward sufficient evidence. — **nonsuit,** *vb.*

nonsupport. The failure to provide support to a person one is legally obliged to provide for, such as a child, spouse, or other dependent; nonsupport is a crime in most states.

nontenure (non-**ten**-yər). An archaic pleading form in a real-property action whereby the defendant denies holding the land in question.

nonuser. The failure to use a right (such as a franchise or easement), as a result of which the person having the right might lose it <the government may not revoke a citizen's voting right because of nonuser>. Cf. USER (1).

nonvoluntary euthanasia. See EUTHANASIA.

nonvoting stock. See STOCK.

non vult contendere (non-vəlt-kən-**ten**-də-ree). [Latin "he will not contest it"] NO CONTEST.

nonwaiver agreement. In insurance law, a contract (supplementing a liability-insurance policy) in which the insured acknowledges that the insurer's investigating or defending against a claim against the insured does not waive the insurer's right to contest coverage later. —Also termed *reservation of rights*.

no-par stock. See STOCK.

no-pass, no-play rule. A state law requiring public-school students who participate in extracurricular activities (such as sports or band) to maintain a minimum grade-point average.

no-retreat rule. The criminal-law doctrine holding that the victim of a murderous assault may stand his or her ground and use deadly force in self-defense if there is no reasonable alternative to avoid the assailant's threatened harm; a majority of American jurisdictions have adopted this rule. Cf. RETREAT RULE.

normative, *adj.* Establishing or conforming to a norm or standard <Rawls's theory describes normative principles of justice>.

North American Free Trade Agreement. A trilateral treaty—entered into on January 1, 1994 between the U.S., Canada, and Mexico—that phases out all tariffs and eliminates many nontariff barriers (such as quotas) inhibiting the free trade of goods between the participating nations. —Abbr. NAFTA.

noscitur a sociis (**nos**-ə-tər-ah-**soh**-see-əs). [Latin "it is known by its associates"] A canon of construction holding that the meaning of an unclear word or phrase should be determined by the words immediately surrounding it. Cf. EJUSDEM GENERIS; INCLUSIO UNIUS EST EXCLUSIO ALTERIUS.

no-shop provision. A stipulation prohibiting one or more parties to a commercial contract from pursuing or entering into a more favorable agreement with a third party.

no-strike clause. A labor-agreement provision that prohibits employees from striking for any reason and establishes instead an arbitration system for resolving disputes.

nota bene (nohd-ə-**ben**-ee). See N.B.

notarial protest certificate. PROTEST CERTIFICATE.

notarial record. JOURNAL OF NOTARIAL ACTS.

notarial register. JOURNAL OF NOTARIAL ACTS.

notary public (**noh**-də-ree), *n.* A person authorized by a state to administer oaths, certify documents, attest to the authenticity of signatures, and perform official acts in commercial matters, such as protesting negotiable instruments. —Often shortened to *notary.* Pl. **notaries public. —notarize,** *vb.*—**notarial,** *adj.*

notary record book. JOURNAL OF NOTARIAL ACTS.

notary seal. 1. The imprint or embossment made by a notary public's seal. **2.** A device, usu. a stamp or embosser, that makes an imprint on a notarized document. —Also termed *notarial seal.*

embossed seal. **a.** A notary seal that is impressed onto a document so that it is raised above the surface; required in some states and often on documents notarized for federal purposes, this type of seal is at best only faintly reproducible, so that original documents are amply safeguarded. **b.** The embossment made by the seal.

rubber-stamp seal. **a.** In most states, a notary public's official seal, which is ink-stamped onto documents and is therefore photographically reproducible; it typically includes the notary's name, the state seal, the words "Notary Public," the name of the county where the notary's bond is filed, and the expiration date of the notary's commission. **b.** The imprint made by the seal.

note, *n.* **1.** A written promise by one party (the *maker*) to pay money to another party (the *payee*) or to bearer. —Also termed *promissory note.* Cf. DRAFT (1).

balloon note. A note requiring small periodic payments but a very large final payment; usu. the periodic payments only cover interest, while the final payment (the balloon payment) represents the entire principal.

bank note. A note that is issued by a bank, payable to the bearer on demand, and intended to circulate as money.

circular note. LETTER OF CREDIT.

cognovit note. See COGNOVIT CLAUSE.

demand note. A note payable whenever the creditor wants to be paid. Cf. *call loan* under LOAN.

installment note. A note payable at regular intervals. —Also termed *serial note.*

inverse-floating-rate note. A note structured in such a way that its interest rate moves in the opposite direction from the underlying index (such as the London Interbank Offer Rate); many such notes are risky investments because if interest rates rise, the securities lose their value and their coupon earnings fall. —Also termed *inverse floater.*

mortgage note. A note evidencing a loan for which real property has been offered as security.

negotiable note. See NEGOTIABLE INSTRUMENT.

reissuable note. A note that may again be put into circulation after having once been paid.

sale note. A broker's memorandum on the terms of a sale, given to the buyer and seller.

savings note. A short-term, interest-bearing paper issued by a bank or the U.S. Government.

secured note. A note backed by a pledge of real or personal property as collateral. —Also termed *collateral note.*

time note. A note payable only at a specified time and not on demand.

treasury note. See TREASURY NOTE.

unsecured note. A note not backed by collateral.

2. A scholarly legal essay shorter than an article and restricted in scope, explaining or criticizing a particular set of cases or a general area of the law, and usu. written by a student for publication in a law review. —Also termed *comment*; *lawnote.* Cf. ANNOTATION.

not-for-profit corporation. See *nonprofit corporation* under CORPORATION.

not guilty. 1. In a criminal case, a defendant's plea denying the crime charged. **2.** In a criminal case, a jury verdict acquitting the defendant because the prosecution failed to prove its case beyond a reasonable doubt.

not guilty by reason of insanity. A not-guilty verdict, based on the insanity defense, that usu. does not release the defendant but instead commits him or her to a mental institution. —Abbr. NGRI. See INSANITY DEFENSE.

notice, *n.* **1.** Legal notification required by law or agreement, or imparted by operation of law as a result of some fact (such as the recording of instruments) <under the lease, the tenant must give the landlord written notice 30 days before vacating the premises>. **2.** The condition of being so notified, whether or not actual awareness exists <all prospective buyers were on notice of the

judgment lien>. **3.** A written or printed announcement <the notice of sale was posted on the courthouse bulletin board>. Cf. KNOWLEDGE.

actual notice. Notice given to a party directly or presumed to be received personally because the evidence within the party's knowledge is sufficient to put him or her on inquiry.

constructive notice. Notice presumed by law to have been acquired by a person and thus imputed to that person.

due notice. Sufficient and proper notice that is intended to and likely to reach a particular person or the public.

implied notice. Notice inferred from facts that a person had means of knowing and thus imputed to that person.

inquiry notice. Notice attributed to a person when the information would lead an ordinarily prudent person to investigate the matter further.

judicial notice. See JUDICIAL NOTICE.

record notice. Constructive notice of the contents of an instrument, such as a deed or mortgage, that has been properly recorded.

notice, *vb.* To give legal notice to or of <the plaintiff's lawyer noticed depositions of all the experts that the defendant listed>.

notice act. NOTICE STATUTE.

notice-and-comment period. In administrative law, the statutory time frame during which an administrative agency publishes a proposed regulation and receives public feedback on the regulation; after this period expires, the regulation can take effect. —Often shortened to *comment period.*

notice of appearance. 1. A party's written notice filed with the court or oral announcement on the record informing the court and the other parties that the party wants to participate in the case. **2.** In bankruptcy law, a written notice filed with the court or oral announcement in open court by a person who wants to receive all pleadings in a particular case; this notice is usu. filed by the attorney for a creditor who requests that his or her name be added to the official service list.

notice of deficiency. NINETY-DAY LETTER.

notice of dishonor. Notice to the indorser of an instrument that acceptance or payment has been refused; this notice—along with presentment and actual dishonor—is a condition of an indorser's secondary liability. U.C.C. § 3-503(a).

notice of lis pendens. LIS PENDENS (3).

notice of pendency. LIS PENDENS (3).

notice pleading. See PLEADING (2).

notice-race statute. RACE-NOTICE STATUTE.

notice statute. A recording act providing that the person with the most recent valid claim, and who purchased without notice, has priority; about half the states have notice statutes. —Also termed *notice act.* Cf.

RACE STATUTE; RACE-NOTICE STAT-UTE.

notice to creditors. In bankruptcy law, formal notice to creditors that a creditors' meeting will be held, that proofs of claim must be filed, or that an order for relief has been granted.

notice to produce. REQUEST FOR PRODUCTION.

notice to quit. A notice by either a landlord or a tenant to vacate the leased premises.

notorious, *adj.* **1.** Generally known and spoken of. **2.** (Of the possession of property) so conspicuous as to impute notice to the true owner. —Also termed (in sense 2) *open and notorious*. See ADVERSE POSSESSION.

notorious cohabitation. See CO-HABITATION.

notorious possession. See *open possession* under POSSESSION.

not proven. An archaic jury verdict—now used only in Scots criminal law—legally equivalent to not guilty, but carrying with it a strong suspicion of wrongdoing. —Also termed *Scotch verdict*.

not sufficient funds. The notation of dishonor (of a check) indicating that there are not enough funds in the drawer's account to cover payment. —Abbr. NSF. —Also termed *insufficient funds*.

notwithstanding, *prep.* Despite; in spite of <notwithstanding the conditions listed above, the landlord can terminate the lease if the tenant defaults>.

n.o.v. *abbr.* NON OBSTANTE VERE-DICTO.

nova causa interveniens. See *intervening cause* under CAUSE (1).

novation (noh-**vay**-shən), *n.* The act of substituting for an old contract a new one that either replaces an existing obligation with a new obligation or replaces an original party with a new party; today, a novation may substitute (1) a new obligation between the same parties, (2) a new debtor, or (3) a new creditor. —**novate,** *vb.*—**novatory** (**noh**-və-tor-ee), *adj.* Cf. SUBROGATION (1).

Novels. A collection of 168 constitutions issued by the Roman emperor Justinian and his immediate successors; taken together, the Novels make up one of four component parts of the *Corpus Juris Civilis*. —Also termed *Novellae*; *Novellae Constitutiones*. See CORPUS JURIS CIVILIS.

novelty. 1. In patent law, the fact that an invention is new in form and in function or performance. **2.** The requirement that this fact must be demonstrated for an invention to be patentable; if the invention was previously patented, described in a publication, or known or used by others, it is not novel. 35 U.S.C. § 102. Cf. NONOBVIOUSNESS.

novus actus interveniens. See *intervening cause* under CAUSE (1).

N.O.W. *abbr.* NEGOTIABLE ORDER OF WITHDRAWAL.

now comes. *Jargon.* COMES NOW.

noxal (**nok**-səl), *adj. Archaic.* Of or relating to a cause of action against an owner of an animal or slave for damage done by the animal or slave.

NPV. See *net present value* under PRESENT VALUE.

NSF. *abbr.* NOT SUFFICIENT FUNDS.

nudum pactum (n[y]oo-dəm-**pak**-təm). [Latin "nude pact"] An agreement that is unenforceable as a contract because it is not "clothed" with consideration. —Also termed *naked contract*.

nugatory (n[y]oo-gə-tor-ee), *adj.* Of no force or effect; useless; invalid <the Supreme Court rendered the statute nugatory by declaring it unconstitutional>.

nuisance. 1. Anything that annoys or disturbs the use or enjoyment of property. **2.** Use of one's own property in a way that annoys or disturbs others' use or enjoyment of property.

abatable nuisance. A nuisance so easily removable that the aggrieved party may lawfully cure the problem without notice to the liable party, such as overhanging tree branches.

anticipatory nuisance. An activity that, although not yet at the level of a nuisance, is very likely to become one, so that a party may obtain an injunction prohibiting the activity.

attractive nuisance. A dangerous condition that may attract children onto land, thereby causing a risk to their safety. See ATTRACTIVE-NUISANCE DOCTRINE.

legalized nuisance. A nuisance created by legislation and therefore immune from lawsuit, such as a city park.

mixed nuisance. A nuisance that is both a private nuisance and a public nuisance.

nuisance in fact. A nuisance existing because of the circumstances of the use or the particular location; for example, a machine emitting high-frequency sound may be a nuisance only if dogs live nearby to hear the noise and be disturbed by it. —Also termed *nuisance per accidens*.

nuisance per se. A nuisance existing regardless of location or circumstances of use, such as a leaky nuclear-waste storage facility.

permanent nuisance. A nuisance that cannot readily be abated at reasonable expense.

private nuisance. A nuisance that interferes with a person's own land or premises and that may allow the person to recover damages or obtain an injunction.

public nuisance. A nuisance that interferes with a communal right and that may lead to civil injunction or criminal prosecution. —Also termed *common nuisance*.

nulla bona (nəl-ə-**boh**-nə). [Latin "no goods"] A form of return by a sheriff or constable upon an execution when the judgment debtor has no property to be seized. Cf. NIHIL EST.

nulla poena sine lege (nəl-ə-**peen**-ə-sI-nee-**lee**-jee *or* -si-nay-**le**-gay). [Latin] No punishment without a law authorizing it.

nullification, *n.* **1.** The act of making something void. **2.** The state or condition of being void. —**nullify,** *vb.* See JURY NULLIFICATION.

nullification doctrine. The theory—espoused by southern states before the Civil War—advocating a state's right to declare a federal law unconstitutional and therefore void.

nullity. 1. Something that is legally void <the forged commercial transfer is a nullity>. **2.** The fact of being legally void <she filed a petition for nullity of marriage>.

nul tiel (nəl-teel). [Law Latin] No such; this phrase typically denotes a plea that denies the existence of something <the defendant entered a plea of *nul tiel* record>.

nunc pro tunc (**nuungk**-proh-**tu-ungk**). [Latin "now for then"] Having retroactive legal effect <the court entered a *nunc pro tunc* order to correct a clerical error in the record>.

nuncupative will. See WILL.

nuptial (**nəp**-shəl), *adj.* Of or relating to marriage.

NYSE. *abbr.* NEW YORK STOCK EXCHANGE.

O

oath. A solemn pledge by which the person swearing to a statement implicitly invites punishment from a supreme being if the person is untruthful. Cf. AFFIRMATION.

assertory oath. An oath by which one attests to some factual matter, rather than making a promise about one's future conduct; a courtroom witness typically takes such an oath.

extrajudicial oath. An oath that, although formally sworn, is taken outside a legal proceeding or outside the authority of law.

oath ex officio. At common law, an oath under which a member of the clergy who was accused of a crime could swear to his innocence before an ecclesiastical court.

oath of allegiance. An oath by which one promises to maintain fidelity to a particular sovereign or government; such an oath is most often administered to high public officers, to soldiers and sailors, and to aliens applying for naturalization. —Also termed *loyalty oath*; *test oath*.

oath of office. An oath taken by a person about to enter into the duties of public office, by which the person promises to perform the duties of that office in good faith.

pauper's oath. An affidavit or verification of poverty by a person requesting public funds or services. See *poverty affidavit* under AFFIDAVIT; IN FORMA PAUPERIS.

promissory oath. An oath that binds the party to observe a specified course of conduct in the future; both the oath of office and the oath of allegiance are types of promissory oaths.

obiit sine prole (**oh**-bit-sI-nee-**proh**-lee *or* -si-nay-**prohl**). [Latin] He died without issue. —Abbr. OSP.

obiter (**oh**-bid-ər), *adv.* [Latin "by the way"] Incidentally; in passing.

obiter dictum (**oh**-bid-ər-**dik**-təm). [Latin "something said in passing"] A judicial comment made during the course of delivering a judicial opinion, but one that is unnecessary to the decision in the case and therefore not precedential (though it may be considered persuasive). —Often shortened to *dictum* or, less commonly, *obiter*. Pl. **obiter dicta.** See DICTUM. Cf. HOLDING (1); RATIO DECIDENDI.

objectant. CONTESTANT.

objection, *n.* A formal statement by counsel that he or she protests something that has occurred in court and seeks the judge's immediate ruling on the point; the person objecting must usu. state the basis for the objection in order to preserve the right to appeal an adverse ruling. —**object** (əb-**jekt**), *vb.*—**objector,** *n.*

objective ethics. MORAL ABSOLUTISM.

objective standard. A legal standard that is based on conduct and perceptions external to a particular person; in tort law, for example, the reasonable-person standard is considered an objective standard because it does not require a determination of what the defendant was thinking. Cf. SUBJECTIVE STANDARD.

object offense. See OFFENSE.

obligation, *n.* **1.** A legal or moral duty to do or not do something. **2.** A formal, binding agreement or acknowledgment of a liability to pay a certain amount or to do a certain thing. —**obligate, oblige,** *vb.*— **obligatory** (ə-**blig**-ə-tor-ee), *adj.* See DUTY; LIABILITY.

accessory obligation. A duty, promise, or undertaking that is incident to a primary obligation.

primary obligation. In contract law, a fundamental term imposing a requirement on a contracting party from which other obligations may spring.

obligation, mutuality of. See MUTUALITY OF OBLIGATION.

obligee (ob-li-**jee**). One to whom an obligation is owed; a promisee or creditor.

obligor (ob-li-**gor**). One who has undertaken an obligation; a promisor or debtor.

obloquy (**ob**-lə-kwee). **1.** Foul language directed to a person; abusive words. **2.** Disgrace; bad repute.

obscenity, *n.* **1.** The quality or state of being repulsive, loathsome, morally abhorrent, or regarded as taboo; under the Supreme Court's three-part test, material is legally obscene—and therefore not protected under the First Amendment—if, taken as a whole, the material (1) appeals to the prurient interest in sex, as determined by the average person applying contemporary community standards; (2) portrays sexual conduct, as specifically defined by the applicable state law, in a patently offensive way; and (3) lacks serious literary, political, or scientific value. *Miller v. California*, 413 U.S. 15 (1973). **2.** Something (such as an expression or act) that has this quality. —**obscene,** *adj.* Cf. INDECENCY.

obsolescence (ob-sə-**les**-[ə]n[t]s), *n.* The process of falling into disuse or the condition of being nearly obsolete, esp. due to technological advances. —**obsolesce,** *vb.*—**obsolescent,** *adj.*

obstruction of justice. Interference with the orderly administration of law (such as by withholding evidence or intimidating a witness); obstruction of justice is a crime in most jurisdictions.

obviate (**ob**-vee-ayt), *vb.* **1.** To dispose of or do away with (a thing); to anticipate and prevent from arising <they obviated the growing problem through legislation>. **2.** To make unnecessary <the movant obviated the all-night drafting session by getting the opponent to agree to an extension>. —**obviation,** *n.*—**obviator,** *n.*

occupancy, *n.* **1.** The act of taking or fact of having possession of property; esp., the act of taking possession of something having no owner, with a view to acquiring it as property. See ADVERSE POSSESSION. **2.** The period during which a person owns, rents, or otherwise occupies real property or premises. —**occupant,** *n.*

occupation. In international law, the condition of territory that has been placed under the authority of a hostile army.

occupational disease. A disease that is contracted as a result of exposure to debilitating conditions or substances in the course of employment <black lung in coal miners is one of the many occupational diseases recognized by OSHA>.

occupational hazard. A danger or risk that is peculiar to a particular calling or occupation; for example, asbestosis is an occupational hazard for persons who work with insulation.

Occupational Safety and Health Administration. A federal agency that establishes and enforces health and safety standards in various industries; this agency, created under the Occupational Safety and Health Act of 1970, routinely conducts inspections of businesses and issues citations for noncompliance with its standards. —Abbr. OSHA.

occupational tax. See *occupation tax* under TAX.

occupation tax. See TAX.

occupying-claimant act. BETTERMENT ACT.

occurrence policy. See INSURANCE POLICY.

occurrence rule. In civil procedure, the rule that a limitations period begins to run when the alleged wrongful act or omission occurs, rather than when the plaintiff discovers the injury; this rule applies, for example, to most breach-of- contract claims. See STATUTE OF LIMITATIONS. Cf. DISCOVERY RULE.

odd lot. See LOT (3).

odd-lot doctrine. In workers'-compensation law, the doctrine that permits a finding of total disability for an injured claimant who, though able to work sporadically, cannot obtain regular employment and steady income and is thus considered an "odd lot" in the labor market.

of counsel. See COUNSEL.

of course. 1. Following the ordinary procedure <the writ was issued as a matter of course>. **2.** Naturally; obviously; clearly <we'll appeal that ruling, of course>.

offender. A person who has committed a crime.

adult offender. **a.** A person who has committed a crime after reaching the age of majority. **b.** A person who, having committed a crime while a minor, has been convicted after reaching the age of majority. **c.** A juvenile who has committed a crime and is tried as an adult rather than as a juvenile.

first offender. A person who authorities believe has committed a crime but who has never before been convicted of a crime; such a person is often treated leniently at sentencing or in plea negotiations.

repeat offender. See RECIDIVIST.

youthful offender. **a.** A person in late adolescence or early adulthood who has been convicted of a crime; such an offender is often eligible for special programs not available to older offenders, including community supervision, the successful completion of which may lead to erasing the conviction from the offender's record. **b.** JUVENILE DELINQUENT.

offense (ə-**fen(t)s**). A violation of the law; a crime, often a minor one. See CRIME.

capital offense. A crime for which the death penalty may be imposed. — Also termed *capital crime.*

civil offense. **a.** A statutory violation that amounts to an act of public nuisance. **b.** An offense that is malum prohibitum; an act that violates a statute, but is not actually considered a bad act. See *civil wrong* under WRONG.

cognate offense. A lesser offense that is related to the greater offense because it shares several of the elements of the greater offense and is of the same class or category; for example, shoplifting is a cognate offense of larceny because both crimes require the elements of taking another's property with the intent to deprive the rightful owner of that property. Cf. *lesser included offense.*

continuing offense. A crime that is committed over a period of time, such as a conspiracy, so that the last act of the crime controls for the commencement of the statute of limitations.

divisible offense. A crime that includes one or more crimes of lesser grade; for example, murder is a divisible offense comprising assault, battery, and assault with intent to kill.

extraneous offense. An offense beyond or unrelated to the offense for which a defendant is on trial.

graded offense. A crime that is divided into various degrees of severity with corresponding levels of punishment, such as murder (first-degree and second-degree) or assault (simple and aggravated). See DEGREE (2).

inchoate offense. A step toward the commission of another crime, the step in itself being serious enough to merit punishment; in criminal law, the three inchoate offenses are attempt, conspiracy, and solicitation. —Also termed *anticipatory offense; inchoate crime.*

index offense. One of eight classes of crimes reported annually by the FBI in the Uniform Crime Report; the eight classes are murder (and nonnegligent homicide), rape, robbery, aggravated assault, burglary, larceny-theft, arson, and auto theft. —Also termed *index crime.*

indictable offense. A crime that can be prosecuted only by indictment; in federal court, such an offense is one punishable by death or by imprisonment for more than one year or at hard labor. Fed. R. Crim. P. 7(a). See INDICTMENT.

lesser included offense. A crime that is composed of some, but not all, of the elements of a more serious crime and that is necessarily committed in carrying out the greater crime <battery is a lesser included offense of murder>; for double-jeopardy purposes, a lesser included offense is considered the "same offense" as the greater offense, so that acquittal or conviction of either offense precludes a separate trial for the other. —Also termed *included offense; necessarily included offense.* Cf. *cognate offense.*

multiple offense. An offense that violates more than one law but that may require different proof so that an acquittal or conviction under one statute does not exempt the defendant from prosecution under another.

object offense. The crime that is the object of the defendant's attempt, solicitation, conspiracy, or complicity; for example, murder is the object offense in a charge of attempted murder. —Also termed *target offense.*

petty offense. A minor or insignificant crime.

political offense. See POLITICAL OFFENSE.

regulatory offense. **a.** A statutory crime, as opposed to a common-law crime. **b.** A minor criminal offense (such as a traffic violation) that does not require criminal intent but instead imposes strict liability. —Also termed *public-welfare offense.*

same offense. **a.** For purposes of the Fifth Amendment, the same criminal act, omission, or transaction for which the person has already stood trial. See DOUBLE JEOPARDY. **b.** In connection with punishing a repeat offender, an identical offense or one similar in nature.

unnatural offense. See *crime against nature* under CRIME.

unrelated offense. A crime that is independent from the charged offense.

offensive collateral estoppel. See COLLATERAL ESTOPPEL.

offer, *n.* **1.** The act or an instance of presenting something for acceptance <the prosecutor's offer of immuni-

ty>. **2.** A display of willingness to enter into a contract on specified terms, made in a way that would lead a reasonable person to understand that an acceptance, having been sought, will result in a binding contract <she accepted the $500 offer on the Victorian armoire>.

irrevocable offer. An offer that includes a promise to keep it open for a specified period, during which the offer cannot be withdrawn without the offeror's becoming subject to liability for breach of contract; traditionally, such a promise must be supported by consideration to be enforceable, but under U.C.C. § 2-205, a merchant's signed, written offer giving assurances that it will be held open— but lacking consideration—is nonetheless irrevocable for the stated time period (or, if not stated, for a reasonable time not exceeding three months). —Also termed (in the U.C.C.) *firm offer.*

two-tier offer. See TWO-TIER OFFER.

3. A price at which one is ready to buy or sell; BID <she lowered her offer to $200>. **4.** ATTEMPT (2) <an offer to commit battery>. —**offer,** *vb.*—**offeror,** *n.*—**offeree,** *n.*

offering, *n.* **1.** The act of making an offer; something offered for sale. **2.** The sale of an issue of securities. See ISSUE (2).

all-or-none offering. An offering that allows the issuer to terminate the distribution if the entire block of offered securities is not sold.

initial public offering. A company's first public sale of stock. —Abbr. IPO.

primary offering. An offering of newly issued securities.

private offering. An offering made only to a small group of interested buyers.

public offering. An offering made to the general public.

registered offering. A public offering of securities registered with the SEC and with appropriate state securities commissions. —Also termed *registered public offering.*

secondary offering. An offering of previously issued securities. See *secondary distribution* (a) under DISTRIBUTION.

offer of proof. In trial procedure, a presentation of evidence for the record (but outside the jury's presence) after the judge has sustained an objection to the admissibility of that evidence, so that the evidence can be preserved on the record for an appeal of the judge's ruling; such an offer may be made of tangible evidence, of testimony through questions and answers, or of testimony through the lawyer's own narrative description. Fed. R. Evid. 103(a)(2). —Also termed *avowal.*

office audit. See AUDIT.

officer. A person who holds an office of trust, authority, or command; esp., in corporate law, a person elected or appointed by the board of directors to manage the daily operations of a corporation, such as a president, CEO, secretary, or treasurer. Cf. DIRECTOR (2).

officer of the court. A person who is charged with upholding the law and the judicial system; typically, of-

ficer of the court refers to a judge, clerk, bailiff, sheriff, or the like, but the term also applies to a lawyer, who is obliged to obey court rules and who owes a duty of candor to the court.

officer of the peace. PEACE OFFICER.

official corruption. See *official misconduct* under MISCONDUCT.

official misconduct. See MISCONDUCT.

officious intermeddler. A person who confers a benefit on another without being requested or having a legal duty to do so, and who therefore has no legal grounds to demand restitution for the benefit conferred.

off point. Not discussing the precise issue at hand; irrelevant. Cf. ON POINT.

offset, *n.* **1.** A deduction; a counterclaim. **2.** In accounting, an entry that counters the effect of a previous entry. —**offset,** *vb.* See SETOFF.

of record. 1. Recorded in the appropriate records <counsel of record>. See ATTORNEY OF RECORD. **2.** (Of a court) that has proceedings taken down stenographically or otherwise documented <court of record>. See *court of record* under COURT.

of the essence. (Of a contractual requirement) so important that if the requirement is not met, the promisor will be held to have breached the contract and a rescission by the promisee will be justified <time is of the essence>.

oligarchy (**ohl**-ə-gahr-kee *or* **ol**-), *n.* A government in which a small group of persons exercises control; the persons who constitute such a government. —**oligarchic, oligarchical,** *adj.*

oligopoly (ohl-ə-**gop**-ə-lee *or* ol-), *n.* Control or domination of a market by a few large sellers, creating high prices and low output similar to those found in a monopoly. —**oligopolistic,** *adj.*—**oligopolist,** *n.* See MONOPOLY.

oligopsony (ohl-ə-**gop**-sə-nee *or* ol-), *n.* Control or domination of a market by a few large buyers or customers. —**oligopsonistic,** *adj.*—**oligopsonist,** *n.*

olograph (**ol**-ə-graf). See *holographic will* under WILL.

ombudsman (om-**bədz**-mən *or* om-bədz- *or* om-buudz-). **1.** An official appointed to receive, investigate, and report on private citizens' complaints about the government. **2.** A similar appointee in a nongovernmental organization (such as a university). — Often shortened to *ombuds.*

omission, *n.* **1.** A failure to do something; a neglect of duty. **2.** The act of leaving something out; a thing left out. —**omit,** *vb.*—**omissive, omissible,** *adj.*

omnibus (**om**-ni-bəs), *adj.* Relating to or providing for numerous distinct objects at once; containing many items.

omnibus bill. See BILL (3).

omnibus clause. 1. A provision in an automobile-insurance policy that extends coverage to all drivers operating the insured vehicle with the owner's permission. **2.** RESIDUARY CLAUSE.

on all fours. *Jargon.* (Of a law case) squarely on point (with a precedent) on both facts and law; nearly identical in all material ways <our client's case is on all fours with the Supreme Court's most recent opinion>.

on demand. When presented or upon request for payment <this note is payable on demand>. —Also termed *on call.* See PAYABLE.

one-action rule. In debtor-creditor law, the principle that when a debt is secured by real property, the creditor must foreclose on the collateral before proceeding against the debtor's unsecured assets.

one-person, one-vote rule. In constitutional law, the principle that the Equal Protection Clause requires legislative voting districts to be apportioned strictly on the basis of population, rather than on residence or other factors. *Reynolds v. Sims,* 377 U.S. 533 (1964). —Also termed *one-man, one-vote rule.* See APPORTIONMENT.

onerous (**oh**-nər-əs), *adj.* **1.** (Of an obligation) exceeding the advantages to be derived; unreasonably burdensome or one-sided. **2.** In civil law, of, relating to, or supported by valuable consideration. —**onerousness,** *n.*

onomastic (on-ə-**mas**-tik), *adj.* **1.** Of or relating to names or nomenclature. **2.** (Of a signature on an instrument) in a handwriting different from that of the body of the document. —**onomastics** (corresponding to sense 1), *n.*

on or about. Approximately; at or around the time specified—this language is used in pleading to prevent a variance between the pleading and the proof, usu. when there is any uncertainty about the exact date of a pivotal event; when used in non-pleading contexts, the phrase is mere jargon.

on pain of. Followed by punishment inflicted if one does not comply with a command or condition <ordered to cease operations on pain of a $2,000 fine>.

on point. Discussing the precise issue now at hand; apposite <this opinion is not on point as authority in our case>. —Also termed *in point*. Cf. OFF POINT.

on-sale bar. In patent law, a statutory bar prohibiting patent eligibility if an invention was sold or offered for sale more than one year before the filing of a patent application.

on the brief. (Of a lawyer) having participated in preparing a given brief; the names of all the lawyers on the brief are typically listed on the front cover.

on the merits. (Of a judgment) delivered after the court has heard and investigated the substantive arguments of the parties.

on the pleadings. (Of a judgment) rendered without hearing or evaluating the full arguments of the parties. See SUMMARY JUDGMENT.

onus (**oh**-nəs). **1.** A burden; a load. **2.** A disagreeable responsibility; an obligation. **3.** ONUS PROBANDI. —**onerous,** *adj.*

onus probandi (**oh**-nəs-proh-**ban**-dI). [Latin] BURDEN OF PROOF. — Often shortened to *onus*.

OPEC (**oh**-pek). *abbr.* Organization of Petroleum Exporting Countries.

open, *adj.* **1.** Manifest; apparent; notorious. **2.** Visible; exposed to public view; not clandestine. **3.** Not closed, settled, fixed, or terminated. See *open possession* under POSSESSION.

open account. See ACCOUNT.

open and notorious. 1. NOTORIOUS (2). **2.** (Of adultery) known and recognized by the public and flouting the accepted standards of morality in the community.

open and notorious possession. See *open possession* under POSSESSION.

open bid. See BID.

open credit. See *revolving credit* under CREDIT.

open-end fund. See MUTUAL FUND.

open-end mortgage. See MORTGAGE.

open-field doctrine. In criminal procedure, the rule permitting a warrantless search of the area outside a property owner's curtilage, which includes the home and any adjoining land (such as a yard) that is within an enclosure or otherwise protected from public scrutiny. Cf. PLAIN-VIEW DOCTRINE.

opening statement. A lawyer's statement, at the outset of a trial, in which the lawyer gives the fact-finder a preview of the case and of the evidence that will be submitted. — Also termed *opening argument*.

open listing. See LISTING (1).

open market. See MARKET.

open mortgage clause. See MORTGAGE CLAUSE.

open possession. See POSSESSION.

open-public-meeting law. SUN-SHINE LAW.

open seas. HIGH SEAS.

open shop. A business where union membership is not a condition of employment. See RIGHT-TO-WORK LAW. Cf. CLOSED SHOP.

open union. See UNION.

operating expense. See EXPENSE.

operating profit. See PROFIT.

operation of law. The manner in which a right or a liability can be created for a party, regardless of that party's intent <by operation of law, one who attempts to rescue a person but then leaves the scene becomes liable for that person's damages>.

opinion. 1. A court's written statement explaining its decision in a given case, including statements of fact, points of law, rationale, and dicta. — Also termed *judicial opinion*. See DECISION. Cf. JUDGMENT; RULING.

advisory opinion. A nonbinding statement by a court of its interpretation of the law on a matter submitted for that purpose; federal courts are constitutionally prohibited from issuing advisory opinions by the case-or- controversy requirement, but other courts, such as the International Court of Justice, render them routinely. See CASE-OR-CONTROVERSY REQUIREMENT.

concurring opinion. CONCURRENCE (3).

dissenting opinion. An opinion by one or more judges who disagree with the decision reached by the majority. —Often shortened to *dissent.* —Also termed *minority opinion.*

majority opinion. An opinion joined in by more than half of the judges considering a given case. —Also termed *main opinion.*

memorandum opinion. A unanimous opinion stating the decision of the court but not its reasoning. —Also termed *memorandum decision.*

per curiam opinion. An opinion handed down by the court without identifying the individual judge who wrote the opinion. —Sometimes shortened to *per curiam.*

plurality opinion. An opinion lacking enough judges' votes to constitute a majority, but receiving more votes than any other opinion.

seriatim opinions. A series of opinions written individually by each judge on the bench, as opposed to a single opinion speaking for the court as a whole.

slip opinion. **a.** A court opinion that is published individually after it is rendered and then collectively in advance sheets. Cf. ADVANCE SHEETS. **b.** *Archaic.* A preliminary draft of a court opinion not yet ready for publication. —Also termed *slip decision.*

2. A formal expression of judgment or advice based on an expert's special knowledge; esp., a document, usu. prepared at a client's request, containing a lawyer's understanding of the law as applied to a particular case. —Also termed *opinion letter.*

audit opinion. A certified public accountant's opinion regarding the audited financial statements of an entity.

coverage opinion. A lawyer's opinion on whether a particular event is covered by a given insurance policy.

title opinion. A lawyer's or title company's opinion on the state of title for a given piece of real property, usu. describing whether the title is clear and marketable or whether it is encumbered. See TITLE SEARCH.

3. A witness's thoughts, beliefs, or inferences about facts in dispute, as opposed to personal knowledge of the facts themselves. See *opinion evidence* under EVIDENCE.

opinion evidence. See EVIDENCE.

opinion letter. OPINION (2).

opportunity cost. See COST.

oppression. 1. Generally, the act or an instance of unjustly exercising authority or power. **2.** At common law, any harm or injury (other than extortion) that a public officer corruptly causes to a person; oppression in this sense was formerly considered a misdemeanor. **3.** In contract law, coercion to enter into an illegal contract; oppression is grounds for recovery of money paid or property transferred under the illegal contract. See DURESS; UNCONSCIONABILITY. **4.** In corporate law, unfair treatment of minority shareholders (esp. in a close corporation) by the directors or those in control of the corporation. See FREEZE-OUT. —Also termed (in sense 4) *shareholder oppression.* —**oppress,** *vb.* —**oppressive,** *adj.* —**oppressor,** *n.*

opt in, *vb.* To choose to participate in (something) <the plaintiffs opted in the settlement, hoping to avoid a lengthy trial>.

option, *n.* **1.** Generally, the right or power to choose; something that may be chosen <the lawyer was running out of options for settlement>. **2.** A contract made to keep an offer open for a specified period, so that the offeror cannot revoke the offer during that period <the option is valid because it is supported by consideration>. —Also termed *option contract.* See *irrevocable offer* under OFFER. **3.** The right conveyed by such a contract <Phil declined to exercise his first option to buy the house>. **4.** The right—but not the obligation—to buy or sell a given quantity of securities, commodities, or other assets at a fixed price within a specified time <trading stock options is a speculative business>. Cf. FUTURES CONTRACT.

call option. An option to buy something (esp. securities) at a fixed price even if the market rises; the right to require another to sell. — Often shortened to *call.*

cash-value option. The right of a life-insurance policyholder to take the policy's predetermined cash value at a specified point in time.

commodity option. An option to buy or sell a commodity.

naked option. A call option that grants another the right to buy stock even though the option-giver does not own the stock to back up that commitment. —Also termed *uncovered option.*

put option. An option to sell something (esp. securities) at a fixed price even if the market declines; the right to require another to buy. —Often shortened to *put.*

stock option. **a.** An option to buy or sell stock at a designated price for a specified period regardless of shifts in market value during the period. **b.** An option that allows a corporate employee to buy shares of corporate stock at a fixed price; such an option is usu. granted as a form of compensation and can qualify for special tax treatment under the Internal Revenue Code. —Also termed (in sense b) *employee stock option; incentive stock option* (ISO); or (if eligible) *qualified stock option.*

option, *vb.* To grant or take an option on (something) <Ward optioned his first screenplay to the studio for $50,000>.

option agreement. In corporate law, a share-transfer restriction that commits the shareholder to sell, but not the corporation or other shareholders to buy, the shareholder's shares at a fixed price when a specified event occurs. Cf. BUY-SELL AGREEMENT (2); OPTION (2).

optional completeness, rule of. See RULE OF OPTIONAL COMPLETENESS.

optional writ. See WRIT.

option contract. OPTION (2).

optionee (op-shə-**nee**). One who receives an option from another. —Also termed *option-holder.*

optionor (op-shə-**nor**). One who grants an option to another. —Also

spelled *optioner.* —Also termed *option-giver.*

option premium. PREMIUM (4).

opt out, *vb.* To choose not to participate in something <with so many plaintiffs opting out of the class, the defendant braced itself for multiplicitous lawsuits>.

oral, *adj.* Spoken or uttered; not expressed in writing. Cf. PAROL.

oral argument. A lawyer's spoken presentation before a court (esp. an appellate court) supporting or opposing the legal relief at issue.

oral contract. See *parol contract* (a) under CONTRACT.

oral deposition. See DEPOSITION.

oral will. See WILL.

order, *n.* **1.** A command, direction, or instruction. **2.** A written direction or command delivered by a court or judge. —Also termed *court order; judicial order.*

final order. An order that is dispositive of the entire case. See *final judgment* under JUDGMENT.

interlocutory order. An order that relates to some intermediate matter in the case. —Also termed *interlocutory decision; interim order.* See *appealable decision* under DECISION; COLLATERAL-ORDER DOCTRINE.

3. A written instrument (such as a check), made by one person and addressed to another, directing that other to pay money or deliver something to someone named in the instrument. See *order paper* under PAPER. **4.** In securities trading, a customer's instructions to a broker regarding how and when to buy or sell securities.

day order. An order to buy or sell on one particular day only.

discretionary order. An order to buy or sell at any price acceptable to the broker.

limit order. An order to buy or sell at a specified price, regardless of market price.

market order. An order to buy or sell at the best price immediately available on the market.

scale order. An order to buy or sell a security at varying price intervals.

stop-loss order. An order to buy or sell when the security's price reaches a specified level (the *stop price*) on the market; by fixing the price beforehand the investor is cushioned against stock fluctuations. —Also termed *stop order.*

order absolute. See *decree absolute* under DECREE.

order bill of lading. See BILL OF LADING.

order document. See *order paper* under PAPER.

order instrument. See *order paper* under PAPER.

order nisi. See *decree nisi* under DECREE.

Order of the Coif. 1. Formerly, the order of serjeants-at-law, the highest order of counsel at the English Bar; the last serjeant was appointed to the Order in 1875. **2.** An honorary legal fraternity composed of a select few law students with the highest grades. See COIF.

order paper. See PAPER.

order to show cause. See SHOW-CAUSE ORDER.

ordinance. A statute or regulation, esp. one established by a municipal government. —Also termed *bylaw.*

ordinarily prudent person. REASONABLE PERSON.

ordinary, *n.* **1.** At common law, a high-ranking ecclesiastical official (such as a bishop) with jurisdiction over a specified territory or group. **2.** A probate judge; the term is used only in some states. **3.** In civil law, a judge or other official having original rather than delegated jurisdiction.

ordinary annuity. See ANNUITY.

ordinary care. See *reasonable care* under CARE.

ordinary course of business. COURSE OF BUSINESS.

ordinary income. See INCOME.

ordinary law. STATUTORY LAW.

ordinary life insurance. See *whole life insurance* under INSURANCE.

ordinary loss. See LOSS.

ordinary shares. See *common stock* under STOCK.

ore tenus rule (or-ee-ten-əs). [Latin "by word of mouth"] The presumption that a trial court's findings of fact are correct and should not be disturbed unless clearly wrong or unjust.

organic act. See *organic statute* under STATUTE.

organic law. 1. In common-law jurisdictions, the basic law and principles that define and establish a government; FUNDAMENTAL LAW. **2.** In civil-law jurisdictions, decisional law; CASELAW.

organic statute. See STATUTE.

organization. UNION.

organizational expense. See EXPENSE.

organizational meeting. See MEETING.

organized crime. 1. Widespread criminal activities that are coordinated and controlled through a central syndicate. See RACKETEERING. **2.** The persons involved in these criminal activities; a syndicate of criminals who rely on their unlawful activities for income. —Also termed (in sense 2) *the mob*; *the family*; *the syndicate*; *Mafia*; *Cosa Nostra*.

original contractor. See *general contractor* under CONTRACTOR.

original-document rule. BEST-EVIDENCE RULE.

original evidence. See EVIDENCE.

original intent. See INTENT.

original jurisdiction. See JURISDICTION.

originality. In copyright law, the requirement that a work be created independently by an author and that it possess a minimal degree of creativity; a work does not have to be novel or unique in order to be original.

original market. See *primary market* under MARKET.

original-package doctrine. In constitutional law, the principle that imported goods are exempt from state taxation as long as they remain unsold and are contained in their original package; the Supreme Court abolished this doctrine in 1976, holding that states can tax imported goods if the tax is nondiscriminatory. See IMPORT-EXPORT CLAUSE.

original writ. See WRIT.

original-writing rule. BEST-EVIDENCE RULE.

ORP. *abbr.* Ordinary, reasonable, and prudent—the standard on which negligence cases are based.

orphan's court. See *probate court* under COURT.

OSHA (**oh**-shə). *abbr.* OCCUPATIONAL SAFETY AND HEALTH ADMINISTRATION.

OSP. *abbr.* OBIIT SINE PROLE.

ostensible (ah-**sten**-sə-bəl), *adj.* Open to view; declared or professed; apparent.

ostensible agent. See *apparent agent* under AGENT.

ostensible authority. See *apparent authority* under AUTHORITY.

ostensible partner. See *nominal partner* under PARTNER.

ostrich defense. A criminal defendant's claim not to have known of the criminal activities of his or her associates.

ostrich instruction. See JURY INSTRUCTION.

OTC. *abbr.* Over-the-counter <those stocks were traded in the OTC market>. See *over-the-counter market* under MARKET.

our federalism. (*often cap.*) The doctrine holding that federal courts must refrain from hearing constitutional challenges to state action when federal adjudication would be considered an improper intrusion on the state's right to enforce its laws in its own courts. See ABSTENTION. Cf. FEDERALISM.

ouster, *n.* The act or an instance of wrongfully dispossessing someone of property, esp. real property. —**oust,** *vb.* Cf. EJECTMENT.

outcome-determinative test. In civil procedure, a test used to determine whether an issue is substantive for purposes of the *Erie* doctrine by examining the issue's potential effect on the result of the litigation. See ERIE DOCTRINE.

out-of-court settlement. See SETTLEMENT.

out-of-pocket expense. See EXPENSE.

out-of-pocket loss. See LOSS.

output contract. See CONTRACT.

outrage, *n.* See *intentional infliction of emotional distress* under EMOTIONAL DISTRESS.

outrageous conduct. See CONDUCT.

outside director. See DIRECTOR.

outside party. THIRD PARTY.

outstanding capital stock. See STOCK.

outstanding stock. See STOCK.

overbreadth doctrine. In constitutional law, the doctrine holding that if a statute is so broadly written that it deters free expression, then it can be struck down on its face because of this chilling effect—even if it also prohibits acts that may legitimately be forbidden; the Supreme Court has used this doctrine to invalidate a number of laws, including those that prohibit peaceful picketing or require loyalty oaths. Cf. VAGUENESS DOCTRINE.

overdraft. 1. A bank depositor's withdrawal or attempted withdrawal of a sum exceeding the amount on deposit; esp., a check written for more money than is in an account. **2.** The sum overdrawn. **3.** A line of credit extended by a bank to a customer who might overdraw on an account.

overhead, *n.* Business expenses (such as rent, utilities, or support-staff salaries) that cannot be allocated to a particular product or service; fixed or ordinary operating costs.

overinsurance. See INSURANCE.

overlapping jurisdiction. See *concurrent jurisdiction* under JURISDICTION.

overplus. SURPLUS.

overreaching, *n.* **1.** The act or an instance of taking unfair commercial advantage of another, esp. by fraudulent means. **2.** The act or an instance of defeating one's own purpose by going too far. —**overreach,** *vb.*

override, *vb.* To prevail over; to nullify or set aside <Congress mustered enough votes to override the President's veto>.

override, *n.* **1.** A commission paid to a manager on a sale made by his or her subordinate. **2.** A commission paid to a real-estate broker who listed a property if, within a reasonable amount of time after the expiration of the listing, the owner sells that property directly to a buyer with whom the broker had negotiated during the term of the listing. **3.** ROYALTY (2).

overriding royalty. See ROYALTY.

overrule, *vb.* **1.** To rule against; to reject <the judge overruled all of the defendant's objections>. **2.** (Of a superior court) to overturn or set aside (a precedent) by expressly deciding it should no longer be controlling law <in *Brown v. Board of Education*, the Supreme Court overruled *Plessy v. Ferguson*>. Cf. VACATE (1).

overt, *adj.* Open and observable; not concealed or secret <the conspirators' overt acts>.

over-the-counter market. See MARKET.

owelty (oh-əl-tee). **1.** Equality as achieved by a compensatory sum of money given after an exchange of pieces of land having different values or after an unequal partition of real property. **2.** The sum of money so paid.

owner. One who has the right to possess, use, and convey something; a proprietor. See OWNERSHIP.

beneficial owner. **a.** See *equitable owner.* **b.** A corporate shareholder who has the power to buy or sell the shares, but who has not registered the shares on the corporation's books in his or her name.

equitable owner. One recognized in equity as the owner of something because real and beneficial use and title belong to that person, even though legal title may belong to someone else; esp., one for whom property is held in trust. —Also termed *beneficial owner.*

legal owner. One recognized by law as the owner of something; esp., one who holds legal title to property for the benefit of another. See TRUSTEE.

record owner. **a.** A property owner in whose name the title appears in public records. **b.** A corporate shareholder in whose name the shares are registered on the corporation's books.

owners' association. The basic governing entity for condominiums or planned unit developments; usu. it is an unincorporated association or a nonprofit corporation.

owners' equity. The aggregate of the owners' financial interests in the assets of a business entity; the capital contributed by the owners plus any retained earnings. —Also termed (in a corporation) *shareholders' equity; stockholders' equity.*

ownership. The collection of rights allowing one to use and enjoy property, including the right to convey it to others; ownership implies the right to possess a thing, regardless of any actual or constructive control. Cf. POSSESSION; TITLE (1).

owner's policy. In real-estate law, a title-insurance policy covering the owner's title as well as the mortgagee's title. Cf. MORTGAGEE POLICY.

oyer and terminer (oi-ər-and-tər-mə-nər). [Law French *oyer et terminer* "to hear and determine"] **1.** At common law, a commission authorizing a judge to hear a criminal case in special circumstances. **2.** In some states, a court of higher criminal jurisdiction.

oyez (oh-**yez** *or* oh-**yes** *or* **oh**-yay). [Law French] Hear ye; the utterance *oyez, oyez, oyez* is usu. used in court by the public crier to call the courtroom to order when a session begins or when a proclamation is about to be made.

P

P.A. *abbr.* **1.** See *professional association* under ASSOCIATION. **2.** See *participating associate* under ASSOCIATE.

PAC. *abbr.* POLITICAL-ACTION COMMITTEE.

packing a jury. See JURY-PACKING.

Pac-Man defense. An aggressive antitakeover defense by which the target company attempts to take over the acquiring company by making a cash tender offer for the acquiring company's shares; the name derives from a video game popular in the 1980s, the object of which was to gobble up the enemy.

pact. An agreement between two or more parties; esp., an agreement (such as a treaty) between two or more nations or governmental entities.

pacta sunt servanda (pak-tə-sənt-sər-**van**-də). [Latin "agreements must be kept"] The rule that agreements and stipulations, esp. those contained in treaties, must be observed <the Quebec courts have been faithful to the *pacta sunt servanda* principle>.

paid-in capital. See CAPITAL.

paid-in surplus. See SURPLUS.

pain and suffering. Physical discomfort or emotional distress compensable as an element of damages in torts. See DAMAGES.

pain of, on. See ON PAIN OF.

pains and penalties, bill of. See BILL OF PAINS AND PENALTIES.

pais. See IN PAIS.

palimony. A court-ordered allowance paid by one member to the other of a couple that, though unmarried, formerly cohabited. Cf. ALIMONY.

palming off. PASSING OFF.

pandect (**pan**-dekt). **1.** A complete legal code, esp. of a nation or a system of law, together with commentary. **2.** (*cap. & pl.*) The 50 books constituting Justinian's *Digest* (one of the four works making up the *Corpus Juris Civilis*), first published in 533 A.D.—Also termed (in sense 2) *Digest.* Pl. **pandects, pandectae.** See CORPUS JURIS CIVILIS.

pander, *n.* PIMP.

pandering, *n.* **1.** The crime of soliciting customers for a prostitute; pimping. **2.** The act or an instance of catering to others, esp. to win their support or favors. —**pander,** *vb.*

P & L. *abbr.* Profit and loss. See INCOME STATEMENT.

panel. 1. A list of persons summoned as potential jurors. **2.** A group of persons selected for jury duty and from which jurors are chosen; VENIRE. **3.** A set of judges selected from a complete court to decide a specific case; esp., a group of three judges designated to sit for an appellate court.

paper. 1. Any written or printed document or instrument. **2.** A negotiable document or instrument evidencing a debt; esp., commercial documents or negotiable instruments considered as a group. See NEGOTIABLE INSTRUMENT.

accommodation paper. See ACCOMMODATION PAPER.

bearer paper. An instrument payable to the person who holds it rather than to the order of a specific person. —Also termed *bearer document*; *bearer instrument*.

chattel paper. A writing or set of writings evidencing both a monetary obligation and a security interest in, or a lease of, specific goods. U.C.C. § 9-105(1)(b). See *security agreement* under AGREEMENT.

commercial paper. **a.** An instrument, other than cash, for the payment of money; commercial paper—typically existing in the form of a draft (as a check) or a note (as a certificate of deposit)—is governed by Article 3 of the U.C.C. See NEGOTIABLE INSTRUMENT. **b.** Loosely, a short-term unsecured promissory note, usu. issued and sold by one company to meet another company's immediate cash needs.

order paper. An instrument payable to a specific payee or to any person that the payee designates. —Also termed *order document*; *order instrument*.

3. (*pl.*) COURT PAPERS.

paper loss. See LOSS.

paper profit. See PROFIT.

paper title. See TITLE.

par. PAR VALUE.

paralegal, *n.* A person who assists a lawyer in duties related to the practice of law, but who is not a trained or licensed attorney. —Also termed *legal assistant.* —**paralegal,** *adj.*

parallel citation. See CITATION.

paramount title. See TITLE.

parcenary (**pahrs**-[ə]n-er-ee). COPARCENARY.

pardon, *n.* The act or an instance of officially nullifying punishment or other legal consequences of a crime; a pardon is usu. granted by the chief executive of a government <the President has the sole power to issue pardons for federal offenses, while state governors have the power to issue pardons for state crimes>. —Also termed *executive pardon.* —**pardon,** *vb.* See CLEMENCY. Cf. COMMUTATION (2); REPRIEVE.

absolute pardon. A pardon that releases the wrongdoer from punishment and restores the offender's civil rights without qualification. —Also termed *full pardon*; *unconditional pardon.*

conditional pardon. A pardon that does not become effective until the wrongdoer satisfies a prerequisite or that will be revoked upon the occurrence of some specified act.

general pardon. AMNESTY.

partial pardon. A pardon that exonerates the offender from some but not all of the punishment or legal consequences of a crime.

parens patriae (**pa**-renz-**pa**-tree-ee). [Latin "parent of the country"] The state regarded as a sovereign <the attorney general acted as *parens patriae* in the administrative hearing>.

parentage action. PATERNITY SUIT.

Parental Kidnapping Prevention Act. A federal statute, enacted in 1980, providing penalties for child-kidnapping by noncustodial parents and requiring states to recognize and enforce child-custody decisions rendered by courts of other states. 28 U.S.C. § 1738A; 42 U.S.C. §§ 654, 655, 663. —Abbr. PKPA. Cf. UNIFORM CHILD CUSTODY JURISDICTION ACT.

parental-liability law. A statute obliging parents to pay for torts (esp. intentional ones) committed by their minor children; all states have these laws, but most limit the parents' liability to about $3,000 per tort.

parental-responsibility statute. A law imposing criminal sanctions (such as fines) on parents whose minor children commit crimes in part because the parents do not exercise sufficient control over them. —Also termed *control-your-kid law*.

parental rights. A parent's rights concerning his or her child, including the right to educate and discipline the child and the right to control the child's earnings and property.

parent-child immunity. See IMMUNITY (2).

parent company. See *parent corporation* under CORPORATION.

parent corporation. See CORPORATION.

parentelic method. A scheme of computation used to determine the paternal or maternal collaterals entitled to inherit.

Pareto optimality (pə-re-doh *or* -ray-). An economic situation in which no person can be made better off without making someone else worse off. —**Pareto-optimal,** *adj.*

Pareto superiority. An economic situation in which an exchange can

be made that both benefits someone and injures no one; when such exchanges can no longer be made, the situation becomes one of Pareto optimality. —**Pareto-superior,** *adj.*

pari causa, in. See IN PARI CAUSA.

pari delicto, in. See IN PARI DELICTO.

pari materia, in. See IN PARI MATERIA.

pari passu (**pahr**-ee-**pah**-soo *or* par-ee- *or* -**pa**-soo). [Latin "with equal step"] Proportionally; at an equal pace; without preference <creditors of a bankrupt estate will receive distributions *pari passu*>.

parish. In Louisiana, a governmental subdivision analogous to a county in other U.S. states. See COUNTY.

parking. 1. The sale of securities subject to an agreement that they will be bought back by the seller at a later time for a similar price; parking is illegal if done to circumvent securities regulations or tax laws. **2.** The placement of assets in a safe, short-term investment while other investment opportunities are being considered.

parliament. The supreme legislative body of some nations; esp. (cap.), in the United Kingdom, the national legislature consisting of the House of Lords and the House of Commons.

parliamentary law. A body of procedural rules governing legislative assemblies and other deliberative meetings.

parol (**par**-əl *or* pə-**rohl**), *adj.* **1.** Oral; unwritten <parol evidence>. **2.** Not under seal <parol contract>.

parol agreement. See *parol contract* (a) under CONTRACT.

parol arrest. See ARREST.

parol contract. See CONTRACT.

parole (pə-**rohl**), *n.* The release of a prisoner from imprisonment before the full sentence has been served; although not available under some sentences, parole is usu. granted for good behavior on the condition that the parolee regularly report to a law-enforcement officer for a specified period. —**parole,** *vb.* Cf. PARDON; PROBATION (1).

parole board. The state or federal body that decides whether a prisoner may be released from prison before completing his or her sentence. — Also termed *parole commission.*

parolee (pə-roh-**lee**). One who has been released on parole.

parol evidence. See EVIDENCE.

parol-evidence rule. In contract law, the principle that evidence cannot be admitted if it has the effect of adding to, varying, or contradicting a written contract; this rule usu. operates to prevent a party from introducing extrinsic evidence of negotiations that occurred before or while the agreement was being reduced to its final written form. See INTEGRATION (2); MERGER (2). Cf. FOUR-CORNERS RULE.

parricide (**par**-ə-sId), *n.* **1.** The act of killing a close relative, esp. a parent. **2.** One who kills such a relative. —**parricidal,** *adj.* Cf. PATRICIDE.

partial breach. See BREACH OF CONTRACT.

partial disability. See DISABILITY.

partial eviction. See EVICTION.

partial integration. See INTEGRATION.

partially disclosed principal. See PRINCIPAL (1).

partial summary judgment. See SUMMARY JUDGMENT.

partial verdict. See VERDICT.

particeps criminis (**par**-ti-seps-**crim**-i-nis), *n.* [Latin "partner in crime"] An accomplice or accessory. Pl. ***participes criminis.*** See ACCESSORY.

participating associate. See ASSOCIATE.

participating bond. See BOND (1).

participating insurance. See INSURANCE.

participating preferred stock. See STOCK.

participation loan. See LOAN.

participation mortgage. See MORTGAGE.

particular average. See AVERAGE.

particular jurisprudence. See JURISPRUDENCE.

particular lien. See LIEN.

particular malice. See MALICE.

particulars, bill of. See BILL OF PARTICULARS.

partition, *n.* **1.** Something that separates, esp. one part of a space from another. **2.** The action of dividing; esp., a division of real property owned by two or more persons into individually owned interests. —**partition,** *vb.*—**partible,** *adj.*

partner. 1. One who shares or takes part with another, esp. in a venture with shared benefits and shared risks; an associate or colleague <partners in crime>. **2.** One of two or more persons who jointly own and carry on a business for profit <the firm and its partners were sued for malpractice>. See PARTNERSHIP. **3.** One of two persons who are married or who live together; a spouse or companion <my partner in life>.

general partner. A partner who actively takes part in the daily operations of the business, fully shares in the profits and losses, and is personally liable for the partnership's debt. —Also termed *full partner.*

junior partner. A partner whose participation is limited with respect to both profits and management.

limited partner. A partner who receives limited profits from the business and who is not liable for any amount greater than his or her original investment. —Also termed *special partner.* See *limited partnership* under PARTNERSHIP.

liquidating partner. The partner appointed to settle the accounts, collect the assets, adjust the claims, and pay the debts of a dissolving or insolvent firm.

name partner. A partner whose name appears in the name of the partnership <Mr. Tibbs is a name partner in the law firm of Gibbs & Tibbs>. —Also termed *title member.*

nominal partner. A person who is held out as a partner in a firm or business but who has no actual interest in the partnership. —Also termed *ostensible partner.*

senior partner. A high-ranking partner, esp. in a law firm.

silent partner. A partner whose membership in the partnership is concealed from the public and who usu. is not actively involved in the business operations. —Also termed *dormant partner*; *secret partner*; *sleeping partner.*

surviving partner. The partner who, upon the partnership's dissolution because of another partner's death, serves as a trustee to administer the firm's remaining affairs.

partnership. A voluntary association of two or more persons who jointly own and carry on a business for profit; under the Uniform Partnership Act, a partnership is presumed to exist if the persons agree to share proportionally the business's profits or losses. Cf. JOINT VENTURE; STRATEGIC ALLIANCE.

general partnership. A partnership in which all partners participate fully in running the business and share equally in profits and losses (though the partners' monetary contributions may vary).

limited partnership. A partnership composed of one or more persons who control the business and are personally liable for the partnership's debts (called *general partners*), and one or more persons who contribute capital and share profits but who cannot manage the business and are liable only for the amount of their contribution (called *limited partners*). —Abbr.

L.P. —Also termed *special partnership*.

limited-liability partnership. A partnership in which a partner is not liable for a negligent act committed by another partner or by an employee not under the partner's supervision; almost half the states have enacted statutes that allow a business (typically a law firm or accounting firm) to register as this type of partnership. —Abbr. L.L.P.

master limited partnership. A limited partnership whose interests or shares are publicly traded. See *publicly traded partnership*.

partnership at will. A partnership that any partner may dissolve at any time without liability. Cf. *partnership for a term*.

partnership by estoppel. A partnership implied by law when one or more persons represent themselves as partners to a third party who relies on that representation; a person who is deemed a partner by estoppel becomes liable for any credit extended to the partnership by the third party.

partnership for a term. A partnership that exists for a specified duration or until a specified event occurs; such a partnership can be prematurely dissolved by any partner, but that partner may be held liable for breach of the partnership agreement. Cf. *partnership at will*.

publicly traded partnership. A partnership whose interests are traded either over-the-counter or on a securities exchange; such partnerships are treated as corporations for federal income-tax purposes. —Abbr. PTP.

subpartnership. An arrangement between a firm's partner and a nonpartner to share the partner's profits and losses in the firm business, but without forming a legal partnership between the partner and the nonpartner.

tiered partnership. An ownership arrangement consisting of one parent partnership that is a partner in one or more subsidiary partnerships.

universal partnership. A partnership formed by persons who agree to contribute all of their individually owned property to the partnership.

partnership agreement. A contract defining the partners' rights and duties with one another—not the partners' relationship with third parties. —Also termed *articles of partnership*.

partnership association. A business organization that combines the features of a limited partnership and a close corporation; partnership associations are statutorily recognized in only a few states. —Also termed *statutory partnership association*; *limited partnership association*.

partnership distribution. See DISTRIBUTION.

part performance. 1. The accomplishment of some but not all of one's contractual obligations. 2. A party's execution, in reliance on an opposing party's oral promise, of enough of an oral contract's requirements that a court may hold the statute of frauds not to apply. 3. The equitable principle by which a violation of the statute of frauds is so overcome. —Also termed (in sense 3) *part-performance doctrine*.

part-sovereign state. See SOVEREIGN STATE.

party. A person involved in a legal transaction or court proceeding <a party to the contract> <a party to the lawsuit>.

aggrieved party. A party whose personal, pecuniary, or property rights have been adversely affected by another person's actions or by a court's decree or judgment. —Also termed *party aggrieved*.

indispensable party. A party who, having interests that would inevitably be affected by a court's judgment, must be included in the case; if such a party is not, the case must be dismissed. Fed. R. Civ. P. 19(b). Cf. *necessary party*.

necessary party. A party who, being closely connected to a lawsuit, should be included in the case if feasible, but whose absence will not require dismissal of the proceedings. See *compulsory joinder* under JOINDER. Cf. *indispensable party*.

nominal party. A party who, having some interest in the subject matter of a lawsuit, will not be affected by any judgment but is nonetheless joined in the lawsuit to avoid procedural defects; an example is the disinterested stakeholder in a garnishment action. —Also termed *formal party*. Cf. *real party in interest*.

prevailing party. A party in whose favor a judgment is rendered, regardless of the amount of damages awarded <in certain cases, the court will award attorney's fees to the prevailing party>.

proper party. A party who may be joined in a case for reasons of judicial economy but whose presence is not essential to the proceeding. See *permissive joinder* under JOINDER.

real party in interest. A person entitled under the substantive law to enforce the right sued upon and who generally, but not necessarily, benefits from the action's final outcome. Cf. *nominal party*.

third party. See THIRD PARTY.

party of the first part. *Archaic.* The party named first in a contract; esp., the owner or seller.

party of the second part. *Archaic.* The party named second in a contract; esp., the buyer.

party wall. A wall that divides two adjoining, separately owned properties and that is shared by the two property owners as tenants in common.

par value. The value of an instrument or security as shown on its face; esp., the arbitrary dollar amount assigned to a stock share by the corporate charter, or the principal of a bond. —Often shortened to *par*. —Also termed *face value*; *nominal value*; *stated value*.

pass, *vb.* **1.** To pronounce or render an opinion, ruling, sentence, or judgment <the court refused to pass on the constitutional issue, deciding the case instead on procedural grounds>. **2.** To transfer or be transferred <the woman's will passes title to the house to her nephew, much to her

husband's surprise> <title passed when the nephew received the deed>. **3.** To enact (a legislative bill or resolution) <Congress has debated whether to pass a balanced-budget amendment to the Constitution>. **4.** To approve or certify (something) as meeting specified requirements <the mechanic informed her that the car had passed inspection>. **5.** To publish, transfer, or circulate (a thing, often a forgery) <he was found guilty of passing counterfeit bills>.

passbook. A depositor's book in which a bank records all the transactions on an account. —Also termed *bankbook*.

passed dividend. See DIVIDEND.

passim (pas-əm), *adv.* Here and there; throughout (the cited work)— in modern legal writing, the citation signal *see generally* is preferred to *passim* as a general reference, although *passim* can be useful in a brief's index of authorities to show that a given authority is cited throughout the brief.

passing off, *n.* The act or an instance of falsely representing one's own product as that of another in an attempt to deceive potential buyers; passing off is actionable in tort under the law of unfair competition. —Also termed *palming off.* —**pass off,** *vb.* Cf. MISAPPROPRIATION.

passive activity. In tax law, a business activity in which the taxpayer does not materially participate and therefore does not have immediate control over the income; a typical example is the ownership and rental of real property.

passive concealment. See CONCEALMENT.

passive debt. See DEBT.

passive euthanasia. See EUTHANASIA.

passive income. See INCOME.

passive loss. See LOSS.

passive trust. See TRUST.

pass-through taxation. See TAXATION.

past consideration. See CONSIDERATION.

past recollection recorded. In the law of evidence, a document concerning events that a witness once knew about but can no longer remember; the document itself is evidence and, despite being hearsay, may be admitted (or read into the record) if it was prepared when the events were fresh in the witness's memory. Fed. R. Evid. 803(5). —Also termed *recorded recollection*. Cf. PRESENT RECOLLECTION REFRESHED.

pat-down, *n.* FRISK.

patent (pay-t[ə]nt *or* pa-), *adj.* Obvious; apparent <a patent ambiguity>. Cf. LATENT.

patent (pa-t[ə]nt), *n.* **1.** The grant of a right, privilege, or authority by the government; the official document so granting. See LETTERS PATENT.

land patent. An instrument by which the government conveys a grant of public land to a private person.

2. The exclusive right to make, use, or sell an invention for a specified period (usu. 17 years), granted by the federal government to the inventor if the device or process is novel, useful, and nonobvious. 35 U.S.C. §§ 101 et seq.

design patent. A patent granted for a new, original, and ornamental design for an article of manufacture; design patents—which, unlike utility patents, have a term of only 14 years—are similar to copyrights.

plant patent. A patent granted for the invention or discovery of a new and distinct variety of asexually reproducing plant.

utility patent. A patent granted for one of the following types of inventions: a machine, a composition of matter (such as a chemical or pharmaceutical), an article of manufacture, or a process; utility patents are the most commonly issued patents.

patent ambiguity. See AMBIGUITY.

Patent and Copyright Clause. The constitutional provision granting Congress the authority to promote the advancement of science and the arts by establishing a national system for patents and copyrights. U.S. Const. art. I, § 8, cl. 8.

Patent and Trademark Office. The Department of Commerce agency that examines patent and trademark applications, issues patents, registers trademarks, and furnishes patent and trademark information and services to the public. —Abbr. PTO.

patent disclaimer. See DISCLAIMER.

patentee. One to whom a patent has been granted.

patent infringement. See INFRINGEMENT.

patentor. One who grants a patent.

patent pending. The designation given to an invention while the Patent and Trademark Office is processing the patent application; no protection against infringement exists, however, until an actual patent is granted. —Abbr. pat. pend.

paternal, *adj.* Of, relating to, or coming from one's father <paternal property>. Cf. MATERNAL.

paternalism, *n.* A government's policy or practice of taking responsibility for the individual affairs of its citizens, esp. by supplying their needs or regulating their conduct in a heavyhanded manner. —**paternalistic,** *adj.* Cf. SUMPTUARY LAW.

paternal line. See LINE.

paternity. The state or condition of being a father, esp. a biological one; fatherhood.

paternity suit. A court proceeding to determine whether a person is the father of a child born out of wedlock, usu. initiated by the mother in an effort to obtain child support. —Also termed *paternity action; parentage action; bastardy proceeding.*

paternity test. A test, usu. involving DNA identification or tissue-typing, for determining whether a given man is the biological father of a particular child. See DNA IDENTIFICATION; HLA TEST.

pathology, *n.* The branch of medical study that examines the causes, symptoms, and treatments of diseases. —**pathological,** *adj.*—**pathologist,** *n.*

patient-physician privilege. See *doctor-patient privilege* under PRIVILEGE.

pat. pend. *abbr.* PATENT PENDING.

patricide (pa-trə-sīd), *n.* **1.** The act of killing one's own father. **2.** One who kills his or her father. —**patricidal,** *adj.* Cf. PARRICIDE.

patrimony (pa-trə-moh-nee). **1.** An estate inherited from one's father or other ancestor; legacy or heritage. **2.** In civil law, all of a person's assets and liabilities that are capable of monetary valuation and subject to execution for a creditor's benefit.

patronage (pa-trə-nij *or* pay-). **1.** The act or an instance of giving support, sponsorship, or protection. **2.** All the customers of a business; clientele. **3.** The power to appoint persons to governmental positions or to confer other political favors. —Also termed (in sense 3) *political patronage.* See SPOILS SYSTEM.

pattern similarity. See *comprehensive nonliteral similarity* under SUBSTANTIAL SIMILARITY.

paucital (paw-si-təl). *Archaic.* IN PERSONAM.

pauper. A very poor person, esp. one who receives aid from charity or public funds; an indigent. See IN FORMA PAUPERIS.

pauper's affidavit. See *poverty affidavit* under AFFIDAVIT.

pauper's oath. See OATH.

pawn, *n.* **1.** An item of personal property deposited as security for payment of a debt; a pledge or guarantee. **2.** The act of depositing personal property in this manner. **3.** The

condition of being held on deposit as a pledge. —**pawn,** *vb.* Cf. BAILMENT.

pawnbroker, *n.* One who lends money in exchange for personal property that is pledged as security by the borrower. —**pawnbroking,** *n.*

pawnee. One who receives a pledge of personal property as security for a debt.

pawnor. One who pledges an item of personal property as security for a debt. —Also spelled *pawner.*

payable, *adj.* (Of a sum of money or a negotiable instrument) that is to be paid; due.

payable after sight. Payable after acceptance or protest of nonacceptance. See *sight draft* under DRAFT.

payable on demand. Payable when presented or upon request for payment; payable at any time.

payable to bearer. Payable to anyone holding the instrument.

payable to order. Payable only to a specified payee.

payable, *n.* See *account payable* under ACCOUNT (2).

payback method. An accounting procedure that measures the time required to recover a venture's initial cash investment.

payback period. The length of time required to recover a venture's initial cash investment, without accounting for the time value of money.

paydown. A loan payment in an amount less than the total loan principal.

payee. One to whom money is paid or payable; esp., a party named in commercial paper as the recipient of the payment.

payer. PAYOR.

paying quantities. An amount earned from oil production after paying the oil well's drilling, equipping, and operating costs <production in paying quantities>.

payment. 1. Performance of an obligation, usu. by the delivery of money; performance may occur by delivery and acceptance of things other than money, but there is a payment only if money or other valuable things are given and accepted in partial or full discharge of an obligation. **2.** The money or other valuable thing so delivered in satisfaction of an obligation.

balloon payment. A final loan payment that is usu. much larger than the preceding regular payments and that discharges the principal balance of the loan. See *balloon note* under NOTE.

constructive payment. A payment made by the payer but not yet credited by the payee; for example, a rent check mailed on the first of the month is a constructive payment even though the landlord does not deposit the check until ten days later.

down payment. The portion of a purchase price paid in cash (or its equivalent) at the time the sale agreement is executed.

lump-sum payment. A payment of a large amount all at once, as opposed to smaller payments over time.

payment bond. See BOND (2).

payment date. In corporate law, the date on which stock dividends are paid to shareholders.

payment in due course. A payment to the holder of a negotiable instrument at or after its maturity date, made by the payor in good faith and without notice of the holder's defective title. See HOLDER IN DUE COURSE.

payment into court. A party's money or property deposited with a court for distribution after a proceeding according to the parties' settlement or the court's order.

payoff. KICKBACK.

payor. One who pays; esp., a person responsible for paying a negotiable instrument. —Also spelled *payer*. See DRAWEE.

payor bank. See BANK.

payout ratio. The ratio between a corporation's dividends per share and its earnings per share; shareholders generally prefer a high payout ratio because most of them want to consistently receive dividends.

payroll. 1. A company-employee log including all employees' names and the amount owed to each of them. **2.** The total compensation payable to a firm's employees for one pay period.

payroll tax. See TAX.

PBGC. *abbr.* PENSION BENEFIT GUARANTY CORPORATION.

P.C. *abbr.* **1.** See *professional corporation* under CORPORATION. **2.** POLITICAL CORRECTNESS.

PCR action. POSTCONVICTION-RELIEF PROCEEDING.

P.D. *abbr.* PUBLIC DEFENDER.

peace, *n.* A state of public tranquility; freedom from civil disturbance or hostility <breach of the peace>. — **peaceable,** *adj.*

peace, justice of. See JUSTICE OF THE PEACE.

peaceable possession. See POSSESSION.

peace bond. See BOND (2).

peace officer. A civil officer (such as a sheriff or police officer) appointed to preserve and maintain public tranquility and order. —Also termed *officer of the peace; conservator of the peace.*

peace treaty. See TREATY.

peccavi (pə-**kah**-vee), *n.* [Latin "I have sinned"] An acknowledgment or confession of guilt or sin.

peculation (pe-kyə-**lay**-shən), *n.* Embezzlement, esp. by a public official. —**peculate,** *vb.*—**peculative,** *adj.*—**peculator,** *n.*

pecuniary (pi-**kyoo**-nee-er-ee), *adj.* Of or relating to money; monetary <a pecuniary interest in the lawsuit>.

pecuniary benefit. See BENEFIT.

pecuniary bequest. See BEQUEST.

pecuniary loss. See LOSS.

pederasty (**ped**-ə-ras-tee), *n.* Anal intercourse between a man and a boy; pederasty is illegal in all states. —**pederast,** *n.* Cf. SODOMY.

pedigree. A history of family succession; ancestry or lineage.

Peeping Tom. A person who spies on another (as through a window), usu. to gain sexual pleasure; VOYEUR.

peer, *n.* **1.** A person who is of equal status, rank, or character with another. **2.** A member of the British nobility (such as a duke, marquis, earl, viscount, or baron). —**peerage,** *n.*

peer-review organization. A government agency that monitors health-regulation compliance by private hospitals requesting public funds. —Abbr. PRO.

penal (**pee**-n[ə]l), *adj.* Of or relating to penalty or punishment, esp. criminal punishment.

penal action. See ACTION.

penal bill. See *penal bond* under BOND (2).

penal bond. See BOND (2).

penal clause. PENALTY CLAUSE.

penal code. A compilation of a state's criminal laws, usu. categorizing the offenses and their respective punishments. See MODEL PENAL CODE.

penal institution. PRISON.

penal law. See *penal statute* under STATUTE.

penal statute. See STATUTE.

penal sum. The monetary amount specified as a penalty in a penal bond. See *penal bond* under BOND (2).

penalty. 1. Punishment, esp. in the form of death, imprisonment, or fine, for the commission of a crime. **2.** A monetary sum that a contracting party agrees to forfeit if the party fails to comply with specified conditions. **3.** Excessive liquidated damages that a contract purports to impose on a party that breaches; if the damages are excessive enough to be considered a penalty, a court will usu. not enforce that particular provision of the contract. See PENALTY CLAUSE.

penalty clause. A contractual provision that assesses an excessive monetary fine against a defaulting party; penalty clauses are generally unenforceable. —Also termed *penal clause.* Cf. LIQUIDATED-DAMAGES CLAUSE.

pendency, *n.* The state or condition of being pending or continuing undecided. —**pend,** *vb.*—**pendent,** *adj.*

pendens. See LIS PENDENS.

pendente lite (pen-**den**-tee-**li**-tee *or* -tay-**lee**-tay), *adv.* [Latin "while the action is pending"] During the proceeding or litigation; contingent on the outcome of litigation. —Also termed *lite pendente.* Cf. LIS PENDENS.

***pendente lite* administration.** See ADMINISTRATION.

pendent jurisdiction. See JURISDICTION.

pendent-party jurisdiction. See JURISDICTION.

penitentiary, *n.* A correctional facility or other place of long-term confinement for convicted criminals; PRISON. —**penitentiary,** *adj.*

penny stock. See STOCK.

penology (pee-**nol**-ə-jee *or* pi-), *n.* The study of penal institutions, crime prevention, and the punishment and rehabilitation of criminals. —**penological,** *adj.*—**penologist,** *n.* See CRIMINOLOGY.

pen register. A mechanical device that logs dialed telephone numbers, without overhearing the telephone conversation, by monitoring electrical impulses. Cf. WIRETAPPING.

pension. A fixed sum paid regularly to a person (or to the person's beneficiaries), esp. by an employer as a retirement benefit. Cf. ANNUITY.

Pension Benefit Guaranty Corporation. The federal agency that guarantees the payment of retirement benefits covered by private pension plans that lack sufficient assets to pay the promised benefits. —Abbr. PBGC.

pension plan. An employer's plan established to pay long-term retirement benefits to employees or their beneficiaries.

penumbra (pə-**nəm**-brə), *n.* A surrounding area or periphery of uncertain extent; in constitutional law, the Supreme Court has ruled that the specific guarantees in the Bill of Rights have penumbras containing implied rights, esp. the right of privacy. Pl. **penumbras, penumbrae.** —**penumbral,** *adj.*

peonage (pee-ə-nij), *n.* Illegal and involuntary servitude forcing a person to perform labor in satisfaction of a debt. —**peon,** *n.*

People. The citizens of a state as represented by the prosecution in a criminal case <*People v. Manson*>.

people's court. 1. A court in which ordinary people can resolve small disputes. **2.** In totalitarian countries, a group of nonlawyer citizens, often illiterate commoners, convened at the scene of a crime to pass judgment or impose punishment on the accused criminal. **3.** (*cap.*) In Nazi Germany, a tribunal that dealt with political offenses.

peppercorn. A small or insignificant thing or amount; nominal consideration <the contract was upheld despite involving mere peppercorn>. See *nominal consideration* under CONSIDERATION.

per. 1. Through; by <the dissent, per Justice Thomas>. **2.** For each; for every <55 miles per hour>. **3.** *Jargon.* In accordance with the terms of; according to <per the contract>.

per annum (pər-**an**-əm). [Latin] By the year; in each year; annually.

P/E ratio. *abbr.* PRICE-EARNINGS RATIO.

per autre vie (pər-**oh**-dər-**vee** or -trə-**vee**). PUR AUTRE VIE.

per capita (pər-**ka**-pi-tə), *adj.* [Latin "by the head"] **1.** Divided equally among all individuals, usu. in the same class <the court will distribute the bankruptcy estate's remaining assets to the unsecured creditors on a per capita basis>. Cf. PER STIRPES.

per capita with representation. In the law of wills, divided equally among all members of a class of takers, including those who have predeceased the testator, so that no family stocks are cut off by predeceasing takers; for example, if T (the testator) has three children—A, B, and C—and C has two children but predeceases T, C's children would still take C's share when T's estate is distributed.

2. Allocated to each person <the average annual per capita income has increased over the last two years>. —**per capita,** *adv.*

per capita tax. See *poll tax* under TAX.

percentage lease. See LEASE.

per curiam (pər-**kyuur**-ee-əm). [Latin] **1.** *adj. or adv.* By the court. **2.** *n.* See *per curiam opinion* under OPINION (1).

per curiam opinion. See OPINION (1).

per diem (pər-**dee**-əm), *adv.* [Latin "by the day"] Day by day; each day. Cf. IN DIEM.

per diem, *n.* A monetary daily allowance, usu. to cover expenses.

perempt, *vb.* **1.** *Slang.* To exercise a peremptory challenge. **2.** In Louisiana, to quash, do away with, or extinguish. —**peremption** (corresponding to sense 2), *n.*

peremptory (pə-**rem[p]**-tə-ree), *adj.* **1.** Final; absolute; conclusive; incontrovertible <the king's peremptory order>. **2.** Not requiring any shown cause; arbitrary <peremptory challenges>.

peremptory, *n.* See *peremptory challenge* under CHALLENGE (2).

peremptory challenge. See CHALLENGE (2).

peremptory defense. See DEFENSE (1).

peremptory instruction. See JURY INSTRUCTION.

peremptory plea. See PLEA.

peremptory writ. See WRIT.

perfect (pər-**fekt**), *vb.* **1.** To fulfill all legal requirements for (as a security interest) so that one achieves greater rights than those who have not fulfilled these requirements; to consummate or execute (something) without defect <lienholders should promptly perfect their security interests>. **2.** To make (title) clear and marketable <to perfect the property's title, the buyer must record the deed with the county clerk>.

perfect competition. A completely efficient market situation characterized by numerous buyers and sellers, a homogeneous product, perfect information for all parties, and complete freedom to move in and out of the market; perfect competition rarely if ever exists, but antitrust scholars often use the theory as a standard for measuring market performance.

perfection. Validation of a security interest as against other creditors, usu. by filing a statement with some public office or by taking possession of the collateral. Cf. ATTACHMENT (4).

perfect-tender rule. In commercial law, the principle that a buyer may reject a seller's goods if the quality, quantity, or delivery of the goods fails to conform precisely to the contract; although the perfect-tender rule was adopted by the U.C.C. (§ 2-601), other Code provisions—such as the seller's right to cure after rejection—have softened the rule's impact. Cf. SUBSTANTIAL-PERFORMANCE DOCTRINE.

performance, *n.* The successful completion of a contractual duty, usu. resulting in the performer's release from any past or future liability; EXECUTION (2). —**perform,** *vb.* Cf. NONPERFORMANCE.

part performance. See PART PERFORMANCE.

specific performance. See SPECIFIC PERFORMANCE.

performance bond. See BOND (2).

performance right. A copyright holder's exclusive right to recite, play, act, show, or otherwise render the protected work publicly, whether directly or by technological means (as by broadcasting the work on television).

peril, *n.* A risk, hazard, or cause of loss, esp. one covered by an insurance policy. —**perilous,** *adj.*

periodic estate. See ESTATE.

periodic tenancy. See TENANCY.

perjury (pər-jər-ee), *n.* The act or an instance of a person's deliberately making false or misleading statements while under oath. —Also termed *false swearing*; *false oath*; *forswearing.* —**perjure,** *vb.* —**perjured, perjurious,** *adj.*

permanent abode. DOMICILE (1).

permanent alimony. See ALIMONY.

permanent disability. See DISABILITY (1).

permanent employment. See EMPLOYMENT.

permanent financing. See FINANCING.

permanent injunction. See INJUNCTION.

permanent nuisance. See NUISANCE.

permissive counterclaim. See COUNTERCLAIM.

permissive joinder. See JOINDER.

permissive waste. See WASTE.

perpetrate, *vb.* To commit or carry out (something, esp. a crime or tort) <find whoever perpetrated this heinous deed>. —**perpetration,** *n.*—**perpetrator,** *vb.*

perpetual injunction. See *permanent injunction* under INJUNCTION.

perpetuities, rule against. See RULE AGAINST PERPETUITIES.

perpetuity (pər-pə-t[y]oo-ə-tee). **1.** The state of continuing forever. **2.** A restriction limiting an estate so that it will not take effect or vest within the period established by law. **3.** An estate so restricted.

perquisite (pər-kwə-zit). A privilege or benefit given in addition to one's salary or regular wages. —Often shortened to *perk*.

per quod (pər-**kwod**). [Latin "whereby"] Requiring reference to additional facts; (of libel or slander) actionable only on allegation and proof of special damages. See *libel per quod* under LIBEL.

per se (pər-**say**), *adv. or adj.* [Latin] **1.** Of, in, or by itself; standing alone, without reference to additional facts. See *libel per se* under LIBEL. **2.** As a matter of law.

per se rule. In antitrust law, the judicial doctrine holding that a trade practice violates the Sherman Act simply if the practice is a restraint of trade, regardless of whether the practice actually harms anyone. See SHERMAN ANTITRUST ACT. Cf. RULE OF REASON.

persistent price discrimination. See PRICE DISCRIMINATION.

person. An individual or entity possessing legal rights and duties.

artificial person. An entity, such as a corporation, created by law and given the legal rights and duties of a human being.

natural person. A human being, as distinguished from an artificial person created by law.

personal action. See ACTION.

personal defense. See DEFENSE (4).

personal exemption. See EXEMPTION.

personal holding company. See COMPANY.

personal injury. See INJURY.

personal judgment. See JUDGMENT.

personal jurisdiction. See JURISDICTION.

personal knowledge. See KNOWLEDGE.

personal liability. See LIABILITY.

personal property. See PROPERTY.

personal replevin. See REPLEVIN.

personal representative. See REPRESENTATIVE.

personal service. See SERVICE.

personalty (pərs-ən-əl-tee). See *personal property* (a) under PROPERTY.

personam. See IN PERSONAM.

persona non grata (pər-**sohn**-ə-non-**grah**-də), *n.* [Latin] An unwanted person; esp., a diplomat unaccepted by a country as its ambassador. Pl. **personae non gratae.**

per stirpes (pər-**stər**-peez). [Latin "by roots or stocks"] Proportionally divided between beneficiaries according to their deceased ancestor's share. —Also termed *in stirpes*. Cf. PER CAPITA.

persuasion burden. BURDEN OF PERSUASION.

persuasive precedent. See PRECEDENT.

pertinent art. See *analogous art* under ART.

petition, *n.* A formal written request presented to a court or other governmental or official body; some states use this term in place of *complaint* when referring to a lawsuit's first pleading. —**petition,** *vb.* See COMPLAINT.

petitioner. A party who presents a petition to a court or other official body, esp. when seeking relief on appeal. Cf. RESPONDENT (2).

petition in bankruptcy. A formal written request, presented to a bankruptcy court, seeking protection for an insolvent debtor; either the debtor itself (*voluntary bankruptcy*) or the debtor's creditors (*involuntary bankruptcy*) can file such a petition in order to initiate a bankruptcy proceeding. See BANKRUPTCY.

petit jury. See JURY.

petit larceny. See LARCENY.

petitory action. See ACTION.

pettifogger, *n.* **1.** A lawyer lacking in education, ability, sound judgment, or common sense. **2.** A lawyer who clouds an issue with insignificant details. —**pettifoggery,** *n.*

petty jury. See *petit jury* under JURY.

petty larceny. See *petit larceny* under LARCENY.

petty offense. See OFFENSE.

petty treason. See TREASON.

phantom jury. See *shadow jury* under JURY.

phantom stock plan. A long-term benefit plan under which a corporate employee is given units having the same characteristics as the employer's stock shares; it is termed a "phantom" plan because the employee doesn't actually hold any shares but instead holds the right to the value of those shares. —Also termed *shadow stock plan*.

phonorecord. A physical object from which fixed sounds can be perceived, reproduced, or otherwise communicated directly or with a machine's aid, such as a cassette tape or compact disc.

P.H.V. *abbr.* PRO HAC VICE.

physical disability. See DISABILITY (1).

physical-facts rule. The evidentiary principle that a court may disregard a witness's testimony that contradicts the laws of nature. —Also termed *doctrine of incontrovertible physical facts*.

physical harm. See HARM.

physical-impact rule. IMPACT RULE.

physical impossibility. See *factual impossibility* under IMPOSSIBILITY.

physical injury. See *bodily injury* under INJURY.

physical-inventory accounting method. See ACCOUNTING METHOD.

physical-proximity test. In criminal law, a common-law test for the crime of attempt, focusing on how much more the defendant needs to do in order to complete the offense. See DANGEROUS-PROXIMITY TEST; INDISPENSABLE-ELEMENT TEST.

physician-client privilege. See *doctor-patient privilege* under PRIVILEGE.

physician's directive. ADVANCE DIRECTIVE.

P.I. *abbr.* **1.** Personal injury. **2.** Private investigator.

picketing. The gathering of persons outside a business or organization to protest the entity's activities or policies and to pressure the entity to meet the protesters' demands; esp., an employees' demonstration aimed at publicizing a labor dispute and influencing the public to withhold business from the employer. Cf. BOYCOTT; STRIKE.

common-situs picketing. The illegal picketing by union workers of a construction site, stemming from a dispute with one of the subcontractors.

secondary picketing. The picketing of an establishment with which the picketing party has no direct dispute in order to pressure the party with which there is a dispute. See *secondary boycott* under BOYCOTT; *secondary strike* under STRIKE.

pickpocket. A thief who steals money or property from the person of another, usu. by stealth but sometimes by physical diversion such as bumping into or pushing the victim.

piepowder court. In medieval England, a court having jurisdiction over a fair or market presided over by the organizer's steward; the name is a corruption of two French words (*pied* and *poudre*) meaning "dusty feet."— Also termed *court of piepowder.* — Also spelled *piepoudre*; *piedpoudre*; *pipowder*; *py-powder*.

piercing the corporate veil. The judicial act of imposing personal liability on otherwise immune corporate officers, directors, and shareholders for a corporation's fraudulent or wrongful acts. —Also termed *disregarding the corporate entity*. See CORPORATE VEIL.

pilfer, *vb.* To steal. —**pilferage,** *n.*—**pilferer,** *n.* See LARCENY; THEFT.

pillage, *n.* **1.** The forcible seizure of another's property, esp. in war. **2.** The property so seized; BOOTY. — Also termed *plunder*.

pimp, *n.* A person who solicits customers for a prostitute. —Also termed *pander*. —**pimp,** *vb.* See PANDERING.

***Pinkerton* rule.** In criminal law, the doctrine imposing liability on a conspirator for all offenses committed in furtherance of the conspiracy, even if those offenses are actually performed by coconspirators. *Pinkerton v. United States*, 328 U.S. 640 (1946).

pink sheet. A daily report, printed on pink paper, of the prices for over-the-counter securities.

pinpoint citation. See CITATION.

piracy, *n.* **1.** Robbery, kidnapping, or other criminal violence committed at sea. **2.** A similar crime committed aboard a plane or other vehicle; hijacking. **3.** The unauthorized and illegal reproduction or distribution of materials protected by copyright, patent, or trademark law. See INFRINGEMENT; PLAGIARISM. —**pirate,** *vb.*—**piratical,** *adj.*—**pirate,** *n.*

PITI. *abbr.* Principal, interest, taxes, and insurance—the components of a monthly mortgage payment.

P.J. See *presiding judge* under JUDGE.

PKPA. *abbr.* PARENTAL KIDNAPPING PREVENTION ACT.

P.L. *abbr.* PUBLIC LAW.

place-of-wrong rule. LEX LOCI DELICTI.

plagiarism (**play**-jə-riz-əm), *n.* The act or an instance of copying or stealing another's words or ideas and attributing them as one's own. —**plagiarize,** *vb.*—**plagiarist,** *n.* Cf. INFRINGEMENT.

plain error. See ERROR.

plain-language law. Legislation requiring nontechnical, readily comprehensible language in consumer contracts such as residential leases or insurance policies.

plain-language movement. 1. The loosely organized campaign to encourage legal writers and business writers to write clearly and concisely—without legalese—while preserving accuracy and precision. **2.** The body of persons involved in this campaign.

plain-meaning rule. The principle that prohibits the examination of any information not contained in a writing when determining the meaning of a contract, statute, or other document; esp., the statutory-interpretation rule requiring the application of a word's plain and customary meaning, without analyzing legislative intent. Cf. GOLDEN RULE; MISCHIEF RULE.

plaintiff. The party who brings a civil suit in a court of law. Cf. DEFENDANT.

plaintiff in error. *Archaic.* APPELLANT; PETITIONER.

plain-view doctrine. In criminal procedure, the rule permitting a peace officer's warrantless seizure of evidence observed in plain view from a lawful position or during a legal search. —Also termed *clear-view doctrine*; *plain-sight rule*. Cf. OPEN-FIELD DOCTRINE.

PLAM. See *price-level-adjusted mortgage* under MORTGAGE.

plan. BANKRUPTCY PLAN.

planned-unit development. A land area zoned for a single-community subdivision with flexible restrictions on residential, commercial, and public uses. —Abbr. PUD. Cf. RESIDENTIAL CLUSTER.

plan of reorganization. BANKRUPTCY PLAN.

plant patent. See PATENT (2).

plat. 1. A small piece of land; PLOT (1). **2.** A map describing a piece of land and its features, such as boundaries, lots, roads, and easements.

plea. 1. An accused person's formal response of "guilty," "not guilty," or "nolo contendere" to a criminal charge. **2.** At common law, the defendant's responsive pleading in a civil action. Cf. DECLARATION (7). **3.** A factual allegation offered in a case; a pleading. Cf. DEMURRER.

common plea. A common-law plea in a civil action as opposed to a criminal prosecution.

dilatory plea. A plea that does not challenge the merits of a case but that seeks to delay or defeat the action on procedural grounds.

insanity plea. INSANITY DEFENSE.

issuable plea. A plea on the merits presenting a complaint to the court. Cf. *issuable defense* under DEFENSE (1).

jurisdictional plea. A plea asserting that the court lacks jurisdiction either over the defendant or over the subject matter of the case.

nonissuable plea. A plea on which a court ruling will not decide the case on the merits, such as a plea in abatement.

peremptory plea. A plea that responds to the merits of the plaintiff's claim.

plea in abatement. A plea that objects to the place, time, or method of asserting the plaintiff's claim but does not dispute the claim's merits; a defendant who successfully asserts a plea in abatement leaves the claim open for continuation in the current action or reassertion in a later action if the defect is cured.

plea in bar. A plea that seeks to defeat the plaintiff's action completely and permanently.

plea in discharge. A plea alleging that the defendant has previously satisfied and discharged the plaintiff's claim.

special plea. A plea alleging one or more new facts rather than merely disputing the legal grounds of the action or charge.

plea bargain, *n.* An agreement between the prosecutor and criminal defendant to resolve a case without trial, usu. allowing the defendant to plead guilty to a lesser offense or testify against another in return for a less severe punishment. —**plea-bargain,** *vb.*—**plea-bargaining,** *n.*

plead, *vb.* **1.** To draft, file, or deliver a pleading <plead in court>. **2.** To answer a criminal charge <she pleaded no contest to the charges>. **3.** To assert or allege in a legal proceeding <if we don't plead this affirmative defense, it will be waived>.

pleading, *n.* **1.** The document containing the factual allegations that each party is required to communicate to the opponent before trial; in federal civil procedure, the main pleadings are the plaintiff's complaint and the defendant's answer.

accusatory pleading. An indictment or complaint accusing a person of a crime that the government will pursue in court.

amended pleading. A pleading that relates to newly discovered matters that occurred before the filing of an earlier pleading; an amended pleading entirely supersedes the earlier pleading.

anomalous pleading. A pleading that is partly affirmative and partly negative in its allegations.

articulated pleading. A pleading that states each allegation in a separately numbered paragraph.

defective pleading. A pleading that fails to meet minimum standards of sufficiency or accuracy in form or substance.

responsive pleading. A pleading that replies to the merits of an opponent's prior pleading. See ANSWER.

sham pleading. An obviously frivolous or absurd pleading that is made only for purposes of vexation or delay. —Also termed *sham plea*; *false plea.*

supplemental pleading. A pleading that either corrects a defect in an earlier pleading or addresses facts arising since the earlier pleading was filed; unlike an amended pleading, a supplemental pleading merely adds to the earlier pleading and does not supersede it.

2. A system of defining and narrowing the issues in a lawsuit whereby the parties file formal documents alleging their respective positions.

alternative pleading. A form of pleading whereby the pleader alleges two or more independent claims or defenses that are not necessarily consistent with each other, such as alleging both intentional infliction of emotional distress and negligent infliction of emotional distress based on the same conduct. Fed. R. Civ. P. 8(e)(2).

artful pleading. A plaintiff's disguised phrasing of a federal claim as solely a state-law claim in order to prevent a defendant from removing the case from state court to federal court.

code pleading. A procedural system requiring that the pleader allege merely the facts of the case giving rise to the claim, not the legal conclusions necessary to sustain the claim. —Also termed *fact pleading.*

notice pleading. A procedural system requiring that the pleader give only a short and plain statement of the claim showing that the pleader is entitled to relief, and not a complete detailing of all the facts. Fed. R. Civ. P. 8(a).

special pleading. See SPECIAL PLEADING.

pleading the baby act. See BABY ACT, PLEADING THE.

pleading the Fifth. The act or an instance of asserting one's right against self-incrimination under the Fifth Amendment. —Also termed *taking the Fifth.* See RIGHT AGAINST SELF-INCRIMINATION.

plea in abatement. See PLEA.

plea in bar. See PLEA.

plea in discharge. See PLEA.

plea of tender. At common law, a pleading asserting that the defendant has consistently been willing to pay the debt demanded, has offered it to the plaintiff, and has brought the money into court ready to pay the plaintiff. See TENDER.

plebiscite (ple-bə-sIt), *n.* A binding or nonbinding referendum on a proposed law, constitutional amendment, or significant public issue. — **plebiscitary** (ple-**bi**-sə-ter-ee), *adj.* See REFERENDUM.

pledge, *n.* **1.** A bailment or other deposit of personal property to a creditor as security for a debt or obligation; PAWN (2). Cf. LIEN. **2.** The item of personal property so deposited; PAWN (1). **3.** Broadly, the act of providing something as security for a debt or obligation; the thing so provided. —**pledge**, *vb.*—**pledgeable**, *adj.*

pledged account. See ACCOUNT.

pledgee. One with whom a pledge is deposited.

pledgor. One who gives a pledge to another. —Also spelled *pledger*.

plenary (plee-nə-ree *or* **ple**-), *adj.* **1.** Full; complete; entire <plenary authority>. **2.** (Of an assembly) to be attended by all members or participants <plenary session>.

plenary action. See ACTION.

plenary confession. See CONFESSION.

plenary jurisdiction. See JURISDICTION.

plot. 1. A measured piece of land; LOT (1). **2.** A plan forming the basis of a conspiracy.

plunder. PILLAGE.

plurality. A large number or quantity that does not constitute a majority; a number greater than another, regardless of the margin <a four-member plurality of the Supreme Court agreed with this view, which gets more votes than any other>. Cf. MAJORITY (2).

plurality opinion. See OPINION (1).

plural marriage. See MARRIAGE (1).

pluries (pluu-ree-eez), *n.* [Latin "many times"] A third or subsequent writ issued when the previous writs have been ineffective.

PMM. See *purchase-money mortgage* under MORTGAGE.

PMRT. See *purchase-money resulting trust* under TRUST.

PMSI. See *purchase-money security interest* under SECURITY INTEREST.

pocket part. A supplemental pamphlet inserted usu. into the back inside cover of a lawbook, esp. a treatise or code, in order to update the material in the main text until the publisher issues a new edition of the entire work; legal publishers frequently leave a little extra room inside their hardcover books specifically so that pocket parts may later be added <although the main text had nothing on point, the hot-off-the-press pocket part solved the riddle>.

pocket veto. See VETO.

P.O.D. *abbr.* Pay on delivery.

point, *n.* **1.** A pertinent and distinct legal proposition, issue, or argument <point of error>. **2.** One percent of the face value of a loan (esp. a mortgage loan), paid up front to the lender as a service charge or placement fee <the borrower hoped for a two-point discount on the mortgage>. —Also termed *mortgage point*. **3.** A unit used for quoting stock, bond, or commodity prices <the stock closed up a few points today>.

point of error. A mistake by a lower court asserted as a ground for appeal. See ERROR; WRIT OF ERROR.

point of law. A discrete legal proposition at issue in a case.

reserved point of law. An important or difficult point of law that arises during trial but that the judge sets aside for future argument so that testimony can continue.

poisonous-tree doctrine. See FRUIT-OF-THE-POISONOUS-TREE DOCTRINE.

poison pill. *Slang.* A corporation's defense against an unwanted takeover bid whereby shareholders are granted the right to purchase stock at a low price in order to increase the aggressor's acquisition costs. See SHARK REPELLENT. Cf. PORCUPINE PROVISION.

police court. See *magistrate's court* (a) under COURT.

police magistrate. See MAGISTRATE.

police power. 1. A state's Tenth Amendment right, subject to due-process and other limitations, to establish and enforce laws protecting the public's health, safety, and general welfare, or to delegate this right to local governments. **2.** Loosely, the power of the government to intervene in the use of privately owned property, as by subjecting it to eminent domain. See EMINENT DOMAIN.

policy. INSURANCE POLICY.

policyholder. One who owns an insurance policy, regardless of whether that person is the insured party.

policy of insurance. INSURANCE POLICY.

political-action committee. An organization formed by a special-interest group to raise and contribute money to the campaigns of political candidates who the group believes will promote its interests. —Abbr. PAC.

political asylum. ASYLUM (2).

political correctness, *n.* **1.** The doctrine favoring the elimination of language and practices that might offend political sensibilities, esp. in racial or sexual matters. **2.** An instance in which a person conforms to this doctrine. —Abbr. P.C. —**politically correct,** *adj.*

political gerrymandering. GERRYMANDERING (1).

political liberty. See *political right* under RIGHT.

political offense. A crime directed against the security or governmental system of a nation, such as treason, sedition, or espionage; under principles of international law, the perpetrator of such an offense cannot be extradited.

political party. An organization of voters formed to influence the government's conduct and policies by nominating and electing candidates to public office; the U.S. has traditionally maintained a two-party system, which today comprises the Democratic and Republican parties.

political patronage. PATRONAGE (3).

political-question doctrine. The judicial principle that a court should refuse to decide issues involving the exercise of discretionary powers by the executive or legislative branch of government.

political right. See RIGHT.

poll, *vb.* **1.** To ask each member of (a group) to state his or her vote individually <after the verdict was read, the judge polled the jury>. **2.** To question (people) so as to elicit votes, opinions, or preferences <Mr. Byers

polled the history class about taking an essay exam>. **3.** To receive (a given number of votes) in an election <the third-party candidate polled only 250 votes in Fort Bend County>.

poll tax. See TAX.

polygamy (pə-lig-ə-mee), *n.* The state of being simultaneously married to more than one spouse; multiple marriages. —**polygamous,** *adj.*—**polygamist,** *n.* Cf. BIGAMY; MONOGAMY.

polygraph, *n.* A device used to evaluate veracity by measuring and recording involuntary physiological changes in the human body during interrogation; polygraph results are inadmissible as evidence in most states. —Also termed *lie detector.* —**polygraphy,** *n.*—**polygraphic,** *adj.*

Ponzi scheme. A fraudulent investment scheme in which money contributed by later investors generates artificially high dividends for the original investors, whose example attracts even larger investments. Cf. PYRAMID SCHEME.

pool, *n.* **1.** An association of individuals or entities who share resources and funds to promote their joint undertaking; if such an association is formed to eliminate competition throughout a single industry, it is a restraint of trade that violates federal antitrust laws. **2.** A gambling scheme in which numerous persons contribute stakes for betting on a particular event (such as a sporting event).

pooling. COMMUNITIZATION.

pooling agreement. A contractual arrangement among corporate shareholders whereby they agree that their shares will be voted as a unit. —Also termed *voting agreement; shareholder voting agreement.*

porcupine provision. *Slang.* A clause in a corporation's charter or bylaws designed to prevent a takeover without the consent of the board of directors. Cf. SHARK REPELLENT; POISON PILL.

pork-barrel legislation. See LEGISLATION.

pornography, *n.* The depiction of sexual activity or erotic behavior in writing or pictures (as in books, photographs, or films); pornography is protected speech under the First Amendment unless it is legally obscene. —**pornographic,** *adj.* See OBSCENITY.

child pornography. A work or production that depicts children engaged in sexual activity; child pornography is not protected by the First Amendment—even if it falls short of the legal standard for obscenity—and anyone involved in its distribution can be criminally punished.

port authority. A state or federal agency that regulates traffic through a port or that establishes and maintains airports, bridges, tollways, and public transportation.

portfolio. The various securities or other investments held by an investor at any given time, usu. for the purpose of diversifying risk.

market portfolio. A value-weighted portfolio of every asset in a particular market.

positive easement. See *affirmative easement* under EASEMENT.

positive externality. See EXTERNALITY.

positive fraud. See *actual fraud* under FRAUD.

positive law. A system of law implemented and laid down within a particular political community by political superiors, as distinct from moral law or law existing in an ideal community or in some nonpolitical community; positive law typically consists of enacted law—the statutes and regulations that are applied and enforced in the courts. Cf. NATURAL LAW.

positive prescription. PRESCRIPTION (1).

positivism. See LEGAL POSITIVISM; LOGICAL POSITIVISM.

posse comitatus (**pos**-ee-kom-ə-**tah**-təs), *n.* [Latin "power of the county"] A group of citizens who are called together to assist the sheriff in keeping the peace. —Often shortened to *posse.*

possession, *n.* **1.** The fact of having or holding property in one's power; the exercise of dominion over property. **2.** The right under which one may exercise control over something to the exclusion of all others. **3.** (*usu. pl.*) Something that a person owns or controls; PROPERTY (2). —**possess,** *vb.*—**possessor,** *n.* Cf. OWNERSHIP; TITLE (1).

actual possession. Physical occupancy or control over property. Cf. *constructive possession.*

adverse possession. See ADVERSE POSSESSION.

constructive possession. Control or dominion over a property without actual possession or custody of it. Cf. *actual possession.*

exclusive possession. The exercise of exclusive dominion over property, including the use and benefit of the property.

hostile possession. Possession asserted against the claims of all others, including the record owner. See ADVERSE POSSESSION.

open possession. Possession or control that is evident to others. — Also termed *notorious possession; open and notorious possession.* See ADVERSE POSSESSION.

peaceable possession. Possession (as of real property) not disturbed by another's hostile or legal attempts to recover possession. Cf. ADVERSE POSSESSION.

possession unity. See *unity of possession* under UNITY.

possessory action. See ACTION.

possessory interest. The right to control property, including the right to exclude others, by a person who is not necessarily the owner.

possessory lien. See LIEN.

possibility of reverter. A future interest retained by a grantor after conveying a fee simple determinable, so that the grantee's estate terminates automatically and reverts to the grantor if the terminating event ever occurs. —Often shortened to *reverter.* See *fee simple determinable* under FEE SIMPLE. Cf. POWER OF TERMINATION.

post, *vb.* **1.** To publicize or announce by affixing a notice in a public place

<foreclosure notice was posted at the county courthouse>. **2.** To transfer (accounting entries) from an original record to a ledger <post debits and credits>. **3.** To place in the mail <post a letter>. **4.** To make a payment or deposit; to put up <post bail>.

post audit. See AUDIT.

postconviction-relief proceeding. A state or federal procedure for a prisoner to request a court to vacate or correct a conviction or sentence. — Also termed *postconviction-remedy proceeding*; *PCR action*; *postconviction proceeding*.

postdate. To put a date on (something, such as an instrument) that is later than the actual date. Cf. ANTE-DATE; BACKDATE.

postdated check. See CHECK.

postglossators (pohst-**glo**-say-tərz *or* -sə-tərz). (*often cap.*) A group of Italian jurisconsults who were active during the 14th and 15th centuries writing commentaries and treatises that related Roman law to feudal and Germanic law, canon law, and other contemporary bodies of law; the postglossators constituted the second wave of Roman-law study after its revival in the 11th century, the first being that of the glossators. —Also termed *commentators*. See GLOSSA-TORS.

post hoc. [Latin *post hoc, ergo propter hoc* "after this, therefore because of this"] **1.** *adj.* Of or relating to the fallacy of assuming causality from temporal sequence; confusing sequence with consequence. **2.** *adv.* After the fact; consequently.

posthumous (**pos**-chə-məs), *adj.* Occurring or existing after death; esp., (of a child) born after the father's death.

postjudgment discovery. See DIS-COVERY.

postmortem, *adj.* Done or occurring after death.

postmortem, *n.* AUTOPSY.

postnuptial agreement (pohst-**nəp**-shəl). A written agreement entered into after marriage defining each spouse's rights in the event of death or divorce. —Also termed *postnuptial settlement*. Cf. PRENUPTIAL AGREEMENT.

posttrial discovery. See *postjudgment discovery* under DISCOV-ERY.

potential Pareto superiority. WEALTH MAXIMIZATION.

pour out, *vb. Slang.* (Of a claimant) to fail to obtain damages or relief in a lawsuit <the plaintiff was poured out of court by the jury's verdict of no liability>.

pourover trust. See TRUST.

pourover will. See WILL.

poverty affidavit. See AFFIDAVIT.

Powell **doctrine.** CORRUPT-MOTIVE DOCTRINE.

power. 1. The ability to act or not act. **2.** The legal right or authorization to act or not act. **3.** Dominance, control, or influence over another. **4.** A document granting legal authorization. See AUTHORITY.

concurrent power. A political power independently exercisable by both federal and state governments in the same field of legislation.

enumerated power. A political power specifically delegated to a governmental branch by a constitution. — Also termed *express power*.

implied power. A political power that is not enumerated but that nonetheless exists because it is needed to carry out an express power.

incident power. A power that, although not expressly granted, must exist because it is necessary to the accomplishment of an express purpose.

inherent power. A power that necessarily derives from an office, position, or status.

judicial power. The authority vested in courts and judges; esp., the authority to hear and decide cases and to make binding judgments on them.

naked power. The power to exercise rights over something (such as a trust) without having a corresponding interest in that thing.

reserved power. A political power that is not enumerated or prohibited by a constitution, but instead is reserved by the constitution for a specified political authority, such as a state government. See TENTH AMENDMENT.

resulting power. A political power derived from the aggregate powers expressly or impliedly granted by a constitution.

power of appointment. A power conferred on a donee by will or deed to select and nominate one or more recipients of the donor's estate or income.

general power of appointment. A power of appointment by which the donee can appoint—that is, dispose of the donor's property—in favor of anyone the donee chooses.

limited power of appointment. A power of appointment by which the donee can appoint to only the person or class specified in the instrument creating the power. —Also termed *special power of appointment.*

power of attorney. 1. An instrument granting someone authority to act as agent or attorney-in-fact for the grantor. —Also termed *letter of attorney.* **2.** The authority so granted. Pl. **powers of attorney.** See ATTORNEY (1).

durable power of attorney. A power of attorney that remains in effect during the grantor's incompetency; such instruments commonly allow an agent to make healthcare decisions for a patient who has become incompetent.

power-of-sale clause. A provision in a mortgage or deed of trust permitting the mortgagee or trustee to sell the property without court authority if the payments are not made.

power-of-sale foreclosure. See FORECLOSURE.

power of termination. A future interest retained by a grantor after conveying a fee simple subject to a condition subsequent, so that the grantee's estate terminates (upon breach of the condition) only if the grantor exercises the right to retake it. —Also termed *right of entry; right* *of re-entry*; *right of entry for breach of condition*; *right of entry for condition broken*. See *fee simple subject to a condition subsequent* under FEE SIMPLE. Cf. POSSIBILITY OF REVERTER.

PPO. *abbr.* PREFERRED-PROVIDER ORGANIZATION.

practice, *n.* The procedural methods and rules used in a court of law <local practice requires an extra copy of motions to be filed with the clerk>.

praecipe (**pre**-sə-pee), *n.* [Latin "command"] **1.** At common law, a writ ordering a defendant to do some act or to explain why inaction is appropriate. —Also termed *writ of praecipe*. **2.** A written motion or request seeking some court action, esp. a trial setting or an entry of judgment. —Also spelled *precipe*. —**praecipe,** *vb.*

praedial (**pree**-dee-əl). PREDIAL.

praxis (**prak**-sis). [Greek "doing; action"] In critical legal studies, practical action; the practice of living the ethical life in conjunction and in cooperation with others.

prayer for relief. A request addressed to the court and appearing at the end of a pleading; esp., a request for specific relief or damages. —Often shortened to *prayer*. —Also termed *demand for relief*.

preamble, *n.* An introductory statement in a constitution, statute, or other document explaining the document's basis and objective. —**preambular,** *adj.*

precatory (**pre**-kə-tor-ee), *adj.* (Of words) requesting, recommending, or expressing a desire for action, but usu. in a nonbinding way; an example of precatory language is "it is my wish and desire to . . . . "

precedence (**pre**-sə-dən[t]s *or* pri-**seed**-[ə]n[t]s), *n.* The act or state of going before; esp., the order or priority in place or time observed by persons of different statuses (such as political dignitaries) on the basis of rank during ceremonial events.

precedent (pri-**seed**-[ə]nt *or* **pre**-sə-dənt), *adj.* Preceding in time or order <condition precedent>.

precedent (**pre**-sə-dənt), *n.* A decided case that furnishes a basis for determining later cases involving similar facts or issues. —**precedential,** *adj.* See STARE DECISIS.

binding precedent. A precedent that a court must follow; for example, a lower court is bound by an applicable holding of a higher court in the same jurisdiction.

persuasive precedent. A precedent that a court may either follow or ignore; for example, if the case was decided in a neighboring jurisdiction, the court might evaluate the earlier court's reasoning without being bound to decide the same way.

precept (**pree**-sept). **1.** A standard or rule of conduct; a command or principle <several legal precepts govern here>. **2.** A civil or criminal writ or warrant issued by an authorized person demanding another's action, such as a judge's order to an officer to bring a party before the court <the sheriff executed the precept immediately>.

precinct. A geographical unit of government, such as an election district, a police district, or a judicial district.

precipe (**pre**-sə-pee). PRAECIPE.

précis (pray-**see**), *n.* A concise summary of a text's essential points; an abstract.

preconceived malice. MALICE AFORETHOUGHT.

precontract. See CONTRACT.

predate, *vb.* ANTEDATE.

predatory pricing. Unlawful below-cost pricing intended to eliminate specific competitors and reduce overall competition. See ANTITRUST.

predial (**pree**-dee-əl), *adj.* Consisting of, relating to, or attached to land <predial servitude>. —Also spelled *praedial.*

predicate act. In the law of RICO, one of two or more acts of racketeering necessary to establish a pattern. See RACKETEER INFLUENCED AND CORRUPT ORGANIZATIONS ACT.

preemption (pree-**em[p]**-shən), *n.* **1.** The right to buy before others. See RIGHT OF PREEMPTION. **2.** The purchase of something under this right. **3.** An earlier seizure or appropriation. **4.** The occupation of public land so as to establish a preemptive title. **5.** In constitutional law, the principle—derived from the Supremacy Clause—that a federal law supersedes any inconsistent state law or regulation. —Also termed (in sense 5) *federal preemption.* —**preempt,** *vb.*—**preemptive,** *adj.*

preemptive right. A shareholder's privilege to purchase newly issued stock—before the shares are offered to the public—in an amount proportionate to the shareholder's current holdings in order to prevent dilution of the shareholder's ownership inter-

est; this right must be exercised within a fixed period, usu. 30 to 60 days. —Also termed *subscription privilege.* See SUBSCRIPTION RIGHT. Cf. RIGHTS OFFERING.

preexisting duty. See DUTY.

preexisting-duty rule. In contract law, the rule that performance of an act that a party is already contractually bound to perform does not constitute valid consideration for a new promise; for example, if a builder agrees to construct a building for a specified price but later threatens to walk off the job unless the owner promises to pay an additional sum, the owner's new promise would not be enforceable because, under the pre-existing duty rule, there is no consideration for that promise.

preference. 1. The act of favoring one person or thing over another; the person or thing so favored. **2.** Priority of payment given to one or more creditors by a debtor; a creditor's right to receive such priority. **3.** PREFERENTIAL TRANSFER.

liquidation preference. A preferred shareholder's right, once the corporation is liquidated, to receive a specified distribution before common shareholders receive anything.

voidable preference. PREFERENTIAL TRANSFER.

preference shares. See *preferred stock* under STOCK.

preferential transfer. A prebankruptcy transfer made by an insolvent debtor to or for the benefit of a creditor, thereby allowing the creditor to receive more than its proportionate share of the debtor's assets; under the circumstances described in 11 U.S.C. § 547, the bankruptcy trustee may recover—for the estate's benefit—a preferential transfer from the transferee. —Also termed *preference*; *voidable preference*; *voidable transfer*; *preferential assignment*. Cf. FRAUDULENT CONVEYANCE (2).

preferred dividend. See DIVIDEND.

preferred-provider organization. A group of healthcare providers (such as doctors, hospitals, and pharmacies) that agree to provide medical services at a discounted cost to enrolled persons in a given geographic area. —Abbr. PPO. Cf. HEALTH-MAINTENANCE ORGANIZATION.

preferred stock. See STOCK.

prejudice, *n.* **1.** Damage or detriment to one's legal rights or claims. See *dismissal with/without prejudice* under DISMISSAL. **2.** A preconceived judgment formed without a factual basis; a strong bias. —**prejudice,** *vb.*—**prejudicial,** *adj.*

prejudicial error. See *reversible error* under ERROR.

preliminary hearing. A criminal hearing (usu. conducted by a magistrate) to determine whether there is sufficient evidence to prosecute an accused person; if sufficient evidence exists, the case will be bound over for grand-jury review or an information will be filed in the trial court. —Also termed *preliminary examination*; *probable-cause hearing*; *bindover hearing*; *examining trial*. Cf. ARRAIGNMENT.

preliminary injunction. See INJUNCTION.

preliminary letter. INVITATION TO NEGOTIATE.

preliminary prospectus. See PROSPECTUS.

premarital agreement. PRENUPTIAL AGREEMENT.

prematurity. 1. The circumstance existing when the facts underlying a plaintiff's complaint do not yet create a live claim. Cf. RIPENESS. **2.** The affirmative defense based on this circumstance.

premeditated malice. MALICE AFORETHOUGHT.

premeditation, *n.* Conscious consideration and planning that precedes some act (such as committing a crime). —**premeditate,** *vb.*—**premeditated,** *adj.*

premise, *n.* A previous statement or contention from which a conclusion is deduced. —Also spelled (in England) *premiss*. —**premise,** *vb.*

premises. 1. Matters (usu. preliminary facts or statements) previously referred to in the same instrument <wherefore, premises considered, the plaintiff prays for the following relief>. **2.** A house or building, along with its grounds <smoking is not allowed on these premises>.

premises liability. A landowner's or landholder's tort liability for conditions or activities on the premises.

premium. 1. The periodic payment required to keep an insurance policy in effect. —Also termed *insurance premium*.

   earned premium. The portion of an insurance premium applicable to the coverage period that has already expired; for example, if the total premium for a one-year insurance policy is $1200, the earned premium after three months is $300.

unearned premium. The portion of an insurance premium applicable to the coverage period that has not yet occurred; in the same example as above, the unearned premium after three months is $900.

2. A sum of money paid in addition to a regular price, salary, or other amount; a bonus. **3.** The amount by which a security's market value exceeds its face value. Cf. DISCOUNT (3). **4.** The amount paid to buy a securities option. —Also termed (in sense 4) *option premium.*

premium on capital stock. See *paid-in surplus* under SURPLUS.

prenatal tort. See TORT.

prenuptial (pree-**nap**-shəl), *adj.* Made or occurring before marriage; premarital. —Also termed *antenuptial.*

prenuptial agreement. An agreement made before marriage usu. to resolve issues of support and property division if the marriage ends in divorce or by the death of a spouse. —Also termed *antenuptial agreement; premarital agreement; marriage settlement.* See SETTLEMENT (2). Cf. POSTNUPTIAL AGREEMENT.

prenuptial gift. See GIFT.

prenuptial will. See WILL.

prepaid expense. See EXPENSE.

prepaid interest. See INTEREST (3).

prepaid legal services. An arrangement—usu. serving as an employee benefit—that enables a person to make advance payments for future legal services.

prepayment clause. A loan-document provision that permits a borrower to satisfy a debt before its due date usu. without paying a penalty.

prepayment penalty. A charge assessed against a borrower who elects to pay off a loan before it is due.

preponderance, *n.* Superiority in weight, importance, or influence. — **preponderate,** *vb.*—**preponderant,** *adj.*

preponderance of the evidence. The greater weight of the evidence; the burden of proof in a civil trial, in which the jury is instructed to find for the party that, on the whole, has the stronger evidence, however slight the edge may be. —Also termed *preponderance of proof; balance of probability.* Cf. *clear and convincing evidence* under EVIDENCE.

prerogative (pri-**ro**-gə-tiv), *n.* An exclusive right, power, privilege, or immunity, usu. acquired by virtue of office. —**prerogative,** *adj.*

prerogative writ. See *extraordinary writ* under WRIT.

prescription, *n.* **1.** The acquisition of title to a thing (esp. an intangible thing such as the use of real property) by open and continuous possession over a statutory period. —Also termed *positive prescription.* Cf. ADVERSE POSSESSION. **2.** The extinction of a title or right by failure to claim or exercise it over a long period. —Also termed *negative prescription.* **3.** The act of establishing authoritative rules; a rule so established. —**prescribe,** *vb.* Cf. PROSCRIPTION.

prescriptive easement. See EASEMENT.

presentence hearing. A proceeding at which a judge or jury receives and examines all relevant information regarding a convicted criminal and the related offense before passing sentence. —Also termed *sentencing hearing*.

presentence investigation report. A probation officer's detailed account of a convicted defendant's educational, criminal, family, and social background, conducted at the court's request as an aid in passing sentence. —Abbr. PSI. —Often shortened to *presentence report*.

presenting bank. See BANK.

presenting jury. GRAND JURY.

presentment (pri-**zent**-mənt). **1.** The act of presenting or laying before a court or other tribunal a formal statement about a matter to be dealt with legally. **2.** A formal written accusation returned by a grand jury on its own initiative, without a prosecutor's previous indictment request. **3.** The formal production of a negotiable instrument for acceptance or payment.

present recollection refreshed. In the law of evidence, a witness's memory that has been enhanced by showing the witness a document that describes the relevant events; the document itself is merely a memory stimulus and is not admitted in evidence. Fed. R. Evid. 612. —Also termed *refreshing recollection*; *present recollection revived*. Cf. PAST RECOLLECTION RECORDED.

present sense impression. One's perception of an event or condition, formed during or immediately after the fact; a statement containing a present sense impression is admissible even if it is hearsay. Fed. R. Evid. 803(1). Cf. EXCITED UTTERANCE.

present value. The sum of money that, with compound interest, would amount to a specified sum at a specified future date; future value discounted to its value today. —Also termed *present worth*.

adjusted present value. An asset's value determined by adding together its present value and the value added by capital-structure effects. —Abbr. APV.

net present value. The present value of net cash flow from a project, discounted by the cost of capital; this value is used to evaluate the project's investment potential. —Abbr. NPV.

president. 1. The chief political executive of a government; the head of state. **2.** The chief executive officer of a corporation or other organization.

presiding judge. See JUDGE.

presiding juror. See JUROR.

presumption, *n.* A factual or legal assumption drawn from the existence of another fact or group of facts; a presumption shifts the burden of production to the opposing party, who can then attempt to rebut the presumption <the age-old presumption holds that one is considered innocent until proven guilty>. —**presume,** *vb.* See BURDEN OF PRODUCTION.

conclusive presumption. A presumption that cannot be overcome by any additional evidence or argument <it is a conclusive presumption that a child under the age of seven is incapable of committing a felony>. —Also termed *absolute presumption; irrebuttable presumption; mandatory presumption; presumption juris et de jure.* Cf. *rebuttable presumption.*

presumption of fact. A type of rebuttable presumption that may be, but as a matter of law need not be, drawn from another established fact or group of facts <the possessor of recently stolen goods is, by presumption of fact, considered the thief>. —Also termed *factual presumption.*

presumption of law. A legal assumption that a court is required to make if certain facts are established and no contradictory evidence is produced <by presumption of law, a criminal defendant is considered innocent until proven guilty beyond a reasonable doubt>. —Also termed *legal presumption.*

rebuttable presumption. An inference drawn from certain facts that establish a prima facie case, which may be overcome by the introduction of contrary evidence. —Also termed *disputable presumption; presumption juris.* Cf. *conclusive presumption.*

presumption of innocence. The fundamental criminal-law principle that a person may not be convicted of a crime unless the government proves guilt beyond a reasonable doubt, without any burden placed on the accused to prove innocence.

presumption of natural and probable consequences. In criminal law, the presumption that *mens rea* may be derived from proof of the defendant's conduct.

presumptive authority. See *implied authority* under AUTHORITY.

presumptive death. See DEATH.

presumptive evidence. See EVIDENCE.

presumptive heir. See *heir presumptive* under HEIR (1).

pretermission statute. PRETERMITTED-HEIR STATUTE.

pretermit (pree-tər-**mit**), *vb.* **1.** To ignore or disregard purposely <the court pretermitted the constitutional question by deciding the case on procedural grounds>. **2.** To neglect or overlook accidentally <the third child was pretermitted in the will>. —**pretermission,** *n.*

pretermitted child. See *pretermitted heir* under HEIR (1).

pretermitted defense. See DEFENSE (1).

pretermitted heir. See HEIR.

pretermitted-heir statute. A state law that grants a pretermitted heir the right to inherit a share of the testator's estate, usu. by treating the heir as though the testator had died intestate. —Also termed *pretermission statute.*

pretermitted spouse. See *pretermitted heir* under HEIR (1).

pretext, *n.* A false or weak reason or motive advanced to hide the actual or strong reason or motive. —**pretextual,** *adj.*

pretrial conference. An informal meeting at which opposing attorneys confer, sometimes with the judge, to work toward the disposition of the case by discussing matters of evidence and narrowing the issues that will be argued; the conference ordinarily results in a pretrial order. — Often shortened to *pretrial.* —Also termed *pretrial hearing.*

pretrial detention. See DETENTION.

pretrial discovery. See DISCOVERY.

pretrial diversion. DIVERSION PROGRAM.

pretrial intervention. DIVERSION PROGRAM.

pretrial order. An order reciting a trial's procedural rules and stipulations as agreed to by the parties at a pretrial conference.

prevailing party. See PARTY.

prevarication (pri-vair-ə-**kay**-shən), *n.* The act or an instance of lying or avoiding the truth; equivocation. — **prevaricate,** *vb.*—**prevaricator,** *n.*

prevention doctrine. In contract law, the principle that each contracting party has an implied duty to not do anything that prevents the other party from performing its obligation. —Also termed *prevention-of-performance doctrine.*

preventive detention. See DETENTION.

preventive injunction. See INJUNCTION.

price. The amount of money or other consideration asked for or given in exchange for something else; the cost at which something is bought or sold.

asked price. The lowest price at which a seller is willing to sell a security at a given time. See SPREAD (2).

asking price. The value at which a seller lists property for sale, often suggesting a willingness to sell for less. —Also termed *ask price*; *offering price.*

bid price. The highest price that a prospective buyer is willing to pay for a security at a given time. See SPREAD (2).

call price. **a.** The price at which a bond may be retired before its maturity. **b.** See *strike price.*

ceiling price. **a.** The highest price at which a buyer is willing to buy. **b.** The highest price allowed by a government agency or by some other regulatory institution.

floor price. The lowest price at which a seller is willing to sell.

liquidation price. A price that is paid for property sold to liquidate a debt; usu., this price is below market price. —Also termed *liquidation value.*

market price. The prevailing price at which something is sold in a specific market. See FAIR MARKET VALUE.

strike price. The price for which a security will be bought or sold under an option contract if the option is exercised. —Also termed *exercise price*; *call price*; *put price.* See OPTION.

subscription price. See SUBSCRIPTION PRICE.

transfer price. The charge assigned to an exchange of goods or services between a corporation's organizational units.

upset price. The lowest amount a seller is willing to accept for property or goods sold at auction.

price discrimination. Two substantially contemporaneous sales of identical personal property to two different buyers at two different prices; such a scheme violates antitrust laws if the parties intended to reduce competition.

persistent price discrimination. A monopolist's systematic policy of obtaining different rates of return from different sales groupings.

price-earnings ratio. The ratio between a stock's current share price and the corporation's earnings per share for the last year; investors sometimes avoid stocks with high price-earnings ratios because those stocks may be overpriced. —Abbr. P/E ratio.

price-fixing. An unlawful cooperative effort by competitors to interfere with trade by setting prices.

horizontal price-fixing. Price-fixing among competitors on the same level, such as retailers throughout an industry.

vertical price-fixing. Price-fixing among parties in the same chain of distribution, such as manufacturers and retailers attempting to control an item's resale price.

price-level-adjusted mortgage. See MORTGAGE.

priest-penitent privilege. See PRIVILEGE.

prima facie (**prI**-mə-**fay**-shə *or* -shee *or* -shee-ee). [Latin "at first sight"] **1.** *adv.* On its face; apparently. **2.** *adj.* True or valid on first impression; evident without proof.

prima facie case. 1. The establishment of a legally required rebuttable presumption. **2.** The plaintiff's production of enough evidence to allow the fact-trier to infer the fact at issue and rule in the plaintiff's favor.

prima facie evidence. See EVIDENCE.

prima facie tort. See TORT.

primary, *n.* See *primary election* under ELECTION.

primary beneficiary. See BENEFICIARY.

primary boycott. See BOYCOTT.

primary committee. In bankruptcy law, a group of creditors organized to help the debtor draw up a reorganization plan.

primary election. See ELECTION.

primary evidence. See *best evidence* under EVIDENCE.

primary fact. See FACT.

primary-jurisdiction doctrine. A judicial doctrine whereby a court tends to favor allowing an agency an initial opportunity to decide an issue in a case in which the court and the agency have concurrent jurisdiction.

primary liability. See LIABILITY.

primary market. See MARKET.

primary obligation. See OBLIGATION.

primary offering. See OFFERING.

primary reserve ratio. See RE-SERVE RATIO.

prime, *n.* See *prime rate* under IN-TEREST RATE.

prime, *vb.* To take priority over <Watson's preferred mortgage primed Moriarty's lien>.

prime contractor. See *general contractor* under CONTRACTOR.

prime lending rate. See *prime rate* under INTEREST RATE.

prime minister. (*often cap.*) The chief executive of a parliamentary government; the head of a cabinet.

prime rate. See INTEREST RATE.

primogeniture (prī-moh-**jen**-ə-chər). **1.** The state of being the first-born child among siblings. **2.** The common-law right of the firstborn son to inherit his ancestor's estate, usu. to the exclusion of his younger siblings. See BOROUGH ENGLISH.

principal, *n.* **1.** One who authorizes another to act on his or her behalf as an agent. Cf. AGENT (1).

disclosed principal. A principal whose identity is revealed by the agent to a third party; a disclosed principal is always liable on the third-party contract, but the agent is usu. not liable.

partially disclosed principal. A principal whose existence—but not his or her actual identity—is revealed by the agent to a third party.

undisclosed principal. A principal whose identity is kept secret by the agent; an undisclosed principal and the agent are both liable on the third-party contract.

2. One who commits or participates in a crime. Cf. ACCESSORY (2).

principal in the first degree. The perpetrator of a crime.

principal in the second degree. One who helped the perpetrator at the time of the crime. —Also termed *accessory at the fact.*

3. The person who has primary responsibility on an obligation, as opposed to a surety or indorser. **4.** The corpus of an estate or trust. **5.** The amount of a debt, investment, or other fund, not including interest or profits.

principal, *adj.* Chief; primary; most important.

principle, *n.* A fundamental truth, law, or doctrine; a rule or code of conduct.

principle of legality. LEGALITY (2).

prior-appropriation doctrine. The rule that, among the persons whose property borders on a waterway, the earliest users of the water have the right to take all they can use before anyone else has a right to it. Cf. RIPARIAN-RIGHTS DOCTRINE.

prior art. See ART.

prior inconsistent statement. A witness's earlier statement that conflicts with the witness's testimony at trial; in federal practice, extrinsic evidence of a prior inconsistent statement is admissible—if the witness is given an opportunity to explain or deny the statement—for impeachment purposes only. Fed. R. Evid. 613(b).

priority. 1. The status of being earlier in time, degree, or rank; precedence. **2.** An established right to such precedence; esp., a creditor's right to have a claim paid before other creditors of the same debtor receive payment.

priority lien. See *prior lien* under LIEN.

priority of invention. See INVENTION.

prior lien. See LIEN.

prior restraint. A governmental restriction on speech or publication before its actual expression; prior restraints violate the First Amendment unless the speech is either obscene or defamatory, or creates a clear and present danger to society.

prior-use bar. PUBLIC-USE BAR.

prior-use doctrine. The principle that, without legislative authorization, a government agency may not appropriate property already devoted to a public use.

prison. A state or federal facility of confinement for convicted criminals, esp. felons. —Also termed *penitentiary*; *penal institution*; *adult correctional institution*. Cf. JAIL.

prisoner's dilemma. A logic problem—often used by law-and-economics scholars to illustrate—the effect of cooperative behavior—involving two prisoners who are being separately questioned about their participation in a crime: (1) if both confess, they will each receive a 5-year sentence; (2) if neither confesses, they will each receive a 3-year sentence; and (3) if one confesses but the other does not, the confessing prisoner will receive a 1-year sentence while the silent prisoner will receive a 10-year sentence. See EXTERNALITY.

privacy, invasion of. See INVASION OF PRIVACY.

privacy, right of. See RIGHT OF PRIVACY.

privacy law. A federal or state statute that protects a person's right to be left alone and restricts public access to personal information such as tax returns and medical records. — Also termed *privacy act*.

private, *adj.* **1.** Relating or belonging to an individual, as opposed to the public or the government. **2.** (Of a company) not having shares that are freely available on an open market. **3.** Confidential; secret.

private carrier. See CARRIER.

privateer, *n.* **1.** A vessel owned and operated by private persons, but authorized by a nation on certain conditions to damage the commerce of the enemy by acts of piracy; privateers are forbidden by the Declaration of Paris of 1856, which has been observed by nearly all nations since that time. **2.** A sailor on such a vessel. —**privateer,** *vb.*

private international law. See INTERNATIONAL LAW.

private judging. A type of alternative dispute resolution whereby the parties hire a private individual to hear and decide a case; this process may occur as a matter of contract between the parties or in connection with a statute authorizing such a process. —Also termed *rent-a-judge*.

private law. 1. The body of law dealing with private persons and their property and relationships. Cf. PUBLIC LAW (1). **2.** SPECIAL LAW.

private necessity. See NECESSITY.

private nuisance. See NUISANCE.

private offering. See OFFERING.

private placement. 1. The placement of a child for adoption by a parent, lawyer, or doctor, but not by an agency. —Also termed *direct placement.* **2.** See *private offering* under OFFERING.

private property. See PROPERTY.

private prosecutor. PROSECUTOR (2).

private reprimand. See REPRIMAND.

private trust. See TRUST.

privatization (prI-və-tə-**zay**-shən), *n.* The act or process of converting a business or industry from governmental ownership or control to private enterprise. —**privatize,** *vb.*

privies. See PRIVY.

privilege. 1. A special legal right, exemption, or immunity granted to a person or class of persons. **2.** An affirmative defense by which a defendant acknowledges at least part of the conduct complained of but asserts that the defendant's conduct was authorized or sanctioned by law; esp., in tort law, a circumstance justifying or excusing an intentional tort. See JUSTIFICATION (2). Cf. IMMUNITY (2). **3.** In the law of evidence, the right to prevent disclosure of certain information in court, esp. when the information was originally communicated in a professional or confidential relationship.

accountant-client privilege. The protection afforded to a client from unauthorized disclosure by his or her accountant of materials submitted to or prepared by the accountant.

attorney-client privilege. The client's right to refuse to disclose and to prevent any other person from disclosing confidential communications between the client and his or her attorney. —Also termed *client's privilege.*

doctor-patient privilege. The statutory right to exclude from evidence in a legal proceeding communications a person made to his or her physician unless that person consents to the disclosure. —Also termed *physician-client privilege; patient-physician privilege.*

executive privilege. A privilege, based on the constitutional separation of power, that exempts the executive branch of the federal government from usual disclosure requirements when the matter to be disclosed involves national security or foreign policy. Cf. *executive immunity* under IMMUNITY (1).

joint-defense privilege. The rule that a defendant can assert the attorney-client privilege to protect confidential communications made to a codefendant's lawyer if the communications were related to the defense of both defendants. —Also termed *common-interest doctrine.*

journalist's privilege. **a.** A reporter's protection, under constitutional or statutory law, from being compelled to testify about confidential information or sources. —Also termed *reporter's privilege; newsman's privilege.* See SHIELD LAW (1). **b.** A publisher's protection against defamation lawsuits when the publication makes fair comment on the actions of public officials in matters of public concern. —Also termed *editorial privilege*. See FAIR COMMENT.

marital privilege. **a.** The privilege allowing a spouse not to testify about confidential communications made with the other spouse during the marriage. —Also termed *marital-communications privilege.* **b.** The privilege allowing a spouse not to testify in a criminal case as an adverse witness against the other spouse, regardless of the subject matter of the testimony. —Also termed (in sense b) *privilege against adverse spousal testimony*; *antimarital-facts privilege.* —Also termed (in both senses) *spousal privilege*; *husband-wife privilege.*

priest-penitent privilege. The bar against clergy members' testifying about a confessor's communications.

state-secrets privilege. A privilege that the government may invoke against discovery of materials that, if divulged, could compromise national security. —Also termed *national-security privilege.*

work-product privilege. See WORK PRODUCT.

privilege against self-incrimination. RIGHT AGAINST SELF-INCRIMINATION.

privileged communication. See COMMUNICATION.

privileged subscription. RIGHTS OFFERING.

Privileges and Immunities Clause. The constitutional provision (U.S. Const. art. IV, § 2, cl. 1) prohibiting a state from favoring its own citizens by discriminating against nonresidents who come within its borders.

Privileges or Immunities Clause. The constitutional provision (U.S. Const. amend. XIV, § 1) prohibiting state laws that abridge the privileges or immunities of U.S. citizens; the clause was effectively nullified by the Supreme Court in the *Slaughter-House Cases*, 83 U.S. (16 Wall.) 36 (1873). Cf. DUE PROCESS CLAUSE; EQUAL PROTECTION CLAUSE.

privity (**pri**-və-tee). The relationship between two contracting parties, each having a legally recognized interest in the subject matter of the contract; mutuality of interest <the buyer and seller are in privity>. — Also termed *privity of contract.*

horizontal privity. In commercial law, the legal relationship between a party and a nonparty who is related to the party (such as a buyer and a member of the buyer's family).

vertical privity. In commercial law, the legal relationship between parties in a product's chain of distribution (such as a manufacturer and a seller).

privy (**pri**-vee), *n.* (*usu. pl.*) A person having a legal interest of privity in any action, matter, or property. Pl. **privies.**

prize. 1. Something of value awarded in recognition of a person's achievement. **2.** A vessel or cargo captured at sea or seized in port by the forces of a nation at war, and therefore liable to being condemned or appropriated as enemy property.

prize court. See COURT.

prize goods. See GOODS.

PRO. *abbr.* PEER-REVIEW ORGANIZATION.

probable cause. A reasonable ground to suspect that a person has committed a particular crime or that a place contains specific items connected with a crime; under the Fourth Amendment, probable cause—which amounts to more than a bare suspicion but less than legal evidence—must be shown before an arrest warrant or search warrant may be issued. —Also termed *reasonable cause*; *sufficient cause*. Cf. REASONABLE SUSPICION.

probable-cause hearing. PRELIMINARY HEARING.

probable-desistance test. In criminal law, a common-law test for the crime of attempt, focusing on the whether the defendant has exhibited dangerous behavior indicating that he or she will likely commit the crime. Cf. PHYSICAL-PROXIMITY TEST; SUBSTANTIAL-STEP TEST.

probate (**proh**-bayt), *n.* **1.** The judicial procedure by which a testamentary document is established to be a valid will; the proving of a will to the satisfaction of the court. **2.** Loosely, a personal representative's actions in handling a decedent's estate.

probate, *vb.* **1.** To admit (a will) to proof. **2.** To administer (a decedent's estate). **3.** To grant probation to (a criminal); to reduce (a sentence) by means of probation.

probate asset. See *legal asset* under ASSET.

probate code. A collection of statutes setting forth the law (substantive and procedural) of decedents' estates and trusts.

probate court. See COURT.

probate distribution. See DISTRIBUTION.

probate estate. A decedent's property subject to administration by his or her personal representative. See *decedent's estate* under ESTATE.

probate homestead. A homestead, exempt from creditors' claims, set apart for use by a decedent's surviving spouse and minor children. See HOMESTEAD.

probate judge. A judge having jurisdiction over probate, inheritance, guardianships, and the like. —Also termed *surrogate*; *register*.

probation. 1. A court-imposed criminal sentence that, subject to stated conditions, releases a convicted person into the community instead of sending the criminal to prison. Cf. PAROLE. **2.** The act of judicially proving a will.

probationer. A convicted criminal who is on probation.

probation officer. A court-appointed officer who supervises the conduct of a probationer.

probative (**proh**-bə-tiv), *adj.* Tending or serving to prove (or disprove); courts can exclude relevant evidence if its probative value is substantially outweighed by the danger of unfair prejudice. Fed. R. Evid. 403. —**probativeness,** *n.*

probative fact. See FACT.

probatum (proh-**bayd**-əm). [Latin] Something proved or conclusively established; proof. Pl. *probata*.

pro bono (proh-**boh**-noh), *adj.* [Latin *pro bono publico* "for the public good"] Of or relating to uncompensated legal services performed esp. for the public good.

procedendo (proh-sə-**den**-doh). [Latin] A higher court's order directing a lower court to determine and enter a judgment in a previously removed case.

procedural due process. See DUE PROCESS.

procedural law. The rules that prescribe the steps for having a right or duty judicially enforced, as opposed to the law that defines the specific rights or duties themselves. —Also termed *adjective law.* Cf. SUBSTANTIVE LAW.

procedure. 1. A specific method or course of action. 2. The judicial rule, mode, or manner for carrying on a civil lawsuit or criminal prosecution. See CIVIL PROCEDURE; CRIMINAL PROCEDURE.

proceeding. 1. The regular and orderly progression of a lawsuit, including all acts and events between the time of commencement and judgment. 2. Any procedural means for seeking redress from a tribunal or administrative agency. 3. An act or step that is part of a larger action. 4. The business conducted by a court or other official body; a hearing.

collateral proceeding. A proceeding brought to address an incidental issue, not to attack a previous judgment.

core proceeding. See CORE PROCEEDING.

ex parte proceeding. Any judicial or quasi-judicial hearing in which only one party is heard.

informal proceeding. A trial conducted in a more relaxed manner, such as an administrative hearing or a trial in small-claims court.

judicial proceeding. Any court proceeding.

related proceeding. See RELATED PROCEEDING.

summary proceeding. A nonjury proceeding that settles a controversy or disposes of a case in a relatively prompt and simple manner.

proceeds (proh-**seedz**), *n.* The value of land, goods, or investments when converted into money; the amount of money received from a sale <the proceeds are subject to attachment>.

process, *n.* 1. The proceedings in any action or prosecution <due process of law>. 2. The summons or writ by which a person is cited to appear in court <service of process>. —Also termed *judicial process; legal process.*

compulsory process. **a.** A process, with a warrant to arrest or attach included, that compels a person to attend court as a witness. **b.** A defendant's constitutional right to compel the attendance of a favorable witness.

mesne process. A process issued between the commencement of a lawsuit and the final judgment or determination.

process, abuse of. See MALICIOUS ABUSE OF PROCESS.

process server. A person authorized by law or by a court to formally deliver process to a defendant or respondent. See SERVICE.

procès-verbal (proh-say-vər-**bahl**). [French "verbal trial"] PROTOCOL (2).

prochein ami (proh-**shayn**-a-**mee** *or* **proh**-shen-). [Law French] NEXT FRIEND.

proclamation. A formal public announcement made by the government.

procuracy (**prok**-yə-rə-see). The document that grants power to an attorney-in-fact; a letter of agency.

procuration (prok-yə-**ray**-shən). **1.** The act of appointing someone as an agent or attorney-in-fact. **2.** The authority vested in a person so appointed; the function of an attorney. **3.** PROCUREMENT.

procurator (**prok**-yə-ray-tər). An agent or attorney-in-fact.

procurement (proh-**kyuur**-mənt), *n*. **1.** The act of getting or obtaining something. —Also termed *procuration*. **2.** The act of persuading or inviting another, esp. a woman or child, to have illicit sexual intercourse. —**procure,** *vb*.

procuring cause. See CAUSE (1).

producing cause. See *proximate cause* under CAUSE (1).

product. Something that is distributed commercially for use or consumption and that is usu. (1) tangible personal property, (2) the result of fabrication or processing, and (3) an item that has passed through a chain of commercial distribution before ultimate use or consumption. See PRODUCTS LIABILITY.

product defect. See DEFECT.

production burden. BURDEN OF PRODUCTION.

product market. See MARKET.

products liability, *n*. **1.** A manufacturer's or seller's tort liability for any damages or injuries suffered by a buyer, user, or bystander as a result of a defective product; products liability can be based on theories of negligence, strict liability, or breach of warranty. **2.** The legal theory by which liability is imposed on the manufacturer or seller of a defective product; the field of law dealing with this theory. —**product-liability,** *adj*. See LIABILITY.

product test. DURHAM RULE.

profession. 1. A vocation requiring advanced education and training. **2.** Collectively, the members of such a vocation.

professional association. See ASSOCIATION.

professional corporation. See CORPORATION.

proffer (**pro**-fər), *vb*. To offer or tender (something, esp. evidence) for immediate acceptance. —**proffer,** *n*.

profit, *n*. The excess of revenues over expenditures in a business transaction; GAIN (2). Cf. EARNINGS; INCOME.

gross profit. Total sales revenue less the cost of the goods sold, excluding additional expenses and taxes. Cf. *net profit*.

mesne profits. The profits of an estate received by a tenant in wrongful possession between two dates.

net profit. Total sales revenue less the cost of the goods sold and all additional expenses. Cf. *gross profit*.

operating profit. Total sales revenue less all operating expenses, excluding any nonoperating income and expenses, such as interest payments.

paper profit. An increase in the value of an investment (such as a stock), but an increase that remains unrealized until the investment is sold. —Also termed *unrealized profit.*

undistributed profit. See *retained earnings* under EARNINGS.

profit-and-loss statement. INCOME STATEMENT.

profit à prendre (**prah**-fət-ah-**prahn**-dər *or* -drə). [Law French] (*usu. pl.*) The right exercised by one person to enter another's land and take away some part of the soil, as by cutting hay or harvesting crops. — Also termed *right of common.* See EASEMENT.

profit margin. 1. The difference between the cost of something and the price for which it is sold. **2.** The ratio, expressed as a percentage, between this difference and the selling price; for example, a widget costing a retailer $10 and selling for $15 has a profit margin of 33% ($5 difference divided by $15 selling price). —Often shortened to *margin.*

profit-sharing plan. An employer's benefit plan that allows an employee to share in the company's profits.

pro forma, *adj.* [Latin "for form"] **1.** Made or done as a formality. **2.** (Of an invoice or financial statement) provided in advance to describe items, predict results, or secure approval.

progeny (**pro**-jə-nee), *n. pl.* **1.** Children or descendants; offspring <only one of their progeny attended law school>. **2.** A group of successors; esp., a line of opinions succeeding a leading case <*Erie* and its progeny>.

program trading. A form of computerized securities trading that usu. involves buying or selling large amounts of stocks while simultaneously selling or buying index futures in offsetting amounts.

progressive tax. See TAX.

pro hac vice (proh-hak-**vIs**[-ee] *or* proh-hahk-**vee**-chay). [Latin] For this occasion or particular purpose; the phrase usu. refers to a lawyer who has not been admitted to practice in a particular jurisdiction but who is admitted there temporarily for the purpose of conducting a particular case. —Abbr. P.H.V.

prohibition, writ of. See WRIT OF PROHIBITION.

prohibitory injunction. See INJUNCTION.

promise, *n.* A declaration by which a person agrees to perform or refrain from doing a specified act; a binding promise—that is, a promise that the law will enforce—is the essence of a contract. —**promise,** *vb.*—**promissory,** *n.* See CONTRACT (4).

illusory promise. A promise that appears on its face to be so insubstantial as to impose no obligation on the promisor; a promise in form but not in substance.

naked promise. A promise for which the promisee has given nothing in return; naked promises are not legally unenforceable. —Also termed *bare promise.*

promisee. One to whom a promise is made.

promisor. One who makes a promise; esp., one who undertakes a contractual obligation.

promissory estoppel. See ESTOPPEL.

promissory fraud. See FRAUD.

promissory note. NOTE (1).

promissory oath. See OATH.

promissory warranty. See WARRANTY (3).

promoter. 1. A person who encourages or incites. **2.** A founder or organizer of a corporation or business venture.

promulgate (**prah**-məl-gayt *or* prə-**məl**-gayt), *vb.* **1.** To publicly declare or announce; to proclaim. **2.** To put (a law or decree) into force or effect. —**promulgation,** *n.*

proof, *n.* **1.** The establishment or denial of an alleged fact by evidence; the result of evidence. **2.** Evidence that determines the judgment of the court. **3.** An attested document that constitutes legal evidence.

proof, burden of. See BURDEN OF PROOF.

proof of acknowledgment. See ACKNOWLEDGMENT.

proof of claim. A creditor's written statement that is submitted (esp. in a bankruptcy proceeding) to show the basis and amount of the creditor's claim. Pl. **proofs of claim.**

proof of loss. An insured's formal statement of loss required by an insurance company before it will determine whether the policy covers the loss.

proof of service. Evidence that a process server has successfully served a defendant or witness. —Also termed *return of service.* See SERVICE (3).

pro per. PRO PERSONA.

proper care. See *reasonable care* under CARE.

proper party. See PARTY.

pro persona (proh-pər-**sohn**-ə). [Latin] For one's own person; on one's own behalf <a *pro persona* brief>. —Sometimes shortened to *pro per.* See PRO SE.

property. 1. The right to possess, use, and enjoy a determinate thing (either a tract of land or a chattel); the right of ownership <the institution of private property is protected from undue governmental interference>. **2.** Any external thing over which the rights of possession, use, and enjoyment are exercised <the airport is city property>.

abandoned property. Property that the owner voluntarily surrenders, relinquishes, or disclaims. Cf. *lost property*; *mislaid property.*

common property. **a.** Property that is held jointly by two or more persons. **b.** See COMMON AREA.

community property. See COMMUNITY PROPERTY.

distressed property. Property that must be sold because of mortgage foreclosure or because it is part of an insolvent estate.

intangible property. Property that lacks a physical existence; examples include bank accounts, stock options, and business goodwill.

intellectual property. See INTELLECTUAL PROPERTY.

literary property. See LITERARY PROPERTY.

lost property. Property that the owner no longer possesses due to accident, negligence, or carelessness, and that cannot be located by an ordinary, diligent search. Cf. *abandoned property*; *mislaid property*.

marital property. Property that is acquired from the time when a marriage begins until one spouse files for divorce (assuming a divorce decree actually results); in equitable-distribution states, the phrase *marital property* is the rough equivalent of *community property*. See COMMUNITY PROPERTY; EQUITABLE DISTRIBUTION.

mislaid property. Property voluntarily relinquished by the owner with an intent to recover it later—but which cannot now be found. Cf. *abandoned property*; *lost property*.

mixed property. Property with characteristics of both real property and personal property—such as heirlooms and fixtures.

personal property. **a.** Any movable or intangible thing that is subject to ownership and not classified as real property. —Also termed *personalty*. **b.** Property not used in a taxpayer's trade or business or held for income production or collection. Cf. *real property*.

private property. Property—protected from public appropriation—over which the owner has exclusive and absolute rights.

public property. State- or community-owned property not restricted to any one individual's use or possession.

real property. Land and anything growing on, attached to, or erected on it, excluding anything that may be severed without injury to the land; real property can be either corporeal (soil and buildings) or incorporeal (easements). —Also termed *realty*; *real estate*. Cf. *personal property*.

separate property. See SEPARATE PROPERTY.

tangible property. Property that has physical form and characteristics.

property crimes. CRIMES AGAINST PROPERTY.

property dividend. See *asset dividend* under DIVIDEND.

property settlement. 1. A judgment in a divorce case determining the distribution of the marital property between the divorcing parties. **2.** MARITAL AGREEMENT.

property tax. See TAX.

prophylactic (proh-fə-**lak**-tik), *adj.* Formulated to prevent something <a

prophylactic rule>. —**prophylactic,** *n.*

proportional representation. An electoral system that allocates legislative seats to each political group in proportion to its popular voting strength.

proportional tax. See *flat tax* under TAX.

propound, *vb.* **1.** To offer for consideration or discussion. **2.** To make a proposal. **3.** To put forward (a will) as authentic.

proprietary (prə-**prī**-ə-ter-ee), *adj.* **1.** Of or relating to a proprietor <the licensee's proprietary rights>. **2.** Of, relating to, or holding as property <the software designer sought to protect its proprietary data>.

proprietor, *n.* An owner, esp. one who runs a business. —**proprietorship,** *n.* See SOLE PROPRIETORSHIP.

pro rata (proh-**rah**-tə *or* -**ra**-tə *or* -**ray**-tə), *adv.* Proportionately; according to an exact rate, measure, or interest <the liability will be assessed pro rata between the defendants>. —**pro rata,** *adj.* See RATABLE.

prorate (proh-**rayt**), *vb.* To divide, assess, or distribute proportionately. —**proration,** *n.*

prorogue (proh-**rohg** *or* prə-**rohg**), *vb.* **1.** To postpone or defer. **2.** To discontinue the meetings of (a legislative assembly, usu. British Parliament) for a definite or indefinite time without dissolving it. **3.** To discontinue meeting until the next session.

proscription, *n.* **1.** The act of prohibiting; the state of being prohibited. **2.** A prohibition or restriction. —

proscribe, *vb.* —**proscriptive,** *adj.* Cf. PRESCRIPTION.

pro se (proh-say). [Latin] For oneself; on one's own behalf <the pro se defendant acted as his own counsel during the trial>. —Also termed *pro persona; in propria persona.*

prosecute, *vb.* **1.** To commence and carry out a legal action <because the plaintiff failed to prosecute its contractual claims, the court dismissed the suit>. **2.** To institute and pursue a criminal action against (a person) <the notorious felon has been prosecuted in seven states>. **3.** To engage in; carry on <the company prosecuted its business for 12 years before going bankrupt>. —**prosecutory,** *adj.*

prosecuting attorney. DISTRICT ATTORNEY.

prosecuting witness. See WITNESS.

prosecution. 1. The commencement and carrying out of any action or scheme <the prosecution of a long, bloody war>. **2.** A criminal proceeding in which an accused person is tried <the conspiracy trial involved the prosecution of seven defendants>. **3.** The government attorneys who initiate and maintain a criminal action against an accused defendant <the prosecution rests>.

prosecution history. The complete record of proceedings in the Patent and Trademark Office from the initial application to the issued patent. —Also termed *file wrapper.*

prosecution-history estoppel. In patent law, the doctrine preventing a patent holder from invoking the doctrine of equivalents if the holder, during the application process, surrendered certain claims or interpretations of the invention. —Also termed *file-wrapper estoppel*. See DOCTRINE OF EQUIVALENTS.

prosecutor, *n.* **1.** A legal officer who represents the government in criminal proceedings. See DISTRICT ATTORNEY; UNITED STATES ATTORNEY; ATTORNEY GENERAL.

public prosecutor. DISTRICT ATTORNEY.

special prosecutor. A lawyer appointed to investigate and, if justified, seek indictments in a particular case. See *independent counsel* under COUNSEL.

2. A private person who institutes and carries on a legal action, esp. a criminal action. —Also termed (in sense 2) *private prosecutor*. —**prosecutorial,** *adj.*

prosecutorial discretion. See DISCRETION.

prospective, *adj.* **1.** Effective or operative in the future <prospective application of the new statute>. Cf. RETROACTIVE. **2.** Anticipated or expected; likely to come about <prospective clients>.

prospective heir. See HEIR.

prospectus. A printed document that describes the main features of an enterprise (esp. a corporation's business) and that is distributed to prospective buyers or investors; under SEC regulations, a publicly traded corporation must provide a prospectus before anyone can buy stock in the corporation. Pl. **prospectuses.** See REGISTRATION STATEMENT.

preliminary prospectus. In securities law, a prospectus for a stock issue that has not yet been approved by the SEC; the SEC requires these prospectuses to contain a notice—printed in distinctive red lettering—that the document is not complete or final. —Also termed *red-herring prospectus*; *red herring.*

prostitution, *n.* **1.** The act or practice of engaging in sexual activity for money. **2.** The act of debasing. — **prostitute,** *vb.*—**prostitute,** *n.*

pro tanto (proh-**tahn**-toh *or* -**tan**-toh). [Latin] *Jargon.* To that extent; for so much; as far as it goes <a pro tanto payment>.

protection order. A temporary court order issued on an emergency basis in domestic-violence matters to protect a spouse or child from physical harm. Cf. PROTECTIVE ORDER.

protective custody. See CUSTODY (1).

protective order. A court order issued to protect a person from abusive service or discovery methods or other types of legal harassment. Cf. PROTECTION ORDER.

protective sweep. A police officer's quick and limited search—conducted after the officer has lawfully entered the premises—based on a reasonable belief that a search is necessary to protect the officer or others from harm. See SEARCH.

protective tariff. See TARIFF.

protectorate (prə-**tek**-t[ə]-rət). **1.** In international law, the relationship between a weaker nation and a stronger one when the weaker nation has transferred the management of its more important international affairs to the stronger nation. **2.** The weaker or dependent nation within such a relationship. **3.** (*usu. cap.*) The period in British history—from 1653 to 1659—during which Oliver Cromwell and Richard Cromwell governed; also, the British government during that period.

pro tempore (proh-**tem**-pə-ree), *adv.* [Latin] For the time being; temporarily <judge pro tempore>. — Abbr. **pro tem.**

protest, *n.* **1.** A formal statement or action expressing dissent or disapproval. **2.** A notary public's written statement that, upon presentment, a negotiable instrument was neither paid nor accepted. **3.** A formal statement, usu. in writing, disputing a debt's legality or validity but agreeing to make payment while reserving the right to recover the amount at a later time; the disputed debt is described as *under protest.* —**protest,** *vb.*

protest certificate. *Archaic.* A notarial certificate declaring (1) that a holder in due course has recruited the notary public to re-present a previously refused or dishonored negotiable instrument, (2) that the notary has presented the instrument to the person responsible for payment or acceptance (the *drawee*), (3) that the instrument was presented at a given time and place, and (4) that the drawee refused or dishonored the instrument; under former practice, the notary would issue a protest certificate, which could then be presented to the drawee and any other liable parties as notice that the holder could seek damages for the dishon-

ored negotiable instrument. —Also termed *notarial protest certificate.* See NOTICE OF DISHONOR.

prothonotary (prə-**thon**-ə-ter-ee *or* proh-thə-**nod**-ə-ree). The chief clerk of a court of law. —Also spelled *protonotary.*

protocol. 1. A summary of a document or treaty. **2.** The formal record of the proceedings of a conference or congress. —Also termed *procès-verbal.* **3.** The minutes of a meeting, usu. initialed by all participants after confirming accuracy. **4.** The rules of diplomatic etiquette; the practices that nations observe in the course of their contacts with one another.

prove up. To present or complete the proof of (something); to show that one has fulfilled the legal requirements <deciding not to put a doctor on the stand, the plaintiff attempted to prove up his damages with medical records only>.

provisional director. See DIRECTOR.

provisional remedy. See REMEDY.

proviso (prə-**vI**-zoh *or* proh-). **1.** A limitation, condition, or stipulation upon whose compliance a legal or formal document's validity or application may depend. **2.** In drafting, a provision that begins with the words *provided that* and supplies a condition, exception, or addition.

provocation, *n.* Something (such as words or actions) that arouses anger or animosity in another, causing that person to respond in the heat of passion; "adequate" provocation can reduce a murder charge to voluntary manslaughter. —**provoke,** *vb.* —**provocative,** *adj.* See MANSLAUGHTER.

proximate cause. See CAUSE (1).

proxy, *n.* **1.** One who is authorized to act as a substitute for another; esp., in corporate law, a person who is authorized to vote another's stock shares. **2.** The grant of authority by which a person is so authorized. **3.** The document granting this authority.

proxy contest. A struggle between two corporate factions to obtain the votes of uncommitted shareholders; a proxy contest usu. occurs when a group of dissident shareholders mounts a battle against the corporation's managers.

proxy marriage. See MARRIAGE (2).

proxy solicitation. The act of a corporate shareholder's asking another shareholder for his or her voting rights.

proxy statement. In securities law, an informational document that must accompany a solicitation of proxies under SEC regulations.

prudent person. REASONABLE PERSON.

prudent-person rule. In the law of trusts, the principle that a fiduciary must invest in only those securities that a reasonable person would buy.

prurient (**pruur**-ee-ənt), *adj.* Characterized by or arousing inordinate or unusual sexual desire <films appealing to prurient interests>. — **prurience,** *n.* See OBSCENITY.

pseudo-foreign-corporation statute. A state law regulating foreign corporations that either derive a specified high percentage of their income from that state or have a high percentage of their stock owned by people living in that state.

pseudonym, *n.* A fictitious name or identity. —**pseudonymous,** *adj.*— **pseudonymity,** *n.*

PSI. *abbr.* PRESENTENCE INVESTIGATION REPORT.

psychopath (**sI**-kə-path), *n.* **1.** A person with a mental disorder characterized by an extremely antisocial personality that often leads to aggressive, perverted, or criminal behavior. **2.** Loosely, a person who is mentally ill or unstable. —Also termed *sociopath*. —**psychopathy** (sI-**ko**-pə-thee), *n.*—**psychopathic,** *adj.*

PTO. *abbr.* PATENT AND TRADEMARK OFFICE.

PTP. See *publicly traded partnership* under PARTNERSHIP.

Pub. L. *abbr.* PUBLIC LAW (2).

public, *adj.* **1.** Relating or belonging to an entire community, state, or nation. **2.** Open or available for all to use, share, or enjoy. **3.** (Of a company) having shares that are available on an open market.

public administration. See ADMINISTRATION.

public advocate. See ADVOCATE.

public agency. AGENCY (3).

public agent. See AGENT.

publication, *n.* **1.** Generally, the act of declaring or announcing to the public. **2.** In copyright law, the distribution of copies of a work to the public; at common law, publication marked the dividing line between state and federal protection, but the Copyright Act of 1976 superseded most of common-law copyright and thereby diminished the significance of publication. **3.** In the law of defamation, the communication of defamatory words to someone other than the person defamed. **4.** In the law of wills, the formal declaration made by a testator when signing the will that it is the testator's will. —**publish,** *vb.*

public carrier. See *common carrier* under CARRIER.

public corporation. See CORPORATION.

public debt. See DEBT.

public defender. A lawyer or staff of lawyers, usu. publicly appointed, whose duty is to represent indigent criminal defendants. —Abbr. P.D.

public disclosure of private facts. The public revelation of some aspect of a person's private life; the disclosure is actionable in tort if the publicized facts would be highly objectionable to a reasonable person. See INVASION OF PRIVACY.

public domain. 1. Government-owned land. **2.** The realm of publications, inventions, and processes that are not protected by copyright or patent; things in the public domain can be appropriated by anyone without liability for infringement.

public easement. See EASEMENT.

public figure. A person who has achieved fame or notoriety or who has voluntarily become involved in a public controversy; a public figure (or public official) suing for defamation must prove that the defendant acted with actual malice. *New York*

Times Co. v. Sullivan, 376 U.S. 254 (1964).

public forum. In constitutional law, public property where people traditionally gather to express ideas and exchange views; to be constitutional, government regulation of a public forum must be narrowly tailored to serve a significant government interest and must usu. be limited to time, place, and manner restrictions. Cf. NONPUBLIC FORUM.

public-function rationale. GOVERNMENTAL-FUNCTION THEORY.

public international law. INTERNATIONAL LAW.

public intoxication. See INTOXICATION.

public law. 1. The body of law dealing with the relations between private individuals and the government, and with the operation of the government itself; constitutional law, criminal law, and administrative law taken together. Cf. PRIVATE LAW (1). **2.** A statute affecting the general public; federal public laws are first published in *Statutes at Large* and are eventually collected by subject in the United States Code. —Abbr. Pub. L.; P.L.

publicly held corporation. See *public corporation* (a) under CORPORATION.

publicly traded partnership. See PARTNERSHIP.

public necessity. See NECESSITY.

public nuisance. See NUISANCE.

public offering. See OFFERING.

public office. A position whose occupant possesses legal authority to exercise a government's sovereign powers for a fixed time period.

public official. A person elected or appointed to carry out some portion of a government's sovereign powers.

public policy. 1. Broadly, principles and matters regarded by the legislature or by the courts as being of fundamental concern to the state and the whole of society; courts sometimes use the term to justify their decisions, such as when declaring a contract void because it undermines the public good. **2.** More narrowly, the principle that a person should not be allowed to do anything that would tend to injure the public at large.

public property. See PROPERTY.

public prosecutor. DISTRICT ATTORNEY.

public reprimand. See REPRIMAND.

public seal. See SEAL.

public security. See SECURITY.

public service. 1. A service provided or facilitated by the government for the general public's convenience and benefit. **2.** Government employment; work performed for or on the government's behalf.

public statute. See *general statute* under STATUTE.

public stock. See STOCK.

public trust. See *charitable trust* under TRUST.

public use. See USE (1).

public-use bar. In patent law, a statutory bar that prevents the granting of a patent for an invention that was publicly used or sold in the U.S. more than one year before the application date. 35 U.S.C. § 102(b). —Also termed *prior-use bar*.

public welfare. A society's well-being in matters of health, safety, order, morality, economics, and politics.

public-welfare offense. See *regulatory offense* under OFFENSE.

PUC. *abbr.* Public Utilities Commission.

PUD. *abbr.* PLANNED-UNIT DEVELOPMENT.

puffing. 1. The act or an instance of expressing an exaggerated opinion— as opposed to a factual representation—with the intent to sell a good or service. —Also termed *puffery*; *sales puffery*. **2.** Secret bidding at an auction by or on behalf of a seller.

***Pullman* abstention.** See ABSTENTION.

punishment, *n.* A sanction—such as a fine, penalty, confinement, or loss of property, right, or privilege—assessed against a person who has violated the law. —**punish,** *vb.* See SENTENCE.

capital punishment. DEATH PENALTY.

corporal punishment. Physical punishment; punishment that is inflicted upon the body (including imprisonment).

cruel and unusual punishment. Punishment that is torturous, disproportionate to the crime in question, degrading, inhuman, or otherwise shocking to the moral sense of the community; such punishment is prohibited by the Eighth Amendment.

cumulative punishment. Punishment that increases in severity when a person is convicted of the same offense more than one time.

excessive punishment. Punishment that is not justified by the gravity of the offense or the defendant's criminal record.

infamous punishment. Punishment by imprisonment, usu. in a penitentiary. See *infamous crime* under CRIME.

punitive damages. See DAMAGES.

pur autre vie (pər-**oh**-dər-**vee** *or* -trə-vee). [Law French "for another's life"] For or during a period measured by another's life <a life estate *pur autre vie*>. —Also spelled *per autre vie.*

purchase, *n.* **1.** The act or an instance of buying. **2.** The acquisition of real property by one's own or another's act (as by will or gift) rather than by descent or inheritance. Cf. DESCENT (1).

purchase, words of. See WORDS OF PURCHASE.

purchase agreement. A sales contract. Cf. REPURCHASE AGREEMENT.

purchase-money interest. See *purchase-money security interest* under SECURITY INTEREST.

purchase-money mortgage. See MORTGAGE.

purchase-money resulting trust. See TRUST.

purchase-money security interest. See SECURITY INTEREST.

purchaser. **1.** One who obtains property for money or other valuable consideration; a buyer.

bona fide purchaser. One who buys something for value without notice of another's claim to the item or of any defects in the seller's title. — Abbr. BFP. —Also termed *good-faith purchaser*; *innocent purchaser.*

2. One who acquires real property by means other than descent or inheritance.

pure annuity. See *nonrefund annuity* under ANNUITY.

pure easement. See *easement appurtenant* under EASEMENT.

pure race statute. RACE STATUTE.

purport (pər-port), *n.* The idea or meaning that is conveyed or expressed, esp. by a formal document.

purport (pər-**port**), *vb.* To profess or claim falsely; to seem to be <the document purports to be a will, but it is neither signed nor dated>.

purported, *adj.* Reputed; rumored.

purpose clause. In legislation, an introductory clause that explains the background of the enactment and shows the reasons for the statute's enactment.

pursuant to. *Jargon.* **1.** In compliance with; in accordance with; under <she filed the motion pursuant to the court's order>. **2.** As authorized by; under <pursuant to Rule 56, the plaintiff moves for summary judgment>. **3.** In carrying out <pursuant to his responsibilities, he ensured that all lights had been turned out>.

purview (pər-vyoo). **1.** Scope; area of application. **2.** The body of a statute following the preamble.

put, *n.* See *put option* under OPTION.

putative (**pyoo**-də-tiv), *adj.* Reputed; believed; supposed.

putative father. The alleged father of a child born out of wedlock.

putative marriage. See MARRIAGE (1).

putative spouse. A spouse who believes in good faith that his or her invalid marriage is legally valid. See *putative marriage* under MARRIAGE.

put option. See OPTION.

put price. See *strike price* under PRICE.

pyramiding. A speculative method used to finance a large purchase of stock or a controlling interest by pledging an investment's unrealized profit. See LEVERAGE; MARGIN.

pyramiding inferences, rule against. The evidentiary rule that prohibits a fact-finder from piling one inference on another to arrive at a conclusion; today this rule is followed in only a few jurisdictions. Cf. REASONABLE-INFERENCE RULE.

pyramid scheme. A property-distribution scheme in which a participant pays for the chance to receive compensation for introducing new persons to the scheme, as well as for when those new persons themselves introduce participants; pyramid schemes are illegal in most states. — Also termed *endless-chain scheme; chain-referral scheme; multilevel-distribution program.* Cf. PONZI SCHEME.

Q

Q.B. *abbr.* QUEEN'S BENCH.

Q.B.D. *abbr.* QUEEN'S BENCH DIVISION.

Q.C. *abbr.* QUEEN'S COUNSEL.

q.c.f. *abbr.* QUARE CLAUSUM FREGIT.

Q.E.D. *abbr.* [Latin *quod erat demonstrandum*] Which was to be demonstrated or proved.

Q.E.F. *abbr.* [Latin *quod erat faciendum*] Which was to be done.

qq.v. See Q.V.

QTIP trust. See TRUST.

qua (kwah *or* kway). [Latin] In the capacity of; as <the fiduciary, qua fiduciary, is not liable for fraud, but he may be liable as an individual>.

qualified, *adj.* **1.** Possessing the necessary qualifications; capable or competent <a qualified medical examiner>. **2.** Limited; restricted <qualified permission>. —**qualify,** *vb.*

qualified disclaimer. See DISCLAIMER.

qualified fee. 1. See *fee simple defeasible* under FEE SIMPLE. **2.** See *fee simple determinable* under FEE SIMPLE.

qualified immunity. See IMMUNITY (1).

qualified indorsement. See INDORSEMENT.

qualified stock option. See *stock option* (b) under OPTION.

qualifying share. A share of common stock purchased by someone in order to become a director of a corporation that requires its directors to be shareholders. See SHARE (2).

quality-of-products legislation. LEMON LAW (2).

quantum (kwahn-təm). The required, desired, or allowed amount; portion or share <a quantum of evidence>. Pl. **quanta.**

quantum meruit (kwahn-təm-**mer**-ə-wit). [Latin "as much as he or she has deserved"] **1.** The reasonable value of services; damages awarded in an amount considered reasonable to compensate a person who has rendered services in a quasi-contractual relationship. **2.** At common law, a count in an assumpsit action to recover payment for services rendered to another; *quantum meruit* is still used today as an equitable remedy to provide restitution for another's unjust enrichment. See *implied-in-law contract* under CONTRACT.

quantum valebant (kwahn-təm-**val**-ə-bant *or* -bənt *or* -və-**lay**-bənt). [Latin "as much as they were worth"] **1.** The reasonable value of goods and materials. **2.** At common law, a count in an assumpsit action to recover payment for goods sold and delivered to another; *quantum valebant*—although less common than *quantum meruit*—is still used today as an equitable remedy to provide restitution for another's unjust enrichment.

quarantine, *n.* The temporary isolation of a person or animal afflicted with a contagious or infectious disease. —**quarantine,** *vb.*

quare clausum fregit (kwer-ee-kloz-əm-frej-it). [Latin] Whereas he or she broke the close. —Abbr. *qu. cl. fr.*; *q.c.f.* See TRESPASS QUARE CLAUSUM FREGIT.

quarter, *n.* In the law of war, the act of showing mercy to a defeated enemy by sparing his or her life and accepting a surrender <to give no quarter>.

quarterly report. A financial report issued by a corporation every three months.

quash, *vb.* **1.** To annul or make void; to terminate <quash an indictment> <quash proceedings>. **2.** To suppress or subdue; to crush out <quash a rebellion>.

quasi (**kwah**-zee *or* **kway**-zI). [Latin "as if"] Seemingly but not actually; in some sense; resembling; nearly.

quasi-admission. See ADMISSION.

quasi-contract. See *implied-in-law contract* under CONTRACT.

quasi-corporation. See CORPORATION.

quasi-domicile. See *commercial domicile* under DOMICILE.

quasi-easement. See EASEMENT.

quasi-estoppel. See ESTOPPEL.

quasi in rem. See IN REM.

quasi-in-rem jurisdiction. See JURISDICTION.

quasi-judicial, *adj.* Of, relating to, or involving an executive or administrative official's adjudicative acts; quasi-judicial acts, which are valid if there is no abuse of discretion, often determine the fundamental rights of citizens—they are subject to review by courts.

quasi-public corporation. See CORPORATION.

quasi-suspect classification. See SUSPECT CLASSIFICATION.

qu. cl. fr. *abbr.* QUARE CLAUSUM FREGIT.

Queen's Bench. Historically, the highest common-law court in England, presided over by the reigning monarch; now the jurisdiction of this court lies with the Queen's Bench Division of the High Court of Justice; when a king begins to reign, the name automatically changes to *King's Bench.* —Abbr. Q.B. —Also termed *Court of Queen's Bench.*

Queen's Bench Division. The English court, formerly known as the Queen's Bench or King's Bench, that presides over tort and contract actions, applications for judicial review, and some magistrate-court appeals. —Abbr. Q.B.D.

Queen's Counsel. An elite, senior-level barrister appointed to serve as counsel to the queen. —Abbr. Q.C. Cf. KING'S COUNSEL.

question of fact. A disputed issue to be resolved by the jury in a jury trial or by the judge in a bench trial. —Also termed *fact question.* See FACT-FINDER.

question of law. A question, to be decided by the judge, concerning the application or interpretation of the law. —Also termed *legal question.*

quia timet (**kwee**-ə-**tim**-it *or* -**teem**-it). [Latin "because he (or she) fears"] A legal doctrine that allows a person to seek equitable relief from future probable harm to a specific right or interest.

quia-timet **injunction.** See IN-JUNCTION.

quick asset. See *current asset* under ASSET.

quick-asset ratio. The ratio between an entity's current or liquid assets (such as cash and accounts receivable) and its current liabilities. —Also termed *quick ratio*; *acid-test ratio*.

quick condemnation. See CON-DEMNATION.

quid pro quo (kwid-proh-**kwoh**). [Latin "this for that"] The exchange of one valuable thing for another of more or less equal value; tit for tat.

quiet, *vb.* To make (a title) secure by freeing from dispute or litigation.

quiet enjoyment. See ENJOYMENT.

quiet-title action. See *action to quiet title* under ACTION.

qui tam action (k[w]ee-tam *or* -tahm). [Latin *qui tam pro domino rege quam pro se ipso in hac parte sequitur* "who as well for the King as for himself sues in this matter"] An action brought under a statute that allows a private person to sue for a penalty, part of which the government or some specified public institution will receive.

quitclaim, *n.* **1.** A formal release of one's claim or right. **2.** See *quitclaim deed* under DEED.

quitclaim, *vb.* **1.** To relinquish or release (a claim or right). **2.** To convey all of one's interest in (property), to whatever extent one has an interest.

quitclaim deed. See DEED.

quittance. 1. A release or discharge from a debt or obligation. **2.** The document serving as evidence of such release. See ACQUITTANCE.

quo animo (kwoh-**an**-ə-moh), *adv.* [Latin] With what intention or motive. See ANIMUS.

quod erat demonstrandum (kwod-er-aht-dem-ən-**strahn**-dəm). See Q.E.D.

quod erat faciendum (kwod-er-aht-fays-ee-en-dəm). See Q.E.F.

quod vide (kwod-**vee**-day *or* -**vI**-dee). See Q.V.

quorum. The minimum number of members (usu. a majority) who must be present for a body to transact business or take a vote. Pl. **quorums.**

quota. 1. A proportional share assigned to a person or group; an allotment <the company's affirmative-action program established a quota for minority positions>. **2.** A quantitative restriction; a minimum or maximum number <Faldo met his sales quota for the month>.

quotation. 1. A statement or passage that is repeated, attributed, and cited. **2.** The amount stated as a stock's or commodity's current price. **3.** A contractor's estimate for a given job. —Sometimes shortened to *quote.*

quotient verdict. See VERDICT.

quo warranto (kwoh-**wor**-ən-toh *or* -wə-**rahn**-toh). [Law Latin "by what authority"] **1.** A common-law writ used to inquire into the authority by which a public office is held or a franchise is claimed. **2.** An action by which the state seeks to revoke a corporation's charter.

q.v. *abbr.* [Latin *quod vide*] Which see—used in non-*Bluebook* citations for cross-referencing. Pl. **qq.v.**

R

R. *abbr.* **1.** REX. **2.** REGINA.

race act. RACE STATUTE.

race-notice statute. A recording act providing that the person who records first, without notice of prior unrecorded claims, has priority; about half the states have race-notice statutes. —Also termed *race-notice act*; *notice-race statute*. Cf. RACE STATUTE; NOTICE STATUTE.

race of diligence. In bankruptcy law, a first-come, first-served disposition of assets.

race statute. A recording act providing that the person who records first, regardless of notice, has priority; only Louisiana and North Carolina have race statutes. —Also termed *pure race statute*; *race act*. Cf. NOTICE STATUTE; RACE-NOTICE STATUTE.

Racketeer Influenced and Corrupt Organizations Act. A federal or state law designed to investigate, control, and prosecute organized crime; a RICO statute usu. provides for public enforcement by criminal prosecution and private enforcement by civil lawsuit. 18 U.S.C. §§ 1961-68. —Abbr. RICO.

racketeering, *n.* **1.** A system of organized crime traditionally involving the extortion of money from businesses by intimidation, violence, or other illegal methods <everyone in the community knew the drug lord was involved in racketeering>. **2.** The practice of engaging in a fraudulent scheme or enterprise <convicted of racketeering>. —**racketeer,** *vb.*—**racketeering,** *adj.*—**racketeer,** *n.*

raider. CORPORATE RAIDER.

rainmaker, *n.* A lawyer who generates a large amount of business for a law firm, usu. through wide contacts within the business community <the law firm fell on hard times when the rainmaker left and took his clients with him>. —**rainmaking,** *n.*

raised check. See CHECK.

raising an instrument. The act of fraudulently altering a negotiable instrument, esp. a check, to increase the sum stated as being payable. See *raised check* under CHECK.

rake-off, *n.* An illegal bribe, payoff, or skimming of profits. —**rake off,** *vb.*

RAM. See *reverse annuity mortgage* under MORTGAGE.

Rambo lawyer. A lawyer, esp. a litigator, who uses aggressive, unethical, or illegal tactics in representing a client and who lacks courtesy and professionalism in dealing with other lawyers. —Often shortened to *Rambo.*

ransom, *n.* **1.** Money or other consideration paid or demanded for the release of a captured (usu. kidnapped) person. **2.** In international law, money or other consideration paid to regain captured property.

rape, *n.* **1.** At common law, unlawful sexual intercourse with a woman without her consent. **2.** Under modern statutes, unlawful sexual intercourse with a person without his or her consent. —**rape,** *vb.*—**rapist,** *n.* Cf. *sexual assault* under ASSAULT.

date rape. Rape committed by someone known to the victim, esp. by the victim's social companion.

marital rape. A husband's sexual intercourse with his wife by force or without her consent; marital rape was not a crime at common law, but under modern statutes the marital exemption no longer applies, and in most jurisdictions a husband can be convicted for raping his wife.

statutory rape. Unlawful sexual intercourse with a person under the age of consent (as defined by statute), regardless of whether it is against that person's will. See AGE OF CONSENT.

rape shield law. SHIELD LAW (2).

rapprochement (ra-prohsh-**mo[n]**). The establishment or restoration of cordial relations between two or more nations. —Also spelled *rapprochment.*

rasure (**ray**-shər). The act of scraping the surface of a written instrument to remove writing from it.

ratable (**rayd**-ə-bəl), *adj.* **1.** Proportionate <ratable distribution>. **2.** Capable of being estimated, appraised, or apportioned <because hundreds of angry fans ran onto the field at the same time, blame for the goalpost's destruction is not ratable>. **3.** Taxable <the government assessed the widow's ratable estate>. See PRO RATA.

ratchet theory. In constitutional law, the principle that Congress—in exercising its enforcement power under the Fourteenth Amendment—can increase, but cannot dilute, the scope of Fourteenth Amendment guarantees as previously defined by the Supreme Court; thus, the enabling

clause works in only one direction, like a ratchet.

rate, *n.* **1.** Proportional or relative value; the proportion by which quantity or value is adjusted <rate of inflation>. **2.** An amount paid or charged for a good or service <the rate for a two-bedroom apartment is $550 per month>. **3.** INTEREST RATE <the rate on the loan increases by 2% after 5 years>. —**rate,** *vb.*

rate base. The investment amount or property value on which a company, esp. a public utility, is allowed to earn a particular rate of return.

rate of interest. INTEREST RATE.

rate of return. The annual income from an investment, expressed as a percentage of the investment.

internal rate of return. In accounting, a discounted-cashflow method of evaluating a long-term project, used to determine the actual return on an investment. —Abbr. IRR.

ratification, *n.* **1.** Confirmation and acceptance of a previous act, thereby making the act valid from the moment it was done <the board of directors' ratification of the president's resolution>. **2.** In contract law, a person's binding adoption of an act already completed but either not done in a way that originally produced a legal obligation or done by a stranger having at the time no authority to act as the person's agent <an adult's ratification of a contract signed during childhood is necessary to make the contract enforceable>. **3.** In international law, the final confirmation by the parties to an international treaty, usu. including the documents reflecting the confirmation <the ratification of the nuclear-weapons treaty>. —**ratify,** *vb.* Cf. CONFIRMATION.

ratiocination (raht-ee-ohs-[ə]n-**ay**-shən *or* rat- *or* rash-), *n.* The process or an act of reasoning. —**ratiocinate,** *vb.*—**ratiocinative,** *adj.*

ratio decidendi (**ray**-shee-oh-des-i-**den**-dee *or* **ray**-shoh-). [Latin "the reason for deciding"] **1.** The rule of law on which a court says its decision is founded <many poorly written judicial opinions do not contain a clearly ascertainable *ratio decidendi*>. **2.** The rule of law on which a later court thinks that a previous court founded its decision <this opinion recognizes the Supreme Court's *ratio decidendi* in the school desegregation cases>. —Often shortened to *ratio.* Pl. *rationes decidendi.* Cf. OBITER DICTUM.

ratio legis (**ray**-shee-oh-**lee**-jəs). [Latin] The reason or purpose for making a law <the Senator argued that the rapid spread of violent crime was a compelling *ratio legis* for the gun-control statute>.

rational-basis test. In constitutional law, a principle whereby a court will uphold a law as valid under the Equal Protection Clause if it bears a reasonable relationship to the attainment of some legitimate governmental objective. —Also termed *rational-purpose test.* Cf. STRICT SCRUTINY; INTERMEDIATE SCRUTINY.

ravishment, *n. Archaic.* Rape; this term is widely considered inappropriate for modern usage, given its romantic connotations of ecstasy and delight. —**ravish,** *vb.*

re. [Latin] Regarding; in the matter of; the term is often used as a signal or introductory title announcing the subject of business correspondence. See IN RE.

rea (**ree**-ə). [Latin] In civil and canon law, a female defendant. Pl. *reae.*

reacquired stock. See *treasury stock* under STOCK.

readjustment, *n.* Voluntary reorganization of a financially troubled corporation by the shareholders themselves and without a trustee's or a receiver's intervention. —**readjust,** *vb.*

reaffirmation, *n.* Approval of something previously agreed to; renewal <the bankruptcy court authorized the debtor's reaffirmation of prepetition debts that otherwise would have been discharged>. —**reaffirm,** *vb.*

real action. See ACTION.

real authority. See *actual authority* under AUTHORITY.

real chattel. See *chattel real* under CHATTEL.

real covenant. See *covenant running with the land* under COVENANT (4).

real defense. See DEFENSE (4).

real estate. See *real property* under PROPERTY.

real-estate investment trust. A company that invests in and manages a portfolio of real estate, with the majority of the trust's income distributed to its shareholders; such a trust may qualify for special income-tax treatment if it distributes 95 percent of its income to its shareholders. —

Abbr. REIT. See *investment company* under COMPANY.

real estate owned. Property acquired by a lender, usu. through foreclosure, in satisfaction of a debt. —Abbr. REO.

Real Estate Settlement Procedures Act. A federal law that requires lenders to provide home buyers with information about known or estimated settlement costs. 12 U.S.C. §§ 2601 et seq. —Abbr. RESPA.

real evidence. See *demonstrative evidence* under EVIDENCE.

realignment (ree-ə-lIn-mənt), *n.* The process by which a court, in determining diversity jurisdiction, identifies and rearranges the parties as plaintiffs and defendants according to their ultimate interests. —**realign,** *vb.*

real income. See INCOME.

realization, *n.* **1.** Conversion of noncash assets into cash assets. **2.** In tax law, an event or transaction, such as the sale or exchange of property, that substantially changes a taxpayer's economic position so that income tax may be imposed or a tax allowance granted. Cf. RECOGNITION (3). —**realize,** *vb.*

real party in interest. See PARTY.

real property. See PROPERTY.

real rate. See INTEREST RATE.

realtor (ree[ə]l-tər). **1.** (*cap.*) *Servicemark.* A member of the National Association of Realtors. **2.** Loosely, any real-estate agent or broker.

realty. See *real property* under PROPERTY.

reapportionment, *n.* Realignment of a legislative district's boundaries to reflect changes in population; reapportionment is mandated by U.S. Const. art. I, § 2, cl. 3. —Also termed *redistricting.* —**reapportion,** *vb.* Cf. GERRYMANDERING.

reargument, *n.* The presentation of additional arguments, which often suggest that a controlling legal principle has been overlooked, to a court (usu. an appellate court) that has already heard initial arguments. —**reargue,** *vb.* Cf. REHEARING.

reasonable, *adj.* **1.** Fair, proper, or moderate under the circumstances <reasonable pay>. **2.** According to reason <your argument is reasonable but not convincing>. **3.** (Of a person) having the faculty of reason <a reasonable person would have looked both ways before crossing the street>. —**reasonableness,** *n.*

reasonable care. See CARE.

reasonable cause. See PROBABLE CAUSE.

reasonable diligence. DUE DILIGENCE (1).

reasonable doubt. The doubt that prevents one from being firmly convinced of a defendant's guilt, or the belief that there is a real possibility that a defendant is not guilty; "beyond a reasonable doubt" is the standard used by a jury to determine whether a criminal defendant is guilty, based on the presumption of innocence. See BURDEN OF PERSUASION.

reasonable-expectation doctrine. In insurance law, the doctrine that resolves insurance-policy ambiguities in favor of the insured's reasonable expectations.

reasonable force. See FORCE.

reasonable-inference rule. An evidentiary principle providing that a jury, in deciding a case, may properly consider any reasonable inferences drawn from the evidence presented at trial.

reasonable person. A hypothetical person used as a legal standard, esp. to determine whether someone acted with negligence; the reasonable person acts sensibly, does things without serious delay, and takes proper but not excessive precautions. —Also termed *prudent person*; *ordinarily prudent person*. See *reasonable care* under CARE.

reasonable suspicion. A particularized and objective basis, supported by specific and articulable facts, for suspecting a person of criminal activity; a police officer must have a reasonable suspicion to stop a person in a public place. *Terry v. Ohio*, 392 U.S. 1 (1968). See STOP-AND-FRISK RULE; TERRY STOP. Cf. PROBABLE CAUSE.

reasonable time. 1. In contract law, the time needed to conveniently do what a contract requires to be done, based on subjective circumstances; if the contracting parties do not fix a time for performance, the law will usu. presume a reasonable time. **2.** In commercial law, the time during which the U.C.C. permits a party to accept an offer, inspect goods, substitute conforming goods for rejected goods, and the like.

reasonable-use theory. In property law, the principle that owners of riparian land may make reasonable use of their water if this use does not affect the water available to lower riparian owners.

reassurance. See *reinsurance* under INSURANCE.

rebate. A discount, deduction, or refund of money.

rebus sic stantibus (**ree**-bəs-sik-**stan**-ti-bəs). [Latin "things standing so"] In international law, the weak principle that treaties are concluded with the implied condition that they are binding only as long as there are no major changes in the circumstances. —Also termed *clausula rebus sic stantibus*.

rebuttable presumption. See PRESUMPTION.

rebuttal, *n.* **1.** In-court contradiction of an adverse party's evidence. **2.** The time given to a party to present contradictory evidence or arguments. —**rebut,** *vb.*

rebuttal evidence. See EVIDENCE.

rebutter. 1. In common-law pleading, the defendant's answer to a plaintiff's surrejoinder; the pleading that followed the rejoinder and surrejoinder, and that might in turn be answered by the surrebutter. **2.** One who rebuts.

recall, *n.* **1.** Removal of a public official from office by popular vote. **2.** A manufacturer's request to consumers for the return of defective products for repair or replacement. **3.** Revocation of a judgment for factual, as opposed to legal, reasons. —**recall,** *vb.*

recapitalization, *n.* An adjustment or recasting of a corporation's capital structure—that is, its stocks, bonds, or other securities—through amendment of the articles of incorporation or merger with a parent or subsidiary <the recapitalization eliminates unpaid preferred dividends and creates a new class of senior securities>. —**recapitalize**, *vb.* Cf. REORGANIZATION (1).

leveraged recapitalization. Recapitalization whereby the corporation substitutes debt for equity in the capital structure, usu. to make the corporation less attractive as a target for a hostile takeover. —Also termed *leveraging up*.

recaption. 1. At common law, lawful seizure of another's property for a second time to secure the performance of a duty; a second distress. See DISTRESS. **2.** Peaceful retaking, without legal process, of one's own property that has been wrongfully taken.

recapture, *n.* Recovery by the I.R.S. of a tax benefit, such as a deduction or a credit, previously taken by a taxpayer <the tax code's rules for recapture of depreciation do not apply when the property is sold at a loss>. —**recapture**, *vb.*

recapture clause. 1. A contract provision that limits prices or allows for the recovery of goods if market conditions greatly differ from what the contract anticipated. **2.** A commercial-lease provision that grants the landlord both a percentage of the tenant's profits above a fixed amount of rent and the right to terminate the lease—and thus recapture the property—if those profits are too low.

receipt, *n.* **1.** The act of receiving something <my receipt of the document was delayed by 2 days>. **2.** A written acknowledgment that something has been received <keep the receipt for the gift>. **3.** (*usu. pl.*) Something received; INCOME <post the daily receipts in the ledger>.

receipt, *vb.* **1.** To acknowledge in writing the receipt of (something, esp. money) <the bill must be receipted>. **2.** To give a receipt for (something, esp. money) <the bookkeeper receipted the payments>.

receivable, *n.* See *account receivable* under ACCOUNT (2).

receiver. A disinterested person appointed by a court, or by a corporation or other person, for the protection or collection of property that is the subject of diverse claims (for example, because it belongs to a bankrupt or is otherwise being litigated).

receivership. 1. A legal proceeding in which a court appoints a receiver. **2.** The state or condition of a business or property over which a receiver has been appointed.

receiving stolen property. The criminal offense of acquiring or controlling property known to have been stolen by another person; some jurisdictions require the additional element of wrongful intent. See FENCE.

recess, *n.* **1.** A brief break in judicial proceedings <the court granted a two-hour recess for lunch>. Cf. CONTINUANCE (3). **2.** An interval between sittings of the same legislative body <Congress took a month-long recess for the winter>. —**recess**, *vb.*

recession. A period characterized by a sharp slow-down in economic activity, declining employment, and a decrease in investment and consumer spending. Cf. DEPRESSION.

recidivism (ri-**sid**-ə-viz-əm), *n.* The tendency to relapse into criminal activity or behavior. —**recidivous,** *adj.*—**recidivate,** *vb.*

recidivist, *n.* One who has been convicted of numerous criminal offenses; a repeat offender <proponents of prison reform argue that prisons don't cure the recidivist>. —Also termed *habitual offender*; *habitual criminal*; *repeater*.

reciprocal contract. See *bilateral contract* under CONTRACT.

reciprocal-dealing arrangement. A business plan between two parties whereby the first party agrees to buy goods from the second party only if the second party also buys goods from the first party; this type of arrangement often violates antitrust laws. Cf. TYING ARRANGEMENT.

reciprocal insurance. See INSURANCE.

reciprocal negative easement. See EASEMENT.

reciprocal trust. See TRUST.

reciprocal wills. See *mutual wills* under WILL.

reciprocity (res-ə-**pros**-i-tee). **1.** Mutual or bilateral action <the Arthurs stopped receiving social invitations from friends because of their lack of reciprocity>. **2.** The mutual concession of advantages or privileges for purposes of commercial or diplomatic relations <Texas and Louisiana grant reciprocity to each other's citizens with respect to in-state tuition rates>.

recision. RESCISSION.

recital. 1. An account or description of some fact or thing <the recital of

the events leading up to the accident>. **2.** A preliminary statement in a contract or deed explaining the background of the transaction or showing the existence of particular facts <the recitals in the settlement agreement should describe the underlying dispute>. —**recite,** *vb.*

reckless disregard. 1. Conscious indifference to the consequences (of an act). **2.** In libel law, serious indifference to truth or accuracy (of a publication); "reckless disregard for the truth" is the standard in proving the defendant's actual malice toward the plaintiff.

reckless driving. The criminal offense of operating a motor vehicle in a manner that shows conscious indifference to the safety of others.

reckless endangerment. The criminal offense of putting another person at substantial risk of death or serious injury.

reckless homicide. See HOMICIDE.

reckless negligence. See *gross negligence* under NEGLIGENCE.

recklessness, *n.* **1.** Conduct whereby the actor does not desire the consequence but nonetheless foresees the possibility and consciously takes the risk; recklessness involves a greater degree of fault than negligence but a lesser degree of fault than intentional wrongdoing. **2.** The state of mind in which a person does not care about the consequences of his or her actions. —**reckless,** *adj.*

reclamation (rek-lə-**may**-shən), *n.* **1.** The act or an instance of improving the value of economically useless land by physically changing the land, such as irrigating a desert. **2.** In commercial law, a seller's limited right to retrieve goods delivered to a buyer when the buyer is insolvent. U.C.C. § 2-702(2). **3.** The act or an instance of obtaining valuable materials from waste materials. —**reclaim,** *vb.*

recognition, *n.* **1.** Confirmation that an act done by another person was authorized. See RATIFICATION. **2.** The formal admission that a person, entity, or thing has a particular status; esp., a nation's act in formally acknowledging the existence of another nation or national government. **3.** In tax law, the act or an instance of accounting for a taxpayer's realized gain or loss for the purpose of income-tax reporting. Cf. REALIZATION (2). —**recognize,** *vb.*

recognitor (ree-**kog**-ni-tor). An empaneled juror at an assize or inquest.

recognizance (ri-**kog**-nə-zən[t]s). A bond or obligation, made in court, by which a person promises to perform some act or observe some condition, such as to appear when called, to pay a debt, or to keep the peace; most commonly, a recognizance takes the form of a bail bond that guarantees an unjailed criminal defendant's return for a court date <the defendant was released on his own recognizance>. Cf. BAIL (2).

recollection, *n.* The act of recalling something to mind, esp. through conscious effort; something recalled in this manner. —**recollect,** *vb.* See PAST RECOLLECTION RECORDED; PRESENT RECOLLECTION REFRESHED.

recompensable. COMPENSABLE.

recompense (**re**-kəm-pen[t]s), *n.* Repayment, compensation, or retri-

bution for something, esp. an injury or loss. —**recompense,** *vb.*

reconciliation (re-kən-sil-ee-**ay**-shən), *n.* **1.** Renewal of amicable relations between two persons who had been in conflict <a reconciliation between the plaintiff and defendant is unlikely even if the lawsuit settles before trial>. **2.** In family law, voluntary resumption, after a separation, of full marital relations <the child's grades improved after her parents' reconciliation>. **3.** In bookkeeping, adjustment of account records to make them agree with a financial statement <reconciliation of the cash account>. —**reconcile** (**rek**-ən-sɪl), *vb.*

reconduction, *n.* **1.** In international law, the forcible return of aliens—esp. illegal aliens, destitute or diseased aliens, or alien criminals who have served their punishment—to their country of origin. —Also termed *renvoi.* **2.** In civil law, the renewal of a lease. —**reconduct,** *vb.*

record, *n.* **1.** A written account of past events, usu. designed to memorialize those events. **2.** The official report of the proceedings in a case, including the filed papers, verbatim transcript, and tangible exhibits. —Also termed (in Texas) *transcript.* See DOCKET (1).

recordation (re-kor-**day**-shən), *n.* The act or process of recording an instrument, such as a deed or mortgage, in a public registry. —**record** (ri-**kord**), *vb.*

record date. The date on which corporate shareholders must be registered on the corporation's books to be entitled to vote and receive dividends.

recorded recollection. PAST REC-OLLECTION RECORDED.

recorder. 1. A municipal judge who hears minor criminal and sometimes civil cases. 2. A municipal or county officer who keeps public records such as deeds, liens, judgments, and the like.

recording act. In property law, a statute determining priorities between persons claiming an interest in the same (usu. real) property; recording acts—the three main types of which are a *race statute*, *race-notice statute*, and a *notice statute*—are designed to protect subsequent bona fide purchasers from prior unrecorded interests.

recording agent. See INSURANCE AGENT.

record notice. See NOTICE.

record on appeal. The record of a trial-court proceeding as presented to the appellate court for review. —Also termed *appellate record*.

record owner. See OWNER.

record title. See TITLE.

recoupment (ri-**koop**-mənt). 1. An act or an instance of recovering something, esp. money, that was once owned. 2. An act or an instance of withholding, for equitable reasons, something that is due. 3. Reduction of a plaintiff's damages because of the plaintiff's failure to perform an obligation under the transaction that is the subject of the lawsuit. Cf. SET-OFF. 4. The obsolete pleading equivalent to a counterclaim. —**recoup,** *vb.*

recourse (ree-kors). 1. The act of seeking help or advice. 2. Enforcement of, or a method for enforcing, a

right. 3. A right to repayment, esp., the right of a holder of a negotiable instrument to repayment from the drawer and indorsers when the first liable party defaults. See WITH RE-COURSE; WITHOUT RECOURSE.

recourse loan. See LOAN.

recovery, *n.* 1. A thing secured by legal process, esp. a judgment. 2. The amount of money in a judgment. —**recover,** *vb.*

recrimination (ri-krim-ə-**nay**-shən), *n.* A charge made by an accused person against the accuser, esp. a charge of adultery or cruelty made by a spouse charged with the same offense in a divorce suit. —**recriminatory,** *adj.*

recross-examination. A second cross-examination, after redirect examination. —Often shortened to *recross.* See CROSS-EXAMINATION.

rectification (rek-ti-fi-**kay**-shən), *n.* A court's equitable correction of a contractual term that is misstated, such as when the rent is wrongly recorded in a lease or the area of land is incorrectly cited in a deed. —**rectify,** *vb.* See REFORMATION.

recusal (ri-**kyoo**-zəl), *n.* Removal of oneself as judge in a particular case, esp. because of a conflict of interest. —Also termed *recusation; recusement.* —**recuse,** *vb.* Cf. DISQUAL-IFICATION.

redaction (ri-**dak**-shən), *n.* 1. The careful editing (of a document), esp. to remove confidential references or offensive material. 2. A revised or edited document. —**redact,** *vb.*—**redactional,** *adj.*

redeemable bond. See BOND (1).

redeemable security. See SECURI-
TY.

redemption, *n.* **1.** The act or an
instance of reclaiming or regaining
possession by paying a specific price.
2. In bankruptcy, a debtor's right to
repurchase property from a buyer
who obtained the property at a forced
sale initiated by a creditor. **3.** In corporate law, the reacquisition of a security by the issuer; redemption usu.
refers to the repurchase of a bond
before maturity, but it may also refer
to the repurchase of stock and mutu-
al-fund shares. —Also termed (in reference to stock) *stock redemption.* **4.**
In property law, the payment of a
defaulted mortgage debt by a borrower who does not want to lose the
property. —**redeem,** *vb.*—**redeemable, redemptive, redemptional**
adj.

equity of redemption. The right of a
mortgagor in default to recover
property before a foreclosure sale
by paying the principal, interest,
and other costs that are due and
owing. —Also termed *right of redemption.* See CLOG ON THE EQUI-
TY OF REDEMPTION.

redemption period. The statutory
period during which a defaulting
mortgagor may recover property after a foreclosure or tax sale by paying
the outstanding debt or charges.

red herring. 1. An irrelevant legal
or factual issue <law students should
avoid discussing the red herrings
that professors raise in exams>. **2.**
See *preliminary prospectus* under
PROSPECTUS.

red-herring prospectus. See *preliminary prospectus* under PROSPEC-
TUS.

redhibition (red-[h]ə-**bish**-ən), *n.* In
Louisiana, the voidance of a sale as
the result of an action brought on
account of some defect in a thing
sold, on grounds that the defect renders the thing either useless or so
imperfect that the buyer would not
have originally purchased it. —**red-
hibitory** (red-**hib**-ə-tor-ee), *adj.*

redirect examination. A second direct examination, after cross-examination, the scope ordinarily being
limited to testimony covered during
cross- examination. —Often shortened to *redirect.* —Also termed (in
England) *re-examination.* See DI-
RECT EXAMINATION.

rediscount rate. See INTEREST
RATE.

redistricting. REAPPORTIONMENT.

redlining, *n.* **1.** Unlawful credit discrimination by financial institutions
that refuse to make loans on properties in allegedly bad neighborhoods.
2. The process of creating a new
draft of a document showing suggest-
ed revisions explicitly alongside the
text of an earlier version. —**redline,**
vb.

redraft, *n.* A second negotiable instrument offered by the drawer after
the first instrument has been dishonored. —**redraft,** *vb.*

redress (ri-**dres** *or* **ree**-dres), *n.* **1.**
Relief; remedy <money damages, as
opposed to equitable relief, is the
only redress available>. **2.** A means
of seeking relief or remedy <if the
statute of limitations has run, the
plaintiff is without redress>. —**redress** (ri-**dres**), *vb.*

reductio ad absurdum (ri-**dək**-
shee-oh-ad-əb-**sərd**-əm). [Latin "re-

duction to the absurd"] In logic, disproof of an argument by showing that it leads to a ridiculous conclusion.

reduction to practice. In patent law, the physical construction of an inventor's conception into actual working form, the date of which is critical in determining priority between inventors competing for a patent on the same invention. See INVENTION.

reenactment rule. In statutory construction, the principle that when reenacting a law, the legislature implicitly adopts well-settled judicial or administrative interpretations of the law.

re-entry, *n.* The act or an instance of retaking possession of land by a person who formerly held the land and who reserved the right to retake the land when he or she let it go. — **re-enter,** *vb.* See POWER OF TERMINATION.

re-examination, *n.* **1.** REDIRECT EXAMINATION <the attorney focused on the defendant's alibi during re-examination>. **2.** In patent law, a procedure whereby a party can seek review of a patent on the basis of additional references to prior art not originally considered by the U.S. Patent Office <the alleged infringer, hoping to avoid liability, sought re-examination of the patent to narrow its scope>. —**re-examine,** *vb.*

referee. A type of master appointed by a court to assist with certain proceedings. See MASTER (2).

referee in bankruptcy. A federal judicial officer who administers bankruptcy proceedings; abolished by the Bankruptcy Reform Act of 1978, these referees were replaced by bankruptcy judges. See BANKRUPTCY JUDGE.

reference, *n.* **1.** The act of referring, esp. sending a case to a master. **2.** Submission of a contractual dispute to arbitration. **3.** Direction (in a document) to where information may be found. —**refer,** *vb.*

referendum. **1.** The process of referring state legislative acts or state constitutional amendments to the people for final approval by popular vote. **2.** A vote taken by this method. Pl. **referendums, referenda.** Cf. INITIATIVE.

refinancing, *n.* An exchange of an old debt for a new debt, as by negotiating a different interest rate or by repaying the existing loan with money acquired from a new loan. —**refinance,** *vb.*

reformation (ref-ər-**may**-shən), *n.* An equitable remedy by which a court will modify a written agreement to reflect the actual intent of the parties, usu. to correct fraud or mutual mistake, such as an incomplete property description in a deed. —**reform,** *vb.* See RECTIFICATION.

refoulement (ri-**fowl**-mənt). [French] Expulsion or return of a refugee from one state to another, esp. to one where his or her life or liberty would be threatened.

refreshing recollection. PRESENT RECOLLECTION REFRESHED.

refugee. A person who has fled from or been expelled or deported by his or her home country.

refund, *n.* **1.** The return of money to a person who overpaid, such as a taxpayer who overestimated tax liability or whose employer withheld too much tax from earnings; the money so returned. **2.** The act of refinancing, esp. by replacing outstanding securities with a new issue of securities. —**refund,** *vb.*

refund annuity. See ANNUITY.

refute, *vb.* To prove a statement false. Cf. REBUTTAL.

Regina. [Latin] Queen. —Abbr. R.

regional securities exchange. See SECURITIES EXCHANGE.

register, *n.* **1.** A governmental officer who keeps official records <each county employs a register of deeds and wills>. Cf. REGISTRAR. **2.** A book or other record in which entries are made during the course of business or public affairs <the Federal Register lists recent agency regulations>. —Also termed *registry*. **3.** PROBATE JUDGE.

registered agent. See AGENT.

registered bond. See BOND (1).

registered check. See CHECK.

registered corporation. See CORPORATION.

registered mail. See MAIL.

registered offering. See OFFERING.

registered public offering. See *registered offering* under OFFERING.

registered representative. See REPRESENTATIVE.

registered stock. See *registered security* under SECURITY.

registered voter. A person who is qualified to vote and whose name is recorded in the voting district where he or she resides.

registrar. A person who keeps official records, esp. a school official who maintains academic and enrollment records. Cf. REGISTER (1).

registration, *n.* **1.** The act of recording or enrolling <the county clerk handles registration of voters>.

criminal registration. The requirement in some communities that any felon who spends any time in the community must register his or her name with the police.

2. In securities law, the complete process of preparing to sell a newly issued security to the public <the security is currently in registration>. —**register,** *vb.*

shelf registration. Registration with the SEC of several securities, to be sold over a long time period, for the purpose of avoiding the delays of individual registration.

registration statement. A document containing detailed information required by the SEC for the public sale of corporate securities; it includes the prospectus to be supplied to prospective buyers. See PROSPECTUS.

registry. REGISTER (2).

regnal (**reg**-nəl), *adj.* Of or relating to a monarch's reign <Queen Elizabeth II is in her forty-third regnal year since accession to the throne in 1952>.

regress (ree-gres), *n.* The right or liberty of going back; re-entry. See EGRESS; INGRESS.

regressive tax. See TAX.

regular course of business. COURSE OF BUSINESS.

regular meeting. See *annual meeting* under MEETING.

regulation, *n.* **1.** The act or process of controlling by rule or restriction <the federal regulation of the airline industry>. **2.** BYLAW (1) <the CEO referred to the corporate regulation>. **3.** A rule or order, having legal force, issued by an administrative agency or a local government <Treasury regulations explain and interpret the Internal Revenue Code>. —Also termed (in sense 3) *agency regulation*; *subordinate legislation*. —**regulate,** *vb.* —**regulatory, regulable,** *adj.* See MERIT REGULATION.

Regulation A. An SEC regulation that permits small stock offerings to be registered with the SEC under a cheaper and more simplified process than normal registration.

Regulation D. An SEC regulation that exempts small stock offerings (those limited in dollar amount or in the number of investors) from registration under the Securities Act of 1933.

Regulation J. A Federal Reserve Board regulation that governs the collection of checks by and the transfer of funds through member banks.

Regulation Q. A Federal Reserve Board regulation that sets interest-rate ceilings and regulates advertising of interest on savings accounts; this regulation, which applies to all commercial banks, was created by the Banking Act of 1933.

Regulation T. An SEC regulation that limits the amount of credit that securities brokers and dealers may extend to customers who wish to buy securities; the Federal Reserve Board sets the limit, which usu. requires the customer to provide between 40 and 60 percent of the purchase price.

Regulation U. A Federal Reserve Board regulation that limits the amount of credit that banks may extend to customers who wish to buy securities.

Regulation Z. A Federal Reserve Board regulation that implements the provisions of the federal Consumer Credit Protection Act. See CONSUMER CREDIT PROTECTION ACT.

regulatory agency. AGENCY (3).

regulatory offense. See OFFENSE.

rehabilitation, *n.* **1.** In criminal law, the improvement a criminal's character so that he or she can function in society without committing crimes in the future <rehabilitation is a traditional theory of criminal punishment, along with deterrence and retribution>. Cf. DETERRENCE; RETRIBUTION (1). **2.** In evidence, the restoration of a witness's credibility after the witness has been impeached on cross-examination <the inconsistencies were explained away during the prosecution's rehabilitation of the witness>. **3.** In bankruptcy law, the process of reorganizing a debtor's financial affairs—under Chapter 11, 12, or 13 of the Bankruptcy Code—so that the debtor may continue to exist as a financial entity, with creditors satisfying their claims from the debtor's future earnings <the corporation's

rehabilitation was successful>. — Also termed *debtor rehabilitation*. Cf. LIQUIDATION (4). —**rehabilitate,** *vb.*—**rehabilitative,** *adj.*

rehabilitative alimony. See ALIMONY.

rehearing. A second or subsequent hearing of a case or an appeal, usu. held to review an error or omission in the first hearing <the petitioner, dissatisfied with the appellate court's ruling, filed a motion for rehearing>. Cf. REARGUMENT.

reification (ree-ə-fi-**kay**-shən *or* ray-), *n.* **1.** Mental conversion of an abstract concept into a material thing. **2.** In civil procedure, identification of the disputed thing in a non-personal action and attribution of an in-state situs to it for jurisdictional purposes. **3.** In commercial law, embodiment of a right to payment in a writing (such as a negotiable instrument) so that a transfer of the writing also transfers the right. —**reify** (ree-ə-fī *or* ray-), *vb.*

reinstate, *vb.* To place again in a former state or position; to restore <the judge reinstated the judgment that had been vacated>. —**reinstatement,** *n.*

reinsurance. See INSURANCE.

reissuable note. See NOTE.

REIT (reet). *abbr.* REAL-ESTATE INVESTMENT TRUST.

rejection, *n.* Refusal of a contract offer or of tendered goods. Cf. REPUDIATION; RESCISSION. —**reject,** *vb.*

rejoinder, *n.* In common-law pleading, the defendant's answer to the plaintiff's reply (or replication). —**rejoin,** *vb.*

related good. In trademark law, a good that infringes a trademark because it appears to come from the same source as the marked good, despite not competing with the marked good; for example, a cutting tool named "McKnife" might infringe the "McDonald's" trademark as a related good.

related proceeding. In bankruptcy law, a proceeding involving claims that will affect the administration of the debtor's estate (such as a tort action between the debtor and a third party); such a proceeding must be adjudicated in federal district court unless the parties consent to bankruptcy-court jurisdiction or unless the district court refers the matter to the bankruptcy court or to state court. Cf. CORE PROCEEDING.

relation back, *n.* **1.** The doctrine that an act done at a later time is considered to have occurred at an earlier time; for example, in civil procedure, an amended pleading relates back, for purposes of the statute of limitations, to the time when the original pleading was filed. Fed. R. Civ. P. 15(c). **2.** A judicial application of that doctrine. —**relate back,** *vb.*

relative, *n.* A person connected with another by blood or affinity; a kinsman.

relative fact. See FACT.

relator. 1. The real party in interest in whose name a state or an attorney general brings a lawsuit. See EX REL. **2.** The applicant for a writ, esp. a writ of mandamus or quo warranto. **3.** A person who furnishes information on which a civil or criminal case is based; an informer.

release, *n.* **1.** Liberation from an obligation, duty, or demand; the act of giving up a right or claim to the person against whom it could have been enforced <the ex-husband asked his ex-wife for a release from the payment of alimony>. **2.** A written discharge, acquittance, or receipt <Jones signed the release before accepting the cash from Hawkins>. **3.** A written authorization or permission for publication <the newspaper obtained a release from the witness before printing his picture on the front page>. **4.** The act of conveying an estate or right to another, or of legally disposing of it <the release of the easement on February 14>. **5.** A deed or document effecting a conveyance <the legal description in the release was defective>. See *deed of release* under DEED. **6.** The action of freeing or the fact of being freed from restraint or confinement <he became a model citizen after his release from prison>. **7.** A document giving formal discharge from custody <after the sheriff signed the release, the prisoner was free to go>. —**release,** *vb.*

releasee. 1. One who is released, either physically or by contractual discharge. **2.** One to whom an estate is released.

release of mortgage. A written document that discharges a mortgage upon full payment by the mortgagor and that is publicly recorded to show that the mortgagor has full equity in the property.

release to uses. Conveyance of property, by deed of release, by one party to a second party for the use of the first party or a third party. See *deed of release* under DEED; STATUTE OF USES.

releasor. One who releases property or a claim to another.

relevant, *adj.* Logically connected and tending to prove or disprove a matter in issue; pertinent. —**relevance,** *n.* Cf. MATERIAL.

relevant evidence. See EVIDENCE.

relevant market. See MARKET.

reliance, *n.* Dependence or trust by a person, esp. when combined with action based on that dependence or trust. —**rely,** *vb.*

detrimental reliance. Reliance by one party on the acts or representations of another, causing a worsening of the first party's position; detrimental reliance may serve as a substitute for consideration and thus make a promise enforceable as a contract. See *promissory estoppel* under ESTOPPEL.

relict (**rel**-ikt). A widow or widower.

reliction (ri-**lik**-shən). **1.** A process by which a river or stream shifts its location, causing the recession of water from its bank. **2.** The alteration of a boundary line due to the gradual removal of land by a river or stream. See ACCRETION; DERELICTION.

relief. 1. A payment made by an heir of a feudal tenant to the feudal lord for the privilege of taking possession of the ancestor's estate. **2.** Aid or assistance given to those in need, esp., financial aid provided by the state. **3.** The redress or benefit, esp. equitable in nature (such as an injunction or specific performance), that a party asks of a court. Cf. REMEDY.

affirmative relief. The relief sought by a defendant by raising a counterclaim or cross-claim that could have been maintained independently of the plaintiff's action.

alternative relief. Judicial relief that is mutually exclusive with another form of judicial relief; in pleading, a party may request alternative relief, such as by asking for both a monetary judgment and an injunction. Fed. R. Civ. P. 8(a). Cf. ELECTION OF REMEDIES.

coercive relief. Active judicial relief, either legal or equitable, that the government will enforce.

therapeutic relief. The relief, esp. in a settlement, that requires the defendant to take remedial measures as opposed to paying damages; an example is a defendant-corporation (in an employment-discrimination suit) that agrees to undergo sensitivity training. —Often shortened to *therapeutics*.

religion, freedom of. See FREEDOM OF RELIGION.

relinquishment, *n.* The abandonment of a right or thing. —**relinquish,** *vb.*

rem. See IN REM.

remainder. A future interest arising in a third person—that is, someone other than the creator of the estate or the creator's heirs—who is intended to take after the natural termination of the preceding estate; for example, if a grant is "to A for life, and then to B," B's future interest is a remainder. Cf. EXECUTORY INTEREST; REVERSION; POSSIBILITY OF REVERTER.

alternative remainder. A remainder in which the disposition of property is to take effect only if another disposition does not take effect.

charitable remainder. A remainder, usu. from a life estate, that is given to a charity; for example, "to Jane for life, and then to the American Red Cross."

contingent remainder. A remainder that is either given to an unascertained person or made subject to a condition precedent; for example, "to A for life, and then, if B has married before A dies, to B."—Also termed *executory remainder*; *remainder subject to a condition precedent*.

defeasible remainder. A vested remainder that will be eliminated if a condition subsequent occurs; for example, "to A for life, and then to B, but if B ever sells liquor on the land, then to C."—Also termed *remainder subject to divestment*.

indefeasible remainder. A vested remainder that is not subject to a condition subsequent. —Also termed *indefeasibly vested remainder*.

remainder subject to open. A vested remainder that is given to one person but that may later have to be shared with others; for example, "to A for life, and then equally to all of B's children."—Also termed *remainder subject to partial divestment*.

vested remainder. A remainder that is given to an ascertained person and that is not subject to a condition precedent; for example, "to A for life, and then to B."—Also termed *executed remainder*.

remainder bequest. See *residuary bequest* under BEQUEST.

remainderman. A person to whom a remainder is devised. —Also termed *remainderer*; *remainor*; *remainderperson*.

remainder subject to a condition precedent. See *contingent remainder* under REMAINDER.

remainder subject to divestment. See *defeasible remainder* under REMAINDER.

remainder subject to open. See REMAINDER.

remainder subject to partial divestment. See *remainder subject to open* under REMAINDER.

remainor. REMAINDERMAN.

remand (ri-**mand**), *vb.* **1.** To send (a case) back to the court from which it came for some further action <the appellate court reversed the trial court's opinion and remanded the case for new trial>. Cf. REMOVAL (2). **2.** To recommit (an accused) to custody after a preliminary examination <the magistrate, after denying bail, remanded the defendant to custody>. —**remand** (ri-**mand** *or* ree-mand), *n.*

remargining, *n.* In securities law, the act or process of depositing additional cash or collateral with a broker when the equity in a margin account falls to an insufficient level. —**remargin,** *vb.* See *margin account* under ACCOUNT (2).

remedial law. 1. A statute providing a means to enforce rights or redress injuries. **2.** A law passed to

correct or modify an existing law; esp., a law that gives a party a new or different remedy in cases where the existing remedy, if any, is inadequate.

remedy, *n.* The enforcement of a right or the redress of an injury, esp. monetary damages, that a party asks of a court. —**remedy,** *vb.*—**remedial,** *adj.* Cf. RELIEF.

administrative remedy. A nonjudicial remedy provided by an administrative agency; ordinarily, all administrative remedies must be exhausted before a court will hear a case. See EXHAUSTION OF REMEDIES.

cumulative remedy. A statutory remedy available to a party in addition to another remedy that still remains in force.

equitable remedy. A nonmonetary remedy—such as an injunction or specific performance—obtained when monetary damages cannot adequately redress the injury. See IRREPARABLE-INJURY RULE.

extrajudicial remedy. A remedy not obtained from a court, such as repossession. —Also termed *self-help remedy.*

extraordinary remedy. A remedy—such as a writ of mandamus or habeas corpus—not available to a party unless necessary to preserve rights that cannot be protected by standard legal or equitable remedies.

provisional remedy. A temporary remedy—such as attachment or a temporary restraining order—incidental to the primary action and available to a party while the action is pending.

remedy, mutuality of. See MUTUALITY OF REMEDY.

remise (ri-**mīz**), *vb.* To give up, surrender, or release (a right, interest, etc.) <the quitclaim deed provides that the grantor remises any rights in the property>.

remit, *vb.* **1.** To pardon or forgive <the wife could not remit her husband's infidelity>. **2.** To abate or slacken; to mitigate <the receipt of money damages remitted the embarrassment of being fired>. **3.** To refer (a matter for decision) to some authority, esp. to send back (a case) to a lower court <the appellate court remitted the case to the trial court for further factual determinations>. See REMAND. **4.** To send or put back to a previous condition or position <a landlord's breach of a lease does not justify the tenant's refusal to pay rent; instead, the tenant is remitted to the right to recover damages>. **5.** To transmit (as money) <upon receiving the demand letter, she promptly remitted the amount due>. —**remission** (corresponding to senses 1-4), *n.*—**remittance** (corresponding to sense 5), *n.*

remittee. One to whom money is sent by somebody else.

remitter. 1. One who sends money to somebody else. **2.** A principle by which a person having two titles to an estate, and entering on it by the later or more defective of these titles, is deemed to hold it by the earlier or more valid title. **3.** The act of sending back a case to a lower court.

remittitur (ri-**mit**-i-tər). The process by which a court reduces the damages awarded in a jury verdict; a court's order reducing an award of damages <the defendant sought a remittitur of the $100 million judgment>. Cf. ADDITUR.

remittitur of record. The action of sending the transcript of a case back from an appellate court to a trial court; the notice for doing so.

remonstrance   (ri-**mon**[t]-strən[t]s), *n.* **1.** Presentation of reasons for grievance or opposition. **2.** A formal protest against governmental policy, actions, or officials. —**remonstrate** (ri-**mon**-strayt *or* **rem**-ən-strayt), *vb.*

remote, *adj.* **1.** Far removed or separated in time, space, or relation. **2.** Slight. **3.** In property law, beyond the 21 years after some life in being by which a devise must vest. See RULE AGAINST PERPETUITIES.

remote cause. See CAUSE (1).

removal, *n.* **1.** The transfer or moving of a person or thing from one location, position, or residence to another. **2.** The transfer of an action from a court on one jurisdictional level to a court on another level, esp. from a state court to a federal court. —**remove,** *vb.* Cf. REMAND.

civil-rights removal. Removal of a case from state to federal court for any of the following reasons: (1) because a person has been denied or cannot enforce a civil right of equality in state court, (2) because a person is being sued for performing an act under color of authority derived from a law providing for equal rights, or (3) because a person is being sued for refusing to perform an act that would be inconsistent with equal rights.

remuneration (ri-myoo-nə-**ray**-shən), *n.* **1.** Payment; compensation. **2.** The act of paying or compensating. —**remunerate,** *vb.*—**remunerative,** *adj.*

rendition, *n.* **1.** The action of making, delivering, or giving out, such as a legal decision. **2.** The return of a fugitive from one state to the state where the fugitive is accused or convicted of a crime. See EXTRADITION. —**render,** *vb.*

rendition of judgment. The judge's oral or written ruling containing the judgment entered. Cf. ENTRY OF JUDGMENT.

renege (ri-**nig** *or* ri-**neg**), *vb.* To fail to keep a promise or commitment; to back out of a deal.

renegotiation, *n.* A subsequent negotiation of terms previously bargained for, esp. a review of contracts by a government to determine whether contractors have made excessive profits. —**renegotiate,** *vb.*

renewal, *n.* **1.** The act of restoring or reestablishing. **2.** The re-creation of a legal relationship or the replacement of an old contract with a new contract, as opposed to the mere extension of a previous relationship or contract. —**renew,** *vb.* Cf. EXTENSION; REVIVAL (1).

rent, *n.* Consideration paid, usu. periodically, for the use or occupation of property. —**rent,** *vb.*

economic rent. See ECONOMIC RENT.

ground rent. **a.** Rent paid by a tenant under a long-term lease for the use of undeveloped land, usu. for the construction of a commercial building. See *ground lease* under LEASE. **b.** An inheritable interest, in rental income from land, reserved by a grantor who conveys the land in fee simple.

rent-a-judge. PRIVATE JUDGING.

rental, *n.* **1.** The amount received as rent. **2.** The income received from rent. **3.** A record of payments received from rent. —**rental,** *adj.*

rent charge. The right to receive an annual sum from the income of land, usu. in perpetuity, and to retake possession if the payments are in arrears.

rent control. A restriction imposed, usu. by municipal legislation, on the maximum rent that a landlord may charge for rental property, and often on a landlord's power of eviction.

renunciation (ri-nən[t]-see-**ay**-shən), *n.* **1.** The express or tacit abandonment of a right without transferring it to another. **2.** In criminal law, complete and voluntary abandonment of criminal purpose—sometimes coupled with an attempt to thwart the activity's success—before a crime is committed; renunciation can be an affirmative defense to attempt, conspiracy, and the like. Model Penal Code § 5.01(4). —Also termed *withdrawal; abandonment.* **3.** In wills and estates, the act of waiving a right under a will and claiming instead a statutory share. See RIGHT OF ELECTION. —**renounce,** *vb.*—**renunciative, renunciatory,** *adj.*

renvoi (ron-vwah), *n.* [French "sending back"] **1.** The doctrine under which a court in resorting to foreign law adopts as well the foreign law's conflict-of-laws principles, which may in turn refer the court back to the law of the forum. **2.** The problem arising when one state's rule on conflict of laws refers a case to the law of another state, and that second state's conflict-of-law rule refers the case either back to the law of the first state or to a third state. See CONFLICT OF LAWS. **3.** RECONDUCTION (1).

REO. *abbr.* REAL ESTATE OWNED.

reorganization, *n.* **1.** In corporate tax law, a restructuring of a corporation, such as by a merger or recapitalization; the Internal Revenue Code classifies the different types of reorganizations for tax purposes. I.R.C. § 368(a)(1) <a Class A reorganization>. See RECAPITALIZATION. **2.** In bankruptcy law, a financial restructuring of a corporation, esp. in the repayment of debts, under a plan created by a trustee and approved by a court. See CHAPTER 11. —**reorganize,** *vb.*

haircut reorganization. Slang. In bankruptcy, a restructuring of the indebtedness that remains after a creditor forgives a portion of the debtor's loan.

reorganization bond. See *adjustment bond* under BOND (1).

reparation (rep-ə-**ray**-shən). **1.** The act of making amends for a wrong. **2.** (*usu. pl.*) Compensation for an injury or wrong, esp. for wartime damages or breach of an international obligation.

reparative injunction. See INJUNCTION.

repeal, *n.* Abrogation of an existing law by legislative act. —**repeal,** *vb.*

express repeal. Repeal effected by specific declaration in a new statute.

implied repeal. Repeal effected by irreconcilable conflict between an old law and a new law.

repealer. 1. A legislative act abrogating an earlier law. **2.** One who repeals.

repeater. RECIDIVIST.

replacement cost. See COST.

replacement-cost depreciation method. See METHOD.

repleader. In common-law pleading, a court order or judgment—issued on the motion of a party who suffered an adverse verdict—requiring the parties to file new pleadings because of some defect in the original pleadings. —Also termed *judgment of repleader.*

replevin (ri-**plev**-ən), *n.* **1.** An action for the repossession of personal property wrongfully taken or detained by the defendant, whereby the plaintiff gives security for and holds the property until the court decides who owns it. **2.** A writ obtained from a court authorizing the retaking of personal property wrongfully taken or detained. —Also termed (in sense 2) *writ of replevin.* —**replevy** (ri-**plev**-ee), *vb.* Cf. DETINUE; TROVER.

personal replevin. At common law, an action to replevy a person out of prison or out of another's custody; personal replevin has been largely superseded by the writ of habeas corpus as a means of investigating the legality of an imprisonment. See HABEAS CORPUS.

replevin in cepit (in-**kay**-pit *or* in-**see**-pət). An action for the repossession of property that is both wrongfully taken and wrongfully detained.

replevin in detinet (in-**det**-ə-nət). An action for the repossession of property that is rightfully taken but wrongfully detained.

replication. REPLY (2).

reply, *n.* **1.** In federal practice, the plaintiff's response to the defendant's counterclaim (or, by court order, to the defendant's or a third-party's answer). Fed. R. Civ. P. 7(a). **2.** In common-law pleading, the plaintiff's response to the defendant's plea or answer; the reply is the plaintiff's second pleading and it is followed by the defendant's rejoinder. —Also termed (in sense 2) *replication.* —**reply,** *vb.*

repo (**ree**-poh). **1.** REPOSSESSION. **2.** REPURCHASE AGREEMENT.

report, *n.* **1.** A formal oral or written presentation of facts <according to the treasurer's report, there is $300 in the bank>. **2.** A written account of a court proceeding and judicial decision <the law clerk sent the court's report to counsel for both sides>. **3.** (*usu. pl.*) A published volume of judicial decisions by a particular court or group of courts <U.S. Reports>. —Also termed (in sense 3) *reporter.* —**report,** *vb.*

reporter. 1. A person responsible for making and publishing a report; esp., a lawyer-consultant who prepares drafts of official or semi-official writings such as court rules or Re-

statements <the reporter to the Advisory Committee on Bankruptcy Rules explained the various amendments>. **2.** REPORTER OF DECISIONS. **3.** REPORT (3) <Supreme Court Reporter>.

reporter of decisions. The person responsible for publishing a court's opinions; the reporter of decisions often has duties that include verifying citations, correcting spelling and punctuation, and suggesting minor editorial improvements before judicial opinions are released or published. —Often shortened to *reporter.* —Also termed *court reporter.*

reporter's privilege. See *journalist's privilege* (a) under PRIVILEGE.

reporting company. A company that, because it issues securities, must comply with the reporting requirements of the Securities Exchange Act of 1934.

report of proceedings. TRANSCRIPT (1).

repose (ri-**pohz**), *n.* **1.** Cessation of activity; temporary rest. **2.** A statutory period after which an action cannot be brought in court, even if it expires before the plaintiff suffers any injury. See STATUTE OF REPOSE.

repossession, *n.* The act or an instance of retaking property; esp., a seller's retaking of goods sold on credit when the buyer has failed to pay for them. —Often shortened to *repo.* —**repossess,** *vb.* Cf. FORECLOSURE.

representation, *n.* **1.** A presentation of fact—either by words or by conduct—made to induce someone to act, esp. to enter into a contract <the buyer relied on the seller's represen-

tation that the roof did not leak>. Cf. MISREPRESENTATION.

false representation. MISREPRESENTATION.

material representation. A representation that relates directly to the matter in issue or that actually causes an event to occur (such as a party's relying on the representation in entering into a contract); material representation is a necessary element of an action for fraud.

2. The act or an instance of standing for or acting on behalf of another, esp. by a lawyer on behalf of a client <Johnnie Cochran's representation of O.J. Simpson>. **3.** The assumption by an heir of the rights and obligations of his or her predecessor <each child takes a share by representation>. See PER STIRPES. —**represent,** *vb.*

representative, *n.* **1.** One who stands for or acts on behalf of another <the owner was the football team's representative at the labor negotiations>. See AGENT.

accredited representative. With respect to service of process, a person with general authority to act.

class representative. A person who sues on behalf of a group of plaintiffs in a class action. —Also termed *named plaintiff.* See CLASS ACTION.

personal representative. A person who manages the legal affairs of another because of incapacity or death, such as the executor of an estate. —Also termed *legal representative.*

registered representative. A person approved by the SEC and stock exchanges to sell securities to the public.

2. A member of a legislature, esp. of the lower house <senators and representatives>.

representative action. 1. CLASS ACTION. **2.** DERIVATIVE ACTION (1).

representee. One to whom a representation is made.

representor. One who makes a representation.

repressive tax. See *sin tax* under TAX.

reprieve (ri-preev), *n.* Temporary postponement of the execution of a criminal sentence, esp. a death sentence. —Also termed *respite.* —**reprieve,** *vb.* Cf. COMMUTATION (2); PARDON.

reprimand, *n.* In professional responsibility, a form of disciplinary action—imposed after trial or formal charges—that declares the lawyer's conduct improper but does not limit his or her right to practice. —**reprimand,** *vb.*

private reprimand. A reprimand that is not published but instead communicated only to the lawyer, or that is published without identifying the lawyer by name.

public reprimand. A reprimand that is published, usu. in a bar journal or legal newspaper.

reprise (ri-prIz), *n.* An annual deduction, duty, or payment out of a manor or estate, such as an annuity.

reprisal. (*usu. pl.*) **1.** A nation's use of force, short of war, to redress an injury caused by another nation. **2.** A nation's retaliatory action during wartime in response to a belligerent's war crimes, such as the execution of prisoners of war.

reproduction right. A copyright holder's exclusive right to make copies or phonorecords of the protected work; unauthorized copying by others constitutes infringement.

republic, *n.* A system of government in which the people hold sovereign power and elect representatives who exercise that power. —**republican,** *adj.* Cf. DEMOCRACY.

republication, *n.* In wills and estates, the act or an instance of re-establishing the validity of a previously revoked will by repeating the formalities of execution or by using a codicil. —Also termed *revalidation.* —**republish,** *vb.* Cf. REVIVAL (2).

repudiation (ri-pyood-ee-**ay**-shən), *n.* A contracting party's words or actions that indicate an intention not to perform the contract in the future; a threatened breach of contract. —**repudiate,** *vb.*—**repudiatory, repudiable,** *adj.* Cf. REJECTION; RESCISSION.

anticipatory repudiation. Repudiation of a contractual duty before the time for performance, giving the injured party an immediate right to damages for total breach, as well as discharging the injured party's remaining duties of performance. See *anticipatory breach* under BREACH OF CONTRACT.

repugnant (ri-**pəg**-nənt), *adj.* **1.** Inconsistent with; contrary or contradictory to <the court's interpretation is repugnant to the express terms of the contract>. **2.** Causing distaste or aversion <his bad breath was repugnant>. —**repugnance,** *n.*

repurchase agreement. A short-term loan agreement by which one party sells a security to another party but promises to buy back the security on a specified date at a specified price. —Often shortened to *repo.*

reputation, *n.* The esteem in which a person is held by others; evidence of reputation may be introduced as proof of character whenever character evidence is admissible. Fed. R. Evid. 405. —**reputational,** *adj.*

reputation evidence. See EVIDENCE.

request for admission. In pretrial discovery, a party's written factual statements served on another party who must admit, deny, or object to the substance of each statement; the admitted statements will be treated by the court as established, and therefore do not have to be proved at trial. Fed. R. Civ. P. 36.

request for instructions. During trial, a party's written request that the court instruct the jury on the law as set forth in the request. Fed. R. Civ. P. 51. —Also termed *request to charge.*

request for production. In pretrial discovery, a party's written request that another party present specified documents or other tangible things for inspection and copying by the requesting party. Fed. R. Civ. P. 34. — Also termed *notice to produce.*

request to charge. REQUEST FOR INSTRUCTIONS.

required reserve. See RESERVE.

requirements contract. See CONTRACT.

requisition (rek-wə-**zish**-ən), *n.* **1.** An authoritative, formal demand <a state governor's requisition for another state's surrender of a fugitive>. **2.** A governmental seizure of property <the state's requisition of the shopping center during the weather emergency>. See TAKING. —**requisition,** *vb.*

requisitory letter. LETTER OF REQUEST.

res (rays *or* reez *or* rez). [Latin "thing"] **1.** The subject matter of a trust; CORPUS (2) <the stock certificate is the res of the trust>. **2.** A thing or object; a status <jurisdiction of the res—the real property in Texas>. Pl. **res.**

res adjudicata. RES JUDICATA.

resale, *n.* **1.** The act of selling goods or property—previously sold to a buyer who breached the sales contract—to someone else. U.C.C. § 2-706. **2.** A retailer's selling of goods, previously purchased from a manufacturer or wholesaler, to consumers. —**resell,** *vb.*

resale-price maintenance. An agreement between a manufacturer and a retailer—or the manufacturer's unilateral requirement—that the retailer will not sell the manufacturer's product below a specified minimum price. See *vertical price-fixing* under PRICE-FIXING.

rescission (ri-**sizh**-ən), *n.* **1.** A party's unilateral unmaking of a contract for a legally sufficient reason, such as the other party's material breach; apart from a few limitations, rescission is generally available as a

remedy or defense for a nondefaulting party and restores the parties to their precontract positions. **2.** An agreement by contracting parties to discharge all remaining duties of performance and terminate the contract. —Also termed (in sense 2) *agreement of rescission; mutual rescission; abandonment.* —Also spelled *recision.* —**rescind,** *vb.*—**rescissory,** *adj.* Cf. REJECTION; REPUDIATION.

rescript (**ree**-skript), *n.* **1.** A judge's written order to a court clerk explaining how to dispose of a case. **2.** An appellate court's written decision, usu. unsigned, that is sent down to the trial court. **3.** A Roman emperor's or a pope's written answer to a legal inquiry or petition.

rescue, *n.* **1.** The act or an instance of saving or freeing someone from danger or captivity. **2.** At common law, the act or an instance of forcibly and unlawfully freeing a prisoner or recovering distrained goods. —**rescue,** *vb.*

rescue doctrine. In tort law. the principle holding a tortfeasor liable for injuries to his or her victim's rescuer, and preventing the rescuer from being charged with contributory negligence unless the rescue was conducted recklessly. Cf. EMERGENCY DOCTRINE; GOOD SAMARITAN DOCTRINE.

res derelicta (rays-der-ə-**lik**-tə). [Latin] An abandoned chattel.

reservation. 1. The retention of a right or interest in property being conveyed <the deed's reservation of rights provides for a permanent easement>. **2.** A nation's formal declaration, upon signing or ratifying a treaty, that its willingness to become a party to the treaty is conditioned on certain additional terms that will limit the effect of the treaty in some way <the U.S. reservation to the nuclear arms treaty>. **3.** Land that is set aside for a particular use; esp., land owned and used by American Indians <the Hopi Indian Reservation>. —Also termed (in sense 3) *reserve*.

reservation of rights. NONWAIVER AGREEMENT.

reserve, *n.* **1.** RESERVATION (3). **2.** Something retained or stored for future use; esp., a fund of money set aside by a bank or an insurance company to cover future liabilities. —**reserve,** *vb.*

bad-debt reserve. A reserve to cover losses on uncollectible accounts receivable.

legal reserve. The amount of liquid assets that a bank or an insurance company must maintain in order to meet depositors' or claimants' demands.

mean reserve. In insurance, the average of the beginning reserve (after the premium has been paid for the policy year) and the ending reserve of the policy year.

required reserve. The minimum amount of money, as required by the Federal Reserve Board, that a bank must hold in the form of vault cash and deposits with regional Federal Reserve Banks.

sinking-fund reserve. A reserve used to pay long-term debt. See SINKING FUND.

reserve account. See *impound account* under ACCOUNT (2).

reserve bank. See *member bank* under BANK.

reserve clause. A clause in a professional athlete's contract restricting the athlete's right to change teams, even after the contract expires; reserve clauses are uncommon in modern professional sports. Cf. FREE AGENCY.

reserved easement. See EASEMENT.

reserved point of law. See POINT OF LAW.

reserved power. See POWER.

reserve ratio. The Federal Reserve Board's measurement of a member bank's required reserves. See *required reserve* under RESERVE.

primary reserve ratio. The ratio between a bank's required reserves (cash in vault plus deposits with Federal Reserve Banks) and its demand and time deposits.

secondary reserve ratio. The ratio between a bank's government securities and its demand and time deposits.

res gestae (rays-**jes**-tI *or* -tay *or* -tee), *n. pl.* [Latin "things done"] The events at issue, or other events contemporaneous with them; in evidence law, words and statements about the res gestae are usu. admissible under a hearsay exception (such as present sense impression or excited utterance).

residence, *n.* **1.** The act or fact of living in a particular place for a time <one year of residence in Texas is required before you are eligible for

in-state tuition>. **2.** The locale in which one actually or officially lives <she has now made Oregon her residence>. **3.** A house or other fixed abode <a three-story residence>. **4.** DOMICILE (1). —Also termed (in senses 2 & 4) *residency*. —**residential,** *adj.*—**resident,** *n.*

resident agent. See *registered agent* under AGENT.

resident alien. See ALIEN.

residential cluster. An area of land developed as a unit with group housing and open common space. Cf. PLANNED-UNIT DEVELOPMENT.

residential community treatment center. HALFWAY HOUSE.

residual, *n.* **1.** A remainder. **2.** The profit on a sale. **3.** The cash available after the refinancing of an investment.

residual, *adj.* **1.** Of or relating to residue; left over <residual claim>. **2.** Of or relating to a person's capabilities and functions remaining after an injury <residual functional disability>.

residual value. The value of an asset after depreciation charges have been deducted from the original cost. See DEPRECIATION.

residuary bequest. See BEQUEST.

residuary clause. A testamentary clause that disposes of any estate property remaining after the satisfaction of specific bequests and devises.

residuary devise. See DEVISE.

residuary estate. The property remaining in a decedent's estate after all debts, expenses, and previous bequests and devises have been satisfied. —Also termed *residue*.

residuary legacy. See LEGACY.

residue. RESIDUARY ESTATE.

residuum (ri-**zij**-ə-wəm *or* -**zid**-yoo-əm). That which remains; a residue, esp. in chemical contexts. Pl. **residua.**

residuum rule. An administrative-law principle holding that an agency decision based partly on hearsay evidence will be upheld on judicial review only if the decision is founded on at least some competent evidence; federal courts have generally rejected the residuum rule.

res integra (rays-in-**teg**-rə). [Latin "an entire thing"] RES NOVA.

res inter alios acta (rays-in-tər-ah-lee-ohs-**ak**-tə). [Latin "a thing done between others"] **1.** The evidentiary rule prohibiting the admission in evidence of collateral facts. **2.** The common-law doctrine holding that a contract cannot unfavorably affect the rights of a person who is not a party to the contract.

res ipsa loquitur (rays-ip-sə-**loh**-kwə-tər). [Latin "the thing speaks for itself"] **1.** In tort law, the doctrine providing that, in some circumstances, the mere fact of an accident's occurrence raises an inference of negligence so as to establish a prima facie case. —Often shortened to *res ipsa*. —Also termed *resipsy*. **2.** In criminal law, a test used to determine whether a defendant has gone beyond preparation and committed an attempt, based on whether the defendant's act itself indicated to an observer what the defendant intended to do. —Also termed (in sense 2) *equivocality*.

resisting arrest. The crime of obstructing or opposing a police officer who is making an arrest.

res judicata (rays-joo-di-**kah**-tə *or* -**kay**-tə). [Latin "a thing adjudicated"] **1.** An issue that has been definitively settled by judicial decision. **2.** An affirmative defense barring the same parties from litigating a second lawsuit on the same claim; the three essential elements are (1) an earlier decision on the identical issue, (2) a final judgment on the merits, and (3) the involvement of the same parties or parties in privity with the original parties. —Also termed *res adjudicata*; *claim preclusion*. Cf. COLLATERAL ESTOPPEL.

res nova (rays-**noh**-və). [Latin "a new thing"] **1.** An undecided question of law. **2.** A case of first impression. —Also termed *res integra*. See *case of first impression* under CASE.

resolution, *n.* A formal expression of an official body's opinion or decision <the corporate resolution declared a stock dividend>. —**resolve,** *vb.*

concurrent resolution. A congressional resolution passed by one house and agreed to by the other; it expresses the opinion of Congress on a subject, but does not have the force of law.

joint resolution. A congressional resolution passed by both houses; it has the force of law and is subject to presidential veto.

simple resolution. A congressional resolution passed by one house only; it expresses the opinion or

affects the internal affairs of the passing house, but does not have the force of law.

Resolution Trust Corporation. A federal agency established to act as a receiver for insolvent federal savings-and-loan associations and to transfer or liquidate those associations' assets; the agency was created when the Federal Savings and Loan Insurance Corporation was abolished in 1989. —Abbr. RTC.

resort, *n.* Something that one turns to for refuge or aid <court of last resort>. —**resort,** *vb.*

RESPA (**res**-pə). *abbr.* REAL ESTATE SETTLEMENT PROCEDURES ACT.

respite. REPRIEVE.

respondeat superior (ri-**spon**-dee-aht-soo-**peer**-ee-or). [Latin "let the master respond"] The common-law doctrine holding an employer or principal liable for the employee's or agent's actions (including torts) committed during the scope of employment. —Also termed *master-servant rule*. See SCOPE OF EMPLOYMENT.

respondent. 1. The party against whom an appeal is taken and who resists that appeal; APPELLEE. **2.** The party against whom a motion or petition is filed. Cf. PETITIONER. **3.** At common law, the defendant in an equity proceeding. **4.** In civil law, one who answers for another or acts as another's security.

responsibility, *n.* **1.** LIABILITY (1). **2.** In criminal law, a person's mental fitness to answer in court for his or her actions. See COMPETENCY. **3.** In criminal law, guilt. —Also termed (in senses 2 & 3) *criminal responsibility*. —**responsible,** *adj.*

responsive. Giving or constituting a response; answering <the witness's testimony is not responsive>.

responsive pleading. See PLEADING (1).

rest, *vb.* (Of a litigant) to voluntarily conclude presenting evidence in a trial <after the police officer's testimony, the defense rested>.

Restatement. One of a number of influential treatises, published by the American Law Institute, describing the law in a particular area and guiding its development <Restatement of the Law of Torts>.

restitution, *n.* **1.** Return or restoration of some specific thing or condition. **2.** Compensation, reimbursement, indemnification, or reparation for benefits derived from or loss caused to another; a remedy available in tort and contract law, and sometimes ordered as a condition of probation in criminal law. —**restitutionary,** *adj.*

restraining order. 1. TEMPORARY RESTRAINING ORDER. **2.** A court order restricting or prohibiting a person from contacting or approaching another specified person; this type of order is issued most commonly in domestic disputes.

restraint, *n.* **1.** Confinement, abridgment, or limitation <a restraint on the freedom of speech>. **2.** Prohibition of action; holding back <the victim's family exercised no restraint—they told the suspect exactly what they thought of him>.

restraint of trade. An agreement between or combination of businesses that eliminates competition, creates a monopoly, artificially raises prices, or otherwise adversely affects the free market; restraints of trade are usu. illegal, but may be declared reasonable if they are in the best interests of both the parties and the public. See PER SE RULE; RULE OF REASON.

horizontal restraint. In antitrust law, a restraint imposed by agreement between competitors.

vertical restraint. In antitrust law, a restraint imposed by agreement between firms at different levels of distribution (as between manufacturer and retailer).

restraint on alienation. 1. A restriction, usu. in a deed of conveyance, on a grantee's ability to sell or transfer real property; restraints on alienation are generally unenforceable as against public policy favoring the free alienability of land. —Also termed *unreasonable restraint on alienation.* **2.** A trust provision that prohibits or penalizes alienation of the trust corpus.

restricted security. See SECURITY.

restricted stock. See *restricted security* under SECURITY.

restrictive covenant. See COVENANT (4).

restrictive indorsement. See INDORSEMENT.

resulting power. See POWER.

resulting trust. See TRUST.

resulting use. See USE (4).

retail, *n.* The sale of goods or commodities to ultimate consumers, as opposed to the sale for further distribution or processing. —**retail,** *vb.*— **retail,** *adj.* Cf. WHOLESALE.

retail installment contract. See CONTRACT.

retainage (ri-**tayn**-ij). A percentage of what a landowner pays a contractor, withheld until the construction has been satisfactorily completed and all mechanic's liens are released or have expired.

retained earnings. See EARNINGS.

retainer, *n.* **1.** A client's authorization for a lawyer to act in a case <the attorney must obtain a retainer before filing the motion>. **2.** A fee paid to a lawyer to secure legal representation <he requires a $100,000 retainer>. —**retain,** *vb.*

general retainer. A retainer for a specific length of time rather than for a specific project.

special retainer. A retainer for a specific case or project.

retaining lien. See *attorney's lien* under LIEN.

retaliatory eviction. See EVICTION.

retaliatory law. A state law restraining another state's businesses—such as by levying taxes—in response to similar restraints imposed by the second state on the first state's businesses.

retaliatory tariff. See TARIFF.

retired stock. See *treasury stock* under STOCK.

retirement, *n.* **1.** Voluntary termination of one's own employment or career, esp. upon reaching a certain age <she travelled around the world after her retirement>. **2.** Withdrawal from action or for privacy <Janie's retirement to her house by the lake>. **3.** Withdrawal from circulation; payment of a debt <retirement of a series of bonds>. See REDEMPTION (3). —**retire,** *vb.*

retirement-income insurance. See INSURANCE.

retirement plan. A benefit plan—such as a pension plan or Keogh plan—provided by an employer (or a self-employed person) for an employee's retirement.

retorsion (ri-**tor**-shən). In international law, retaliation in kind for unfair or discourteous acts, such as high tariffs or discriminatory duties, and even such serious actions as detaining vessels and blockading commercial trade. —Also spelled *retortion.*

retraction, *n.* **1.** The act of taking or drawing back <retraction of anticipatory repudiation before breach of contract>. **2.** The act of recanting; a statement in recantation <retraction of a defamatory remark>. **3.** In wills and estates, a withdrawal of a renunciation <because of her retraction, she took property under her uncle's will>. See RENUNCIATION (3). —**retract,** *vb.*

retraxit (ri-**trak**-sit). At common law, a plaintiff's voluntary abandonment of a lawsuit and a cause of action; in modern practice, retraxit is called *voluntary dismissal* or *dismissal with prejudice.* See *judgment in retraxit* under JUDGMENT.

retreat rule. The criminal-law doctrine holding that the victim of a murderous assault must choose a safe retreat instead of resorting to deadly force in self-defense, unless (1) the victim is in his or her own home or place of business (the so-called *castle doctrine*), or (2) the assailant is a person whom the victim is trying to arrest; this is the minority rule among American jurisdictions. Cf. NO-RETREAT RULE.

retrial, *n.* A new trial of an action that has already been tried. **—retry,** *vb.* See TRIAL DE NOVO.

retribution, *n.* **1.** In criminal law, the theory that a criminal should be punished in proportion to the harm that he or she caused. Cf. DETERRENCE; REHABILITATION. **2.** Repayment; reward. **—retribute,** *vb.* **—retributive,** *adj.*

retroactive, *adj.* (Of a statute, ruling, etc.) extending in scope or effect to matters that have occurred in the past. —Also termed *retrospective*. Cf. PROSPECTIVE (1).

return, *n.* **1.** A court officer's bringing back of an instrument to the court that issued it <a sheriff's return of citation>. **2.** A court officer's indorsement on an instrument brought back to the court, reporting what the officer did or found <a return of *nulla bona*>. See FALSE RETURN (1). **3.** TAX RETURN <file your return before April 15>. **4.** (*usu. pl.*) An official report of voting results <election returns>. **5.** Yield or profit <return on an investment>. See RATE OF RETURN. **—return,** *vb.*

return day. The date by which a court officer must make a return. See RETURN.

return of service. PROOF OF SERVICE.

reus (**ree**-əs). [Latin] In civil and canon law, a male defendant. Pl. **rei.**

revalidation. REPUBLICATION.

revaluation, *n.* The increase in the value of one currency in relation to another currency. **—revalue,** *vb.* Cf. DEVALUATION.

revaluation surplus. See SURPLUS.

revenue. Gross income or receipts from a given source.

marginal revenue. The amount of revenue earned from the sale of one additional unit.

revenue bill. See BILL (3).

revenue bond. See BOND (1).

Revenue Procedure. An official statement by the I.R.S. regarding the administration and procedures of the tax laws. —Abbr. Rev. Proc.

Revenue Ruling. An official interpretation by the I.R.S. of the proper application of the tax law to a specific transaction; Revenue Rulings carry some authoritative weight and may be relied on by the taxpayer. —Abbr. Rev. Rul.

reversal, *n.* An appellate court's overturning of a lower court's decision. **—reverse,** *vb.*

reverse annuity mortgage. See MORTGAGE.

reverse contingent fee. See CONTINGENT FEE.

reverse discrimination. See DISCRIMINATION.

reverse doctrine of equivalents. See DOCTRINE OF EQUIVALENTS.

reverse FOIA suit. A lawsuit by the owner of a trade secret to prevent an agency from releasing that secret to the general public. See FREEDOM OF INFORMATION ACT.

reverse stock split. See STOCK SPLIT.

reverse subsidiary merger. See *reverse triangular merger* under MERGER.

reverse triangular merger. See MERGER.

reversible error. See ERROR.

reversion, *n*. A future interest in land arising by operation of law whenever an estate owner grants to another a particular estate, such as a life estate or a term of years, but does not dispose of the entire interest; a reversion occurs automatically upon termination of the prior estate, such as when a life tenant dies. — Also termed *reversionary estate*; *estate in reversion*. —**revert,** *vb*.—**reversionary,** *adj*. Cf. POSSIBILITY OF REVERTER; REMAINDER.

reversioner. One who possesses the reversion to an estate; the grantor or heir in reversion.

reverter. POSSIBILITY OF REVERTER.

review, *n*. Consideration, inspection, or re-examination of a subject or thing. —**review,** *vb*.

appellate review. Examination of a lower court's decision by a higher court, which can affirm, reverse, or modify the decision.

discretionary review. The form of appellate review that is not a matter of right but that occurs only at the judgment of the appellate courts. See CERTIORARI.

judicial review. See JUDICIAL REVIEW.

reviewable issue. See *appealable decision* under DECISION.

revised statutes. A collection of existing statutes that have been reorganized and reenacted as a whole. — Abbr. Rev. Stat.; R.S. See CODE (1).

revival, *n*. **1.** Restoration to current use or operation, esp., the act of restoring the validity or legal force of an expired contract or dormant judgment. —Also termed (as to dormant judgments) *revival of judgment*. Cf. RENEWAL. **2.** In wills and estates, reestablishing the validity of a revoked will by revoking the will that invalidated the original will. Cf. REPUBLICATION. —**revive,** *vb*.

revival statute. See STATUTE.

revivor. A proceeding to revive an action ended because of the death of one of the parties or other circumstance.

revocable trust. See TRUST.

revocation (rev-ə-**kay**-shən), *n*. **1.** An annulment, cancellation, or reversal, usu. of an act or power. **2.** In contract law, withdrawal of an offer by the offeror. **3.** In wills and estates, invalidation of a will by the testator, either by destroying the will or executing a new one. —**revoke,** *vb*.—**revocable** (rev-ə-kə-bəl), *adj*.

revolution. An overthrow of a government, usu. resulting in fundamental political change; a successful rebellion.

revolver loan. See LOAN.

revolving charge account. See *revolving credit* under CREDIT.

revolving credit. See CREDIT.

revolving fund. See FUND.

Rev. Proc. *abbr.* REVENUE PROCE-DURE.

Rev. Rul. *abbr.* REVENUE RULING.

Rev. Stat. *abbr.* REVISED STAT-UTES.

reward, *n.* Something of value, usu. money, given in return for some service or achievement, such as recovering property or providing information that leads to the capture of a criminal. **—reward,** *vb.*

Rex. [Latin] King. —Abbr. R.

rhadamanthine (rad-ə-**man**-thən), *adj.* (Of a judge) rigorous and inflexible <the judge's rhadamanthine interpretation of procedural requirements makes it essential to study the local rules before appearing in his court>.

RICO (**ree**-koh). *abbr.* RACKETEER INFLUENCED AND CORRUPT ORGA-NIZATIONS ACT.

rider. An attachment to some document, such as a legislative bill or an insurance policy, that describes an amendment to that document.

rigging the market. The practice of artificially inflating stock prices, by a series of bids, so that the demand for those stocks appears to be high and investors will therefore be enticed into buying the stocks. See MANIPU-LATION.

right, *n.* An interest or expectation guaranteed by law; for every right that a person has, somebody else has a corresponding duty.

acquired right. A right that a person does not naturally enjoy, but that is instead procured, such as the right to own property.

civil right. See CIVIL RIGHT.

fundamental right. See FUNDAMEN-TAL RIGHT.

inalienable right. A right that cannot be transferred or surrendered, esp. a natural right such as the right to property. —Also termed *inherent right.*

natural right. A right that is conceived as part of natural law and that is therefore thought to exist independently of rights created by government or society, such as the right to life, liberty, and property. See NATURAL LAW.

political right. The right to participate in the establishment or administration of government, such as the right to vote or the right to hold public office. —Also termed *political liberty.*

right against self-incrimination. A criminal defendant's or a witness's constitutional right—under the Fifth Amendment, but waivable under specific conditions—guaranteeing that a person cannot be compelled by the government to testify if the testimony might result in that person being criminally punished; although this right is most often asserted during criminal prosecutions, a person can also "plead the Fifth" in civil, legislative, administrative, and grand-jury proceedings. —Also termed *privilege against self-incrimination; right to remain silent.* See SELF-INCRIMINA-TION.

right-and-wrong test. MCNAGHT-EN RULES.

rightful, *adj.* **1.** (Of an action) equitable; fair <a rightful dispossession>. **2.** (Of a person) legitimately entitled to a position <a rightful heir>. **3.** (Of an office or piece of property) that one is entitled to <her rightful inheritance>.

right of action. 1. The right to bring a specific case to court. **2.** A right that can be enforced by legal action; a chose in action. Cf. CAUSE OF ACTION.

right of assembly. The constitutional right—guaranteed by the First Amendment—of the people to gather peacefully for public expression of political ideas and grievances. —Also termed *freedom of assembly.* Cf. FREEDOM OF ASSOCIATION; *unlawful assembly* under ASSEMBLY.

right of common. PROFIT A PRENDRE.

right of contribution. CONTRIBUTION (1).

right of dissent and appraisal. APPRAISAL REMEDY.

right of election. In wills and estates, a spouse's statutory right to choose, upon the other spouse's death, either the share under the deceased spouse's will or a share of the estate as defined in the probate statute, which usu. amounts to what the spouse would have received if the deceased spouse had died intestate. —Also termed *widow's election.* See ELECTION (3).

right of entry. POWER OF TERMINATION.

right of entry for breach of condition. POWER OF TERMINATION.

right of entry for condition broken. POWER OF TERMINATION.

right of first refusal. A potential buyer's contractual right to meet the terms of a third party's offer if the seller intends to accept that offer; for example, if Beth has a right of first refusal on the purchase of Sam's house, and if Sam intends to accept Terry's offer to buy the house for $300,000, Beth can match this offer and prevent Terry from buying it. Cf. RIGHT OF PREEMPTION.

right of preemption. A potential buyer's contractual right to have the first opportunity to buy, at a specified price, if the seller chooses to sell; for example, if Beth has a right of preemption on Sam's house for 5 years at $100,000, Sam can either keep the house for 5 years (in which case Beth's right expires) or, if he wishes to sell during those 5 years, offer the house to Beth who can either buy it for $100,000 or refuse to buy, but if she refuses, Sam can sell to someone else. —Also termed *first option to buy.* Cf. RIGHT OF FIRST REFUSAL.

right of privacy. 1. The right to personal autonomy; the U.S. Constitution does not explicitly provide for a right of privacy, but the Supreme Court has repeatedly ruled that this right is implied in the "zones of privacy" created by specific constitutional guarantees. **2.** The right of a person and his or her property to be free from unwarranted public scrutiny or exposure. —Also termed *right to privacy.* Cf. INVASION OF PRIVACY.

right of publicity. The right to the commercial value of a person's identity, including the person's name, likeness, voice, or other indicators of identity.

right of redemption. See *equity of redemption* under REDEMPTION.

right of re-entry. POWER OF TERMINATION.

right of search. In international law, the right to stop and visit and overhaul vessels on the high seas in order to discover whether they or the goods they carry are liable to capture; this right carries with it no right to destroy without full examination, unless those on a given vessel actively resist.

right of survivorship. A joint tenant's right to succeed to the whole estate upon the death of the other joint tenant. See SURVIVORSHIP; *joint tenancy* under TENANCY.

right of visitation. VISITATION RIGHT.

right of way. 1. A person's legal right, established by usage or by contract, to pass through grounds or property owned by another. Cf. EASEMENT. **2.** The right to build and operate a railway line or a highway on land belonging to another, or the land so used. **3.** The right to take precedence in traffic.

rights-consciousness. See CLAIMS-CONSCIOUSNESS.

rights offering. An issue of stock-purchase rights allowing shareholders to buy newly issued stock at a fixed price, usu. below market value, and in proportion to the number of shares they already own. —Also termed *privileged subscription*. Cf. PREEMPTIVE RIGHT.

right to bear arms. The constitutional right of persons to own firearms; the right is qualified by the Second Amendment as necessary for securing freedom through a well-regulated militia.

right-to-convey covenant. See *covenant of seisin* under COVENANT (4).

right to counsel. A criminal defendant's constitutional right, guaranteed by the Sixth Amendment, to representation by a court-appointed lawyer if the defendant cannot afford to hire one. —Also termed *access to counsel*. See ASSISTANCE OF COUNSEL.

right to die. The right of a terminally ill person to refuse life-sustaining treatment. —Also termed *right to refuse treatment*. See ADVANCE DIRECTIVE.

right to petition. The constitutional right—guaranteed by the First Amendment—of the people to make formal requests to the government, such as by lobbying or writing letters to public officials. —Also termed *freedom of petition*.

right to privacy. RIGHT OF PRIVACY.

right to refuse treatment. RIGHT TO DIE.

right to remain silent. RIGHT AGAINST SELF-INCRIMINATION.

right to travel. A person's constitutional right—guaranteed by the Privileges and Immunities Clause—to travel freely between states.

right-to-work law. A state law that prevents labor-management agreements requiring a person to join a union as a condition of employment. See OPEN SHOP.

rigor mortis (rig-ər-**mor**-dəs). The temporary stiffening of a body's joints and muscles after death; the onset of rigor mortis can vary from 15 minutes to several hours after death, depending on the body's condition and on atmospheric factors.

riot, *n.* An unlawful assembly that has begun to fulfill its common purpose of breaching the peace and terrorizing the public; some states require participation by three or more persons. —**riot,** *vb.* Cf. *unlawful assembly* under ASSEMBLY.

riparian (ri-**pair**-ee-ən), *n.* Of or relating to the bank of a river or stream <a landowner's riparian rights to the use of the water>. Cf. LITTORAL.

riparian-rights doctrine. The rule that owners of land bordering on a waterway have equal rights to use the water passing through or by their property. Cf. PRIOR-APPROPRIATION DOCTRINE.

ripeness, *n.* **1.** The circumstance existing when a case has reached, but has not passed, the point when the facts have developed sufficiently to permit an intelligent and useful decision to be made. **2.** The requirement that this circumstance must exist before a court will decide a controversy. —**ripen,** *vb.*—**ripe,** *adj.* See JUSTICIABILITY. Cf. MOOTNESS DOCTRINE; PREMATURITY (1).

rising of court. 1. A court's final adjournment of a term. **2.** A recess or temporary break in court's business, such as at the end of the day.

risk, *n.* **1.** The hazard of property loss covered by an insurance contract, or the degree of such a hazard. **2.** A person or thing that an insurer considers a hazard.

assigned risk. One who is a poor risk for insurance but whom an insurance company is forced to insure because of state law; for example, an accident-prone driver is an assigned risk in a state with a compulsory motor-vehicle insurance statute.

3. A known danger to which a person assents, thus foreclosing recovery for injuries suffered. See ASSUMPTION OF THE RISK. —**risk,** *vb.*

risk arbitrage. See ARBITRAGE.

risk-averse. (Of a person) tending to avoid speculating and taking chances.

risk capital. See CAPITAL.

risk of nonpersuasion. BURDEN OF PERSUASION.

robbery, *n.* The illegal taking of property from the person of another, or in the person's presence, by violence or intimidation; aggravated larceny. —**rob,** *vb.* See LARCENY; THEFT. Cf. BURGLARY.

aggravated robbery. Robbery committed by a person who either carries a dangerous weapon—often called *armed robbery*—or inflicts bodily harm on someone during the robbery.

armed robbery. Robbery committed by a carrying a dangerous weapon, regardless of whether the weapon is revealed or used; most states punish armed robbery as an aggravated form of robbery rather than as a separate crime.

Robinson-Patman Act. A federal statute (specifically, an amendment to the Clayton Act) prohibiting price discrimination that hinders competition or tends to create a monopoly. 15 U.S.C. § 13. See ANTITRUST LAW; CLAYTON ACT.

rogatory letter (**roh**-gə-tor-ee). LETTER OF REQUEST.

roll, *n.* **1.** A record of a court's or public office's proceedings. **2.** A list of the persons and property subject to a tax. —Also termed (in sense 2) *tax roll.*

rolling over, *n.* **1.** The extending or renewing of a short-term loan for another term. **2.** The transfer of funds, esp. retirement-plan funds, from one type of investment to another. —**roll over,** *vb.*

Roman law. 1. CIVIL LAW (1). **2.** CIVIL LAW (2).

root of title. The recorded land transaction, usu. at least 40 years old, that is used to begin a title search. See CHAIN OF TITLE; TITLE SEARCH.

round lot. See LOT (3).

royalty. 1. A payment made to an author or inventor for each copy of a work or article sold under a copyright or patent. **2.** A share of the product or profit from real property, reserved by the grantor of a mineral lease, in exchange for the lessee's right to mine or drill on the land. —Also termed (in sense 2) *override.*

overriding royalty. A royalty retained by a mineral lessee when the property is subleased.

shut-in royalty. A payment made by an oil-and-gas lessee to the lessor to keep the lease in force when a well capable of producing is not utilized because there is no market for the oil or gas; generally, without such a payment, the lease will terminate at the end of the pri-

mary term unless actual production has begun.

R.S. *abbr.* REVISED STATUTES.

RTC. *abbr.* RESOLUTION TRUST CORPORATION.

rubber check. See *bad check* under CHECK.

rubber-stamp seal. See NOTARY SEAL.

rubric (**roo**-brik). **1.** The title of a statute or code <the rubric of the relevant statute is the Civil Rights Act of 1964>. **2.** A category or designation <assignment of rights falls under the rubric of contract law>. **3.** An authoritative rule, esp. for conducting a public worship service <the rubric dictates whether the audience should stand or kneel>. **4.** An introductory or explanatory note; a preface <a well-known scholar wrote the rubric to the book's fourth edition>. **5.** An established rule, custom, or law <what is the rubric in the Northern District of Texas regarding appearance at docket call? >.

rule, *n.* **1.** An established and authoritative standard or principle <rule of thumb>. **2.** A regulation governing a court's or an agency's internal procedures <rule of civil procedure>.

rule, *vb.* **1.** To command or require; to exert control <the dictator ruled the country>. **2.** To decide a legal point <the court ruled on the issue of admissibility>.

rule, the. An evidentiary and procedural rule by which all witnesses are excluded from the courtroom while another witness is testifying <invok-

ing "the rule">; the rule is used chiefly in the American South and Southwest.

Rule 10b-5. In securities law, the rule prohibiting false statements of material fact or material omissions in connection with the buying or selling of securities. —Also termed *antifraud rule*.

Rule 11. 1. In federal practice, the procedural rule requiring the attorney of record or the party (if not represented by an attorney) to sign all pleadings, motions, and other papers filed with the court and—by this signing—to represent that the paper is filed in good faith after an inquiry that is reasonable under the circumstances; this rule provides for the imposition of sanctions, upon a party's or the court's own motion, if an attorney or party violates the conditions stated in the rule. Fed. R. Civ. P. 11. **2.** In Texas practice, the procedural rule requiring agreements between attorneys or parties concerning a pending suit to be in writing, signed, and filed in the court's record or made on the record in open court. Tex. R. Civ. P. 11.

rule absolute. See *decree absolute* under DECREE.

rule against accumulations. See ACCUMULATIONS, RULE AGAINST.

rule against perpetuities. In property law, the rule prohibiting a grant of an estate unless the interest must vest, if at all, no later than 21 years after the death of some person alive when the interest is created. —Sometimes written *Rule Against Perpetuities*.

rule in Heydon's case. MISCHIEF RULE.

Rule in Shelley's Case. In property law, the rule that if—in a single grant—a freehold estate is given to a person and a remainder is given to the person's heirs, the remainder belongs to the named person and not the heirs, so that the person is held to have a fee simple absolute; the rule, which dates from the 14th century but draws its name from the famous 16th-century case, has been abolished in most states. *Wolfe v. Shelley*, 76 Eng.Rep. 206 (K.B. 1581).

Rule in Wild's Case. In property law, the rule construing a grant to "A and A's children" as a fee tail if A's children do not exist at the effective date of the instrument, and as a joint tenancy if A's children do exist at the effective date; the rule has been abolished along with the fee tail in most states.

rulemaking, *n.* The process used by an administrative agency to formulate, amend, or repeal a rule or regulation. —Also termed *administrative rulemaking.* —**rulemaking,** *adj.*

rule nisi. See *decree nisi* under DECREE.

rule of 72. A method for determining how many years it takes to double money invested at a compound interest rate; for example, at a compound rate of 6 percent, it takes 12 years (72 divided by 6) for principal to double.

rule of 78. A method for computing the amount of interest that a borrower saves by paying off a loan early, when the interest payments are higher at the beginning of the loan period; for example, to determine how much interest is saved by prepaying a 12-month loan after 6 months, divide the sum of the digits for the remaining six payments (21) by the sum of the digits for all twelve payments (78) and multiply that percentage by the total interest. —Also termed *rule of the sum of the digits*.

rule of capture. In property law, the principle that migratory substances (such as minerals) or wild animals belong to the person who captures them, regardless of whether they were originally on another person's land. —Also termed *law of capture*.

rule of four. The convention that for certiorari to be granted by the U.S. Supreme Court, four justices must vote in favor of the grant. See CERTIORARI.

rule of law. 1. A substantive legal principle. **2.** The supremacy of regular as opposed to arbitrary power; the wielders of that regular power in a society. **3.** The doctrine that every person is subject to the ordinary law of the area. **4.** The doctrine that general constitutional principles are the result of judicial decisions determining the rights of private individuals in the courts.

rule of lenity (le-nə-tee). The judicial doctrine holding that a court, in construing an ambiguous criminal statute that sets out multiple or inconsistent punishments, should resolve the ambiguity in favor of the more lenient sentence. —Also termed *lenity rule*.

rule of marshaling assets. An equitable doctrine that requires a senior creditor, having two or more funds to satisfy its debt, to first dispose of the fund not available to a junior creditor; it prevents the inequity that would result if the senior creditor could choose to satisfy its debt out of the only fund available to the junior creditor and thereby exclude the junior creditor from any satisfaction. —Also termed *rule of marshaling securities*; *rule of marshaling remedies*.

rule of marshaling liens. INVERSE-ORDER-OF-ALIENATION DOCTRINE.

rule of optional completeness. The rule of evidence providing that when a party uses deposition testimony in trial, the opposing party may require that more of the passage be read to establish the full context.

rule of reason. In antitrust law, the judicial doctrine holding that a trade practice violates the Sherman Act only if the practice is an unreasonable restraint of trade, based on economic factors. See SHERMAN ANTITRUST ACT. Cf. PER SE RULE.

rule of the last antecedent. An interpretative principle by which a court determines that qualifying words or phrases modify the words or phrases immediately preceding them and not words or phrases more remote, unless the extension is necessary from the context or the spirit of the entire writing; for example, an application of this rule might mean that, in the phrase *Texas courts, New Mexico courts, and New York courts in the federal system*, the words *in the federal system* might be held to modify only *New York courts* and not *Texas courts* or *New Mexico courts*.

rule of the sum of the digits. RULE OF 78.

Rules of Decision Act. A federal statute (28 U.S.C. § 1652) providing that a federal court, when exercising diversity jurisdiction, must apply the substantive law of the state in which the court sits. See *diversity jurisdiction* under JURISDICTION.

ruling, *n.* The outcome of a court's decision either on some point of law or on the case as a whole. —**rule,** *vb.* Cf. JUDGMENT; OPINION (1).

ruling case. LEADING CASE (3).

run, *vb.* **1.** To expire after a prescribed time period <the statute of limitations had run, so the plaintiff's lawsuit was barred>. **2.** To accompany a conveyance or assignment of (land) <the covenant runs with the land>. **3.** To apply <the injunction runs against only one of the parties in the dispute>.

runner. **1.** A law-office employee who delivers papers between offices and files papers in court. **2.** One who solicits personal-injury cases for a lawyer.

running account. See ACCOUNT.

S

s. *abbr.* **1.** Statute. **2.** SECTION (1). **3.** (*usu. cap.*) Senate.

Sabbath law. BLUE LAW.

sabotage (**sab**-ə-tahzh), *n.* **1.** The intentional hindrance or destruction of national-defense premises, utilities, production, or materials. **2.** The malicious interference with an employer's normal operations, or destruction of its property, esp. during a labor dispute. —**sabotage,** *vb.*—**saboteur** (sab-ə-t[y]**oor**), *n.*

safe-berth clause. SAFE-PORT CLAUSE.

safe-conduct, *n.* A permission to travel given by a belligerent government to subjects of an enemy nation, or to the movables that they bring with them.

safe-deposit box. A lockbox stored in a bank's vault and used by a customer to secure valuables; it usu. takes two keys (one held by the bank and one held by the customer) to open the box. —Often shortened to *deposit box.* —Also termed *safety-deposit box.*

safe harbor. 1. Generally, an area or means of protection. **2.** A provision in a statute, rule, or regulation whereby a person who has made a good-faith attempt to comply is protected even if the attempt to comply has failed.

safe-port clause. An agreement by which the charterer of a shipping vessel assumes responsibility for any harm done to the ship as a result of its entering or berthing at an unsafe port. —Also termed *safe-berth clause.*

safety-deposit box. SAFE-DEPOSIT BOX.

said, *adj.* AFORESAID.

sailor's will. See *soldier's will* under WILL.

salable (**say**-lə-bəl), *adj.* Fit for sale in the usual course of trade at the usual selling price. —**salability** (say-lə-**bil**-ə-tee), *n.*

sale, *n.* The transfer of property for a price; the agreement by which such a transfer takes place.

bootstrap sale. **a.** A sale in which the purchase price is paid from earnings and profits of the property sold; esp., a leveraged buyout. See BUYOUT. **b.** A seller's tax-saving conversion of a business's ordinary income into a capital gain from the sale of corporate stock.

bulk sale. BULK TRANSFER.

conditional sale. **a.** A sale in which the buyer gains immediate possession but the seller retains title until the buyer performs a condition, esp. payment of the full purchase price. See *conditional sales contract* under CONTRACT. **b.** A sale accompanied by an agreement to resell upon specified terms.

consignment sale. A sale of an owner's property (such as clothing or furniture) by a third party entrusted to make the sale.

distress sale. **a.** A form of liquidation in which the seller receives less for the goods than what would be received under normal sales conditions; esp., a going-out-of-business sale. **b.** A foreclosure or tax sale.

execution sale. A forced sale of a debtor's property by a government official carrying out a writ of execution. —Also termed *forced sale*; *judgment sale*; *sheriff's sale*. See EXECUTION.

forced sale. **a.** See *execution sale*. **b.** A hurried sale by a debtor because of financial hardship or a creditor's action.

foreclosure sale. The sale of mortgaged property authorized by court decree or a power-of-sale clause, the proceeds of which are used to satisfy the debt. See *deficiency judgment* under JUDGMENT.

installment sale. A conditional sale in which the buyer makes a down payment followed by periodic payments and the seller retains the title until all payments are received. —Also termed *installment plan*.

isolated sale. An infrequent or one-time sale that does not carry an implied warranty of merchantability.

judicial sale. A sale conducted under the authority of a judgment or an order, or under the supervision of a court, such as an execution sale.

lumping sale. A court-ordered sale in which several distinct pieces of property are sold together for a single sum.

memorandum sale. A conditional sale in which the buyer takes possession but does not accept title until he or she approves the property.

sale and leaseback. LEASEBACK.

sale as is. A sale in which the buyer must accept the property for better or for worse unless the seller has misrepresented its quality. —Also termed *sale with all faults*.

sale in gross. A sale by lot with no warranty as to quantity or size.

sale on approval. A sale whose completion hinges on the buyer's satisfaction, regardless of whether the goods conform to the contract. U.C.C. § 2-326(1)(a). —Also termed *approval sale*.

sale or return. A sale in which the buyer may return the goods to the seller, regardless of whether they conform to the contract, if the goods were delivered primarily for resale. U.C.C. § 2-326(1)(b). —Also termed *sale and return*.

sale with right of redemption. A sale in which the seller reserves the right to retake the goods by refunding the purchase price.

short sale. In securities law, a sale of a security that the seller must borrow in order to deliver; such a sale is usu. made when the seller expects the security's value to decline.

short sale against the box. In securities law, a short sale of a security by a seller who owns enough shares of that security to cover the borrowed shares; because delivery may be made with either the owned or the borrowed shares, it is less risky than an ordinary short sale.

simulated sale. A contrived sale lacking consideration and intended to put property beyond the reach of creditors.

wash sale. The simultaneous, or nearly simultaneous, selling and buying of the same asset, esp. stock, by the same person to create the impression of market activity. See MANIPULATION.

sale note. See NOTE.

sale-of-business doctrine. The outmoded rule holding that the transfer of stock incident to the sale of a business does not constitute a transfer of securities; this doctrine was rejected by the U.S. Supreme Court in *Landreth Timber Co. v. Landreth,* 471 U.S. 681 (1985), and its companion case, *Gould v. Ruefenacht,* 471 U.S. 701 (1985).

sales load. LOAD.

sales puffery. PUFFING (1).

sales tax. See TAX.

salting, *n. Slang.* In labor law, a union tactic that involves a paid union employee going to work for a targeted non-union employer with the intention of organizing the workforce; the union agent (known as a *salt*) is considered an employee of the non-union company and is protected by the National Labor Relations Act.

salvage, *n.* **1.** The rescue of property. **2.** The property saved or remaining after a fire or other loss, sometimes retained by an insurance company that has compensated the owner for the loss. **3.** A compensation allowed, under certain conditions, to people who help save a ship or its cargo. —**salvage,** *vb.*

salvage loss. See LOSS.

salvage value. The value of an asset after it has become useless to the owner; this value is used, under some depreciation methods, to determine the allowable tax deduction for depreciation.

same, *pron. Jargon.* It or them <two days after receiving the goods, Mr. Siviglio returned same>.

same-evidence test. In criminal procedure, a test of whether the facts alleged in a given case are essentially identical to those alleged in a previous case; if they are the same, the Fifth Amendment's prohibition against double jeopardy will bar the subsequent action.

same offense. See OFFENSE.

sanction, *n.* **1.** A recognized authority's official approval or confirmation of an action <the committee gave sanction to Leonard's proposal>. **2.** An enforcement mechanism used to ensure compliance with the law, international agreements, or court rules and orders by either imposing a penalty for violations or offering a reward for observances; the penalty imposed or reward offered under such a mechanism <Rule 11 sanctions>.

sanction, *vb.* **1.** To approve, authorize, or support <the court will sanction the trust disposition if it is not against public policy>. **2.** To punish (a person) by imposing a penalty, such as a fine; to deter (conduct) by punishing the person who engages in it <the court sanctioned the attorney for violating the gag order>.

sanctions tort. A means of recovery for another party's discovery abuse, whereby the judge orders the abusive party to pay the injured party a fine for the discovery violations; this is not a tort in the traditional sense, but rather a form of punishment that results in monetary gain for the injured party.

S & L. SAVINGS-AND-LOAN ASSOCIATION.

sandpapering. *Jargon.* A lawyer's general preparation of a witness before trial. Cf. HORSESHEDDING.

sandwich lease. See LEASE.

sanitary code. A set of ordinances regulating the food and healthcare industries.

sanity hearing. 1. An inquiry into the mental competency of a person to stand trial. **2.** A proceeding to determine whether a person should be institutionalized.

sans recours. WITHOUT RECOURSE.

satellite litigation. 1. One or more lawsuits related to a major piece of litigation that is being conducted in another court. <the satellite litigation in state court prevented the federal judge from ruling on the issue>. **2.** Peripheral skirmishes involved in the prosecution of a lawsuit <the plaintiffs called the sanctions satellite litigation, drummed up by the defendants to deflect attention from the main issues in the case>.

satisfaction, *n.* **1.** The fulfillment of an obligation; esp., the payment in full of a debt. **2.** SATISFACTION PIECE. —**satisfy,** *vb.* See ACCORD AND SATISFACTION.

satisfaction piece. A written statement of satisfaction between the parties, stating that one party has been satisfied and the other has discharged its obligation. —Also termed *certificate of discharge*; *satisfaction*.

Saturday-night special. 1. A handgun that is easily obtained and con-

cealed. **2.** In corporate law, a tender offer held open for only one week in order to capitalize on the shareholders' panic and haste; now effectively prohibited by section 14(e) of the Williams Act. 15 U.S.C. § 78n(e).

save harmless. HOLD HARMLESS.

save-harmless agreement. HOLD-HARMLESS AGREEMENT.

saving clause. 1. A statutory provision exempting from coverage something that would otherwise be included; generally used in a repealing act to preserve rights and claims that would otherwise be lost. **2.** SAVING-TO-SUITORS CLAUSE. **3.** SEVERABILITY CLAUSE.

savings-account trust. See *Totten trust* under TRUST.

savings-and-loan association. A financial institution—often organized and chartered like a bank—that is primarily designed to make home-mortgage loans but that also usu. maintains checking accounts and provides other banking services. — Often shortened to *S & L.* —Also termed *thrift institution*; *thrift.* Cf. BUILDING-AND-LOAN ASSOCIATION.

savings bank. See BANK.

savings bond. See BOND (1).

savings note. See NOTE.

saving-to-suitors clause. In maritime law, a federal statutory provision that allows a party to bring suit in either state or federal court, but requires both courts to apply federal substantive law. —Also termed *saving clause*.

S.B. *abbr.* SENATE BILL.

SBA. *abbr.* SMALL BUSINESS ADMINISTRATION.

sc. *abbr.* SCILICET.

S.C. *abbr.* **1.** SUPREME COURT. **2.** Same case; in former practice, if put between two citations, it indicated that the same case is reported in both places.

scab. A person who works under conditions contrary to the union contract, esp. a worker who crosses a union picket line to replace a union worker during a strike. —Also termed *strikebreaker*.

scale order. See ORDER (4).

scalping, *n.* **1.** The purchase of a security by an investment adviser before recommending that a customer buy the same security; this practice is usu. considered unethical because the customer's purchase will increase the security's price, thereby enabling the investment adviser to sell at a profit. **2.** The excessive markup or markdown on a transaction by a market-maker; this action violates NASD guidelines. **3.** The practice of selling something (esp. tickets) at a price above face value. —**scalp,** *vb.*

scandalous matter. In pleading, a matter that is both grossly disgraceful (or defamatory) and irrelevant to the action or defense; a federal court—upon a party's or its own motion—can order a scandalous matter stricken from a pleading. Fed. R. Civ. P. 12(f). Cf. IMPERTINENT MATTER.

scarlet-letter punishment. A criminal sanction that stigmatizes or shames the convicted offender <he was also assessed the scarlet-letter punishment of having a sign—"Convicted Child Molester Living Here"— posted in his front yard>. —Also termed *scarlet-letter sentence*; *shaming sentence*.

scènes à faire (senz-ah-**fair**). [French "scenes for action"] In copyright law, standard or general themes that are common to a wide variety of works and are therefore not copyrightable.

schedule, *n.* A written list or inventory; esp., a statement that is attached to a document and that gives a detailed showing of the matters referred to in the document <Schedule B to the title policy lists the encumbrances on the property>. —**schedule,** *vb.*—**scheduled,** *adj.*

scheduled injury. See INJURY.

scienter (see-**en**-tər *or* sI-), *n.* [Latin "knowingly"] **1.** The fact of an act's having been done knowingly, esp. as a ground for damages or criminal punishment. **2.** Prior knowledge or intention. **3.** Loosely, guilty knowledge; intent to defraud.

sci. fa. *abbr.* SCIRE FACIAS.

scil. *abbr.* SCILICET.

scilicet (**sil**-i-set *or* -sət). [Latin "to wit"] That is to say; namely. —Abbr. sc.; scil.

scintilla (sin-**til**-ə). A spark or trace <the standard is that there must be more than a scintilla of evidence>. Pl. **scintillas.**

scintilla-of-evidence rule. A common-law doctrine holding that if even the slightest amount of relevant and substantive evidence favors the nonmovant in a motion for summary judgment or for directed verdict, the motion cannot be granted and the factual issues must to go to the jury. —Also termed *scintilla rule*.

scire facias (sI-ree-**faysh**-[ee-]əs). A writ founded upon a matter of record and requiring the person against whom it is issued to appear and show cause why the record should not be annulled or vacated, or why a dormant judgment against that person should not be revived. —Abbr. sci. fa.

scofflaw. *Slang.* One who treats the law with contempt; esp., one who avoids various laws that are not easily enforced <some scofflaws carry mannequins in their cars in order to drive in the carpool lane>.

scope of employment. The reasonable and foreseeable activities that an employee engages in while carrying out the employer's business. See RESPONDEAT SUPERIOR. Cf. ZONE OF EMPLOYMENT.

scorched-earth defense. An antitakeover device by which a target corporation sells its most valuable assets or divisions, or otherwise destroys the character of the corporation, in order to defeat the bidder's tender offer. See CROWN JEWEL.

S corporation. See CORPORATION.

Scotch verdict. NOT PROVEN.

screening grand jury. See GRAND JURY.

scrip. 1. A document that entitles the holder to receive something of value. **2.** Paper money issued for temporary use.

scrip dividend. See DIVIDEND.

S.D. *abbr.* Southern District, in reference to U.S. judicial districts.

seal, *n.* **1.** An impression or sign that has legal consequence when applied to an instrument.

corporate seal. A seal adopted by a corporation for executing and authenticating its corporate and legal instruments.

public seal. A seal that is used to certify documents belonging to a public authority or government bureau.

2. A fastening that must be broken before access can be obtained. —**seal,** *vb.*—**sealed,** *adj.*

sealed bid. See BID.

sealed contract. See *contract under seal* under CONTRACT.

sealed verdict. See VERDICT.

seaman's will. See *soldier's will* under WILL.

search, *n.* The examination of persons or their property with the intention of finding evidence not in plain view; often, in constitutional law, a visual observation or invasive action that may infringe on a person's reasonable expectation of privacy. —**search,** *vb.*

border search. A search conducted by immigration or customs officials at the border of a country to detect and prevent illegal entries of people or things; such a search requires no warrant.

consent search. A search of a person who has consented to the search, making a warrant unnecessary.

inventory search. A complete search of an arrestee's person before being booked into jail; all possessions found are typically held in police custody.

search incident to arrest. A search of a detained suspect and his or her immediate surroundings to secure the safety of the arresting police officer.

unreasonable search. In constitutional law, a search made without legal authority. —Also termed *illegal search*.

search warrant. A judge's written order, on behalf of the state, authorizing an officer to search for and seize evidence at a specified address. See WARRANT (1).

anticipatory search warrant. A search warrant based on an affidavit showing probable cause that evidence of a certain crime (such as the delivery of illegal drugs) will be located at a specific place in the future.

blanket search warrant. **a.** A single search warrant that authorizes the search of more than one area. **b.** An unconstitutional warrant that authorizes the seizure of everything found at a given location, without specifying which items may be seized.

seasonable, *adj.* Within the time agreed upon; within a reasonable time <seasonable performance of the contract>.

seasonal employment. See EMPLOYMENT.

SEC. *abbr.* SECURITIES AND EXCHANGE COMMISSION.

Second Amendment. The constitutional amendment, ratified with the Bill of Rights in 1791, guaranteeing

the right to keep and bear arms; the Supreme Court has narrowly defined this right so as not to prevent the state and federal governments from enacting gun-control legislation.

secondary beneficiary. See *contingent beneficiary* under BENEFICIARY.

secondary boycott. See BOYCOTT.

secondary distribution. See DISTRIBUTION.

secondary evidence. See EVIDENCE.

secondary liability. See LIABILITY.

secondary market. See MARKET.

secondary offering. See OFFERING.

secondary picketing. See PICKETING.

secondary reserve ratio. See RESERVE RATIO.

secondary strike. See STRIKE.

second chair, *n.* A lawyer who helps the lead attorney in court, usu. by examining some of the witnesses, arguing some of the points of law, and handling parts of the voir dire, opening statement, and closing argument <the young associate was second chair for the fraud case>. —**second-chair,** *vb.*

second-degree murder. See MURDER.

secondhand evidence. HEARSAY.

second lien. See LIEN.

second-look doctrine. 1. WAIT-AND-SEE PRINCIPLE. **2.** An approach that courts use to monitor the continuing effectiveness or validity of an earlier order; for example, family courts may reconsider waivers of alimony, and federal courts may reconsider a law that Congress has passed a second time after the first such law was struck down as unconstitutional.

second mortgage. See MORTGAGE.

secretary. In a corporation, the person in charge of official correspondence and the keeping of records. — Also termed *clerk of the corporation*.

secretary of state. 1. (*usu. cap.*) The cabinet member who heads the State Department and directs foreign policy; the secretary of state is fourth in line of succession to the presidency after the Vice President, the Speaker of the House, and the President pro tempore of the Senate. **2.** A state government official who is responsible for the licensing and incorporation of businesses, the administration of elections, and other formal duties; the secretary of state is elected in some states and appointed in others.

secret partner. See *silent partner* under PARTNER.

Secret Service. A federal law-enforcement agency—organized as a division of the Treasury Department—primarily responsible for preventing counterfeiting and protecting the President and other public officials.

section. 1. A distinct part or division of a writing, esp. a legal instrument. —Abbr. § or s. **2.** In real-estate law, an area of 640 acres; traditionally, public lands in the U.S. were divided into 640-acre squares, each one called a "section."

secured bond. See BOND (1).

secured claim. See CLAIM (4).

secured creditor. See CREDITOR.

secured debt. See DEBT.

secured loan. See LOAN.

secured note. See NOTE.

secured party. See *secured creditor* under CREDITOR.

secured transaction. A business arrangement by which a buyer or borrower gives collateral to the seller or lender to guarantee payment of an obligation. See SECURITY AGREEMENT.

Securities Act of 1933. The federal securities act regulating the initial public offering of securities, with an emphasis on full disclosure. 15 U.S.C. §§ 77a et seq.

Securities and Exchange Commission. The presidentially appointed five-member board that regulates and oversees stock trading and enforces federal securities statutes; established by the Securities Exchange Act of 1934. —Abbr. SEC.

securities exchange. 1. A facility for the organized purchase and sale of securities, esp. stocks. **2.** A group of individuals and entities that are members of such a facility. —Often shortened to *exchange*.

regional securities exchange. A securities exchange that focuses on stocks and bonds of local interest, such as the Boston, Philadelphia, and Midwest stock exchanges.

Securities Exchange Act of 1934. The federal securities act regulating the public trading of securities; this legislation established the Securities and Exchange Commission. 15 U.S.C. §§ 78a et seq.

security, *n.* **1.** An instrument given to secure the performance of an obligation; the assurance that a creditor will be repaid (usu. with interest) any money or credit extended to a debtor. **2.** Collateral given or pledged to guarantee the fulfillment of an obligation. **3.** A person who is bound by some type of guaranty; SURETY. **4.** An instrument that evidences the holder's ownership rights in a firm (such as a stock), the holder's creditor relationship with a firm or government (such as a bond), or the holder's other ownership rights (such as an option). Cf. SHARE (2); STOCK (4).

adjustment security. A stock or bond that is issued during a corporate reorganization; the security holders' relative interests are readjusted during this process.

collateral security. A security, subordinate to and given in addition to a primary security, that is intended to guarantee the validity or convertibility of the primary security.

conversion security. The security into which a convertible security may be converted, usu. common stock.

convertible security. A security (usu. a bond or preferred stock) that may be exchanged by the owner for another security, esp. common stock from the same company, and usu. at a fixed price on a specified date.

debt security. A security representing funds borrowed by the corporation from the holder of the debt obligation; esp., a bond, note, or debenture. See BOND.

equity security. A security representing an ownership interest in the corporation, such as a share of stock, rather than a debt interest, such as a bond.

exempt security. A security that is not required to be registered under the provisions of the Securities Act of 1933 and is exempt from the margin requirements of the Securities Exchange Act of 1934.

government security. A security whose principal or interest is guaranteed by the government or its agents.

listed security. A security accepted for trading on a securities exchange; the issuing company must have met the SEC's registration requirements and complied with the rules of the particular exchange. —Also termed *listed stock.* See DELISTING.

long-term security. **a.** A new securities issue with an initial maturity of ten years or more. **b.** On a balance sheet, a security with a remaining maturity of one year or more.

marginable security. A security that can be bought on margin. See MARGIN.

margined security. A security that is bought on margin and that serves as collateral in a margin account. See MARGIN.

marketable security. A security that the holder can readily sell on a stock exchange or an over-the-counter market.

noncallable security. A security that cannot be redeemed, or bought back, at the issuer's option.

public security. A negotiable or transferable security that is evidence of government debt.

redeemable security. Any security, other than a short-term note, that, when presented to the issuer, entitles the holder to receive a share of the issuer's assets or the cash equivalent. —Also termed *callable security.*

registered security. **a.** A security with the owner's name printed on the face of the certificate; the issuer keeps a record of the current owners for purposes of sending checks, proxies, and the like. —Also termed (depending on the type of security) *registered stock*; *registered bond.* **b.** A security that was registered with the SEC at the time of its initial sale, or was subsequently sold publicly in accordance with SEC rules. —Also termed *registered stock.*

restricted security. A security that is not registered with the SEC and therefore may not be sold publicly; usu. such stock is acquired in a nonpublic transaction in which the buyer gives the seller a letter stating the buyer's intent to hold the stock as an investment rather than resell it. —Also termed *letter security*; *letter stock.*

short-term security. A bond or note that matures and is payable within a brief period (often one year).

treasury security. See *treasury stock* under STOCK.

unlisted security. An over-the-counter security that is not registered with a stock exchange. —Also termed *unlisted stock.*

voting security. See *voting stock* under STOCK.

when-issued security. A security that can be traded even though it has not yet been issued; any transactions do not become final until the security is issued.

zero-coupon security. A security (esp. a bond) that is issued at a large discount but that pays no interest.

security agreement. An agreement that creates or provides for an interest in specified real or personal property to guarantee the performance of an obligation.

security for costs. Money, property, or a bond given to a court by a plaintiff or an appellant to secure the payment of court costs if that party loses.

security interest. A property interest created by agreement or by operation of law to secure performance of an obligation (esp. repayment of a debt).

purchase-money security interest. A security interest that is created when a buyer uses the lender's money to make the purchase and immediately gives the lender security. U.C.C. § 9-107. —Abbr. PMSI. —Also termed *purchase-money interest.*

sedition, *n.* An agreement, communication, or other preliminary activity aimed at inciting treason or some lesser commotion against public authority. —**seditious,** *adj.* Cf. TREASON.

seditious libel. See LIBEL.

seed money. Start-up money for a business venture. —Also termed *front-end money.*

segregation, *n.* **1.** The act or process of separating. **2.** The unconstitutional policy of separating people on the basis of color, nationality, religion, or the like. —**segregate,** *vb.*— **segregative,** *adj.*

de facto segregation. Segregation that occurs without state authority, usu. on the basis of socioeconomic factors.

de jure segregation. Segregation that is sanctioned by law.

seise (seez), *vb.* To invest with seisin or establish as a holder in fee simple; to put in possession <in 1995, he became seised of half a section of farmland near Tulia>.

seisin (**seez**-[ə]n *or* **sIz**-), *n.* Possession of a freehold estate in land; ownership. —Also spelled *seizin.*

covenant of seisin. See COVENANT (4).

livery of seisin. See LIVERY OF SEISIN.

seisin in deed. Actual possession of a freehold estate in land, by oneself or by one's tenant or agent. —Also termed *seisin in fact; actual seisin.*

seisin in law. The right to immediate possession of a freehold estate in land, as when an heir inherits land but has not yet entered it.

seizure, *n.* The act or an instance of taking possession of a person or property by legal right or process; esp., in constitutional law, a confiscation or arrest that may interfere with a person's reasonable expectation of privacy. —**seize,** *vb.*

selective incorporation. See INCORPORATION.

Selective Service System. An executive agency charged with maintaining records of all persons eligible for military service. —Abbr. SSS.

self-authentication. See AUTHENTICATION.

self-crimination. SELF-INCRIMINATION.

self-dealing, *n.* The act or an instance of a fiduciary's using another's property for his or her own benefit. —**self-deal,** *vb.*

self-defense, *n.* **1.** The use of force to protect oneself, one's family, or one's property from a real or threatened attack; generally, a person is justified in using a reasonable amount of force in self-defense if he or she believes that the danger of bodily harm is imminent and that force is necessary to avoid this danger.

imperfect self-defense. The use of force by one who makes an honest but unreasonable mistake that force is necessary to repel an attack; in some jurisdictions, such a self-defender will be charged with a lesser offense than the one committed.

2. The right of a state to defend itself against a real or threatened attack. —**self-defender,** *n.*

self-employed retirement plan. KEOGH PLAN.

self-employment tax. See TAX.

self-executing, *adj.* Effective immediately without the need of any type of implementing action <the wills

had self-executing affidavits attached>.

self-help. An attempt to redress a perceived wrong outside the normal legal process.

self-help remedy. See *extrajudicial remedy* under REMEDY.

self-incrimination. An act or declaration by which a party explicitly or implicitly admits a personal connection with a crime. —Also termed *self-crimination; self-inculpation.*

compulsory self-incrimination. Any sort of physical or psychological coercion that makes a confession or admission to a crime involuntary, and that therefore violates the Fifth Amendment. See RIGHT AGAINST SELF-INCRIMINATION.

self-induced intoxication. See *voluntary intoxication* under INTOXICATION.

self-insurance. See INSURANCE.

self-killing. SUICIDE.

self-liquidating mortgage. See *amortized mortgage* under MORTGAGE.

self-proved will. See WILL.

self-proving affidavit. See AFFIDAVIT.

self-serving declaration. See DECLARATION (6).

seller's market. See MARKET.

selling agent. The real-estate broker's representative who sells the property, as opposed to the agent who lists the property for sale. Cf. LISTING AGENT.

senate. 1. The upper chamber of a bicameral legislature. **2.** (*cap.*) The upper house of the U.S. Congress, composed of 100 members—two from each state—who are elected to six-year terms.

Senate Bill. A legislative bill in the process of going through a senate before being enacted as a statute. — Abbr. S.B. See BILL (2).

senior counsel. See *lead counsel* under COUNSEL.

senior judge. See JUDGE.

senior lien. See LIEN.

senior mortgage. See MORTGAGE.

senior partner. See PARTNER.

sentence, *n.* The judgment that a court formally pronounces after finding a criminal defendant guilty; the punishment imposed on a criminal wrongdoer <he received a sentence of 10 years in prison>. —**sentence,** *vb.*

concurrent sentences. Sentences to be served at the same time as each other; for example, if a defendant receives concurrent sentences of 5 years and 15 years, the full amount of the term is 15 years.

conditional sentence. A sentence of confinement if the defendant fails to perform the conditions of probation.

consecutive sentences. Separate sentences that are to be served in sequence; for example, if a defendant receives consecutive sentences of 20 years and 5 years, the full amount of the term is 25 years. — Also termed *cumulative sentences.*

death sentence. A sentence that imposes the death penalty. See DEATH PENALTY.

determinate sentence. A sentence that is set by law, but that gives the judge some discretion to individualize punishment. —Also termed *definite sentence*; *fixed sentence*; *flat sentence.*

indeterminate sentence. **a.** A sentence of an unspecified duration, such as one for a term of 10 to 20 years. **b.** A maximum prison term that the parole board can reduce, through statutory authorization, after the inmate has served the minimum time required by law. —Also termed *indefinite sentence.*

life sentence. A sentence that puts the criminal in prison for life— though in some jurisdictions the prisoner may become eligible for release on good behavior, rehabilitation, or the like.

mandatory sentence. A sentence set by law with no discretion for the judge to individualize punishment. —Also termed *mandatory penalty*; *mandatory punishment.*

multiple sentences. Concurrent or consecutive sentences, if a defendant is found guilty of more than one offense.

noncustodial sentence. A criminal sentence (such as probation) not requiring prison time.

split sentence. A sentence in which part of the time is served in confinement—to expose the offender to the unpleasantness of prison— and the rest is served out on probation.

suspended sentence. A sentence that is withheld or postponed either immediately after conviction or during the term; the court may, in its discretion, reinstate the sentence if the defendant is arrested for another crime.

sentencing guidelines. A set of standards for determining the level of punishment that a convicted criminal should receive, based on the nature of the crime and the offender's criminal history; the federal government, as well as several states, has adopted sentencing guidelines in an effort to make judicial sentencing more consistent.

sentencing hearing. PRESENTENCE HEARING.

separability clause. SEVERABILITY CLAUSE.

separate action. See ACTION.

separate-but-equal doctrine. The now-defunct doctrine that blacks may be segregated if they are provided with equal opportunities and facilities in education, public transportation, and jobs; this rule was established in *Plessy v. Ferguson,* 163 U.S. 537 (1896), but overturned in *Brown v. Board of Educ.,* 347 U.S. 483 (1954).

separate property. Property that a spouse owned before marriage or acquired during marriage through an inheritance or by gift from a third party, or property acquired during marriage but after the spouses have entered into a separation agreement and begun living apart. Cf. COMMUNITY PROPERTY; *marital property* under PROPERTY.

separate return. See TAX RETURN.

separate-sovereigns rule. In criminal procedure, the principle that a person may be tried twice for the same offense—despite the Double Jeopardy Clause—if the prosecutions are conducted by separate sovereigns, such as by the federal government and a state government or by two different states. See DOUBLE JEOPARDY.

separation. **1.** An arrangement whereby a married couple lives apart from each other while remaining married, either by mutual consent or judicial decree; the act of carrying out such an arrangement. —Also termed *legal separation*; *judicial separation*. **2.** The status of a husband and wife having begun such an arrangement, or the judgment or contract that brought the arrangement about.

separation agreement. An agreement between spouses in the process of a divorce or legal separation concerning alimony, property division, child custody and support, and the like.

separation of powers. The division of governmental authority into three branches of government—legislative, executive, and judicial—each with specified duties on which neither of the other branches can encroach; the constitutional doctrine of checks and balances by which the people are protected against tyranny. Cf. DIVISION OF POWERS.

sequential journal. JOURNAL OF NOTARIAL ACTS.

sequester, *n.* **1.** In legislative parlance, an across-the-board cut in domestic spending. **2.** A person with whom litigants deposit property being contested until the case has concluded; a sequestrator.

sequestration (see-kwes-**tray**-shən), *n.* **1.** The process by which property is removed from the possessor pending the outcome of a dispute in which two or more parties contend for it. Cf. ATTACHMENT (1); GARNISHMENT. **2.** The setting apart of a decedent's personal property when no one has been willing to act as a personal representative for the estate. **3.** A judicial writ commanding the sheriff or other officer to seize the goods of a person named in the writ; this writ is sometimes issued against a civil defendant who has defaulted or has acted in contempt of court. **4.** The court-ordered seizure of a bankrupt's estate for the benefit of creditors. **5.** The confiscation of private property for public use; esp., in international law, the seizure by a belligerent power of property owed by its own citizens to an enemy power. **6.** The freezing of a government agency's funds. **7.** Custodial isolation of a trial jury to prevent tampering and exposure to publicity, or of witnesses to prevent them from hearing the testimony of others. —**sequester** (si-**kwes**-tər), *vb.* —**sequestrator** (see-kwes-**tray**-tər), *n.*

serial bond. See BOND (1).

serial note. See *installment note* under NOTE.

seriatim (seer-ee-**ay**-dəm), *adv.* [Latin] One after another; in a series; successively <the court disposed of the issues seriatim>.

seriatim opinions. See OPINION (1).

series bonds. See BOND (1).

servant. *Archaic.* EMPLOYEE.

service, *n.* **1.** The formal delivery of a writ, summons, or other legal process <after three attempts, service still had not been accomplished>. — Also termed *service of process*. **2.** The formal delivery of some other legal notice, such as a pleading <be sure that a certificate of service is attached to the motion>. —**serve,** *vb.*

constructive service. **a.** See *substituted service.* **b.** Service accomplished by a method not intended to give notice.

personal service. Actual delivery of the notice or process to the person to whom it is directed. —Also termed *actual service.*

service by publication. The service of process on an absent or nonresident defendant by publishing the process in a specified publication, usu. a newspaper.

sewer service. In bankruptcy law, the fraudulent service of process on a debtor by a creditor seeking to obtain a default judgment.

substituted service. Any method of service allowed by law in place of personal service, such as service by mail. —Also termed *constructive service.*

service, *vb.* **1.** To provide service for <the copy machine needed servicing>. **2.** To pay interest on <service a debt>. **3.** To perform services for <the firm focused on servicing its new clients>.

servicemark. A name, phrase, or other device used to identify and distinguish the services of a certain provider. —Often shortened to *mark.* — Also spelled *service mark*; *servicemark.* Cf. TRADEMARK (1).

service of process. SERVICE (1).

servient estate. See ESTATE.

servient tenant. The person who holds a servient estate and is therefore burdened by an easement. Cf. DOMINANT TENANT.

servient tenement. See *servient estate* under ESTATE.

servitude. **1.** A charge or burden on an estate for another's benefit <the easement by necessity is an equitable servitude>. See EASEMENT. **2.** The condition of being a servant or slave <under the 15th Amendment, an American citizen's right to vote cannot be denied on account of race, color, or previous condition of servitude>. **3.** The condition of a prisoner who has been sentenced to forced labor <penal servitude>.

session. **1.** The sitting of a court, legislature, or other deliberative body so that it may carry on its business <the court's spring session>. See TERM (4).

joint session. The combination of two legislative bodies (such as the House of Representatives and the Senate) to pursue a common agenda.

lame-duck session. A post-election legislative session in which some of the participants are voting during their last days as elected officials. See LAME DUCK.

special session. A legislative session, usu. called by the executive, that meets outside its regular term to consider a specific issue or to reduce backlog. —Also termed *extra session*; *extraordinary session.*

2. The period within any given day during which such a body is assembled and performing its duties <court is in session>.

session laws. A body of statutes enacted by a legislature during a particular annual or biennial session; the softbound booklets containing these statutes.

set-aside, *n.* Something (such as a percentage of funds) that is reserved or put aside for a specific purpose.

set aside, *vb.* (Of a court) to annul or vacate (a judgment, order, etc.) <the judge refused to set aside the default judgment>.

setback, *n.* In real-estate law, the minimum amount of space required between a lot line and a building line; usu. contained in zoning ordinances or deed restrictions, setbacks are designed to ensure that enough light and ventilation reach the property and to keep buildings from being erected too close to property lines <the setback is 10 feet in this subdivision>.

setoff, *n.* **1.** A defendant's counterdemand against the plaintiff, arising out of a transaction independent of the plaintiff's claim. **2.** A debtor's right to reduce the amount of a debt by any sum the creditor owes the debtor; the counterbalancing sum owed by the creditor. —**set off,** *vb.* See COUNTERCLAIM; OFFSET. Cf. RECOUPMENT (3).

setting, *n.* The date and time established by a court for a trial or hearing <the plaintiff sought a continuance of the imminent setting>.

special setting. A preferential setting on a court's calendar, usu. reserved for older cases or cases given priority by law, made either on a party's motion or the court's own motion; for example, some jurisdictions authorize a special setting for cases involving a party over the age of 70. —Also termed *special trial setting*; *trial-setting preference*.

settlement, *n.* **1.** The colonizing of a region; the place colonized <the settlement of Jamestown>. **2.** The conveyance of property—or of interests in property—to provide for one or more beneficiaries, usu. members of the settlor's family, in a way that differs from what the beneficiaries would receive as heirs under the statutes of descent and distribution <in marriage settlements, historically, the wife waived her right to claim dower or to succeed to her husband's property>. **3.** The process of coming to a political or financial agreement, esp. to end a dispute or lawsuit; the oral or written agreement so arrived at <the parties reached a settlement two hours before voir dire was scheduled to begin>. **4.** Payment, satisfaction, or final adjustment <the seller shipped the goods after confirming the buyer's settlement of the account>. **5.** CLOSING <the settlement on their first home is next Friday>. **6.** In the law of wills and estates, the complete execution of an estate by the executor <the settlement of the tycoon's estate was long and complex>. —**settle,** *vb.*

final settlement. In the law of wills, the court order discharging the executor's duties after the estate's execution.

out-of-court settlement. The settlement and termination of a pending suit, arrived at without the court's participation.

strict settlement. A property settlement that aims to keep the estate within the family by creating successive interests.

structured settlement. A settlement in which the defendant agrees to pay periodic sums to the plaintiff for a specified time.

voluntary settlement. A property settlement made without valuable consideration—other than love and affection—from the beneficiary.

settlement class. See CLASS (4).

settlement sheet. CLOSING STATEMENT (2).

settlement statement. CLOSING STATEMENT (2).

settlor. 1. A person who makes a settlement of property; esp., one who sets up a trust. —Also termed *creator*; *donor*; *trustor*; *grantor*. 2. A party to an instrument.

set up, *vb.* To raise (as a defense) <the defendant set up the insanity defense on the murder charge>.

Seventeenth Amendment. The constitutional amendment, ratified in 1913, transferring the power to elect U.S. Senators from the state legislatures to the states' voters.

Seventh Amendment. The constitutional amendment, ratified with the Bill of Rights in 1791, guaranteeing the right to a jury trial in federal civil cases that are traditionally considered to be suits at common law and that have an amount in controversy exceeding twenty dollars.

severability clause. A provision that keeps the remaining provisions of a contract or statute in force if that contract or statute is judicially

declared void or unconstitutional. —Also termed *saving clause*; *separability clause*. See *severable contract* under CONTRACT.

severable contract. See CONTRACT.

severable statute. See STATUTE.

several, *adj.* 1. More than one <the judge gave several reasons for her decision>. 2. Separate; distinct <joint and several liability>.

several liability. See LIABILITY.

severalty. The condition of being separate or distinct <the individual landowners held the land in severalty, not as joint tenants>.

severance, *n.* 1. The act of cutting off; the state of being cut off. 2. The separation of claims, by the court, of multiple parties either to permit separate actions on each claim or to allow certain interlocutory orders to become final. —Also termed *severance of actions*; *severance of claims*. Cf. *bifurcated trial* under TRIAL. 3. The termination of a joint tenancy, usu. by converting it into a tenancy in common. 4. The removal of anything (such as crops or minerals) attached or affixed to real property, making it personal property rather than a part of the land. —**sever,** *vb.*—**severable,** *adj.*

severance damages. Compensation awarded to a landowner for the loss in value of the tract that remains after a partial taking of the land.

severance pay. Money (apart from back wages or salary) paid by an employer to an employee who is dismissed; such a payment is often made in exchange for a release of any claims that the employee might have against the employer.

severance tax. See TAX.

sewer service. See SERVICE.

sexual abuse. See ABUSE.

sexual assault. See ASSAULT.

sexual harassment. A type of employment discrimination consisting in verbal or physical abuse of a sexual nature. See HARASSMENT.

SF. *abbr.* SINKING FUND.

SG. *abbr.* SOLICITOR GENERAL.

shadow jury. See JURY.

shadow stock plan. PHANTOM STOCK PLAN.

shall, *vb.* **1.** Has a duty to; more broadly, is required to <the requester shall send notice> <notice shall be sent>. **2.** Should (as often interpreted by courts) <all claimants shall request mediation>. **3.** May <no person shall enter the building without first signing the roster>. **4.** Will (as a future-tense verb) <the debtor shall then be released from all debts>. **5.** Is entitled to <the secretary shall be reimbursed for all expenses>. —Only sense 1 is acceptable under strict standards of drafting.

sham, *n.* **1.** Something that is not what it seems; a counterfeit. **2.** A faker; a person who pretends to be something that he or she is not. — **sham,** *vb.*—**sham,** *adj.*

shaming sentence. SCARLET-LETTER PUNISHMENT.

sham marriage. See MARRIAGE (1).

sham plea. See *sham pleading* under PLEADING (1).

sham pleading. See PLEADING (1).

share, *n.* **1.** An allotted portion owned by, contributed by, or due to someone <Sean's share of the partnership's profits>. **2.** A single unit of capital that represents an ownership interest in a corporation or in its equity <the broker advised his customer to sell the stock shares when the price reaches $29>. Cf. SECURITY (4); STOCK (4).

share acquisition. The acquisition of a corporation by purchasing all or most of its outstanding shares directly from the shareholders; TAKEOVER. —Also termed *share-acquisition transaction*; *stock acquisition*; *stock-acquisition transaction*. Cf. ASSET ACQUISITION.

share certificate. STOCK CERTIFICATE.

shared custody. See *joint custody* under CUSTODY.

shared-equity mortgage. See MORTGAGE.

share draft. See DRAFT.

shareholder. The person in whose name stock is issued and registered by the corporation. —Also termed *stockholder*; *shareowner*. Cf. STAKEHOLDER (3).

dummy shareholder. A shareholder who owns stock in name only for the benefit of the true owner whose identity is generally concealed.

majority shareholder. A shareholder who owns or controls more than 50 percent of the corporation's stock.

minority shareholder. **a.** Generally, a shareholder who owns less than 50 percent of the total shares outstanding. **b.** A shareholder who holds such a small percentage of the total shares outstanding that he or she cannot control the corporation's management or single-handedly elect directors.

shareholder derivative suit. DERIVATIVE ACTION (1).

shareholder oppression. OPPRESSION (4).

shareholder proposal. A proposal by one or more corporate stockholders to change company policies or procedures; ordinarily, the corporate managers inform all stockholders about the proposal before the next shareholder meeting.

shareholders' equity. OWNERS' EQUITY.

shareholder voting agreement. POOLING AGREEMENT.

shareowner. SHAREHOLDER.

shares outstanding. See *outstanding stock* under STOCK.

share split. STOCK SPLIT.

shark repellent. *Slang.* A measure, such as issuing new shares of stock or making a significant acquisition, taken by a corporation to discourage unwanted takeover attempts. —Also termed *takeover defense.* See POISON PILL. Cf. PORCUPINE PROVISION.

shelf issue. See ISSUE (2).

shelf registration. See REGISTRATION (2).

shell corporation. See CORPORATION.

Shelley's Case, Rule in. See RULE IN SHELLEY'S CASE.

shelter, *n.* TAX SHELTER <the shelter saved the taxpayer over $2,000 in taxes>. —**shelter,** *vb.*

shepardize, *vb.* **1.** (*often cap.*) To determine the subsequent history of (a case) by using a printed or computerized version of *Shepard's Citators.* **2.** Loosely, to check the precedential value of (a case) by the same or similar means. —**shepardization, shepardizing,** *n.*

sheriff. A county's chief peace officer, usu. elected, who in most jurisdictions acts as custodian of the county jail, executes civil and criminal process, and carries out judicial mandates within the county.

sheriff's deed. See DEED.

sheriff's sale. See *execution sale* under SALE.

Sherman Antitrust Act. A federal act, passed in 1890, that prohibits direct or indirect interference with the freely competitive interstate movement of goods; amended by the Clayton Act in 1914. 15 U.S.C. §§ 1-7. —Often shortened to *Sherman Act.*

shield law. **1.** A statute that affords journalists the privilege not to reveal confidential sources. See *journalist's privilege* under PRIVILEGE. **2.** A statute that restricts or prohibits the use, in rape or sexual assault cases, of evidence about the past sexual conduct of the victim. —Also termed (in sense 2) *rape shield law.*

shifting use. See USE (4).

shingle theory. In securities law, the notion that broker-dealers must be held to a high standard of conduct because by the very act of engaging in the securities business ("hanging out a shingle"), the broker-dealer implicitly represents to the world that the conduct of all its employees will be fair and meets professional norms.

shipper. **1.** One who ships goods to another. **2.** One who tenders goods to a carrier for transportation.

shipping document. Any paper that covers a shipment in trade, such as a bill of lading or letter of credit.

shop-book rule. An exception to the hearsay rule permitting the admission into evidence of original bookkeeping records if the books' entries were made in the ordinary course of business and the books are introduced by somebody who maintains their custody.

shoplifting, *n.* Theft of merchandise from a store or business. —**shoplift,** *vb.*

shop steward. STEWARD (2).

short-form merger. See MERGER.

short sale. See SALE.

short sale against the box. See SALE.

short summons. See SUMMONS.

short-swing profits. Profits made by an insider on the purchase and sale (or sale and purchase) of company stock within a six-month period; these profits are subject to being returned to the company.

short-term debt. See DEBT.

short-term security. See SECURITY.

short-term trust. See *Clifford trust* under TRUST.

shotgun instruction. ALLEN CHARGE.

show-cause order. An order directing a party to appear in court and explain why the party took (or failed to take) some action or why the court should or should not grant some relief.

show trial. A trial, usu. in a nondemocratic country, that is staged primarily for propagandistic purposes, with the outcome predetermined.

show-up, *n.* A pretrial identification procedure in which a suspect is confronted with a witness to or the victim of a crime; unlike a lineup, a show-up is a one-on-one confrontation. Cf. LINEUP.

shut-in royalty. See ROYALTY.

sic. [Latin "so; thus"] Spelled or used as written; *sic,* invariably put in brackets, is used to indicate that a preceding word or phrase in a quoted passage is reproduced as it erroneously appeared in the original document <"that case peeked [*sic*] the young lawyer's interest">.

sidebar. **1.** A position at the side of a judge's bench where counsel can confer with the judge beyond the jury's earshot <the judge called the attorneys to sidebar>. **2.** SIDEBAR CONFERENCE <during the sidebar, the prosecutor accused the defense attorney of misconduct>. **3.** A short, secondary article within or accompanying a main story in a publication <the sidebar contained information on related topics>.

sidebar conference. **1.** A discussion among the judge and counsel, usu. over an evidentiary objection, outside the jury's hearing. —Also termed *bench conference.* **2.** A discussion, esp. during voir dire, between the judge and a juror or venire-member. —Often shortened to *side-bar*.

sight draft. See DRAFT.

signatory (sig-nə-tor-ee), *n.* A party that signs a document, personally or via an agent, and thereby becomes a party to an agreement <eight countries are signatories to the treaty>. —**signatory,** *adj.*

signature. 1. A person's name or mark written by that person or at his or her direction. **2.** In commercial law, any name, mark, or writing used with the intention of authenticating a document. U.C.C. §§ 1-201(39), 3-401(b). —Also termed *legal signature.*

signature loan. See LOAN.

significant-relationship theory. CENTER-OF-GRAVITY DOCTRINE.

silent partner. See PARTNER.

silver parachute. TIN PARACHUTE.

silver-platter doctrine. In criminal procedure, the principle that federal courts could allow the admission of evidence obtained illegally by state police officers, as long as federal officers did not participate in or request the search; the Supreme Court rejected this doctrine in *Elkins v. United States*, 364 U.S. 206 (1960).

similiter (sə-mil-i-tər). A party's written acceptance of an opponent's issue or argument. See JOINDER OF ISSUE (2).

simple, *adj.* **1.** (Of a crime) not accompanied by aggravating circumstances. Cf. AGGRAVATED. **2.** (Of an estate or fee) inheritable by the owner's heirs with no conditions concern-

ing tail. **3.** (Of a contract) not made under seal.

simple average. See *particular average* under AVERAGE.

simple battery. See BATTERY.

simple contract. See *parol contract* (b) under CONTRACT.

simple interest. See INTEREST (3).

simple listing. See *open listing* under LISTING (1).

simple majority. See MAJORITY.

simple mortgage clause. See *open mortgage clause* under MORTGAGE CLAUSE.

simple resolution. See RESOLUTION.

simple trust. See TRUST.

simplex dictum. See DICTUM.

simulated sale. See SALE.

simultaneous death. See DEATH.

simultaneous-death act. A statute providing that when two persons die under circumstances making it impossible to determine the order of their deaths (as in a common disaster), each person is presumed to have survived the other for purposes of distributing their respective estates; many states' simultaneous-death acts have been amended to require that a person survive the decedent by at least 120 hours to qualify as an heir or beneficiary.

sine die (sI-nee-**dI**[-ee] *or* si-nay-**dee**-ay). [Latin "without day"] With no day being assigned (as for resumption of a meeting or hearing). See GO HENCE WITHOUT DAY.

sine qua non (sI-nee-kway-**non** *or* si-nay- *or* -kwah-), *n.* [Latin "without which not"] An indispensable condition or thing; something on which something else necessarily depends.

single-juror instruction. See JURY INSTRUCTION.

single-name paper. *Slang.* A negotiable instrument signed by only one maker and not backed by a surety.

single-publication rule. The doctrine that a plaintiff in a libel suit against a publisher has only one claim for each mass publication, not a claim for every book or issue in that run.

sinking fund. A fund consisting of regular deposits that are accumulated with interest to pay off a long-term corporate or public debt. — Abbr. SF.

sinking-fund debenture. See DEBENTURE.

sinking-fund depreciation method. See DEPRECIATION METHOD.

sinking-fund reserve. See RESERVE.

sin tax. See TAX.

sister corporation. See CORPORATION.

sistren, *n. pl.* Sisters, esp. those considered spiritual kin (such as female colleagues on a court). Cf. BRETHREN.

sit. 1. (Of a judge) to occupy a judicial seat <Justice Breyer sits on the U.S. Supreme Court>. **2.** (Of a judge) to hold court or perform official functions <is the judge sitting this week?>. **3.** (Of a court or legislative body) to hold proceedings <the U.S. Supreme Court sits from October to June>.

sit-down strike. See STRIKE.

situs (sI-təs). [Latin] The location or position (of something) for legal purposes.

Sixteenth Amendment. The constitutional amendment, ratified in 1913, allowing Congress to tax income.

Sixth Amendment. The constitutional amendment, ratified with the Bill of Rights in 1791, guaranteeing in criminal cases the right to a speedy and public trial by jury, the right to be informed of the nature of the accusation, the right to confront witnesses, the right to counsel, and the right to compulsory process for obtaining favorable witnesses.

skilled witness. See *expert witness* under WITNESS.

skip bail. JUMP BAIL.

S.L. *abbr.* **1.** Session law. See SESSION LAWS. **2.** Statute law.

slander, *n.* **1.** A false, defamatory statement expressed in a transitory form, esp. speech; unlike libel, damages from slander are not presumed and thus must be proved by the plaintiff (unless the defamation is slander per se). **2.** The act of making such a statement. —**slander,** *vb.*— **slanderous,** *adj.* See DEFAMATION. Cf. LIBEL.

slander per se. Slander for which special damages need not be proved because it imputes to the plaintiff any one of the following: (1) a crime involving moral turpitude, (2) a loathsome disease (such as a sexually transmitted disease), (3) conduct that would adversely affect one's business or profession, or (4) unchastity (esp. of a woman); if the defamation does not fall into one of these four categories, it is called *slander per quod* and the plaintiff must prove special damages.

slander of title. A false statement, made orally or in writing, that casts doubt on another person's ownership of property. See DISPARAGEMENT.

SLAPP. *abbr.* Strategic Lawsuit Against Public Participation—a suit brought by a developer, corporate executive, or elected official to stifle those who protest against some type of high-dollar initiative (often involving the environment). —Also termed *SLAPP suit.*

slavery, badge of. See BADGE OF SLAVERY.

slayer's rule. The doctrine that neither a person who kills another nor the killer's heirs can share in the decedent's estate.

sleeping partner. See *silent partner* under PARTNER.

slight care. See CARE.

slight negligence. See NEGLIGENCE.

slip-and-fall case. 1. A lawsuit brought by a plaintiff for injuries sustained in slipping and falling, usu. on the defendant's property. **2.** Loosely, any minor case in tort.

slip decision. See *slip opinion* under OPINION (1).

slip law. A legislative enactment that is separately and promptly published after its passage, so that it is used and cited in this temporary form until it is published in a more permanent form—first in session laws and later in a hardbound statute book.

slip opinion. See OPINION (1).

slowdown. An organized effort by workers to decrease production to pressure the employer to take some desired action.

slush fund. Money that is set aside for undesignated purposes, often corrupt ones.

Small Business Administration. A federal agency that assists and protects the interests of small businesses, usu. by making low-interest loans. —Abbr. SBA.

small-claims court. See COURT.

smart money. 1. Funds held by sophisticated, usu. large investors who are considered capable of minimizing risks and maximizing profits <the smart money has now left this market>. **2.** See *punitive damages* under DAMAGES <although the jury awarded only $7,000 in actual damages, it also awarded $500,000 in smart money>.

smuggling, *n.* The crime of importing or exporting illegal articles or articles on which duties have not been paid. —**smuggle,** *vb.* See CONTRABAND.

sobriety checkpoint. A public place at which police officers maintain a roadblock to detain motorists in order to determine whether the drivers are intoxicated.

sobriety test. A method of determining whether a person is intoxicated, including coordination tests and mechanical devices that measure the blood- alcohol content of a person's breath sample. See BREATHALYZER.

field sobriety test. A motor-skills test administered by a peace officer during a stop to determine whether a suspect was driving while intoxicated; the test usu. involves checking the suspect's speaking ability or coordination (as by reciting the alphabet or walking in a straight line).

social cost. The cost to society of any particular practice or rule <although automobiles are undeniably beneficial to society, they carry a certain social cost in the lives that are lost every year on the road>.

social guest. See GUEST.

Social Security Administration. A federal agency created by the Social Security Act (42 U.S.C. §§ 301 et seq.) to institute a national program of contributory insurance. —Abbr. SSA.

sociological jurisprudence. See JURISPRUDENCE.

sociopath, *n.* PSYCHOPATH. —**sociopathy,** *n.*—**sociopathic,** *adj.*

sodomy, *n.* **1.** Oral or anal copulation between humans, esp. homosexuals. **2.** Oral or anal copulation between a human and an animal; bestiality. —Also termed *crime against nature*; *abominable and detestable crime against nature*; *unnatural offense*; *unspeakable crime.* —**sodomize,** *vb.*—**sodomitic,** *adj.*—**sodomist, sodomite,** *n.* Cf. PEDERASTY.

soft dollars. 1. In the security industry, the credits that brokers give their clients in return for the investor's stock-trading business. **2.** The portion of an equity investment that is tax-deductible in the first year. Cf. HARD DOLLARS.

soldier's will. See WILL.

sole-actor doctrine. In the law of agency, the rule charging a principal with knowledge of the agent's actions, even if the agent acted fraudulently.

sole cause. See *superseding cause* under CAUSE (1).

sole custody. See CUSTODY (2).

solemnity of contract. The concept that two people may enter into any contract they wish and that the resulting contract is enforceable if formalities are observed and no defenses exist.

solemnize (sol-əm-nIz), *vb.* To enter into (a marriage, contract, etc.) by a formal act, usu. before witnesses. —**solemnization** (sol-əm-ni-**zay**-shən), *n.*

sole practitioner. A lawyer who practices law without any partners or associates. —Also termed *solo practitioner.* —Often shortened to *solo.*

sole proprietorship. A form of business in which one person owns all the assets, owes all the liabilities, and conducts affairs in his or her own capacity, often under an assumed name. —Also termed *individual proprietorship.*

solicitation, *n.* **1.** The act or an instance of requesting or seeking to obtain something; entreaty or petition <a solicitation for volunteers to handle at least one pro bono case per year>. **2.** The act or an instance of urging, advising, commanding, or otherwise enticing or inciting another to commit a crime; solicitation is an inchoate offense distinct from the solicited crime. <convicted of solicitation of murder>. —Also termed *incitement*. **3.** An offer of sexual favors in exchange for money <the prostitute was charged only with solicitation>. **4.** A lawyer's aggressive attempts to gain business; the Model Rules of Professional Conduct place certain prohibitions on direct solicitation <the personal-injury attorney's solicitation consisted of television commercials>. —**solicit,** *vb.*

solicitation of bids. INVITATION TO NEGOTIATE.

solicitor. 1. A person who seeks business or contributions from others; an advertiser or promoter. **2.** A person who conducts matters on another's behalf; an agent or representative. **3.** The chief law officer of a governmental body or a municipality. **4.** In England, a legal adviser who consults with clients and prepares legal documents but is not heard in court. Cf. BARRISTER.

solicitor general. The second-highest ranking legal officer in a government (after the attorney general); esp., the chief courtroom lawyer for the executive branch. —Abbr. SG. Pl. **solicitors general.**

solidary, *adj.* (Of a liability or obligation) joint and several. See JOINT AND SEVERAL.

solidary liability. See *joint and several liability* under LIABILITY.

solitary confinement. Separate confinement that gives a prisoner extremely limited access to other people; esp., the complete isolation of a prisoner.

solo, *n.* SOLE PRACTITIONER.

solo practitioner. SOLE PRACTITIONER.

solvency, *n.* The ability to pay debts as they come due. —**solvent,** *adj.* Cf. INSOLVENCY.

S-1. An SEC form that a company must file before the company may list and trade its securities on a national exchange; used primarily by first-time issuers of securities, this form is the basic, full-length registration statement that requires a great deal of information about the issuer. —Also termed *Form S-1*.

Son-of-Sam law. A statute that prevents a convicted criminal from profiting by selling his or her story rights to a publisher or moviemaker, usu. by authorizing prosecutors to seize royalties from convicted criminals and to place the money in an escrow account for the crime victim's benefit; in 1991, the U.S. Supreme Court declared New York's Son-of-Sam law unconstitutional as a content-based speech regulation, prompting many states to amend their laws in an attempt to avoid constitutionality problems. *Simon & Schuster, Inc. v. New York State Crime Victims Bd.*, 502 U.S. 105 (1991).

sound, *vb.* To be actionable (in) <her claims for physical injury sound in tort, not in contract>.

sovereign immunity. See IMMUNITY (1).

sovereign power. The power to make and enforce laws.

sovereign state. A political community whose members are bound together by the tie of common subjection to some central authority, whose commands the bulk of those members must habitually obey. See STATE.

part-sovereign state. A political community in which part of the powers of external sovereignty are exercised by the home government, and part are vested in or controlled by some other political body or bodies; such a state is not fully independent because by the conditions of its existence it is not allowed full freedom of action in external affairs.

sovereignty. 1. Supreme dominion, authority, or rule. 2. The supreme political authority of an independent state. 3. The state itself.

external sovereignty. The power of dealing on a nation's behalf with other national governments.

internal sovereignty. The power that rulers exercise over their own subjects.

space arbitrage. ARBITRAGE.

speaking demurrer. See DEMURRER.

speaking motion. A motion that requires consideration of matters outside the pleadings.

special act. SPECIAL LAW.

special administration. See ADMINISTRATION.

special agency. See AGENCY.

special appearance. See APPEARANCE.

special assessment. See ASSESSMENT.

special attorney. See *special counsel* under COUNSEL.

special benefit. See BENEFIT.

special calendar. See CALENDAR.

special case. See *case reserved* under CASE.

special-circumstances rule. SPECIAL-FACTS RULE.

special contract. See CONTRACT.

special counsel. See COUNSEL.

special count. See COUNT.

special court-martial. See COURT-MARTIAL.

special damages. See DAMAGES.

special demurrer. See DEMURRER.

special deterrence. See DETERRENCE.

special dividend. See *extraordinary dividend* under DIVIDEND.

special election. See ELECTION.

special exception. 1. A party's objection to the form rather than the substance of an opponent's claim, such as an objection for vagueness or ambiguity. See DEMURRER. 2. An allowance in zoning ordinances for special uses that are considered essential and are not fundamentally incompatible with the original zoning regulations. Cf. VARIANCE (2).

special execution. See EXECUTION.

special executor. See EXECUTOR.

special-facts rule. In corporate law, the principle that a director or officer has a fiduciary duty to disclose inside information to a shareholder when engaging in stock transactions under special circumstances, such as when the shareholder lacks business acumen, the shares are closely held with no readily ascertainable market value, or the director or officer instigated the transaction; this is an exception to the "majority rule."—Also termed *special-circumstances rule.* Cf. MAJORITY RULE (2).

special guardian. GUARDIAN AD LITEM.

special indorsement. See INDORSEMENT.

special instruction. See JURY INSTRUCTION.

special-interest group. A group of persons or organizations that, because they share a particular interest, band together to lobby the government on a specific issue. —Also termed *special interest.*

special interrogatory. See INTERROGATORY.

special issue. See ISSUE (1).

specialist. 1. A lawyer who has been board-certified in a specific field of law. See BOARD OF LEGAL SPECIALIZATION. **2.** A securities-exchange member who makes a market in one or more listed securities; the exchange assigns securities to various specialists and expects them to maintain a fair and orderly market as provided by SEC standards.

special jurisdiction. See *limited jurisdiction* under JURISDICTION.

special jury. See JURY.

special law. A law that pertains to and affects a particular case, person, place, or thing, as opposed to the general public. —Also termed *special act; private law.*

special legacy. See *specific legacy* under LEGACY.

special lien. See *particular lien* under LIEN.

special limitation. See LIMITATION.

special litigation committee. In corporate law, a committee of independent corporate directors assigned to investigate the merits of a shareholder derivative suit and, if appropriate, to recommend maintaining or dismissing the suit. See DERIVATIVE ACTION.

special malice. See *particular malice* under MALICE.

special master. See MASTER.

special matter. See MATTER.

special meeting. See MEETING.

special-needs analysis. In constitutional criminal procedure, a balancing test used by the Supreme Court to determine whether certain searches (such as administrative, civil-based, or public-safety searches) impose unreasonably on individual rights.

special partner. See *limited partner* under PARTNER.

special partnership. See *limited partnership* under PARTNERSHIP.

special permit. SPECIAL-USE PERMIT.

special plea. See PLEA.

special pleading. 1. The common-law system of pleading under which no case could be brought to trial until the lawyers on either side had exchanged a series of court papers (such as replications, rebutters, and surrebutters) setting out their rival contentions in accordance with hypertechnical rules; often, therefore, cases were decided on points of pleading and not on the merits. **2.**

The art of drafting pleadings under this system. **3.** An instance of drafting such a pleading. **4.** A responsive pleading that does more than merely deny allegations, as by introducing new matter to justify an otherwise blameworthy act. **5.** An argument that is unfairly slanted toward the speaker's viewpoint because it omits unfavorable facts or authorities and develops only favorable ones.

special power of appointment. See *limited power of appointment* under POWER OF APPOINTMENT.

special prosecutor. See PROSECUTOR.

special retainer. See RETAINER.

special-sensitivity rule. EGGSHELL-SKULL RULE.

special session. See SESSION.

special setting. See SETTING.

special term. See TERM.

special traverse. See TRAVERSE.

special trial setting. See *special setting* under SETTING.

special trust. See *active trust* under TRUST.

specialty. See *contract under seal* under CONTRACT.

specialty contract. See *contract under seal* under CONTRACT.

special-use permit. A permit that allows a property owner to use the property in a way ordinarily permitted by zoning regulations if specified conditions are met. —Also termed *special permit*; *conditional-use permit*. See SPECIAL EXCEPTION (2).

special-use valuation. See VALUATION.

special verdict. See VERDICT.

special warranty. See WARRANTY (1).

special warranty deed. See DEED.

specie (**spee**-shee). See IN SPECIE.

specification, *n.* **1.** The act of making a detailed statement; the statement so made. **2.** In patent law, an applicant's written description of how an invention is constructed and used. Cf. CLAIM (5). **3.** In military law, a statement of charges against one who is accused of a military offense. **4.** In property law, the acquisition of title to materials belonging to another person by converting those materials into a new and different form, as by changing grapes into wine, lumber into shelving, or corn into liquor; the effect is that the original owner of the materials loses the property rights in them and is left with a right of action for their original value. —**specify,** *vb.*

specific bequest. See BEQUEST.

specific denial. See DENIAL.

specific devise. See DEVISE.

specific intent. See INTENT.

specific-intent crime. See CRIME.

specific jurisdiction. See JURISDICTION.

specific legacy. See LEGACY.

specific performance. A court-ordered remedy that requires precise fulfillment of a legal or contractual obligation when monetary damages are inappropriate or inadequate, such as when the sale of real estate or rare articles is involved. —Also termed *specific relief*.

speculation, *n.* **1.** The buying or selling of something with the expectation of profiting by price fluctuations <he engaged in speculation in the stock market>. **2.** The act or practice of theorizing about matters over which there is no certain knowledge <the public's speculation about the assassination of John F. Kennedy>. —**speculate,** *vb.*—**speculator,** *n.*

speech. The expression or communication of thoughts or opinions in spoken words; something spoken or uttered. See FREEDOM OF SPEECH.

commercial speech. Communication (such as advertising and marketing) that involves only the commercial interests of the speaker and the audience, and is therefore afforded lesser First Amendment protection than social, political, or religious speech.

corporate speech. Speech deriving from a corporation and protected under the First Amendment; it does not lose protected status simply because of its corporate source.

hate speech. See SPEECH.

speech-plus. Speech that is joined with conduct, and that is not accorded the same degree of protection under the First Amendment as speech without conduct is.

symbolic speech. Conduct that expresses opinions or thoughts, such as a hunger strike or the wearing of a black armband; symbolic speech does not enjoy the same constitutional protection that pure written expression does.

Speech and Debate Clause. The constitutional provision (art. I, § 6, cl. 1) granting members of Congress immunity for any speech or debate delivered in either the House or the Senate; this immunity is extended to other areas where it is necessary to prevent impairment of deliberations and other legitimate legislative activities, such as subpoenaing bank records for an investigation. See *congressional immunity* under IMMUNITY (1).

speech-plus. See SPEECH.

speedy trial. A criminal trial that the prosecution, with reasonable diligence, begins promptly and conducts expeditiously; in determining whether the accused has been deprived of the Sixth Amendment right to a speedy trial, courts generally consider the length of the delay, the reason for the delay, and the prejudice to the defendant.

spendthrift trust. See TRUST.

spillover. EXTERNALITY.

spin-off, *n.* **1.** A corporate divestiture in which a division of a corporation becomes an independent company and stock of the new company is distributed to the original corporation's shareholders. **2.** The corporation created by this divestiture. Cf. SPLIT-OFF; SPLIT-UP.

spirit. General meaning or purpose, as opposed to literal content <the spirit of the law>. Cf. LETTER (3).

spiritual court. See *ecclesiastical court* under COURT.

spite fence. A fence erected solely to annoy a neighbor <the court enjoined the completion of the 25-foot spite fence>.

split income. See INCOME.

split-off, *n.* **1.** The creation of a new corporation by an existing corporation that gives its shareholders stock in the new corporation in return for their stock in the original corporation. **2.** The corporation created by this process. Cf. SPIN-OFF; SPLIT-UP.

split sentence. See SENTENCE.

split-up, *n.* The division of a corporation into two or more new corporations; the shareholders in the original corporation typically receive shares in the new corporation, and the original corporation goes out of business. Cf. SPIN-OFF; SPLIT-OFF.

spoils of war. BOOTY (1).

spoils system. The practice of awarding government jobs to supporters and friends of the victorious political party. Cf. MERIT SYSTEM.

spoliation (spoh-lee-**ay**-shən), *n.* **1.** The intentional destruction, mutilation, alteration, or concealment of evidence, usu. a document; if proved, this action may be used to establish that the evidence was unfavorable toward the party responsible. **2.** The seizure of personal or real property by violent means; the act of pillaging. **3.** The taking of a benefit properly belonging to another. —**spoliate,** *vb.*—**spoliator,** *n.*

spontaneous declaration. In evidence, a statement that is made without time to reflect or fabricate and that is related to the circumstances of the perceived occurrence. —Also termed *spontaneous statement.* See EXCITED UTTERANCE; PRESENT SENSE IMPRESSION.

spot zoning. See ZONING.

spousal abuse. See ABUSE.

spousal allowance. See ALLOWANCE (1).

spousal privilege. See *marital privilege* under PRIVILEGE.

spousal support. ALIMONY.

spray trust. See *sprinkling trust* under TRUST.

spread, *n.* **1.** In banking, the difference between the interest rate that a financial institution must pay to attract deposits and the rate at which money can be loaned. **2.** In securities law, the difference between the highest price a buyer is willing to pay for a security (the *bid price*) and the lowest price at which a seller is willing to sell a security (the *asked price*). **3.** In securities law, the simultaneous buying and selling of one or more options or futures contracts on the same security in order to profit from the price differential. **4.** In investment banking, the difference between the price the underwriter pays the issuer of the security and the price paid by the public in the initial offering. **5.** In gambling, a winning margin.

spread eagle. STRADDLE.

springing use. See USE (4).

sprinkling trust. See TRUST.

spurious (**spyuur**-ee-əs), *adj.* **1.** Deceptively suggesting an erroneous origin; fake <spurious trademarks>. **2.** Of doubtful or low quality <spurious goods that fell apart>. **3.** *Archaic.* Of illegitimate birth <spurious offspring>.

square, *n.* **1.** A certain portion of land within a city limit. —Also termed *block.* **2.** A space set apart for public use. **3.** In a government survey, an area measuring 24 by 24 miles. See...

squatter. 1. A person who settles on property without any legal claim or license. **2.** A person who settles on public land under a government regulation allowing that person to acquire upon fulfilling certain conditions.

squeeze-out, *n.* An action taken in an attempt to eliminate or reduce the minority interest in a corporation.

SSA. *abbr.* SOCIAL SECURITY ADMINISTRATION.

SSS. *abbr.* SELECTIVE SERVICE SYSTEM.

stagflation, *n.* A period of slow economic growth or recession characterized by high inflation, stagnant consumer demand, and high unemployment. —**stagflationary,** *adj.*

staggered board of directors. See BOARD OF DIRECTORS.

stakeholder. 1. One who holds the money or valuables placed as bets when people are wagering. **2.** A disinterested third party who holds money or property, the right or possession of which is disputed between two other parties. See INTERPLEADER. **3.** A member of a group having an interest (or stake) in a company's actions, though not as owners; in this sense, *stakeholder* is opposed to *shareholder.* Cf. SHAREHOLDER.

stale check. See CHECK.

stale claim. A claim that is barred by the statute of limitations or the defense of laches. —Also termed *stale demand.*

stamp tax. See TAX.

standard, *n.* **1.** A model accepted as correct by custom, consent, or authority <what is the standard in the ant-farm industry? >. **2.** A criterion for measuring acceptability, quality, or accuracy <the attorney was making a nice living—even by New York standards>. —**standard,** *adj.*

objective standard. See OBJECTIVE STANDARD.

subjective standard. See SUBJECTIVE STANDARD.

standard deduction. See DEDUCTION.

standard mortgage clause. See MORTGAGE CLAUSE.

standard of care. In the law of negligence, the degree of care that a reasonable person should exercise. See CARE (2).

standard of proof. The degree or level of proof demanded in a specific case, such as "beyond a reasonable doubt" or "by a preponderance of the evidence." See BURDEN OF PERSUASION.

standard policy. See INSURANCE POLICY.

standby commitment. An arrangement between an underwriter and an issuer of securities whereby the underwriter agrees, for a fee, to buy any unsold shares remaining after the public offering. —Also termed *standby underwriting agreement.* See *standby underwriting* under UNDERWRITING.

standby letter of credit. See LETTER OF CREDIT.

standby underwriting. See UNDERWRITING.

standby underwriting agreement. STANDBY COMMITMENT.

standing, *n.* **1.** A party's right to make a legal claim or seek judicial enforcement of a duty or right; to have standing in federal court, a plaintiff must show (1) that the challenged conduct has caused him or her injury in fact, and (2) that the interest sought to be protected is within the zone of interests meant to be regulated by the statutory or constitutional guarantee in question. — Also termed *standing to sue.* **2.** One's place in a community in the estimation of others; reputation.

standi master. See MASTER.

standing mortgage. See *interest-only mortgage* under MORTGAGE.

standing order. A rule adopted by a particular court to govern practice before it, though not embodied in local rules.

stand mute. (Of a defendant) to refuse to enter a plea in a criminal trial; standing mute is treated as a plea of not guilty.

stand trial. To defend oneself in a lawsuit, esp. in criminal proceedings.

Star Chamber, Court of. In 16th- and early-17th-century England, an equity court having jurisdiction over breaches of the peace such as libel, perjury, jury-packing, contempt of court, and conspiracy to pervert justice; the court was abolished in 1641 for abuse of its power.

star-chamber proceeding. An unfair judicial proceeding in which the outcome is predetermined.

stare decisis (stahr-ee-də-**sI**-səs *or* stair-), *n.* [Latin "to stand by things decided"] The doctrine of precedent, under which it is necessary for courts to follow earlier judicial decisions when the same points arise again in litigation. See PRECEDENT. Cf. RES JUDICATA.

star paging, *n.* **1.** A method of referring to a page in an earlier edition of a book, esp. a legal source; this method correlates the pagination of the later edition with that of the earlier edition. **2.** By extension, the method of displaying on a computer screen the page breaks that occur in printed documents such as law reports and law reviews. —Also termed *star pagination.* —**star page,** *n.*

state, *n.* **1.** The system of rules by which jurisdiction and authority are exercised over a politically organized body of people; the political organization or the body of people itself <separation of church and state>. Cf. NATION. **2.** An institution of self-government within a larger political entity; esp., one of the constituent parts of a nation having a federal government <the 50 states>. **3.** The prosecution as the representative of the people <the state rests its case>.

state action. Anything done by a government; esp., in constitutional law, an intrusion on a person's rights (esp. civil rights) either by a governmental entity or by a private requirement that can be enforced only by governmental action (such as a racially restrictive covenant, which requires judicial action for enforcement).

state bank. See BANK.

state court. See COURT.

stated capital. See CAPITAL.

stated interest rate. See *nominal rate* under INTEREST RATE.

stated meeting. See *annual meeting* under MEETING.

stated value. PAR VALUE.

statement. 1. In the rules of evidence, a verbal assertion or nonverbal conduct intended as an assertion. 2. A formal and exact presentation of facts.

statement of claim. COMPLAINT (1).

statement of facts. 1. A party's presentation of the facts leading up to or surrounding a legal dispute, usu. recited at the beginning of a brief. 2. In Texas, TRANSCRIPT (1).

agreed statement of facts. A narrative statement of facts that is stipulated to be correct by the parties and is submitted to a tribunal for a ruling; when the narrative statement is filed on appeal instead of a report of the trial proceedings, it is called an *agreed statement on appeal.*

statement of financial affairs. In bankruptcy, a document that an individual or corporate debtor must file to answer questions about its past and present financial status.

statement of financial condition. BALANCE SHEET.

statement of financial position. BALANCE SHEET.

statement of income. INCOME STATEMENT.

statement of particulars. BILL OF PARTICULARS.

state of mind. 1. The condition or capacity of a person's mind; MENS

REA. 2. Loosely, a person's reasons or motives for committing an act, esp. a criminal act.

state-of-mind exception. In the law of evidence, the principle that an out-of-court declaration of an existing motive is admissible, even when the declarant cannot testify in person; this doctrine constitutes an exception to the hearsay rule.

state police power. The power of a state to enforce laws for the health, welfare, morals, and safety of the citizens, if enacted so that the means are reasonably calculated to protect those legitimate state interests.

state's attorney. DISTRICT ATTORNEY.

state-secrets privilege. See PRIVILEGE.

state's evidence, turn. See TURN STATE'S EVIDENCE.

states' rights. Under the Tenth Amendment, all rights not conferred on the federal government or not forbidden to the states.

status crime. See CRIME.

status quo (stay-dəs-**kwoh** *or* sta-). [Latin] The situation that currently exists. Cf. IN STATU QUO.

status quo ante. [Latin] The situation that existed before something else (being discussed) occurred.

statutable (sta-chə-də-bəl), *adj.* 1. Prescribed or authorized by statute. 2. Conformed to the legislative requirements for quality, size, amount, or the like. 3. (Of an offense) punishable by law. See STATUTORY.

statute. The law passed by a legislative body.

codifying statute. A statute that purports to be exhaustive in restating the whole of the law on a particular topic, including prior caselaw as well as legislative provisions; courts generally presume that a codifying statute supersedes prior caselaw. Cf. *consolidating statute.*

consolidating statute. A statute that collects the legislative provisions on a particular topic and embodies them in a single statute, often with minor amendments and drafting improvements; courts generally presume that a consolidating statute leaves prior caselaw intact. Cf. *codifying statute.*

declaratory statute. A statute enacted to clarify prior law by reconciling conflicting judicial decisions or by explaining the meaning of a prior statute.

directory statute. A statute that indicates only what should be done, with no provision for enforcement. Cf. *mandatory statute.*

disabling statute. A statute that limits or curbs certain rights.

enabling statute. A statute that permits what was previously prohibited or that creates new powers; esp., a congressional statute conferring powers on executive agencies to carry out various delegated tasks. —Also termed *enabling act.*

general statute. A statute pertaining to an entire community or all persons generally. —Also termed *public statute.*

imperfect statute. A statute that prohibits, but does not render void, an objectionable transaction; such a statute provides a penalty for disobedience without depriving the violative transaction of its legal effect.

mandatory statute. A statute that requires a course of action as opposed to merely permitting it. Cf. *directory statute.*

organic statute. A statute that establishes an administrative agency or local government. —Also termed *organic act.* Cf. ORGANIC LAW.

penal statute. A statute that defines a criminal offense and prescribes its corresponding fine, penalty, or punishment. —Also termed *penal law.*

revival statute. A statute that provides for the renewal of actions, of wills, and of the legal effect of documents.

severable statute. A law that remains operative as to the remaining provisions even though a portion of the law is declared unconstitutional.

statute law. STATUTORY LAW.

statute of frauds. 1. (*cap.*) An English statute enacted in 1677 declaring certain contracts judicially unenforceable (but not void) if they are not committed to writing and signed by the parties. **2.** A statute—based on the English Statute of Frauds—that, in order to prevent fraud and perjury, requires certain contracts to be in writing and signed by the parties; the statute applies to the following types of contracts: (1) a contract of an executor or administrator to answer for a decedent's debt, (2) a contract to guarantee the debt or duty of another, (3) a contract made in consideration of marriage, (4) a contract for the sale or transfer of an interest in land, (5) a contract that cannot be performed within one year of its making, and (6) a contract for the sale of goods valued at $500 or more (U.C.C. § 2-201(1)). —Also termed (in sense 2) *statute of frauds and perjuries*.

statute of limitations. A statute establishing a time limit for suing or for prosecuting a crime, based on the date when the claim accrues (usu. when the injury occurs); the purpose of such a statute is to require diligent prosecution of known claims, thereby providing finality and predictability in legal affairs and ensuring that claims will be resolved while evidence is reasonably available and fresh. Cf. STATUTE OF REPOSE.

statute of repose. A statute that bars a suit a fixed number of years after the defendant acts in some way (such as by designing or manufacturing a product), even if this period ends before the plaintiff suffers any injury. Cf. STATUTE OF LIMITATIONS.

Statute of Uses. An English statute (enacted in 1535) that discouraged the granting of property subject to another's use by deeming the person who enjoys the use to have legal title with the right of absolute ownership and possession; for example, if A conveys land to B subject to the use of C, then C becomes the legal owner of the land in fee simple.

statute of wills. 1. (*cap.*) An English statute (enacted in 1540) that established the right of persons to devise real property by will. —Also termed *Wills Act.* **2.** A state statute, usu. derived from the English stat-

ute, providing for testamentary disposition in that jurisdiction.

Statutes at Large. An official compilation of the acts and resolutions of each session of Congress, printed in chronological order.

statutory, *adj.* **1.** Of or relating to legislation <statutory interpretation>. **2.** Legislatively created <the law of patents is purely statutory>. **3.** Conformable to a statute <a statutory act>.

statutory agent. See AGENT.

statutory construction. The act or process of interpreting a statute. See CONSTRUCTION (2).

statutory deed. See DEED.

statutory foreclosure. See *power-of-sale foreclosure* under FORE-CLOSURE.

statutory law. The body of law derived from statutes rather than from constitutions or judicial decisions. — Also termed *statute law; legislative law; ordinary law.* Cf. COMMON LAW (1); CONSTITUTIONAL LAW.

statutory lien. See LIEN.

statutory partnership association. PARTNERSHIP ASSOCIATION.

statutory rape. See RAPE.

stay, *n.* **1.** The postponement or halting of a proceeding, judgment, or the like. **2.** An order to suspend all or part of a judicial proceeding or judgment resulting from that proceeding. —Also termed *stay of execution.* —**stay,** *vb.* —**stayable,** *adj.*

automatic stay. In bankruptcy, a bar to all judicial and extrajudicial collection efforts against the debtor or the debtor's property; the bar is effective upon the filing of the bankruptcy petition. —Also termed *automatic suspension.*

stay law. A statute that suspends execution or some other legal procedure.

STB. *abbr.* Surface Transportation Board. See INTERSTATE COMMERCE COMMISSION.

steal, *vb.* **1.** To take (personal property) illegally with the intent to keep it unlawfully. **2.** To take (something) by larceny, embezzlement, or false pretenses.

stepped-up basis. See BASIS.

steward. 1. A person appointed in place of another. **2.** A union official who represents union employees and who oversees the carrying out of union contracts. —Also termed (in sense 2) *union steward; shop steward.*

stickering. In securities law, the practice of updating an SEC registration statement to account for material changes; the prospectus supplement is termed a "sticker," hence the name for this practice. See REGISTRATION STATEMENT.

stipulated damages. See *liquidated damages* under DAMAGES.

stipulation, *n.* **1.** A material condition or requirement in an agreement <breach of the stipulation regarding payment of taxes>. **2.** A voluntary agreement between opposing parties concerning some relevant point <the plaintiff and defendant entered into a stipulation on the issue of liability>. —**stipulate,** *vb.*—**stipulative,** *adj.*

stirpes (stər-peez). See PER STIRPES.

stirps (stərps), *n.* [Latin "stock or stem"] The descendants of a common ancestor; branch of a family. Pl. **stirpes. —stirpital** (stər-pi-təl), *adj.* See PER STIRPES.

stock, *n.* **1.** In the law of descent, the original progenitor of a family <George Harper, Sr. was the stock of the Harper line>. **2.** A merchant's goods that are kept for sale or trade <the car dealer put all of last year's models on sale to reduce its stock>. **3.** The capital or principal fund raised by a corporation through subscribers' contributions or the sale of shares <the value of XYZ Corporation's stock has increased by 35% over the last five years>. **4.** A proportional part of a corporation's capital, represented by the number of units (or shares) that one owns, and granting the holder the right to participate in the company's general management and to share in its net profits or earnings <Dale sold his stock in Walt Disney Co.>. See SHARE (2). Cf. SECURITY (4).

authorized stock. The total number of shares of stock that the charter or articles of incorporation permit a corporation to sell; a corporation may increase the amount of authorized stock if a majority of its shareholders consent. —Also termed *authorized shares; authorized capital stock; authorized stock issue.*

blue-chip stock. See BLUE CHIP.

bonus stock. A stock share that is issued for no consideration, as an enticement to buy some other type or class of security; considered a type of watered stock. —Also termed *bonus share.*

capital stock. **a.** The total amount of stock authorized for issue by a corporation, including common stock and preferred stock. **b.** The total par value or stated value of this stock.

common stock. Ownership shares in a corporation entitling the holder to vote and to receive dividends after other claims and dividends have been paid (esp. to preferred shareholders); often called *capital stock* if it is the corporation's only class of stock outstanding. —Also termed *ordinary shares.* Cf. *preferred stock.*

convertible stock. See *convertible security* under SECURITY.

cumulative preferred stock. Preferred stock that must pay dividends in full before common shareholders may receive any dividend; if the corporation passes a dividend in a particular year or period, it is carried over to the next year or period and must be paid before the common shareholders receive any payment. —Also termed *cumulative stock.*

deferred stock. Stock whose dividends are paid only after the corporation meets some other specified obligation, such as the discharge of a liability or the payment of a dividend to preferred shareholders.

discount stock. A stock share issued for less than par value; considered a type of watered stock, the issuance of which may impose liability on the recipient for the difference between the par value and the cash

amount paid. —Also termed *discount share.*

hot stock. See *hot issue* under ISSUE (2).

letter stock. See *restricted security* under SECURITY.

listed stock. See *listed security* under SECURITY.

nonassessable stock. Stock owned by a holder whose potential liability is limited to the amount paid for the stock and who cannot be charged additional funds to pay the issuer's debts; most stock issued in the U.S. is nonassessable.

noncumulative preferred stock. A type of preferred stock that does not have to pay dividends that are in arrears; once a period's dividends are passed, they will not be paid.

nonparticipating preferred stock. A type of preferred stock that does not give the shareholder the right to additional earnings—usu. surplus common- stock dividends—beyond those stated in the preferred contract.

nonvoting stock. Stock that has no voting rights attached to it under most situations.

no-par stock. Stock issued without a specific value assigned to it; for accounting purposes, it is given a legal or stated value that has little or no connection to the stock's market value.

outstanding stock. Stock that is held by an investor and has not been redeemed by the issuing corporation. —Also termed *outstanding capital stock; shares outstanding.*

participating preferred stock. Preferred stock whose holder is entitled to priority in receiving stated dividends or in sharing with the common shareholders in any additional distributions of earnings.

penny stock. Highly speculative stock that can be purchased for under a dollar a share.

preferred stock. Stock that gives its holders a preferential claim to a company's earnings and to its assets on liquidation; usu. preferred stock is nonvoting stock. —Also termed *preference shares.* Cf. *common stock.*

public stock. **a.** See *public security* under SECURITY. **b.** Stock of a publicly traded corporation.

registered stock. See *registered security* under SECURITY.

restricted stock. See *restricted security* under SECURITY.

treasury stock. Stock issued by a company but then reacquired and either canceled or held as an asset; some states have eliminated this classification and treat such stock as if it is authorized but unissued. —Also termed *reacquired stock*; *retired stock.*

unissued stock. Stock that is authorized by the corporate charter, but not yet distributed.

unlisted stock. See *unlisted security* under SECURITY.

voting stock. Stock that entitles the holder to vote in the corporation's election of its officers and on other matters put to a vote.

watered stock. Stock issued for no or little consideration, usu. in exchange for overvalued property or services.

stock acquisition. SHARE ACQUISITION.

stock association. See *joint-stock company* under COMPANY.

stock attribution. ATTRIBUTION.

stockbroker. One who buys or sells stock as the agent of another.

stock certificate. An instrument evidencing ownership of a bond or shares of stock. —Also termed *certificate of stock*; *share certificate.*

stock clearing. The actual physical delivery of money and stocks between buyer and seller.

stock corporation. See CORPORATION.

stock dividend. See DIVIDEND.

stock exchange. See SECURITIES EXCHANGE.

stockholder. SHAREHOLDER.

stockholder derivative suit. DERIVATIVE ACTION (1).

stockholders' equity. OWNERS' EQUITY.

stock insurance company. An insurance company operated as a private corporation and owned by stockholders who share in the company's profits and losses. Cf. MUTUAL INSURANCE COMPANY.

stockjobber. JOBBER (2).

stock market. See MARKET (4) & (5).

stock merger. See MERGER.

stock option. See OPTION.

stock redemption. REDEMPTION (3).

stock right. SUBSCRIPTION RIGHT.

stock split. The issuing of a number of new shares in return for each old share without changing the proportional ownership interests of each shareholder; for example, a 3-for-1 split would give an owner of 100 shares an additional 200 shares, or 3 shares for each share previously owned. —Also termed *share split*.

reverse stock split. The reduction in the number of shares outstanding when a corporation calls in its stocks and reissues a smaller number.

stock subscription. SUBSCRIPTION (2).

stock swap. See SWAP.

stock-transfer agent. See AGENT.

stock warrant. SUBSCRIPTION WARRANT.

stop, *n.* Under the Fourth Amendment, a temporary restraint that prevents a person from walking away.

stop-and-frisk rule. The constitutional doctrine that a police officer may, without a warrant or probable cause, stop and search a person for a concealed weapon if the officer reasonably suspects the person is a criminal or on the verge of committing a crime. *Terry v. Ohio*, 392 U.S. 1 (1968). See TERRY STOP.

stop-loss order. See ORDER (4).

stop order. **1.** See *stop-loss order* under ORDER (4). **2.** An SEC order that suspends a registration statement containing false, incomplete, or misleading information. **3.** A bank customer's order instructing the bank not to honor one of the custom-

er's checks. —Also termed (in sense 3) *stop-payment order*.

straddle, *n.* In securities and commodities trading, a situation in which an investor holds contracts to buy and to sell the same security or commodity, thus ensuring a loss on one of the contracts; the aim of this strategy is to defer gains and use losses to offset other taxable income. —Also termed *spread eagle*. — **straddle,** *vb.*

straight annuity. See ANNUITY.

straight bankruptcy. See CHAPTER 7.

straight bill of lading. See BILL OF LADING.

straight life annuity. See *nonrefund annuity* under ANNUITY.

straight life insurance. See *whole life insurance* under INSURANCE.

straight-line depreciation method. See DEPRECIATION METHOD.

straight-term mortgage. See *interest-only mortgage* under MORTGAGE.

straight voting. See *noncumulative voting* under VOTING.

straw bond. See BOND (2).

straw man. **1.** A fictitious person, esp. one that is weak or flawed. **2.** A tenuous and exaggerated counterargument that an advocate puts forward for the sole purpose of disproving it. —Also termed *straw-man argument*. **3.** In some transactions, a third party used as a temporary transferee to allow the principal parties to accomplish something that is otherwise impermissible. **4.** A person hired to post a worthless bail bond for the release of an accused.

stranger. **1.** One who is not party to a given transaction <she was a stranger to the agreement>. **2.** One not standing toward another in some relation implied in the context <the trustee was negotiating with a stranger>.

strategic alliance. A coalition—less structured than a joint venture—formed by two or more persons in the same or complementary businesses to gain long-term financial, operational, and marketing advantages without jeopardizing competitive independence <through their strategic alliance, the manufacturer and distributor of a co-developed product shared development costs>. Cf. JOINT VENTURE; PARTNERSHIP.

street name. The registered name of securities that are held in the name of the broker instead of in the name of the owner.

strict construction. See CONSTRUCTION.

strict constructionism, *n.* The doctrinal view of judicial construction holding that judges should apply the literal words of a statute or document without looking to the purpose behind them. —Also termed *literal canon*; *literal rule*. —**strict constructionist,** *n.*

strict foreclosure. See FORECLOSURE.

strict liability. See LIABILITY.

strict-liability crime. See CRIME.

strict scrutiny. In constitutional law, the standard applied to suspect classifications (such as race) in equal-protection analysis and to fundamental rights (such as voting rights) in due-process analysis; under strict scrutiny, the state must establish that it has a compelling interest that justifies and necessitates the law in question. See COMPELLING-STATE-INTEREST TEST; SUSPECT CLASSIFICATION; FUNDAMENTAL RIGHT. Cf. INTERMEDIATE SCRUTINY; RATIONAL-BASIS TEST.

strict settlement. See SETTLEMENT.

strike, *n.* An organized cessation or slowdown of work by employees to compel the employer to meet the employees' demands. —**strike,** *vb.* Cf. LOCKOUT; BOYCOTT; PICKETING.

general strike. A strike organized to affect an entire industry.

secondary strike. A strike against another employer who has business dealings with the employer involved in a dispute with the union. See *secondary boycott* under BOYCOTT; *secondary picketing* under PICKETING.

sit-down strike. A strike in which employees appear at the workplace but do not work.

sympathy strike. A strike by union members who have no grievances against their employer, but who want to show solidarity with another union.

wildcat strike. A strike not authorized by a union or in violation of a collective-bargaining agreement.

strike, *vb.* **1.** (Of an employee or employees) to engage in a strike against <the flight attendants struck the airline>. **2.** To reject (a venire-member) by a peremptory challenge <the prosecution struck the panelist who indicated an opposition to the death penalty>. **3.** To expunge, as from a record <motion to strike the prejudicial evidence>.

strikebreaker. SCAB.

strike down. To invalidate (a statute).

strike price. See PRICE.

strike suit. See SUIT.

striking a jury. The selecting of a jury out of all the candidates available to serve on the jury; esp., the selecting of a special jury. See *special jury* (a) under JURY.

struck jury. See *special jury* (a) under JURY.

structured settlement. See SETTLEMENT.

study release. A program that allows a prisoner to be released for a few hours at a time to attend classes at a nearby college or technical institution. —Also termed *study furlough*.

style. A case name or designation <the style of the opinion is *Connor v. Gray*>.

suable, *adj.* **1.** Capable of being sued <a suable party>. **2.** Capable of being enforced <a suable contract>. — **suability,** *n.*

sua sponte (**soo**-ə-**spon**-tee). [Latin "of one's own accord; voluntarily"] Without prompting or suggestion; on its own motion <the court took notice sua sponte that it lacked jurisdiction over the case>.

subagent. See AGENT.

subchapter-C corporation. See *C corporation* under CORPORATION.

subchapter-S corporation. See *S corporation* under CORPORATION.

subcontract. See CONTRACT.

subcontractor. See CONTRACTOR.

subdivision, *n.* **1.** The division of a thing into smaller parts. **2.** A parcel of land in a larger development. — **subdivide,** *vb.*

subdivision exaction. A charge that a community imposes on a subdivider as a condition for permitting recordation of the subdivision map and sale of the subdivided parcels.

subdivision map. A map that shows how a parcel of land is to be divided into smaller lots, and generally showing the layout and utilities.

subinfeudation (səb-in-fyoo-**day**-shən), *n.* The system under which the tenants in a feudal system granted smaller estates to their tenants who in turn did the same from their piece of land. —**subinfeudate** (sə-bin-**fyoo**-dayt), **subinfeud** (sə-bin-**fyood**), *vb.* —**subinfeudatory** (sə-bin-**fyoo**-də-tor-ee), *adj.* Cf. INFEUDATION.

subjacent, *adj.* Located underneath or below <the land's subjacent support>.

subjacent support. See SUPPORT.

subject, *n.* **1.** One who owes allegiance to a sovereign and is governed by that sovereign's laws <the monarchy's subjects>. **2.** The matter of concern over which something is created <the subject of the statute>. — Also termed (in sense 2) *subject matter*.

subject, *adj. Jargon.* Referred to above; having relevance to the current discussion <the subject property was then sold to Smith>.

subjective ethics. MORAL RELATIVISM.

subjective standard. A legal standard that is peculiar to a particular person and based on the person's individual views and experiences; in criminal law, for example, premeditation is determined by a subjective standard because it depends on the defendant's mental state. Cf. OBJECTIVE STANDARD.

subject-matter jurisdiction. See JURISDICTION.

subject to open. Denoting the future interest of a class of people when this class is subject to a possible increase or decrease in number.

sub judice (səb-**joo**-di-see *or* -**yoo**-di-kay). [Latin] *Jargon.* Before a court or judge for determination; legal writers sometimes use "case sub judice" where "the present case" would suffice more comprehensibly <in the case sub judice, there have been no out-of-court settlements>.

sublease, *n.* A lease by a lessee to a third party, conveying some or all of the leased property for a shorter term than that of the lessee, who retains a reversion in the lease. — Also termed *subtenancy* and (esp. in England) *underlease.* —**sublease, sublet,** *vb.*

sublessee. A third party who receives by lease some or all of the leased property from a lessee. —Also termed *subtenant* and (esp. in England) *undertenant.*

sublessor. A lessee who leases some or all of the leased property to a third party. —Also termed (esp. in England) *underlessor.*

submission, *n.* **1.** A yielding to authority or will of another <his resistance ended in an about-face: complete submission>. **2.** A contract in which the parties agree to refer dispute to a third party for resolution <in their submission to arbitration, they referred to the rules of the American Arbitration Association>. **3.** An advocate's argument <neither the written nor the oral submissions were particularly helpful>. —**submit,** *vb.*

sub modo (səb-**moh**-doh). [Latin] Subject to conditions or qualifications <the riparian landowner enjoys the property *sub modo,* i.e., subject to the right of the public to reserve enough space for levees, public roads, and the like>.

submortgage. See MORTGAGE.

sub nomine (səb-**nom**-ə-nee). [Latin] Under the name—this phrase, in a case citation, indicates that there has been a name change from one stage of the case to another, as in *Guernsey Memorial Hosp. v. Secretary of Health and Human Servs.,* 996 F.2d 830 (6th Cir.1993), *rev'd sub nom. Shalala v. Guernsey Memorial Hosp.,* 115 S.Ct. 1232 (1995). —Abbr. *sub nom.*

subordinate, *adj.* Inferior in nature, power, or order. —**subordinate,** *vb.*—**subordinate,** *n.*

subordinate debenture. See DEBENTURE.

subordinate legislation. REGULATION (2).

subordination, *n.* The act or process of moving something to a lower rank, position, or priority, esp. a person's rights <subordination of a first lien to a second lien>. —**subordinate,** *vb.*—**subordinate, subordinative,** *adj.*—**subordinate,** *n.*

subordination agreement. An agreement by which one who holds an otherwise senior interest agrees to subordinate that interest to a normally lesser interest; frequently used when a seller agrees to subordinate his or her purchase-money mortgage so that the buyer can obtain a first-mortgage loan to improve the property.

subordination clause. A covenant in a junior mortgage enabling the first lien to keep its priority in case of renewal or refinancing.

suborn (sə-**born**), *vb.* **1.** To induce (a person) to commit an unlawful or wrongful act, esp. in a secret or underhanded manner. **2.** To induce (a person) to commit perjury. **3.** To obtain (perjured testimony) from another. —**subornation,** (sə-bor-**nay**-shən), *n.*

subpartnership. See PARTNERSHIP.

subpoena (sə-**pee**-nə), *n.* A court order commanding the appearance of a witness, subject to penalty for noncompliance. —Also termed *subpoena ad testificandum.* Pl. **subpoenas.** —**subpoena,** *vb.*

alias subpoena. A subpoena issued after an initial subpoena has failed.

subpoena duces tecum (doo-səs-**tee**-kəm *or* -**tay**-kəm). A subpoena ordering the witness not only to ap-

pear but also to bring specified books, papers, or records.

subpoenal (sə-**pee**-nəl), *adj.* Required or done under penalty, esp. in compliance with a subpoena.

subrogation (səb-roh-**gay**-shən), *n.* **1.** The substitution of one party for another whose debts the party pays, entitling the paying party to rights, remedies, or securities that would otherwise go to the debtor. **2.** The principle under which an insurer that has paid the loss under an indemnity policy is entitled to take on all the rights and remedies belonging to the insured against a third party with respect to any injuries or breaches covered by the policy. —**subrogate** (səb-roh-gayt), *vb.*—**subrogative** (səb-roh-gay-div), *adj.*

conventional subrogation. Subrogation that arises by contract or by express acts of the parties.

legal subrogation. Subrogation that arises by operation of law or by implication in equity to prevent fraud or injustice; such subrogation usu. arises when: (1) the paying party has a liability, claim, or fiduciary relationship with the debtor, (2) the party pays to fulfill a legal duty or because of public policy, (3) the paying party is a secondary debtor, (4) the paying party is a surety, or (5) the party pays to protect its own rights or property.

subrogee (səb-rə-**jee**). One who is substituted for another in having a right, duty, or claim.

subrogor (səb-rə-**gor**). One who allows another to be substituted for oneself as creditor, with a transfer of rights and duties.

subscribed capital. See CAPITAL.

subscribing witness. See WITNESS.

subscription, *n.* **1.** The act of signing one's name on a document; the signature so affixed. **2.** In securities law, a written contract to purchase newly issued shares of stock or bonds. —Also termed (in connection with stock) *stock subscription.* **3.** An oral or written agreement to contribute a sum of money or property, gratuitously or with consideration, to a specific person or for a specific purpose. —**subscribe,** *vb.*

subscription price. The price at which investors can buy shares in a new stock offering before the shares are offered to the public.

subscription privilege. PREEMPTIVE RIGHT.

subscription right. A certificate evidencing a shareholder's right (known as a *preemptive right*) to purchase newly issued stock before the stock is offered to the public; subscription rights have a market value and are actively traded because they allow the holder to purchase stock at favorable prices. —Also termed *stock right.* See PREEMPTIVE RIGHT.

subscription warrant. An instrument granting the holder a long-term (usu. a five- to ten-year) option to buy shares at a fixed price; commonly attached to preferred stocks or bonds. —Also termed *warrant*; *stock warrant.*

subsequent remedial measure. (*usu. pl.*) In the law of evidence, an action taken after an event, which, if taken before the event, would have reduced the likelihood of the event's occurrence; evidence of such an action is not admissible to prove negligence, but may be admitted to prove ownership, control, feasibility, or the like. Fed. R. Evid. 407.

subservant. See *subagent* under AGENT.

subsidiary, *n.* See *subsidiary corporation* under CORPORATION.

subsidiary corporation. See CORPORATION.

subsidiary merger. See *triangular merger* under MERGER.

subsidy, *n.* A grant, usu. made by the government, to any enterprise whose promotion is considered to be in the public interest. —**subsidize,** *vb.*

sub silentio (səb-si-**len**-sh[ee]-oh or -t[ee]-oh). [Latin] Under silence; without notice being taken.

substantial-capacity test. In criminal law, the Model Penal Code's test for the insanity defense, stating that a person is not criminally responsible for an act if, as a result of a mental disease or defect, the person lacks substantial capacity either to appreciate the criminality of the conduct or to conform the conduct to the law; this test was formerly used by the federal courts and many states, but since 1984 most jurisdictions—in reaction to would-be presidential assassin John Hinckley's acquittal by reason of insanity—have narrowed the insanity defense and adopted a test resembling the *McNaghten* rules. Model Penal Code § 4.01. Cf. MCNAGHTEN RULES.

substantial-certainty test. In copyright law, the test for deciding whether a second work was copied from the first; the question is whether a reasonable observer would conclude with substantial certainty that the second work is a copy.

substantial-compliance rule. SUBSTANTIAL-PERFORMANCE DOCTRINE.

substantial evidence. See EVIDENCE.

substantial-evidence rule. The principle that a reviewing court should uphold an administrative body's ruling if it is supported by evidence on which the administrative body could reasonably base its decision.

substantial-performance doctrine. The equitable rule that, if a good-faith attempt to perform does not precisely meet the terms of the agreement, the agreement will still be considered complete if the substantial purpose of the contract is accomplished; courts may allow a remedy for minimal damages caused by the deviance. —Also termed *substantial-compliance rule*.

substantial similarity. In copyright law, a strong resemblance between a copyrighted work and an alleged infringement, thereby creating an inference of unauthorized copying; the standard for substantial similarity is whether an ordinary person would conclude that the alleged infringement has appropriated nontrivial amounts of the copyrighted work's expressions. See DERIVATIVE WORK.

comprehensive nonliteral similarity. Similarity evidenced by the copying of the protected work's general ideas or structure (such as a movie's plot) without using the precise words or phrases of the work. — Also termed *pattern similarity*.

fragmented literal similarity. Similarity evidenced by the copying of verbatim portions of the protected work.

substantial-step test. The Model Penal Code's test for determining whether a person is guilty of attempt, based on the extent of the defendant's preparation for the crime, the criminal intent shown, and the defendant's statements as they bear on his or her actions. Model Penal Code § 5.01(1)(c). Cf. DANGEROUS-PROXIMITY TEST; INDISPENSABLE-ELEMENT TEST.

substantive due process. See DUE PROCESS.

substantive evidence. See EVIDENCE.

substantive law. The part of the law that creates, defines, and regulates the rights, duties, and powers of parties. Cf. PROCEDURAL LAW.

substitute, *n.* In civil law, a person named in a will as heir to an estate after the estate has been held and then passed on by another specified person (called the *institute*).

substituted basis. See BASIS.

substituted executor. See EXECUTOR.

substituted-judgment doctrine. The rule allowing a court to exercise the imagined judgment of an incompetent or unconscious person, as when there is a question about withdrawing life support, administering medicine, or approving an estate plan designed to produce tax savings.

substituted service. See SERVICE.

substitution of parties. The replacement of one party to an action by another party due to some event such as death, incompetency, transfer of interest or, in the case of a public official, separation from office.

subsurface right. A landowner's right to the minerals and water below his or her property. See MINERAL RIGHT. Cf. SURFACE RIGHT.

subtenancy. SUBLEASE.

subtenant. SUBLESSEE.

subversive activity. An act aimed at overthrowing the government, such as treason or sedition.

succession, *n.* **1.** The act or right of legally or officially taking over a predecessor's office, rank, or duties. **2.** The acquisition of rights or property by inheritance under the laws of descent and distribution. See INTESTATE SUCCESSION; TESTATE SUCCESSION. **3.** The right by which one group, in replacing another group, acquires all the goods, movables, and other chattels of a corporation. — **successional** (corresponding to sense 2), *adj.*—**successor,** *n.*

succession tax. See *inheritance tax* (a) under TAX.

successor in interest. One who follows another in ownership or control of property; a successor in interest retains the same rights as the original owner, with no change in substance.

such, *adj.* **1.** Of this or that kind <she collects a variety of such things>. **2.** *Jargon.* That or those; having just been mentioned <a newly discovered Fabergé egg will be on auction next week; such egg is expected to sell for more than $500,-000>.

sudden-emergency doctrine. EMERGENCY DOCTRINE (1).

sudden heat of passion. HEAT OF PASSION.

sudden-peril doctrine. EMERGENCY DOCTRINE (1).

sue, *vb.* To institute a legal proceeding against (another party).

sue out, *vb.* To apply to a court for the issuance of (a court order or writ).

sufferance (səf-[ə-]rən[t]s). **1.** Toleration; passive consent. **2.** The state of one who holds land without the owner's permission. See *tenancy at sufferance* under TENANCY. **3.** A license implied from the omission to enforce a right.

sufficiency-of-evidence test. The guideline for a grand jury considering whether to indict a suspect: if all the evidence presented were uncontradicted and unexplained, it would warrant a conviction by the fact-trier. — Also termed *sufficiency-of-the-evidence test.*

sufficient cause. 1. See *good cause* under CAUSE (2). **2.** PROBABLE CAUSE.

suffrage (səf-rəj). **1.** The right or privilege of casting a vote at a public election. **2.** A vote; the act of voting.

suggestibility, *n.* The readiness with which a person accepts another's suggestion. —**suggestible,** *adj.*

suggestion, *n.* **1.** An indirect presentation of an idea <the client agreed with counsel's suggestion to reword the warranty>. **2.** In litigation practice, a statement of some fact or circumstance that will materially affect the further proceedings in the case <suggestion for rehearing en banc>. —**suggest** (corresponding to sense 1), *vb.*

suicide, *n.* **1.** The act of taking one's own life. —Also termed *self-killing*.

assisted suicide. The intentional act of providing a person with the medical means or the medical knowledge to commit suicide. — Also termed *assisted self-determination*.

2. A person who has taken his or her own life. —**suicidal,** *adj.*

sui generis (soo-ee-**jen**-ə-rəs). [Latin "of its own kind"] Of its own kind or class; unique or peculiar.

sui juris (soo-ee-**juur**-əs). [Latin "of one's own right"] **1.** Of full age and capacity. **2.** Possessing full social and civil rights.

suit. Any proceeding by a party or parties against another in a court of law; CASE. —Also termed *lawsuit*.

ancillary suit. An action, either in law or in equity, that grows out of and is auxiliary to another suit and is filed to aid the primary suit, to enforce a prior judgment, or to impeach a prior decree. —Also termed *ancillary bill*; *ancillary proceeding*; *ancillary process*.

blackmail suit. A suit filed by a party having no genuine claim but hoping to extract a favorable settlement from a defendant who would rather avoid the expenses and hassles of litigation.

class suit. CLASS ACTION.

derivative suit. DERIVATIVE ACTION.

strike suit. A derivative action brought against a corporation either for nuisance value or to obtain a favorable settlement.

suit money. The payment by one party of the attorney's fees and court costs of the opposing party, esp. the husband's payment of the wife's attorney's fees in a divorce action.

suitor. **1.** The party that brings an action; the plaintiff or petitioner. **2.** A man who seeks to marry a woman; a wooer. **3.** A corporation or individual who offers to buy the corporation's voting stock in order to take over the corporation.

suit papers. COURT PAPERS.

sum certain. **1.** Any amount that is fixed, settled, or exact. **2.** In negotiable instruments, a sum that is agreed upon in the instrument or a sum that can be ascertained from the document.

summary, *n.* **1.** An abridgement or brief. **2.** A short application to a court without the formality of a full proceeding.

summary, *adj.* **1.** Short; concise <a summary account of the events on March 6>. **2.** Without the usual formalities; esp., without a jury <summary trial>. **3.** Immediate; done without delay <the new weapon was

put to summary use by the military>.

summary adjudication. See *partial summary judgment* under SUMMARY JUDGMENT.

summary court-martial. See COURT-MARTIAL.

summary disposition. SUMMARY JUDGMENT.

summary judgment. A judgment granted on a claim about which there is no genuine issue of material fact and upon which the movant is entitled to prevail as a matter of law; this procedural device allows the speedy disposition of a controversy without the need for trial. Fed. R. Civ. P. 56. —Also termed *summary disposition*. See JUDGMENT.

partial summary judgment. A summary judgment that is limited to certain issues in a case and that disposes of only a portion of the whole case. —Also termed *summary adjudication*.

summary-judgment motion. MOTION FOR SUMMARY JUDGMENT.

summary jury trial. See TRIAL.

summary proceeding. See PROCEEDING.

summation. See CLOSING ARGUMENT.

summer associate. CLERK (4).

summing up. CLOSING ARGUMENT.

summon, *vb.* To command (a person) by service of a summons to appear in court. —Also termed *summons*.

summons, *n.* **1.** Formerly, a writ directing a sheriff to summon a de-

fendant to appear in court. **2.** A writ or process commencing the plaintiff's action and requiring the defendant to appear and answer. **3.** A notice requiring a person to appear in court as a juror or witness. Pl. **summonses.**

John Doe summons. A summons to someone whose name is unknown.

short summons. A summons having a response time less than that of an ordinary summons, usu. served on a fraudulent or nonresident debtor.

summons, *vb.* **1.** SUMMON. **2.** To request (information) by summons.

sum-of-the-years'-digits depreciation method. See DEPRECIATION METHOD.

sumptuary law. 1. A statute, ordinance, or regulation that limits the expenditures that people can make for personal gratification or ostentatious display. **2.** More broadly, any law whose purpose is to regulate conduct thought to be immoral, such as prostitution, gambling, or the purchase and sale of mind- and mood-altering drugs.

Sunday-closing law. BLUE LAW.

Sunday law. BLUE LAW.

sunk cost. See COST.

sunset law. A statute under which a governmental agency or program automatically terminates at the end of a fixed period unless it is formally renewed.

sunshine law. A statute requiring a governmental department or agency to open its meetings and its records to public access. —Also termed *open-public-meeting law*.

suo nomine (soo-oh-**nom**-ə-nee). [Latin] In his or her own name.

Superfund. 1. The program that funds and administers the clean up of hazardous waste sites through a trust fund (financed by taxes on petroleum and chemicals and a new tax on corporations) created to pay for clean up pending reimbursement from the liable parties. **2.** The popular name for the act that established this program—the Comprehensive Environmental Response, Compensation, and Liability Act of 1980 (CERCLA). See CERCLA.

superior court. See COURT.

supermajority. See MAJORITY.

superpriority. In bankruptcy, the special priority status granted by the court to a creditor for extending credit to a debtor or trustee that cannot obtain unsecured credit from a willing lender; this priority may be either an administrative claim outranking other administrative claims or, if certain statutory requirements are met, a security interest in property.

supersede, *vb.* **1.** To annul, make void, or repeal by taking the place of <the 1996 statute supersedes the 1989 act>. **2.** To invoke or make applicable the right of supersedeas against (an award of damages) <what is the amount of the bond necessary to supersede the judgment against her? >. —**supersession** (corresponding to sense 1), *n.*

supersedeas (soo-pər-**seed**-ee-əs), *n.* [Latin "you shall desist"] A writ or bond that suspends a judgment creditor's power to levy execution, usu. pending appeal. Pl. **supersedeases.**

supersedeas bond. See BOND (2).

superseding cause. See CAUSE (1).

supervening cause. See *intervening cause* under CAUSE (1).

supervisor, *n.* **1.** One having authority over others; a manager or overseer. **2.** The chief administrative officer of a town or county. —**supervise,** *vb.*—**supervisory, supervisorial,** *adj.*

supplemental claim. See CLAIM (3).

supplemental complaint. See COMPLAINT.

supplemental jurisdiction. See JURISDICTION.

supplemental pleading. See PLEADING (1).

supplementary proceeding. A proceeding held in connection with the enforcement of a judgment, for the purpose of identifying and locating the debtor's assets available to satisfy the judgment.

supplier, *n.* A person engaged, directly or indirectly, in the business of making a product available to consumers. —**supply,** *vb.*

supply, *n.* The amount of goods produced or available at a given price.

supply curve. A line on a price-output graph showing the relationship between a good's price and the quantity supplied at a given time.

support, *n.* **1.** Sustenance or maintenance; esp., articles such as food and clothing that allow one to live in the degree of comfort to which one is accustomed. See MAINTENANCE (2); NECESSARIES. **2.** Basis or foundation. **3.** The right to have one's ground braced so that it does not cave in due to another landowner's actions. —**support**, *vb.*

lateral support. The right to have one's land supported by the land that lies next to it.

subjacent support. The right to have one's land supported by the earth that lies underneath it.

support trust. See TRUST.

supposition, *n.* An assumption that something is true, without proof of its veracity; the act of supposing. —**suppose**, *vb.*—**supposable**, *adj.*

suppress, *vb.* To put a stop to, put down, or prohibit; to prevent (something) from being seen, heard, known, or discussed <the defendant tried to suppress the incriminating evidence>. —**suppression**, *n.*—**suppressible**, *adj.*—**suppressive**, *adj.*

suppression hearing. A pretrial proceeding in which a criminal defendant seeks to prevent the introduction of evidence alleged to have been seized illegally.

suppression of evidence. 1. A trial judge's ruling that evidence sought to be admitted should be excluded because it was illegally acquired. **2.** The destruction of evidence or the refusal to give evidence or testify at a criminal proceeding; this is usu. considered a crime. **3.** The prosecution's withholding from the defense of evidence that is favorable to the defendant.

supra (**soo**-prə). [Latin "above"] Earlier in this text; used as a citational signal to refer to a previously cited authority. Cf. INFRA.

Supremacy Clause. The clause—contained in Art. VI of the U.S. Con-

stitution—declaring that all laws made in pursuance of the Constitution and all treaties made under the authority of the United States are the "supreme law of the land" and enjoy legal superiority over any conflicting provision of a state constitution or law. See PREEMPTION.

supreme court. 1. (*cap.*) SUPREME COURT OF THE UNITED STATES. **2.** An appellate court existing in most states, usu. as the court of last resort. **3.** In New York, a court of general jurisdiction with trial and appellate divisions; the Court of Appeals is the court of last resort in New York. —Abbr. S.C.; S.Ct.

Supreme Court of the United States. The court of last resort in the federal system, whose members are appointed by the President and approved by the Senate; the Court was established in 1789 by Art. III, § 1 of the U.S. Constitution, which vests the Court with the "judicial [p]ower of the United States."—Often shortened to *Supreme Court.* — Also termed *United States Supreme Court.*

Supreme Judicial Court. The highest appellate court in Maine and Massachusetts.

surcharge, *n.* **1.** An additional tax, charge, or cost, usu. one that is excessive. **2.** An additional load or burden. **3.** A second or further mortgage. **4.** The amount that a court may charge a fiduciary who has breached its duty. **5.** An overprint on a stamp, esp. one that changes its face value. **6.** The overstocking of an area with animals. —**surcharge**, *vb.*

surety (**shuur**[-ə]-tee). **1.** A person who is primarily liable for the payment of another's debt or the performance of another's obligation. **2.** A formal assurance; esp., a pledge, bond, guarantee, or security given for the fulfillment of an undertaking. **3.** The state of being sure, confident, or secure.

surety bond. See *performance bond* under BOND (2).

suretyship. 1. The contractual relationship among a debtor (known as the *principal*), a creditor, and a surety who becomes answerable for the debtor's debt or obligation. **2.** The position or status of a surety.

surface right. A landowner's right to the land's surface and to all substances below the surface that are not defined as minerals; the surface right is subject to the mineral owner's right to use the surface. —Also termed *surface interest*. Cf. MINERAL RIGHT.

Surface Transportation Board. See INTERSTATE COMMERCE COMMISSION.

surplus. 1. The remainder of a thing; the residue or excess. **2.** The excess of receipts over disbursements. **3.** Funds that remain after a partnership has been dissolved and all its debts paid. **4.** A corporation's net worth, beyond the par value of capital stock. —Also termed *overplus*.

acquired surplus. The surplus gained by the purchase of another business.

earned surplus. See *retained earnings* under EARNINGS.

paid-in surplus. The surplus gained by the sale, exchange, or issuance of capital stock at a price above par

value. —Also termed *capital surplus*; *premium on capital stock*.

revaluation surplus. Surplus that is gained when assets are reappraised at a higher value. —Also termed *appreciation surplus*.

surplusage (sər-plə-sij). **1.** Redundant words in a statute or other drafted document; language that does not add meaning <the court must give effect to every word, read­ing nothing as mere surplusage>. **2.** Extraneous matter in a pleading <because these allegations were ir­relevant to the case, they will be treated as surplusage>.

surplus earnings. See EARNINGS.

surrebutter (sər-[r]i-**bət**-ər). In common-law pleading, the plaintiff's answer of fact to the defendant's rebutter.

surrejoinder (sər-[r]i-**join**-dər). In common-law pleading, the plaintiff's answer of fact to the defendant's rejoinder.

surrender, *n.* **1.** The act of yielding to another's power or control. **2.** In property law, the return of an estate to the person who has a reversion or remainder, so as to merge the estate into a larger estate. **3.** In commercial law, the delivery of an instrument so that the delivery releases the deliverer from all liability. **4.** In landlord-tenant law, the tenant's relinquishment of possession before the lease has expired, allowing the landlord to take possession and treat the lease as terminated. —**surrender,** *vb.*

surrender value. In insurance, the current cash value of a life-insurance policy; this amount is paid to the policyholder if he or she cancels the policy.

surrogate (sər-ə-gət), *n.* **1.** A substitute; esp., a person appointed to act in the place of another <in his absence, Sam's wife acted as a surrogate>. **2.** PROBATE JUDGE <the surrogate held that the will was valid>. **—surrogacy** (sər-ə-gə-see), **surrogateship,** *n.*

surrogate court. See *probate court* under COURT.

surrogate mother. 1. A woman who carries a child to term on behalf of another woman and then assigns her parental rights to that woman and the father. **2.** A person who carries out the role of a mother.

surrogate parent. A person who carries out the role of a parent by court appointment or the voluntary assumption of parental responsibilities.

surrogate-parenting agreement. An agreement in which the surrogate mother agrees to carry a child to term on behalf of another woman and then assign her parental rights to that woman and the father.

surtax. See TAX.

surveillance (sər-vay-lən[t]s), *n.* Close observation or listening of a person or place in the hope of gathering evidence. **—surveil** (sər-vay[ə]l), *vb.*

survey, *n.* **1.** A general consideration of something; appraisal <a survey of the situation>. **2.** The measuring of a tract of land and its boundaries and contents; a map indicating the results of such measurements <the lender requires a survey of the property before it will issue a loan>. **3.** A governmental department that carries out such measurements <please obtain the boundaries from survey>. **4.** A poll or questionnaire, esp. one examining popular opinion <the radio station took a survey of the concert audience>. **—survey,** *vb.*

surveyor, *n.* One who surveys land and buildings. **—surveyorship,** *n.*

survival action. A lawsuit brought on behalf of a decedent's estate for injuries or damages incurred by the decedent immediately before death. Cf. WRONGFUL-DEATH ACTION.

survival statute. A law that modifies the common law by allowing certain actions to continue in favor of a personal representative after the death of the party who could have originally brought the action; esp., a law that provides for the estate's recovery of damages incurred by the decedent immediately before death. Cf. DEATH STATUTE.

surviving partner. See PARTNER.

surviving spouse. A spouse who outlives the other spouse.

survivor. 1. One who outlives another. **2.** A trustee who administers a trust after the cotrustee has been removed, has refused to act, or has died.

survivorship. 1. The state or condition of being the one person out of two or more who remains alive after the others die. **2.** The right of a surviving party having a joint interest with others in an estate to take the whole. See RIGHT OF SURVIVORSHIP.

survivorship annuity. See ANNUITY.

suspect, *n.* Someone believed to have committed a wrong.

suspect classification. In constitutional law, a statutory classification based on race, national origin, or alienage, and thereby subject to strict scrutiny under equal-protection analysis; examples of suspect classifications are a law permitting only U.S. citizens to receive welfare benefits and a law setting quotas for the government's hiring of minority contractors. See STRICT SCRUTINY.

quasi-suspect classification. In constitutional law, a statutory classification based on gender or legitimacy, and therefore subject to intermediate scrutiny under equal-protection analysis; examples of quasi-suspect classifications are a law permitting alimony for women only and a law providing for an all-male draft. See INTERMEDIATE SCRUTINY.

suspend, *vb.* **1.** To interrupt; postpone; defer <the fire alarm suspended the prosecutor's opening statement>. **2.** To temporarily keep (a person) from performing a function, occupying an office, holding a job, or exercising a right or privilege <the attorney's law license was suspended for violating the Model Rules of Professional Conduct>. —**suspension,** *n.*

suspended sentence. See SENTENCE.

suspension of arms. TRUCE.

suspicious character. In some states, a person who is strongly suspected or known to be a habitual criminal and therefore may be arrested or required to give security for good behavior.

sustain, *vb.* **1.** To support or maintain, esp. over a long period <enough oxygen to sustain life>. **2.** To nourish and encourage; lend strength to <she helped sustain the criminal enterprise>. **3.** To undergo; suffer <Charles sustained third-degree burns>. **4.** (Of a court) to uphold or rule in favor of <objection sustained>. **5.** To substantiate or corroborate <several witnesses sustained Ms. Sipes's allegation>. **6.** To persist in making (an effort) over a long period <he sustained his vow of silence for the last 16 years of his life>. —**sustainment, sustentation,** *n.*—**sustainable,** *adj.*

suzerainty (sooz-[ə-]rən-tee *or* -ə-rayn-tee). **1.** The power of a feudal overlord to whom fealty is due. See FEALTY. **2.** The dominion of a nation that controls the foreign relations of another nation but allows it autonomy in its domestic affairs.

swap, *n.* An exchange of one security for another.

currency swap. An agreement to swap specified payment obligations denominated in one currency for specified payment obligations denominated in a different currency.

stock swap. In a corporate reorganization, an exchange of one corporation's stock for the stock of another corporation.

swearing contest. A dispute in which determining a vital fact involves the credibility choice between one interested witness's word and another's—the two being irreconcilably in conflict and there being no other evidence; in such a dispute, the fact-finder is generally thought to believe the more reputable witness, such as a police officer over a convicted drug-dealer, or a nun over a law student. —Also termed *swearing match*.

swear out, *vb.* To obtain the issue of (an arrest warrant) by making a charge under oath <Franklin swore out a complaint against Sutton>.

sweat equity. Financial equity created in property by the owner's labor in improving the property <the lender required the homeowner to put 300 hours of sweat equity into the property>.

sweatshop. A business where the employees are overworked and underpaid in extreme conditions; esp., in lawyer lingo, a law firm that requires associates to work so hard that they barely (if at all) maintain a family or social life—though the firm may, in return, pay higher salaries.

swindle, *vb.* **1.** To cheat (a person) out of property <Johnson swindled Norton out of his entire savings>. **2.** To cheat a person out of (property) <Johnson swindled Norton's entire savings out of him>. —**swindle,** *n.*— **swindling,** *n.*

swing vote. The vote that determines an issue when all other voting parties, such as appellate judges, are evenly split.

syllabus (**sil**-ə-bəs). **1.** An abstract or outline of a topic or course of study. **2.** HEADNOTE. Pl. **syllabuses, syllabi.**

symbiotic relationship (sim-bee-ah-dik). A relationship between state and private actors in which mutual advantages are so interwoven that the private actor may be held liable for constitutional violations.

symbolic delivery. See DELIVERY.

symbolic speech. See SPEECH.

sympathy strike. See STRIKE.

syndicalism (**sin**-di-kə-liz-əm), *n.* A direct plan or practice implemented by trade-union workers seeking to control the means of production and distribution, esp. by using a general strike. —**syndicalist,** *n.*

criminal syndicalism. Any doctrine that advocates or teaches the use of illegal methods as a means to change industrial or political control.

syndicate (**sin**-di-kət), *n.* A group organized for some common purpose; esp., an association formed to promote a common interest, carry out some particular business transaction, or (in a negative sense) organize criminal enterprises. —**syndicate** (**sin**-də-kayt), *vb.*—**syndication** (sin-də-**kay**-shən), *n.* See ORGANIZED CRIME.

synergism (**sin**-ər-jiz-əm), *n.* In patent law, a combination of known elements or functions that create a result greater than the sum of the individual elements or functions; demonstrating that synergism exists is sometimes useful in proving nonobviousness. —Also termed *synergy.* —**synergistic, synergetic,** *adj.*

synopsis (si-**nop**-sis), *n.* A brief or partial survey; a summary or outline; HEADNOTE. —**synopsize,** *vb.*

T

TAB. *abbr.* TAX-ANTICIPATION BILL.

table, *vb.* To postpone consideration of (a pending bill or proposal) for a later time.

tabula rasa (tab-yə-lə-**rahs**-ə). [Latin "scraped tablet"] A blank tablet ready for writing; a clean slate. Pl. *tabulae rasae* (tab-yə-lee-**rahs**-I).

tacit (**tas**-it), *adj.* Implied by silence or silent acquiescence; implied by the circumstances, in the absence of an express agreement <they had a tacit understanding>.

tacit admission. See *implied admission* under ADMISSION.

tacking, *n.* **1.** The act of adding one's own period of land possession to that of a prior possessor in order to establish continuous adverse possession for the statutory period. See ADVERSE POSSESSION. **2.** The joining of a junior lien with the first lien in order to acquire priority over an intermediate one. **—tack,** *vb.*

Taft-Hartley Act. LABOR-MANAGEMENT RELATIONS ACT.

tail, *n.* The limitation of an estate so that it can be inherited only by the owner's issue or class of issue. See FEE TAIL; ENTAIL (2).

taint, *vb.* **1.** To imbue with a noxious quality or principle. **2.** To contaminate or corrupt. **3.** To tinge or affect slightly for the worse. **—taint,** *n.*

tainted evidence. See EVIDENCE.

take, *vb.* **1.** To get into one's possession or control, whether legally or illegally <it's a felony to take that property without the owner's consent>. **2.** To seize with authority; to confiscate or apprehend <take the suspect into custody>. **3.** To acquire possession by virtue of a grant of title, the use of eminent domain, or other legal means; esp., to receive property by will or intestate succession <the probate code indicates the proportions according to which each heir will take>. See TAKING.

take-it-or-leave-it contract. See *adhesion contract* under CONTRACT.

take-nothing judgment. See JUDGMENT.

take-or-pay contract. See CONTRACT.

takeover. In corporate law, the act or an instance of assuming ownership or control of another corporation; a takeover is typically accomplished by a purchase of shares, a sale of assets, a tender offer, or a merger.

friendly takeover. A takeover that is favored or approved by the corporation being acquired.

hostile takeover. A takeover that is resisted by the corporation being acquired.

takeover bid. An attempt by an outside corporation or group to wrest control away from the incumbent management of a target corporation.

takeover defense. SHARK REPELLENT.

taking, *n.* **1.** In criminal and tort law, the act of seizing an article, with or without removing it, but with an implicit transfer of possession or control.

constructive taking. An act that does not equal actual appropriation of a chattel but that does show an intention to convert it; an example is when a person entrusted with the possession of goods starts using them contrary to the owner's instructions.

2. In constitutional law, the government's actual or effective acquisition of private property either by ousting the owner and claiming title or by destroying the property or severely impairing its utility. See CONDEMNATION (2); EMINENT DOMAIN.

Takings Clause. The Fifth Amendment provision that prohibits the government from taking private property for public use without fairly compensating the owner. See EMINENT DOMAIN.

taking the Fifth. PLEADING THE FIFTH.

talesman (**taylz**-mən *or* **tay**-leez-mən). *Archaic.* **1.** A person selected from among the bystanders in court to serve as a juror in a case in which the original jury panel has become deficient in number. **2.** VENIRE-MEMBER. —Also termed *tales-juror.*

talisman (**tal**-əs-mən), *n.* A charm, amulet, or other thing supposedly capable of working wonders <private property is not some sacred talisman that can never be touched by the state; it can be taken for public use as long as the owner is justly compensated>. —**talismanic,** *adj.*

TAM. *abbr.* TECHNICAL ADVICE MEMORANDUM.

tampering, *n.* The act or an instance of engaging in improper or underhanded dealings, esp. in an attempt to influence; tampering with a witness or jury is a criminal offense. —**tamper,** *vb.* See OBSTRUCTION OF JUSTICE; EMBRACERY.

tangible evidence. See *demonstrative evidence* under EVIDENCE.

tangible property. See PROPERTY.

target corporation. See CORPORATION.

target offense. See *object offense* under OFFENSE.

target witness. See WITNESS.

tariff, *n.* **1.** A schedule or system of duties imposed by a government on imported or exported goods; in the U.S., tariffs are imposed on imported goods only. **2.** A duty imposed on imported or exported goods under such a system. —**tariff,** *vb.* See DUTY (5).

antidumping tariff. A tariff equaling the difference between the price at which the product is sold in the exporting country and the price at which the importer will sell the product in the importing country; these tariffs are designed to prevent foreign corporations from artificially lowering their prices and gaining unfair advantages outside their home market. See ANTIDUMPING LAW.

discriminatory tariff. A tariff containing duties that are applied unequally to different countries or manufacturers.

protective tariff. A tariff designed primarily to give domestic manufacturers economic protection against price competition from abroad, rather than to generate revenue.

retaliatory tariff. A tariff imposed to pressure another country into removing its own tariffs or making trade concessions.

tax, *n.* A monetary charge imposed by the government on persons, entities, or property to yield public revenue. —**tax,** *vb.*

accumulated-earnings tax. A penalty tax imposed on a corporation that retains its earnings, rather than distributing them to shareholders as dividends, to avoid income taxes paid by the shareholders on those dividends.

ad valorem tax. A tax imposed proportionally on the value of something (esp. real property), rather than on its quantity or some other measure.

alternative minimum tax. A flat tax potentially imposed on corporations and high-income individuals to ensure that those taxpayers do not fully avoid income-tax liability by using exclusions, deductions, and credits. —Abbr. AMT. —Also termed *minimum tax.*

capital-gains tax. A tax on income derived from the sale of a capital asset; the federal income tax on capital gains typically has a more favorable maximum tax rate—28% for individuals and 34% for corporations—than the tax on ordinary income has. See CAPITAL GAIN.

collateral-inheritance tax. A tax levied on the transfer of property by will or intestate succession to persons other than the spouse, parents, or descendants of the decedent.

death tax. An estate tax or inheritance tax.

estate tax. A tax imposed on the estate of a decedent who transfers property by will or by intestate succession. Cf. *inheritance tax.*

estimated tax. A tax paid quarterly by taxpayers not subject to withholding (such as self-employed persons) based on either the previous year's tax liability or an estimation of the current year's tax liability.

excise tax. A tax imposed on the manufacture, sale, or use of goods (such as a cigarette tax), or on an occupation or activity (such as a license tax). Cf. *income tax*; *property tax.*

flat tax. A tax in which the tax rate remains fixed regardless of the amount of the tax base; most sales taxes are flat taxes. —Also termed *proportional tax.* Cf. *progressive tax*; *regressive tax.*

franchise tax. A tax imposed on the privilege of carrying on a business (esp. as a corporation), usu. measured by the business's income. See FRANCHISE.

gift tax. A tax imposed when property is voluntarily and gratuitously transferred; under federal law, the gift tax is imposed on the donor, while in some states, the tax is imposed on the donee.

hidden tax. A tax that is unknowingly paid by someone other than the person or entity on whom it is levied; esp., a tax imposed on a manufacturer or seller (such as a gasoline producer) who passes it on to consumers in the form of a higher sales price.

income tax. A tax on an individual's or entity's net income; the federal income tax—governed by the Internal Revenue Code—is the federal government's primary source of revenue, and many states have income taxes as well. Cf. *excise tax*; *property tax*.

inheritance tax. **a.** A tax imposed on a person who inherits property from another (unlike an estate tax, which is imposed on the decedent's estate); there is no federal inheritance tax, but some states provide for one (though it is deductible under the federal estate tax). —Also termed *succession tax*. Cf. *estate tax*. **b.** Loosely, an estate tax.

kiddie tax. A federal tax imposed on a child's unearned income at the parents' tax rate if the parents' rate is higher and if the child is under 14 years of age.

luxury tax. An excise tax imposed on high-priced items that are not necessities (such as cars costing more than $30,000). Cf. *sin tax*.

nanny tax. A federal tax imposed on the employer of a domestic worker if the employer pays domestic employees more than $1000 in total wages in a year; the term was popularized when several of President Clinton's nominees were found not to have paid the social-security tax for their nannies.

occupation tax. An excise tax imposed on persons for the privilege of carrying on a business, trade, or profession; for example, many states require lawyers to pay an occupation tax. —Also termed *occupational tax*.

payroll tax. **a.** A tax owed by an employer on its payroll (such as social-security tax and unemployment tax). **b.** A tax collected by an employer from its employees' paychecks (such as income tax and social-security tax). See *withholding tax*.

poll tax. A fixed tax levied on each person within a jurisdiction; the Twenty-Fourth Amendment prohibits the federal and state governments from imposing poll taxes as a condition for voting. —Also termed *per capita tax*; *capitation tax*; *capitation*.

progressive tax. A tax structured so that the tax rate increases as the tax base increases; most income taxes are progressive, meaning that those with higher income pay at a higher rate. —Also termed *graduated tax*. Cf. *regressive tax*; *flat tax*.

property tax. A tax levied on the owner of property (esp. real property), usu. based on the property's value; local governments often impose property taxes to finance school districts, municipal projects, and the like. Cf. *income tax*; *excise tax*.

regressive tax. A tax structured so that the tax rate decreases as the tax base increases; a flat tax (such as the typical sales tax) is usu. considered regressive—despite its constant rate—because it is more burdensome for low-income taxpayers than high-income taxpayers. Cf. *progressive tax*; *flat tax*.

sales tax. A tax imposed on the sale of goods and services, usu. measured as a percentage of their price. See *flat tax*.

self-employment tax. The social-security tax imposed on the net earnings of a self-employed person.

severance tax. A tax imposed on the value of oil, gas, timber, or other natural resources extracted from the earth.

sin tax. An excise tax imposed on goods or activities that are considered harmful or immoral (such as cigarettes, liquor, or gambling). — Also termed *repressive tax.* Cf. *luxury tax.*

stamp tax. A tax imposed by requiring the purchase of revenue stamps that must be affixed to legal documents (such as deeds or notes) before the documents can be recorded. —Also termed *documentary stamp tax.*

surtax. An additional tax imposed on the thing being taxed or on the primary tax itself.

transfer tax. A tax imposed on the transfer of property, esp. by will, inheritance, or gift; the federal estate-and-gift tax is sometimes referred to as the *unified transfer tax* (or the *unified estate-and-gift tax*) because lifetime gifts and death gifts are treated equally under the same tax laws.

use tax. A tax imposed on the use of certain goods that are bought outside of the taxing authority's jurisdiction; it is designed to discourage the purchase of products that are not subject to the sales tax.

value-added tax. A tax assessed at each step in the production process of a commodity, based on the value added at each step by the difference between the commodity's pro-

duction cost and its selling price; value-added taxes—which are popular in several European countries—effectively act as a sales tax on the ultimate consumer. —Abbr. VAT.

withholding tax. A portion of income tax that is deducted from salary, wages, dividends, or other income before the earner receives payment; the most common example is the income tax and social-security tax withheld by an employer from an employee's paycheck.

taxable, *adj.* **1.** Subject to taxation <interest earned on a checking account is taxable income>. **2.** (Of legal costs or fees) assessable <expert-witness fees are not taxable court costs>.

taxable income. See INCOME.

taxable year. TAX YEAR.

tax-anticipation bill. A short-term obligation issued by the U.S. Treasury to meet the cash-flow needs of the government; corporations can tender these bills at par value to make quarterly tax payments. — Abbr. TAB.

taxation. The imposition or assessment of a tax.

double taxation. **a.** The imposition of two taxes on the same property during the same period and for the same taxing purpose. **b.** The imposition of two taxes on one corporate profit; esp., the structure of taxation employed by Subchapter C, under which corporate profits are first taxed to the corporation when earned and also taxed to the shareholders when the earnings are distributed as dividends.

pass-through taxation. The taxation of an entity's owners for the entity's income without taxing the entity itself; partnerships and S corporations are taxed under this method. —Also termed *conduit taxation.*

tax audit. See AUDIT.

tax avoidance. The act of taking advantage of legally available tax-planning opportunities in order to minimize one's tax liability. Cf. TAX EVASION.

tax base. The total property, income, or wealth subject to taxation in a given jurisdiction; the aggregate amount being taxed by a particular tax. Cf. BASIS (2).

tax basis. BASIS (2).

tax-benefit rule. The principle that if a taxpayer recovers a loss or expense that was deducted in a previous year, the recovery must be included in the current year's gross income to the extent that it was previously deducted. —Also termed *tax-benefit doctrine.*

tax bracket. A categorized level of income subject to a particular tax rate under federal or state law <28% tax bracket>.

Tax Court, U.S. A federal legislative court that hears appeals by taxpayers from adverse IRS rulings regarding tax deficiencies; the Tax Court was created in 1942, replacing the Board of Tax Appeals. —Abbr. T.C.

tax credit. An amount subtracted directly from one's total tax liability, dollar for dollar, as opposed to a deduction from gross income. —Often shortened to *credit.* Cf. DEDUCTION (2).

child- and dependent-care tax credit. A tax credit available to persons who are employed full-time and who maintain a household for a dependent child or a disabled spouse or dependent.

earned-income credit. A federal tax credit on earned income of low-income workers with dependent children; the credit is paid to the taxpayer even if it exceeds the total tax liability.

foreign tax credit. A tax credit against U.S. income taxes for taxpayers who earn income overseas and have paid foreign taxes on that income.

unified credit. A tax credit applied against the federal unified transfer tax; in 1995, the credit is $192,-800, meaning that an estate worth up to $600,000 passes to the heirs free of any federal estate tax. —Also termed *unified estate-and-gift tax credit.*

tax deduction. See DEDUCTION (2).

tax evasion. The act of willfully attempting to defeat or circumvent the tax law in order to minimize one's tax liability; tax evasion is punishable by both civil and criminal penalties. —Also termed *tax fraud.* Cf. TAX AVOIDANCE.

tax-exempt, *adj.* **1.** Excluded by law from taxation <a tax-exempt charity>. **2.** Bearing interest that is free from income tax <tax-exempt municipal bonds>. —Also termed *tax-free.*

tax fraud. TAX EVASION.

tax lease. See *leveraged lease* under LEASE.

tax liability. The amount that a taxpayer legally owes after multiplying his or her tax base by the applicable tax rate.

taxpayer. One who pays or is subject to a tax.

taxpayer-standing doctrine. In constitutional law, the principle that a taxpayer has no standing to sue the government for allegedly misspending the public's tax money unless the taxpayer can demonstrate a personal stake and show some direct injury.

tax rate. The proportion at which a tax base is taxed, usu. expressed as a percentage.

marginal tax rate. In a progressive-tax scheme, the rate applicable to the last dollar of income earned by the taxpayer. See TAX BRACKET.

tax return. An income-tax form on which a person or entity reports income, deductions, and exemptions and on which tax liability is calculated. —Often shortened to *return.* —Also termed *income-tax return.*

amended return. A return filed after the original return, usu. to correct an error in the original.

consolidated return. A return that reflects the combined financial interests of a group of affiliated corporations.

false return. A return on which taxable income is incorrectly reported or the tax is incorrectly computed.

information return. A return filed by an entity to report some economic information other than tax liability.

joint return. A return filed together by spouses; a joint return can be filed even if only one spouse had income, but each spouse is individually liable for tax payment.

separate return. A return filed separately by spouses, showing separate income and liability; unlike with a joint return, each spouse is individually liable for only his or her tax payment.

tax roll. ROLL (2).

tax shelter, *n.* A financial operation or investment strategy (such as a limited partnership or real-estate investment trust) that is created primarily for the purpose of reducing or deferring income-tax payments; the Tax Reform Act of 1986—by restricting the deductibility of passive losses—sharply limited the effectiveness of tax shelters. —Often shortened to *shelter.* —**tax-sheltered,** *adj.*

tax year. The period used for computing federal or state income-tax liability, usu. either the calendar year or a fiscal year of 12 months ending on the last day of a month other than December. —Also termed *taxable year.*

T-bill. *abbr.* TREASURY BILL.

T-bond. *abbr.* TREASURY BOND.

T.C. *abbr.* TAX COURT.

Technical Advice Memorandum. A publication issued by the national office of the IRS, usu. at a taxpayer's request, to explain some complex or novel tax-law issue. —Abbr. TAM.

technical error. See *harmless error* under ERROR.

telecopier. FAX (2).

temporary disability. See DISABILITY (1).

temporary frustration. See FRUSTRATION.

temporary injunction. See *preliminary injunction* under INJUNCTION.

temporary insanity. See INSANITY.

temporary insider. See INSIDER.

temporary judge. See *visiting judge* under JUDGE.

temporary restraining order. A court order preserving the status quo until the plaintiff's application for a preliminary or permanent injunction can be heard; a temporary restraining order may be granted without notifying the defendant in advance. —Abbr. TRO. —Often shortened to *restraining order*. Cf. INJUNCTION.

tenancy. **1.** The possession or occupancy of land by right or title, esp. under a lease; a leasehold interest in real estate. **2.** The period of such possession or occupancy. See ESTATE.

cotenancy. A tenancy with two or more co-owners who have unity of possession; examples are a joint tenancy and a tenancy in common.

joint tenancy. A tenancy with two or more co-owners who take identical interests simultaneously by the same instrument and with the same right of possession; a joint tenancy differs from a tenancy in common in that joint tenants each have a right of survivorship to the other's share (in some states, this right must be clearly expressed in the conveyance—otherwise the tenancy will be presumed to be a

tenancy in common). See UNITY (2); RIGHT OF SURVIVORSHIP. Cf. *tenancy in common.*

life tenancy. See *life estate* under ESTATE.

periodic tenancy. A tenancy that automatically continues for successive periods—usu. month to month or year to year—unless terminated at the end of a period by notice; a typical example is a month-to-month apartment lease. —Also termed *tenancy from period to period, periodic estate,* or *estate from period to period*; or, more specifically, *month-to-month tenancy* (or *estate*) or *year-to-year tenancy* (or *estate*).

tenancy at sufferance. A tenancy in which a person takes lawful possession of the property but then wrongfully remains as a holdover after his or her interest is terminated. —Also termed *holdover tenancy; estate at sufferance.* See HOLDING OVER.

tenancy at will. A tenancy in which the tenant holds possession with the landlord's consent but without fixed terms (as for duration or rent); such a tenancy may be terminated by either party upon fair notice. —Also termed *at-will tenancy; estate at will.*

tenancy by the entireties. A joint tenancy between husband and wife, arising when a single instrument conveys realty to the husband and wife but nothing is said in the deed or will about the character of their ownership; this type of tenancy exists in only a few common-law states. —Also termed *tenancy by the entirety*; *estate by the entireties*; *estate by the entirety*.

tenancy for a term. A tenancy whose duration is known in years, weeks, or days from the moment of its creation. —Also termed *tenancy for a period*; *tenancy for years*; *term for years*; *term of years*; *estate for a term*; *estate for years*.

tenancy in common. A tenancy by two or more persons, in equal or unequal undivided shares, who each have an equal right to possess the whole property but no right of survivorship. —Also termed *common tenancy*. Cf. *joint tenancy*.

tenancy in tail. FEE TAIL.

tenant, *n.* **1.** One who holds or possesses lands or tenements by any kind of right or title. See TENANCY. **2.** One who pays rent for the temporary use and occupation of another's land under a lease or similar arrangement. See LESSEE. **3.** *Archaic.* The defendant in a real action (the plaintiff being called a *demandant*). See *real action* under ACTION.

tenantry. A body or group of tenants.

tender, *n.* **1.** An unconditional offer of money or performance to satisfy a debt or obligation; the tender may save the tendering party from a penalty for nonpayment or nonperformance or may, if the other party unjustifiably refuses the tender, place the other party in default <the desperate buyer accepted the seller's tender of delivery even though it was imperfect>. **2.** An offer or bid put forward for acceptance <a tender for the construction contract>. **3.** Something that serves as a means of payment, such as coin, bank notes, or other circulating medium; money <legal tender>. —**tender,** *vb.*

tender, plea of. See PLEA OF TENDER.

tender offer. A public offer to buy a minimum number of shares from a corporation's shareholders at a fixed price, usu. at a substantial premium over the market price, in an effort to take control of the corporation.

cash tender offer. A tender offer in which the corporation offers to pay cash for the shares (as opposed to trading for the shares); most tender offers involve cash.

creeping tender offer. The gradual purchase of a corporation's stock at varying prices in the open market; this takeover method does not involve a formal tender offer, although the SEC may classify it as such for regulatory purposes.

tender-years doctrine. In family law, the doctrine holding that custody of very young children (usu. five years of age and younger) should generally be awarded to the mother in a divorce unless she is found to be unfit; this doctrine has been rejected in most states and replaced by a presumption of joint custody.

tenement. **1.** A house or other building used as a residence. **2.** Property (esp. land) held by freehold; an estate or holding of land.

dominant tenement. See *dominant estate* under ESTATE.

servient tenement. See *servient estate* under ESTATE.

10-K. A financial report filed annually with the SEC by registered corporations; the report typically includes audited financial statements, a description of the corporation's business and financial condition, and summaries of other financial data. — Also termed *Form 10-K*. Cf. 8-K.

10-Q. A financial report filed quarterly with the SEC by registered corporations. —Also termed *Form 10-Q*.

tentative trust. See *Totten trust* under TRUST.

Tenth Amendment. The constitutional amendment, ratified with the Bill of Rights in 1791, providing that any powers not constitutionally delegated to the federal government, nor prohibited to the states, are reserved for the states or the people.

tenure (ten-yər), *n.* **1.** A right, term, or mode of holding or occupying; esp., the feudal system of holding lands in subordination to a superior. **2.** A particular feudal mode of holding lands, such as socage, gavelkind, villeinage, and frankalmoign. **3.** A status afforded to a teacher or professor as a protection against summary dismissal without sufficient cause; this status has long been considered a cornerstone of academic freedom. **4.** More generally, the legal protection of a long-term relationship, such as employment. —**tenurial** (ten-**yuur**-ee-əl), *adj.*

term, *n.* **1.** A word or phrase; esp., an expression that has a fixed meaning in some field <term of art>. **2.** (*pl.*) Provisions that define an agreement's scope; conditions or stipulations <terms of sale>. **3.** A fixed or definite period of time; esp., a limitation or extent of time for which an estate is granted <term for years>. **4.** The period during which a court sits in session <the most recent term was busy indeed>. —Also termed (in sense 4) *term of court.* See SESSION.

general term. A regular term of court—that is, the period during which a court ordinarily sits.

special term. A term of court scheduled outside the general term, usu. for conducting extraordinary business.

term bond. See BOND (1).

term for years. See *tenancy for a term* under TENANCY.

terminable interest. An interest that terminates upon the lapse of time or upon the occurrence of some condition.

termination, *n.* **1.** The act of bringing something to an end <termination of the partnership by winding up its affairs>. **2.** The end of something in time or existence; conclusion or discontinuance <the insurance policy's termination left the doctor without liability coverage>. — **terminate,** *vb.*—**terminable,** *adj.*

terminer. See OYER AND TERMINER.

term life insurance. See INSURANCE.

term loan. See LOAN.

term of art. 1. A word or phrase having a specific, precise meaning in a given specialty, apart from its general meaning in ordinary contexts; examples in law include *and his heirs* and *res ipsa loquitur.* **2.** Loosely, a jargonistic word or phrase. —Also termed *word of art.*

term of court. TERM (4).

term of years. See *tenancy for a term* under TENANCY.

termor (tər-mər). A person who holds lands or tenements for a term of years or for life.

terre-tenant (ter-ten-ənt *or* tər-). **1.** One who has actual possession of land; the occupant of land. **2.** One who has an interest in a judgment debtor's land after the judgment creditor's lien has attached to the land (such as a subsequent purchaser). —Also spelled *tertenant*. —Also termed *land-tenant*.

territorial court. See COURT.

territorialism. The traditional approach to choice of law, whereby the place of injury or contract determines which state's law will be applied in a case. See CHOICE OF LAW.

territorial jurisdiction. See JURISDICTION.

territorial waters. The waters under a state's or nation's jurisdiction, including both inland waters and surrounding sea (traditionally within three miles of the coastline).

territory, *n.* A geographical area included within a particular government's jurisdiction; esp., a part of the U.S. not included within any state but organized with a separate legislature (such as Guam and the U.S. Virgin Islands). —**territorial,** *adj.* Cf. COMMONWEALTH; DEPENDENCY.

terrorism, *n.* The use of violence to intimidate or cause panic, esp. as a means of affecting political conduct. —**terrorist,** *adj.* & *n.*

Terry stop. The act of a police officer's stopping a person whose behav-ior is reasonably considered suspicious and frisking that person for weapons; the term takes its name from *Terry v. Ohio*, 392 U.S. 1 (1968), in which the Supreme Court determined such stops to be constitutional.

tertenant. TERRE-TENANT.

tertius gaudens (tər-sh[ee]əs-**gaw**-dənz). [Latin "a rejoicing third"] A third party who profits when two others dispute.

test action. See *test case* under CASE.

testable, *adj.* **1.** Capable of being put to a test <a testable hypothesis>. **2.** Capable of making a will <an 18-year-old person is testable in this state>. **3.** Capable of being transferred by will <today virtually all property is considered testable>.

testacy (**tes**-tə-see), *n.* The fact or condition of leaving a valid will at one's death. —**testate,** *adj.* Cf. INTESTACY.

testament. 1. A will disposing of personal property. Cf. DEVISE (3). **2.** WILL (1).

testamentary, *adj.* **1.** Of or relating to a will or testament <testamentary intent>. **2.** Provided for or appointed by a will <testamentary guardian>. **3.** Created by a will <testamentary gift>.

testamentary capacity. See CAPACITY (3).

testamentary class. See CLASS (3).

testamentary gift. See GIFT.

testamentary trust. See TRUST.

testate (**tes**-tayt), *adj.* Having left a will at death <she died testate>. Cf. INTESTATE.

testate, *n.* TESTATOR.

testate succession. The passing of rights or property by will. Cf. INTESTATE SUCCESSION.

testation. The disposal of property by will; the power of disposing property by will.

testator (**tes**-tay-tər). **1.** A person who dies leaving a will. **2.** A person who makes or has made a will. —Also termed *testate*. Cf. INTESTATE.

testatrix (tes-**tay**-triks). *Archaic.* A female testator; in modern usage, a person who leaves a will is called a testator, regardless of sex.

test case. See CASE.

teste (**tes**-tee). [Latin *teste meipso* "I myself being a witness"] In drafting, the clause that states the name of a witness and evidences the act of witnessing.

testify, *vb.* **1.** To give evidence as a witness <she testified that the Ford Bronco was at the defendant's home at the critical time>. **2.** (Of a person or thing) to bear witness <the incomplete log entries testified to his sloppiness>.

testifying expert. See EXPERT.

testimonial evidence. See EVIDENCE.

testimonial immunity. See IMMUNITY (3).

testimonium clause. A provision at the end of an instrument (esp. a will) reciting the date when the instrument was signed, by whom it was signed, and in what capacity; testimonium clauses traditionally begin with the phrase "In witness whereof." Cf. ATTESTATION CLAUSE.

testimony, *n.* Evidence that a competent witness under oath or affirmation gives at trial or in an affidavit or deposition. —**testimonial,** *adj.*

test oath. See *oath of allegiance* under OATH.

theft, *n.* **1.** The felonious taking and removing of another's personal property with the intent of depriving the true owner of it; larceny. **2.** Broadly, any act or instance of stealing, including larceny, burglary, embezzlement, and false pretenses; many modern penal codes have consolidated such property offenses under the name "theft."—**thieve,** *vb.*—**thief,** *n.* See LARCENY.

therapeutic relief. See RELIEF.

thereabout, *adv. Jargon.* Near that time or place <Schreuer was seen in Rudolf Place or thereabout>.

thereafter, *adv. Jargon.* Afterward; later <Skurry was thereafter arrested>.

thereby, *adv.* By that means; in that way <Blofeld stepped into the embassy and thereby found protection>.

therefor, *adv. Jargon.* For it or them; for that thing or action; for those things or actions <she lied to Congress but was never punished therefor>.

therefore, *adv.* **1.** For that reason; on that ground or those grounds <a quorum was not present; therefore, no vote was taken>. **2.** To that end <she wanted to become a tax lawyer, and she therefore applied for the uni-

versity's renowned L.L.M. program in tax>. —Also termed *thereupon*.

therefrom, *adv. Jargon.* From that, it, or them <Hofer had several financial obligations to Ricks, who refused to release Hofer therefrom>.

therein, *adv. Jargon.* **1.** In that place or time <the Dallas/Fort Worth metroplex has a population of about 3 million, and some 20,000 lawyers practice therein>. **2.** Inside or within that thing; inside or within those things <there were 3 school buses with 108 children therein>.

thereinafter, *adv. Jargon.* Later in that thing (such as a speech or document) <the book's first reference was innocuous, but the five references thereafter were libelous per se>.

thereof, *adv. Jargon.* Of that, it, or them <although the disease is spreading rapidly, the cause thereof is unknown>.

thereon, *adv. Jargon.* On that or them <Michaels found the on-line reports of the cases and relied thereon instead of checking the printed books>. —Also termed *thereupon*.

thereto, *adv. Jargon.* To that or them <the jury award granted over $750,000 in actual damages, and added thereto was another $250,000 in punitive damages>. —Also termed *thereunto*.

theretofore, *adv.* Up to that time <theretofore, the highest award in such a case has been $450,000>.

thereunder, *adv. Jargon.* Under that or them <on the top shelf were three books, and situated thereunder was the missing bank note> <§ 1988

was the relevant fee statute, and the plaintiffs were undeniably proceeding thereunder>.

thereunto, *adv. Jargon.* THERETO.

thereupon, *adv. Jargon.* **1.** Immediately; without delay; promptly <the writ of execution issued from the court, and the sheriff thereupon sought to find the judgment debtor>. **2.** THEREON. **3.** THEREFORE.

***Thibodaux* abstention.** See ABSTENTION.

thief. One who steals, esp. without force or violence; one who commits theft or larceny. See THEFT.

common thief. A thief who has been convicted of theft or larceny more than once. —Also termed *common and notorious thief.*

thin capitalization. See CAPITALIZATION.

thin corporation. See CORPORATION.

thing in action. See *chose in action* under CHOSE.

thin market. See MARKET.

thin-skull rule. EGGSHELL-SKULL RULE.

Third Amendment. The constitutional amendment, ratified with the Bill of Rights in 1791, prohibiting the quartering of soldiers in private homes except during wartime.

third degree, *n.* The process of extracting a confession or information from a prisoner by prolonged questioning, the use of threats, or physical torture <the police gave the suspect the third degree>.

third-degree instruction. ALLEN CHARGE.

third party, *n.* One who is not a party to a lawsuit, agreement, or other transaction but who is somehow involved in the transaction; one other than the principal parties. —Also termed *outside party.* —**third-party,** *adj.* See PARTY.

third-party, *vb.* To bring (a person or entity) into litigation as a third-party defendant <seeking indemnity, the defendant third-partied the surety>.

third-party action. See ACTION.

third-party beneficiary. See BENEFICIARY.

third-party complaint. See COMPLAINT.

third-party defendant. A party brought into a lawsuit by the original defendant.

third-party equity lease. See *leveraged lease* under LEASE.

third-party insurance. See *liability insurance* under INSURANCE.

third-party plaintiff. A defendant who files a third-party complaint in an effort to bring a third party into the lawsuit. See *third-party complaint* under COMPLAINT.

third-party practice. IMPLEADER.

Thirteenth Amendment. The constitutional amendment, ratified in 1865, that abolished slavery and involuntary servitude.

threat, *n.* **1.** A communicated intent to inflict harm or loss on another or on another's property, esp. one that might diminish a person's freedom to act voluntarily or with lawful consent

<the kidnapper's threat was that if the magnate did not meet the demands, his son would never be seen again>. **2.** An indication of an approaching menace <the threat of bankruptcy>. **3.** A person or thing that might well cause harm <Mrs. Gambino testified that she had never viewed her husband as a threat>. — **threaten,** *vb.*—**threatening,** *adj.*

341 meeting. See *creditors' meeting* under MEETING.

three-strikes law. A criminal-law statute prescribing harsh punishment, usu. life imprisonment, for a repeat offender's third felony conviction; about a third of the states have enacted a statute of this kind. —Also termed *three-strikes-and-you're-out law.*

thrift institution. SAVINGS-AND-LOAN ASSOCIATION.

tied product. See TYING ARRANGEMENT.

tiered partnership. See PARTNERSHIP.

TILA. *abbr.* Truth in Lending Act. See CONSUMER CREDIT PROTECTION ACT.

time arbitrage. See ARBITRAGE.

time-bar, *n.* A bar to a legal claim arising from the lapse of a defined length of time, esp. one contained in a statute of limitations. —**time-barred,** *adj.*

time charter. See CHARTER.

time deposit. See DEPOSIT.

time draft. See DRAFT.

time immemorial. 1. A point in time so far back that no living person has knowledge or proof contradicting the right or custom alleged to have existed since then; at common law, that time was fixed as being the year 1189. Cf. LEGAL MEMORY. **2.** A very long time.

time is of the essence. See OF THE ESSENCE.

time loan. See *term loan* under LOAN.

time note. See NOTE.

time, place, or manner restriction. In constitutional law, a government's limitation on when, where, or how a public speech or assembly may occur, but not on the content of that speech or assembly; as long as such restrictions are narrowly tailored to achieve a legitimate governmental interest, they do not violate the First Amendment. See PUBLIC FORUM.

timesharing, *n.* Joint ownership or rental of property (such as a vacation condominium) by several persons who take turns occupying the property for short periods. —Also termed *timeshare.* —**time-share,** *vb.*

timesheet. An attorney's daily record of his or her billable hours, used to generate a client's bill. See BILLABLE HOUR.

time unity. See *unity of time* under UNITY.

tin parachute. An employment-contract provision that grants a corporate employee (esp. one below executive level) severance benefits in the event of a takeover; these benefits are typically less lucrative than those provided under a golden parachute. —Also termed *silver parachute.* Cf. GOLDEN PARACHUTE.

tip, *n.* **1.** A piece of special information; esp., in securities law, advance or inside information passed from one person to another. See INSIDE INFORMATION; INSIDER TRADING. **2.** A gratuity for service given.

tippee. In securities law, a person who acquires material nonpublic information from someone who enjoys a fiduciary relationship with the company to which that information pertains.

tipper. In securities law, a person who possesses material inside information and who selectively discloses that information for trading or other personal purposes <the tippee traded 5,000 shares after her conversation with the tipper>.

tipstaff. A court crier. Pl. **tipstaves, tipstaffs.** See CRIER.

tithe (tīth), *n.* **1.** A tenth of one's income, esp. in reference to a religious or charitable gift. **2.** A small tax or assessment, esp. in the amount of one tenth. —**tithe,** *vb.*

title. 1. The union of all elements (as ownership, possession, and custody) constituting the legal right to control and dispose of property; the legal link between a person and some object of property <no one has title to that land>. **2.** Legal evidence of a person's ownership rights in property; an instrument (such as a deed) that constitutes such evidence <record your title with the county clerk>. **3.** The heading of a legal document or proceeding <the appellate rules require the party's name to appear in the brief's title>. **4.** A subdivision of a statute or code <Title IX>.

after-acquired title. See AFTER-AC-QUIRED-TITLE DOCTRINE.

bad title. **a.** See *defective title.* **b.** See *unmarketable title.*

clear title. **a.** Title that is free from any encumbrances, burdens, or other limitations. **b.** See *marketable title.* —Also termed *good title.*

defective title. Title that cannot legally convey the property to which it applies, usu. because of some conflicting claim to that property. — Also termed *bad title.*

doubtful title. Title that exposes the party holding it to the risk of litigation with an adverse claimant. See *unmarketable title.*

equitable title. Title that indicates a beneficial interest in property and that gives the holder the right to receive formal legal title. Cf. *legal title.*

good title. **a.** Title that is legally valid or effective. **b.** See *clear title.*

legal title. Title that evidences apparent ownership but does not necessarily signify full and complete title or a beneficial interest. Cf. *equitable title.*

marketable title. Title that a reasonable buyer would accept because it appears to lack any defects and to cover the entire property that the seller has purported to sell. —Also termed *merchantable title*; *clear title*; *good title.*

paper title. Title supported by a mere series of conveyances rather than by a proper chain of title. See CHAIN OF TITLE.

paramount title. **a.** *Archaic.* Title that is the source of the current title; original title. **b.** Title that is superior to another title or claim on the same property.

record title. Title as it appears in the public records after being properly recorded. —Also termed *title of record.*

unmarketable title. Title that a reasonable buyer would refuse to accept because of possible conflicting interests in or litigation over the property. —Also termed *bad title.*

title, abstract of. See ABSTRACT OF TITLE.

title, action to quiet. See *action to quiet title* under ACTION.

title, chain of. See CHAIN OF TITLE.

title, covenant for. See *covenant for title* under COVENANT (4).

title, document of. See DOCUMENT OF TITLE.

title, muniment of. See MUNIMENT OF TITLE.

title, root of. See ROOT OF TITLE.

title company. See COMPANY.

title deed. See DEED.

title insurance. See INSURANCE.

title member. See *name partner* under PARTNER.

title of record. See *record title* under TITLE.

title opinion. See OPINION (2).

title search. An examination of the public records to determine whether any defects or encumbrances exist in a given property's chain of title; title searches are typically conducted by title companies or real-estate lawyers at a prospective buyer's or mortgagee's request.

title theory. In real-property law, the idea that a mortgage transfers legal title of the property to the mortgagee, who retains it until the mortgage has been either satisfied or foreclosed; only a few American states—known as *title states, title jurisdictions,* or *title-theory jurisdictions*—have adopted this theory. Cf. LIEN THEORY.

title unity. See *unity of title* under UNITY.

T-note. *abbr.* TREASURY NOTE.

toll, *vb.* **1.** *Archaic.* To annul or take away <toll a right of entry>. **2.** (Of a time period, esp. a statutory one) to stop the running of; to abate <the limitations period is tolled while Webb is out of the country but resumes immediately upon her return>.

tolling agreement. An agreement between a potential plaintiff and a potential defendant whereby the defendant agrees to extend the statutory limitations period on the plaintiff's claim, usu. so that both parties will have more time to resolve their dispute without litigation.

tolling statute. A statute that interrupts the running of a statute of limitations in certain situations, such as when the defendant cannot be served with process in the forum jurisdiction.

tombstone. An advertisement (esp. in a newspaper) for a public securities offering, stating some of the security's details as well as the parties who are selling the issue; the term gets its name from the ad's tradition-al black border and plain print. — Also termed *tombstone advertisement; tombstone ad.* Cf. PROSPECTUS.

tonnage duty. A charge or impost for bringing a ship into port, usu. assessed on the basis of the ship's weight; U.S. Const. art. I, § 10, cl. 3 prohibits the states from levying tonnage duties. —Also termed *tonnage.* See DUTY (5).

top lease. See LEASE.

Torrens system. A system for establishing title to real estate, whereby a claimant first acquires an abstract of title and then applies to a court for issuance of a title certificate, which serves as conclusive evidence of ownership; this system—named after Sir Robert Torrens, a 19th-century reformer of Australian land laws—has been adopted in the U.S. by several counties with large metropolitan areas. —Also termed *Torrens title system.*

tort. 1. A civil wrong for which a remedy may be obtained, usu. in the form of damages; a breach of a duty that the law imposes on everyone. **2.** (*pl.*) The branch of law dealing with such wrongs.

constitutional tort. A violation of one's constitutional rights by a government officer, redressable by a damages suit filed directly against the officer; constitutional torts committed under color of state law (such as civil-rights violations) are actionable under 42 U.S.C. § 1983.

intentional tort. A tort committed by someone acting with general or specific intent; examples include battery, false imprisonment, and trespass to land. —Also termed *willful tort*. Cf. NEGLIGENCE.

maritime tort. A tort committed on navigable waters. See JONES ACT.

mass tort. A large number of tort claims with a common cause that has injured many victims; examples include a single-accident disaster, a defective product that injures many people, or environmental contamination at a single site.

prenatal tort. **a.** A tort committed against a fetus; if born alive, a child can sue for injuries resulting from tortious conduct predating the child's birth. **b.** Loosely, any of several torts relating to reproduction, such as those giving rise to wrongful-birth actions, wrongful-life actions, and wrongful-pregnancy actions.

prima facie tort. The infliction of intentional harm on another person, resulting in damages, by one or more acts that would otherwise be lawful; some jurisdictions have established this tort to provide a remedy for malicious deeds—esp. in business and trade contexts— that are not covered under traditional tort law.

sanctions tort. See SANCTIONS TORT.

toxic tort. A tort caused by exposure to a toxic substance, such as asbestos, radiation, or hazardous waste; toxic torts can be remedied by civil lawsuits (esp. class actions) or administrative actions.

tortfeasor. One who commits a tort; a wrongdoer.

concurrent tortfeasors. Two or more tortfeasors whose simultaneous ac-

tions cause injury to a third party; such tortfeasors are jointly and severally liable.

consecutive tortfeasors. Two or more tortfeasors whose actions, while occurring at different times, combine to cause a single injury to a third party; such tortfeasors are jointly and severally liable.

joint tortfeasors. Two or more tortfeasors who are vicariously liable for their concerted action, and who may be joined as defendants in the same lawsuit. See *joint and several liability* under LIABILITY.

tortious (tor-shəs), *adj*. **1.** Constituting a tort; wrongful <tortious conduct>. **2.** In the nature of a tort <tortious cause of action>.

tortious interference with contractual relations. A third party's intentional inducement for a contracting party to break a contract, causing damage to the relationship between the contracting parties. — Also termed *interference with a contractual relationship*.

tortious interference with prospective advantage. An intentional, damaging intrusion on another's potential business relationship, such as the opportunity of obtaining customers or employment. —Also termed *interference with a business relationship*.

tort reform. A movement to reduce the amount of tort litigation in the judicial system, usu. involving legislation that restricts legal theories in tort or that caps damages awards (esp. for punitive damages); advocates of tort reform argue that it lowers insurance and healthcare costs, while opponents contend that it denies plaintiffs the recovery they deserve for their injuries.

total disability. See DISABILITY (1).

total incorporation. See INCORPORATION.

totality-of-the-circumstances test. In criminal procedure, a standard for determining whether hearsay (such as an informant's tip) is sufficiently reliable to establish probable cause for an arrest or search warrant; under this test—which replaced *Aguilar-Spinelli*'s two-pronged approach—the reliability of the hearsay is weighed by focusing on the entire situation as described in the probable-cause affidavit, and not on any one specific factor. *Illinois v. Gates*, 462 U.S. 213 (1983). Cf. AGUILAR-SPINELLI TEST.

Totten trust. See TRUST.

to wit, *adv. Archaic.* That is to say; namely <the district attorney amended the complaint to include prostitution, to wit, "solicited sexual acts for a fee">. —Sometimes spelled *to-wit*; *towit*.

town meeting. 1. A legal meeting of a town's qualified voters for the administration of local government or the enactment of legislation; town meetings of this type are common in some New England states. **2.** More generally, any assembly of a town's citizens for the purpose of discussing political, economic, or social issues. **3.** Modernly, a televised event in which one or more politicians meet and talk with representative citizens about current issues.

toxic tort. See TORT.

tracing, *n.* The process of tracking a given property's ownership or characteristics from the time of its origin to the present. —**trace,** *vb.*

tract. A specified parcel of land <a 40-acre tract>.

tract index. See INDEX.

trade, *n.* **1.** The business of buying and selling or bartering goods or services; COMMERCE. **2.** A transaction or swap. **3.** A business or industry occupation; a craft or profession. —**trade,** *vb.*

trade acceptance. See ACCEPTANCE.

trade deficit. See DEFICIT.

trade dress. The overall appearance and image of a product (such as its packaging and labeling) or commercial enterprise (such as its design and decor) in the marketplace; if a trade dress is distinctive and nonfunctional, it may be protected under trademark law.

trade fixture. See FIXTURE.

trade gap. See *trade deficit* under DEFICIT.

trade libel. A false statement that disparages the quality or reputation of another's product or business.

trademark, *n.* **1.** A word, phrase, logo, or other graphic symbol used by a manufacturer or seller to distinguish its products from those of others; to receive federal protection, a trademark must be (1) distinctive rather than merely descriptive, (2) affixed to a product that is actually sold in the marketplace, and (3) registered with the U.S. Patent and Trademark Office. —Often shortened to *mark*. Cf. SERVICEMARK. **2.** The body of law dealing with how businesses distinguish their products from those of others. See LANHAM ACT.

tradename. A name, style, or symbol used to distinguish a company, partnership, or business (as opposed to a product or service); the name under which a business operates.

trade secret. A formula, process, device, or other business information that is kept confidential in order to maintain an advantage over competitors.

trade usage. See USAGE.

traditionary evidence. See EVIDENCE.

traduce, *vb.* To slander; calumniate. —**traducement,** *n.*

transaction, *n.* **1.** The act or an instance of conducting business or other dealings. **2.** Something performed or carried out; a business agreement or exchange. **3.** Any activity involving two or more persons. —**transact,** *vb.*—**transactional,** *adj.*

transaction cost. See COST.

transactional immunity. See IMMUNITY (3).

transcript, *n.* **1.** A handwritten, printed, or typed copy; esp., the official copy of the record of proceedings in a trial or hearing, as taken down by the court reporter. —Also termed *report of proceedings* or (in Texas) *statement of facts.* **2.** In Texas, RECORD (2). —**transcribe,** *vb.*

transcription. The act or process of producing a transcript.

transfer, *n.* A conveyance of property or title from one person to another. —**transfer,** *vb.*

transferee. One to whom an interest in property is conveyed.

transfer in contemplation of death. See *gift causa mortis* under GIFT.

transfer of venue. CHANGE OF VENUE.

transferor. One who conveys an interest in property.

transfer payment. (*usu. pl.*) Governmental payment to a person who has neither provided goods or services nor invested money in exchange for the payment; examples include unemployment compensation and welfare payments.

transfer price. See PRICE.

transferred-intent doctrine. The rule that if one person intends to harm a second person but instead unintentionally harms a third, the first person's criminal or tortious intent toward the second applies to the third as well; thus, the offender may be prosecuted for an intent crime or sued by the third person for an intentional tort. See INTENT.

Transfers to Minors Act. UNIFORM TRANSFERS TO MINORS ACT.

transfer tax. See TAX.

transient jurisdiction. See JURISDICTION.

transitory action. See ACTION.

transnational law. 1. General principles of law recognized by civilized nations. Cf. INTERNATIONAL LAW. **2.** The amalgam of common principles of domestic and international law dealing esp. with problems arising from agreements made between sovereign states and foreign private parties; the problems to which such principles apply.

trashing. DECONSTRUCTION.

travaux préparatoires (tra-**voh**-pray-par-ə-**twah[r]z**). [French "preparatory works"] Materials used in preparing the ultimate form of an agreement or statute, and esp. of an international treaty; materials constituting a legislative history. See LEGISLATIVE HISTORY.

traverse (tra-vərs), *n.* At common law, a formal denial of a factual allegation made in the opposing party's pleading <Smith filed a traverse to Allen's complaint, asserting that he did not knowingly provide false information>. —**traverse** (trə-**vərs**), *vb.* See DENIAL.

general traverse. A denial of all the facts in an opponent's pleading.

special traverse. A denial of one material fact in an opponent's pleading.

traverse jury. See *petit jury* under JURY.

treason, *n.* The offense of attempting to overthrow the government of the state to which one owes allegiance, either by levying war against the state or by materially supporting its enemies—Also termed *high treason.* —**treasonable, treasonous,** *adj.* Cf. SEDITION.

petty treason. Archaic. Murder of one's employer or husband; until 1828, this act was considered treason under English law.

Treas. Reg. *abbr.* TREASURY REGULATION.

treasure trove. [Law French "treasure found"] Valuables (usu. gold or silver) found hidden in the ground or other private place, the owner of which is unknown; at common law, the finder of a treasure trove was entitled to title against all except the true owner.

Treasury bill. A short-term debt security issued by the federal government, with a maturity of 13, 26, or 52 weeks; these bills—auctioned weekly or quarterly—pay interest in the form of the difference between their discounted purchase price and their par value at maturity. —Abbr. T-bill.

Treasury bond. A long-term debt security issued by the federal government, with a maturity of 10 to 30 years; these bonds are considered risk-free, but they pay little interest. —Abbr. T-bond.

Treasury note. An intermediate-term debt security issued by the federal government, with a maturity of 2 to 10 years; these notes are considered risk- free, but they pay little interest. —Abbr. T-note.

Treasury Regulation. A regulation promulgated by the U.S. Treasury Department to explain or interpret a section of the Internal Revenue Code; Treasury Regulations are binding on all taxpayers. —Abbr. Treas. Reg.

treasury stock. See STOCK.

treasury warrant. See WARRANT (2).

treaty. A formally signed and ratified agreement between two nations or sovereigns; a treaty is not only the law in each state but also a contract between the signatories. —Also termed *accord*; *convention*; *covenant*; *declaration*; *pact*. Cf. EXECUTIVE AGREEMENT.

peace treaty. A treaty signed by at least two heads of state to end a war. —Also termed *treaty of peace*.

treble damages. See DAMAGES.

trespass (**tres**-pas *or* **tres**-pəs), *n.* **1.** An unlawful act committed against the person or property of another; esp., wrongful entry on another's real property. **2.** At common law, a legal action for injuries resulting from an unlawful act of this kind. — **trespass,** *vb.* — **trespassory,** *adj.*

continuing trespass. A trespass in the nature of a permanent invasion on another's rights, such as a sign that overhangs one's property.

criminal trespass. **a.** A trespass on property that is clearly marked against trespass by signs or fences. **b.** A trespass in which the trespasser remains on the property after being ordered off by a person authorized to do so.

innocent trespass. A trespass committed either unintentionally or in good faith.

trespass de bonis asportatis (də-**boh**-nəs-as-pər-**tay**-təs *or* -**tah**-təs). [Latin "for goods taken away"] At common law, an action to recover damages for the wrongful taking of chattels. —Often shortened to *trespass de bonis*.

trespasser. One who commits a trespass; in tort law, a landholder

owes no duty to unforeseeable trespassers. Cf. INVITEE; LICENSEE (2).

trespass on the case. At common law, an action to recover damages that are not the immediate result of a wrongful act but rather a later consequence; this action was the precursor to a variety of modern-day tort claims, including negligence, nuisance, and business torts. —Often shortened to *case*. —Also termed *action on the case*.

trespass quare clausum fregit (**kwer**-ee-**kloz**-əm-**frej**-it). [Latin "whereas he or she broke the close"] At common law, an action to recover damages resulting from another's unlawful entry on one's land that is visibly enclosed. See TRESPASS VI ET ARMIS.

trespass to try title. 1. In some states, a cause of action for the recovery of property unlawfully withheld from an owner who has the immediate right to possession. **2.** A procedure under which a rival claim to title may be adjudicated.

trespass vi et armis (vee-et-**ahr**-mis *or* vI-). [Latin "with force and arms"] **1.** At common law, an action for damages resulting from an intentional injury to person or property, esp. if by violent means. **2.** TRESPASS QUARE CLAUSUM FREGIT; in this sense, the "force" is implied by the "breaking" of the close (that is, an enclosed area), even if no real force was used.

trial. A formal judicial examination and determination of evidence and legal issues.

bench trial. A trial before a judge without a jury; the judge decides questions of fact as well as questions of law. —Also termed *trial to the bench*; *nonjury trial*.

bifurcated trial. A trial that is divided into two stages, such as for guilt and punishment or for liability and damages. —Also termed *two-stage trial*. Cf. SEVERANCE (2).

fair trial. See TRIAL.

jury trial. A trial in which the fact issues are determined by a jury, not by the judge. —Also termed *trial by jury*.

mock trial. See MOCK TRIAL.

show trial. See SHOW TRIAL.

speedy trial. See SPEEDY TRIAL.

summary jury trial. A settlement technique whereby the parties argue before a mock jury who then reaches a nonbinding verdict that will guide the judge.

trifurcated trial. A trial that is divided into three stages, such as for liability, general damages, and special damages.

trial by the record. A trial in which one party insists that a record exists to support its claim and the opposing party denies the existence of such a record; if the record can be produced, the court will consider it in reaching a verdict—otherwise it will rule for the opponent.

trial court. See COURT.

trial de novo. A new trial on the entire case—that is, on both questions of fact and issues of law—conducted as if there had been no trial in the first instance.

trial jury. See *petit jury* under JURY.

trial on the merits. A trial on the substantive issues of a case, as opposed to a motion hearing or interlocutory matter.

trial-setting preference. See *special setting* under SETTING.

trial to the bench. See *bench trial* under TRIAL.

triangular merger. See MERGER.

tribunal. 1. A court or other adjudicatory body. **2.** The seat, bench, or place where a judge sits.

trier of fact. FACT-FINDER.

trifurcated trial. See TRIAL.

tripartite (trI-**pahr**-tIt), *adj.* Involving, composed of, or divided into three parts or elements <a tripartite agreement>.

triple damages. See *treble damages* under DAMAGES.

TRO (tee-ahr-oh). *abbr.* TEMPORARY RESTRAINING ORDER.

trover (**troh**-vər). A common-law action for the recovery of damages for conversion of personal property, the damages generally being measured by the value of the property. Cf. DETINUE; REPLEVIN.

truancy (**troo**-ən-see), *n.* The act or state of shirking responsibility; esp., willful and unjustified failure to attend school by one who is required to attend. —**truant,** *adj. & n.*

truce. In international law, a suspension or temporary cessation of hostilities by agreement between belligerent powers. —Also termed *armistice*; *ceasefire*; *suspension of arms*.

true and correct. *Jargon.* Authentic; accurate; unaltered <we have

forwarded a true and correct copy of the expert's report>. —Also termed *true and exact*.

true bill, *n.* A grand jury's notation that a criminal charge should go before a petty jury for trial <the grand jury returned a true bill, and the state prepared to prosecute>. —Also termed *billa vera*. —**true-bill,** *vb.* <the grand jury true-billed the indictment>. Cf. NO BILL.

trust. 1. A property interest held by one person (the *trustee*) at the request of another (the *settlor*) for the benefit of a third party (the *beneficiary*); for a trust to be valid, it must involve specific property, reflect the settlor's intent, and be created for a lawful purpose. **2.** The confidence placed in a trustee who so holds the property, together with the trustee's obligations toward the property and the beneficiary. See FIDUCIARY RELATIONSHIP. **3.** The property so held; TRUST FUND. **4.** A business combination that aims at monopoly. See ANTITRUST.

active trust. A trust in which the trustee has some affirmative duty of management or administration besides the obligation to transfer the property to the beneficiary. — Also termed *special trust*. Cf. *passive trust*.

blended trust. A trust in which the beneficiaries are a group, with no member of the group having a separable individual interest; courts rarely recognize these trusts.

blind trust. A trust in which the settlor places investments under the control of an independent trustee, usu. to avoid a conflict of interest.

business trust. A form of business organization, similar to a corporation, in which investors receive transferable certificates of beneficial interest (instead of stock shares). —Also termed *Massachusetts trust*; *common-law trust*.

bypass trust. A trust into which a decedent's estate passes, so that the surviving heirs get a life estate in the trust rather than the property itself, in order to avoid estate taxes on an estate larger than the tax-credit-sheltered amount ($600,000). —Also termed *credit-shelter trust*. See *unified credit* under TAX CREDIT.

charitable trust. A trust created to benefit a specific charity or the general public rather than a private individual or entity; charitable trusts are often eligible for favorable tax treatment. —Also termed *public trust*. See CY PRES. Cf. *private trust*.

Clifford trust. An irrevocable trust, set up for at least ten years and a day, whereby income from the trust property is paid to the beneficiary but the property itself reverts back to the settlor when the trust expires; these trusts were often used by parents—with their children as beneficiaries—to shelter investment income, but the Tax Reform Act of 1986 eliminated the tax advantage by imposing the kiddie tax and by taxing the income of settlors with a reversionary interest that exceeds 5% of the trust's value. —Named from *Helvering v. Clifford*, 309 U.S. 331 (1940). — Also termed *short-term trust*.

complex trust. A trust that may either distribute or accumulate its income.

constructive trust. A trust imposed by a court on equitable grounds against one who has obtained property by wrongdoing, thereby preventing the wrongful holder from being unjustly enriched; such a trust creates no fiduciary relationship. —Also termed *involuntary trust*; *trust de son tort*; *trust ex delicto*; *trust ex maleficio*. Cf. *resulting trust.*

discretionary trust. A trust in which the trustee alone decides whether or how to distribute the trust property or its income to the beneficiary; the beneficiary, in other words, has no say in the matter.

express trust. A trust created with the settlor's express intent, usu. declared in writing. —Also termed *direct trust.*

fixed trust. A trust in which the trustee may not exercise any discretion over the trust's management or distributions. —Also termed *directory trust*; *nondiscretionary trust.*

grantor trust. A trust in which the settlor retains control over the trust property or its income to such an extent that the settlor is taxed on the trust's income. See *Clifford trust.*

honorary trust. A trust that is legally invalid and unenforceable because it lacks a proper beneficiary; examples include trusts that honor dead persons, maintain cemetery plots, or benefit animals.

indestructible trust. A trust that, because of the settlor's wishes, cannot be prematurely terminated by the beneficiary. —Also termed *Claflin trust.*

inter vivos trust. A trust that is created and takes effect during the settlor's lifetime. —Also termed *living trust.* Cf. *testamentary trust.*

investment trust. See *investment company* under COMPANY.

irrevocable trust. A trust that cannot be terminated by the settlor once it is created; in most states, a trust will be deemed irrevocable unless the settlor specifies otherwise.

land trust. A land-ownership arrangement by which a trustee holds both legal and equitable title to land while the beneficiary retains the power to direct the trustee, manage the property, and draw income from the trust. —Also termed *Illinois land trust.*

life-insurance trust. A trust consisting of one or more life-insurance policies payable to the trust when the insured dies.

liquidating trust. A trust designed to be liquidated as soon as possible; an example is a trust into which a decedent's business is placed to safeguard the business until it can be sold off.

passive trust. A trust in which the trustee has no duty other than to transfer the property to the beneficiary. —Also termed *dry trust*; *nominal trust*; *simple trust.* Cf. *active trust.*

pourover trust. An inter vivos trust that receives property (usu. the residual estate) from a will upon the testator's death.

private trust. A trust created for the financial benefit of one or more designated beneficiaries rather than for the public benefit. Cf. *charitable trust.*

purchase-money resulting trust. A resulting trust that arises when one person buys property but directs the seller to transfer the property and its title to another; the buyer is the beneficiary, and the holder is the trustee. —Abbr. PMRT.

QTIP trust (**kyoo**-tip). A testamentary trust established to transfer assets between spouses when one spouse dies; under this trust, the assets—referred to as the qualified-terminable-interest property (QTIP)—are considered part of the surviving spouse's estate and are therefore not subject to the estate tax on the decedent spouse's estate.

real-estate investment trust. See REAL-ESTATE INVESTMENT TRUST.

reciprocal trust. A trust arrangement between two parties whereby one party is beneficiary of a trust established by the other party, and vice versa; such trust are common between husband and wife.

resulting trust. A trust imposed by law when someone transfers property under circumstances suggesting that he or she did not intend the transferee to have the beneficial interest in the property. —Also termed *implied trust.* Cf. *constructive trust.*

revocable trust. A trust in which the settlor reserves the right to terminate the trust and recover the corpus.

simple trust. **a.** A trust that must distribute all income as it accrues. **b.** See *passive trust.*

spendthrift trust. A trust that prohibits the beneficiary from assigning his or her equitable interest and also prevents a creditor from attaching that interest.

sprinkling trust. A trust that delegates to the trustee the discretion to decide how much will be given to each beneficiary. —Also termed *spray trust.*

support trust. A trust in which the trustee pays to the beneficiary only so much trust income that the trustee believes is needed for the beneficiary's support; as with a spendthrift trust, the beneficiary's interest cannot be assigned or reached by creditors.

testamentary trust. A trust that is created by a will and takes effect when the settlor (testator) dies. —Also termed *trust under will.* Cf. *inter vivos trust.*

Totten trust. A revocable trust created by one's deposit of money in one's own name as a trustee for another; such a trust is commonly used to indicate a successor to the account without having to create a will. —Also termed *tentative trust; bank-account trust; savings-account trust.*

voting trust. A trust in which corporate shareholders transfer their shares to a trustee for the purpose of creating a voting bloc; the shareholders still receive dividends under such an arrangement.

wasting trust. A trust in which the corpus is gradually depleted by periodic payments to the beneficiary.

trust agreement. See *declaration of trust* (b) under DECLARATION.

trust company. See COMPANY.

trust deed. 1. See *declaration of trust* (b) under DECLARATION. 2. See *deed of trust* under DEED.

trust de son tort. See *constructive trust* under TRUST.

trust distribution. See DISTRIBUTION.

trustee (trəs-**tee**), *n.* One who, having legal title to property, holds it in trust for the benefit of another and owes a fiduciary duty to that beneficiary.

trustee ad litem (ad-**lī**-təm). A trustee appointed by the court.

trustee de son tort (də-**sohn-tor[t]**). A person who, without legal authority, administers a living person's property to the detriment of the property owner. See *constructive trust* under TRUST.

trustee ex maleficio (eks-mal-ə-**fish**-[i-]oh *or* -mahl-ə-**fik**-ee-oh). A person who is guilty of wrongful or fraudulent conduct and is held by equity to the duty of a trustee, in relation to the subject matter, to prevent him or her from profiting from the wrongdoing.

trustee, *vb.* 1. To serve as trustee. 2. To place (a person or property) in the hands of one or more trustees. 3. To appoint (a person) trustee, often of a bankrupt's estate in order to restrain a creditor from collecting moneys due. 4. To attach (the effects of a debtor) in the hands of a third person.

trustee, U.S. See UNITED STATES TRUSTEE.

trustee in bankruptcy. BANKRUPTCY TRUSTEE.

trusteeship. 1. The office, status, or function of a trustee. 2. In international law, administration or supervision of a territory by one or more countries, esp. under a United Nations commission. Cf. MANDATE (6).

trust estate. CORPUS (2).

trust ex delicto. See *constructive trust* under TRUST.

trust ex maleficio. See *constructive trust* under TRUST.

trust fund. CORPUS (2).

trust indenture. See INDENTURE.

trustor. One who creates a trust; SETTLOR (1).

trust property. CORPUS (2).

trust res. CORPUS (2).

trust under will. See *testamentary trust* under TRUST.

trusty, *n.* A convict or prisoner who is considered trustworthy by prison authorities and therefore given special privileges

truth. In the law of defamation, an affirmative defense whereby the defendant asserts that the alleged defamatory statement is not in any way false.

Truth in Lending Act. CONSUMER CREDIT PROTECTION ACT. —Abbr. TILA.

try title. The judicial examination of a title. See TRESPASS TO TRY TITLE; *action to quiet title* under ACTION.

turnkey, *adj.* **1.** Provided in a state of being ready for immediate use <a turnkey computer network>. **2.** Of or relating to something provided in this manner <a turnkey contract>.

turn state's evidence, *vb.* To cooperate with prosecutors and testify against other criminal defendants <after hours of intense negotiations, the suspect accepted a plea bargain and agreed to turn state's evidence>.

turntable doctrine. ATTRACTIVE-NUISANCE DOCTRINE; this term gets its name from the enticing yet dangerous qualities of railroad turntables, which have frequently been the subject of litigation.

turpitude (tər-pə-t[y]ood). See MORAL TURPITUDE.

Twelfth Amendment. The constitutional amendment, ratified in 1804, that altered the electoral-college system by separating the balloting for presidential and vice-presidential candidates.

Twentieth Amendment. The constitutional amendment, ratified in 1933, that established the date for presidential inauguration as January 20 and the date for congressional convention as January 3.

Twenty-fifth Amendment. The constitutional amendment, ratified in 1967, that established rules of succession for the presidency and vice presidency in the event of death, resignation, or incapacity.

Twenty-first Amendment. The constitutional amendment, ratified in 1933, that repealed the Eighteenth Amendment (which established national Prohibition) and returned the power to regulate alcohol to the states.

Twenty-fourth Amendment. The constitutional amendment, ratified in 1964, that prohibits the federal and state governments from restricting the right to vote in federal elections because of one's failure to pay a poll tax or other tax.

Twenty-second Amendment. The constitutional amendment, ratified in 1951, that prohibits a person from being elected president more than twice (or, if the person succeeded to the office with more than half the predecessor's term remaining, more than once).

Twenty-seventh Amendment. The constitutional amendment, ratified in 1992, that prevents a pay raise for senators and representatives from taking effect until a new Congress convenes; this amendment was proposed as part of the original Bill of Rights in 1789, but it took 203 years for the required three-fourths of the states to ratify it.

Twenty-sixth Amendment. The constitutional amendment, ratified in 1971, that sets the minimum voting age at 18 for all state and federal elections.

Twenty-third Amendment. The constitutional amendment, ratified in 1961, that allows District of Columbia residents to vote in presidential elections.

two-dismissal rule. The rule that a notice of voluntary dismissal operates as an adjudication on the merits—not merely as a dismissal without prejudice—when filed by a plaintiff who has already dismissed the same claim in another court.

two-issue rule. The rule that if multiple issues were submitted to a trial jury and at least one of them is error-free, the appellate court should presume that the jury based its verdict on the proper issue—not on an erroneous one—and should therefore affirm the judgment.

two-stage trial. See *bifurcated trial* under TRIAL.

two-tier offer. A two-step technique by which a bidder tries to acquire a target corporation, the first step involving a cash tender offer and the second usu. a merger in which the target company's remaining shareholders receive securities from the bidder (these securities ordinarily being less favorable than the cash given in the first step).

two-witness rule. The rule that, to support a perjury conviction, two independent witnesses (or one witness along with corroborating evidence) must establish that the alleged perjurer gave false testimony.

tying arrangement. In antitrust law, an arrangement by which a seller will let a buyer obtain a desired product (the *tying product*) only if the buyer agrees to take an additional product (the *tied product*) that may or may not be desired; tying arrangements may be illegal under the Sherman or Clayton Acts if their effect is too anticompetitive. Cf. RECIPROCAL-DEALING ARRANGEMENT.

U

U.3C. *abbr.* UNIFORM CONSUMER CREDIT CODE.

ubi (oo-bee). [Latin] Where.

ubi supra (oo-bee-**soo**-prə). [Latin] Where stated above.

U.C.C. *abbr.* UNIFORM COMMERCIAL CODE.

UCCC. *abbr.* UNIFORM CONSUMER CREDIT CODE.

UCCJA. *abbr.* UNIFORM CHILD CUSTODY JURISDICTION ACT.

UCMJ. See CODE OF MILITARY JUSTICE.

UCR. *abbr.* UNIFORM CRIME REPORTS.

UGMA. See UNIFORM TRANSFERS TO MINORS ACT.

ultimate fact. See FACT.

ultimate issue. See ISSUE (1).

ultimatum (əl-tə-**may**-dəm). The final and categorical proposition made in negotiating a treaty, contract, or the like; an ultimatum implies that a rejection might lead to a break-off in negotiations or, in international law, to a cessation of diplomatic relations or even to war. Pl. **ultimatums.**

ultrahazardous activity. In tort law, an activity (such as dynamiting) for which the actor is held strictly liable because the activity (1) involves the risk of serious harm to persons or property; (2) cannot be performed without this risk, regardless of the precautions taken; and (3) does not ordinarily occur in the community. —Also termed *abnormally dangerous activity.* See *strict liability* under LIABILITY.

ultra vires (əl-trə-**veer**-eez *or* -**vI**-reez), *adj.* Unauthorized; beyond the scope of power allowed or granted by a corporate charter or by law <the officer was liable for the firm's ultra vires actions>. —Also termed *extra vires.* —**ultra vires,** *adv.* Cf. INTRA VIRES.

umbrella policy. See INSURANCE POLICY.

umpire. A third party selected to independently render a decision, usu. in labor disputes, when arbitrators have disagreed.

U.N. *abbr.* UNITED NATIONS.

unavoidable-accident doctrine. In tort law, the rule holding no party liable for an accident that was not foreseeable and that could not have been prevented by the exercise of reasonable care; the modern trend is for courts to ignore this doctrine and instead rely on the basic concepts of duty, negligence, and proximate cause.

unborn-widow rule. The legal fiction, assumed under the rule against perpetuities, that a beneficiary's widow is not alive at the testator's death, and thus a succeeding life estate to her voids any remainders because the interest would not vest within the perpetuities period. See RULE AGAINST PERPETUITIES.

unclean-hands doctrine. CLEAN-HANDS DOCTRINE.

unconditional pardon. See *absolute pardon* under PARDON.

unconscionability, doctrine of. The principle that courts may refuse to enforce contracts that are unfair or oppressive because of procedural abuses during contract formation or because of overreaching contractual terms, esp. terms that are unreasonably favorable to one party while precluding meaningful choice for the other party.

unconscionable (ən-**konsh**-[ə-]nə-bəl), *adj.* **1.** (Of persons) having no conscience; unscrupulous <an unconscionable criminal>. **2.** (Of actions) showing no regard for conscience; not in accordance with what is just or reasonable <the contract is void as unconscionable>. —**unconscionability, unconscionableness,** *n.* Cf. CONSCIONABLE.

unconstitutional, *adj.* Contrary to or in conflict with a constitution, esp. the U.S. Constitution <the law is unconstitutional because it violates the First Amendment's free-speech guarantee>. Cf. NONCONSTITUTIONAL.

unconstitutional-conditions doctrine. The principle that a government may not condition the receipt of government benefits on the recipient's surrender of constitutional rights (esp. First Amendment rights); for example, a television station that receives public funds cannot be forced to refrain from endorsing political candidates.

uncovered option. See *naked option* under OPTION.

undercapitalization. See CAPITALIZATION.

underinsurance. See INSURANCE.

underlease. SUBLEASE.

underlessor. SUBLESSOR.

under protest. See PROTEST.

under submission. Being considered by the court; under advisement <the case was under submission in the court of appeals for more than two years>.

undertake, *vb.* **1.** To take on an obligation or task <he has undertaken to chair the committee on legal aid for the homeless>. **2.** To give a formal promise; guarantee <the merchant undertook that the goods were waterproof>. **3.** To act as surety for (another); to make oneself responsible for (a person, fact, or the like) <her husband undertook for her appearance in court>.

undertaking, *n.* A promise, pledge, or engagement.

undertenant. SUBLESSEE.

under the influence. (Of a driver, pilot, etc.) in a condition in which drugs or intoxicating liquor have affected the nervous system in a way that deprives the person of the clearness of mind and the self-control that he or she would otherwise possess. See DRIVING UNDER THE INFLUENCE.

underwriter. 1. INSURER. **2.** A person or entity, esp. an investment banker, who guarantees the sale of newly issued securities by purchasing all or part of the shares for resale to the public.

underwriting, *n.* **1.** The act of assuming a risk by insuring it; the insurance of life or property. See INSURANCE. **2.** The act of agreeing to buy all or part of a new issue of securities to be offered for public sale. —**underwrite,** *vb.*

best-efforts underwriting. Underwriting whereby an investment banker agrees to direct, but not guarantee, the public sale of the issuer's securities.

firm-commitment underwriting. Underwriting whereby the underwriter agrees to purchase all the shares to be issued and remain financially responsible for any securities not purchased.

standby underwriting. Underwriting whereby the underwriter agrees, for a fee, to buy from the issuer any unsold shares remaining after the public offering.

undisclosed agency. See AGENCY (1).

undisclosed principal. See PRINCIPAL (1).

undistributed profit. See *retained earnings* under EARNINGS.

undivided interest. An interest held by the same title by two or more persons, whether their rights are equal or unequal as to value or quantity. —Also termed *undivided right*; *undivided title*. See *joint tenancy* and *tenancy in common* under TENANCY.

undocumented alien. See *illegal alien* under ALIEN.

undue-burden test. In constitutional law, the Supreme Court test stating that a law regulating abortion will be struck down if it places a substantial obstacle in the path of a woman's right to obtain an abortion; this test replaced the "trimester analysis," set forth in *Roe v. Wade*, in which the state's ability to restrict abortion increased during each trimester of pregnancy. *Planned Par-*

enthood of Southeastern Pa. v. Casey, 505 U.S. 833 (1992).

undue influence. 1. The unfair or improper persuasion of one person by another who has attained a position of domination or power; consent to a contract, transaction, relationship, or conduct is voidable if the consent is obtained through undue influence. **2.** In the context of wills, coercion that destroys the testator's free will and substitutes another's objectives in its place; when a beneficiary actively procures the execution of a will, a presumption of undue influence is raised, based on the confidential relationship between the influencer and the testator.

unearned income. See INCOME.

unearned premium. See PREMIUM.

unethical, *adj.* Not in conformity with moral norms or standards of professional conduct. See LEGAL ETHICS.

unfair competition. 1. Dishonest or fraudulent rivalry in trade and commerce; esp., the practice of endeavoring to substitute one's own goods or products in the market for those of another by means of imitating or counterfeiting the name, brand, size, shape, or other distinctive characteristic of the article or packaging. **2.** The body of law protecting the first user of such a name, brand, size, shape, or other distinctive characteristic against an imitating or counterfeiting competitor.

unfair labor practice. Any act by a union or employer in violation of the National Labor Relations Act; for example, an employer's act that interferes with or restrains the ability of its workers to organize or bargain collectively, or a union's coercion of employers to discriminate against employees.

unfit, *adj.* **1.** Unsuitable; not adapted or qualified for a particular use or service <the buyer returned the unfit goods to the seller and asked for a refund>. **2.** In family law, morally unqualified; incompetent <the judge found her to be an unfit mother and awarded custody to the father>.

unfriendly suitor. CORPORATE RAIDER.

unified bar. See *integrated bar* under BAR ASSOCIATION.

unified credit. See TAX CREDIT.

unified estate-and-gift tax. See *transfer tax* under TAX.

unified estate-and-gift tax credit. See *unified credit* under TAX CREDIT.

unified transfer tax. See *transfer tax* under TAX.

uniform act. A statute drafted by the National Conference of Commissioners on Uniform State Laws and proposed as legislation for all the states to adopt exactly as written; examples of uniform acts include the Uniform Partnership Act and the Uniform Child Custody Jurisdiction Act. Cf. MODEL ACT.

Uniform Child Custody Jurisdiction Act. An act, in force in all states, that sets out a standard (based on the child's residence in and connections with the state) by which a state court determines whether it has jurisdiction over a particular child-custody matter or whether it must recognize a custody decree issued by another state's court. —

Abbr. UCCJA. Cf. PARENTAL KIDNAPPING PREVENTION ACT.

Uniform Code of Military Justice. CODE OF MILITARY JUSTICE.

Uniform Commercial Code. A uniform law—adopted in whole or in part in most states—that governs commercial transactions, including sales of goods, secured transactions, and negotiable instruments. —Abbr. U.C.C.

Uniform Consumer Credit Code. A uniform law, adopted by some states, designed to simplify and modernize the consumer credit and usury laws, to further consumer understanding of the terms of credit transactions, to protect consumers against unfair practices, and the like. —Abbr. UCCC; U.3C. —Also termed *Consumer Credit Code.* Cf. CONSUMER CREDIT PROTECTION ACT.

Uniform Crime Reports. A series of annual criminological studies (each entitled *Crime in the United States*) prepared by the FBI; the reports include data on eight index offenses, statistics on arrests, and information on offenders, crime rates, and the like. —Abbr. UCR.

Uniform Deceptive Trade Practices Act. A type of Baby FTC Act that provides monetary and injunctive relief for a variety of unfair and deceptive acts, such as false advertising and disparagement. See BABY FTC ACT.

Uniform Enforcement of Foreign Judgments Act. A uniform state law giving the holder of a foreign judgment the right to levy and execute as if it were a domestic judgment.

Uniform Gifts to Minors Act. UNIFORM TRANSFERS TO MINORS ACT.

Uniform Law Commissioners. NATIONAL CONFERENCE OF COMMISSIONERS ON UNIFORM STATE LAWS.

Uniform Reciprocal Enforcement of Support Act. A uniform law providing a procedure by which alimony and child-support decrees issued by one state can be established and enforced against a former spouse who resides in another state. —Abbr. URESA.

Uniform Transfers to Minors Act. A uniform law—adopted by most states—providing for the transfer of property to a minor, whereby a custodian acting in a fiduciary capacity can act on behalf of the minor by managing investments and applying the income from the property to the minor's support. —Abbr. UTMA. —Also termed *Transfers to Minors Act.* —Formerly also termed *Uniform Gifts to Minors Act* (UGMA); *Gifts to Minors Act.*

unilateral, *adj.* One-sided; relating to only one of two or more persons or things <unilateral mistake>.

unilateral contract. See CONTRACT.

unilateral mistake. See MISTAKE.

unimproved land. 1. Land that has never been improved. **2.** Land that was once improved but has now been cleared of all buildings and structures.

union, *n.* A workers' organization formed to collectively negotiate with employers about such issues as salary, benefits, hours, and working conditions. —Also termed *labor union;* *labor organization; organization.* — **unionize,** *vb.* —**unionist,** *n.*

closed union. A union with restrictive membership requirements, such as high dues and long apprenticeship periods. Cf. CLOSED SHOP.

company union. **a.** A union whose membership is limited to the employees of a single company. **b.** A union under company domination.

craft union. A union composed of workers in the same trade or craft, such as carpentry or plumbing, regardless of the industry in which they work. —Also termed *horizontal union.*

independent union. A union that is not affiliated with a national or international union.

industrial union. A union composed of workers in the same industry, such as shipbuilding or automobile manufacturing, regardless of their particular trade or craft. —Also termed *vertical union.*

local union. A union that serves as the local bargaining unit for a national or international union.

open union. A union with minimal membership requirements. Cf. OPEN SHOP.

union certification. The determination by the National Labor Relations Board or a state agency that a particular union qualifies as the bargaining unit for a company's or an industry's workers because it has the support of a majority of the workers. —Also termed *certification of bargaining agent.*

union mortgage clause. See *standard mortgage clause* under MORTGAGE CLAUSE.

union shop. CLOSED SHOP.

union steward. STEWARD.

unissued stock. See STOCK.

unit depreciation method. See DEPRECIATION METHOD.

United Nations. An international organization formed in 1945 to establish a global community with the goals of preventing war, providing justice, and promoting human rights and welfare. —Abbr. U.N.

United States Attorney. A lawyer appointed by the President to represent, under the direction of the Attorney General, the federal government in civil and criminal cases in a federal judicial district. —Also termed *United States District Attorney*. Cf. DISTRICT ATTORNEY.

United States Code. A multivolume published codification of federal statutory law; in citation form, it is abbreviated as U.S.C., as in 42 U.S.C. § 1983.

United States Code Annotated. A multivolume publication of the complete text of the United States Code with historical notes, cross-references, and casenotes of federal and state decisions construing specific Code sections. —Abbr. U.S.C.A.

United States court. A court having federal jurisdiction, including the U.S. Supreme Court, courts of appeals, district courts, bankruptcy courts, tax courts, and the like.

United States Court of Appeals for the Armed Forces. The primary civilian appellate tribunal responsible for reviewing court-martial convictions from all the military services. 10 U.S.C. §§ 941 et seq. —Formerly also termed *Court of Military Appeals*.

United States District Attorney. UNITED STATES ATTORNEY.

United States District Court. A federal trial court having jurisdiction within its judicial district. —Abbr. U.S.D.C.

United States Magistrate Judge. A federal judicial officer who hears civil and criminal pretrial matters and who conducts either civil trials or criminal misdemeanor trials. 28 U.S.C. §§ 631-639. —Also termed *federal magistrate* and (before 1990) *United States Magistrate*.

United States Marshal. See MARSHAL.

United States Reports. The official printed record of U.S. Supreme Court cases; in citation form, it is abbreviated as U.S., as in 715 U.S. 68 (2018).

United States Supreme Court. SUPREME COURT OF THE UNITED STATES.

United States Tax Court. See TAX COURT, U.S.

United States trustee. A federal official who is appointed by the Attorney General to perform administrative tasks in the bankruptcy process, such as appointing bankruptcy trustees in Chapter 7 and Chapter 11 cases. See BANKRUPTCY TRUSTEE.

unitization (yoo-ni-tə-**zay**-shən), *n.* In oil-and-gas law, the aggregation of two or more separately owned oil-producing properties to form a single property that can be operated as a single entity under an arrangement for sharing costs and revenues. — **unitize (yoo**-nə-tIz), *vb.* Cf. COMMU-NITIZATION.

units-of-output depreciation method. See DEPRECIATION METHOD.

unity, *n.* **1.** The fact or condition of being one in number; oneness. **2.** At common law, a requirement for the creation of a joint tenancy; the four unities are interest, possession, time, and title. —**unitary,** *adj.* See *joint tenancy* under TENANCY.

unity of interest. The requirement that all joint tenants' interests must be identical in nature, extent, and duration. —Also termed *interest unity.*

unity of possession. The requirement that each joint tenant must be entitled to possession of the whole property. —Also termed *possession unity.*

unity of time. The requirement that all joint tenants' interests must vest at the same time. —Also termed *time unity.*

unity of title. The requirement that all joint tenants must acquire their interests under the same instrument. —Also termed *title unity.*

universal agent. See AGENT.

universal defense. See *real defense* under DEFENSE (4).

universal malice. See MALICE.

universal partnership. See PARTNERSHIP.

unjust enrichment. 1. A benefit obtained from another, not intended as a gift and not legally justifiable, for which the beneficiary must make restitution or recompense. **2.** The area of law dealing with unjustifiable benefits of this kind.

unlawful, *adj.* **1.** Unauthorized by law; illegal <in some cities, jaywalking is unlawful>. **2.** Criminally punishable <unlawful entry>. **3.** Involving moral turpitude <the preacher spoke to the congregation about the unlawful activities of gambling and drinking>.

unlawful assembly. See ASSEMBLY.

unlawful detainer. See DETAINER.

unlawful entry. 1. The crime of entering another's property, by fraud or other illegal means, without the owner's consent. **2.** An alien's crossing of a border into a country without proper documents.

unlawful force. See FORCE.

unliquidated, *adj.* Not previously specified or determined <unliquidated damages>.

unliquidated claim. See CLAIM (2).

unliquidated debt. See DEBT.

unlisted security. See SECURITY.

unlisted stock. See *unlisted security* under SECURITY.

unmarketable title. See TITLE.

unnatural offense. SODOMY.

unnatural will. See WILL.

unnecessary hardship. In zoning law, a ground for granting a variance, based on the impossibility or prohibitive expense of conforming the property or its use to the zoning regulation. See VARIANCE (2).

unprofessional conduct. See CONDUCT.

unrealized profit. See *paper profit* under PROFIT.

unrealized loss. See *paper loss* under LOSS.

unreasonable compensation. See COMPENSATION.

unreasonable restraint on alienation. RESTRAINT ON ALIENATION (1).

unreasonable search. See SEARCH.

unrelated business income. See INCOME.

unrelated offense. See OFFENSE.

unsecured bond. DEBENTURE (2).

unsecured claim. See CLAIM (4).

unsecured creditor. See CREDITOR.

unsecured debt. See DEBT.

unsecured note. See NOTE.

unspeakable crime. SODOMY.

untenantable (ən-**ten**-ən-tə-bəl), *adj.* Not capable of being occupied or lived in <the city closed the untenantable housing project>.

unvalued policy. See INSURANCE POLICY.

unwritten law. 1. Law that, although never enacted in the form of a statute or ordinance, has the sanction of custom. —Also termed *jus non scriptum*; *jus ex non scripto*. **2.** CASELAW.

upper chamber. See CHAMBER.

upper court. See *court above* under COURT.

upset price. See PRICE.

upstreaming. A parent corporation's use of a subsidiary's cash flow or assets for purposes unrelated to the subsidiary.

upstream merger. See MERGER.

URESA. *abbr.* UNIFORM RECIPROCAL ENFORCEMENT OF SUPPORT ACT.

usage. A well-known, customary, and uniform practice, usu. in a specific profession or business. See CUSTOM (1).

trade usage. A customary practice or set of practices relied on by persons conversant in, or connected with, a trade or business. —Also termed *usage of trade*.

U.S.C. *abbr.* UNITED STATES CODE.

U.S.C.A. *abbr.* UNITED STATES CODE ANNOTATED.

U.S.D.C. *abbr.* UNITED STATES DISTRICT COURT.

use (yoos), *n.* **1.** The application, employment, or enjoyment of something <the neighbors complained to the city about the owner's use of the building as a dance club>.

accessory use. In zoning law, a use that is dependent on or pertains to a main use.

beneficial use. The right to use and enjoy property and all that makes that property desirable or habitable, such as light, air, and access, even if someone else owns the legal title to the property.

collateral use. The legal use of a trademark by someone other than the trademark owner, whereby the other party must clearly identify itself, the use of the trademark, and the absence of affiliation with the trademark owner.

conforming use. In land-use planning, the use of a structure or of the land in conformity with the uses permitted under the zoning classifications of a particular area, such as the building of a single-family dwelling in a residential zone.

exclusive use. **a.** In trademark law, the right to use a specific mark without exception, and to prevent another from using a confusingly similar mark. **b.** In property law, the right of an adverse user to a property, exercised independently of any similar rights held by others; one of the elements of a prescriptive easement.

experimental use. **a.** In patent law, the use or sale of an invention by the inventor for experimental purposes. **b.** A defense to liability for infringement of a patent, where the infringement took place only to satisfy curiosity or to complete an experiment, rather than for profit.

highest and best use. In valuing real property, the use that will generate the most profit; esp. used to determine the fair market value of property subject to eminent domain. — Often shortened to *best use.* —Also termed *most suitable use.*

incidental use. In zoning law, land use that is dependent on or affiliated with the land's primary use.

nonconforming use. Land use that is impermissible under current zoning restrictions but that is allowed because the use existed lawfully before the restrictions took effect.

public use. **a.** The public's beneficial right to use or actual use of property or facilities subject to condemnation. See CONDEMNATION (2). **b.** In patent law, any use or offer to use a completed or operative invention in a nonsecret, natural, and intended manner; a patent is invalid if the invention was in public use more than one year before the patent's application date.

2. A habitual or common practice <drug use>. **3.** A purpose or end served <the tool had several uses>. **4.** A benefit or profit—esp., the right to take profits from land owned and possessed by another; the equitable ownership of land the legal title to which another person holds <*cestui que use*>. See CESTUI QUE USE. — **use** (yooz), *vb.*

resulting use. A use created by implication and remaining with the grantor when the conveyance lacks consideration.

shifting use. A use arising from the occurrence of a certain event that terminates the preceding use; in the following example, C has a shifting use that arises when D makes the specified payment: "to A for the use of B, but then to C when D pays $1,000 to E."

springing use. A use that arises on the occurrence of a future event; in the following example, B has a springing use that vests when B marries: "to A for the use of B when B marries."

use/derivative-use immunity. See *use immunity* under IMMUNITY (3).

useful life. The estimated length of time that depreciable property will generate income; useful life is used to calculate depreciation and amortization deductions. See DEPRECIATION METHOD.

use immunity. See IMMUNITY (3).

user. 1. The exercise or enjoyment of a right or property <the neighbor argued that an easement arose by his continuous user over the last 15 years>. Cf. NONUSER. **2.** Someone who uses a thing <the stapler's last user did not put it away>.

Uses, Statute of. See STATUTE OF USES.

use tax. See TAX.

use variance. See VARIANCE (2).

usucaption (yoo-zə-**kap**-shən), *n.* In civil law, the acquisition of ownership by prescription. —Also termed *usucapion; usucapio.* —**usucapt,** *vb.* See PRESCRIPTION (1).

usufruct (**yoo**-zə-frəkt *or* **yoo**-zoo-), *n.* A right to use and enjoy another's property without damaging or diminishing the property. —**usufructuary,** *adj.*—**usufructuary,** *n.*

usurpation (yoo-zər-**pay**-shən), *n.* The unlawful seizure and assumption of another's position, office, or authority by force. —**usurp** (yoo-**sərp** *or* yoo-**zərp**), *vb.*

usury (**yoo**-zə-ree *or* **yoozh**-[ə-]ree) *n.* **1.** Historically, the lending of money with interest. **2.** Today, the charging of an illegal rate of interest. **3.** An illegally high rate of interest. — **usurious** (yoo-**z[h]uur**-ee-əs), *adj.*— **usurer** (**yoo**-zhər-ər), *n.*

utility. The quality of serving some function that benefits society; in patent law, utility—in addition to nonobviousness and novelty—is one of the three basic requirements of patentability.

utility patent. See PATENT (2).

UTMA. *abbr.* UNIFORM TRANSFERS TO MINORS ACT.

utter, *vb.* **1.** To say, express, or publish <don't utter another word until your attorney is present>. **2.** To put or send (a document) into circulation; esp., to circulate (a forged note) as if genuine <she uttered a counterfeit fifty-dollar bill at the grocery store>. —**utterance** (corresponding to sense 1), **uttering** (corresponding to sense 2), *n.*

uttering. The crime of presenting a false or worthless instrument with the intent to harm or defraud. See FORGERY.

uxor (**ək**-sor). [Latin] Wife. —Abbr. *ux.* See ET UX.

V

v. *abbr.* VERSUS.

VA. *abbr.* VETERANS AFFAIRS, DEPARTMENT OF.

vacate, *vb.* **1.** To nullify or cancel <the court vacated the judgment>. Cf. OVERRULE. **2.** To physically surrender occupancy or possession; to leave <the tenant vacated the premises>. —**vacation,** *n.*

vagrancy (**vay**-grən-see), *n.* **1.** The state or condition of wandering from place to place without a home, job, or means of support. **2.** An instance of such wandering; many state laws prohibiting vagrancy have been declared unconstitutionally vague. — **vagrant,** *adj.* & *n.* Cf. LOITERING.

vagueness doctrine. In constitutional law, the doctrine—based on the Due Process Clause—requiring that a criminal statute state explicitly and definitely what acts are prohibited, so as to provide fair warning and preclude arbitrary enforcement. —Also termed *void-for-vagueness doctrine.* Cf. OVERBREADTH DOCTRINE.

valid, *adj.* **1.** Legally sufficient; binding <a valid contract>. **2.** Meritorious <that is a valid conclusion based on the facts presented in this case>. —**validate,** *vb.*—**validation, validity,** *n.*

valuable consideration. See *good consideration* (a) under CONSIDERATION.

valuation, *n.* **1.** The act of determining the value of a thing or entity. **2.** The estimated worth of a thing or entity. —**value, valuate,** *vb.*

special-use valuation. An executor's option of valuating real property in an estate, esp. farmland, at its current use rather than for its highest potential value.

valuation date. See ALTERNATE VALUATION DATE.

value, *n.* **1.** The monetary worth or price of something. **2.** The amount of goods, services, or money that something will command in an exchange. **3.** The significance, desirability, or utility of something. **4.** Sufficient contractual consideration. —**value,** *vb.*—**valuation,** *n.*

value-added tax. See TAX.

vandalism, *n.* **1.** Willful or ignorant destruction of public or private property, esp. of artistic, architectural, or literary treasures. **2.** The actions or attitudes of one who maliciously or ignorantly destroys or disfigures public or private property; active hostility to anything that is venerable or beautiful. —**vandalize,** *vb.*—**vandal,** *n.*

variable annuity. See ANNUITY.

variable cost. See COST.

variable rate. See INTEREST RATE.

variable-rate mortgage. See *adjustable-rate mortgage* under MORTGAGE.

variance. 1. A difference or disparity between two statements or documents that ought to agree; esp., in criminal procedure, a difference between the allegations in a charging instrument and the proof actually introduced at trial.

fatal variance. A variance that either deprives the defendant of fair notice of the charges or exposes the defendant to the risk of double jeopardy; such a variance is grounds for reversing a conviction.

immaterial variance. A variance that is too slight to mislead or prejudice the defendant, and is thus harmless error.

2. A license or official authorization to depart from a zoning law. —Also termed (in sense 2) *zoning variance.* Cf. SPECIAL EXCEPTION (2).

area variance. A variance that permits deviation from zoning requirements as to construction and placement, but not from requirements as to use.

use variance. A variance that permits deviation from zoning requirements as to use.

VAT. See *value-added tax* under TAX.

vehicular homicide. See HOMICIDE.

vel non (vel-non). [Latin "or not"] *Jargon.* Or the absence of it (or them) <this case turns solely on the finding of discrimination vel non>.

vendee. A purchaser, usu. of real property; a buyer.

vendor. A seller, usu. of real property.

vendor's lien. See LIEN.

venire (və-**neer** *or* və-**nī**-ree). **1.** A panel of persons selected for jury duty and from which the jurors are to be chosen. —Also termed *array*; *jury panel.* **2.** VENIRE FACIAS.

venire facias. (-**faysh**-[ee]əs). A writ directing a sheriff to assemble a jury. —Often shortened to *venire.*

venire facias de novo. A writ for summoning a jury panel anew because of some impropriety or irregularity in the original jury's return or verdict so that no judgment can be given on it. —Often shortened to *venire de novo.*

veniremember (və-**neer**-mem-bər *or* və-**nī**-ree-). A prospective juror; a member of a jury panel. —Also termed *venireperson*; *venireman*; *talesman.*

venture capital. See CAPITAL.

venue (**ven**-yoo). [Law French "coming"] **1.** The proper or a possible place for the trial of a lawsuit, usu. because the place has some connection with the events that have given rise to the lawsuit. **2.** The county or other territory over which a trial court has jurisdiction. **3.** Loosely, the place where a conference or meeting is being held. Cf. JURISDICTION.

venue, change of. See CHANGE OF VENUE.

veracity (və-**ras**-ət-ee), *n.* **1.** Truthfulness <the witness's fraud conviction supports the defense's challenge to his veracity>. **2.** Accuracy <you called into question the veracity of Murphy's affidavit>. —**veracious** (və-**ray**-shəs), *adj.*

verdict. 1. A jury's finding or decision on the factual issues of a case. **2.** Loosely, in a nonjury trial, a judge's resolution of the issues of a case.

chance verdict. A now-illegal verdict, arrived at by hazard or lot.

compromise verdict. A verdict that is reached when jurors concede some

issues so they can settle other issues in their favor.

directed verdict. A judgment entered
on the order of a trial judge who
takes over the fact-finding role of
the jury because the evidence is so
compelling that only one decision
can reasonably follow or because it
fails to establish a prima facie
case. —Also termed *instructed verdict.*

excessive verdict. A verdict that results from the jury's passion or
prejudice and thereby shocks the
court's conscience.

false verdict. A verdict so contrary to
the evidence and so unjust that the
judge may set it aside.

general verdict. A verdict by which
the jury finds in favor of one party
or the other, as opposed to resolving specific fact questions. Cf. *special verdict.*

guilty verdict. A jury's formal pronouncement that a defendant is
guilty of the charged offense.

partial verdict. A verdict by which a
jury finds a criminal defendant innocent of some charges and guilty
of other charges.

quotient verdict. An improper verdict
that a jury arrives at by totalling
their individual damage awards
and dividing by the number of jurors.

sealed verdict. A verdict put into
writing and sealed in an envelope
for delivery to the court; such a
verdict is sometimes used in order
to avoid detaining the jury until
the next session of court, so that
the jury is allowed to separate be-

fore the verdict is read in open
court.

special verdict. A verdict that gives a
written finding for each issue, leaving the application of the law to
judge. Cf. *general verdict.*

veredicto. See NON OBSTANTE VE-
REDICTO.

verification, *n.* **1.** A formal declaration made in the presence of an authorized officer, such as a notary
public, by which one swears to the
truth of the statements in the document. Cf. ACKNOWLEDGMENT (1). **2.**
An oath or affirmation that an authorized officer administers to an affiant or deponent. **3.** Loosely, AC-
KNOWLEDGMENT (2). **4.** See *certified
copy* under COPY. **5.** CERTIFICATE OF
AUTHORITY. **6.** Any act of notariz-
ing. —**verify,** *vb.*—**verifier,** *n.* Cf.
JURAT (1).

verified copy. See *certified copy* under COPY.

versus. Against. —Abbr. v.; vs.

vertical integration. INTE-
GRATION (4).

vertical merger. See MERGER.

vertical price-fixing. See PRICE-
FIXING.

vertical privity. See PRIVITY.

vertical restraint. See RESTRAINT
OF TRADE.

vertical union. See *industrial union* under UNION.

vest, *vb.* **1.** To confer ownership of
(property) upon a person. **2.** To invest (a person) with the full title to
property. **3.** To give (a person) an
immediate, fixed right of present or
future enjoyment. —**vesting,** *n.*

vested, *adj.* Not contingent; unconditional; absolute <a vested interest in the estate>.

vested estate. See ESTATE.

vested interest. An immediate, fixed right of present or future enjoyment.

vested remainder. See REMAINDER.

Veterans Affairs, Department of. An independent federal agency that administers benefit programs for veterans and their families. —Abbr. V.A. —Also termed *Veterans Administration.*

veto, *n.* A power of one governmental branch to prohibit an action by another branch; esp., a chief executive's refusal to sign into law a bill passed by the legislature. —**veto,** *vb.*—**vetoer,** *n.*

legislative veto. A veto that allowed Congress to block a federal executive or agency action taken under congressionally delegated authority; the Supreme Court held the legislative veto unconstitutional in *INS v. Chadha,* 462 U.S. 919 (1983). See DELEGATION DOCTRINE.

line-item veto. The power to veto some provisions in a legislative bill without affecting other provisions. —Also termed *item veto.*

pocket veto. A veto resulting from the President's failure to sign a bill passed within the last 10 days of the legislative session.

vexatious (vek-**say**-shəs), *adj.* Harassing; annoying. —**vexation,** *n.*

vexatious litigation. One or more lawsuits filed without reasonable or probable cause. See MALICIOUS PROSECUTION.

viable (**vI**-ə-bəl), *adj.* **1.** Capable of living, esp. outside the womb <a viable fetus>. **2.** Capable of independent existence or standing <a viable lawsuit>. —**viability,** *n.*

vicarious (vI-**ker**-ee-əs), *adj.* Performed or suffered by one person as substitute for another; indirect; surrogate.

vicarious infringement. See INFRINGEMENT.

vicarious liability. See LIABILITY.

vice crime. See CRIME.

vicinage (**vis**-[ə]-nij). [Law French "neighborhood"] **1.** Vicinity; proximity. **2.** The place where a crime is committed or a trial is held.

victim, *n.* A person harmed by a crime, tort, or other wrong. —**victimize,** *vb.*—**victimization,** *n.*

victim allocution. See ALLOCUTION.

victim-impact statement. A statement read into the record during sentencing to inform the judge or jury of the financial, physical, and psychological impact of the crime on the victim and the victim's family.

victimless crime. See CRIME.

videlicet. See VIZ.

vi et armis (vee-et-**ahr**-mis *or* vI-). [Latin] By or with force and arms. See TRESPASS VI ET ARMIS.

villein (**vil**-ən). In feudal law, a person entirely subject to a lord or attached to a manor, but free in relation to all others; a serf.

villeinage (vil-ə-nij *or* -nayj). **1.** The holding of property through servitude to a feudal lord. **2.** A villein's status or condition.

vindicate, *vb.* **1.** To clear (a person or thing) from suspicion, criticism, blame, or doubt <the serial killer will never be vindicated in the minds of the victims' families>. **2.** To assert, maintain, or affirm (one's interest) by action <the claimants sought to vindicate their rights through a class-action proceeding>. **3.** To defend (one's interest) against interference or encroachment <the borrower vindicated its interest in court when the lender attempted to foreclose>. —**vindication,** *n.*—**vindicator,** *n.*

vindictive damages. See *punitive damages* under DAMAGES.

violation, *n.* **1.** An infraction or breach of the law. **2.** The act of breaking or dishonoring the law. **3.** A penal code's noncriminal classification for public-welfare offenses. —**violate,** *vb.*—**violative,** *adj.*—**violator,** *n.*

violence, *n.* Physical behavior or treatment forcefully and unjustly exercised with the intent to harm. —**violent,** *adj.*

virtual adoption. See *adoption by estoppel* under ADOPTION.

virtual-representation doctrine. The principle that a judgment may bind a person who is not a party to the litigation if one of the parties is so closely aligned with the nonparty's interests that the nonparty has been adequately and effectively represented by the party in court; under this doctrine, for instance, a judgment in a case naming only the husband as a party can be binding on his wife as well. See RES JUDICATA.

visa (vee-sə). A notation or indorsement printed on a passport by an official who grants entry into a country. —Also termed *visé.*

vis-à-vis (veez-ə-vee). [French "face to face"] **1.** *prep.* In relation to; opposite to <the creditor established a preferred position vis-à-vis the other creditors>. **2.** *adv.* Facing each other; opposite <that defense is possible in all intrafamilial legal relationships, esp. parent vis-à-vis child>.

visitation right. 1. A parent's court-ordered privilege of spending time with his or her child who is living with another person, usu. the divorced spouse. **2.** In international law, a belligerent nation's right to go upon and search a neutral vessel to find out whether it is carrying contraband or is otherwise engaged in nonneutral service; if it is doing either of these things, the searchers may seize the contraband and carry out an appropriate punishment. —Also termed *right of visitation.*

visiting judge. See JUDGE.

vis major (vees-**may**-jər *or* vis-). [Latin "a superior force"] FORCE MAJEURE.

vitiate (vish-ee-ayt), *vb.* **1.** To impair the quality of (something). **2.** To invalidate either completely or in part; to render of no effect. **3.** To corrupt morally. —**vitiation,** *n.*—**vitiator,** *n.*

viz. (viz). *abbr.* [Latin *videlicet*] Namely; that is to say <the defendant engaged in fraudulent activities, *viz.,* misrepresenting his gross in-

come, misrepresenting the value of his assets, and forging his wife's signature>.

void, *adj.* Of no legal effect; null; unenforceable. —**void, avoid,** *vb.*— **voidness,** *n.*

voidable, *adj.* Capable of being annulled. —**voidability,** *n.*

voidable marriage. See MARRIAGE (1).

voidable preference. PREFERENTIAL TRANSFER.

voidable transfer. PREFERENTIAL TRANSFER.

voidance, *n.* The act of annulling, canceling, or making void. —Also termed *avoidance.* —**void,** *vb.*

void-for-vagueness   **doctrine.** VAGUENESS DOCTRINE.

void marriage. See MARRIAGE (1).

voir dire (vwah-**deer** *or* vor-**dIr**), *n.* [Law French "to speak the truth"] **1.** A preliminary examination of a prospective juror by a judge or lawyer to decide if the prospect is qualified and suitable to serve on a jury. **2.** A preliminary examination to test the competence of a witness or evidence. —Also spelled *voire dire.*— Formerly also termed *examination on the voir dire.* —**voir dire,** *vb.*

volenti non fit injuria (voh-**len**-tee-non-fit-in-**juur**-[i-]yə *or* -tI-). [Latin "a person cannot be harmed by that to which he or she consents"] The principle that a person who knowingly and voluntarily risks danger cannot recover for any resulting injury. See ASSUMPTION OF THE RISK.

volition (voh-**li**-shən), *n.* **1.** The ability to make a choice or determine something. **2.** The act of making a choice or determining something. **3.** The choice or determination someone makes. —**volitional,** *adj.*

volitional test. IRRESISTIBLE-IM-PULSE TEST.

voluntary, *adj.* **1.** Decided or accomplished by personal choice or impulse; not required, coerced, or prompted by another person or thing. **2.** Gratuitous; without consideration. —**voluntariness,** *n.*

voluntary appearance. See APPEARANCE.

voluntary assignment. See *general assignment* under ASSIGNMENT.

voluntary bankruptcy. See BANKRUPTCY.

voluntary dismissal. See DISMISSAL.

voluntary dissolution. See DISSOLUTION.

voluntary euthanasia. See EUTHANASIA.

voluntary intoxication. See INTOXICATION.

voluntary manslaughter. See MANSLAUGHTER.

voluntary waste. See *commissive waste* under WASTE.

voluntary settlement. See SETTLEMENT.

vote, *n.* **1.** The expression of one's preference or opinion by ballot, show of hands, or other type of communication <the Republican candidate received more votes than the Democratic candidate>. **2.** The total number of votes cast in an election <the incumbent received 60% of the vote>. **3.** The act of voting, usu. by a legislative body <the Senate postponed the vote on the gun-control bill>. —**vote,** *vb.*

vote dilution. DILUTION (3).

voting. The action of giving a vote; deciding by vote.

absentee voting. Participation in an election by a qualified voter who is unable to appear at the polls on election day; the practice of allowing voters to participate in this way.

class voting. A method of shareholder voting by which different classes of shares vote separately on fundamental corporate changes that adversely affect the rights and privileges of that class. —Also termed *voting by class; voting by voting group.*

cumulative voting. A system for electing corporate directors whereby a shareholder may multiply his or her number of shares by the number of open directorships and cast the total for a single candidate or a select few candidates.

majority voting. A system for electing corporate directors whereby each shareholder is allowed one vote for each director, who can win with a simple majority.

noncumulative voting. A corporate voting system in which a shareholder is limited in board elections to voting no more than the number

of shares he or she owns for a single candidate; the result is that a majority shareholder will elect the entire board of directors. — Also termed *straight voting.*

voting   agreement.   POOLING AGREEMENT.

voting group. A categorization of shareholders by the type of stock held for voting on corporate matters.

Voting Rights Act. The federal law that guarantees—without discrimination—a citizen's right to vote.

voting security. See *voting stock* under STOCK.

voting stock. See STOCK.

voting trust. See TRUST.

vouch, *vb.* **1.** To answer for (another); to personally assure <the suspect's mother vouched for him>. **2.** To call upon, rely on, or cite as authority; to substantiate with evidence <counsel vouched the mathematical formula for determining the statistical probability>.

voucher, *n.* **1.** Confirmation of the payment or discharge of a debt; a receipt. **2.** A written or printed authorization to disburse money.

vouching-in. IMPLEADER.

voyeur (voi-**yər** *or* vwah-**yər**), *n.* A person who observes something without participating; esp., one who gains sexual pleasure by secretly observing another's sexual acts. —**voyeuristic,** *adj.*—**voyeurism,** *n.*

vs. *abbr.* VERSUS.

W

Wade **hearing.** In criminal law, a pretrial hearing in which the defendant contests the validity of his or her out-of-court identification; if the court finds that the identification was tainted by unconstitutional methods, the prosecution cannot use the identification and must link the defendant to the crime by other means. *United States v. Wade,* 388 U.S. 218 (1967).

wage, *n.* (*usu. pl.*) Payment for labor or services, usu. based on time worked or quantity produced.

front wages. Prospective compensation paid to a victim of job discrimination until the denied position becomes available.

minimum wage. The lowest hourly rate of compensation for labor, as established by federal statute and required of employers engaged in interstate commerce. 29 U.S.C. § 206.

wage-and-hour law. A law, such as the federal Fair Labor Standards Act, governing the minimum wages and maximum working hours for employees.

wage-earner's plan. See CHAPTER 13.

wager, *n.* Money or other consideration risked on an uncertain event; a bet or gamble. —**wager,** *vb.* —**wagerer,** *n.*

wager of law. COMPURGATION.

wager policy. See INSURANCE POLICY.

wait-and-see principle. A modification to the rule against perpetuities allowing a court to determine the validity of a contingent future interest based on whether it actually does vest within the perpetuities period, rather than on whether it possibly could have vested outside the period. —Also termed *second-look doctrine.*

waiting period. A time period that must expire before some legal right or remedy can be enjoyed or enforced; for example, many states have waiting periods for the issuance of marriage licenses or the purchase of handguns.

waiver, *n.* **1.** The voluntary relinquishment or abandonment—express or implied—of a legal right or advantage; the party alleged to have waived a right must have had both knowledge of the existing right and the intention of forgoing it <waiver of notice>. Cf. ESTOPPEL. **2.** The instrument by which a person relinquishes or abandons a legal right or advantage <the plaintiff must sign a waiver when the funds are delivered>. —**waive,** *vb.*

waiver of immunity. The act of giving up the right against self-incrimination and proceeding to testify. See IMMUNITY (3).

waiver of tort. The election to sue in quasi-contract to recover the defendant's unjust benefit, instead of suing in tort to recover damages. See *implied-in-law contract* under CONTRACT.

want of consideration. The lack of consideration for a contract. See CONSIDERATION. Cf. FAILURE OF CONSIDERATION.

want of jurisdiction. The lack of jurisdiction over a person or the subject matter of a lawsuit.

want of prosecution. Failure of a litigant to pursue the case <dismissal for want of prosecution>. —Also termed *lack of prosecution*.

wanton misconduct. See MISCONDUCT.

wanton negligence. See *gross negligence* under NEGLIGENCE.

wantonness, *n.* Conduct that indicates the actor is aware of the risks but indifferent to the results; wantonness usu. suggests a greater degree of culpability than recklessness, and it often connotes malice in criminal-law contexts. —**wanton,** *adj.* Cf. RECKLESSNESS.

war. 1. Hostile conflict by means of armed forces, carried on between nations, states, or rulers, or sometimes between parties within the same nation or state; a period of such conflict <the Gulf War>.

civil war. An internal armed conflict between people of the same nation; esp. (usu. cap.), the war between the states from 1861 to 1865, resulting from the Confederate states' attempted secession from the Union.

2. A dispute or competition between adversaries <fare wars are common in the airline industry>. **3.** A struggle to solve a pervasive problem <America's war against drugs>.

war crime. Conduct that violates international laws governing war; examples of war crimes are the killing of hostages, abuse of civilians in occupied territories, abuse of prisoners of war, and devastation not justified by military necessity.

ward. 1. A person, usu. a minor, who is under a guardian's charge or protection. See GUARDIAN. **2.** A territorial division in a city, usu. defined for purposes of city government.

warehouseman. WAREHOUSER.

warehouseman's lien. See *warehouser's lien* under LIEN.

warehouser. A person hired to receive and store another's goods. —Also termed *warehouseman.* See BAILEE.

warehouse receipt. A document evidencing title to goods stored with someone else; a warehouse receipt may be a negotiable instrument and is often used for financing with inventory as security. See BAILMENT.

warehouser's lien. See LIEN.

warehousing. 1. A mortgage banker's holding of mortgages until the resale market improves. **2.** A corporation's giving of advance notice of a tender offer to institutional investors, who can then buy stock in the target company before public awareness of the takeover inflates the stock's price. See TENDER OFFER.

war power. The constitutional authority of Congress to declare war and maintain armed forces (U.S. Const. art. I, § 8, cl. 11-14), and of the President to conduct war as commander-in-chief (U.S. Const. art. II, § 2, cl. 1).

warrant, *n.* **1.** A writ directing or authorizing someone to do an act, esp. one directing a law enforcer to make an arrest, a search, or a seizure.

arrest warrant. A warrant, issued only on probable cause, directing a law enforcer to arrest a person and to bring him or her to court. —Also termed *warrant of arrest.*

bench warrant. A warrant issued directly by a judge to a law enforcer, esp. for the arrest of a person who has been held in contempt, has been indicted, or has disobeyed a subpoena.

distress warrant. A warrant authorizing a court officer to distrain property. See DISTRESS.

search warrant. See SEARCH WARRANT.

2. A document conferring authority, esp. to pay or receive money.

dock warrant. See DOCK RECEIPT.

treasury warrant. An order in the form of a check on which government disbursements are paid.

3. SUBSCRIPTION WARRANT.

warrant, *vb.* **1.** To justify <the conduct warrants a presumption of negligence>. **2.** To guarantee the security of (realty or personalty, or a person) <the store warranted the safety of the customer's jewelry>. **3.** To give warranty of (title); to give warranty of title to (a person) <the seller warrants the property's title to the buyer>. **4.** To authorize <the manager warranted the search of the premises>.

warrantee. A person to whom a warranty is given.

warrantless arrest. See ARREST.

warrantor. A person who gives a warranty.

warranty, *n.* **1.** In property law, a covenant by which the grantor in a deed binds himself or herself, as well as any heirs, to secure to the grantee the estate conveyed in the deed, and pledges to compensate the grantee with other land if the grantee is evicted by someone possessing paramount title. See COVENANT (4). Cf. *quitclaim deed* under DEED.

general warranty. A warranty against the claims of all persons.

special warranty. A warranty against the claims of persons claiming by, through, or under the grantor or the grantor's heirs.

2. In contract law, an express or implied undertaking that something in furtherance of the contract is guaranteed by one of the contracting parties; esp., a seller's undertaking that the thing being sold is as represented or promised. Cf. CONDITION (3).

express warranty. A warranty created by the overt words or actions of the seller.

implied warranty. A warranty arising by operation of law because of the circumstances of a sale, rather than by the seller's express promise.

implied warranty of fitness for a particular purpose. A warranty—implied by law if the seller has reason to know of the buyer's special purposes for the property—that the property is suitable for those purposes.

implied warranty of habitability. In a residential lease, a warranty from the landlord to the tenant that the leased property is fit to live in and that it will remain so during the term of the lease. —Also termed *covenant of habitability*.

implied warranty of merchantability. A warranty that the property is fit for the ordinary purposes for which it is used.

limited warranty. A warranty that does not fully cover labor and materials for repairs; under federal law, a limited warranty must be clearly labeled as such on the face of the warranty.

3. In insurance law, a pledge or stipulation by the insured that the facts relating to the person insured, the thing insured, or the risk insured are as stated.

affirmative warranty. A warranty that facts are as stated at the beginning of the policy period.

promissory warranty. A warranty that facts will continue to be as stated throughout the policy period, such that a failure of the warranty provides the insurer with a defense to claims under the policy. —Also termed *continuing warranty*.

warranty deed. See DEED.

wash sale. See SALE.

waste, *n.* Permanent harm to real property committed by a tenant (for life or for years) to the prejudice of the heir, the reversioner, or the remainderman; in the law of mortgages, any of the following acts by the mortgagor may constitute waste: (1) physical damage, whether intentional or negligent, (2) failure to maintain and repair, except for repair of casualty damage or damage caused by

third-party acts, (3) failure to pay property taxes or governmental assessments secured by a lien having priority over the mortgage, so that the payments become delinquent, (4) the material failure to comply with mortgage covenants concerning physical care, maintenance, construction, demolition, or casualty insurance, or (5) keeping the rents to which the mortgagee has the right of possession.

ameliorating waste (ə-**meel**-[i]yə-ray-ding). A lessee's unauthorized change to the physical character of a lessor's property—technically constituting waste, but in fact resulting in improvement of the property; generally, equity will not enjoin such waste. —Also termed *ameliorative waste*.

commissive waste. Waste caused by the affirmative acts of the tenant. —Also termed *active waste*; *affirmative waste*; *voluntary waste*.

equitable waste. Waste caused by a life tenant who, although ordinarily not responsible for permissive waste, flagrantly damages or destroys the property.

permissive waste. A tenant's failure to make normal repairs to property so as to protect it from substantial deterioration.

wasting asset. See ASSET.

wasting property. A right to or an interest in something that is consumed in its normal use, such as a wasting asset, a leasehold interest, or a patent right.

wasting trust. See TRUST.

watered stock. See STOCK.

water right. The right to use water from a natural stream or from an artificial canal for irrigation, power, domestic use, and the like.

waybill. BILL OF LADING.

ways-and-means committee. A legislative committee that determines how money will be raised for various governmental projects.

W.D. *abbr.* Western District, in reference to U.S. judicial districts.

wealth maximization. An economic situation in which a change in the allocation of resources benefits the winner—i.e., the one who gains from the allocation—more than it harms the loser. —Also termed *Kaldor-Hicks efficiency*; *potential Pareto superiority*.

wear and tear. Deterioration caused by ordinary use <the tenant is not liable for normal wear and tear to the leased premises>. —Also termed *fair wear and tear*.

wedding. MARRIAGE CEREMONY.

weight of the evidence. The persuasiveness of some evidence relative to other evidence <because the verdict is against the great weight of the evidence, a new trial should be granted>. See BURDEN OF PERSUASION. Cf. PREPONDERANCE OF THE EVIDENCE.

Welfare Clause. GENERAL WELFARE CLAUSE.

welfare state. A nation in which the government undertakes various social insurance programs, such as unemployment compensation, old-age pensions, family allowances, food stamps, and aid to the blind or deaf. —Also termed *welfare-regulatory state*.

well-pleaded complaint. See COMPLAINT.

Westlaw. A West Publishing Company database for computer-assisted legal research, providing on-line access to legal resources including federal and state caselaw, statutes, regulations, and legal periodicals. Cf. LEXIS.

Wharton rule. The criminal-law doctrine preventing conspiracy prosecution for a crime that necessarily involves the participation of two or more persons, such as illegal gambling; named after the criminal-law author, Francis Wharton. —Also termed *concert-of-action rule*. See CONSPIRACY.

wheel conspiracy. See CONSPIRACY.

when-issued security. See SECURITY.

whereabouts, *n.* The general locale where a person or thing is <her whereabouts are unknown> <the Joneses' present whereabouts is a closely guarded secret>; as the examples illustrate, this noun, though plural in form, may be construed with either a plural or a singular verb. —**whereabouts,** *adv. & conj.*

whereas, *conj.* **1.** While by contrast; although <McWilliams was stopped at 10:08 p.m. wearing a green hat, whereas the assailant was identified at 10:04 p.m. wearing a black hat>. **2.** Given the fact that; since <Whereas, the parties have found that their 1994 agreement did not adequately address incidental expenses ... ; and Whereas, the par-

ties have now decided in an equitable sharing of those expenses ... ; Now, Therefore, the parties agree to amend the 1994 agreement as follows.... >; in sense 2, *whereas* is used to introduce contractual recitals and the like, but modern drafters increasingly prefer a simple heading, such as "Recitals" or "Preamble," and in that way avoid the legalistic *whereases*. —**whereas** (recital or preamble), *n.*

whereat, *conj. Jargon.* **1.** At or toward which <the point whereat he was aiming>. **2.** As a result of which; whereupon <Pettrucione called Bickley a scurrilous name, whereat a fistfight broke out>.

whereby, *conj.* By which; through which; in accordance with which <the treaty whereby the warring nations finally achieved peace>.

wherefore, premises considered. *Jargon.* For all these reasons; for the reason or reasons mentioned above.

wherefrom, *conj. Jargon.* From which <the students sent two faxes to the president's office, wherefrom no reply ever came>.

wherein, *conj. Jargon.* **1.** In which; where <the jurisdiction wherein Lynn practices>. **2.** During which <they listened intently to the concert, wherein both of them became convinced that the composer's "new" work was a fraud>. **3.** How; in what respect <Fallon demanded to know wherein she had breached any duty>. —**wherein,** *adv.*

whereof, *conj.* **1.** Of what <Judge Wald knows whereof she speaks>. **2.** *Jargon.* Of which <citations whereof even the most responsible are far

afield from the true issue>. **3.** *Jargon.* Of whom <judges whereof only the most glowing words might be said>.

whereon, *conj. Jargon.* On which <the foundation whereon counsel bases this argument>. —Also termed *whereupon.*

whereto, *conj. Jargon.* To what place or time <at first, Campbell did not know whereto he was being taken>. —Also termed *whereunto.* —**whereto,** *adv.*

whereupon, *conj. Jargon.* **1.** WHEREON <the precedent whereupon the defense bases its argument>. **2.** Soon after and as a result of which; and then <they sped away from the scene, whereupon a riot erupted>.

wherewith, *conj. Jargon.* By means of which <the plaintiff lacked a form of action wherewith to state a compensable claim>.

whistleblower, *n.* An informant, esp. an employee who reports employer misconduct; employer retaliation against the employee is prohibited by federal and state statutes. —**whistleblowing,** *n.*

white-collar crime. A nonviolent crime usu. involving cheating or dishonesty in commercial matters; examples include fraud, bribery, and insider trading.

whitehorse case. *Slang.* A reported case with facts virtually identical to those of the instant case, so that the disposition of the reported case should determine the outcome of the instant case. —Also termed *horse case; goose case; gray mule case.* Cf. ON ALL FOURS.

white knight. *Slang.* A person or corporation that rescues the target of an unfriendly corporate takeover, esp. by acquiring a controlling interest in the target corporation or by making a competing tender offer. — Also termed *friendly suitor.* See TAKEOVER. Cf. CORPORATE RAIDER.

white slavery. The practice of forcing a female (or, rarely, a boy) to engage in commercial prostitution; trafficking in white slavery is prohibited by the federal Mann Act (18 U.S.C. §§ 2421-2424).

whole law. The law applied by a forum court in a multistate or multinational case after referring to its own choice-of-law rules.

whole life insurance. See INSURANCE.

wholesale, *n.* The sale of goods or commodities usu. for resale by retailers, as opposed to a sale to the ultimate consumer. —**wholesale,** *vb.*— **wholesale,** *adj.* Cf. RETAIL.

wholesaler. One who buys large quantities of goods and resells them in smaller quantities to retailers or other merchants who in turn sell to the ultimate consumer.

widower's allowance. See *spousal allowance* under ALLOWANCE.

widow's allowance. See *spousal allowance* under ALLOWANCE.

widow's election. RIGHT OF ELECTION.

wildcat strike. See STRIKE.

wild deed. See DEED.

Wild's Case, Rule in. See RULE IN WILD'S CASE.

will, *n.* **1.** Wish; desire; choice <employment at will>. **2.** A document by which a person directs his or her estate to be distributed upon death <there was no mention of his estranged brother in the will>. —Also termed *testament*; *will and testament.* —**will,** *vb.*

conditional will. A will that depends on the occurrence of an uncertain event for the will to take effect.

holographic will (ho-lə-**graf**-ik). A will that is entirely handwritten by the testator; in many states, such a will is valid even if not witnessed. —Also termed *holograph*; *olograph.*

invalid will. A will that fails to make an effective disposition of property.

joint will. A single will executed by two or more testators, usu. disposing of their common property. — Also termed *conjoint will.*

living will. See LIVING WILL.

lost will. An executed will that cannot be found at the testator's death; its contents can be proved by parol evidence in many jurisdictions, but in some states a lost will creates a rebuttable presumption that it has been revoked.

mutual wills. Separate wills in which two or more persons, usu. a husband and wife, establish identical testamentary provisions disposing of their estates in favor of each other. —Also termed *reciprocal wills*; *double wills.*

nonintervention will. A will that authorizes the executor to settle and distribute the estate without court supervision.

nuncupative will (nəng-**kyoo**-pə-tiv *or* **nəng**-kyə-pay-div). An oral will made in contemplation of imminent death from an injury recently incurred; nuncupative wills are invalid in most states, but in those states allowing them, the amount that may be conveyed is usu. limited by statute.

oral will. A will made by the verbal declaration of the testator and usu. dependent on oral testimony for proof.

pourover will. A will giving money or property to an existing trust. Cf. *pourover trust* under TRUST.

prenuptial will. A will executed before marriage; at common law, marriage automatically revoked a spouse's will, but modern statutes usu. provide that marriage does not revoke a will (although divorce does). Unif. Probate Code § 2-508. —Also termed *antenuptial will.*

self-proved will. A will proved by the testator's affidavit instead of by the live testimony of attesting witnesses.

soldier's will. An oral will made by a soldier heading off for battle. — Also termed (in relation to a sailor at sea) *sailor's will; seaman's will; mariner's will.*

unnatural will. A will that distributes the testator's estate to strangers rather than to the testator's relatives, without apparent reason.

will contest. In probate law, the litigation of a will's validity, usu. based on allegations that the testator lacked capacity or was under undue influence.

willful, *adj.* Voluntary and intentional, but not necessarily malicious. —Sometimes spelled *wilful.* — **willfulness,** *n.* Cf. MALICE.

willful blindness. In criminal law, a defendant's intentional avoidance of incriminating knowledge.

willful negligence. See *gross negligence* under NEGLIGENCE.

willful tort. See *intentional tort* under TORT.

Williams Act. A 1968 federal statute that amended the Securities Exchange Act of 1934; the Williams Act established rules for tender offers.

Wills Act. 1. STATUTE OF WILLS (1). **2.** An 1837 English statute that allowed people to dispose of every type of property interest by will and that required every will to be attested by two witnesses. —Also termed (in sense 2) *Lord Langdale's Act.*

will substitute. A document or instrument that attempts to dispose of an estate in the same or similar manner as a will, such as a trust or a life-insurance plan.

winding up, *n.* The process of settling accounts and liquidating assets in anticipation of a partnership's or a corporation's dissolution. Cf. DISSOLUTION (3). —**wind up,** *vb.*—**wind up,** *n.*

wiretapping, *n.* Electronic or mechanical eavesdropping, usu. done by law enforcers, under court order, to listen to private conversations; wiretapping is regulated by federal and state statutes. —**wiretap,** *vb.*—**wiretap,** *n.* See BUGGING; EAVESDROPPING. Cf. PEN REGISTER.

with all deliberate speed. See DELIBERATE SPEED, WITH ALL.

with all faults. See AS IS.

withdrawal, *n.* **1.** The act of taking back or away; removal <withdrawal of consent>. **2.** The act of retreating from a place, position, or situation <withdrawal from the moot-court competition>. **3.** The removal of money from a depository <withdrawal of funds from the checking account>. **4.** RENUNCIATION (2) <withdrawal from the conspiracy to commit arson>. —**withdraw,** *vb.*

withholding, *n.* The practice of deducting a certain amount from a person's salary, wages, dividends, winnings, or other income, usu. for tax purposes; esp., an employer's practice of taking out a portion of an employee's gross earnings and paying that portion to the government for income-tax and social-security purposes. —**withhold,** *vb.*

withholding tax. See TAX.

without day. See GO HENCE WITHOUT DAY.

without prejudice, *adv.* Without loss of any rights; in a way that does not harm or cancel the legal rights or privileges of a party <dismissed without prejudice>. See *dismissal without prejudice* under DISMISSAL.

without recourse, *adv.* (In an indorsement) with no liability to subsequent holders; with this stipulation, one who indorses an instrument repudiates any liability to anyone who may later hold the instrument. — Also termed *sans recours.* See *qualified indorsement* under INDORSEMENT.

without reserve. Of or relating to an auction in which an item will be sold for the highest bid price.

with prejudice, *adv.* With loss of all rights; in a way that finally disposes of a party's claim and bars any future action on that claim <dismissed with prejudice>. See *dismissal with prejudice* under DISMISSAL.

with recourse, *adv.* (In an indorsement) with liability to subsequent holders; with this stipulation, one who indorses an instrument indicates that he or she remains liable to the holder for payment.

with reserve. Of or relating to an auction in which an item will not be sold unless the highest bid exceeds a minimum price.

witness, *n.* **1.** One who sees, knows, or vouches for something <a witness to the accident>. **2.** One who gives testimony under oath or affirmation, either orally or by affidavit or deposition <the prosecution called its next witness>. —**witness,** *vb.*

attesting witness. One who vouches for the authenticity of another's signature by affixing his or her name to an instrument the other has signed <proof of the will requires two attesting witnesses>.

character witness. A witness who testifies about another person's character traits or community reputation. See *character evidence* under EVIDENCE.

competent witness. A witness who is legally qualified to testify; a lay witness is competent if he or she has personal knowledge of the subject matter of the testimony. Fed. R. Evid. 601-602.

credible witness. A witness whose testimony is believable.

expert witness. A witness qualified by knowledge, skill, experience, training, or education to provide scientific, technical, or other specialized opinions about the evidence or a fact issue. Fed. R. Evid. 702-706. — Also termed *skilled witness.* See EXPERT.

hostile witness. A witness who is biased against the examining party or who is unwilling to testify; hostile witnesses may be asked leading questions on direct examination. Fed. R. Evid. 611(c). —Also termed *adverse witness.*

lay witness. A witness who does not testify as an expert and who therefore may only give opinions or make inferences that are based on firsthand knowledge and helpful in understanding the testimony or in determining facts. Fed. R. Evid. 701.

material witness. A witness who can testify about matters having some logical connection with the consequential facts, esp. if few others, if any, know about those matters.

prosecuting witness. A person who files the complaint that triggers a criminal prosecution and whose testimony the prosecution usu. relies on to secure a conviction.

subscribing witness. One who witnesses the signatures on an instrument and signs at the end of the instrument to that effect.

target witness. **a.** The person who has the knowledge that an investigating body seeks. **b.** A witness who is called before a grand jury and against whom the government is also seeking an indictment.

witnesseth. *Jargon.* Take notice of; this term, usu. set in all capitals, commonly separates the preliminaries in a contract, up through the recitals, from the contractual terms themselves, but modern drafters increasingly avoid it as an antiquarian relic.

witness jurat. See JURAT.

witness stand. The space in a courtroom, usu. an enclosure, occupied by a witness while testifying. —Often shortened to *stand.* —Also termed *witness box.*

woodshedding. HORSESHEDDING.

word of art. TERM OF ART.

words of limitation. Language in a deed or will—often nonliteral language—describing the extent or quality of the estate; for example, under long-standing principles of property law, the phrasing "to A and her heirs" creates a fee simple and does not give anything to A's heirs. See LIMITATION (4).

words of purchase. Language in a deed or will designating the persons who are to receive the grant; for example, the phrasing "to A for life with a remainder to her heirs" creates a life estate in A and a remainder in A's heirs. See PURCHASE (2).

workers' compensation. A system of providing benefits to an employee for injuries occurring in the scope of employment; most workers'-compensation statutes both hold the employer strictly liable and bar the employee from suing in tort. —Also termed *workmen's compensation; employers' liability.*

work for hire. In copyright law, a copyrightable work produced either by an employee within the scope of employment or by an independent contractor under a written agreement; the employer or commissioning party owns the copyright.

workhouse. A jail for criminals who committed minor offenses and are serving short sentences.

working capital. See CAPITAL.

workmen's compensation. WORKERS' COMPENSATION.

workout, *n.* **1.** The act of restructuring or refinancing overdue loans. **2.** In bankruptcy law, a debtor's agreement, negotiated out of court, with a creditor or creditors to discharge debt. —**work out,** *vb.*

work product. Tangible material or its intangible equivalent—in unwritten or oral form—that was either prepared by or for a lawyer or prepared for litigation then in progress or contemplated as soon to be initiated; work product is generally exempt from discovery or other compelled disclosure. Fed. R. Civ. P. 26(b)(3). —Also termed *attorney work product.*

work-release program. A correctional program allowing prison inmates—primarily those who are being readied for discharge—to hold jobs outside prison. —Also termed *work-furlough program.* See HALFWAY HOUSE.

World Bank. A U.N. bank established in 1945 to provide loans that aid in economic development, through economically sustainable enterprises; its capital derives from U.N. member states' subscriptions and by loans on the open market. —Also termed *International Bank for Reconstruction and Development.*

World Court. INTERNATIONAL COURT OF JUSTICE.

worthier-title doctrine. 1. At common law, the doctrine holding that if a beneficiary of a will would receive an identical interest as an heir under the laws of intestacy, the person takes the interest as an heir rather than as a beneficiary; the doctrine has been abolished in most states. **2.** In real-property law, the doctrine that favors a grantor's intent by construing a grant as a reversion in the grantor instead of as a remainder in the grantor's heirs. See REMAINDER; REVERSION.

worthless check. See *bad check* under CHECK.

wraparound mortgage. See MORTGAGE.

writ. A court's written order, in the name of a state or other competent legal authority, commanding the addressee to do or refrain from doing some specified act.

alternative writ. A common-law writ commanding the person against whom it is issued either to do a specific thing or to show cause to the court why he or she should not be compelled to do it.

extraordinary writ. A writ issued by a court exercising unusual or discretionary power; examples are certiorari, habeas corpus, mandamus, and prohibition. —Also termed *prerogative writ.*

optional writ. At common law, an original writ issued when the plaintiff seeks specific damages, such as payment of a liquidated debt; the writ commands the defendant either to do a specified thing or to show why the thing has not been done.

original writ. A writ commencing an action and directing the defendant to appear and answer; in the U.S., this writ has been largely superseded by the summons. See SUMMONS.

peremptory writ. At common law, an original writ issued when the plaintiff seeks only general damages, as in an action for trespass; the writ, which is issued only after the plaintiff gives security for costs, directs the sheriff to have the defendant appear in court.

writ of assistance. 1. An equitable remedy enforcing a court's decree transferring real property, the title of which has been previously adjudicated. **2.** An ancient document issuing from the Court of Exchequer ordering sheriffs to assist in the collection of debts owed the Crown.

writ of attachment. ATTACHMENT (3).

writ of capias. CAPIAS.

writ of certiorari. CERTIORARI.

writ of course. A writ issued as a matter of course or granted as a matter of right. —Also termed *writ of right.*

writ of debt. DEBT (4).

writ of deliverance. DELIVERANCE (3).

writ of entry. A writ that allows a person wrongfully dispossessed of real property to enter and retake the property.

writ of error. A writ, issued by an appellate court, directing a lower court to deliver the record in the case for review. Cf. ASSIGNMENT OF ERROR.

writ of error coram nobis. CORAM NOBIS.

writ of error coram vobis. CORAM VOBIS.

writ of execution. EXECUTION (4).

writ of habeas corpus. HABEAS CORPUS.

writ of mandamus. MANDAMUS.

writ of possession. A writ issued to recover the possession of land.

writ of prohibition. An extraordinary writ issued by an appellate court to prevent a lower court from exceeding its jurisdiction or to prevent a nonjudicial officer or entity from exercising a power.

writ of praecipe. PRAECIPE (1).

writ of replevin. REPLEVIN (2).

writ of right. WRIT OF COURSE.

writ of second deliverance. DELIVERANCE (4).

writ system. The common-law procedural system under which plaintiffs commenced most actions by obtaining the appropriate type of original writ.

written directive. ADVANCE DIRECTIVE.

written law. Statutory law, together with constitutions and treaties, as opposed to judge-made law. —Also termed *jus scriptum.*

wrong, *n.* Breach of one's legal duty; violation of another's legal right. — **wrong,** *vb.*

civil wrong. A violation of noncriminal law, such as a tort, a breach of contract or trust, a breach of statutory duty, or a defect in performing public duties.

wrongdoer, *n.* One who violates the law <both criminals and tortfeasors are wrongdoers>. —**wrongdoing,** *n.*

wrongful, *adj.* **1.** Characterized by unfairness or injustice <wrongful military invasion>. **2.** Contrary to law; unlawful <wrongful termination>. **3.** (Of a person) not entitled to the position occupied <wrongful possessor>.

wrongful-birth action. A lawsuit brought by parents against a doctor for failing to advise them prospectively about the risks of their having a child with birth defects.

wrongful-conception action. WRONGFUL-PREGNANCY ACTION.

wrongful-death action. A lawsuit brought on behalf of a decedent's survivors for their damages resulting from a tortious injury that caused the decedent's death. —Also termed *death action; death case.* Cf. SURVIVAL ACTION.

wrongful-death statute. A statute establishing a claim that a decedent's personal representative may bring for the benefit of certain beneficiaries against the party who negligently caused the death.

wrongful-discharge action. A lawsuit brought by a person against his or her former employer, alleging that the person's termination from employment violated a contract or statute. —Also termed *wrongful-termination action.*

wrongful-life action. A lawsuit brought by or on behalf of a child with birth defects, alleging that but for the doctor-defendant's negligent advice, the parents would not have conceived the child, or if they had, they would have aborted the fetus to avoid the pain and suffering resulting from the child's congenital defects; most jurisdictions reject these claims.

wrongful-pregnancy action. A lawsuit brought by a parent for damages resulting from a pregnancy following a failed sterilization. —Also termed *wrongful-conception action.*

wrongful-termination action. WRONGFUL-DISCHARGE ACTION.

X

X. A mark serving as the signature of a person who is physically handicapped or illiterate; usu. the signer's name appears near the mark, and if the mark is to be notarized as a signature, two signing witnesses are ordinarily required in addition to the notary public.

XYY-chromosome defense. In criminal law, a defense (usu. asserted as the basis for an insanity plea) whereby a male defendant argues that his criminal behavior is due to the genetic abnormality of having an extra Y chromosome, which causes him to have uncontrollable aggressive impulses; most courts have rejected this defense because its scientific foundations are uncertain. See INSANITY DEFENSE.

Y

year-and-a-day rule. In criminal law, the common-law principle that an act causing death is not homicide if the death occurs more than a year and a day after the act was committed.

year-end dividend. See DIVIDEND.

year-to-year tenancy. See *periodic tenancy* under TENANCY.

yeas and nays. The affirmative and negative votes on a bill or resolution before a legislature.

yellow-dog contract. An employment contract forbidding membership in a labor union; such a contract is generally illegal under federal and state statutes.

yield, *n.* Profit expressed as a percentage of investment. —Also termed *return.* —**yield,** *vb.* See RATE OF RETURN.

current yield. The annual interest paid on a security (esp. a bond) divided by the security's current market price.

earnings yield. The earnings per share of a security divided by its market price; the higher the ratio, the better the investment yield. — Also termed *earnings-price ratio.* Cf. PRICE-EARNINGS RATIO.

nominal yield. The annual income received from a security (esp. a bond) divided by the security's par value.

yield to maturity. The rate of return from an investment if the investment is held until it matures.

York-Antwerp rules. A set of rules relating to the settlement of maritime losses and disputes arising from bills of lading; although these rules have no statutory authority, they are incorporated into almost all bills of lading.

***Younger* abstention.** See ABSTENTION.

youthful offender. See OFFENDER.

Z

zap. INTERSUBJECTIVE ZAP.

zero-bracket amount. A tax deduction formerly available to all individual taxpayers, regardless of whether they itemized their deductions; in 1944 this was replaced by the standard deduction. See *standard deduction* under DEDUCTION.

zero-coupon security. See SECURITY.

zero-rate mortgage. See MORTGAGE.

zipper clause. MERGER CLAUSE.

zone-of-danger rule. In tort law, the doctrine allowing recovery of damages for negligent infliction of emotional distress if the plaintiff was both located in the dangerous area created by the defendant's negligence and frightened by the risk of harm.

zone of employment. In workers'-compensation law, the physical place of employment within which an employee, if injured there, can receive compensation. Cf. SCOPE OF EMPLOYMENT.

zone of privacy. In constitutional law, a range of fundamental privacy rights that are implied in the express guarantees of the Bill of Rights. See PENUMBRA; RIGHT OF PRIVACY.

zoning, *n.* The legislative division of a region, esp. a municipality, into separate districts with different regulations within the districts as to land use, building size, and the like. — **zone,** *vb.*

cluster zoning. Zoning that favors planned-unit development by allowing a modification in lot size and frontage requirements under the condition that other land in the development be set aside for parks, schools, or other public needs. — Also termed *density zoning.* See PLANNED-UNIT DEVELOPMENT.

cumulative zoning. A method of zoning in which any use permitted in a higher-use, less-intensive zone is permissible in a lower-use, more-intensive zone; for example, under this method, a house could be built in an industrial zone but a factory could not be built in a residential zone.

Euclidean zoning. Zoning by specific and uniform geographical division.

exclusionary zoning. Zoning that excludes a specific class of people or type of business from a district.

floating zoning. Zoning that creates exceptional-use districts, as needed, within ordinary zoned districts.

inverse zoning. Zoning that attempts to disperse particular types of property use rather than concentrate them.

spot zoning. Zoning of a particular piece of land without regard for the zoning of the larger area surrounding the land.

zoning variance. VARIANCE (2).

APPENDIX

THE CONSTITUTION OF THE UNITED STATES OF AMERICA

We the People of the United States, in Order to form a more perfect Union, establish Justice, insure domestic Tranquility, provide for the common defence, promote the general Welfare, and secure the Blessings of Liberty to ourselves and our Posterity, do ordain and establish this Constitution for the United States of America.

Article I

Section 1. All legislative Powers herein granted shall be vested in a Congress of the United States, which shall consist of a Senate and House of Representatives.

Section 2. The House of Representatives shall be composed of Members chosen every second Year by the People of the several States, and the Electors in each State shall have the Qualifications requisite for Electors of the most numerous Branch of the State Legislature.

No Person shall be a Representative who shall not have attained to the Age of twenty five Years, and been seven Years a Citizen of the United States, and who shall not, when elected, be an Inhabitant of that State in which he shall be chosen.

Representatives and direct Taxes shall be apportioned among the several States which may be included within this Union, according to their respective Numbers, which shall be determined by adding to the whole Number of free Persons, including those bound to Service for a Term of Years, and excluding Indians not taxed, three fifths of all other Persons. The actual Enumeration shall be made within three Years after the first Meeting of the Congress of the United States, and within every subsequent Term of ten Years, in such Manner as they shall by Law direct. The Number of Representatives shall not exceed one for every thirty Thousand, but each State shall have at Least one Representative; and until such enumeration shall be made, the State of New Hampshire shall be entitled to chuse three, Massachusetts eight, Rhode Island and Providence Plantations one, Connecticut five, New York six, New Jersey four, Pennsylvania eight, Delaware one, Maryland six, Virginia ten, North Carolina five, South Carolina five, and Georgia three.

When vacancies happen in the Representation from any State, the Executive Authority thereof shall issue Writs of Election to fill such Vacancies.

The House of Representatives shall chuse their Speaker and other Officers; and shall have the sole Power of Impeachment.

Section 3. The Senate of the United States shall be composed of two Senators from each State, chosen by the Legislature thereof, for six Years; and each Senator shall have one Vote.

Immediately after they shall be assembled in Consequence of the first Election, they shall be divided as equally as may be into three Classes. The Seats of the Senators of the first Class shall be vacated at the Expiration of the Second Year, of the second Class at the Expiration of the fourth Year, and of the third Class at the Expiration of the sixth Year, so that one third may be chosen every second Year; and if Vacancies happen by Resignation, or otherwise, during the Recess of the Legislature of any State, the Executive thereof may make temporary Appointments until the next Meeting of the Legislature, which shall then fill such Vacancies.

No Person shall be a Senator who shall not have attained to the Age of thirty Years, and been nine Years a Citizen of the United States, and who shall not, when elected, be an Inhabitant of that State for which he shall be chosen.

The Vice President of the United States shall be President of the Senate, but shall have no Vote, unless they be equally divided.

The Senate shall chuse their other Officers, and also a President pro tempore, in the Absence of the Vice President, or when he shall exercise the Office of President of the United States.

The Senate shall have the sole Power to try all Impeachments. When sitting for that Purpose, they shall be on Oath or Affirmation. When the President of the United States is tried, the Chief Justice shall preside: And no Person shall be convicted without the Concurrence of two thirds of the Members present.

Judgment in Cases of Impeachment shall not extend further than to removal from Office, and disqualification to hold and enjoy any Office of honor, Trust, or Profit under the United States: but the Party convicted shall nevertheless be liable and subject to Indictment, Trial, Judgment, and Punishment, according to Law.

Section 4. The Times, Places and Manner of holding Elections for Senators and Representatives, shall be prescribed in each State by the Legislature thereof; but the Congress may at any time by Law make or alter such Regulations, except as to the Places of chusing Senators.

The Congress shall assemble at least once in every Year, and such Meeting shall be on the first Monday in December, unless they shall by Law appoint a different Day.

Section 5. Each House shall be the Judge of the Elections, Returns, and Qualifications of its own Members, and a Majority of each shall constitute a Quorum to do Business; but a smaller Number may adjourn from day to day, and may be authorized to compel the Attendance of absent Members, in such Manner, and under such Penalties as each House may provide.

Each House may determine the Rules of its Proceedings, punish its Members for disorderly Behavior, and, with the Concurrence of two thirds, expel a Member.

Each House shall keep a Journal of its Proceedings, and from time to time publish the same, excepting such Parts as may in their Judgment require Secrecy; and the Yeas and Nays of the Members of either House on any question shall, at the Desire of one fifth of those Present, be entered on the Journal.

Neither House, during the Session of Congress, shall, without the Consent of the other, adjourn for more than three days, nor to any other Place than that in which the two Houses shall be sitting.

Section 6. The Senators and Representatives shall receive a Compensation for their Services, to be ascertained by Law, and paid out of the Treasury of the United States. They shall in all Cases, except Treason, Felony and Breach of the Peace, be privileged from Arrest during their Attendance at the Session of their respective Houses, and in going to and returning from the same; and for any Speech or Debate in either House, they shall not be questioned in any other Place.

No Senator or Representative shall, during the Time for which he was elected, be appointed to any civil Office under the Authority of the United States, which shall have been created, or the Emoluments whereof shall have been increased during such time; and no Person holding any Office under the United States, shall be a member of either House during his Continuance in Office.

Section 7. All Bills for raising Revenue shall originate in the House of Representatives; but the Senate may propose or concur with Amendments as on other Bills.

Every Bill which shall have passed the House of Representatives and the Senate, shall, before it become a Law, be presented to the President of the United States; If he approve he shall sign it, but if not he shall return it, with his Objections to the House in which it shall have originated, who shall enter the Objections at large on their Journal, and proceed to reconsider it. If after such Reconsideration two thirds of that House shall agree to pass the Bill, it shall be sent together with the Objections, to the other House, by which it shall likewise be reconsidered, and if approved by two thirds of that House, it shall become a Law. But in all such Cases the Votes of both Houses shall be determined by Yeas and Nays, and the Names of the Persons voting for and against the Bill shall be entered on the Journal of each House respectively. If any Bill shall not be returned by the President within ten Days (Sundays excepted) after it shall have been presented to him, the Same shall be a Law, in like Manner as if he had signed it, unless the Congress by their Adjournment prevent its Return in which Case it shall not be a Law.

Every Order, Resolution, or Vote, to Which the Concurrence of the Senate and House of Representatives may be necessary (except on a question of Adjournment) shall be presented to the President of the United States; and before the Same shall take Effect, shall be approved by him, or being disapproved by him, shall be repassed by two thirds of the Senate and House of Representatives, according to the Rules and Limitations prescribed in the Case of a Bill.

Section 8. The Congress shall have Power to lay and collect Taxes, Duties, Imposts and Excises, to pay the Debts and provide for the common Defence and general Welfare of the

United States; but all Duties, Imposts and Excises shall be uniform throughout the United States;

To borrow money on the credit of the United States;

To regulate Commerce with foreign Nations, and among the several States, and with the Indian Tribes;

To establish an uniform Rule of Naturalization, and uniform Laws on the subject of Bankruptcies throughout the United States;

To coin Money, regulate the Value thereof, and of foreign Coin, and fix the Standard of Weights and Measures;

To provide for the Punishment of counterfeiting the Securities and current Coin of the United States;

To Establish Post Offices and Post Roads;

To promote the Progress of Science and useful Arts, by securing for limited Times to Authors and Inventors the exclusive Right to their respective Writings and Discoveries;

To constitute Tribunals inferior to the supreme Court;

To define and punish Piracies and Felonies committed on the high Seas, and Offenses against the Law of Nations;

To declare War, grant Letters of Marque and Reprisal, and make Rules concerning Captures on Land and Water;

To raise and support Armies, but no Appropriation of Money to that Use shall be for a longer Term than two Years;

To provide and maintain a Navy;

To make Rules for the Government and Regulation of the land and naval Forces;

To provide for calling forth the Militia to execute the Laws of the Union, suppress Insurrections and repel Invasions;

To provide for organizing, arming, and disciplining, the Militia, and for governing such Part of them as may be employed in the Service of the United States, reserving to the States respectively, the Appointment of the Officers, and the Authority of training the Militia according to the discipline prescribed by Congress;

To exercise exclusive Legislation in all Cases whatsoever, over such District (not exceeding ten Miles square) as may, by Cession of particular States and the Acceptance of Congress, become the Seat of the Government of the United States, and to exercise like Authority over all Places purchased by the Consent of the Legislature of the State in which the Same shall be, for the Erection of Forts, Magazines, Arsenals, dock-Yards, and other needful Buildings;—And

To make all Laws which shall be necessary and proper for carrying into Execution the foregoing Powers, and all other Powers vested by this Constitution in the Government of the United States, or in any Department or Officer thereof.

Section 9. The Migration or Importation of Such Persons as any of the States now existing shall think proper to admit, shall not be prohibited by the Congress prior to the Year one thousand eight hundred and eight, but a Tax or duty may be imposed on such Importation, not exceeding ten dollars for each Person.

The privilege of the Writ of Habeas Corpus shall not be suspended, unless when in Cases of Rebellion or Invasion the public Safety may require it.

No Bill of Attainder or ex post facto Law shall be passed.

No Capitation, or other direct, Tax shall be laid, unless in Proportion to the census or Enumeration herein before directed to be taken.

No Tax or Duty shall be laid on Articles exported from any State.

No Preference shall be given by any Regulation of Commerce or Revenue to the Ports of one State over those of another: nor shall Vessels bound to, or from, one State be obliged to enter, clear, or pay Duties in another.

No money shall be drawn from the Treasury, but in Consequence of Appropriations made by Law; and a regular Statement and Account of the Receipts and Expenditures of all public Money shall be published from time to time.

No Title of Nobility shall be granted by the United States: And no Person holding any Office of Profit or Trust under them, shall, without the Consent of the Congress, accept of any present, Emolument, Office, or Title, of any kind whatever, from any King, Prince, or foreign State.

Section 10. No State shall enter into any Treaty, Alliance, or Confederation; grant Letters of Marque and Reprisal; coin Money; emit Bills of Credit; make any Thing but gold and silver Coin a Tender in Payment of Debts; pass any Bill of Attainder, ex post facto Law, or Law impairing the Obligation of Contracts, or grant any Title of Nobility.

No State shall, without the Consent of the Congress, lay any Imposts or Duties on Imports or Exports, except what may be absolutely necessary for executing its inspection Laws: and the net Produce of all Duties and Imposts, laid by any State on Imports or Exports, shall be for the Use of the Treasury of the United States; and all such Laws shall be subject to the Revision and Controul of the Congress.

No State shall, without the Consent of Congress, lay any Duty of Tonnage, keep Troops, or Ships of War in time of Peace, enter into any Agreement or Compact with another State, or with a foreign Power or engage in War, unless actually invaded, or in such imminent Danger as will not admit of delay.

Article II

Section 1. The executive Power shall be vested in a President of the United States of America. He shall hold his Office during the Term of four Years, and, together with the Vice President, chosen for the same Term, be elected, as follows:

Each State shall appoint, in such Manner as the Legislature thereof may direct, a Number of Electors, equal to the whole Number of Senators and Representatives to which the State may be entitled in the Congress; but no Senator or Representative, or Person holding an Office of Trust or Profit under the United States, shall be appointed an Elector.

The Electors shall meet in their respective States, and vote by Ballot for two Persons, of whom one at least shall not be an Inhabitant of the same State with themselves. And they shall make a List of all the Persons voted for, and of the Number of Votes for each; which List they shall sign and certify, and transmit sealed to the Seat of the Government of the United States, directed to the President of the Senate. The President of the Senate shall, in the Presence of the Senate and House of Representatives, open all the Certificates, and the Votes shall then be counted. The Person having the greatest Number of Votes shall be the President, if such Number be a Majority of the whole Number of Electors appointed; and if there be more than one who have such Majority, and have an equal Number of Votes, then the House of Representatives shall immediately chuse by Ballot one of them for President; and if no Person have a Majority, then from the five highest on the List the said House shall in like Manner chuse the President. But in chusing the President, the Votes shall be taken by States, the Representation from each State having one Vote; A quorum for this Purpose shall consist of a Member or

Members from two thirds of the States, and a Majority of all the States shall be necessary to a Choice. In every Case, after the Choice of the President, the Person having the greater Number of Votes of the Electors shall be the Vice President. But if there should remain two or more who have equal Votes, the Senate shall chuse from them by Ballot the Vice President.

The Congress may determine the Time of chusing the Electors, and the Day on which they shall give their Votes; which Day shall be the same throughout the United States.

No person except a natural born Citizen, or a Citizen of the United States, at the time of the Adoption of this Constitution, shall be eligible to the Office of President; neither shall any Person be eligible to that Office who shall not have attained to the Age of thirty five Years, and been fourteen Years a Resident within the United States.

In case of the removal of the President from Office, or of his Death, Resignation or Inability to discharge the Powers and Duties of the said Office, the Same shall devolve on the Vice President and the Congress may by Law provide for the Case of Removal, Death, Resignation or Inability, both of the President and Vice President, declaring what Officer shall then act as President, and such Officer shall act accordingly, until the Disability be removed, or a President shall be elected.

The President shall, at stated Times, receive for his Services, a Compensation, which shall neither be increased nor diminished during the Period for which he shall have been elected, and he shall not receive within that Period any other Emolument from the United States, or any of them.

Before he enter on the Execution of his Office, he shall take the following Oath or Affirmation: "I do solemnly swear (or affirm) that I will faithfully execute the Office of President of the United States, and will to the best of my Ability, preserve, protect and defend the Constitution of the United States."

Section 2. The President shall be Commander in Chief of the Army and Navy of the United States, and of the militia of the several States, when called into the actual Services of the United States; he may require the Opinion, in writing, of the principal Officer in each of the Executive Departments, upon any Subject relating to the Duties of their respective Offices and he shall have Power to grant Reprieves and Pardons for Offenses against the United States, except in Cases of Impeachment.

He shall have Power, by and with the Advice and Consent of the Senate, to make Treaties, provided two thirds of the Senators present concur; and he shall nominate, and by and with the Advice and Consent of the Senate, shall appoint Ambassadors, other public Ministers and Consuls, Judges of the supreme Court, and all other Officers of the United States, whose Appointments are not herein otherwise provided for, and which shall be established by Law; but the Congress may by Law vest the Appointment of such inferior Officers, as they think proper, in the President alone, in the Courts of Law, or in the Heads of Departments.

The President shall have Power to fill up all Vacancies that may happen during the Recess of the Senate, by granting Commissions which shall expire at the End of their next Session.

Section 3. He shall from time to time give to the Congress Information of the State of the Union, and recommend to their Consideration such Measures as he shall judge necessary and expedient; he may, on extraordinary Occasions, convene both Houses, or either of them, and in Case of Disagreement between them, with Respect to the Time of Adjournment, he may adjourn them to such Time as he shall think proper; he shall receive Ambassadors and other public Ministers; he shall take Care that the Laws be faithfully executed, and shall Commission all the Officers of the United States.

Section 4. The President, Vice President and all civil Officers of the United States, shall be removed from Office on Impeachment for, and Conviction of, Treason, Bribery, or other high Crimes and Misdemeanors.

Article III

Section 1. The judicial Power of the United States, shall be vested in one supreme Court, and in such inferior Courts as the Congress may from time to time ordain and establish. The Judges, both of the supreme and inferior Courts, shall hold their Offices during good Behaviour, and shall, at stated Times, receive for their Services a Compensation, which shall not be diminished during their Continuance in Office.

Section 2. The judicial Power shall extend to all Cases, in Law and Equity, arising under this Constitution, the Laws of the United States, and Treaties made, or which shall be made, under their Authority;—to all Cases affecting Ambassadors, other public Ministers and Consuls;—to all Cases of admiralty and maritime Jurisdiction;—to Controversies to which the United States shall be a Party;—to Controversies between two or more States;—between a State and Citizens of another State;—between Citizens of different States;—between Citizens of the same State claiming Lands under the Grants of different States, and between a State, or the Citizens thereof, and foreign States, Citizens or Subjects.

In all Cases affecting Ambassadors, other public Ministers and Consuls, and those in which a State shall be a Party, the supreme Court shall have original Jurisdiction. In all the other Cases before mentioned, the supreme Court shall have appellate Jurisdiction, both as to Law and Fact, with such Exceptions, and under such Regulations as the Congress shall make.

The trial of all Crimes, except in Cases of Impeachment, shall be by Jury; and such Trial shall be held in the State where the said Crimes shall have been committed; but when not committed within any State, the Trial shall be at such Place or Places as the Congress may by Law have directed.

Section 3. Treason against the United States, shall consist only in levying War against them, or, in adhering to their Enemies, giving them Aid and Comfort. No Person shall be convicted of Treason unless on the Testimony of two Witnesses to the same overt Act, or on Confession in open Court.

The Congress shall have Power to declare the Punishment of Treason, but no Attainder of Treason shall work Corruption of Blood, or Forfeiture except during the Life of the Person attainted.

Article IV

Section 1. Full Faith and Credit shall be given in each State to the public Acts, Records, and judicial Proceedings of every other State. And the Congress may by general Laws prescribe the Manner in which such Acts, Records and Proceedings shall be proved, and the Effect thereof.

Section 2. The Citizens of each State shall be entitled to all Privileges and Immunities of Citizens in the several States.

A Person charged in any State with Treason, Felony, or other Crime, who shall flee from Justice, and be found in another State, shall on demand of the executive Authority of the State from which he fled, be delivered up, to be removed to the State having Jurisdiction of the Crime.

No Person held to Service or Labour in one State, under the Laws thereof, escaping into another, shall, in Consequence of any Law or Regulation therein, be discharged from such Service or Labour, but shall be delivered up on Claim of the Party to whom such Service or Labour may be due.

Section 3. New States may be admitted by the Congress into this Union; but no new State shall be formed or erected with the Jurisdiction of any other State; nor any State be formed by the Junction of two or more States, or Parts of States, without the Consent of the Legislatures of the States concerned as well as of the Congress.

The Congress shall have Power to dispose of and make all needful Rules and Regulations respecting the Territory or other Property belonging to the United States; and nothing in this Constitution shall be so construed as to Prejudice any Claims of the United States, or of any particular State.

Section 4. The United States shall guarantee to every State in this Union a Republican Form of Government, and shall protect each of them against Invasion; and on Application of the Legislature, or of the Executive (when the Legislature cannot be convened) against domestic Violence.

Article V

The Congress, whenever two thirds of both Houses shall deem it necessary, shall propose Amendments to this Constitution, or, on the Application of the Legislatures of two thirds of the several States, shall call a Convention for proposing Amendments, which, in either Case, shall be valid to all Intents and Purposes, as part of this Constitution, when ratified by the Legislatures of three fourths of the several States, or by Conventions in three fourths thereof, as the one or the other Mode of Ratification may be proposed by the Congress; Provided that no Amendment which may be made prior to the Year One thousand eight hundred and eight shall in any Manner affect the first and fourth Clauses in the Ninth Section of the first Article; and that no State, without its consent, shall be deprived of its equal Suffrage in the Senate.

Article VI

All Debts contracted and Engagements entered into, before the Adoption of this Constitution, shall be as valid against the United States under this Constitution, as under the Confederation.

This Constitution, and the Laws of the United States which shall be made in Pursuance thereof; and all treaties made, or which shall be made, under the Authority of the United States, shall be the supreme Law of the Land; and the Judges in every State shall be bound thereby, any Thing in the Constitution or Laws of any State to the Contrary notwithstanding.

The Senators and Representatives before mentioned, and the Members of the several State Legislatures, and all executive and judicial Officers, both of the United States and of the several States, shall be bound by Oath or Affirmation, to support this Constitution; but no religious Test shall ever be required as a Qualification to any Office or public Trust under the United States.

Article VII

The Ratification of the Conventions of nine States shall be sufficient for the Establishment of this Constitution between the States so ratifying the Same.

ARTICLES IN ADDITION TO, AND AMENDMENT OF, THE CONSTITUTION OF THE UNITED STATES OF AMERICA, PROPOSED BY CONGRESS, AND RATIFIED BY THE LEGISLATURES OF THE SEVERAL STATES PUR-

SUANT TO THE FIFTH ARTICLE OF THE ORIGINAL
CONSTITUTION.

Amendment I [1791]

Congress shall make no law respecting an establishment of
religion, or prohibiting the free exercise thereof; or abridging
the freedom of speech, or of the press; or the right of the people peaceably to assemble, and to petition the Government for
a redress of grievances.

Amendment II [1791]

A well regulated Militia, being necessary to the security of
a free State, the right of the people to keep and bear Arms,
shall not be infringed.

Amendment III [1791]

No Soldier shall, in time of peace be quartered in any
house, without the consent of the Owner, nor in time of war,
but in a manner to be prescribed by law.

Amendment IV [1791]

The right of the people to be secure in their persons, houses, papers, and effects, against unreasonable searches and
seizures, shall not be violated, and no Warrants shall issue,
but upon probable cause, supported by Oath or affirmation,
and particularly describing the place to be searched, and the
persons or things to be seized.

Amendment V [1791]

No person shall be held to answer for a capital, or otherwise infamous crime, unless on a presentment or indictment
of a Grand Jury, except in cases arising in the land or naval
forces, or in the Militia, when in actual service in time of War

or public danger; nor shall any person be subject for the same offence to be twice put in jeopardy of life or limb; nor shall be compelled in any criminal case to be a witness against himself, nor be deprived of life, liberty, or property, without due process of law; nor shall private property be taken for public use, without just compensation.

Amendment VI [1791]

In all criminal prosecutions, the accused shall enjoy the right to a speedy and public trial, by an impartial jury of the State and district wherein the crime shall have been committed, which district shall have been previously ascertained by law, and to be informed of the nature and cause of the accusation; to be confronted with the witnesses against him; to have compulsory process for obtaining witnesses in his favor, and to have the Assistance of Counsel for his defence.

Amendment VII [1791]

In Suits at common law, where the value in controversy shall exceed twenty dollars, the right of trial by jury shall be preserved, and no fact tried by jury, shall be otherwise re-examined in any Court of the United States, than according to the rules of the common law.

Amendment VIII [1791]

Excessive bail shall not be required, nor excessive fines imposed, nor cruel and unusual punishments inflicted.

Amendment IX [1791]

The enumeration in the Constitution, of certain rights, shall not be construed to deny or disparage others retained by the people.

Amendment X [1791]

The powers not delegated to the United States by the Constitution, nor prohibited by it to the States, are reserved to the States respectively, or to the people.

Amendment XI [1798]

The Judicial power of the United States shall not be construed to extend to any suit in law or equity, commenced or prosecuted against one of the United States by Citizens of another State, or by Citizens or Subjects of any Foreign State.

Amendment XII [1804]

The Electors shall meet in their respective states and vote by ballot for President and Vice President, one of whom, at least, shall not be an inhabitant of the same state with themselves; they shall name in their ballots the person voted for as President, and in distinct ballots the person voted for as Vice President, and they shall make distinct lists of all persons voted for as President, and of all persons voted for as Vice President, and of the number of votes for each, which lists they shall sign and certify, and transmit sealed to the seat of the government of the United States, directed to the President of the Senate;—The President of the Senate shall, in the presence of the Senate and House of Representatives, open all the certificates and the votes shall then be counted;—The person having the greatest number of votes for President, shall be the President, if such number be a majority of the whole number of Electors appointed; and if no person have such majority, then from the persons having the highest numbers not exceeding three on the list of those voted for as President, the House of Representatives shall choose immediately, by ballot, the President. But in choosing the President, the votes shall be taken by states, the representation from each state having one vote; a quorum for this purpose shall consist of a member or members from two-thirds of the states, and a majority of all the states shall be necessary to a choice. And if the House of Representatives shall not choose a President whenever the right of choice shall devolve upon them before the fourth day of March next following, then the Vice President shall act as President, as in the case of the death or other constitutional disability of the President.—The person having the greatest number of votes as Vice President, shall be the Vice President, if such number be a majority of the whole number of Electors appointed, and if no person have a majority, then from the two highest numbers on the list, the Senate shall choose the Vice President; a quorum for the purpose shall consist of two-thirds of the whole number of Senators, and a majority of the whole number shall be necessary to a choice. But no person constitutionally ineligible to the office of President shall be eligible to that of Vice President of the United States.

Amendment XIII [1865]

Section 1. Neither slavery nor involuntary servitude, except as a punishment for crime whereof the party shall have been duly convicted, shall exist within the United States, or any place subject to their jurisdiction.

Section 2. Congress shall have power to enforce this article by appropriate legislation.

Amendment XIV [1868]

Section 1. All persons born or naturalized in the United States, and subject to the jurisdiction thereof, are citizens of the United States and of the State wherein they reside. No State shall make or enforce any law which shall abridge the privileges or immunities of citizens of the United States; nor shall any State deprive any person of life, liberty, or property, without due process of law; nor deny to any person within its jurisdiction the equal protection of the laws.

Section 2. Representatives shall be apportioned among the several States according to their respective numbers, counting the whole number of persons in each State, excluding Indians not taxed. But when the right to vote at any election for the choice of electors for President and Vice President of the United States, Representatives in Congress, the Executive and Judicial officers of a State, or the members of the Legislature thereof, is denied to any of the male inhabitants of such State, being twenty-one years of age, and citizens of the United States, or in any way abridged, except for participation in rebellion, or other crime, the basis of representation therein shall be reduced in the proportion which the number of such male citizens shall bear to the whole number of male citizens twenty-one years of age in such State.

Section 3. No person shall be a Senator or Representative in Congress, or elector of President and Vice President, or hold any office, civil or military, under the United States, or under any State, who having previously taken an oath, as a member of Congress, or as an officer of the United States, or as a member of any State legislature, or as an executive or judicial officer of any State, to support the Constitution of the United States, shall have engaged in insurrection or rebellion against the same, or given aid or comfort to the enemies thereof. But Congress may by a vote of two-thirds of each House, remove such disability.

Section 4. The validity of the public debt of the United States, authorized by law, including debts incurred for payment of pensions and bounties for services in suppressing insurrection or rebellion, shall not be questioned. But neither the United States nor any State shall assume or pay any debt or obligation incurred in aid of insurrection or rebellion against the United States, or any claim for the loss or emancipation of any slave; but all such debts, obligations and claims shall be held illegal and void.

Section 5. The Congress shall have power to enforce, by appropriate legislation, the provisions of this article.

Amendment XV [1870]

Section 1. The right of citizens of the United States to vote shall not be denied or abridged by the United States or by any State on account of race, color, or previous condition of servitude.

Section 2. The Congress shall have power to enforce this article by appropriate legislation.

Amendment XVI [1913]

The Congress shall have power to lay and collect taxes on incomes, from whatever source derived, without apportionment among the several States, and without regard to any census or enumeration.

Amendment XVII [1913]

[1] The Senate of the United States shall be composed of two Senators from each State, elected by the people thereof, for six years; and each Senator shall have one vote. The electors in each State shall have the qualifications requisite for electors of the most numerous branch of the State legislatures.

[2] When vacancies happen in the representation of any State in the Senate, the executive authority of such State shall issue writs of election to fill such vacancies: Provided, that the legislature of any State may empower the executive thereof to make temporary appointments until the people fill the vacancies by election as the legislature may direct.

695

[3] This amendment shall not be so construed as to affect the election or term of any Senator chosen before it becomes valid as part of the Constitution.

Amendment XVIII [1919]

Section 1. After one year from the ratification of this article the manufacture, sale, or transportation of intoxicating liquors within, the importation thereof into, or the exportation thereof from the United States and all territory subject to the jurisdiction thereof for beverage purposes is hereby prohibited.

Section 2. The Congress and the several States shall have concurrent power to enforce this article by appropriate legislation.

Section 3. This article shall be inoperative unless it shall have been ratified as an amendment to the Constitution by the legislatures of the several States, as provided in the Constitution, within seven years from the date of the submission hereof to the States by the Congress.

Amendment XIX [1920]

[1] The right of citizens of the United States to vote shall not be denied or abridged by the United States or by any State on account of sex.

[2] Congress shall have power to enforce this article by appropriate legislation.

Amendment XX [1933]

Section 1. The terms of the President and Vice President shall end at noon on the 20th day of January, and the terms of Senators and Representatives at noon on the 3d day of January, of the years in which such terms would have ended if this article had not been ratified; and the terms of their successors shall then begin.

Section 2. The Congress shall assemble at least once in every year, and such meeting shall begin at noon on the 3d day of January, unless they shall by law appoint a different day.

Section 3. If, at the time fixed for the beginning of the term of the President, the President elect shall have died, the Vice President elect shall become President. If the President shall not have been chosen before the time fixed for the beginning of his term, or if the President elect shall have failed to qualify, then the Vice President elect shall act as President until a President shall have qualified; and the Congress may by law provide for the case wherein neither a President elect nor a Vice President elect shall have qualified, declaring who shall then act as President, or the manner in which one who is to act shall be selected, and such person shall act accordingly until a President or Vice President shall have qualified.

Section 4. The Congress may by law provide for the case of the death of any of the persons from whom the House of Representatives may choose a President whenever the right of choice shall have devolved upon them, and for the case of the death of any of the persons from whom the Senate may choose a Vice President whenever the right of choice shall have devolved upon them.

Section 5. Sections 1 and 2 shall take effect on the 15th day of October following the ratification of this article.

Section 6. This article shall be inoperative unless it shall have been ratified as an amendment to the Constitution by the legislatures of three-fourths of the several States within seven years from the date of its submission.

Amendment XXI [1933]

Section 1. The eighteenth article of amendment to the Constitution of the United States is hereby repealed.

Section 2. The transportation or importation into any State, Territory, or possession of the United States for delivery or use therein of intoxicating liquors, in violation of the laws thereof, is hereby prohibited.

Section 3. This article shall be inoperative unless it shall have been ratified as an amendment to the Constitution by conventions in the several States, as provided in the Constitution, within seven years from the date of the submission hereof to the States by the Congress.

Amendment XXII [1951]

Section 1. No person shall be elected to the office of the President more than twice, and no person who has held the office of President, or acted as President, for more than two years of a term to which some other person was elected President shall be elected to the office of President more than once. But this Article shall not apply to any person holding the office of President when this Article was proposed by the Congress, and shall not prevent any person who may be holding the office of President, or acting as President, during the term within which this Article becomes operative from holding the office of President or acting as President during the remainder of such term.

Section 2. This article shall be inoperative unless it shall have been ratified as an amendment to the Constitution by the legislatures of three-fourths of the several States within seven years from the date of its submission to the States by the Congress.

Amendment XXIII [1961]

Section 1. The District constituting the seat of Government of the United States shall appoint in such manner as the Congress may direct:

A number of electors of President and Vice President equal to the whole number of Senators and Representatives in Congress to which the District would be entitled if it were a State, but in no event more than the least populous state; they shall be in addition to those appointed by the states, but they shall be considered, for the purposes of the election of President and Vice President, to be electors appointed by a state; and they shall meet in the District and perform such duties as provided by the twelfth article of amendment.

Section 2. The Congress shall have power to enforce this article by appropriate legislation.

Amendment XXIV [1964]

Section 1. The right of citizens of the United States to vote in any primary or other election for President or Vice President, for electors for President or Vice President, or for Senator or Representative in Congress, shall not be denied or abridged by the United States or any State by reason of failure to pay any poll tax or other tax.

Section 2. The Congress shall have power to enforce this article by appropriate legislation.

Amendment XXV [1967]

Section 1. In the case of the removal of the President from office or of his death or resignation, the Vice President shall become President.

Section 2. Whenever there is a vacancy in the office of the Vice President, the President shall nominate a Vice President who shall take office upon confirmation by a majority vote of both Houses of Congress.

Section 3. Whenever the President transmits to the President pro tempore of the Senate and the Speaker of the House of Representatives his written declaration that he is unable to discharge the powers and duties of his office, and until he transmits to them a written declaration to the contrary, such powers and duties shall be discharged by the Vice President as Acting President.

Section 4. Whenever the Vice President and a majority of either the principal officers of the executive departments or of such other body as Congress may by law provide, transmit to the President pro tempore of the Senate and the Speaker of the House of Representatives, their written declaration that the President is unable to discharge the powers and duties of his office, the Vice President shall immediately assume the powers and duties of the office as Acting President.

Thereafter, when the President transmits to the President pro tempore of the Senate and the Speaker of the House of Representatives his written declaration that no inability exists, he shall resume the powers and duties of his office unless the Vice President and a majority of either the principal officers of the executive department or of such other body as Congress may by law provide, transmit within four days to the President pro tempore of the Senate and the Speaker of the House of Representatives their written declaration that the President is unable to discharge the powers and duties of his office. Thereupon Congress shall decide the issue, assembling within forty-eight hours for that purpose if not in session. If the Congress, within twenty-one days after receipt of the latter written declaration, or, if Congress is not in session, within twenty-one days after Congress is required to assemble, determines by two-thirds vote of both Houses that the President is unable to discharge the powers and duties of his office, the

Vice President shall continue to discharge the same as Acting President; otherwise, the President shall resume the powers and duties of his office.

Amendment XXVI [1971]

Section 1. The right of citizens of the United States, who are eighteen years of age or older, to vote shall not be denied or abridged by the United States or by any State on account of age.

Section 2. The Congress shall have power to enforce this article by appropriate legislation.

Amendment XXVII [1992]

No Law, varying the compensation for the services of the Senators and Representatives, shall take effect, until an election of Representatives shall have intervened.

†